T0338239

Developing Econometrics

Developing Econometrics

Hengqing Tong

Department of Mathematics
Wuhan University of Technology, P.R. China

T. Krishna Kumar

Indian Institute of Management
Samkhya Analytica India Private Limited, Bangalore, India

Yangxin Huang

Department of Epidemiology and Biostatistics
University of South Florida, USA

A John Wiley & Sons, Ltd., Publication

Registered Office
John Wiley & Sons Ltd, The Atrium, Southern Gate, Chichester, West Sussex, PO19 8SQ, United Kingdom

For details of our global editorial offices, for customer services and for information about how to apply for permission to reuse the copyright material in this book please see our website at www.wiley.com.

Library of Congress Cataloging-in-Publication Data

Tong, Hengqing, 1971–
    Developing econometrics / Hengqing Tong, T. Krishna Kumar, Yangxin Huang.
      p. cm.
    Includes bibliographical references and index.
    ISBN 978-0-470-68177-0 (cloth) – ISBN 978-1-119-96090-4
 1. Econometrics. 2. Econometric models. 3. Data mining. I. Kumar, T. Krishna. II. Huang, Yang Xin. III. Title.
    HB139.T66 2011
    330.01′5195–dc23

                                    2011024956

A catalogue record for this book is available from the British Library.

Print ISBN: 978-0-470-68177-0
ePDF ISBN: 978-1-119-95424-8
oBook ISBN: 978-1-119-95423-1
ePub ISBN: 978-1-119-96090-4
Mobi ISBN: 978-1-119-96091-1

Set in 10/12pt Times by SPi Publisher Services, Pondicherry, India
Printed and bound in Singapore by Markono Print Media Pte Ltd

Contents

Foreword

Econometrics was defined by the Econometric Society as a science devoted to the advancement of economic theory in relation to mathematics and statistics. With mathematical statistics as theoretical basis, and with the regression model as basic framework, econometrics provides a quantitative description of economic phenomenon by describing the internal relationships among economic data. It is also used to predict or forecast the economic scene under alternate hypothetical scenarios in order to aid us in designing economic policies. Econometrics is the better half, and the scientific half, of economics. It is a science like other sciences such as physics and chemistry, a Nobel Prize in economics has been awarded since 1969, and most of the works of the awardees happened to be in econometrics.

More recently, using new data mining tools, econometrics enabled companies to squeeze the last bit of knowledge from information to gain a competitive advantage over other companies competing with them. So far, many of the econometrics books in the English language at advanced undergraduate and graduate levels have been aimed at the graduate students and researchers of the western countries. The competition for the knowledge industry is throwing up vast opportunities for econometrics in the academic and business worlds of the emerging Asian countries. Only some of the successful books have been brought out as Asian editions with Asian co-authors who tend to be teachers and not researchers. At present, the teaching and research level on econometrics in countries like China, India, Singapore, and South Korea has improved significantly, and a number of high-level econometrics research works come from this part of the world. There is some time lag in adapting the latest developments in statistical theories and methods into econometrics. Brazil, Russia, India, and China (BRIC Countries) are emerging as the new growth centers. There is therefore a need to have a different kind of book that not only bridges the gap between recent statistical theories and methods and econometrics but also provides examples from problems arising in these emerging economies.

The contents and quality of this book are comparable approximately to some classical econometrics books that are currently available. With particular emphasis on mathematical analysis of econometric models, and a focus on robust modeling and Bayesian methods, this book covers advanced developments to an extent that they are relevant to econometrics.

The book draws heavily from the teaching and research experience of all the authors in China, India, and the United States. In particular it draws from the extensive teaching, research, and consultancy experience of some of the authors in India and China. It is commendable that almost all of the statistical theories and methods discussed in the book are illustrated through computer software prepared by the principal author. This book is a much revised and updated version of a similar book written by some of these authors in the Chinese language that was well received in China. I hope the book will be well received and found useful by graduate students, researchers, and teachers not only in the Asian countries but also in the advanced industrialized countries of the west. I congratulate the authors and the publisher for the timely introduction of this kind of book.

As a person who founded the Indian Econometric movement in India in 1960, and who made contributions to statistical science expounded in this book it gives me immense pleasure to write the foreword for this book.

C. R. Rao

October 2011   (Calyampudi Radhakrishna Rao)

Preface

The economies of the world are developing, and so are the theories and methods of econometrics. This book, called *Developing Econometrics*, written by authors coming from the developing countries, makes a sincere effort to reflect these developments.

In recent years countries have been grouped differently and are being given different names, as new industrialized economies, emerging economies and BRIC (Brazil, Russia, India, and China). They are creating a competitive spirit amongst themselves and are trading with the advanced industrialized countries. With increasing globalization and trade, increasing world competition, and increasing availability of large volumes of data, the need is being felt more and more to unlock the mysteries of uncertainty hidden in the chest of statistical tools and data.

Besides, there is a new emerging econometrics that is called by different names, business analytics being the most popular. In this book we attempt to realign econometrics with business analytic needs, and with recent trends in statistical theories and methods. The practitioner applying econometrics to business and public policy will thus, we hope, be equipped with the best possible tools for the pattern-recognition and predictions required for policy intervention so as to make our world a better place to live in.

Importance of econometrics for business analytics

'Uncertain knowledge plus knowledge of the amount of uncertainty equals usable knowledge' observed C.R. Rao. All decision makers in scientific investigations, business and public policy search continuously for better and better usable knowledge. Rajeeva Karandikar, the Director of the Chennai Mathematics Institute, advised graduate students of statistics in Bangalore to learn economics not only to apply statistics to economic problems but also to enrich statistics through the development of new statistical tools designed to address economic issues. Nothing can give a better fillip to developing cutting-edge statistical theories and methods than the need to use them for competitive advantage in a globally competitive business world. In recent years, and under recessionary conditions, businesses the world over have been looking for new ways of reducing costs and increasing revenues in the face of uncertainty. One such way is to squeeze as much useful information (usable knowledge) as possible from the volumes of data on consumer preferences and consumer complaints on product quality, production, sales, as well as operations data from various companies over time.

How this book came into being

There are several econometric textbooks that deal mostly with econometrics as statistical methods applied to the domain of economics. Most of these books covered the subject quite well both in depth and breadth. Courses on econometrics in business schools mostly use some of these textbooks written primarily for graduate students in economics departments. There are a few exceptions. Most of these texts are written by authors who teach and do research in the western industrialized countries. With globalization and the growth of the emerging economies western countries as well as emerging economies have felt a need to have some business applications from these emerging economies, preferably from those who had taught and done research in those countries. It is in this context that one of us, Tong, felt that he should write an English language textbook on econometrics, building upon his successful Chinese textbook on econometrics. Huang, co-author of Tong's Chinese language book, who teaches in the United States, agreed to join him in this new venture. Their proposal went before James Murphy of Wiley. On the basis of a preliminary review Murphy realized that most of the examples were drawn from China and a few from the US, but another major emerging economy, India, had been left out. He felt it desirable to have some examples from India, and to have a broader perspective. He thus felt it desirable to involve an Indian author who had been teaching econometrics to business students in India. This is how Kumar was asked to join the team.

For whom the book is written

The book is ideally suited as a graduate text to a course in a business school on econometrics or business analytics. It can serve as a textbook on econometrics for graduate students in the economics department of a typical school of arts and sciences. It can also serve as a reference book for mathematicians and statisticians who look for financially lucrative opportunities in the business world in the area of business analytics. Teachers, students, and researchers in the emerging economies such as the BRIC countries (Brazil, Russia, India, and China) may find the book a welcome addition to the existing textbooks. Teachers, students, and researchers in the western countries will also find it useful. The book presents a unified approach to statistical modeling in economics and business. This unified approach treats data as sample information, with the truth behind the data being known only partially. Such a perspective makes it necessary to specify a probability distribution for the observed data. Inferences regarding that distribution can be drawn either using the classical approach or the Bayesian approach, or as the authors prefer an eclectic approach. The classical approach presumes the existence of a prior knowledge that is deterministic while the Bayesian approach assumes the prior knowledge to be stochastic. If you are a teacher and want to have a text that incorporates Bayesian econometrics and nonparametric inference you will find this book useful.

Various recent developments in statistical theories and methods, such as nonparametric and semi-parametric methods, are more general versions of specifying the underlying probability distribution of the observed data than the purely parametric specification. This unified treatment brings home the importance of entertaining alternate specifications of the econometric models and of choosing the best among them for squeezing the most information from the observed data. If you are a teacher who is interested in teaching econometrics with a business perspective so that the students have a ready use, soon after their graduation, for the skills developed in the course, you will find this book useful.

Some special features of the book

There is a tendency among many econometrics teachers and students to treat econometrics as an already developed statistical tool that can be applied to economics and business, and hence emphasize which statistical tool should be used in a given specific situation. From the same perspective the standard statistical computing software required to practice econometrics is almost always imported from outside. In this book we make a sincere attempt to integrate economic problems with mathematical and statistical modeling and developing computer software. In this process we hope we have been able to help the reader to modify, and even build new models, methods and computer software to solve a variety of new problems that cannot be adequately solved employing present day methods. Such an approach is needed in order to arrive at better and better models if business analytics is to succeed in a competitive world. This is why this book can be of immense use to consultants in business analytics.

The book comes with computer software called Data Analysis and Statistical Computing (DASC). The architecture of DASC is different from other statistical software. It is simple to learn and to use. There is an illustrative example and an illustrative data set for each menu function in DASC. It is made user-friendly with menus that help accomplish various statistical computations needed for statistical inference/decision making. Some of the specialized topics are delegated to Electronic References that are available on the website created for the readers of this book. Each chapter is preceded by a chapter summary that presents a brief preview of what one can find in that chapter. As a ready reference, at the end of each chapter, there is a list of contents of the Electronic References that are pertinent to that chapter.

Software DASC and the Electronic References can be downloaded from website http://public.whut.edu.cn/slx/English/Login1.htm

The organization of the book

Keeping in mind the economic and business as the domain of the application of statistics, Chapter 1 gives a broad overview of the types of problems one might encounter, and the types of data that each such problem context will throw up.

The linear regression model is the work horse of econometrics. Which variables are to be used in standard linear multiple regressions and in what functional forms are discussed in Chapter 2. Normally if the model is properly chosen one would expect the errors to have a Normal distribution with constant variance. In general when the model is specified a priori it may happen that the conditional variance will be non-constant. How to handle that situation is the topic of Chapter 3. What are normally termed as a dummy variable or limited dependent variable models are termed discrete or categorical variable models in this book. This is because that is how the variables appear in econometric models. These models are discussed in Chapter 4. In econometrics some situations call for models that are nonlinear in parameters. These are also discussed in Chapter 4. A general specification of the conditional distribution and conditional mean may lead one to specify the econometric models as non-parametric or semi-parametric models. This topic engages us in Chapter 5.

Economic models can be classified into three major segments, partial equilibrium models, general equilibrium models, and disequilibrium models. Formulating an economic problem in any of these forms requires econometric models that involve a system of regression equations, one each for each simultaneously determined endogenous economic variable. Disequilibrium models deal with adjustment towards the equilibrium. These adjustment mechanisms, such as adaptive expectations and partial adjustment involve formulation of models with distributed lags. Chapter 6 deals with simultaneous equation models and models with distributed lags.

As explained in Chapter 1 the econometric models we build depend on the form in which the data come to us. Most economic data, and especially high frequency financial data, come to us in the form of time series. Chapter 7 covers univariate stationary time series models. Chapter 8 deals with both non-stationary time series and multivariate time series (to capture the general equilibrium approach to economic modeling). In Chapter 9 we cover a variety of topics, such as the General Linear Model with error distributions belonging to non-Normal distributions, robust regression, multivariate analysis, analysis of variance, causal modeling and path analysis, etc.

The conditional probability distribution of a dependent variable, conditional on the assigned values of the independent variables, can be characterized by its moments. It is for this reason that one normally focuses attention in econometrics on the conditional mean of that distribution as a single parametric multiple regression model. With the business analytic perspective in mind there is a need to have in our tool kit a variety of models, Bayesian, non-Bayesian, parametric and non-parametric, etc., so as to allow for the possibility that the pattern in data is in a flexible form to fit the data better than a single parametric model. Chapter 10 provides this integrated view of all the material covered in the book.

It is the prerogative of an instructor to structure a course as he or she wishes and hence we do not intend to suggest how these chapters can be structured to suit different types of courses.

Hengqing Tong
(*Department of Mathematics, Wuhan University of Technology, China*)

T. Krishna Kumar
(*Samkhya Analytica India Pvt Ltd., Bangalore, and Adjunct Professor, Indian Institute of Management, Bangalore, India*)

Yangxin Huang
(*Department of Epidemiology and Biostatistics at the University of South Florida, USA*)

August 20, 2011

Acknowledgements

Many people contributed to this work. We are most indebted to the major original contributors to statistical science and economic theory who inspired us. We are indebted to our teachers. We thank Professor C.R. Rao, a living legend in statistics, for agreeing to see various chapter outlines and a few sample chapters and write a Foreword for the book. We thank B.L.S. Prakasa Rao for going through the first draft of Chapter 10 and offering his comments and suggestions for improvement. We thank our students who helped us in checking the mathematical derivations and numerical statistical computations. Special mention may be made here of Kumar's doctoral students of Indian Institute of Management, Bangalore, Jayarama Holla and Puja Guha, of Tong's doctoral and postgraduate students of Wuhan University of Technology, Yuan Wan, Yang Ye, Yichao Pan, Fangmei Wang, Yan Gong, Yingbi Zhang, Yajie Cheng, Shudan Lu, Wei Wan, Wenjuan Wang and Li Guo, and of Huang's student and associate of University of South Florida, Ralph Carpenter and Ren Chen. Special thanks are due to Dr Qiaoling Tong, Dr Tianzhen Liu, Dr Qiaohui Tong, Dr Xing Xie and Sha Wang for programing the DASC software. Kumar thanks Nirmala for her help during the last stage of proof reading the galley proofs. Kumar thanks Ramarao Annavarapu for his valuable comments on the drafts of various parts of the manuscript written by him. Kumar's contribution is based on the graduate course in econometrics taught by him for several years at Indian Institute of Management as an Adjunct Professor. He thanks various batches of students who provided excellent feedback on what is relevant and what is not. He thanks Indian Institute of Management for providing him the necessary infrastructure. Kumar also thanks Cranes Software International Limited for supplying him with SYSTAT 12 free of cost to check the calculations used in our illustrative examples using our own DASC software.

We thank the editorial support and encouragement provided to us by editors James Murphy, Richard Davies, and Susan Barclay, along with other editorial staff working in the Statistics division of Wiley, Kathryn Sharples, Ilaria Meliconi and Heather Kay. Special thanks are due to James Murphy for bringing together the authors, Tong and Kumar, from two different countries who had not known each other. Ilaria Meliconi and Kathryn Sharples deserve thanks for bearing the pressures from the authors and the difficulties in getting the technical reviews of the manuscript as quickly as the authors wanted it. Our sincere thanks go to Richard Davies who managed so efficiently the tight time schedule and technical processing of the manuscript for printing. The final stages of print-setting and print-layout are quite crucial in the making of a book. The authors thank Prachi Sinha Sahay and Britto Fleming Joe for an excellent and speedy job of print-setting and publishing.

We thank our wives – Pingxi Cai (Tong), Usha (Kumar), and Liuyan Yan (Huang) for bearing with our preoccupation with our work on the manuscript, subtracting time from the family. No words are adequate to express Kumar's gratitude to his wife Usha for the encouragement she gave him to go ahead with the writing for this book. Usha's encouragement is our source of strength for the success of this book.

Kumar thanks the Department of Information and Decision Sciences, College of Business Administration, University of Illinois, Chicago for availing him of its library facilities as a Visiting Scholar. This facility became critically important as Kumar moved to Chicago during the final phases of preparing the manuscript.

The research work of Tong reported in this book was supported by the National Natural Science Foundation of China (30570611, 60773210).

1

Introduction

As mentioned in the preface, this book is a graduate text and a reference book for those who are interested in statistical theories and methods with economic and business applications. The role of econometrics has changed significantly during the last decade. Businesses and governments are now made accountable for making knowledge-based decisions. This requirement, coupled with the development in information and communication technology, has generated an enormous amount of data as a major source of information. This voluminous data is also coupled with some subjective but still useful knowledge in the hands of the decision makers. All of this information needs to be converted into meaningful and useful knowledge. The field of statistical knowledge itself, which came into existence barely a century ago, has expanded during the last few decades. Thus any new book such as this in econometrics must address itself as to how to handle large amounts of data and how to use cutting-edge statistical tools in order to discover the patterns in the data.

Gathering the right data, deciding which data are useful and which are not, data cleaning, data editing, combining quantitative data with other pieces of information and discovering patterns in all that information, etc are the building blocks of useful knowledge. It is that knowledge which is needed for making better business and economic decisions.

Fortunately there has also been a remarkable degree of acceptance in recent years of quantitative analysis in business and economics. The fear of mathematics and statistics, that was a characteristic feature of top management in business and government in the past, has now given way to an appreciation of their usefulness in making knowledge-based decisions. This is due mainly to the developments in computing software with graphics that have made mathematics and statistics a part of a black box. Their importance, however, is demonstrated by innovative graphics in terms of the end results of productivity gains, revenues, profits, reduced risk, etc that such methods can generate. This last part, an effective communication system between the quantitative analyst and the decision makers, is still in its infancy, and needs a great deal more development. We hope that the illustrative examples we give in this book, and the graphics that are built into our software, will go a long way in this direction. There is nevertheless a great danger of excessive use of such software without a proper understanding of

Developing Econometrics, First Edition. Hengqing Tong, T. Krishna Kumar and Yangxin Huang.
© 2011 John Wiley & Sons, Ltd. Published 2011 by John Wiley & Sons, Ltd.

the underlying statistical procedures. A misuse by incompetent people of the analytic tools, which can be easily implemented through the click of a mouse, using freely available open source software, might bring more discredit to analytics than credit. It is the main aim of this book to provide that link between business analytics, analytics software, and the required statistical knowledge. From that perspective this book differs in its scope from several other econometrics books, in the sense that it is aimed at the practitioner of business analytics or an applied econometrician. By providing a new orientation it also helps an academically oriented scholar to pursue academic interests in econometrics with a practical orientation.

We assume that the reader has had an introductory course on probability distributions and statistics, and also on the basic principles of statistical inference. This chapter introduces the types of economic problems and data that require quantitative analysis for business and public policy decisions. The competitive business environment requires that the analysis be done using the best possible statistical tools. Extensive treatment of these statistical methods will engage us in the subsequent chapters of this book. This chapter emphasizes the need to understand clearly the domain of application; as such knowledge is vital to understanding the data generating process or mechanism. Such an understanding is necessary for obtaining the best possible model.

1.1   Nature and scope of econometrics

1.1.1   What is econometrics and why study econometrics?

This book deals with the application of mathematical models, statistical theories and methods, to economic problems. This is an area of both economics and statistics which is called econometrics. When the International Econometric Society was founded in 1930 it defined econometrics as a science devoted to the advancement of economic theory in relation to mathematics and statistics. It was meant to be an interaction between economic theory or mathematical economics and measurement of economic variables, with the theory guiding the attempts at measurement, and measurement in turn modifying theory. Statistical methods become relevant in economics in two different ways. First, there is some variation in the observed economic data that needs to be understood through **exploratory data analysis**. Second, by making certain assumptions regarding the stochastic mechanism that generated the economic data one can attempt to specify and estimate an underlying statistical pattern in the data of the sample to make statements about the **data generating process**. It is this which constitutes the quantitative knowledge regarding the domain of application.

The development of econometrics, however, became unbalanced and leaned more towards mathematical theories and models that were divorced from reality. Fortunately econometrics today has another entirely different meaning and purpose that will amend this lack of relevance. Econometrics today is known simply as knowledge based on quantitative economic data and its analysis. It is this knowledge that businesses are seeking to exploit so as to gain an edge over their competitors. In the new age of digital on-line information firms gain competitive advantage by leveraging knowledge gained from data, such as optically scanned bar code data at the point of sale, or information on peoples' socioeconomic background and their preferences that can be mined from social network data. According to Davenport, the **business analytics** Guru, business analytics (econometrics), is about using '...sophisticated data-collection technology and analysis to wring every last drop of value from all your business processes' (Davenport, 2006: p. 1).

There is a value chain from information to knowledge, and knowledge to decision making based on that knowledge. Econometrics deals with processing information to filter out noise and redundant information and to discover patterns in the information so gathered. It is this **pattern recognition** that constitutes knowledge in business analytics. This book is about: (i) exploratory data analysis (including processing of raw data, data reduction, and data classification), and pattern recognition that separates signals from noise (**signal extraction**)[1]; (ii) model building and choice between alternate models; and (iii) prediction or forecasts based on the selected and estimated or calibrated model, along with probabilistic statements on the credibility of those predictions and forecasts. All of this is achieved through mathematical models, statistical theories, and numerical computations. These are the constituent molecules this book is made of.

It is estimated that in the year 2007 the average daily volume of traditional market transactions (spot, forward, and swaps) in foreign exchange markets globally was $3.21 trillion. For the same year the foreign exchange derivatives markets recorded an average daily turnover of $2.1 trillion. It is estimated that the ten most active traders account for almost 73% of the trading volume. One can imagine the importance of the econometric modeling of the foreign exchange markets for these ten traders, as well as for the other traders who wish to encroach on the privileged territory of these ten by leveraging the knowledge gained from econometric models. While the economic theory of **efficient capital markets** postulates that stock prices follow a **random walk**[2] it is also clear that there are asymmetries in information and knowledge available to the investors and asset management companies. Such asymmetries can lead to value addition for those who have better knowledge of how the market behaves under such asymmetries. Various asset management companies manage several thousands of individual accounts of corporations and families, each account maintaining a longitudinal database pertaining to the account holders' characteristics, their preferences, and how their portfolios performed in the market over time. This extensive database is not fully exploited for the knowledge inherent in that information. To quote T.S. Elliott, 'Where is the knowledge lost in the information?' Asset management companies can do better by using a better knowledge extraction from such information. Retail sales data, collected all over the world using bar codes and optical scanners and computers, includes data on consumer preferences.

Consumer feedback received by customer service departments has some textual information. This information can be exploited through data mining and **text mining** to gather knowledge on product quality, individual preferences, and individual willingness to pay so as to improve product design and advertising strategies. Click stream data stored on servers offer excellent information on peoples' preferences regarding the products and services available on the worldwide web. Using knowledge from that data one can do target marketing to improve sales, as is being done by Amazon.com.[3] These

---

[1] All these constitute what is now called data mining. Data mining is a specialized subject and is not discussed in detail here. Our discussion here is limited to some preliminary methods of pattern recognition through correlations and scatter plots. However, in Chapter 9 we discuss the methods of factor analysis and principal component analysis which form a part of data mining. For a more detailed description of data mining one may see Section 1.1 of the electronics references for Chapter 1 and Han and Kamber (2006).

[2] A random walk is achieved by taking successive random steps.

[3] Michael Lynch, a Bayesian with a Ph.D. degree in Engineering from Cambridge University, exploited his computational and statistical skills to discover patterns in a variety of digitized data such as text, visual, and numerical data employing Bayesian principles of searching for useful information. He is regarded as Bill Gates of Europe and started Autonomy Inc, a company specializing in meaning-based computing in 1996.

are just a few examples of the application of econometrics in business. More examples mentioned subsequently in this chapter will substantiate this point.

1.1.2   Econometrics and scientific credibility of business and economic decisions

There is an increasing tendency among business firms to base their decisions on credible knowledge. Knowledge derived from an arbitrarily chosen model, however scientific the subsequent statistical analysis might be, suffers from a lack of credibility to the extent that the basis for choosing the model is not made explicit and defended. Credibility of knowledge is being judged by scientific approaches used in generating knowledge, including evaluating the performance of alternate models and testing the chosen model. Scientific credibility is to be achieved through objectivity, reproducibility, testability or falsifiability, efficiency in use of information, closeness to reality of the assumptions made and results obtained.[4] There are two kinds of information, beneficial information or signalling information, and non-beneficial information or noise. The first question is: 'Is all beneficial information used?' The second question is: 'Is all available information classified into beneficial and non-beneficial information?' The third question is: 'What is the knowledge gathered or pattern discovered from the beneficial information?'

Not all information is in the form of quantitative information of comparable quality. When information comes from sources of different quality or reliability, scientific credibility calls for the best way of pooling such information. When information needed for analysis is not available one may have to collect it, if the resources permit it, or obtain it using some proxy variable. Alternately, one may obtain the value of such a crucial unavailable variable by eliciting its likely value from experts. Not using such a relevant variable in a model, as data on it were not available, is equivalent to ignoring that variable altogether! The question then arises as to what is the most credible way to combine such subjectively ascertained information with objectively collected information. **Bayesian analysis** deals with this method of credible ways of combining the subjective non-sample information with sample information. Bayesian analysis is explained in some detail in Chapter 10. Ultimately we must try to extract the maximum possible credible knowledge from *all* the available and *useful* information.

Most situations in economics call for using data generated by either a designed **random experiment** or a **sample survey** or a naturally occurring economic process that is viewed as a random data generation process. Scientific credibility in the former two cases can be established through design of economic experiments using the statistical theory of **design of experiments**, and design of sample surveys. In the third type of non-experimental situation credibility of econometric knowledge depends on how convincing the model is in reflecting the truth of the underlying data generating process. Where the sample data used is not from a random experiment or a random sample we need a much greater degree of effort to establish statistical credibility for modeling. To summarize: achieving credibility through pattern recognition is the essence of this book. We might quote the famous Indian poet and Nobel Laureate in literature, Rabindranath Tagore, who wrote this to inaugurate the launching of *Sankhya*, the Indian journal of statistics:

---

[4] Carl Sagan (1996) calls the scientific method the most effective 'baloney detector' ever invented.

The enchantment of rhythm is obviously felt in music, the rhythm which is inherent in the notes and their groupings. It is the magic of mathematics, this rhythm, which is in the heart of all creation, which moves in the atom and in its different measures fashions gold and lead, the rose and the thorn, the sun and the planets, the variety and vicissitudes of man's history. These are the dance steps of numbers in the arena of time and space, which weave the maya of appearance, the incessant flow of changes that ever is and is not. *What we know as intellectual truth, is that also not a perfect rhythm of the relationship of facts that produce a sense of convincingness to a person who somehow feels that he knows the truth?* We believe any fact to be true because of harmony, a rhythm in reason, the process of which is analysed by the logic of mathematics. (*Sankhya*, Vol. 2, Part 1, Page 1, 1935. Emphasis in italics is by the authors).

1.2   Types of economic problems, types of data, and types of models[5]

1.2.1   Experimental data from a marketing experiment

Practical situations often arise where the questions that are of interest to us are such that there are no data that are actually available to answer the questions. We may have to generate the required data. We give a simple example. A coffee powder manufacturer would like to design a packaging and pricing strategy for the product that maximizes his revenue. He knows that using a plastic bag with color has a positive effect on the consumer's choice, while a colored plastic bag is more costly than a plain plastic cover. He needs to estimate the net benefit he would have in introducing a colored plastic bag. He also knows that consumers prefer to have fresh coffee powder and thus depending on the weekly rate of consumption they choose the size of the packet. The larger the size of the packet that a household wants the lower is its willingness to pay, but smaller packets will increase the cost of packaging. He would like to know what would be the net benefits to the firm of different sizes of the packets at different levels of prices he could fix for them given different types of demand.

To introduce more realism and more complexity let us assume that there is a cost saving coffee substitute, called chicory, that when mixed with coffee brings thickness and bitterness to coffee that some people may like. But too much chicory is not liked by many consumers. As a result the manufacturer expects that the greater the content of chicory the lower the price the customer is willing to pay. Are consumers willing to trade a part of their preference for colored plastic bag for the optimal size of the packet? Historically collected data on coffee sales may be of no use to answer these questions as colored plastic bags were not used in the past. The manufacturer cannot go ahead and introduce the new colored package incurring higher cost. The coffee manufacturer wishes to conduct a small-scale pilot **marketing experiment** to estimate the effects on net revenue of different types of packaging, different levels of chicory and different sizes of the packets. How should one conduct the experiment? How should one analyze the data collected through such an experiment? Designing economic

---

[5] The authors have some managerial and statistical consultancy experience. They are also fortunate to have students with industry experience who bring practical problems to the classroom for discussion. The examples given below are drawn from such teaching and consultancy experience.

Table 1.1 The kind of data from marketing experiment.

Design Point	Chicory Content	Size of Packet	Colour of Packet	Mean Price (Customer's Willingness to Pay for 100 grams)
1	L(−)	L(−)	L(−)	15
2	H(+)	L(−)	L(−)	14
3	L(−)	H(+)	L(−)	12
4	H(+)	H(+)	L(−)	10
5	L(−)	L(−)	H(+)	17
6	H(+)	L(−)	H(+)	15
7	L(−)	H(+)	H(+)	16
8	H(+)	H(+)	H(+)	15

experiments and their analysis has become a new econometric tool widely used in recent years. Data in Table 1.1 summarizes the kind of data obtained for one such marketing experiment when each of the factors is set at two levels labeled Low (L) and High (H) for chicory content of 10%, size of packet 100 gms and 200 gms, plain cover and colored cover.

The questions of interest are: 1. How to choose the factors and assign them to the experimental subjects of the pilot experiment? 2. How do the changes in the three factors affect people's willingness to pay for 100 gms of coffee powder? 3. Is the relation between these factors and willingness to pay linear or nonlinear? 4. How can we estimate the effects? These questions can be answered using the statistical theory of design of experiments and the statistical method of **analysis of variance**. The first question is discussed in specialized texts on the design of experiments (see Anderson and Whitcomb (2000) for details on how to design **factorial experiments**).[6] The rest of the topics on the statistical analysis of experimental data are discussed in greater detail in Chapter 3 and Chapter 9.

1.2.2   Cross-section data: national sample survey data on consumer expenditure

The National Sample Survey Organization of India conducts nation-wide sample surveys of households to record their consumption expenditure pattern. This is a very rich database that was initiated to aid Indian planners to plan economic development. It is now an excellent data base for understanding consumer behavior in India in order to develop retail marketing strategies. The data is now made available at a reasonable cost and is at the household level, by means of a fine grid of geographic strata both in the rural and urban regions of India. One can delineate market areas and for each such a market estimate the consumer demand patterns. Typical information available from the NSSO database is presented in Table 1.2. Data presented in the table are only representative of the original data.

---

[6] In the field of marketing research there are very sophisticated designs of experiment. These are intended to meet the needs of a marketing researcher so as to perform a choice based conjoint analysis. For example, see Raghavarao, Wiley, and Chitturi (2011).

Table 1.2 National sample survey data on consumer expenditure (representative).

Sl. No	State	Region	Sub Sample	House hold Number	Multiplier	House hold Size	Cereal Consumption		Total Expenditure
							Quantity	Value	
1	2	1	1	1	13291	1	14.5	184	1023
2	2	1	1	3	13291	4	56	672	1744
3	2	1	1	5	13291	3	42	500	1476
4	2	1	1	7	13291	5	70.5	846	2630
5	2	1	1	1	2492	4	54	800	3760
6	2	1	1	3	2492	1	14.5	184	1028
7	2	1	1	1	35165	5	45.75	553	2145
8	2	1	1	3	35165	3	40	480	1068
9	2	1	1	5	35165	4	40.5	406	1536
10	2	1	1	7	35165	4	43	559	2860
11	2	1	1	9	35165	6	73	1062	4608
12	2	1	1	11	35165	5	60	550	1875
13	2	1	1	1	4786	2	14	192	2474
......	2	1	1	3	4786	2	27.5	405	10008
N	2	1	1	1	10608	3	35	362	1695

Source: Unit level data from National Sample Survey Organization, Government of India, used in a research study on consumption deprivation reported in Kumar, Mallick, and Holla (2009).

Sample surveys such as this are usually multi-stage stratified samples, giving different weights to different strata. Unit level data such as these cannot all be regarded as equivalent, ignoring the different over- and under-sampling of strata. The column labeled multiplier gives the weight one must attach to each observation to convert it into what would have been the case, if the sample was a simple random sample that gives an equal chance for every sampled unit to be included in the sample. These multipliers are derived from the sample design chosen. Sampling is a specialized topic and one may see Thompson (2002) for the details. These multipliers must be used as weights for the recorded observations before any modeling is attempted. Given this sample information one might want to know (i) if there is any pattern implied by the theory of consumer behavior that relates expenditure on cereals to household size and total expenditure; (ii) if such a relation is linear or nonlinear; (iii) how to estimate alternate specifications; and (iv) how to choose between alternate specifications. This type of data is called cross-section multivariate data. The data analyses of such cross-sectional data will be discussed in detail in Chapters 2–5, 9, and 10.

Another recently popular way of generating data for analysis is through web surveys. Before using such data for analyzing the underlying pattern one must make sure whether the analysis pertains to only that sample of respondents and their behavior or refers to a wider population of which the web survey is only a sample. If the latter is the case one must determine the probability that a unit is selected for web survey, and the probability that a selected unit responds. Based on these two probabilities one must make a sample selection correction. In order to have a credible model this kind of data adjustment must be made before modeling.

1.2.3   Non-experimental data taken from secondary sources: the case of pharmaceutical industry in India

An advertising company noted that the pharmaceutical industry is poised for rapid growth in India owing to several factors such as switching over to a new product patenting regime, economic reforms that permitted foreign direct investment, low cost of doing research and development work in India, and the large pool of scientific and technical manpower that exists in India. It wanted to make a pitch for new customer accounts from some of the major pharmaceutical companies. It examined the data on sales and advertisement expenditure and wished to demonstrate that advertisement expenditure pays rich dividends in terms of generating a substantial increase in sales. The data the agency collected from an industry data-base, such as PROWESS from the Centre for Monitoring the Indian Economy, is presented below in Table 1.3. The figures quoted in the table are in Rs Crore (Rs. 10 million) per year. The advertising agency found a simple relationship between advertising expenditure and sales and argued in favour of spending on advertising. The marketing and **supply-chain** manager of the company argued that the results demonstrated by the advertisement agency referred to all the pharmaceutical companies in India, while they themselves were different from the typical average pharmaceutical company. He also said that sales were also affected by marketing effort and through supply-chain management, of which the distribution expenses were a proxy. He thus said that he was not convinced that the effect of advertising on sales *in his company* was what was suggested by the advertising company. The issues to be examined are: 1. Is the effect of advertising on sales the same for all companies in the database? 2. Do all companies in the database have the same structural pattern so as to be treated as one sample? 3. What are the various drivers of sales? 4. What is the most plausible

Table 1.3   The data collected from an industry database (PROWESS).

Sl. No	Company Name	Sales	Advertising	Marketing	Distribution
1	A C E Laboratories Ltd.	133.02	0.28	1.04	0.71
2	Aarey Drugs & Pharmaceuti	–	–	–	–
3	Aarti Drugs Ltd.	230.79	0.46	2	6.86
4	Abbott India Ltd.	274.17	4.29	39.28	6.65
5	Add-Life Pharma Ltd.	0.46	0	0	0
6	Adinath Bio-Labs Ltd.	12.02	0.01	0.06	0
7	Aditya Medisales Ltd.	0	0	45.38	0
8	Advik Laboratories Ltd.	15.25	0	4.68	0.48
9	Aesculapius Remedies Ltd.	–	–	–	–
10	Ahlcon Parenterals (India	21.13	0.15	0.05	0.4
11	Ajanta Pharma Ltd.	101.62	1.6	10.08	4.81
12	Albert David Ltd.	124.41	0	30.32	0
13	Alembic Ltd.	608.66	0	57.39	10.87
14	Alpha Drug India Ltd.	22.7	0	0.23	0.4
15	Alta Laboratories Ltd.	12.28	0	0.01	0.01
16	Ambalal Sarabhai Enterpri	120.44	0	3.4	0.46
17	American Remedies Ltd. [M	94.3	6.84	1.18	1.52
18	Amit Alcohol & Carbon Dio	20.25	0	0.32	0
19	Amol Drug Pharma Ltd.	2.49	0	0.04	0

Source: Company level data extracted from PROWESS: A company level data base of the Indian economy from the Centre for Monitoring the Indian Economy (CMIE).

functional form for the multivariate relation between sales and these drivers? 5. How does one estimate the separate effect of each of these factors on sales? These questions can be answered using the multiple regression methods for cross-sectional data, discussed in Chapters 2–5, 9 and 10.

1.2.4   Loan default risk of a customer and the problem facing decision on a loan application[7]

When a customer submits an application to a bank for a loan he or she provides personal information in the application, and the person's case is then referred by the bank to a credit rating agency to get a credit rating based on his or her credit history. These two sets of data are used by the bank to determine the credit risk. The bank wishes to examine the past history of several such loan applications and the loan default histories in order to develop a risk score – the probability of default on a loan given the personal information and the information from the credit rating agency. It would also be interested in examining the effects of choosing different thresholds of credit risk score for rejecting the application.

---

[7] This example is based on a term paper submitted for an econometrics course at Indian Institute of Management-Bangalore, in March 2008 by Abhishek Agarwal, Amit Gupta, Dhilip Krishna, and S. Karthik.

1.2.4.1   Some data mining issues[8]

The actual data may pertain to several thousand applicants, and not all of them are similar. There can be information on more than a hundred variables. Actual data provided by the applicants could be of two types, one that can be easily verified with supporting documents and the other, that cannot be easily verified. One may regard some of those variables as variables that have some information on the default risk of the applicant and hence are signaling variables, while there are other variables that have no such information on loan default risk and hence are noisy variables. There may be some missing observations and there can be recording errors.

The first job of an analyst in this case is to clean the data for errors and decide on how to treat the missing data. If data were missing on one variable to throw away the entire observation is an inefficient way of using sample information. Another recommended procedure for replacing the missing value by means of a sample consisting of all non-missing values is also not an efficient way of using the information. One may instead replace the missing value by some kind of an appropriate mean. One way of doing it is to take all the observations that have no missing values and arrange them into data clusters with default risk being of 20 intervals between 0 and 1. Then one can arrange the missing value sample into similar clusters with the default risk being in the same 20 intervals. The missing values in each of these 20 clusters may then be replaced by the mean values observed in a matching cluster of default risk for the earlier sample that had no missing values.

The variables that have contributed to very little variation in default risk can be treated as noisy variables and dropped. The remaining variables can be treated as the signaling variables. Even then the number of variables could be too large, about 100, giving rise to difficulties in estimation due to correlations among such a large number of variables. This issue of problems associated with high correlations among the independent variables is discussed in detail in Section 2.4 of Chapter 2. The number of variables can be reduced through data reduction techniques such as **principal component analysis** discussed in detail in Chapter 9. Finally the model chosen must be the one that is best suited to dealing with binomial variable, default or no default. This is a special case of regression with a categorical dependent variable discussed in detail in Chapter 4. The data of the loan default example is provided in the Electronic References. Two alternate models were evaluated in terms of their performance in predicting the default risk with the historic data.

1.2.5   Panel data: performance of banks in India by the type of ownership after economic reforms

Several interesting questions arise with respect to the banking sector in India as a result of the financial sector reforms: 1. Do the private sector banks perform better than the public sector banks? 2. Are the public sector banks improving their performance relative to the

---

[8] Most of the issues mentioned here regarding the cleaning and editing of data and exploratory analysis are issues dealt with in data mining. Although data mining is not covered in detail in this book, given its importance we give some description of it in this example and in section 1.3. Section 1.1 of the Electronic References to this chapter and Chapter 9 provide some additional details about data mining. This book deals mostly with pattern recognition or statistical modeling of data that are already pre-cleaned and explored through exploratory data analysis. The reader may see Han and Kamber (2006) for more detail on data mining.

Table 1.4   Data of performance of banks in India.

Year	Panel	Size	ROA	NPA RATIO	Op Profit Ratio	CAR	Ownership
1999	_BOB	10.86	0.0066	7.70	1.95	13.30	0
1999	_BOI	10.90	0.0037	7.30	1.41	10.60	0
1999	__BOP	7.66	0.0153	3.70	2.36	14.60	1
1999	_BOR	8.16	−0.0202	9.50	−0.31	0.80	1
1999	_CUB	7.26	0.0087	8.00	1.79	14.30	1
1999	__CB	9.61	0.0117	2.00	2.28	13.20	0
1999	_DB	9.61	0.0055	7.70	1.59	11.10	0
1999	_DLB	7.23	0.0028	12.30	1.07	10.10	1
1999	_FB	9.00	0.0003	7.50	0.69	10.30	1
1999	_HDFC	8.38	0.0189	0.70	3.52	11.90	2
1999	_ICICI	8.85	0.0091	2.90	2.57	11.10	2
1999	_ISB	8.73	0.0056	7.20	2.29	15.20	2
1999	__JKB	8.93	0.0114	3.80	2.74	24.50	1
1999	_OBC	9.84	0.0123	4.50	2.30	14.10	0
1999	_SIB	8.18	0.0007	11.10	1.08	10.40	1
1999	_SBBJ	9.23	0.0090	10.50	1.79	12.30	0
1999	_SBI	12.31	0.0046	7.20	1.55	12.50	0
1999	_SBM	8.84	0.0049	10.60	1.79	10.20	0
1999	_SBT	9.29	0.0040	10.80	1.30	10.30	0
1999	_UTI	8.27	0.0069	6.30	2.14	11.60	2
1999	_UWB	8.27	0.0095	8.30	2.06	11.60	1
2000	_BOB	10.98	0.0086	7.00	1.93	12.10	0
2000	_BOI	10.93	0.0031	8.60	1.24	10.60	0

(ROA: return on Assets; NPA Ratio: Ratio of non-performing assets to all assets; Op Profit ratio: Operating profit divided by non-operating profit; CAR: Capital Adequacy Ratio, Ownership = 0 for scheduled public sector bank, = 1 for scheduled private sector bank, = 2 other kind of bank).

private sector banks after the introduction of financial sector reforms? 3. Is the performance of all banks improving after the introduction of financial sector reforms? In order to answer these questions one may acquire data from the official source, the Reserve Bank of India. Table 1.4 presents the data so collected. Complete data are provided in the Electronic References.

There are several public sector banks while there are only a few private banks. The data on banks' economic operations are available for several years. The data thus consists of a time series of cross-sections or is **panel data**. Regression models for such panel data have some special characteristics of their own and ordinary multiple regression models must be suitably modified so as to address the special features of the data. The statistical modeling of panel data using the **Stochastic Frontier Model** is discussed in Chapter 9 and Chapter 5, and using the **Self Modelling Regression Model** is discussed in the Electronic References for Chapter 5.

1.2.6   Single time series data: The Bombay Stock Exchange (BSE) index[9]

One of the areas where quantitative analysis has been used extensively in recent years is the field of finance. In one of its basic forms the efficiency hypothesis of the capital markets assumes that stock prices follow a random walk model. The six year daily BSE Index (Bombay Stock Exchange Index) data from April 2, 1996 until March 31, 2002 was used by Singhal (2005) to test this hypothesis. This data set is univariate time series data. Many financial time series come like this. Financial institutions require an econometric analysis of such a financial time series. Statistical analysis of univariate time series can be carried out if one can either assume that the series is stationary which means that the series has the same mean, variance, and other higher moments in different segments of time, or if one can find a deterministic transformation of the nonstationary series that will make it stationary. Modeling of time series is taken up in Chapters 7 and 8. Chapter 7 in particular deals with modeling a single time series or a univariate time series that is stationary, while Chapter 8 deals with multiple time series and nonstationary time series. If one plots the closing values of the BSE Sensex on a particular day against the closing value on the previous day in a scatter plot, the scatter does seem to confirm the random walk hypothesis. This is shown in Figures 1.1 and 1.2.

Figure 1.1 can be shown in Data Analysis and Statistical Computing (DASC for short) software by clicking the menu items just three times. Readers can substitute their own data or modify the data given in our example to gain experience with DASC and with this kind of example. The detailed method can be seen in Electronic References for this chapter.

Software for DASC and the Electronic References can be downloaded from the website http://public.whut.edu.cn/slx/English/Login1.htm.

We note that there are two pictures in Figure 1.1 which are drawn simultaneously by DASC. The user can select one of the two pictures to save. In fact, there are two figure systems in DASC for all models, but we will show only one of them in subsequent paragraphs.

Figure 1.2 above plots the daily difference in BSE Sensex against time. The raw data in the figures above give one the impression that the stock prices do follow a random walk and that there is little one can do to make gains in the stock market, contrary to the gains many people do make on the stock market. One very common problem with many econometric analyses is that they tend to model the series as given. The given data may have considerable noise built into them and it may be necessary to smooth the series through some kind of averaging so as to discern the patterns that might exist. This is illustrated by this example. It will be shown a little later in this chapter that a detailed exploratory data analysis using such averaging does provide a scope for making short-term gains in the Indian stock market through a strategy.

1.2.7   Multiple time series data: Stock prices in BRIC countries[10]

Four countries, Brazil, Russia, India, and China, nicknamed the BRIC countries, are gaining importance as possible destination countries for portfolio investment by investors in countries that had a head start in industrial development. Two economic questions are

---

[9]This example draws from Singhal (2005). We are grateful to Paras Singhal and the editor of the *IIMB Management Review* who provided us the raw data used by Singhal.

[10]This example is taken from the term paper submitted for an econometrics course at Indian Institute of Management-Bangalore in 2008 by Akash Agrawal, Hrishikesh Patil, Udayan Sarkar, and Vikram Balan.

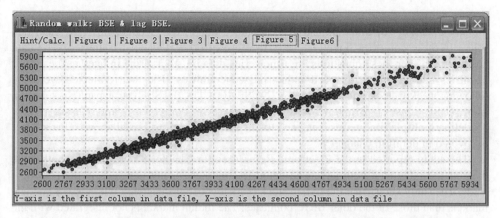

Figure 1.1 (a) Random walk: BSE & lag BSE.

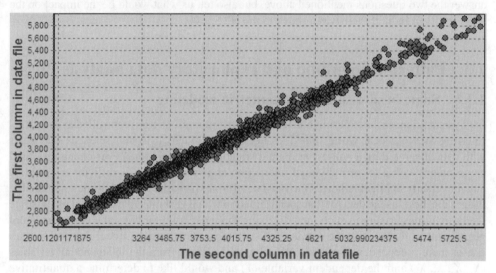

(b) Random walk: BSE & lag BSE.

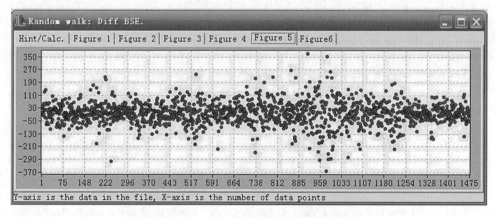

Figure 1.2 First Difference of BSE Index.

important in this context. First, are the stock markets in these four countries integrated with the stock markets of other industrially advanced countries? Second, how are the stock prices in these countries linked causally to those of other advanced countries? The data needed to answer these questions are time series data on stock price indices in these four countries and in other advanced industrialized countries. The data collected were the following weekly stock price indices: US (NYSE-100), UK (FTSE-100), Japan (Nikkei-225), India (BSE-Sensex), Brazil (Bovespa), China (SSE composite), and Russia (RTS). Modeling multiple time series is needed to answer the questions raised above. This subject is covered in detail in Chapter 8.

The study reported in the Electronic References for Chapter 8 reveals that whether the markets are integrated with advanced countries' markets or not depends on the period of study. The study shows that the Indian stock market is better integrated with the US and UK markets than those of the other BRIC countries. The Indian market is not integrated with the Japanese market. The statistical model and its analysis developed in Chapter 8 not only answer the two questions mentioned above, but also tell us what would be the impact on the stock prices in India if there was a shock to the NYSE100.

1.3   Pattern recognition and exploratory data analysis

1.3.1   Some basic issues in econometric modeling

In physical sciences the experimental data refer to observations from controlled experiments referring to a physical world that does not change much. In social sciences one deals with data generated by a non-experimental situation and refers to an ever-changing social environment with a lot of individual interaction and variation.[11] It is difficult to establish any universally applicable laws. One must determine, from the non-experimental data, the pattern that best fits the data for that social situation which generated the data. Let us illustrate the basic issues arising in such models, using the most commonly used econometric tool **regression,** and also with the simplest of such regression models, linear regression with one or more independent variables. We take observations from the independent variables $(X_1, X_2, ..., X_k)$ and the dependent variable (Y) and would like to determine a quantitative relationship between them that is best in some sense. We assume that the variables have a **joint probability distribution** and that the dependent variable has a **conditional probability distribution** given the independent variables. The regression model is supposed to be the conditional mean of the dependent variable given the independent variables.

The issues confronting the analyst in this situation can be summarized as:

(1) Should one use the raw data as given or should one use processed or derived (smooth) data?

(2) Do the observations come from the same population? Or does the sample seem to come from a mixture of two or more populations?

---

[11] This is what must have prompted Murray Gell-Man, a Nobel Laureate in physics, to remark: 'Imagine how hard physics would be if electrons could think' (quoted by Page, 1999).

(3) What transformation of variable X should one use? Linear in X, piece-wise linear in X, non-linear function of X, or Nonlinear in X with non-linearity appearing in parameters?

(4) Should one give equal or unequal importance to all the observations in the minimization of errors?

(5) If there are several possible models, how should one choose one from among them?

(6) Finally is the chosen model good or should one look for additional information?

The question we may ask is 'If our interest is the **conditional mean** of the distribution of the dependent variable, given the independent variables, what should be the most appropriate model we choose for it?' A model most appropriate with the entire sample may not be the one that is most appropriate if one is interested in a portion of that sample. The answer of course depends on what use we put the model to. If we want to explain the observed data, including the extreme values, we may include all observations in the sample. Even then the same pattern of relation may not fit all sections of the distribution of the dependent variable Y. If we are more interested in explaining the middle portions of the distributions of the variables we can use the standard multiple regression models discussed in detail in Chapters 2–5. If we are interested in different segments of the sample then fractile regression discussed in Chapters 9 and 10 will be useful.

One can say that whatever is the regression model such model can be regarded as a signal or pattern that we are trying to discover, and the rest is noise. The criterion for the best fitting model is maximizing the signal and minimizing the noise or maximizing the **signal to noise ratio** as the communication engineers say.[12] Thus, if there are alternative models the choice between them should be made using this criterion. In Chapter 10 we describe in greater detail how this is done. It is also possible that the same model or pattern may not fit equally well with all data points in the chosen sample. Different portions of the sample may have different patterns.

The application of statistics must give importance to an understanding of the phenomenon to which the statistics are applied. Hence statistical modeling necessarily requires an understanding of the domain of application that generated the data, economics in this case. In any model building we would encounter two types of drivers that determine the dependent variable. First, there are those factors that are quite general to the domain area and are suggested by the existing theories in the domain area, and others which are specific to the particular or specific situation that actually generated the data. The knowledge of those specific factors that affect the dependent variable must come from a thorough examination of the sample data itself. That is what we call **exploratory data analysis**. Exploratory data analysis is a special and important component of data mining. Again, as our focus is more on pattern recognition or statistical modeling or what is also called **predictive analytics** in business analytics, we cannot dwell much on data mining. However, given its importance, we are compelled to cover some basic features and refer the reader to the data mining book referred to earlier. Exploratory data analysis must precede identifying possible alternate models.

---

[12] It is said that Florence Nightingale, who was made an honorary member of the American Statistical Association, said that a statistician's work is the work of discovering God. To elaborate, by reducing our ignorance through statistics we improve our knowledge and get closer to the truth.

1.3.2   Exploratory data analysis using correlations and scatter diagrams: The relative importance of managerial function and labor

One might trace the origins of econometrics to exploring the quantitative relations between economic variables using correlations and **scatter diagrams** (Frisch, 1929).[13] Frisch suggested looking at all possible pairs of variables and drawing the scatter diagrams and calculating the correlation coefficients so as to understand the relations between variables. We would like to illustrate this with an example. A company was facing a situation where the workers' union was demanding a productivity-linked bonus year after year, attributing the increase in profits to their hard work. The management undertook a study of the relation between profits after taxes on three other variables. These were: 1. labour productivity, measured as output per unit labour; 2. managerial effectiveness, measured through a scale based on a battery of questions put to workers, managers, and managerial professionals outside the company (on the number of managerial decisions and their perception of whether they made any significant positive or negative impact on the company); and 3. cost of raw materials. The aim was to determine the best fitting statistical relationship between profit after taxes and the other three variables. Here, we are in search of a function that is linear in parameters and possibly involving nonlinear functions of the three explanatory variables that maximizes the explained variation in profits after taxes. As the regression coefficients of the linear regression model are related to the correlation and partial correlations, we can examine scatters and correlations to explore what model is to be chosen. Figures 1.3a to 1.3c provide the scatter plots of the three variables with profit after tax.

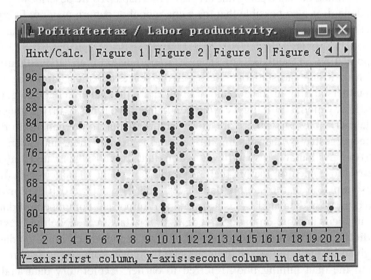

Figure 1.3 (a)   Profit after tax/Labor productivity.

---

[13] Ragnar Frisch is one of the founders of the International Econometric Society that was founded in 1930. He is the one who coined the word econometrics. His first work on econometric, Frisch (1929), outlined the usefulness of such data exploration in determining the true structure of the data generating process.

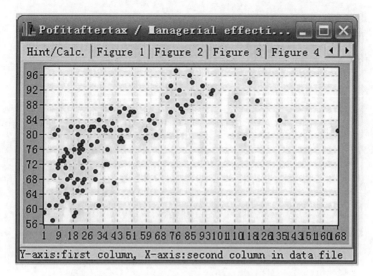

(b)   Profit after tax/Managerial effectiveness.

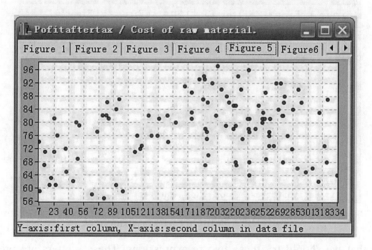

(c)   Profit after tax/Cost of raw material.

Figures 1.3a to 1.3c can be shown in the DASC software. From these scatter diagrams we get the impression that profit after tax is positively related to managerial effectiveness and negatively related to labour productivity, and possibly not related to cost of raw material. From these scatter plots it is also apparent that managerial effectiveness has a nonlinear relationship with profit after tax. We now re-express the relationship through a scatter with the log of managerial effectiveness, and the square root of managerial effectiveness. We find that the scatter with log managerial effectiveness is still exhibiting nonlinearity and seems to indicate a quadratic relation.

We plotted the scatter with the square of the log of managerial effectiveness. The scatters of the square root and the square of the logarithm seem to be quite similar and good

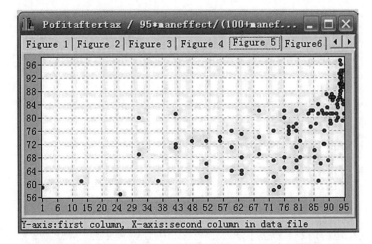

Figure 1.4   Profit after tax/95*maneffect/(100+maneffect).

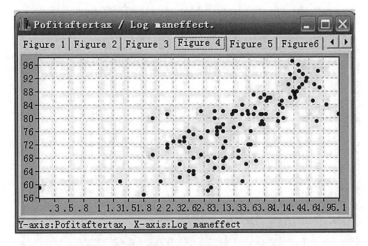

Figure 1.5   Pofitaftertax/Log maneffect.

suggesting that we should try these two re-expressions. These scatters are presented in Figures 1.4 to 1.7.[14]

Figure 1.7 is similar to the previous figure in visual appearance, but their X-axises are not the same.

We then calculated the **zero-order correlations** between profit after tax and these re-expressions of managerial effectiveness and the other two variables, and these are presented in Table 1.5. From this table it is clear that the square of log managerial effectiveness has the highest correlation with profit after tax. While the correlations of other variables are also significant we observe inter-correlations between them. So we wish to know if the other two variables are important after introducing square of log of managerial effectiveness as an

---

[14] Figure 1.4 shows the scatter with respect to a nonlinear transformation of variable maneffect = 95*maneffect/ (100+maneffect).

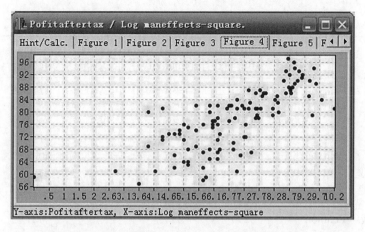

Figure 1.6   Pofitaftertax/Log maneffects-square.

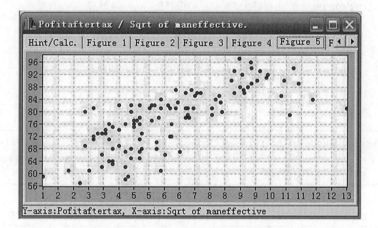

Figure 1.7   Pofitaftertax/Sqrt of maneffective.

explanatory variable. To answer this question we calculate the **partial correlations** after controlling for square of log managerial effectiveness.

These partial correlations are shown in Table 1.6 below.

From this table it is clear that labor productivity is the next most significant variable and that the cost of raw material is possibly not important. However, economic reasoning would suggest that the cost of raw materials must be an explanatory variable for profits after tax.

We are now ready to specify the **regression model** as:

$$y = \beta_0 + \beta_1 X_1 + \beta_2 X_2 + \beta_3 X_3 + \varepsilon \tag{1.1}$$

where X_1 is variable Ln Managerial effectiveness square, X_2 is variable Labor productivity, X_3 is variable Cost of raw material, and ε is the random errors. The results of the least squares estimation of the regression above are presented below in Table 1.7.

Table 1.5   Correlations between variables.

		Profit after tax	Labor productivity	Cost of raw material	In man effect sq	Sqrt man effect
Profit after tax	Pearson Correlation	1	−.497**	.294**	.755**	.746**
	Sig. (2-tailed)		.000	.002	.000	.000
	N	111	111	111	111	111
Labor productivity	Pearson Correlation	−.497**	1	−.127	−.602**	−.609**
	Sig. (2-tailed)	.000		.183	.000	.000
	N	111	111	111	111	111
Cost of raw material	Pearson Correlation	.294**	−.127	1	.421**	.403**
	Sig. (2-tailed)	.002	.183		.000	.000
	N	111	111	111	111	111
In man effect sq	Pearson Correlation	.755**	−.602**	.421**	1	.996**
	Sig. (2-tailed)	.000	.000	.000		.000
	N	111	111	111	111	111
Sqrt man effect	Pearson Correlation	.746**	−.609**	.403**	.996**	1
	Sig. (2-tailed)	.000	.000	.000	.000	
	N	111	111	111	111	111

**Correlation is significant at the 0.01 level (2-tailed).

Table 1.6   Partial correlations.

Control Variables			Profit after tax	Cost of raw material	Labor productivity
In man effect sq	Profit after tax	Correlation	1.000	−.040	−.082
		Significance	.	.681	.396
		(2-tailed) df	0	108	108
	Cost of raw material	Correlation	−.040	1.000	.174
		Significance	.681	.	.069
		(2-tailed)df	108	0	108
	Labor productivity	Correlation	−.082	.174	1.000
		Significance	.396	.069	.
		(2-tailed) df	108	108	0

While the **adjusted R²** (this term and its meaning will be explained in Chapter 2) was only 0.486 without using the transformation of the managerial effectiveness variable, after using lnmaneffectsq the adjusted R^2 has improved to 0.5677. As revealed by the partial correlations both labor productivity and cost of raw material have regression coefficients which are not significantly different from zero.

Table 1.7 Least squares estimation.

Variable	Regression Coefficient	Standard Error	t-statistic	Significance
Constant (Intercept)	63.2426	5.9168	10.6887	0.0000
Labor productivity	−0.1373	0.0931	1.4746	0.0716
Cost of raw material	−3.3053	4.7436	0.6968	0.2437
Ln Managerial effectiveness square	2.5481	1.1595	2.1975	0.0151
R^2	0.5795			
Adj R^2	0.5677			

Dependent variable: Profit after tax.

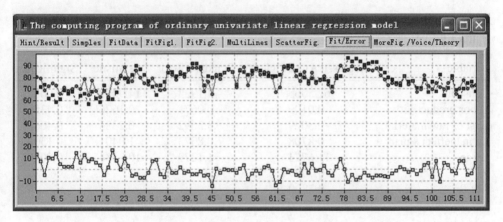

Figure 1.8 Actual and fitted values of profits after tax along with the residuals.

Once such correlations are calculated and scatter diagrams are drawn a potentially useful set of independent variables can be prepared. As we explain in greater detail, from that list one can select a final linear multiple regression using various variable selection methods. Thus, Chapter 2 also can be regarded as a major component of data mining or exploratory data analysis.

Often, we are tempted to specify a regression relation without examining or exploring the sample data to see what story it tells. It pays to look at the data more carefully. This is what we demonstrate next. Figure 1.8 presents the graph of actual and fitted values of profits after tax along with the residuals and can be shown in DASC software. The curve below represents the residual errors.

We note that the top part of figure shows the goodness of fit by plotting the actual and fitting values of the dependent variable, while the bottom part shows the plot of residual errors. Figure 1.9 is the same.

We note from the figure above that the estimated errors have a systematic pattern suggesting that for smaller companies there is an over-estimation and for larger companies there is an underestimation. We therefore introduced a new dummy variable labeled 'large' which is

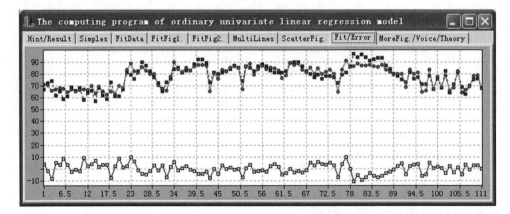

Figure 1.9   Fitted and actual values with a new dummy variable.

Table 1.8   Dependent variable: profit after tax.

Variable	Regression Coefficient	Standard Error	t-statistic	Significance
Constant	62.5065	4.1923	14.9099	0.0000
Labor productivity	−0.0109	0.0671	0.1626	0.4356
Cost of raw material	−0.8029	3.3692	0.2383	0.4061
Ln maneffect square	0.8708	0.8373	1.0401	0.1503
Large	11.6774	1.1279	10.3534	0.0000
R^2	0.7909			
Adj R^2	0.7830			

equal to 1 if the company has a profit after tax of Rs 75 Crores and zero otherwise. The adjusted R^2 has increased from 0.5677 to 0.783. The final results obtained are presented below in Table 1.8 followed by the graph of fitted and actual values and the estimated residuals in Figure 1.9.

What was shown above is the special case of a more general method. Here we have shown that the sample can be classified into two clusters, one for small firm with after tax profits of less than Rs. 75 Crores. A standard data mining technique is to see if the sample can be grouped into several clusters using cluster analysis so that one could try a different model specification for each cluster. Section 9.2.1 of Chapter 9 deals with discriminant analysis and cluster analysis. One can perform the scatter and correlation analysis separately for each cluster of samples.

1.3.3   Cleaning and reprocessing data to discover patterns: BSE index data

Singhal (2005) examined the overnight gains and losses in the stock prices on the Bombay Stock Exchange, along with day gains and losses. The BSE Index and individual stock prices did show the random walk type pattern. He asked two questions:

Table 1.9   BSE index data.

X	Y	X	Y
74.34	−31.67	2.53	2.24
27.67	−13.72	−0.39	−2.78
16.77	−9.32	−4.2	−5.89
10.68	5.94	−12.46	−8.18
6.34	−4.63	−58.34	11.27

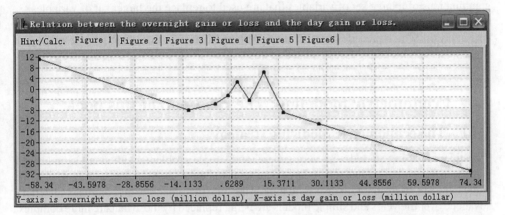

Figure 1.10   Relationship between the overnight gain or loss and the day gain or loss.

(1) Is it possible to predict the value of the day-time gain using the value of the over-night gain?

(2) Is it possible to get significantly more returns by over-night trading or day trading as compared to long-term trading?

He found that if the data were smoothed and some averages were derived for different ranges of gains and losses then the noise in individual daily series is removed and there emerges a definite pattern. That pattern can be used to make gains on the market from the knowledge that there was a substantial gain or loss overnight. The data were arranged in the increasing order of overnight gain and grouped into ten deciles, each of the deciles having about 148 points. The means of these deciles are presented below in Table 1.9.

Based on the processed data above we can see a relationship between the overnight gain or loss (Y) and the day gain or loss (X) as given in Figure 1.10.

The pattern observed with this processed data is different from the raw data observed earlier in this chapter (Section 1.2.6). The raw data only shows a random walk type of relationship between the overnight gain and day gain, the grouped data shows such random walk behavior only for the small ranges of gains or losses. When such gains or losses are substantial there is a negative relationship between them. Based on the pattern above Singhal developed a buy-sell strategy at the beginning of the day that takes into account the observed pattern above, and through simulation showed that short-run gains from the strategy exceeded the gains from day trading (by 100 times) and long-term trading (by 35 times). He found similar gains in trading on individual stocks, the latter based on a similar observed patterns for individual stock prices.

The example given above is a special case of processing the data to form an aggregation of samples and data condensation. There are other methods of data mining (exploratory data analysis) such as reducing the number of variables into a smaller set. This aspect was already mentioned in the loan default example of Section 1.2.4. A more general approach is to use **principal components** and factor analysis methods to reduce the dimensions of the vector of independent variables. Under that approach the **multivariate analysis** of factor and principal components analysis, described more fully in Chapter 9, is used to determine fewer linear combinations of a large set of variables that are used to replace the larger set of variables.

We have thus given a brief tour of a more specialized subject of data mining (exploratory data analysis) which precedes specification of alternate models that constitute the main grist of the statistical modeling issues treated in this book.

1.4   Econometric modeling: The roadmap of this book

1.4.1   The econometric modeling strategy

Statistical modeling started with very general and simple problems with small samples and has now advanced to a stage where large data sets are being stored in data warehouses in the clouds and are used for statistical modeling. The statistical theories and methods also have advanced over the years and simple models are being replaced by those that are more complex. Models remained simple in the earlier years in order to keep the computation tasks manageable. With advances in computing statisticians were able to introduce more complexity into modeling. Unfortunately amongst a section of people who seek statistical applications an impression has been created that the more sophisticated or complex a model is the better it is. This is unfortunate. Model selection must be based not on sophistication or complexity but on its performance in obtaining a good fit to the sample data. Thus, the modeling strategy must consist of:

(1) Getting the state of the art of the domain knowledge so as to know a priori which variables could be related to which variables and how (or get the broad general structure of the model).

(2) Doing exploratory data analysis in order to refine the general model to suit the problem at hand (to refer to the population to which the sample belongs).

(3) Specifying alternate models and estimating (calibrating) them.

(4) Choosing one of the models as the best model based on some credible statistical criteria.

(5) Examining if the chosen model is acceptable.

(6) If not looking for new data that could have been omitted or doing further exploration of data or both to come up with better models, and repeating the process all over again.

The econometric modeling strategy above is described schematically in Figure 1.11.

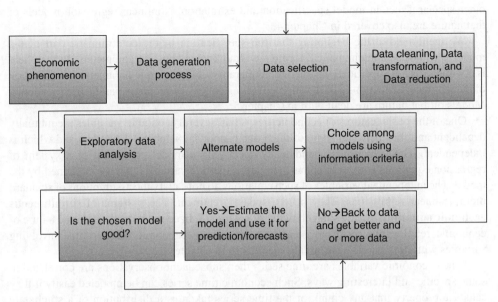

Figure 1.11   Econometric modeling process.

1.4.2   Plan of the book

After the exploratory data analysis we will arrive at one or more alternate specifications of the statistical model to represent the data generation process of the observations we have made. Each of those specifications will have, in general, a dependent variable and several dependent variables and an error in equations that has a probability distribution. The deterministic part is the signal and the equation error is the noise.

Strictly speaking the first part, signal, needs to be a computational procedure that will generate a unique value of the dependent variable, given the values assumed by each, of let us say, m independent variables. If that computational procedure is in terms of a mathematical function with possibly a few unknown constant parameters represented by a p-dimensional vector θ we can write the model as:

$$y_i = f(x_i; \theta) + \varepsilon_i, \quad i = 1, 2, \ldots, n \tag{1.2}$$

If the function f is linear and y is a continuous variable and the error term has a distribution with mean zero and constant variance we get ordinary **linear multiple regression models** with homoscedasticity. Such models are discussed in Chapter 2. Chapter 2 has an extensive discussion on statistical criteria for the selection of variables in linear multiple regressions. It also deals with problems associated with correlated independent variables (multicollinearity and how to cope with that problem).

If the function f of equation (1.2) is linear and the error term has a mean zero but non-constant variance then we get linear multiple regression models with heteroscedasticity. These models are treated in Chapter 3. If the variables are not continuous but categorical then certain problems arise both in interpreting the regressions and in estimating them. These issues engage us in Chapter 4. If the function $f(x; \theta)$ is nonlinear in parameters we get some other special issues in model specification and estimation. Nonlinear regression models of that nature are also covered in Chapter 4.

We mentioned at the beginning that the specification of the deterministic part of the model need not be a mathematical formula with unknown constant parameters. In fact there is a whole class of specifications that are nonparametric or a simple parametric combination of nonparametric functions (like a weighted average of two or more nonparametric functions). Models of that nature are dealt with in Chapter 5.

One of the basic features of econometrics is that several economic variables are mutually dependent and thus between some of them one cannot say which is dependent and which is independent. That situation is handled by specifying a model consisting of a system of regression equations with as many as there are economic variables that are explained by the model. The independent variables of such equations do not satisfy the assumptions of standard multiple linear regressions. They need a special treatment. The **systems of simultaneous economic equations** are the subject matter of Chapter 6. In economics the dynamic nature of economic relationships is usually captured by having economic relationships involving variables with time lags. These are also dealt with in Chapter 6.

When economic variables are time series then subsequent observations are correlated in some specific and interesting ways. Such economic time series can be modeled easily if they satisfy a property that any chunk of the time series taken as a distribution of a **stochastic process** has the same distribution as that of any other chunk. Such time series are called **stationary time series**. Economic modeling of a single stationary economic time series is the topic covered in Chapter 7. Reading Chapter 7 after reading Chapter 6 one might ask what if we have a system of simultaneous equations but with time series data with lags? This topic is covered in Chapter 8 under multiple time series analysis. Even when economic time series are not stationary it is possible that some transformations of them are stationary. If we know what those transformations are we can model the transformed time series as stationary time series, and retransform them to get the original series. This way of analysis of **non-stationary time series** is also covered in Chapter 8.

Chapter 9 covers some very important multivariate analysis tools such as Analysis of Variance of single and multifactor types. It also covers path analysis, factor analysis, principal component analysis, partial least squares. It has an interesting application of **structural equation modeling** using **path analysis** applied to analysis of the consumer satisfaction index. It also presents panel data analysis.

An inquisitive reader would perhaps look at all the statistical theories and methods ranging from classical inference, Bayesian inference, parametric regression, non-parametric regression, and quantile regression and wonder how they all fit together. To quench the thirst of such a reader the last chapter, Chapter 10, offers a unified treatment that is based primarily on the intuitive notion that statistical modeling covered in the book is based on harnessing the information contained in various types of information in the underlying structure of the data generating process.

Now here is a final word for the student reader. If you want to learn the theories and methods of econometrics, you can read this book, because this book offers statistical theories and methods in the form of a good collection of theorems. If you want to go deeper into the theories of statistics and mathematics in econometrics, you can read the Electronic References in this book. If you only want to use the methods of econometrics to deal with economic data, fit a suitable model to the data and make some predictions or forecasting, you can read the data examples in this book and use the computation software DASC, and do not hesitate to skip the mathematical derivations. But such a reader is reminded that the scientific credibility of the results requires that the application of statistical tools be appropriate from the theoretical and methodological perspective. Then you may consult a statistician for advice.

Electronic references for Chapter 1

References

Andersen, F.M., Celov D., Grinderslev D. & Kazlauskas A. (2005) A macro-econometric model of Lithuania LITMOD. *Economic Modeling* **22**, 707–19.

Anderson M.J. & Whitcomb P.J. (2000) *DOE Simplified: Practical Tools for Effective Experimentation*, Productivity Incorporated, Portland, Oregon, USA.

Beenstock M. (1995) An econometric model of the oil importing developing countries. *Economic Modeling* **12**, 3–14.

Bozdogan H. (1990) On the information-based method of covariance complexity and its applications to the evaluation of multivariate linear models. *Communications in Statistics Theory and Methods* **19**, 221–78.

Breeden J.L. (2007) Modeling data with multiple time dimensions. *Computational Statistics & Data Analysis* **51**, 4761–85.

Brownlees C.T. & Gallo G.M. (2006) Financial econometric analysis at ultra-high frequency: Data handling concerns. *Computational Statistics & Data Analysis* **51**, 2232–45.

Busemeyer J.R., Forsyth B. & Nozawa G. (1988) Comparisons of elimination by aspects and suppression of aspects choice models based on choice response time. *Journal of Mathematical Psychology* **32**, 341–49.

Chong J. (2005) The forecasting abilities of implied and econometric variance–covariance models across financial measures. *Journal of Economics and Business* **57**, 463–90.

Costantini M. & Destefanis S. (2009) Cointegration analysis for cross-sectionally dependent panels: The case of regional production functions. *Economic Modeling* **26**, 320–7.

D'Enza A.I., Palumbo F. & Greenacre M. (2008) Exploratory data analysis leading towards the most interesting simple association rules. *Computational Statistics & Data Analysis* **52**, 3269–81.

Dolk D.R. & Kridel D.J. (1991) An active modeling system for econometric analysis. *Decision Support Systems* **7**, 315–28.

Farebrother R.W. (1996) The role of chaotic processes in econometric models. *Journal of Statistical Planning and Inference* **49**, 163–76.

Frisch R. (1929) Correlation and scatter in statistical variables. *Nordic Statistical Journal* **1**, 36–108. Reproduced in Bjerkholt, Olav (1995) (Editor) *Foundations of Modern Econometrics: The Selected Essays of Ragnar Frisch* (in 2 Vols), Aldershot: Edward Elgar.

Han, J., & Kamber M. (2006), *Data Mining: Concepts and Techniques*, Elsevier, Second Edition.

Hendry D.F. (2001) Achievements and challenges in econometric methodology. *Journal of Econometrics* **100**, 7–10.

Kang I.-B. (2003) Multi-period forecasting using different models for different horizons: an application to U.S. economic time series data. *International Journal of Forecasting* **19**, 387–400.

Kumar T. Krishna, Sushanta K. Mallick & Jayarama H. (2009) Estimating consumption deprivation in India using survey data: A state-level rural-urban analysis before and during reform period, *Journal of Development Studies* **45**(4), 441–70.

Li Q. (1999) Consistent model specification tests for time series econometric models. *Journal of Econometrics* **92**, 101–47.

Li T. (2009) Simulation based selection of competing structural econometric models. *Journal of Econometrics* **148**, 114–23.

Lin K.-P. & Farley A.M. (1995) Causal reasoning in econometric models. *Decision Support Systems* **15**, 167–77.

Pagan A. (1997) Whatever happened to optimal control of econometric models. *Control Engineering Practice* **5**, 527–33.

Page, S.E. (1999) Computational models from A to Z. *Complexity* 5(1), 35–41.

Raghavarao, D., Wiley J.B., and Chitturi P. (2011) *Choice Based Conjoint Analysis: Models and Designs*, CRC Books, A Chapman and Hall Book, Boca Raton, London, and New York.

Ridder G. & Moffitt R. (2007) The econometrics of data combination. *Handbook of Econometrics* **6**, 5469–547.

Patterson K.D. (2003) Exploiting information in vintages of time-series data. *International Journal of Forecasting* **19**, 177–97.

Pesaran M.H. & Smith R.P. (1985) Evaluation of macroeconometric models. *Economic Modeling* **2**, 125–34.

Pesaran, M.H. & Smith R. (1995) The role of theory in econometrics. *Journal of Econometrics* **67**, 61–79.

Posse C. (1995) Projection pursuit exploratory data analysis. *Computational Statistics & Data Analysis* **20**, 669–87.

Sagan C. (1996) *Demon Haunted World: Science as a Candle in the Dark*. Ballantine, a Division of Random House, New York.

Sandiford P.J. and Seymour D. (2007) A discussion of qualitative data analysis in hospitality research with examples from an ethnography of English public houses. *International Journal of Hospitality Management* **26**, 724–42.

Singhal P. (2005) Inefficiencies in Indian capital markets: can overnight gain be used as a predictor of day gain? *IIMB Management Review* **17**, 23–30.

Thompson S.K. (2002) *Sampling*. John Wiley and Sons Inc, New York.

von Natzmer W. (1985) Econometric policy evaluation and expectations. *Economic Modeling* **2**, 52–8.

Wallbäcks L. (2007) Multivariate data analysis of multivariate populations. *Chemometrics and Intelligent Laboratory Systems* **86**, 10–16.

Wojciech W.C. (1991) Large econometric models of an East European economy: A critique of the methodology. *Economic Modeling* **8**, 45–62.

Zellner A. (1996) Past, present and future of econometrics. *Journal of Statistical Planning and Inference* **49**, 3–8.

Zheng X. (2008) Testing for discrete choice models. *Economics Letters* **98**, 176–84.

2

Independent variables in linear regression models

In this chapter we will discuss some topics on independent variables in linear regression models. These include the selection of independent variables and stepwise regression, multiple data transformations and polynomial regression, column multicollinearity in design matrix and ridge regression, and recombination of independent variables and principal component regression. These topics are very useful.

More advanced topics on this aspect, such as hierarchical regression, orthogonal polynomial regression, the general solution of least squares, latent root regression, uniform compression estimation of regression parameters, and geometric interpretations of biased estimation, occupy a lot of space. We placed them in the Electronic References for Chapter 2.

As a prerequisite to this discussion we first present some basic principles of univariate and multivariate linear regression.

2.1 Brief review of linear regression

2.1.1 Brief review of univariate linear regression

We mentioned in the previous chapter that an introductory course in probability and statistics is a prerequisite for this book. Given the importance of the linear model in this book this section provides a brief review of the basic statistical results associated with a simple univariate linear regression. A reader familiar with univariate linear regression may go directly to Section 2.1.2.

The general form of **univariate linear regression model** is

$$Y_i = \beta_0 + \beta_1 X_i + \varepsilon_i, \quad i = 1, \ldots, n \tag{2.1}$$

Developing Econometrics, First Edition. Hengqing Tong, T. Krishna Kumar and Yangxin Huang.
© 2011 John Wiley & Sons, Ltd. Published 2011 by John Wiley & Sons, Ltd.

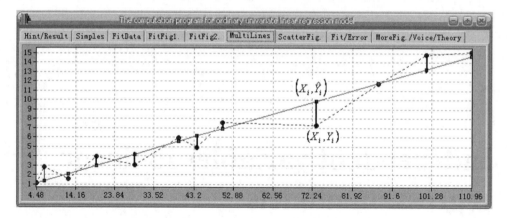

Figure 2.1   Scatter points of univariate linear regression.

where Y_i takes the numerical value of the **response variable** Y (called **dependent variable**) and X_i takes the numerical value of **prediction variable** X (called **independent variable**). Therefore the univariate linear regression model can also be written in a vector representation as

$$Y = \beta_0 + \beta_1 X + \varepsilon \tag{2.2}$$

where β_0, β_1 and the **random disturbance term** ε are unknown. The random variable, ε changes with every observation. β_0 and β_1 are fixed values (parameters). Let $\hat{\beta}_0, \hat{\beta}_1$ be the estimators of β_0, β_1.

For a pair of observed values (X_i, Y_i), there is a pair of values $(X_i, \hat{Y}_i)$ that lies on the regression line $\hat{Y} = \hat{\beta}_0 + \hat{\beta}_1 X$. We would like the error sum of squares to be minimum:

$$\sum_{i=1}^{n} (Y_i - \beta_0 - \beta_1 X_i)^2 \rightarrow \min \tag{2.3}$$

This is the **least squares method**, and its visual image is shown in Figure 2.1.

Now we consider the estimation of parameters β_0, β_1. Let

$$S(\beta_0, \beta_1) = \sum_{i=1}^{n} (Y_i - \beta_0 - \beta_1 X_i)^2$$

In order to obtain the minimum value of the function, we calculate the partial derivatives and equate them to zero, as those are the necessary conditions for a minimum:

$$\begin{cases} \dfrac{\partial S}{\partial \beta_0} = -2 \sum_{i=1}^{n} (Y_i - \beta_0 - \beta_1 X_i) = 0 \\ \dfrac{\partial S}{\partial \beta_1} = -2 \sum_{i=1}^{n} X_i (Y_i - \beta_0 - \beta_1 X_i) = 0 \end{cases}$$

Rearranging the above equations, we can obtain **normal equations** as:

$$\begin{cases} n\beta_0 + \beta_1 \sum_{i=1}^{n} X_i = \sum_{i=1}^{n} Y_i \\ \beta_0 \sum_{i=1}^{n} X_i + \beta_1 \sum_{i=1}^{n} X_i^2 = \sum_{i=1}^{n} X_i Y_i \end{cases}$$

Solving the normal equations we obtain the **least squares estimators (LSE)** as follows:

$$\hat{\beta}_1 = \frac{\sum_{i=1}^{n} X_i Y_i - \frac{1}{n}\left(\sum_{i=1}^{n} X_i\right)\left(\sum_{i=1}^{n} Y_i\right)}{\sum_{i=1}^{n} X_i^2 - \frac{1}{n}\left(\sum_{i=1}^{n} X_i\right)^2} = \frac{\sum_{i=1}^{n}(X_i - \bar{X})(Y_i - \bar{Y})}{\sum_{i=1}^{n}(X_i - \bar{X})^2}$$

$$\hat{\beta}_0 = \bar{Y} - \hat{\beta}_1 \bar{X}$$

where $\bar{X} = \frac{1}{n}\sum_{i=1}^{n} X_i, \bar{Y} = \frac{1}{n}\sum_{i=1}^{n} Y_i$, are called the **sample averages**. Let

$$S_{XX} = \sum_{i=1}^{n}(X_i - \bar{X})^2 = \sum_{i=1}^{n}(X_i - \bar{X})X_i = \sum_{i=1}^{n} X_i^2 - \frac{1}{n}\left(\sum_{i=1}^{n} X_i\right)^2 = \sum_{i=1}^{n} X_i^2 - n\bar{X}^2$$

$$S_{XY} = \sum_{i=1}^{n}(X_i - \bar{X})(Y_i - \bar{Y}) = \sum_{i=1}^{n}(X_i - \bar{X})Y_i = \sum_{i=1}^{n} X_i(Y_i - \bar{Y})$$

$$= \sum_{i=1}^{n} X_i Y_i - \frac{1}{n}\left(\sum_{i=1}^{n} X_i\right)\left(\sum_{i=1}^{n} Y_i\right) = \sum_{i=1}^{n} X_i Y_i - n\bar{X}\bar{Y}$$

Then the least squares estimator can be simply written as

$$\hat{\beta}_1 = \frac{S_{XY}}{S_{XX}}, \quad \hat{\beta}_0 = \bar{Y} - \hat{\beta}_1 \bar{X} \tag{2.4}$$

To undertake various tests of hypotheses on the regression parameters, we need to make some assumptions first. Mainly we assume that random disturbance term ε follows normal distribution with $E(\varepsilon_i) = 0$, $Var(\varepsilon_i) = \sigma^2$. We also assume that the observed values of random variable Y are independent, that is, when $i \neq j$, ε_i is independent of ε_j. When

$$\varepsilon_i \sim N(0, \sigma^2), \quad i = 1, \ldots, n$$

then

$$Y_i \sim N(\beta_0 + \beta_1 X_i, \sigma^2), \quad i = 1, \ldots, n$$

as

$$\hat{\beta}_1 = \frac{\sum_{i=1}^{n}(X_i - \bar{X})(Y_i - \bar{Y})}{\sum_{i=1}^{n}(X_i - \bar{X})^2} = \sum_{i=1}^{n} \frac{X_i - \bar{X}}{\sum_{i=1}^{n}(X_i - \bar{X})^2} Y_i = \sum_{i=1}^{n} C_i Y_i$$

We know that $\hat{\beta}_1$ is the linear combination of independent normal variables and thus follows normal distribution. For $\sum_{i=1}^{n} C_i X_i = \sum_{i=1}^{n} C_i (X_i - \bar{X}) = 1$, $\sum_{i=1}^{n} C_i = 0$,

$$E(\hat{\beta}_1) = \sum_{i=1}^{n} C_i E(Y_i) = \sum_{i=1}^{n} C_i(\beta_0 + \beta_1 X_i) = \beta_0 \sum_{i=1}^{n} C_i + \beta_1 \sum_{i=1}^{n} C_i X_i = \beta_1$$

$$D(\hat{\beta}_1) = \sum_{i=1}^{n} C_i^2 D(Y_i) = \sum_{i=1}^{n} C_i^2 \sigma^2 = \frac{\sigma^2}{\sum_{i=1}^{n}(X_i - \bar{X})^2}$$

Then

$$\hat{\beta}_1 \sim N\left(\beta_1, \frac{\sigma^2}{S_{XX}}\right) \tag{2.5}$$

under the assumption $\varepsilon_i \sim N(0, \sigma^2)$, $\hat{\beta}_1$ is an **unbiased estimator** of the true value of parameter β_1.

We still have to replace error variance σ^2 by an estimate obtained from the sample data. Let $\hat{Y}_i$ be regression value corresponding to X_i, then

$$\hat{Y}_i = \hat{\beta}_0 + \hat{\beta}_1 X_i = \bar{Y} + \hat{\beta}_1(X_i - \bar{X})$$

Residual deviation between sample point and corresponding regression value is $Y_i - \hat{Y}_i$ (that is the vertical straight segment on the scatter diagram). Considering the sum of squared residuals S_{ES}:

$$S_{ES} = \sum_{i=1}^{n}(Y_i - \hat{Y}_i)^2$$

it can be rearranged as follows:

$$S_{ES} = \sum_{i=1}^{n}[Y_i - \bar{Y} - \hat{\beta}_1(X_i - \bar{X})]^2$$

$$= \sum_{i=1}^{n}(Y_i - \bar{Y})^2 - 2\hat{\beta}_1 \sum_{i=1}^{n}(X_i - \bar{X})(Y_i - \bar{Y}) + \hat{\beta}_1^2 \sum_{i=1}^{n}(X_i - \bar{X})^2$$

$$= \sum_{i=1}^{n}(Y_i - \bar{Y})^2 - \hat{\beta}_1^2 \sum_{i=1}^{n}(X_i - \bar{X})^2$$

$$E\left[\sum_{i=1}^{n}(Y_i - \bar{Y})^2\right] = \sum_{i=1}^{n} E(Y_i^2) - nE(\bar{Y}^2) = \sum_{i=1}^{n}\left\{D(Y_i) + [E(Y_i)]^2\right\} - n\left\{D(\bar{Y}) + [E(\bar{Y})]^2\right\}$$

$$= \sum_{i=1}^{n}\left(\sigma^2 + (\beta_0 + \beta_1 X_i)^2\right) - n\left[\frac{\sigma^2}{n} + (\beta_0 + \beta_1 \bar{X})^2\right]$$

$$= (n-1)\sigma^2 + \beta_1^2\left(\sum_{i=1}^{n} X_i^2 - n\bar{X}^2\right) = (n-1)\sigma^2 + \beta_1^2 \sum_{i=1}^{n}(X_i - \bar{X})^2$$

$$E\left[\hat{\beta}_1^2 \sum_{i=1}^{n}(X_i - \bar{X})^2\right] = E(\hat{\beta}_1^2)\sum_{i=1}^{n}(X_i - \bar{X})^2 = \left\{D(\hat{\beta}_1) + [E(\hat{\beta}_1)]^2\right\}\sum_{i=1}^{n}(X_i - \bar{X})^2$$

$$= \left(\frac{\sigma^2}{\displaystyle\sum_{i=1}^{n}(X_i - \bar{X})^2} + \beta_1^2\right)\sum_{i=1}^{n}(X_i - \bar{X})^2 = \sigma^2 + \beta_1^2 \sum_{i=1}^{n}(X_i - \bar{X})^2$$

Combining the above two equations, we get:

$$E(S_{ES}) = E\left[\sum_{i=1}^{n}(Y_i - \bar{Y})^2 - \hat{\beta}_1^2 \sum_{i=1}^{n}(X_i - \bar{X})^2\right] = (n-1)\sigma^2 - \sigma^2 = (n-2)\sigma^2$$

It shows that the square sum of residual S_{ES} divided by $(n-2)$ is an unbiased estimator of σ^2, expressed as

$$\hat{\sigma}^2 = \frac{1}{n-2}S_{ES} = \frac{1}{n-2}\sum_{i=1}^{n}(Y_i - \hat{Y}_i)^2 \tag{2.6}$$

$\hat{\sigma} = \sqrt{\hat{\sigma}^2}$ is called **standard error of the estimate**.

Now we consider **significance tests** (t test, F test and r test) of the linear regression model:

$$Y = \beta_0 + \beta_1 X + \varepsilon, \quad \varepsilon \sim N(0, \sigma^2 I_n)$$

For testing hypothesis on the regression coefficient β_1, the null hypothesis is

$$H_0 : \beta_1 = 0$$

against $\beta_1 \neq 0$ (or $\beta_1 > 0$ or $\beta_1 < 0$). If H_0 is rejected, the regression coefficient β_1 is not insignificant, which means Y and X are in linear relation: $Y = \beta_0 + \beta_1 X + \varepsilon$. If H_0 is accepted, then we may conclude that the regression effect is not significant and the linear model does not hold. We can use the result above to deduce test statistics.

From (2.6) we know that

$$\frac{\hat{\beta}_1 - \beta_1}{\sqrt{\sigma^2/S_{XX}}} \sim N(0,1) \tag{2.7}$$

Because $\hat{\beta}_0, \hat{\beta}_1$ are the solutions of normal equations, they meet

$$\sum_{i=1}^{n}(Y_i - \hat{Y}_i) = 0, \quad \sum_{i=1}^{n}(Y_i - \hat{Y}_i)X_i = 0$$

This means that there are two independent linear restrictions among the n variables $(Y_1 - \hat{Y}_1), \ldots, (Y_n - \hat{Y}_n)$. The **degrees of freedom**, the number of independent pieces of information on σ contained in $\hat{\sigma}$, are $n-2$, so

$$\frac{(n-2)\hat{\sigma}^2}{\sigma^2} = \frac{S_{ES}}{\sigma^2} \sim \chi^2(n-2) \tag{2.8}$$

It can also be verified that $\hat{\sigma}^2$ is independent of $\hat{\beta}_1$ and $\hat{Y}_i$. So

$$\frac{\hat{\beta}_1 - \beta_1}{\sqrt{\sigma^2/S_{XX}}} \Big/ \sqrt{\frac{\hat{\sigma}^2}{\sigma^2}} \sim t(n-2)$$

That is

$$\frac{\hat{\beta}_1 - \beta_1}{\hat{\sigma}} \sqrt{S_{XX}} \sim t(n-2)$$

If the null hypothesis holds, then

$$t = \frac{\hat{\beta}_1}{\hat{\sigma}} \sqrt{S_{XX}} = \frac{S_{XY}\sqrt{n-2}}{\sqrt{S_{XX}S_{RS}}} \sim t(n-2) \tag{2.9}$$

With the sample data we can calculate $\hat{\beta}_1, \hat{\sigma}, S_{XX}$. For the given **significance level** α, we can get the **critical value** $t_{\alpha/2}(n-2)$ from the table of probability distribution of the t distribution with the degree of freedom $n-2$. If

$$\frac{|\hat{\beta}_1|}{\hat{\sigma}} \sqrt{S_{XX}} > t_{\alpha/2}(n-2)$$

$H_0 : \beta_1 = 0$ is rejected against the alternative $\beta_1 \neq 0$.
Next we discuss the F test of analysis of variance. We can write:

$$Y_i - \hat{Y} = (Y_i - \hat{Y}_i) + (\hat{Y}_i - \bar{Y})$$

Taking the sum of squares on both sides we note that the cross-product term on the right

$$2\sum_{i=1}^{n}(Y_i - \hat{Y}_i)(\hat{Y}_i - \bar{Y}) = 2\sum_{i=1}^{n}[Y_i - \bar{Y} - \hat{\beta}_1(X_i - \bar{X})][\hat{\beta}_1(X_i - \bar{X})]$$
$$= 2\hat{\beta}_1[S_{XY} - \hat{\beta}_1 S_{XX}] = 0$$

From these results we obtain **sum of squares decomposition** as

$$\sum_{i=1}^{n}(Y_i - \bar{Y})^2 = \sum_{i=1}^{n}(Y_i - \hat{Y}_i)^2 + \sum_{i=1}^{n}(\hat{Y}_i - \bar{Y})^2$$

That is, corrected total sum of squares = residual sum of squares + regression sum of squares. It can be written as

$$S_{TS} = S_{ES} + S_{RS} \tag{2.10}$$

Consider constraints on **degrees of freedom** of each sum of squares

$$\sum_{i=1}^{n}(Y_i - \bar{Y}) = 0$$

So the degree of freedom of corrected sum of squares is $n-1$. We know from (2.8) that the degree of freedom of residual sum of squares is $n-2$. We also note that $\hat{Y}_i - \bar{Y} = \hat{\beta}_1(X_i - \bar{X})$, so

$$\sum_{i=1}^{n}(\hat{Y}_i - \bar{Y})^2 = \sum_{i=1}^{n}\hat{\beta}_1^2(X_i - \bar{X})^2 = \hat{\beta}_1^2 S_{XX} = \hat{\beta}_1 S_{XY} \tag{2.11}$$

We know the degree of freedom of regression sum of squares is 1. So the degree of freedom decomposition of (2.10) can be written as $n-1 = n-2+1$. If the null hypothesis $H_0: \beta_1 = 0$ holds, then

$$\frac{1}{\sigma^2}\sum_{i=1}^{n}(Y_i - \bar{Y})^2 \sim \chi^2(n-1)$$

$$\frac{1}{\sigma^2}\sum_{i=1}^{n}(Y_i - \hat{Y}_i)^2 \sim \chi^2(n-2)$$

$$\frac{1}{\sigma^2}\sum_{i=1}^{n}(\hat{Y}_i - \bar{Y}) \sim \chi^2(1)$$

Thus we can construct the statistic:

$$F = \frac{\sum_{i=1}^{n}(\hat{Y}_i - \bar{Y})^2}{\sum_{i=1}^{n}(Y_i - \hat{Y}_i)^2 / (n-2)} = \frac{\hat{\beta}_1^2 S_{XX}}{\hat{\sigma}^2} \sim F_\alpha(1, n-2)$$

For a given **confidence level** $(1-\alpha)$ or for a given level of significance of the test α, we look at the table of probabilities associated with an F distribution with the numerator degree of freedom of 1, and denominator degrees of freedom of $n-2$ to obtain the critical value $F_\alpha(1, n-2)$. We reject the null hypothesis and conclude that there is a linear relation between X and Y when

$$F > F_\alpha(1, n-2)$$

If both X and Y can be taken as random variables, we can define their **correlation coefficient**:

$$\rho_{XY} = \frac{Cov(X,Y)}{[D(X)D(Y)]^{1/2}}$$

here numerator is **covariance** $Cov(X, Y) = E\{[X - E(X)][Y - E(Y)]\}$, and denominator is **Variance** $D(X) = E[X - E(X)]^2$ and $D(Y) = E[Y - E(Y)]^2$. When X and Y have samples $X_1, \ldots, X_n$ and $Y_1, \ldots, Y_n$, we can take **sample correlation coefficient** r_{XY} as the estimator of **parent correlation coefficient**:

$$r_{XY} = \frac{\sum_{i=1}^{n}\left[(X_i - \bar{X})(Y_i - \bar{Y})\right]}{\left[\sum_{i=1}^{n}(X_i - \bar{X})^2\right]^{1/2}\left[\sum_{i=1}^{n}(Y_i - \bar{Y})^2\right]^{1/2}} = \frac{S_{XY}}{\sqrt{S_{XX}S_{YY}}} \tag{2.12}$$

From Cauchy-Schwarz inequality we can prove that $|\rho_{XY}| \leq 1$, $|r_{XY}| \leq 1$, and the necessary and sufficient condition for $|\rho_{XY}| = 1$ is that X and Y are linearly dependent with probability 1. So we can take r_{XY} as a measure of existence of linear regression relation between Y and X, then use r_{XY} as a test statistic for testing the hypothesis of existence of linear regression relation.

On the hypothesis that X and Y follow two-dimensional normal distribution, Fisher (1915) found the exact finite sample distribution of sample correlation coefficient, which only depended on the parent correlation coefficient ρ and the sample size n but did not depend on the mean and variance parameters of normal parent. In particular, under the hypothesis that $\rho = 0$, when $n \geq 3$, the probability density of ρ_{XY} obeys the **Fisher distribution**:

$$
f_\rho(x) = \begin{cases} \dfrac{1}{\sqrt{\pi}} \dfrac{\Gamma\left(\dfrac{\upsilon+1}{2}\right)}{\Gamma\left(\dfrac{\upsilon}{2}\right)} (1-x^2)^{\frac{\upsilon-2}{2}} & |x| < 1 \\[2mm] 0 & |x| \geq 1 \end{cases}
$$

here $\upsilon = n - 2$ is the degrees of freedom, so critical value r_α is related to n. Take critical value $r_\alpha(n)$ on the given significance level to make

$$
P(|r_{XY}| \geq r_\alpha(n)) = 1 - \int_{-r_\alpha}^{r_\alpha} f_r(x)dx = \alpha
$$

When

$$
|r_{XY}| \geq r_\alpha(n)
$$

the null hypothesis $\rho = 0$ is rejected against the alternative $\rho \neq 0$. Then we conclude that X is linearly related to Y.

It needs to be noted that rejection of null hypothesis does not indicate that X and Y have a significant correlation. In fact, when $\alpha = 0.05$, $n = 50$, r_α is only 0.273. It is also important to note that if this test does not reject the null hypothesis $\rho = 0$ one cannot conclude that there is no relation between X and Y. The test only reveals that there is no linear relation between X and Y in this case. One can conceive of a perfect quadratic relation between Y and X and this test reveals an insignificant r_{XY}.

Comparing (2.4) with (2.12), we get

$$
\hat{\beta}_1 = \left(\frac{S_{YY}}{S_{XX}}\right)^{\frac{1}{2}} r_{XY}
$$

It indicates that $\hat{\beta}_1$ is closely related to r_{XY}. Thus, r_{XY} is a measure of linear correlation between X and Y, while $\hat{\beta}_1$ denotes the change in Y when X changes by one unit. Also from (2.11) we know

$$
\sum_{i=1}^{n} (\hat{Y}_i - \bar{Y})^2 = \hat{\beta}_1 S_{XY} = \frac{S_{XY}^2}{S_{XX}}
$$

So

$$r_{XY}^2 = \frac{S_{XY}^2}{S_{XX}S_{YY}} = \sum_{i=1}^{n}(\hat{Y}_i - \bar{Y})^2 \Big/ \sum_{i=1}^{n}(Y_i - \bar{Y})^2 \triangleq R^2 \tag{2.13}$$

As $\hat{Y}_i = \hat{\beta}_0 + \hat{\beta}_1 X_i$, $\bar{Y} = \hat{\beta}_0 + \hat{\beta}_1 \bar{X}$, we obtain $\hat{Y}_i - \bar{Y} = \hat{\beta}_1 (X_i - \bar{X})$, so

$$R = \left| r_{Y\hat{Y}} \right|$$

Here statistic R (R^2) is introduced. It is called the correlation coefficient, also known as the **total correlation coefficient**, which can be extended to the multivariate case.

Now we proceed to the topics of predicting Y given X and giving the confidence intervals for such predictions.

Using the estimated regression equation we can predict dependent variable Y_0 when the observed value of independent variable X_0 is given.

$$\hat{Y}_0 = \hat{\beta}_0 + \hat{\beta}_1 X_0$$

Under the assumption that errors are normally distributed from (2.5), we get

$$\hat{Y}_0 \sim N\left(\beta_0 + \beta_1 X_0, \sigma^2 \left[\frac{1}{n} + \frac{(X_0 - \bar{X})^2}{S_{XX}}\right]\right)$$

$$E(\hat{Y}_0) = \beta_0 + \beta_1 X_0 = Y_0, \text{ or } E(\hat{Y}_0 - Y_0) = 0$$

So $\hat{Y}_0$ is an unbiased estimator of Y_0.

This predicted value of Y_0 is called **point estimator** in statistics, for what it gives is a fixed value (a point). Any such point estimator must have, associated with it, a degree of credibility. The degree of credibility may be represented by giving a small range of values or an interval which includes the point estimator, such that the true value is expected to lie in that interval with a high probability. This is called the **interval estimator**.

As Y_0 is independent of each Y_i, we can obtain

$$D(\hat{Y}_0 - Y_0) = D(\hat{Y}_0) + D(Y_0) = \sigma^2 \left[\frac{1}{n} + \frac{(X_0 - \bar{X})^2}{S_{XX}}\right] + \sigma^2$$

So under the assumption that the errors have a normal distribution we must have

$$\frac{\hat{Y}_0 - Y_0}{\sqrt{D(\hat{Y}_0 - Y_0)}} \sim N(0,1)$$

We also know that $\dfrac{(n-2)\hat{\sigma}^2}{\sigma^2} \sim \chi^2(n-2)$, and it is independent of the statistic $\hat{Y}_0$. Hence the following statistic has a t-distribution with $n-2$ degrees of freedom:

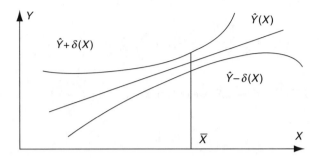

Figure 2.2   Confidence interval of univariate linear regression.

$$\frac{Y_0 - \hat{Y}_0}{\hat{\sigma}\sqrt{1 + \dfrac{1}{n} + \dfrac{(X_0 - \overline{X})^2}{S_{XX}}}} \sim t(n-2)$$

From this distribution we can say that under the confidence level of $1 - \alpha$, the confidence interval of Y_0 is

$$\left[\hat{Y}_0 \pm t_{\alpha/2}(n-2) \cdot \hat{\sigma} \cdot \sqrt{1 + \frac{1}{n} + \frac{(X_0 - \overline{X})^2}{S_{XX}}}\right] = (\hat{Y}_0 \pm \delta(X_0))$$

When the sample is given, we can determine $\hat{\sigma}$, $\overline{X}$, S_{XX} and $\hat{Y}_0$, the latter being related to X_0. When $X_0 = \overline{X}$, the confidence interval is $\hat{Y}_0 \pm t_{\alpha/2}(n-2) \cdot \hat{\sigma} \cdot \sqrt{1 + \frac{1}{n}}$, and it is at its narrowest point. With increasing deviation of X_0 from $\overline{X}$, the confidence interval will be wider as shown in Figure 2.2.

Further discussion on simple univariate linear regression, such as **inverse interval prediction**, **repeated observations** and **fitting deficiency**, linear fitting after data transformation, etc. can be found in the Electronic References for Chapter 2.

2.1.2   Brief review of multivariate linear regression

The **multiple linear regression model** deals with a linear relationship between dependent variable Y and several independent variables $X_1, X_2, \ldots, X_m$,

$$Y = \beta_0 + \beta_1 X_1 + \beta_2 X_2 + \cdots + \beta_m X_m + \varepsilon$$

where $\beta_0, \beta_1, \ldots, \beta_m$ are unknown parameters, $X_1, X_2, \ldots, X_m$ are m general variables that can be measured accurately and given (non-stochastic), and ε is random error. As a rule, we assume that:

$$E(\varepsilon) = 0, \quad Var(\varepsilon) = \sigma^2$$

In many situations such as for tests of significance or Bayesian analysis, etc., we will even assume:

$$\varepsilon \sim N(0, \sigma^2)$$

Let us assume that we have n observations and obtained n groups of observed data: $(Y_i, X_{i1}, X_{i2}, \ldots, X_{im})$, $i = 1, \ldots, n$. Generally $n > m$, and then the regression relationship can be written as follows:

$$\begin{cases} Y_1 = \beta_0 + \beta_1 X_{11} + \beta_2 X_{12} + \cdots + \beta_m X_{1m} + \varepsilon_1 \\ Y_2 = \beta_0 + \beta_1 X_{21} + \beta_2 X_{22} + \cdots + \beta_m X_{2m} + \varepsilon_2 \\ \cdots \\ Y_n = \beta_0 + \beta_1 X_{n1} + \beta_2 X_{n2} + \cdots + \beta_m X_{nm} + \varepsilon_n \end{cases}$$

where $\varepsilon_1, \varepsilon_2, \ldots, \varepsilon_n$ are independently and identically distributed.

We find it convenient to use the vector matrix notation:

$$Y = \begin{pmatrix} Y_1 \\ Y_2 \\ \vdots \\ Y_n \end{pmatrix}, \quad X = \begin{pmatrix} 1 & X_{11} & \cdots & X_{1m} \\ 1 & X_{21} & \cdots & X_{2m} \\ \cdots & \cdots & \ddots & \cdots \\ 1 & X_{n1} & \cdots & X_{nm} \end{pmatrix}, \quad \beta = \begin{pmatrix} \beta_0 \\ \beta_1 \\ \vdots \\ \beta_m \end{pmatrix}, \quad \varepsilon = \begin{pmatrix} \varepsilon_1 \\ \varepsilon_2 \\ \vdots \\ \varepsilon_n \end{pmatrix}$$

Then the multiple linear regression model is

$$Y = X\beta + \varepsilon \tag{2.14}$$

where the matrix X of $n \times (m+1)$ is called **regression design matrix**. Generally we assume that X is of **full column rank**, namely, $rk(X) = m + 1$. For the error, we assume:

$$E(\varepsilon) = 0, \quad Var(\varepsilon) = \sigma^2 I_n \tag{2.15}$$

where I_n is an identity matrix of dimension n. In many cases we can assume:

$$\varepsilon \sim N(0, \sigma^2 I_n) \tag{2.16}$$

The combination of (2.14) and (2.15) or (2.14) and (2.16) is referred to as the standard multiple linear regression model.

We now proceed to compute the least squares estimator (LSE) of the model parameters. The **residual sum of squares** $S(\beta)$ is

$$S(\beta) = (Y - X\beta)'(Y - X\beta) = \sum_{i=1}^{n} (Y_i - \beta_0 - \beta_1 X_{i1} - \cdots - \beta_m X_{im})^2 = \|Y - X\beta\|^2$$

The least squares method requires that $\hat{\beta} = (\hat{\beta}_0, \hat{\beta}_1, \ldots, \hat{\beta}_m)$ is such that

$$S(\hat{\beta}) = \min S(\beta)$$

or write it as:

$$\|Y - X\beta\|^2 \xrightarrow{\beta} \min$$

Since $S(\beta)$ is the twice differentiable function of β, each partial derivative evaluated at the extreme point should be 0. We adopt the **matrix derivative** method to get the partial derivative of $S(\beta)$. The matrix derivative is generally applied to obtain the partial derivative of one vector with respect to another vector, and one of them could be a vector of dimension one or a scalar. For example, the meaning of $\dfrac{\partial S(\beta)}{\partial \beta}$, where $S(\beta)$ is a scalar, is given by

$$\frac{\partial S(\beta)}{\partial \beta} = \left(\frac{\partial S(\beta)}{\partial \beta_0}, \frac{\partial S(\beta)}{\partial \beta_1}, \ldots, \frac{\partial S(\beta)}{\partial \beta_m} \right)$$

When we take the derivative of a vector with respect to another vector the numerator vector is in a column and the denominator vector is in a row (as above).

Some matrix derivative formulas may be obtained after trimming. When A is a constant matrix, we have:

$$\frac{\partial (A\beta)}{\partial \beta} = A$$

$$\frac{\partial (\beta' A' A\beta)}{\partial \beta} = 2A'A\beta$$

Employing the matrix derivative, we may get:

$$\frac{\partial S(\beta)}{\partial \beta} = \frac{\partial}{\partial \beta}[(Y - X\beta)'(Y - X\beta)] = \frac{\partial}{\partial \beta}(Y'Y - 2Y'X\beta + \beta'X'X\beta)$$
$$= \frac{\partial}{\partial \beta}(-2Y'X\beta + \beta'X'X\beta) = -2Y'X + 2X'X\beta$$

To get minimum value of $S(\beta)$ we must have $\dfrac{\partial S(\beta)}{\partial \beta} = 0$, here '0' is zero vector. So we have $-2Y'X + 2X'X\beta = 0$, that is:

$$(X'X)\beta = X'Y \tag{2.17}$$

It is called **normal equation**, and the matrix $X'X$ is called **covariance matrix**. If X is of full column rank, then $X'X$ is a squares matrix, and its inverse matrix exists. Make each side of (2.17) multiplied by the inverse matrix of $X'X$ and get the **least squares solution** of β:

$$\hat{\beta} = (X'X)^{-1} X'Y \tag{2.18}$$

We may examine that (2.18) makes $S(\beta)$ a minimum. Decomposing $S(\beta)$, we get:

$$S(\beta) = (Y - X\beta)'(Y - X\beta) = (Y - X\hat{\beta} + X\hat{\beta} - X\beta)'(Y - X\hat{\beta} + X\hat{\beta} - X\beta)$$
$$= (Y - X\hat{\beta})'(Y - X\hat{\beta}) + (\hat{\beta} - \beta)'X'X(\hat{\beta} - \beta)$$
$$= S(\hat{\beta}) + (\hat{\beta} - \beta)X'X(\hat{\beta} - \beta)$$

This is because the two cross-terms in the middle are 0:

$$(\hat{\beta} - \beta)'X'(Y - X\hat{\beta}) = (\hat{\beta} - \beta)'X'[Y - X(X'X)^{-1}X'Y]$$
$$= (\hat{\beta} - \beta)'[X'Y - X'X(X'X)^{-1}X'Y] = 0$$
$$(Y - X\hat{\beta})'X(\hat{\beta} - \beta) = 0$$

So we find that the second term $(\hat{\beta} - \beta)'X'X(\hat{\beta} - \beta)$ is nonnegative quadratic form. If and only if $\beta = \hat{\beta}$, $S(\beta)$ will have the minimum value 0.

In fact, we can deduce the LSE (2.18) of multiple linear regression model (2.14) more intuitively. We observe the matrix of model $\underset{n\times 1}{Y} = \underset{n\times p}{X} \underset{p\times 1}{\beta} + \underset{n\times 1}{\varepsilon}$, where $p = m + 1$. If we delete the error term ε, we can get contradiction equations $\underset{n\times 1}{Y} \approx \underset{n\times p}{X} \underset{p\times 1}{\beta}$. That is:

$$
\begin{array}{ccc}
\boxed{\begin{array}{c} Y \\[2em] n \end{array}} & \approx & \boxed{\begin{array}{c} X \\[2em] n\times p \end{array}} \boxed{\begin{array}{c} \beta \\ p \end{array}}
\end{array}
$$

We could solve equations with square matrix of coefficients only. So we take a matrix X' to the left multiple of both sides of the equations above. That is:

$$
\boxed{\begin{array}{c} X' \\[1.5em] p\times n \end{array}} \boxed{\begin{array}{c} Y \\[1.5em] n \end{array}} \approx \boxed{\begin{array}{c} X' \\[1.5em] p\times n \end{array}} \boxed{\begin{array}{c} X \\[1.5em] n\times p \end{array}} \boxed{\begin{array}{c} \beta \\ p \end{array}}
$$

Now we get an equation with a square matrix of coefficients

$$
\boxed{\begin{array}{c} X'Y \\[1.5em] p \end{array}} \approx \boxed{\begin{array}{c} X'X \\[1.5em] p\times p \end{array}} \boxed{\begin{array}{c} \beta \\ p \end{array}}
$$

These are normal equations $X'Y = (X' X)\beta$. We can left multiply both sides by inverse matrix $(X'X)^{-1}$ and obtain the solution of LSE $\hat{\beta} = (X'X)^{-1}X'Y$. Of course, this is only an intuitive derivation. We can instead simply say by setting the error equal to zero and premultiplying both sides of the equation by transpose of X we get the normal equations. Then by premultiplying both sides by $(X'X)^{-1}$ we get LSE.

Now we study the basic statistical properties of $\hat{\beta}$. We will do so with the following famous **Gauss Markov Theorem**.

Theorem 2.1 (Gauss Markov): Suppose that the design matrix is of full column rank, and errors are independently and identically distributed with a common variance in linear regression model:

$$Y = X\beta + \varepsilon, \quad E(\varepsilon) = 0, \quad Var(\varepsilon) = \sigma^2 I_n$$

then the least squares solution of the regression coefficient β:

$$\hat{\beta} = (X'X)^{-1}X'Y$$

is the unique linear unbiased minimum variance estimator of β.

Proof. From the expression of $\hat{\beta}$ we know that it is a linear function of Y, and

$$E(\hat{\beta}) = E[(X'X)^{-1}X'Y] = (X'X)^{-1}X'E(Y) = (X'X)^{-1}X'X\beta = \beta$$

establishing that $\hat{\beta}$ is an unbiased estimator of β.

The variance-covariance matrix of $\hat{\beta}$ is

$$\Sigma_{\hat{\beta}} = Cov(\hat{\beta},\hat{\beta}) = (X'X)^{-1}X'Cov(Y,Y)X(X'X)^{-1}$$
$$= (X'X)^{-1}X'\sigma^2 I_n X(X'X)^{-1} = \sigma^2(X'X)^{-1}$$

If $T = C'Y$ is another linear unbiased estimator of β, in accordance with unbiasedness, there should be

$$E(T) = E(C'Y) = C'E(Y) = C'X\beta = \beta$$

which must hold for any β, that implies $C'X = I_{m+1}$, and the variance-covariance matrix of T is

$$\Sigma_T = Cov(T,T) = C'Cov(Y,Y)C = \sigma^2 C'C$$

Note that

$$C'C - (X'X)^{-1} = C'C + (X'X)^{-1} - (X'X)^{-1} - (X'X)^{-1}$$
$$= C'C + (X'X)^{-1} - (X'X)^{-1}X'C - C'X(X'X)^{-1} \quad \text{(Note } C'X = I_{m+1}) \quad (2.19)$$
$$= [C - X(X'X)^{-1}]'[C - X(X'X)^{-1}] \geq 0$$

here matrix ≥ 0 denotes nonnegative definite (semi-positive definite) matrix. Then,

$$C'C \geq (X'X)^{-1}$$

We thus infer that $\Sigma_T - \Sigma_{\hat{\beta}} = (C'C - X'X)\sigma^2 \geq 0$.

As T is any optional linear unbiased estimator, the least squares estimation $\hat{\beta}$ is the minimum variance linear unbiased estimator of β.

Then we demonstrate the uniqueness. We assume that $T = C'Y$ is any minimum variance linear unbiased estimator of β, then we must have $\Sigma_T = \Sigma_{\hat{\beta}}$, namely, $C'C = (X'X)^{-1}$. From (2.19) we may know that $C' = (X'X)^{-1}X'$, namely, $T = C'Y = (X'X)^{-1}X'Y = \hat{\beta}$.

End of Proof

It is necessary to indicate that the minimum variance of LSE of β is when we restrict to the class of linear unbiased estimators. If we consider all unbiased estimators of β, LSE is not necessarily the one with least variance. Moreover, if we consider LSE in the biased estimators of β, and seek the one that has least **mean squared error** (MSE, Variance $+$Bias^2) LSE may not have that property.

Next we look for an estimator of σ^2. Similar to univariate situation, we should relate it to the residual sum of squares. But before we do so we introduce the concept of projection of a vector on a subspace spanned by the columns of a matrix X:

The projection of Y on the subspace spanned by the columns of X is given by $P_X Y$ where matrix P_X is the **projection matrix**, $P_X = X(X'X)^{-1} X'$.

The predicted value of Y can now be recognized as the projection of Y on the subspace spanned by the columns of the design matrix X

$$\hat{Y} = X\hat{\beta} = X(X'X)^{-1} X'Y = P_X Y$$

It is easy to verify that the projection matrix has the following simple characteristics of an idempotent matrix:

$$P_X' = P_X, \; P_X \cdot P_X = P_X$$

and

$$P_X X = X$$

We write for the projection to the space orthogonal to the space spanned by the columns of the matrix X

$$P_{X^\perp} = I_n - X(X'X)^{-1} X'$$

Note that $P_{X^\perp}$ is also an idempotent matrix, i.e.

$$P_{X^\perp}' = P_{X^\perp}, \quad P_{X^\perp} \cdot P_{X^\perp} = P_{X^\perp}$$

and

$$P_{X^\perp} X = (I_n - X(X'X)^{-1} X')X = X - X = 0$$

The residual vector $\hat{\varepsilon} = Y - \hat{Y} = Y - X\hat{\beta}$ is given by

$$\hat{\varepsilon} = Y - \hat{Y} = Y - X\hat{\beta} = Y - X(X'X)^{-1} X'Y = [I_n - X(X'X)^{-1} X']Y = P_{X^\perp} Y$$

The rank of P_X is $m + 1$ when $rk(X) = m + 1$. The rank of $P_{X^\perp}$ is

$$\begin{aligned} rk(P_{X^\perp}) = tr(P_{X^\perp}) &= tr[I_n - X(X'X)^{-1} X'] \\ &= tr(I_n) - tr((X'X)^{-1} X')) = n - tr((X'X)^{-1} X'X) \\ &= n - tr(I_{m+1}) = n - m - 1 \end{aligned}$$

here rk denotes the rank of matrix, and tr denotes the matrix trace. The residual vector $\hat{\varepsilon}$ is uncorrelated with LSE $\hat{\beta}$, because

$$\begin{aligned} Cov(\hat{\varepsilon}, \hat{\beta}) &= Cov(P_{X^\perp} Y, (X'X)^{-1} X'Y) \\ &= P_{X^\perp} Cov(Y, Y)[(X'X)^{-1} X']' = \sigma^2 P_{X^\perp} X(X'X)^{-1} = 0 \end{aligned} \tag{2.20}$$

The mean vector and variance of the residual $\hat{\varepsilon}$ are respectively:

$$E(\hat{\varepsilon}) = E(Y - X\hat{\beta}) = X\beta - X(X'X)^{-1} X'X\beta = 0$$

$$Cov(\hat{\varepsilon}, \hat{\varepsilon}) = P_{X^\perp} Cov(Y,Y) P_{X^\perp} = P_{X^\perp} \sigma^2 I_n P_{X^\perp} = \sigma^2 P_{X^\perp} P_{X^\perp} = \sigma^2 P_{X^\perp}$$

Writing the residual sum of squares as:

$$S_{ES} = \hat{\varepsilon}'\hat{\varepsilon} = Y'P_{X^\perp}Y$$

we get the unbiased estimator of σ^2:

$$\hat{\sigma}^2 = \frac{1}{n-m-1} S_{ES} \tag{2.21}$$

for

$$E(\hat{\sigma}^2) = \frac{1}{n-m-1} E(\hat{\varepsilon}'\hat{\varepsilon}) = \frac{1}{n-m-1} tr[Cov(\hat{\varepsilon}, \hat{\varepsilon})]$$

$$= \frac{1}{n-m-1} tr(\sigma^2 P_{X^\perp}) = \frac{1}{n-m-1} \sigma^2(n-m-1) = \sigma^2$$

We can provide a **geometric interpretation of LSE**. We assume that the column vectors of matrix X are $X_j = (X_{1j}, X_{2j}, \ldots, X_{nj})'$, $j = 0,1,\ldots, m$, where $X_0 = (1,1,\ldots,1)$. $L(X)$ denotes a linear space formed by all linear combinations of $X_j, j = 0,1,\ldots, m$, and $\|Y - X\beta\| \xrightarrow{\beta} \min$ indicates finding a vector $X\beta = \sum_{j=0}^{m} \beta_j X_j$ in $L(X)$ to reach the shortest distance $\|Y - X\beta\|$ between $X\beta$ and Y. From the figure shown below (Figure 2.3) we could see that only if $X\beta$ is the projection of Y on $L(X)$, $\|Y - X\beta\| \xrightarrow{\beta} \min$ can be met.

We may also see that $\hat{\varepsilon}$ and $X\hat{\beta}$ are orthogonal, that is to say the $\hat{\varepsilon}$ is not related to $\hat{\beta}$.

It is necessary to point out that the regression model introduced in this paragraph contains the constant term β_0, thus the design matrix X has $m + 1$ columns, the rank of projection matrix is $n - m - 1$, and the unbiased estimator of σ^2 is $\hat{\sigma}^2 = S_{ES}/(n-m-1)$. If the regression model has no constant term, or when we regard X_1 as the constant term rather than setting it equal to one, the model is still valid. In general if X has p columns, then the rank of projection matrix is $n - p$, $\hat{\sigma}^2 = S_{ES}/(n-p)$, which we will adopt uniformly in the next paragraph. We hope that readers understand the meanings of $m + 1$ and p.

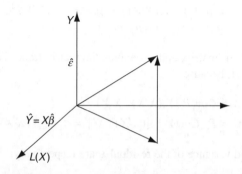

Figure 2.3   Geometric interpretation of LSE.

Now we consider hypothesis testing for the multivariate linear regression model.

In general, for hypothesis testing for multiple linear regression model we make the assumption that the error of the regression model has a Normal distribution with mean zero and a constant variances as in (2.16). All the results of hypothesis testing carry forward with this assumption. While the minimum variance property was established earlier among all linear unbiased estimators, under the additional assumption of normally distributed errors, it follows that the minimum variance property holds for the class of all unbiased estimators, including nonlinear estimators.

We state the following theorem.

Theorem 2.2 We assume there is a linear model:

$$\underset{n\times 1}{Y} = \underset{n\times p}{X}\underset{p\times 1}{\beta} + \underset{n\times 1}{\varepsilon}, \quad \varepsilon \sim N_n(0, \sigma^2 I_n)$$

$rk(X) = p$, the least squares solution of β is $\hat{\beta} = (X'X)^{-1}X'Y$, and the estimator of σ^2 is $\hat{\sigma}^2 = (Y - \hat{Y})'(Y - \hat{Y})/(n - p)$, then we have the following distributional results:

(1) $\hat{\beta} \sim N_p(\beta, \sigma^2 (X'X)^{-1})$.

(2) $(\hat{\beta} - \beta)'X'X(\hat{\beta} - \beta)/\sigma^2 \sim \chi^2(p)$.

(3) $\hat{\beta}$ and $\hat{\sigma}^2$ are independent.

(4) $S_{ES}/\sigma^2 \hat{=} (Y - \hat{Y})'(Y - \hat{Y})/\sigma^2 = (n - p)\hat{\sigma}^2/\sigma^2 \sim \chi^2(n - p)$.

Proof. As $\varepsilon \sim N_n(0, \sigma^2 I_n)$, we observe that

$$Y \sim N_n(X\beta, \sigma^2 I_n)$$

(1) Since $\hat{\beta}$ is a linear function of Y, and Y has a multivariate normal distribution, and so is $\hat{\beta}$. According to the proof of Theorem 2.1 we have known $E(\hat{\beta}) = \underset{P\times 1}{\beta}$, and $Var(\hat{\beta}) = \sigma^2 \underset{p\times p}{(X'X)^{-1}}$, thus $\hat{\beta} \sim N_p(\beta, \sigma^2 (X'X)^{-1})$.

(2) If we write $\Sigma = \sigma^2 (X'X)^{-1}$, then $\hat{\beta} \sim N_p(\beta, \Sigma)$ and Σ is positive definite. We can decompose Σ^{-1} into the product of two nonsingular matrices, namely, $\Sigma^{-1} = T'T$, and $\Sigma = T^{-1}(T')^{-1}$. Then $T(\hat{\beta} - \beta)$, being a linear transformation of a multivariate normal distribution, has a normal distribution, and $E(T(\hat{\beta} - \beta)) = T(E(\hat{\beta}) - \beta) = 0$ $Var(T(\hat{\beta} - \beta)) = TVar(\hat{\beta} - \beta)T' = TVar(\hat{\beta})T' = T\Sigma T' = T(T^{-1}T'^{-1})T' = I_p$ thus

$$C = T(\hat{\beta} - \beta) \sim N_p(0, I_p)$$

Thus,

$$(\hat{\beta} - \beta)'X'X(\hat{\beta} - \beta)/\sigma^2 = (\hat{\beta} - \beta)'\left(\frac{1}{\sigma^2}(X'X)\right)(\hat{\beta} - \beta)$$
$$= (\hat{\beta} - \beta)'\Sigma^{-1}(\hat{\beta} - \beta) = (\hat{\beta} - \beta)T'T(\hat{\beta} - \beta) = C'C \sim \chi^2(p)$$

(3) From (2.20) we know that $Cov(\hat{\varepsilon}, \hat{\beta}) = 0$, and under the current normality hypothesis, $\hat{\varepsilon}$ and $\hat{\beta}$ are independent. $\hat{\sigma}^2$ is the measurable function of $\hat{\varepsilon}$, so $\hat{\beta}$ and $\hat{\sigma}^2$ are independent.

(4) As $P_{X^\perp} X = 0$, $Y'P_{X^\perp} Y = (Y - X\beta)'P_{X^\perp}(Y - X\beta)$, therefore $S_{ES} = \hat{\varepsilon}'\hat{\varepsilon} = (P_{X^\perp} Y)'(P_{X^\perp} Y) = Y'P_{X^\perp} Y = \varepsilon'P_{X^\perp}\varepsilon$, here $\varepsilon \sim N_n(0, \sigma^2 I_n)$. $P_{X^\perp}$ is an idempotent symmetric matrix, and its characteristic root is either 0 or 1. From $rk(P_{X^\perp}) = n - p$ we know that the characteristic roots of $P_{X^\perp}$ contain $n - p$ 1s and p 0s, leading to the existence of the orthogonal matrix C, $C'C = I_n$, and

$$CP_{X^\perp}C' = \begin{pmatrix} I_{n-p} & 0 \\ 0 & 0 \end{pmatrix}$$

Making $Z = C\varepsilon$, then $Z \sim N(0, \sigma^2 I_n)$, $\dfrac{1}{\sigma^2}Z_i \sim N(0,1)$, thus

$$S_{ES}/\sigma^2 = \frac{1}{\sigma^2}\varepsilon'C'CP_{X^\perp}C'C\varepsilon = \frac{1}{\sigma^2}Z'\begin{pmatrix} I_{n-p} & 0 \\ 0 & 0 \end{pmatrix}Z$$
$$= \frac{1}{\sigma^2}(Z_1^2 + \cdots + Z_{n-p}^2) \sim \chi^2(n - p)$$

End of Proof

On the basis of Theorem 2.2, we may derive the test of significance of the regression equation. Here, the null hypothesis is

$$H_0: \beta_1 = \beta_2 = \cdots = \beta_p = 0$$

against the alternative that at least one of the betas is not equal to zero.

If H_0 is accepted, then it is not proper to use model $Y = X\beta + \varepsilon$ to describe the relationship between Y and independent variables $X_1, \ldots, X_m$. In order to establish appropriate statistic, we may carry out quadratic sum decomposition:

$$S_{TS} = \sum_{i=1}^{n}(Y_i - \bar{Y})^2 = \sum_{i=1}^{n}(Y_i - \hat{Y}_i)^2 + \sum_{i=1}^{n}(\hat{Y}_i - \bar{Y})^2 = S_{ES} + S_{RS}$$

Under the hypothesis of normality of error, when H_0 is true, $Y_1, \ldots, Y_n$ are independently and identically distributed as $N(0, \sigma^2)$. As S_{ES} and S_{RS} are also mutually independent, we observe that

$$S_{ES}/\sigma^2 \sim \chi^2(n - p), \quad S_{RS}/\sigma^2 \sim \chi^2(p - 1)$$

We thus derive the F statistic:

$$F = \frac{S_{RS}/(p-1)}{S_{ES}/(n-p)} \sim F(p-1, n-p) \tag{2.22}$$

For the given significance level α, we have its critical value $F_\alpha(p - 1, n - p)$. When $F > F_\alpha(p - 1, n - p)$, H_0 is rejected, which means that the idea that there isn't any linear relationship between Y and $X_1, \ldots, X_p$ is rejected suggesting the significance of a regression relationship.

The test given above is about the overall significance of the regression as a whole. We may test the following hypotheses to examine whether the influence of some independent X_j on Y is significant or not:

$$H_0 : \beta_j = 0$$

Theorem 2.2 shows that $\hat{\beta}$ and $\hat{\sigma}^2$ are mutually independent, and $\hat{\beta} \sim N_p(\beta, \sigma^2 (X'X)^{-1})$. We assume the j th component of $\hat{\beta}$ is $\hat{\beta}_j$, the j th component of β is β_j, and the j th element on the diagonal line of $(X'X)^{-1}$ is C_{jj}, then $E(\hat{\beta}_j) = \beta_j, D(\hat{\beta}_j) = C_{jj}\sigma^2$.

$$(\hat{\beta}_j - \beta_j) / \sqrt{C_{jj}\sigma^2} \sim N(0,1)$$
$$(\hat{\beta}_j - \beta_j)^2 / (C_{jj}\sigma^2) \sim \chi^2(1)$$

and $\dfrac{S_{ES}}{\sigma^2} \sim \chi^2(n - p)$, so we obtain the following distributional results:

$$F = \frac{(\hat{\beta}_j - \beta_j)^2 / C_{jj}}{S_{ES} / (n - p)} \sim F(1, n - p)$$

$$t = \frac{(\hat{\beta}_j - \beta_j) / \sqrt{C_{jj}}}{\sqrt{S_{ES} / (n - p)}} \sim t(n - p)$$

Assuming that $H_0 : \beta_j = 0$ is true, we get two statistics:

$$F = \frac{\hat{\beta}_j^2 / C_{jj}}{S_{ES} / (n - p)} \tag{2.23}$$

$$t = \frac{\hat{\beta}_j}{\sqrt{C_{jj} S_{ES} / (n - p)}} \tag{2.24}$$

And they can be used in hypothesis testing to judge whether the effect of X_j on Y is significant or not.

X_j that has no obvious effect on Y may be eliminated in principle. But some interesting anomalies can occur. We will discuss the problem of inclusion and exclusion of variables later in the next section.

In the univariate linear regression case we had introduced a test based on correlation coefficient with the statistic r_{XY}. In (2.13) we deduced the statistic R^2, and showed $R^2 = r_{XY}^2$. The R^2 statistic may be expanded to multivariate regression. In fact, from the normal equation $X'X\hat{\beta} = X'Y$, we may have:

$$\hat{Y}'\hat{Y} = (X\hat{\beta})'(X\hat{\beta}) = \hat{\beta}'X'X\hat{\beta} = \hat{\beta}'X'Y = \hat{Y}'Y$$

Thus, $\displaystyle\sum_{i=1}^{n} \hat{Y}_i^2 = \sum_{i=1}^{n} \hat{Y}_i Y_i$, moreover, from $\overline{\hat{Y}} = \overline{Y}$, we have

$$\sum_{i=1}^{n}(Y_i - \overline{Y})(\hat{Y}_i - \overline{\hat{Y}}) = \sum_{i=1}^{n}(\hat{Y}_i - \overline{Y})^2$$

Similar to (2.13), there is

$$R^2 = \frac{\sum\limits_{i=1}^{n}(\hat{Y}_i - \overline{Y})^2}{\sum\limits_{i=1}^{n}(Y_i - \overline{Y})^2} = \frac{\left(\sum\limits_{i=1}^{n}(Y_i - \overline{Y})(\hat{Y}_i - \overline{\hat{Y}})\right)^2}{\sum\limits_{i=1}^{n}(\hat{Y}_i - \overline{Y})^2 \cdot \sum\limits_{i=1}^{n}(Y_i - \overline{Y})^2} = r_{Y\hat{Y}}^2$$

We have seen the geometric meaning of R^2, which is the square of correlation coefficient between $Y_i(i = 1,\ldots, n)$ and the estimated values $\hat{Y}_i(i = 1,\ldots, n)$ of Y_i. For good regression fit R^2 should be approximate to 1, which means the fitted value $\hat{Y}_i$ nearly coincides with the observation value Y_i. For bad regression effect, R^2 is approximate to 0, which means the fitted value $\hat{Y}_i$ has very little or no connection with the observation value Y_i. Thus R^2 is a very good measure of goodness of fit of a regression. Generally, R is called the multiple correlation coefficient or **total correlation coefficient**.

Next we consider the prediction of the dependent variable based on multivariate linear regression, and also estimation of its confidence intervals (interval estimation) as a measure of the credibility of our prediction. After we find that linear regression relation is significant, we may use that regression equation to predict. For the point prediction, we only need to substitute $X_0 = (X_{01},\ldots, X_{0p})$ into the regression equation to estimate Y_0 by $\hat{Y}_0 = X_0\hat{\beta}$.

To derive the interval estimation of $\hat{Y}_0$, its distribution is needed. Under the assumption that the errors are normally distributed in accordance with (1) of the Theorem 2.2, we know that $\hat{\beta} \sim N_p(\beta, \sigma^2(X'X)^{-1})$, so we get the distribution for Y_0:

$$\hat{Y}_0 = X_0\hat{\beta} \sim N(X_0\beta, \sigma^2 X_0'(X'X)^{-1}X_0)$$

When σ^2 is unknown, substituting it with $\hat{\sigma}^2 = S_{ES}/(n-p)$, we get the following distribution result:

$$\frac{\hat{Y}_0 - X_0\hat{\beta}}{\hat{\sigma}\sqrt{X_0'(X'X)^{-1}X_0}} \sim t(n-p)$$

The interval estimation of $\hat{Y}_0$ can now be derived (with significance level α) as:

$$X_0\hat{\beta} \pm t_{1-a/2}(n-p) \cdot \hat{\sigma} \cdot \sqrt{X_0'(X'X)^{-1}X_0}$$

We now present the interval estimates or confidence intervals for the LSE of individual regression parameters or components of the vector β. When is given, the interval estimation of $\hat{\beta}$ may be worked out directly in line with (1) of Theorem 2.2. Since

$$(\hat{\beta} - \beta)'X'X(\hat{\beta} - \beta)/\sigma^2 \sim \chi^2(p)$$

The ellipsoidal confidence region for significance level α is:

$$(\hat{\beta} - \beta)'X'X(\hat{\beta} - \beta) \leq \sigma^2 \chi_{\alpha/2}^2(p)$$

When σ^2 is unknown, we may make a new statistic through (2) and (4) of Theorem 2.2:

$$F = \frac{(\hat{\beta} - \beta)' X'X(\hat{\beta} - \beta)/(\sigma^2 p)}{(n-p)\hat{\sigma}^2/(\sigma^2(n-p))} = \frac{(\hat{\beta} - \beta)' X'X(\hat{\beta} - \beta)}{p\hat{\sigma}^2} \sim F(p, n-p)$$

Thus the confidence region (at significance level α) is:

$$(\hat{\beta} - \beta)' X'X(\hat{\beta} - \beta) \le p\hat{\sigma}^2 F_\alpha(p, n-p)$$

For the given parameters, we may obtain the confidence interval of each parameter component. If parameter dimension p is large we should note that $0.9^p \to 0$, as $p \to \infty$ and hence the joint distribution presents a small probability event. In such a case the confidence intervals are of little use.

2.2 Selection of independent variable and stepwise regression

From Section 1 of the Electronic References for Chapter 2, we can see that when the hypothesis H_0: $\beta_j = 0$ is true, the variable X_j may be eliminated from regression model. Sometimes we need to consider the contrary situation, such as adding a new variable into the model. Hence we should take the two problems into account together, that of either eliminating a variable or adding a variable. Some of the questions we answer in this chapter are: What are the principles for selection? How do we choose a good linear regression model? In this section, we will answer these questions one by one.

2.2.1 Principles of selection of independent variables

The decision whether to include or exclude a variable X_j from a regression equation is equivalent to carrying out a hypothesis test for H_0: $\beta_j = 0$. If H_0 is acceptable, X_j should be eliminated. There are two customary procedures that are in use. First, use a regression model with all variables and test the above hypothesis for each of the variables so as to eliminate variables one by one. The other is to start with the most relevant variable, as reflected by its correlation with the dependent variable, and keep adding variables that come as the next best variable and so on. These two procedures of adding and eliminating variables may not lead to the same regression equation.

Economic theory might also suggest more than one regressions equation. For instance, in order to forecast the demand for cars, some people choose per capita income, population density, and per capita car(s) to act as the regressors and others choose the output of steel and gas, and the number of trucks. Both are reasonable, depending on the assumptions one makes on the market clearing process, as the first set comes from the demand side and the second set comes from the supply side. The question then arises: how to judge what is the best regression equation among more than one regression equations.

There are different principles that are suggested. Here, we introduce several of those principles.

1. Mean residual sum of squares $\hat{\sigma}^2$

In univariate and multiple regressions, we gave the decomposition of sums of squares: $S_{TS} = S_{RS} + S_{ES}$, namely, the corrected total sum of squares = regression sum of squares + error sum of squares:

$$S_{TS} = \sum_{i=1}^{n}(Y_i - \bar{Y})^2 = \sum_{i=1}^{n}(Y_i - \hat{Y}_i)^2 + \sum_{i=1}^{n}(\hat{Y}_i - \bar{Y})^2 = S_{ES} + S_{RS}$$

It is obvious that $S_{TS} = \sum_{i=1}^{n}(Y_i - \bar{Y})^2$ is unaffected by the choice of variables. Hence the choice must be based on how large S_{RS} is or how low S_{ES} is.

The smallest residual sum of squares RSS or error sum of squares (S_{ES}) could be one criterion for choosing the variables. However, more variables result in smaller RSS, but a satisfactory regression equation should contain as few variables as possible. Therefore, we adopt the estimate of σ^2: $\hat{\sigma}^2 = \dfrac{1}{n-p}\sum_{i=1}^{n}(Y_i - \hat{Y}_i)^2$, that corrects the S_{ES} for adding more variables, and use the minimization of $\hat{\sigma}^2$ as the principle for choosing between alternate regression equations. The smallest $\hat{\sigma}^2$ indicates the best regression equation.

2. Corrected total correlation coefficient R_p

For a univariate case we have:

$$r_{XY}^2 = \frac{S_{XY}^2}{S_{XX}S_{YY}} = \sum_{i=1}^{n}(\hat{Y}_i - \bar{Y})^2 \Big/ \sum_{i=1}^{n}(Y_i - \bar{Y})^2 \triangleq R^2$$

For a multivariate case we have:

$$R^2 = \frac{\sum_{i=1}^{n}(\hat{Y}_i - \bar{Y})^2}{\sum_{i=1}^{n}(Y_i - \bar{Y})^2} = \frac{\left(\sum_{i=1}^{n}(Y_i - \bar{Y})(\hat{Y}_i - \bar{\hat{Y}})\right)^2}{\sum_{i=1}^{n}(\hat{Y}_i - \bar{Y})^2 \cdot \sum_{i=1}^{n}(Y_i - \bar{Y})^2} = r_{Y\hat{Y}}^2$$

$$|R| = \frac{\left|\sum_{i=1}^{n}(Y_i - \bar{Y})(\hat{Y}_i - \bar{\hat{Y}})\right|}{\left[\sum_{i=1}^{n}(Y_i - \bar{Y})^2 \sum_{i=1}^{n}(\hat{Y}_i - \bar{\hat{Y}})^2\right]^{\frac{1}{2}}} = \frac{|S_{Y\hat{Y}}|}{\sqrt{S_{YY}S_{\hat{Y}\hat{Y}}}} = |r_{Y\hat{Y}}|$$

$|R|$ or $|r_{Y\hat{Y}}|$ is called the total correlation coefficient, which may also be used to measure the suitability of regression. The larger the $|R|$ the better is the regression.

In accordance with the decomposition of sum of squared deviations:

$$R^2 = \frac{\sum_{i=1}^{n}(\hat{Y}_i - \bar{Y})^2}{\sum_{i=1}^{n}(Y_i - \bar{Y})^2} = \frac{\left(\sum_{i=1}^{n}(Y_i - \bar{Y})(\hat{Y}_i - \bar{\hat{Y}})\right)^2}{\sum_{i=1}^{n}(\hat{Y}_i - \bar{Y})^2 \cdot \sum_{i=1}^{n}(Y_i - \bar{Y})^2} = r_{Y\hat{Y}}^2$$

$$R^2 = \frac{\sum_{i=1}^{n}(\hat{Y}_i - \bar{Y})^2}{\sum_{i=1}^{n}(Y_i - \bar{Y})^2} = \frac{\sum_{i=1}^{n}(Y_i - \bar{Y})^2 - \sum_{i=1}^{n}(Y_i - \hat{Y})^2}{\sum_{i=1}^{n}(Y_i - \bar{Y})^2} = 1 - \frac{S_{ES}}{S_{TS}}$$

Since S_{TS} is a constant, bigger R^2 means smaller S_{ES} (residual sum of squares), and it is inevitable that more variables lead up to smaller S_{ES}. Thus we need to correct R^2. This is done by dividing the two sums of squares in the expression above by their respective degrees of freedom. We therefore define the corrected total correlation coefficient R_p by the equation:

$$R_p^2 = 1 - (1 - R^2)\frac{n}{n-p} \tag{2.25}$$

And it is used to measure the suitability of regression. Here, p is the number of variables. In (2.25), R_p^2 is smaller with the larger p. In the literature, this term is also referred to as **adjusted** R^2, or $\bar{R}^2$, thus the principle that among two situations with the same S_{ES}, the one that has fewer independent variables should be preferred is captured by R_p.

3. Variance of prediction errors: $(n+p)\hat{\sigma}^2$

Regression equation has n predicted values at the n observation points, and the prediction error of the i-th predicted value is

$$D_i = Y_i - X_i'\hat{\beta}$$

This is a random variable, and the smaller its variance the better it is. We arrange D_i $(i = 1,\ldots, n)$ into the form of vector

$$D = Y - X'\hat{\beta}$$

Then

$$Var(D) = \sigma^2 + X\, Var(\hat{\beta})X' = \sigma^2(1 + X(X'X)^{-1}X')$$

Thus the sum of variances of individual prediction errors is the sum of diagonal entries of $Var(D)$.

$$\sum_{i=1}^{n} Var(D_i) = n\sigma^2 + \sigma^2 tr(X(X'X)^{-1}X')$$
$$= n\sigma^2 + \sigma^2 tr(X'X)^{-1}X'X$$
$$= n\sigma^2 + \sigma^2 tr(I_p) = (n+p)\sigma^2$$

Substituting $\hat{\sigma}^2$ for σ^2, we may get an estimate of the sum of variances of prediction errors: $(n+p)\hat{\sigma}^2$, minimization of which may be used for selection of variables.

4. C_p-statistic

One of the aims of specifying a regression equation is prediction. The C_p-statistic put forward by Mallows (Mallows, 1964) measures the goodness of regression equations in terms of prediction. Take the original regression model into account:

$$Y = X_{n\times k}\beta_{k\times 1} + \varepsilon, \quad \varepsilon \sim N(0, \sigma^2 I_n)$$

Note that here X have k columns. We are using a slightly different notation in this sub-section and using k instead of p, as p is used in a different context in this section.

X is divided into two parts

$$X = (X_p \mid X_q)$$

We divide $\beta_{k \times 1}$ into also into two parts accordingly:

$$\beta = \begin{pmatrix} \beta_p \\ \beta_q \end{pmatrix}$$

here $p + q = k$,

After q variables are eliminated, the new model is:

$$Y = X_{n \times p} \beta_{p \times 1} + \upsilon$$

Assuming that the residual sum of squares of the LSE is S_{ESp}, we get the following so-called C_p-statistic:

$$C_p = \frac{S_{ESp}}{\hat{\sigma}^2} - n + 2p$$

The principle is that smaller C_p results in better new regression equation.

More detailed properties of the C_p-statistic may be found in the Electronic References for Chapter 2, Appendix.

A reader may be interested in knowing if all these different criteria applied to the same problem lead to the same conclusion. The answer is that they may not. Then the question is which of these is best and under what conditions. In fact this problem cannot be answered clearly. However, we are fortunate to have the statistical tool of simulated experiments. We can perform simulations with a variety of known models with alternate methods of choosing the model, and see which model fits the data best, and under what conditions. When we think of this problem and the tests of statistical hypothesis with an arbitrarily chosen level of significance of the test, and specifying a model (or maintained hypothesis or assumed true model), we may realize that statistics is not only a science, but also an art.

2.2.2   Stepwise regression

Stepwise regression procedure screens independent variables step by step, and variables are included or eliminated in the screening process. In the first instance, we carry out univariate regression of the dependent variable with each of the independent variables, and select that univariate linear regression equation that has the closest relationship with Y or the most significant F test statistic. Then we bring in the second variable in accordance with the principle that it has the highest F value. At the same time, we test the original variable to see whether it is still significant, otherwise it may be eliminated. We follow the above procedure until no variables should be brought in or eliminated.

The stepwise regression usually consists of the following steps.

1.   Standardization of data
The standardization of observed data aims to improve computational accuracy and data conversion, and is carried out in columns. Set the original model as:

$$Y = X\beta + \varepsilon, \quad \varepsilon \sim N(0, \sigma^2 I_n)$$

We arrange X into p columns: $(X_1 \vdots X_2 \vdots \cdots \vdots X_p)$, and record the average of each column of datum as:

$$\bar{X}_j = \frac{1}{n}\sum_{i=1}^{n} X_{ij}, \quad j = 1,\ldots,p, \quad \bar{Y} = \frac{1}{n}\sum_{i=1}^{n} Y_i$$

Likewise the variance of each column of datum is

$$\sigma_j^2 = \frac{1}{n}\sum_{i=1}^{n}(X_{ij} - \bar{X}_j)^2, \quad j = 1,\ldots,p, \quad \sigma_Y^2 = \frac{1}{n}\sum_{i=1}^{n}(Y_i - \bar{Y})^2$$

We carry out data standardization

$$Z_{ij} = \frac{X_{ij} - \bar{X}_j}{\sigma_j}, \quad i = 1,\ldots,n, \quad j = 1,\ldots,p$$

$$Y_i^* = \frac{Y_i - \bar{Y}}{\sigma_Y} \quad i = 1,\ldots,n$$

The regression model with standardized data can be written as

$$Y^* = Z\alpha + \varepsilon^*, \quad \varepsilon^* \sim N(0,1)$$

After standardization the parametric estimation of the new model is

$$\hat{\alpha} = (Z'Z)^{-1} Z'Y^*$$

The elements of $p \times p$ square matrix $Z'Z$ are the correlation coefficients of $X_1,\ldots, X_p$

$$(Z'Z)_{kj} = \frac{\sum_{i=1}^{n}(X_{ik} - \bar{X}_k)(X_{ij} - \bar{X}_j)}{\sigma_k \sigma_j} = r_{X_k X_j}$$

The elements of column vector $Z'Y^*$ are the correlation coefficients between $X_1,\ldots, X_p$ and Y:

$$(Z'Y^*)_k = \frac{\sum_{i=1}^{n}(X_{ik} - \bar{X}_k)(Y_i - \bar{Y})}{\sigma_K \sigma_Y} = r_{X_k Y}, \quad k = 1,\ldots,p$$

After the least squares solution $\hat{\alpha}$ of the new model is obtained, we may deduce the solution of the original model:

$$\hat{\beta}_j = \frac{\sigma_Y}{\sigma_j} \hat{\alpha}_j, \quad j = 1,\ldots,p$$

2. Selection of variables

We put the variables outside the model into it one by one, and calculate their F test values, and choose the variable with the highest F value. As we get closer to the true model these F-values become smaller, and we may not wish to include a new variable with a small F value. Hence we usually specify a small significant F- value as a threshold to include a new variable. This is called the critical F-value for the inclusion of a new variable. It is unnecessary to calculate the inverse matrix for the least squares solution at each stage as we introduce a new variable. We need only to correct the original parameter estimates in accordance with a recursion formula. Readers can see the Electronic References for Chapter 2, Section 2-2-7 (The Effect of Adding Variables to a Linear Model), from (2-2-28) to (2-2-30) provided in the first paragraph of that section.

3. Elimination of variables

In general, we adopt the F-test. Assume $\beta_j = 0$, statistic $F = \dfrac{\hat{\alpha}_j^2 / C_{jj}}{S_{ES} / (n-p)} \sim F(1, n-p)$, C_{jj} is the jth element of the main diagonal of $(Z'Z)^{-1}$. We choose the smallest one from p F values, and carry out F-test to decide whether it should be eliminated or not. As in the inclusion of variables case we specify an F-value, called critical F-value for exclusion, and do not exclude a variable unless its F is very small. These F-values associated with each variable keep changing as we keep adding or deleting variables.

4. Summary of results

When no new independent variables may be put in and no original independent variables may be eliminated, we stop the variable selection process and calculate the estimates of parameters, test for their significance, and make predictions or forecasts based on the estimated regression.

The basic principle of stepwise regression is bringing in and eliminating variables in the course of selection of variables. Once a variable is introduced we do not wish to eliminate it quickly because it became marginally insignificant with the presence of a new variable. This is because it could become significant again with additional variables. It is for this reason that the critical F values are usually set at lower levels for elimination of variables, once introduced, than for inclusion of variables. The basic principle is somewhat similar to the story that is described in *The Water Margin*[1]: Wang Lun (X_1) entered the Water Margin in the very beginning and became the castellan; then Lin Chong (X_2) entered and grudgingly acknowledged Wang Lun's position because he was not powerful enough; afterward, Chao Gai (X_3) came, and he with the help of Lin Chong overthrew Wang Lun. The late comers X_2 and X_3 became the dominant ones, and the first comer (X_1) failed to keep his position. A data example can be seen in DASC using simulated data.

The screening of variables in the following real-life example is another situation: One variable has an excessive influence on the dependent variable suppressing the influence of all other variables.

---

[1] *The Water Margin* is one of the great Chinese novels. It narrates stories of a group of heroes who represent different classes of people daring to fight evil.

Example 2.1   Stepwise regression: relation between amount of Chinese imports and exports (foreign trade) and fiscal expenditure   According to Chinese macroeconomic data shown in Table 2.1, taking total value of trade (exports plus imports) in billions of US dollars as dependent variable, we hope to screen the independent variables, all measured in billions of Yuan, for obtaining the best relation to explain the determinants of Chinese foreign trade.

First, we prepare the data for use by the DASC software. We reverse the order of the rows so that a growth trend can be presented in the data; otherwise we will see a declining trend. The following are the main results of computer analysis of the raw data. Needless to say, we delete the first column labeled 'year'. We delete the third column of total fiscal expenditure as it is a sum of the following columns, and if not deleted, it could present perfect multicollinearity. So we make a text data file with 22 rows and six columns. In order to show the effect of stepwise regression, we use just 18 rows to estimate the model and the other four rows to test how good the model is. This requires an adjustment of the row parameter in the B area in DASC software. We note that defense expenditure (X_3) has the largest zero-order Pearson correlation with trade volume (0.992). For the first stepwise regression, we therefore include the independent variable X_3 (defense expenditure) and the equation will be

$$Y = 2.379 + 0.000\,X_1 + 0.000\,X_2 + 3.593\,X_3 + 0.000\,X_4 + 0.000\,X_5$$

A zero value of the regression coefficient indicates that the variable is omitted.

F statistic $= 146.9153$, F critical value $F\,(5,12) = 3.2059$.
Total correlation coefficient $R^2 = 0.9839$ (R $= 0.9919$).

With respect to these five independent variables, no matter what other variable we try to include after including variable X_3, F test significance level is such that no other variable should be added. It seems that Y is related only to X_3. The relation is very strong with good fit as shown in Figure 2.4. This seems to suggest that other macroeconomic indices really are not linearly related to trade volume.

Delete X_3 from the data file to make a new file with 18 rows and five columns, that is, go further to find the relation between the total value of foreign trade (value of imports and exports) (Y) and economic development expenditure (X_1), social culture and education expenditure (X_2), ADM expenditure (X_4) and other expenditures (X_5). We find that the fitted effect is very significant with the selection of another variable X_2, representing social cultural and educational expenditure. We already noted that when X_3 is selected, X_2 had no chance of being selected; when X_3 is present X_2 cannot work at all in the shade of X_3. The regression equation can be expressed as:

$$Y = 6.113 + 0.000\,X_1 + 0.930\,X_2 + 0.000\,X_4 + 0.000\,X_5$$
F statistic $= 103.6711$, F critical value: F $(4, 13) = 3.2791$.
Total correlation coefficient $R^2 = 0.9696$ (R $= 0.9847$).

It is surprising that when X_2 is freed from the influence of X_3, it keeps on carrying on in hegemonic style and suppresses other variables from being selected. Now let us delete X_2 also from the data file to make a new file with 18 rows and four columns. The equation is

$$Y = 2.124 + 0.669\,X_1 + 0.297\,X_4 + 0.000\,X_5.$$

F statistic $= 177.0305$, F critical value F $(3, 14) = 3.4439$.
Total Correlation Coefficient $R^2 = 0.9744$ ($R = 0.9871$).

Table 2.1 Chinese macroeconomic data.

Year	Total Volume of Foreign Trade Y	Total Fiscal Expenditure	Economic Development Expenditure X_1	Social Cultural and Educational Expenditure X_2	Defense Expenditure X_3	ADM Expenditure X_4	Other Expenditures X_5
2006	1760.396	4042.273	1073.563	1084.620	297.938	757.105	829.147
2005	1421.91	3393.028	931.696	895.336	247.496	651.234	667.266
2004	1154.55	2848.689	793.425	749.051	220.001	552.198	534.114
2003	850.988	2464.995	691.205	646.937	190.787	469.126	466.940
2002	620.77	2205.32	667.37	592.458	170.78	410.132	364.577
2001	509.65	1890.26	647.256	521.323	144.204	351.249	226.226
2000	474.29	1588.65	574.836	4384.51	120.75	276.822	177.787
1999	360.63	13187.7	506.146	363.874	107.64	202.06	139.047
1998	323.95	1079.82	417.951	293.078	93.57	160.027	115.292
1997	325.16	923.46	364.733	246.938	81.257	135.885	94.543
1996	289.88	793.76	323.478	208.056	72.006	118.528	71.787
1995	280.86	682.37	285.578	175.672	63.67	99.654	57.796
1994	236.62	579.26	239.369	150.153	55.071	84.768	49.901
1993	195.70	464.23	183.579	117.827	42.58	63.526	56.918
1992	165.53	374.22	161.281	97.012	37.786	46.341	31.8
1991	135.70	338.66	142.847	84.965	33.031	41.401	36.418
1990	115.44	308.36	136.801	73.761	29.03	41.456	27.31
1989	111.68	282.38	129.119	66.844	25.147	38.626	22.642
1988	102.79	249.12	125.839	58.118	21.8	27.16	16.204
1987	82.65	226.22	115.347	50.583	20.962	22.82	16.506
1986	73.85	220.49	115.897	48.509	20.075	22.004	14.006
1985	69.60	200.43	112.755	40.843	19.153	17.106	10.568

Total value of foreign trade measured in billions of US dollars and other variables measured in billion Yuan. Data come from the Annals of China Statistics.

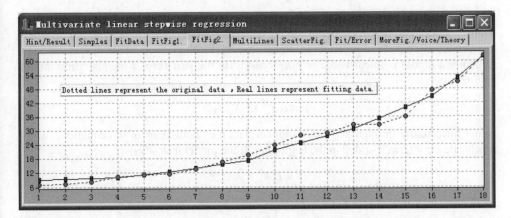

Figure 2.4   Relation between China's value of foreign trade and defense expenditure.

The equation denotes that X_1 has no hegemonic style and it allows the other variable X_4 to work together. The goodness of fit figure is quite similar to the last figure and hence it is omitted here. Readers can input own data in any form (text, Excel, SQL, and other database form) in DASC to perform the calculations involving variable selection using stepwise regression.

2.3   Multivariate data transformation and polynomial regression

We introduced data transformations in Chapter 1 that can convert a curvilinear relation between two variables to a linear relation. Taking a look at the scatter diagram and basic diagrams of different types of functions we can discover what transformation of a variable make that variable linearly related to the dependent variable.

We now discuss a specific case of a multiple regression model that involves transformations of independent variables into polynomials so as to make the regression relation between the independent variables and the dependent variable linear. The procedure also gives us a hint as to whether we should do this for more than one independent variable.

Polynomial regression is obviously a particular case of general data transformation. In principle, any curved surface can be approximated by a sufficiently high degree polynomial, but the high degree of polynomial needed will sometimes causes the problem of instability of parameter estimates and hence of the entire regression itself. Using orthogonal polynomials will often reduce the severity of this instability problem.

2.3.1   Linear regression after multivariate data transformation

The general nonlinear model:

$$Y = f(X, \theta) + \varepsilon, \ E(\varepsilon) = 0$$

It can be classified into two types. One type is where it can be converted into

$$Y = g(X)\beta + \varepsilon* \quad and \quad E(\varepsilon*) = 0$$

where $g(X)$ is $n \times p$ matrix of observations on transformed independent variables. This kind of model can be called linearizing a nonlinear model. The other type is one where the model cannot be converted to linear model through such exact transformation. Whether a model is linearizable or not depends on the structure of the specified model. For example:

$$Y = \alpha X_1^{\beta_1} X_2^{\beta_2} X_3^{\beta_3} + \varepsilon$$

is not linearizable through any exact transformation of both sides of the equation, for the stochastic error term is added in the beginning. If the model instead is:

$$Y = \alpha X_1^{\beta_1} X_2^{\beta_2} X_3^{\beta_3} \varepsilon$$

Taking logarithm on both sides, we have

$$\ln Y = \ln \alpha + \beta_1 \ln X_1 + \beta_2 \ln X_2 + \beta_3 \ln X_3 + \ln \varepsilon$$

This is a trivariate linear regression model, linear in parameters with nonlinear transformation of original variables. It is to be noted that in general we need to test hypotheses requiring some assumptions on the distribution of the error term such as assuming that $\ln \varepsilon \sim N(0, \sigma^2 I)$.

Actually we should add stochastic error term after linearizing the model, which will be more natural. For example, an exponential model is:

$$Y = e^{\beta_0 + \beta_1 X + \beta_2 X_2}$$

Take logarithm and then add in stochastic term,

$$\ln Y = \beta_0 + \beta_1 X_1 + \beta_2 X_2 + \varepsilon$$

This is equivalent to assuming that the model in fact is:

$$Y = e^{\beta_0 + \beta_1 X + \beta_2 X_2 + \varepsilon}$$

For more complicated model such as a Logistic regression:

$$Y = \frac{1}{1 + e^{\beta_0 + \beta_1 X + \beta_2 X_2 + \varepsilon}}$$

It can be transformed into:

$$\ln \left(\frac{1}{Y} - 1 \right) = \beta_0 + \beta_1 X_1 + \beta_2 X_2 + \varepsilon$$

We should have clear identification of the actual distribution of error terms. This can be done through fitting a distribution to the estimated residuals. We discussed linearization of the theoretical model above. In practice we may not know the theoretical model at the beginning. We may have just a few columns of data, the first column is the dependent variable Y, the following columns are independent variables $X_1,..., X_p$ and we need to develop a linear regression. As it is a multivariate relationship, it is natural that there exist intercorrelations among independent variables and can be fitted better with a multiple regression than with a set of simple bivariate regressions, such as between Y and X_1, Y and X_2,..., Y and X_p. We make a decision on what kind of data transformation is needed for each independent variable. If we

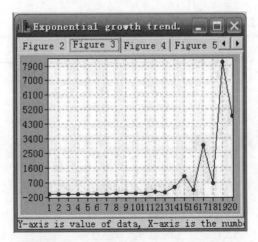

Figure 2.5   Exponential growth Trend.

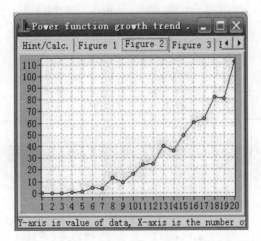

Figure 2.6   Power function growth trend.

can make each transformed independent variable linearly related to Y, we can then run the multiple linear regression with those transformed variables.

Example 2.2   Regression after specific transformation of each column   Given 20 data points of dependent variable Y and the two independent variables X_1, X_2 as shown in the following table, let us analyze the data. Arranging X_1 in an increasing order, we can find that it grows rapidly, seemingly with an exponential growth. So we can consider taking logarithm transformation of X_1. The column X_2 grows fast too, however at a rate less than the column X_1. It is growing seemingly as square function, so square root transformation can be considered. But the transformation relying on the intuition is not necessarily accurate. We can use DASC in order to see Figure 2.5 and observe the dotted pairs (X_{1i}, i) in the rectangular axes. The exponential growth trend is truly discernible.

Likewise when we examine the plot of X_2 the image is quite like curve $X_{2i} = i^2$ as in Figure 2.6. So we take square root function $\sqrt{x} = x^{0.5}$ on column X_2. The original data are

Table 2.2   Raw data for a linearized regression.

Ser No.	Y	X_1	X_2	X_1^*	X_2^*
1	0.4	1.11	0.02	.1044	.1414
2	0.7	1.22	0.04	.1989	.2000
3	2.1	1.64	0.55	.4947	.7416
4	3.3	2.71	1.0	.9969	1.0
5	6.0	4.48	4.55	1.4996	2.1331
6	6.1	7.39	4.0	2.0001	2.0
7	9.0	12.18	13.35	2.4998	3.6401
8	9.8	20.08	9.0	2.9997	3.0
9	12.1	54.59	16.0	3.9999	4.0
10	14.0	33.21	24.25	3.5998	4.9244
11	15.1	148.41	25.0	5.0	5.0
12	18.0	90.0	40.25	4.4998	6.3443
13	18.2	403.52	36.0	6.0	6.0
14	21.0	1096.63	49.0	7.0	7.0
15	21.5	244.69	60.25	5.5000	7.7621
16	23.0	2980.95	64.0	8.0	8.0
17	25.2	665.14	82.25	6.5	9.0692
18	27.0	8103.08	81.0	9.0	9.0
19	28.2	4808.04	112.25	8.478	10.5948
20	32.5	6914.76	144.25	8.8414	12.0104

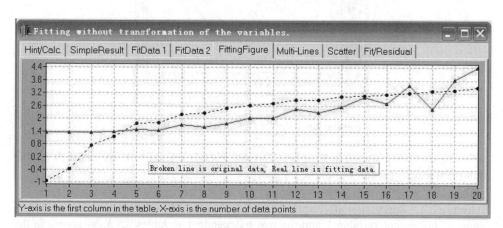

Figure 2.7   Fitting without transformation of the variables.

shown in the left three columns of the following table. The independent variables after transformation are shown with * in the right two columns of Table 2.2.

The regression fitting without transformation of the variables is as shown in Figure 2.7. Its goodness of fit is not good at all.

Readers can see the computation process by clicking DASC→Regression Analysis→Common Linear Regression→Linear Regression with univariate Polynomial. If we modify the first step parameter as 2 in area B of DASC, the second column will be

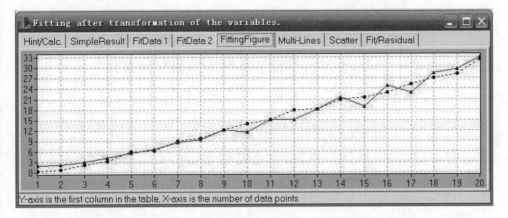

Figure 2.8 Goodness of fit after transformation of the variables.

transformed by the square root function. The regression fit is as shown in Figure 2.8, which is quite acceptable.

$$\text{Regression Equation: } Y = 0.3396 + 0.8618\, X_1^* + 2.0596\, X_2^*.$$

$$\text{Total Correlation Coefficient } R^2 = 0.9772 \; (R = 0.9985).$$

2.3.2 Polynomial regression on an independent variable

From the function approximation theory and Weierstrass's theorem we know that any curve of continuous functions can be approximated to any degree of closeness through a sufficiently high degree of a polynomial. For n observed data pairs, we can use $n-1$ degree polynomial passing through these points exactly. But the estimated polynomial will not be stable in the sense a slight perturbation of the data might give rise to an entirely different $n-1$ degree polynomial. Thus given n observations our main objective is to choose a lower order for the polynomial ($<n-1$) for the regression that may not go through all the n points but that is stable. In general, the higher the degree of the polynomial, the more accurate is the approximation, but the less stable are the estimated coefficients of the polynomial and the predictions based on it. The lower the degrees of the polynomial, the more stable are the estimated coefficients of the polynomial, but the error of approximation could be larger.

Suppose with one independent variable, we take k^{th} degree polynomial as regression model:

$$Y = \beta_0 + \beta_1 X + \beta_2 X^2 + \cdots + \beta_k X^k + \varepsilon$$

Although there is only one explanatory variable X it appears in k different functional forms.

Let:

$$X_{(1)} = X, X_{(2)} = X^2, \ldots, X_{(k)} = X^k$$

Then the model will become:

$$Y = \beta_0 + \beta_1 X_{(1)} + \beta_2 X_{(2)} + \cdots + \beta_k X_{(k)} + \varepsilon$$

It is a k-variate linear regression model. Letting

$$X = \begin{pmatrix} 1 & x_1 & x_1^2 & \cdots & x_1^k \\ 1 & x_2 & x_2^2 & \cdots & x_2^k \\ \cdots & \cdots & \cdots & \cdots & \cdots \\ 1 & x_n & x_n^2 & \cdots & x_n^k \end{pmatrix}, \quad \beta = \begin{pmatrix} \beta_0 \\ \beta_1 \\ \vdots \\ \beta_k \end{pmatrix}, \quad Y = \begin{pmatrix} Y_1 \\ Y_2 \\ \vdots \\ Y_n \end{pmatrix}, \quad \varepsilon = \begin{pmatrix} \varepsilon_1 \\ \varepsilon_2 \\ \vdots \\ \varepsilon_n \end{pmatrix}$$

Then we can express the regression model as:

$$Y = X\beta + \varepsilon$$

Thus the polynomial regression can be converted into general multiple linear regression. Then there is no difficulty in its parametric estimation, significance testing and goodness of fit figure.

Example 2.3   Polynomial fitting of the stock value of Taiwan plastic and the weighted indexes of Taiwan   We select the data of FPC stock[2] and Taiwan weighted index from the website of Yahoo-Finance. The data are shown in Table 2.3. Taking the stock price of FPC as the dependent variable and the Taiwan weighted index as the independent variable, we want to fit the relation between them. Based on exploratory data analysis, as explained in Chapter 1 we found that a quadratic transformation of the Taiwan weighted index is suitable. We select polynomial regression and take quadratic polynomial. The resulting regression results and the computer output are as follows. The goodness of fit figure is shown in Figure 2.9.

We note that the goodness of fit is not good, the total correlation coefficient is too small, and the F statistic does not exceed F critical value. We must improve it. When we take a higher degree polynomial, the goodness of fit should be better in theory. But in fact, it may be worse. In theory, X, X^2, X^3, X^4 are linearly independent mathematically and the Vandermonde determinant will not be zero when $X_i \neq X_j$. But for the data of some examples, X, X^2, X^3, X^4 could be approximately linearly related to make $X'X$ near singular, and the computations cannot go on. The reason for this condition is that column collinearity exists between the rounded of numbers and the machine calculations creates a floating point overflow. In this case the best way is to use ridge regression as discussed in Section 2.3.4. Another way to improve the goodness of fit is to augment the list of independent variables by adding new independent variables, not merely adding polynomial terms. The best way may be to add the lagged variable of a dependent variable as an additional independent variable. These steps will be discussed in subsequent chapters.

2.3.3   Multivariable polynomial regression

If the number of independent variables is more than one, then polynomial regression as well as orthogonal polynomial regression can be built. If there are two variables, we may do surface fitting. The general model is

$$Y = \beta_0 + \beta_1 X_1 + \beta_2 X_1^2 + \cdots + \beta_k X_1^k + \beta_1' X_2 + \beta_2' X_2^2 + \cdots + \beta_m' X_2^m + \varepsilon$$

---

[2]The stock index of Taiwan.

Table 2.3   Stock price of FPC and Taiwan weighted index.

Date	Stock Price of FPC	Taiwan Weighted Index*0.001	Date	Stock Price of FPC	Taiwan Weighted Index*0.001
2009-2-24	45.37	4.43018	2008-12-26	41.83	4.42508
2009-2-23	46.05	4.47778	2008-12-25	40.48	4.41345
2009-2-20	45.66	4.43694	2008-12-24	41.3	4.42309
2009-2-19	46.54	4.52887	2008-12-23	42.08	4.40586
2009-2-18	46.63	4.49837	2008-12-22	43.24	4.53554
2009-2-17	46.73	4.49178	2008-12-19	43.92	4.69452
2009-2-16	46.54	4.59126	2008-12-18	44.26	4.69481
2009-2-13	46.73	4.59250	2008-12-17	43.82	4.64802
2009-2-12	45.95	4.46642	2008-12-16	44.6	4.61689
2009-2-11	47.46	4.57595	2008-12-15	45.37	4.61372
2009-2-10	46.83	4.52610	2008-12-12	45.37	4.48127
2009-2-9	46.34	4.49459	2008-12-11	46.2	4.65557
2009-2-6	45.86	4.47125	2008-12-10	47.6	4.65887
2009-2-5	45.18	4.36325	2008-12-9	46.92	4.47266
2009-2-4	45.95	4.38997	2008-12-8	47.26	4.41833
2009-2-3	46.54	4.37281	2008-12-5	47.26	4.22507
2009-2-2	46.54	4.25998	2008-12-4	47.36	4.25496
2009-1-21	46.1	4.24797	2008-12-3	47.41	4.30726
2009-1-20	44.89	4.24261	2008-12-2	47.41	4.35698
2009-1-19	46	4.36676	2008-12-1	47.51	4.51843
2009-1-16	43.77	4.35370	2008-11-28	47.17	4.46049
2009-1-15	44.01	4.32077	2008-11-27	47.17	4.45375
2009-1-14	45.81	4.52147	2008-11-26	45.95	4.27180
2009-1-13	46.54	4.53236	2008-11-25	45.95	4.26649
2009-1-12	46.54	4.45390	2008-11-24	46.44	4.16054
2009-1-9	46.34	4.50274	2008-11-21	46.44	4.17110
2009-1-8	45.66	4.53579	2008-11-20	49.44	4.08993
2009-1-7	46.68	4.78984	2008-11-19	52.16	4.28409
2009-1-6	43.63	4.72726	2008-11-18	52.35	4.30518
2009-1-5	41.88	4.69831	2008-11-17	52.35	4.43980
2008-12-31	42.27	4.59122	2008-11-14	51.67	4.45270
2008-12-30	43.09	4.58904	2008-11-13	51.48	4.43783
2008-12-29	41.59	4.41616	2008-11-12	51.48	4.61557

Regression equation: Y = 10.5154 + −2.3867 X1 + 2.3623 X2.
Residual sum of squares = 4.18887, Regression sum of squares = 0.197844.
Estimated error variance = 0.06649, Standard Error = 0.257857.
F statistic = 1.48778, F critical value $F(2, 63)$ = 3.9136.
Total correlation coefficient R^2 = 0.0451 (R = 0.2124).

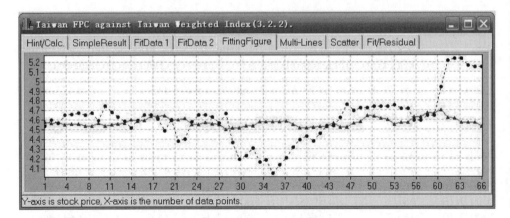

Figure 2.9   Taiwan FPC (dot line) and its fit of the quadratic regression (real line).

One variable polynomial regression is essentially a curve-fitting. A two-variable polynomial regression is essentially surface-fitting.

We give below an example of a bi-variate quadratic polynomial regression.

Example 2.4   Response of individual equity of Yaohua glass and Huaxin cement to plate effect and integral effect of the stock market   Yaohua Glass was listed for transactions on the Shanghai Stock Exchange on July 1, 1996. We wish to forecast the future trends of the Yaohua stock index (Y). Two factors are taken into account: the plate effect of Huaxin Cement- (X_1), and the integral effect of the Shanghai Stock Index of A-shares (X_2). By plate effect we mean the effects of each other in a common plate (Yaohua Glass and Huaxin Cement are together in a building material plate). By integral effect we mean the effect of all business activity of Yaohua Glass. Shanghai Stock Index of A-shares reflects the integral effect. A model using a two variable quadratic polynomial regression as specified below is used:

$$Y = \beta_0 + \beta_1 X_1 + \beta_2 X_1^2 + \beta_3 X_2 + \beta_4 X_2^2 + \varepsilon$$

Twenty-seven observations of the weekly stock prices (from July 1 to December 31 of 1996) of Yaohua Glass, Huaxin Cement and the Shanghai Stock Index of A-shares are presented in Table 2.4 below. In the printed data from the DASC program, not reproduced here (different from the raw data of Table 2.4), the first column is the Yaohua Glass stock price, the dependent variable. The second column is the Huaxin cement index, the third column is the square of the data of Huaxin Cement, the fourth column is the Shanghai composite A Shares index, and the fifth column is the squares of the Shanghai composite A shares index. From the regression output we see: $F = 8.8551$, which is much larger than the critical value of 2.817, and is quite satisfactory for a good fit. The goodness of fit graph (Figure 2.10) is indeed very satisfactory. If the future values of Huaxin Cement and Shanghai composite index of A-shares are given, we can forecast reasonably well the Yaohua Glass stock price. The ultimate regression equation is:

$$Y = 417.5586 - 91.8506 X_1 + 3.1547 X_1^2 + 5.1854 X_2 - 0.0162 X_2^2 + \varepsilon$$

$$\varepsilon \sim N(0, 408.2501 I_n)$$

Table 2.4   Stock prices of Yaohua Glass, Huaxin Cement and Shanghai Stock Index.

Yaohua Glass	Huaxin Cement	Composite Index	Yaohua Glass	Huaxin Cement	Composite Index
Y	X_1	X_2	Y	X_1	X_2
100.0000	11.3370	84.0957	70.5500	14.7540	101.0572
96.9000	11.1050	82.0615	80.0500	14.5560	105.9794
97.8000	11.5080	83.4254	88.4000	15.0310	98.3920
103.2200	12.6020	89.8077	99.3400	14.8290	97.5659
101.2300	11.9260	89.6343	98.4600	14.0840	100.1633
99.3600	12.3690	89.3952	107.3600	14.3860	97.4998
100.8300	12.6700	92.7841	141.3200	14.8150	104.8605
94.4600	12.2080	87.3670	170.3400	14.7910	126.8577
70.0600	12.3350	80.3945	173.5900	18.8920	121.7061
71.9100	12.8540	85.1233	178.2000	18.8920	91.7588
66.9100	12.9530	79.0066	130.7700	13.8200	93.8577
64.9900	13.7400	80.7754	124.7100	13.5240	94.5995
67.9000	14.7960	90.4105	141.4200	14.1290	97.5289
66.3900	14.7650	95.4776			

Sum of squares of residuals = 11010.54, Sum of squares due to regression = 17727.10.
Estimated variance = 407.7978, Standard error = 20.1940.
F statistic = 8.8551, F Critical Value $F(4, 22)$ = 2.817.
Total correlation coefficient R^2 = 0.6597 (R = 0.8122).

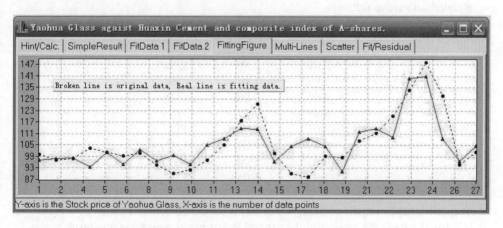

Figure 2.10   Goodness of fit of stock price using two variable quadratic regressions.

2.4   Column multicollinearity in design matrix and ridge regression

2.4.1   Effect of column multicollinearity of design matrix

In the previous sections we assumed that the columns of the X matrix are not linearly related. If they are then $|X'X| = 0$ and the normal equations cannot be solved using the ordinary matrix

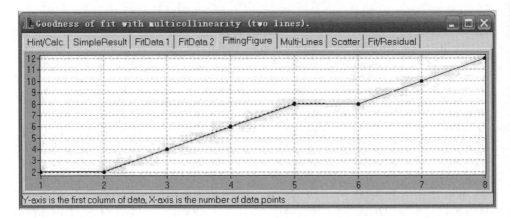

Figure 2.11   Goodness of fitting with multicollinearity (two lines).

theory. Section 2-3-2 of the Electronic References to this chapter introduces the concept of a generalized inverse to take care of that situation. In an actual situation, column vectors of design matrix may be of near-linear correlation (called **multicollinearity**), and $|X' X| \approx 0$. Here, the general least squares method may be used and **generalized inverse** is not needed. However, the sampling distribution of the LSE would have large variances and covariances.

For example, we set a bivariate linear regression model:

$$Y = X_1 + X_2 + \varepsilon \tag{2.26}$$

Related data are as follows:

Y	X_1	X_2
2.01	.99	1.01
1.99	1.02	.99
4.01	2.03	1.99
5.99	2.97	3.01
8.01	3.96	4.01
7.99	4.01	3.99
10.01	5.04	4.99
11.99	6.05	5.99

It approximately satisfies $Y_i = X_{1i} + X_{2i}$, and it should be estimated that $\hat{\beta}_0 = 0$, $\hat{\beta}_1 = 1$, $\hat{\beta}_2 = 1$. But if we use the process of the general least squares regression, the result is

$$Y = 0.0033 + 0.4330X_1 + 1.566X_2 + \varepsilon \tag{2.27}$$

The goodness of fit of the estimated model is good. The predicted values are quite close to the actual values, and two curves showing the predicted and actual values almost run along the same course (Figure 2.11). Total correlation coefficient $R = 1$, but if $X_1 = 0$, $X_2 = 10$ are substituted in (2.27), the expected value is 15.66, which is much different from the expected value 10 of the former model (2.26).

To judge whether an estimator $\hat{\beta}$ is good as an estimate of β, some measure of degree of closeness between $\hat{\beta}$ and β must be defined. For this, a mean squared error of $\hat{\beta}$ may be used:

$$MSE(\hat{\beta}) = E\left(\left\|\hat{\beta} - \beta\right\|^2\right) = E[(\hat{\beta} - \beta)'(\hat{\beta} - \beta)]$$

Then we calculate $MSE(\hat{\beta})$ of the following linear model.

$$Y = X\beta + \varepsilon, \quad E(\varepsilon) = 0, \quad Var(\varepsilon) = \sigma^2 I_n \tag{2.28}$$

Since

$$\hat{\beta} - \beta = (X'X)^{-1}X'Y - \beta = (X'X)^{-1}X'(X\beta + \varepsilon) - \beta = (X'X)^{-1}X'\varepsilon$$

From the formula $E(y'Ay) = (Ey)'A(Ey) + tr[AVar(y)]$ we obtain

$$\begin{aligned}MSE(\hat{\beta}) &= E[(\hat{\beta} - \beta)'(\hat{\beta} - \beta)] = E[\varepsilon X(X'X)^{-2}X'\varepsilon] \\ &= \sigma^2 tr(X(X'X)^{-2}X') = \sigma^2 tr((X'X)^{-2}X'X) = \sigma^2 tr(X'X)^{-1}\end{aligned} \tag{2.29}$$

Since $X'X$ is a positive definite matrix, all of its latent roots are positive numbers, and we set $\lambda_1 \geq \lambda_2 \geq \ldots \geq \lambda_p > 0$, then,

$$tr(X'X)^{-1} = \sum_{i=1}^{p} \frac{1}{\lambda_i}$$

Substituting (2.29), we get

$$MSE(\hat{\beta}) = E\left(\left\|\hat{\beta} - \beta\right\|^2\right) = \sigma^2 \sum_{i=1}^{p} \frac{1}{\lambda_i}$$

If the column vectors of design matrix X are multicollinear, then $\lambda_p \approx 0$, and then $\dfrac{1}{\lambda_p}$ becomes extremely large, which makes the MSE or $E\left(\left\|\hat{\beta} - \beta\right\|^2\right)$ very large. Although $\hat{\beta}$ is an unbiased estimator of β, a mean squared error that is too large could bring about, in any given sample, a very large deviation between the actually estimated value of $\hat{\beta}$ and its true value.

The problem of multicollinearity lies with the near collinearity of the columns of the design matrix, and hence it is a sample phenomenon. It has very little to do with either model specification or with the structure of the regression parameters. Thus there is no meaning that one can attach to the notion of testing for multicollinearity using statistical tests such as the Farrar-Glauber test (Farrar and Glauber, 1967). For a discussion of the inappropriateness of Farrar-Glauber test see Kumar (1975). The severity of multicollinearity can however be measured through some numerical methods such as the size of the eigen values (see Belsley, Kuh, and Welsch, 1980). Some methods are suggested by Silvey (1969) for choosing between data points and altering the design matrix to reduce the extent of multicollinearity or to mitigate the problem.

2.4.2   Ridge regression

The method of ridge regression, suggested by Hoerl in 1962 and systematically developed by Hoerl and Kennard (1970), may significantly improve mean squared error of the least squares estimator when column vectors of design matrix are multicollinear. In numerical mathematics, this method is called damped least squares (Levenberg, 1944). **Ridge regression** artificially adds positive numbers along principal diagonal to an ill-conditioned $(X'\ X)$ matrix to make its eigenvalues $(\lambda_1, \lambda_2, ..., \lambda_p)$ larger. We know that in model (2.28) the least squares estimator of β is

$$\hat{\beta}_L = (X'X)^{-1}X'Y$$

Ridge estimator of β is defined as

$$\hat{\beta}(k) = (X'X + kI_p)^{-1}X'Y, \quad 0 < k < +\infty$$

where k is called the **ridge parameter**.

We see from the equation above, that when $k = 0$, it is the least squares estimator with unbiasedness. As $k \to +\infty$, $\hat{\beta}(k) \to \dfrac{1}{k^p}X'Y \to 0$. It is obvious that k must be chosen to lie between 0 and ∞ so as to make MSE as small as possible. From now on we assume that $0 < k < \infty$.

Property 1. The ridge estimator is a linear function of Y.

Let $S = X'X$, so $(X'X + kI)^{-1} = [S(I + kS^{-1})]^{-1} = (I + kS^{-1})^{-1} S^{-1} = Z_k S^{-1}$, where $Z_k = (I + kS^{-1})^{-1}$. Then

$$\hat{\beta}(k) = (X'X + kI)^{-1}X'Y = Z_k S^{-1}X'Y = Z_k(X'X)^{-1}X'Y = Z_k\hat{\beta}_L$$

where $\hat{\beta}_L$ is the least squares estimator. We can see that $\hat{\beta}(k)$ is not only the linear function of Y, but also the linear function of the least squares estimator $\hat{\beta}_L$.

Property 2. The ridge estimator is not an unbiased estimator, i.e. $E(\hat{\beta}(k)) \neq \beta$ if $k \neq 0$.

Because $E(\hat{\beta}(k)) = E[Z_k\hat{\beta}_L] = Z_kE(\hat{\beta}_L) = Z_k\beta \neq \beta$, if $k \neq 0$.

Unbiasedness is considered a basic property of a good estimator. But when we are confronted with the problem of multicollinearity we have to compromise a bit on unbiasedness in order to improve the stability of the estimator.

Property 3. Latent roots of Z_k are all within $(0, 1)$.

Assume that there are orthogonal matrices P and P' that make

$$PSP' = \begin{pmatrix} \lambda_1 & & \\ & \ddots & \\ & & \lambda_p \end{pmatrix} = \Lambda(\lambda) = diag(\lambda_1, ..., \lambda_p)$$

then it follows that

$$PZ_KP' = P(I + kS^{-1})^{-1}P' = (P')^{-1}(I + kS^{-1})^{-1}(P)^{-1} = (P(I + kS^{-1})P')^{-1} = (I + k\Lambda^{-1})^{-1}$$

$$
= \begin{pmatrix} 1+\dfrac{k}{\lambda_1} & & \\ & \ddots & \\ & & 1+\dfrac{k}{\lambda_p} \end{pmatrix}^{-1} = \begin{pmatrix} \dfrac{\lambda_1}{\lambda_1+k} & & \\ & \ddots & \\ & & \dfrac{\lambda_p}{\lambda_p+k} \end{pmatrix} \triangleq \Lambda\left(\dfrac{\lambda}{\lambda+k}\right)
$$

So the latent roots of Z_k are $\dfrac{\lambda_i}{\lambda_i+k}$, $i = 1,2,\ldots,p$, and lie within $(0,1)$.

Property 4. The ridge estimator is **compression estimator**, i.e. $\left\|\hat{\beta}(k)\right\| \le \left\|\hat{\beta}\right\|$. From Property 2 and Property 3, we have

$$
\left\|\hat{\beta}(k)\right\|^2 = \left\|Z_k\hat{\beta}\right\|^2 = \left\|P'\Lambda(k)P\hat{\beta}\right\|^2 = \left\|\Lambda(k)P\hat{\beta}\right\|^2 < \left\|P\hat{\beta}\right\|^2 = \left\|\hat{\beta}\right\|^2
$$

where P is an orthogonal matrix and $\|P\| = 1$. Certainly, since $\dfrac{\lambda_i}{\lambda_i+k}, i = 1,\ldots,p$ may not always equal to each other, this compression may not be equal compression in all directions.

Property 5. There exist a $k > 0$ to make the mean squared error of ridge estimator smaller than that of least squares estimator, namely,

$$
E\left\|\hat{\beta}(k)-\beta\right\|^2 \le E\left\|\hat{\beta}_L - \beta\right\|^2
$$

Because

$$
Cov(\hat{\beta}(k)) = \sigma^2(X'X+kI_p)^{-1}X'X(X'X+kI_p)^{-1} = \sigma^2(S+kI_p)^{-1}S(S+kI_p)^{-1}
$$

$$
E(\hat{\beta}(k)) = E[Z_k\hat{\beta}_L] = Z_kE(\hat{\beta}_L) = Z_k\beta
$$

From $E\left\|\hat{\beta}(k)-\beta\right\|^2 = \left\|E(\hat{\beta}(k)-\beta\right\|^2 + trCov(\hat{\beta}(k))$ we have

$$
E\left\|\hat{\beta}(k)-\beta\right\|^2 = \left\|E(\hat{\beta}(k)-\beta\right\|^2 + trCov(\hat{\beta}(k))
$$
$$
= \sigma^2 \sum_{i=1}^{p}\frac{\lambda_i}{(\lambda_i+k)^2} + k^2\sum_{i=1}^{p}\frac{\beta_i}{(\lambda_i+k)^2}
$$
$$
\triangleq h_1(k) + h_2(k)
$$

where the symbol $\triangleq$ means equal by definition. Then we have derivative:

$$
\frac{\partial}{\partial k}h_1(k) = -2\sigma^2\sum_{i=1}^{p}\frac{\lambda_i}{(\lambda_i+k)^3}
$$

$$
\frac{\partial}{\partial k}h_2(k) = 2k\sum_{i=1}^{p}\frac{\beta_i}{(\lambda_i+k)^2} - 2k^2\sum_{i=1}^{p}\frac{\beta_i}{(\lambda_i+k)^3} = 2k\sum_{i=1}^{p}\frac{\lambda_i\beta_i}{(\lambda_i+k)^3}
$$

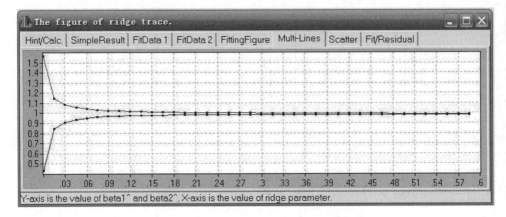

Figure 2.12 The figure of ridge traces.

From the above equation, we know that $h'_1(0) < 0$ and $h'_2(0) = 0$. So

$$\left.\frac{\partial E\left\|\hat{\beta}(k) - \beta\right\|^2}{\partial k}\right|_{k=0} = h'_1(0) + h'_2(0) < 0.$$ Besides, both the $h'_1(k)$ and $h'_2(k)$ are continuous

when $k \geq 0$ and close to zero. Thus $E\left\|\hat{\beta}(k) - \beta\right\|^2$ decreases as k increased when $k > 0$ but close to zero. Therefore, there exist a $k > 0$ to make $E\left\|\hat{\beta}(k) - \beta\right\|^2 < E\left\|\hat{\beta}(0) - \beta\right\|^2$. Because $\hat{\beta}_L$ is $\hat{\beta}(0)$, we have $E\left\|\hat{\beta}(k) - \beta\right\|^2 \leq E\left\|\hat{\beta}_L - \beta\right\|^2$.

2.4.3 Ridge trace analysis and ridge parameter selection

Since ridge estimate

$$\hat{\beta}(k) = (X'X + kI_p)^{-1}X'Y$$

is a function of k, a curve can be drawn by taking k on the horizontal axis and $\hat{\beta}(k)$ on the vertical axis. We call this curve **ridge trace**. We can see a ridge trace figure in Figure 2.12 with curves $\hat{\beta}_1(k)$ and $\hat{\beta}_2(k)$ because the number of columns of matrix X are 2 in our example.

It has been mentioned that, as $k \to 0$, ridge trace reflects the instability of the least squares estimator $\hat{\beta}_L$; and as $k \to +\infty$, ridge trace gets close to 0. Within its range of k from 0 to $+\infty$, $\hat{\beta}(k)$ may exhibit a complex path.

As for the selection of ridge parameter, there is a great deal of discussion in the literature. However, there is no one accepted optimal principle. Most of the suggested methods involve unknown parameters, and one must estimate them. We present below a brief account of some of the methods and principles of selecting the ridge parameter k.

1. Stable ridge trace

Observing ridge trace, we find some range of values for k where $\hat{\beta}(k)$ is stable. In Figure 2.12 we can see the curves decrease and become stable when k is between 0.06 and 0.12, so we can select the ridge parameter between 0.06 and 0.12.

2. Small mean square error

Mean squared error of ridge estimator $MSE(\hat{\beta}(k)) = E\left(\left\|\hat{\beta}(k) - \beta\right\|\right)^2$ also is a function of k, and it may be proved that it can attain the minimum value in some situations. We calculate and plot $MSE(\hat{\beta}(k))$ against k: it falls down in the beginning and then begins to rise from k^*. We take k^* as the ridge parameter. The detailed calculation for k^* can be found in Electronic References for Chapter 2, Appendix.

As it is not difficult to compile a numerical calculation program for ridge estimator and to plot the ridge trace, it is suggested that we use ridge trace figure to determine the ridge parameter k. We can see a ridge trace figure (such as Figure 2.12), and select a small ridge parameter where the ridge trace is stable (such as $k = 0.2$ in Figure 2.12).

Example 2.5   Ridge regression and ridge trace figure   To illustrate the ridge regression we use the data given in the beginning of this section. We use DASC software to perform all calculations. In the figure below (Figure 2.12) there are 2 curves that are two ridge traces of $\hat{\beta}_1$ and $\hat{\beta}_2$ respectively. They tend to stabilize at the same constant 1 because the real values of β_1 and β_2 are 1 exactly.

We see from the data of ridge trace that when ridge parameter k changes from 0 to 0.06, it becomes quite unstable; but when $k = 0.2$, it is rather stable. Therefore we take $k = 0.2$ for formal fitting of regression. Ridge regression equation coefficients, 0.9816 and 1.0060, are quite close to the true values.

Computed ridge regression with ridge parameter, $k = 0.2$.

$$Y = 0.0336 + 0.9816\,X_1 + 1.0060\,X_2.$$

Total correlation coefficient $R^2 = 1.0000$ ($R = 1.0000$).

With ridge regression, the stability of the estimates is established while keeping the actual regression fitting quite satisfactory. The goodness of fit figure is not reproduced as it is almost the same as Figure 2.12. Readers can perform the computation process by clicking DASC→Regression Analysis→Biased/Compress Regress→Ridge Regression.

2.4.4   Generalized ridge regression

We have introduced the **canonical form** of linear regression model above

$$Y = Z\alpha + \varepsilon$$

where $\alpha = P\beta$ is called as **canonical parameter**, $Z = XP'$ is called a **canonical variable**, and P is the orthogonal matrix that makes $P(X'X)P' = \Lambda$. Here ridge estimate of α is

$$\hat{\alpha}(k) = (\Lambda + kI)^{-1} PX'Y$$

Here the same k is added on the principal diagonal. One might expect that if different k_i, $i = 1,\ldots, p$ are added on principal diagonal, the mean square error may reduce further, which it can be shown is the case. Such an estimator is called the **Generalized Ridge Regression Estimator**. The ridge estimator discussed in the previous section turns out to be a special case of generalized ridge estimate. Now we express the Generalized Ridge Regression Estimator formally as follows:

$$\hat{\alpha}(K) = (\Lambda + K)^{-1} PX'Y$$

where

$$K = diag(k_1, k_2, \cdots, k_p)$$

Going back to our original parameters we get

$$\hat{\beta}(K) = P'\hat{\alpha}(K) = P'(\Lambda + K)^{-1} PX'Y$$

The generalized ridge regression may further reduce the mean square error of the ridge regression estimator, but the selection of ridge parameters is more complex. We will perform a demonstration and discuss it in the next chapter in connection with the estimation of the variance component model.

2.5   Recombination of independent variable and principal components regression

The ridge estimator introduced in the last section is a kind of biased estimator compromising on the unbiasedness property. It reduces the mean square error of the estimator greatly and makes it stable while being close to the true parameter values. The ridge estimator is mainly used in a situation where there is a high correlation in independent variables (multicollinearity). In this section we introduce the **principal components estimator** presented by W.F. Massy (1965). The principal components method is also an appropriate alternative to the ridge regression method in dealing with the problem of multicollinearity.

2.5.1   Concept of principal components regression

The method of **principal component regression** is based on two principles. First, as regression explains variation in the dependent variable on the basis of variation in independent variables we can afford to eliminate variables that do not have much variation. Second, as the precision of regression coefficients is best when the independent variables are orthogonal we could find a transformation of variables to make them orthogonal.

Firstly, we shall explain the principle for eliminating a variable. If there is some variable in regression model

$$Y = \beta_0 + X\beta + \varepsilon, \quad E(\varepsilon) = 0, \quad Var(\varepsilon) = \sigma^2 I_n \tag{2.30}$$

with a small variation, for example taking X_1, i.e.

$$\sum_{i=1}^{n}(X_{1i} - \overline{X}_1)^2 \approx 0$$

It is reasonable to merge it into constant term, namely, it is eliminated.

Secondly, we explain the concept of principal components. It includes two steps: forming a set of linear recombination of independent variables that are orthogonal to each other (principal components), and eliminating those principal components with small variations and keeping the other principal components in the regression. Assume that the data of design matrix of model (2.30) has been centralized, namely, $1'X = 0$, where the vector $1' = (1,1,...,1)$.

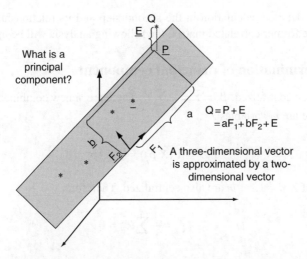

Figure 2.13   Illustration of principal component.

The **latent roots** of **correlated matrix** $X'X$ of the model are $\lambda_1 \geq \lambda_2 \geq \ldots \geq \lambda_m$, which are m solutions of the following characteristic equation

$$|X'X - \lambda I_m| = 0$$

The corresponding eigenvector p_i of latent root λ_i satisfies the following linear equations

$$(X'X - \lambda_i I_m)p_i = 0$$

Select the standardized vector p_i to make $p_i' p_i = 1$. If all these m latent roots are single roots, their corresponding eigenvectors are pairwise orthogonal. If latent roots have repeated roots, we may still make eigenvectors orthogonal as $X'X$ is a real symmetric matrix. We may perform a linear combination on former vectors with these m eigenvectors (each eigenvector is m-dimensional):

$$Z_j = p_{j1}X_1 + p_{j2}X_2 + \cdots + p_{jm}X_m = Xp_j, \quad j = 1,\ldots,m \qquad (2.31)$$

In this way, the first step of principal component regression is a recombination of independent variables.

All $Z_j, j = 1,\ldots, m$ are variables. We order them by value of variation, and then remove Z_j with small variation (say m-r in number) and keep former r variables Z_j with large variations. Then we obtain regression equation of Y in terms of $Z_j, j = 1,\ldots, r$,

$$Y = \alpha_0 + \underset{n \times r \; r \times 1}{Z \; \alpha} + \varepsilon \qquad (2.32)$$

Its regression coefficients are the so-called principal component estimates. Then the second step of principal component regression is completed.

The principal component analysis and the factor analysis are similar in the function of reducing the dimension, but their models and processes are different. The following figure (Figure 2.13) can explain their functions intuitively.

As for the detailed calculation in the second step and its relationship with latent roots $\lambda_1,\ldots, \lambda_m$ of the former correlated matrix, the following analysis will be useful.

2.5.2   Determination of principal component

Since X has been centralized, $\hat{\beta}_0 = \bar{Y} = \dfrac{1}{n}\sum_{i=1}^{n} Y_i$. There are m new combined variables as given by (2.32), there are m variables Z_i.

Since

$$1'Z_j = 1'(X\, p_j) = (1'X)p_j = 0$$

it is known that $Z_j, j = 1,\ldots, m$ are also centralized. Therefore,

$$\bar{Z}_j = \frac{1}{n}\sum_{i=1}^{n} Z_{ij} = 0$$

Accordingly, the variation measures of new variables $Z_j, j = 1,\ldots, m$ are

$$\sum_{i=1}^{n}(Z_{ij} - \bar{Z}_j)^2 = \sum_{i=1}^{n} Z_{ij}^2 = Z_j'Z_j = p_j'X'Xp_j, \quad j = 1,\ldots,m \tag{2.33}$$

What we shall do is to order these m variations above and remove smaller ones. For this, we will describe and demonstrate the following lemma:

Lemma 2.1. Assume that A is a m-order symmetric matrix with latent roots of $\lambda_1 \geq \lambda_2 \geq \ldots \geq \lambda_m$ and corresponding m linear-independent eigenvectors of $p_1, p_2,\ldots, p_m$, and it could be assumed that these eigenvectors have been orthogonally standardized. Then, for any m-dimensional vector b, we have

(1) $\max\limits_{b'b=1} b'Ab = p_1'Ap_1 = \lambda_1$.

(2) $\max\limits_{\left(\substack{b'b=1 \\ b'p_i=0,\, i=1,\ldots,k}\right)} b'Ab = p_{k+1}'Ap_{k+1} = \lambda_{k+1}$.

Proof. (1) Since $p_1,\ldots, p_m$ are standard orthogonal bases, for any $b \in R^m$, b may be expressed as the linear combination of $p_1,\ldots, p_m$. Let $P = (p_1,\ldots, p_m)$, and then P is an orthogonal matrix with $P'P = I_m$, $P'AP = \Lambda$, but $\underset{m\times 1}{b} = \underset{m\times m}{P}\underset{m\times 1}{C}$ and $b'b = C'P'PC = C'C$. Then

$$\max\limits_{b'b=1} b'Ab = \max\limits_{C'C=1} C'P'APC = \max\limits_{C'C=1} C'\begin{pmatrix} \lambda_1 & & \\ & \ddots & \\ & & \lambda_m \end{pmatrix} C$$

$$= \max\limits_{C'C=1}(C_1^2\lambda_1 + \cdots + C_m^2\lambda_m) \leq \max\limits_{C'C=1}(\lambda_1(C_1^2 + \cdots + C_m^2)) = \lambda_1$$

The equality can be reached by letting $C_1 = 1$, $C_2 = \ldots = C_m = 0$, namely, it can be reached in the direction of $b = p_1$.

(2) Since $b'p_i = 0$ and $i = 1,\ldots, k$, $b'P = (b'p_1,\ldots, b'p_k, b'p_{k+1} \ldots b'p_m) = (0,\ldots,0, b'p_{k+1} \ldots b'p_m)$. But $b'P = C'P'P = C'I_m = (C_1 \ldots C_k\ C_{k+1} \ldots C_m)$, so $C_1 = \ldots = C_k = 0$. Then it follows that

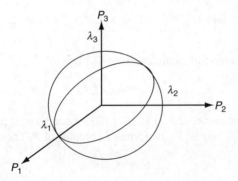

Figure 2.14 Geometric meaning of principal component.

$$\max_{\left(\substack{b'b=1 \\ b'p_i=0,\, i=1,\dots k}\right)} b'Ab = \max_{\left(\substack{C'C=1 \\ C_1=\cdots C_k=0}\right)} C'P'APC$$

$$= \max_{C'C=1}(C_{k+1}^2 \lambda_{k+1} + \cdots + C_m^2 \lambda_m)$$

$$\leq \max_{C'C=1} \lambda_{k+1}(C_{k+1}^2 + \cdots + C_m^2) = \lambda_{k+1}$$

The equality can be reached when letting $C_{k+1} = 1$ and other C_i equals to 0.

The geometric meaning of the conclusion (1) of Lemma 2.1 is shown as Figure 2.14.

The maximum value of quadratic form $b'Ab$ on the spherical surface $b'b = 1$ is the maximum latent root λ_1 of A, and is reached in the direction of $b = p_1$. The geometric meaning of the conclusion (2) is that: on the spherical surface $b'b = 1$, except the direction of p_1, in the linear combination of rest of the directions, the quadratic form $b'Ab$ gets the maximum value λ_2 in the direction of $b = p_2$; further except the direction of p_2, in the linear combination of rest of directions, the quadratic form $b'Ab$ gets the maximum value λ_3 in the direction of $b = p_3$, etc.

Now we turn to the main problem to order variations of new recombined variables expressed by (2.33). Since latent roots of $X'X$ are $\lambda_1 \geq \lambda_2 \geq \dots \geq \lambda_m$ and $p'_j p_j = 1$, in terms of the lemma,

$$\max_{p'_j p_j=1} p'_j(X'X)p_j = \lambda_1, \quad \text{when } p_j = p_1$$

We call $Xp_1 = Z_1 = p_{11}X_1 + \cdots + p_{1m}X_m$ the first principal component of former independent variables $X_1,\dots,X_m$, and its variation is λ_1. Similarly, obtain the second principal component Z_2 with variation of $\lambda_2,\dots$, and the last principal component Z_m with variation of λ_m. To remove variables with small variations is to remove corresponding recombined variables associated with the minimum or minor latent roots. Since $X'X$ is a nonnegative definite matrix, its latent roots are nonnegative and the minor latent roots approach 0. It can be assumed that $m - r$ combined variables are removed and r are left in the regression. Then the model (2.32) becomes

$$Y = \alpha_0 + Z_{(r)}\alpha_{(r)} + \varepsilon \tag{2.34}$$

where, $Z_{(r)} = (Z_1,...,Z_r)$ and $\alpha_{(r)} = (\alpha_1,...,\alpha_r)$. Let $\Lambda_{(r)} = diag(\lambda_1, \lambda_2,...,\lambda_r)$, and centralized

$\underset{n \times r}{}$ $\underset{r \times 1}{}$

Y has $\alpha_0 = 0$.

The least squares solution of canonical form (2.34) is

$$\hat{\alpha}_{(r)} = \Lambda_{(r)}^{-1} Z'_{(r)} Y$$

The expression of the model (2.5.1) $Y = \beta_0 + X\beta + \varepsilon$ can be written as $Y = \beta_0 + XPP'\beta + \varepsilon$. Take $Z = XP$ and $\alpha = P'\beta$, and let $P_{(r)}$ be former r columns of P. Then

$$\hat{\alpha} = (\hat{\alpha}_{(r)} : 0)$$

We can obtain the estimator for the parameter of the original centralized non-transformed model:

$$\hat{\beta}(r) = P\hat{\alpha} = P_{(r)}\hat{\alpha}_{(r)}$$

We call it principal components estimator of β.

The actual calculation process can be concluded as follows:

Basic model: $Y^{(0)} = X^{(0)}\beta^{(0)} + \varepsilon$;

Centralized: $Y = Y^{(0)} - \bar{Y}^{(0)}, X = X^{(0)} - \bar{X}^{(0)}$;

Centralized model: $Y = X\beta + \varepsilon$;

Calculate correlated matrix: $X'X$;

And its latent roots: $\lambda_1 \geq \lambda_2 \geq ... \geq \lambda_m$, $\sum_{i=1}^{m} \lambda_i = \lambda^*$;

Eigenvectors $p_1, p_2,..., p_m$ in accord with $\lambda_1 \geq \lambda_2 \geq ... \geq \lambda_m$;

Take r principal components to make regression model:

$$Y = \alpha_0 + Z_{(r)}\alpha_{(r)} + \varepsilon; \hat{\alpha}(r) = \Lambda_{(r)}^{-1} Z'_{(r)} Y, \Lambda(r) = diag(\lambda_1,...,\lambda_r);$$

Principal components estimator of the former centralized and standardized model: $\hat{\beta}(r) = P_{(r)}\hat{\alpha}_{(r)}$.

Note that the elimination of latent roots corresponding to near zero values and their corresponding principal components corrects for the multicollinearity. The reason is that, if $\lambda_j \approx 0$, $Xp_j \approx 0$, which is $p_{j1}X_1 + \cdots + p_{jm}X_m = 0$, a kind of multicollinearity relationship is removed.

Both ridge regression and principal components regression are intended to resolve the multicollinearity problem. Ridge regression is intended to add a constant along the principal diagonal of correlated matrix to make the minimum latent root larger; principal components regression is intended to eliminate those eigenvalues corresponding to small latent roots. Ridge regression adds information and the principal component regression subtracts information. Both cure the same disease caused by the ill-conditioned information in the sample.

Example 2.6   Economic analysis of gross imports in France   Here, we use the example of economic analysis on gross imports in France performed by Malinvaud which has been cited by Chen Xiru (1984). The reason for the selection of this old example is to check the correctness of our software with a widely known example.

The original data are as follows (Table 2.5):

Table 2.5   Economic data of France from 1949 to 1966.

Year	Y	X_1	X_2	X_3
1949	15.9	149.3	4.2	108.1
1950	16.4	161.2	4.1	114.8
1951	19.0	171.5	3.2	123.3
1952	19.1	175.5	3.2	126.9
1953	18.8	180.8	1.1	132.1
1954	20.4	190.7	2.2	137.7
1955	22.7	202.1	2.1	146.0
1956	26.5	212.4	5.6	154.0
1957	28.1	226.1	5.0	162.3
1958	27.6	231.9	5.1	164.3
1959	26.3	239.0	.7	167.6

The dependent variable Y represents the gross imports of France. There are three independent variables: X_1 involves Gross Domestic Product, X_2 involves National Reserve, and X_3 involves Consumption.

We shall first present the results of fitting principal components regression model.

Latent roots of correlated matrix are: 1.9992, 0.9982, 0.0026.

Latent roots after elimination are: 1.9992 .9982.

Eigenvectors after elimination:

.7064	.0430	.7066
−.0350	.9991	−.0258

So for regular model

$$Y = Za + \varepsilon$$

there are two independent variables, representing first two principal components:

$$Z_1 = 0.7064\, X_1\, 0.0430\, X_2\, 0.7066\, X_3$$

$$Z_2 = 0.0350\, X_1\, 0.9991\, X_2\, 0.0258\, X_3$$

Then the program computes the estimate of $a_1 = 0.6899$ and $a_2 = 0.1920$. It implies that regression equation is

$$Y = 0.6899\, Z_1 + 0.1920\, Z_2 + \varepsilon$$

Subsequently, the program gets back to the original model:

$$Y = X\beta + \varepsilon$$

The program computes the principal components estimates: $\hat{\beta}_1 = 0.4806$, $\hat{\beta}_2 = 0.2215$, $\hat{\beta}_3 = 0.4825$, which are calculated by applying formula $\hat{\beta} = P_{(r)}\hat{\alpha}_{(r)}$. It shows that

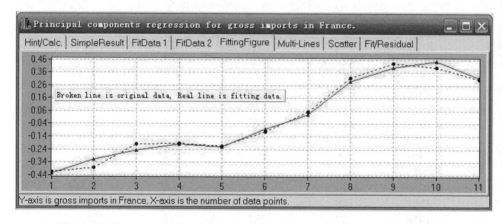

Figure 2.15   Principal components regression for gross imports in France.

$$Y = 0.4806\,X_1\,0.2215\,X_2\,0.4825\,X_3$$

DASC prints the goodness of fit figure (Figure 2.15) of the original model. We can see that the goodness of fit is quite satisfactory. The statistical analysis for regular model is as follows:

F statistics = 336.0713, F critical value $F(2,8)$ = 4.459.

Total correlation coefficient $R^2 = 0.9882$ (R = 0.9941).

In order to compare the principal components regression with the ordinary least squares regression, we perform the least squares regression on these 11 observations with the program of ordinary multivariate linear regression by DASC. Program execution is omitted here. We obtain the regression equation concerning original data:

$$Y^{(0)} = -10.1562 - 0.0528\,X_1^{(0)} + 0.5891\,X_2^{(0)} + 0.2889\,X_3^{(0)}$$

Obviously, it is different from the regression equation with the principal components.

The goodness of fit of this regression equation is almost the same as Figure 2.15, and hence it is omitted. Then what are the advantages of principal components regression over the least squares regression? The main advantage is that, principal components regression abandons one characteristic number closest to 0, namely, removing the one multicollinearity relationship:

$$0.7070\,X_1\,0.0065\,X_2\,0.7072\,X_3 \approx 0$$

which makes this regression model show better stability while fitting future data. Secondly, the number of variables of centralized and standardized model $Y = Za + \varepsilon$ is less than that of former model by one, which gives the model one more degree of freedom and greater precision to OLS estimators.

Readers can verify the computation process by clicking DASC→Regression Analysis→Biased/Compress Regress→Principal Components Regression.

Electronic references for Chapter 2

References

Andrews D.T., Chen L.G., Wentzell P., Hamilton D. & David C. (1996) Comments on the relationship between principal components analysis and weighted linear regression for bivariate data sets. *Chemometrics and Intelligent Laboratory Systems* **34**, 231–44.

Belsley D.A., Kuh E. & Welsch R.E. (1980) *Regression Diagnostics*, John Wiley & Sons, New York.

Bendel R.B. & Afifi A.A. (1977) Comparison of stopping rules in forward 'Stepwise' regression. *J.Amer. Statist. Assoc.* **72**, 46–53.

Bryc W. (2000) Specifying bivariate distributions by polynomial regressions. *Statistics and Probability Letters* **47**, 391–94.

Campbell J.Y., Lo A.W. & Mackinlay C. (1997) *The Econometrics of Financial Markets*. Princeton University Press, Princeton, New Jersey.

Chakraborty B. (2003) On multivariate quantile regression. *Journal of Statistical Planning and Inference* **110**, 109–32.

Chen R.-B. & Lo H.M.-N. (2000) Exact d-optimal designs for weighted polynomial regression model. *Computational Statistics and Data Analysis* **33**, 137–49.

Chen X., Wang S. (1984) *Modern Practical Regression Analysis*, Nanning, China: Guangxi People's Press.

Chipman J.S. (1999) Linear restrictions, rank reduction, and biased estimation in linear regression. *Linear Algebra and its Applications* **289**, 55–74.

Dahl C.M. & González-Rivera G. (2003) Testing for neglected nonlinearity in regression models based on the theory of random fields. *Journal of Econometrics* **114**, 141–64.

Daling J.R. & Tamura H. (1970) Use of orthogonal factors for selection of variables in a regression equation -an illustration. *Applied Statistics* **19**, 260–68.

Doray L.G. & Arsenault M. (2002) Estimators of the regression parameters of the zeta distribution insurance. *Mathematics and Economics* **30**, 439–50.

Dwivedi T.D., Srivastava V.K. & Hall R.L. (1980) Finite sample properties of ridge estimators. *Technometrics* **22**, 205–12.

Dufour J.-M. & Khalaf L. (2002) Simulation-based finite and large sample tests in multivariate regressions. *Journal of Econometrics* **111**, 303–22.

Farrar D.E. & Glauber R.R. (1967) Multicollinearity in regression analysis: the problem revisited. *Review of Economics and Statistics* **49**, 92–107.

Headrick Todd C. & Rotou O. (2001) An investigation of the rank transformation in multiple regression. *Computational Statistics and Data Analysis* **38**, 203–15.

Hoerl A.E. (1962) Applications of ridge analysis to regression problems. *Chemical Engineering Progress* **58**, 54–9.

Hoerl A.E. & Kennard R.W. (1970) Biased Regression of Non-Orthogonal Problems. *Technometrics* **12**, 55–67.

Jackson J.E. (1991) *A User's Guide to Principal Components*. New York: John Wiley & Sons.

Keyes T.K. & Levy M.S. (1996) Optimal control designs using predicting densities for the multivariate linear model. *Communications in Statistics* **26**, 1351–74.

Kumar K.T. (1975) Multicollinearity in Regression Analysis. *Review of Economics and Statistics* **57**, 365–66.

Laskar M.R. & King M.L. (1998) Estimation and testing of regression disturbances based on modified likelihood functions. *Journal of Statistical Planning and Inference* **71**, 75–92.

LeBlanc M. (1997) Restricted polynomial regression. *Computational Statistics & Data Analysis* **24**, 153–67.

Levenberg K. (1944) A Method for the Solution of Certain Non-Linear Problems in Least Squares. *The Quarterly of Applied Mathematics* **2**, 164–8.

Liu S.Z. (2002) Local influence in multivariate elliptical linear regression models. *Linear Algebra and its Applications* **354**, 159–74.

Malinvaud E. (1966) *Statistical Methods of Econometrics*. Rand NcNally, Chicago.

Malinvaud E. (1967) *Decentralized Procedures for Planning, in Malinvaud and Bacharach*, editors, Activity Analysis of Growth and Planning.

Malinvaud E. (1970) The consistency of nonlinear regressions, *The Annals of Mathematical Statistics*, **41**(3) 956–69.

Martínez A., Del Río F.J., Riu J. & Rius X.F. (1999) Detecting proportional and constant bias in method comparison studies by using linear regression with errors in both axes. *Chemometrics and Intelligent Laboratory Systems* **49**, 179–93.

Massy W.F. (1965) Principal Components Regression in Exploratory Statistical Research. *Journal of the American Statistical Association*, **60**(309), 234–56.

Meng X.Y. & Schenker N. (1999) Maximum likelihood estimation for linear regression models with right censored outcomes and missing predictors. *Computational Statistics & Data Analysis* **29**, 471–83.

Ndlovu P. & Preater J. (2001) Calibration using a piecewise simple linear regression model. *Communications in Statistics—Theory and Methods* **30**, 229–42.

Sergent, M., Mathieu D., Phan-Tan-Luu R. & Drava G. (1995) Correct and incorrect use of multilinear regression. *Chemometrics and Intelligent Laboratory Systems* **27**, 153–62.

Silvey S.D. (1969) Multicollinearity and imprecise estimation, *Journal of Royal Statistical Society. Series B* **31**, 539–52.

Wang C.Y. (1999) Robust sandwich covariance estimation for regression calibration estimator in Cox regression with measurement error. *Statistics & Probability Letters* **45**, 371–8.

3

Alternative structures of residual error in linear regression models

The linear model discussed in the previous chapter is:

$$Y = X\beta + \varepsilon, E(\varepsilon) = 0$$

We assumed that their respective residuals (errors) are independent, and have identical distributions with a common variance:

$$Var(\varepsilon) = \sigma^2 I_n$$

Under that condition we concluded (**Gauss Markov Theorem**) that the **ordinary lest squares (OLS)** estimator of the model, $\hat{\beta} = (X'X)^{-1}X'Y$, is the unique **linear unbiased minimum variance estimator** of β.

In this chapter, we continue to discuss the linear model, but relax the condition of residual variance being constant (**homoscedasticity**) and permit it to be different (**heteroscedasticity**). With this modification of the model assumptions one of the basic conditions of the Gauss Markov Theorem is not satisfied. The least squares solution of the linear model is no longer the minimum variance estimator. We need to modify that procedure to obtain the minimum variance estimator under the modified condition. The basic idea of such modification is to transform the observed data so that the transformed model satisfies all the conditions of the Gauss-Markov Theorem. The resulting procedure is called **Generalized Least Squares (GLS)**. Generally, if the residual covariance matrix of linear model is Φ, that is

$$Var(\varepsilon) = \Phi$$

then there exists a matrix P, such that $P'P = \Phi^{-1}$. The new transformed variables can be defined by the following transformation:

$$X^* = PX, \ Y^* = PY, \ \varepsilon^* = P\varepsilon$$

Developing Econometrics, First Edition. Hengqing Tong, T. Krishna Kumar and Yangxin Huang.
© 2011 John Wiley & Sons, Ltd. Published 2011 by John Wiley & Sons, Ltd.

It then follows:

$$Var(\varepsilon^*) = E(\varepsilon^* \varepsilon^{*\prime}) = E(P\varepsilon\varepsilon'P') = PE(\varepsilon\varepsilon')P' = P\Phi P' = I_n$$

We obtain the following model after transformation

$$\begin{cases} Y^* = X^*\beta + \varepsilon^* \\ E(\varepsilon^*) = 0, \quad E(\varepsilon^*\varepsilon^{*\prime}) = I_n \end{cases}$$

This model has constant variance. The least squares solution of the transformed model is:

$$\hat{\beta} = (X^{*\prime} X^*)^{-1} X^{*\prime} Y^*$$

This estimator has all the optimal properties established for the LSE using the Gauss-Markov Theorem. Making the necessary substitutions using the transformation matrix we obtain:

$$\hat{\beta} = (X'\Phi^{-1}X)^{-1} X'\Phi^{-1}Y$$

This is the **generalized least squares** estimator, and it has all the optimal properties.

In this chapter, we will examine different patterns of heteroscedasticity. The variance-covariance matrix Φ may be a constant, either a diagonal matrix, or it could be a constant but non-diagonal matrix, or it could be a stochastic non-diagonal matrix.

In Section 3.1, we discuss the existence of heteroscedasticity and its consequences. In that section we also mention the tests for the null hypothesis of homoscedasticity.

In Section 3.2, we discuss the different cases of heteroscedasticity leading to a constant diagonal matrix Φ such as:

$$Var(\varepsilon) = diag(\sigma_1^2, \ldots, \sigma_n^2), \quad \sigma_i^2, i = 1, \ldots, n \text{ known}$$

$$Var(\varepsilon) = \begin{pmatrix} \sigma_1^2 I_{n_1} & 0 \\ 0 & \sigma_2^2 I_{n_2} \end{pmatrix}, \sigma_1^2, \sigma_2^2 \text{ unknown}$$

$$Var(\varepsilon) = diag(\sigma_1^2, \ldots, \sigma_n^2), \quad \sigma_i^2 = \exp(Z_i'\alpha), \alpha \text{ unknown}$$

The variances of these models are diagonal matrices. In other words, all the errors are independent.

In Section 3.3, we discuss the situation in which errors are not independent, leading to a non-diagonal Φ matrix. In the first part, we discuss the **first order autoregressive linear model** for residuals. These residuals satisfy

$$\varepsilon_i = \rho\varepsilon_{i-1} + \upsilon_i$$

$$E(\upsilon_i) = 0, E(\upsilon_i^2) = \sigma^2, E(\upsilon_i\upsilon_j) = 0, (i \neq j)$$

The resulting Φ matrix is as follows:

$$\Phi = \begin{pmatrix} 1 & \rho & \cdots & \rho^T \\ \rho & 1 & \cdots & \rho^{T-1} \\ \cdots & \cdots & \ddots & \cdots \\ \rho^T & \rho^{T-1} & \cdots & 1 \end{pmatrix}$$

where ρ is unknown.

Here, though the variance of residual ε_i is not a diagonal matrix, it only contains one parameter, and error is random, whereas the error variance is constant.

Then we introduce the **Autoregressive Conditional Heteroscedasticity (ARCH)** model. For this model, we assume that the error variance is random, but no longer a constant and we have the following relation:

$$Var(\varepsilon_i) = \sigma_i^2 = \alpha_0 + \alpha_1 \varepsilon_{i-1}^2 + \alpha_2 \varepsilon_{i-2}^2 + \ldots + \alpha_p \varepsilon_{i-p}^2$$

or

$$\varepsilon_i^2 = \alpha_0 + \alpha_1 \varepsilon_{i-1}^2 + \cdots + \alpha_p \varepsilon_{i-p}^2 + \upsilon_i$$
$$E(\upsilon_i) = 0, E(\upsilon_i^2) = \sigma^2, E(\upsilon_i \upsilon_j) = 0, (i \neq j)$$

where the **Generalized Method of Moments (GMM)** estimation is used for estimating the parameters of the model.

In Section 3.4, we discuss the situations where the errors are dependent. The covariance matrix here is a positive definite one, and there exists the inverse matrix:

$$Var(\varepsilon) = \sigma^2 M > 0, \quad \sigma^2 \text{ unknown}, \quad M \text{ known}$$

We will introduce the relationship between the least squares estimation (LSE) and **the best linear unbiased estimate (BLUE)** of the model.

In Section 3.5, we will discuss the **random effects** of independent variables in regression, that is, the independent variables are not from a predetermined design matrix, but are random variables. This is now a new point of view for the regression with **fixed effects** discussed earlier. Consequently we introduce the **variance component model** to describe this model and offer methods of estimating its parameters. More discussion for variance component model, such as **generalized ridge estimation** of parameters for the variance component model, **empirical Bayes estimation** of the parameters of the variance component model, may be found in Electronic References for Chapter 3.

3.1 Heteroscedasticity: Consequences and tests for its existence

3.1.1 Consequences of heteroscedasticity

The linear regression models in the previous chapters assume that the random errors ε_i are **independent identically distributed (i.i.d.)** and have the same variance (**homoscedasticity**):

$$E(\varepsilon_i) = 0, \quad Var(\varepsilon_i) = \sigma^2, i = 1, 2, \ldots, n$$

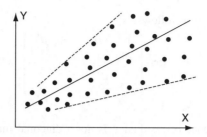

Figure 3.1   Scatter diagram of heteroscedasticity.

However, it is very difficult for any given statistical problem to ensure that the last condition is satisfied. Economic objects differ in thousands of ways and may self-organize themselves into various groups. The economic variables associated with those different groups may give rise to differences in their variances. Hence we must consider **heteroscedasticity** to be defined as follows:

$$E(\varepsilon_i) = 0, \quad Var(\varepsilon_i) = \sigma_i^2, \quad i = 1, 2, \ldots, n$$

which is reflected on the scatter diagram shown in Figure 3.1. It is obvious that the sample variance is related to the point (X_i, Y_i). In this diagram the observations are grouped by increasing variance.

Due to the presence of heteroscedasticity some of the optimal properties of the LSE no longer hold. For instance, in the simple linear regression

$$Y_i = \beta_0 + \beta_1 X_i + \varepsilon_i, \quad i = 1, \ldots, n$$

we have the following least squares estimators

$$\hat{\beta}_1 = \frac{S_{XY}}{S_{XX}} = \frac{\sum_{i=1}^{n} (X_i - \bar{X})(Y_i - \bar{Y})}{\sum_{i=1}^{n} (X_i - \bar{X})^2} = \sum_{i=1}^{n} \frac{X_i - \bar{X}}{S_{XX}} Y_i$$

$$\hat{\beta}_0 = \bar{Y} - \hat{\beta}_1 \bar{X} = \sum_{i=1}^{n} \left[\frac{1}{n} - \frac{\bar{X}(X_i - \bar{X})}{S_{XX}} \right] Y_i$$

We can show that these OLS estimators are linear and unbiased, but they are no longer minimum variance estimators.

We can show easily that

$$Var(\hat{\beta}_1) = \sum_{i=1}^{n} \left(\frac{X_i - \bar{X}}{S_{XX}} \right)^2 Var(Y_i)$$

$$Var(\hat{\beta}_0) = \sum_{i=1}^{n} \left(\frac{1}{n} - \frac{\bar{X}(X_i - \bar{X})}{S_{XX}} \right)^2 Var(Y_i)$$

As $Var(Y_i)$ is not a constant, we cannot prove that $\hat{\beta}_1, \hat{\beta}_0$ are the minimum variance linear unbiased estimators according to Gauss Markov Theorem.

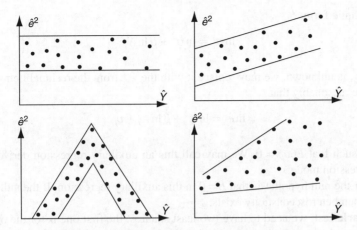

Figure 3.2 Scatter diagram of various residuals.

Besides, the F-test of significance as described earlier cannot be performed, This is so because, as in the originally defined F statistic in the homoscedasticity case, both the numerator and the denominator contain the unknown constant parameter σ^2, which could be cancelled. But now, in the case of heteroscedasticity we cannot cancel the variance terms in the numerator and denominator, as they now assume different values. The originally defined F-statistic thus will not have the F-distribution under heteroscedasticity.

Hence, the previously suggested optimal estimators, their properties, and the originally deduced tests, should all be reconsidered on account of the violation of the homoscedasticity assumption.

Before we discuss the methods for handling heteroscedasticity we must make sure that we do have heteroscedasticity. For this we need a statistical test for heteroscedasticity.

3.1.2   Tests for heteroscedasticity

Generally, to test heteroscedasticity we need a relatively large sample.

The simplest and most directly observable method to detect the presence or absence of heteroscedasticity is to examine the following square sum of residuals:

$$\hat{e}_i^2 = (Y_i - \hat{Y}_i)^2, \quad i = 1,\ldots,n$$

and $\hat{Y}_i$ together in a graph. This graph shows the variation in error variance of the residuals. Except for the first figure, the rest of the figures in Figure 3.2 shows the existence of heteroscedasticity.

There are several tests for the heteroscedasticity problem.

3.1.2.1   Park test

R.E. Park considers a special case of heteroscedasticity that is quite widely applicable, the case where σ_i^2 is considered as a function of the explanatory variable X_i and adopts the following functional form

$$\sigma_i^2 = \sigma^2 X_i^{\beta}$$

or in logarithmic form

$$\ln \sigma_i^2 = \ln \sigma^2 + \beta \ln X_i$$

Since σ_i^2 is unknown, we may replace it with the $\hat{e}_i^2$ from the residual items, as we can assume quite reasonably that

$$\ln \hat{e}_i^2 = \ln \sigma^2 + \beta \ln X_i + \upsilon_i$$

where υ_i is such that $E(\upsilon_i) = 0$. We may call this an auxiliary regression derived from the original regression model.

Consider the null hypothesis that $\beta = 0$ in this auxiliary regression. If the null hypothesis is rejected then heteroscedasticity exists.

In the **Park Test**, we need to have two least squares: the first one is for the original data (X_i, Y_i), and we obtain $\hat{Y}_i$, $\hat{e}_i$; the second is for $(X_i, \hat{e}_i^2)$.

The **Glejser test** is similar in spirit to the Park test, but with different specification of the auxiliary regression equation between Y and X. Instead of using $\hat{e}_i^2$ as the dependent variable in the auxiliary regression it uses $|e_i|$. It also uses the explanatory variables either in their natural form or as their square roots, or as their reciprocals.

3.1.2.2   Breusch- Pagan-Godfrey (BPG) test

We assume that the original data satisfy the following model

$$Y_i = \beta_0 + \beta_1 X_{1i} + \cdots + \beta_m X_{mi} + \varepsilon_i, \quad i = 1, 2, \ldots, n$$

We obtain $\hat{Y}_i$, $\hat{e}_i$ by using the ordinary least squares. We define the maximum likelihood estimator of σ^2

$$\tilde{\sigma}^2 = \frac{1}{n} \sum_{i=1}^{n} \hat{e}_i^2 = \frac{1}{n} \sum_{i=1}^{n} (Y_i - \hat{Y}_i)^2$$

Note that it is not $\hat{\sigma}^2 = \dfrac{1}{n-m-1} \sum_{i=1}^{n} (Y_i - \hat{Y}_i)^2$ normally used in least squares regression analysis. Then we define a new auxiliary variable as follows:

$$p_i = \hat{e}_i^2 / \tilde{\sigma}^2 \tag{3.1}$$

We now define an auxiliary regression with p_i and all the explanatory variables X_{ji},

$$p_i = \alpha_0 + \alpha_1 X_{1i} + \cdots + \alpha_m X_{mi} + \upsilon_i$$

Let the regression sum of squares of this auxiliary regression be S_{ES}. Then we define the statistic as

$$\Theta = \frac{1}{2} S_{ES} = \frac{1}{2} \sum_{i=1}^{n} (\hat{p}_i - \bar{p}_i)^2$$

Table 3.1   Data on consumption (Y) and income (X).

Y	X	Y	X	Y	X
55.	80.	152.	220.	95.	140.
65.	100.	144.	210.	108.	145.
70.	85.	175.	245.	113.	150.
80.	110.	180.	260.	110.	160.
79.	120.	135.	190.	125.	165.
84.	115.	140.	205.	115.	180.
98.	130.	178.	265.	130.	185.
95.	140.	191.	270.	135.	190.
90.	125.	137.	230.	120.	200.
75.	90.	189.	250.	140.	205.
74.	105.	55.	80.	140.	210.
110.	160.	70.	85.	152.	220.
113.	150.	75.	90.	140.	225.
125.	165.	65.	100.	137.	230.
108.	145.	74.	105.	145.	240.
115.	180.	80.	110.	175.	245.
140.	225.	84.	115.	189.	250.
120.	200.	79.	120.	180.	260.
145.	240.	90.	125.	178.	265.
130.	185.	98.	130.	191.	270.

We can prove that under the normality assumption, when the sample size is large enough, Θ has the asymptotic Chi-square distribution with m-1 degrees of freedom:

$$\Theta \sim \chi^2(m-1), (n \to \infty)$$

If the Θ exceeds the critical χ^2 value at the chosen level of significance, one can reject the hypothesis of homoscedasticity and accept the hypothesis of heteroscedasticity. This test is called **Breusch-Pagan-Godfrey (BPG) Test**.

More tests of heteroscedasticity, such as **White Test**, can be seen in the Electronic References and DASC.

Example 3.1   Breusch-Pagan-Godfrey test for heteroscedastic data of consumption
Table 3.1 contains 60 pairs of data on consumption expenditure (Y) and income (X), requiring the heteroscedasticity test.

For optimal use of the page layout the table above is arranged in six columns rather than two columns, as is done in the computer data file of DASC. Using the BPG heteroscedasticity test program developed by us, that forms part of DASC, we estimate the regression equation as:

$$\hat{Y}_i = 9.2903 + 0.6378X_i$$

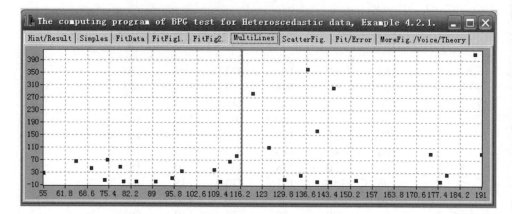

Figure 3.3   BPG test for heteroscedastic data: residual variance plot.

Regressing p_i defined by (3.1) on X_i, we obtain the following:

$$\hat{p}_i = -0.7426 + 0.0101X_i$$

and the test program calculates the statistic as

$$\Theta = 5.2140$$

The critical value of a Chi-square distribution with one degree of freedom at 1% level of significance is 6.6349. The critical value at 5% level of significance is 3.8414. From these we infer that the null hypothesis of homoscedasticity cannot be rejected at 1% level of significance while at 5% level of significance or higher we can reject it and assume that there is heteroscedasticity.

The F-statistic in regression is as high as 1038.9, and the total correlation coefficient R 0.9730, suggesting that the regression fit is very good. But there is no heteroscedasticity according to BPG test. In Figure 3.3 we see the residual variance plot.

It is seen from Figure 3.3 that variances are relatively smaller until $Y = 116.2$ and gradually grow bigger after that. The figures and computation can be seen by clicking on DASC→Hypothesis Test→BPG Test of Heteroscedastic Data.

3.2 Generalized linear model with covariance being a diagonal matrix

3.2.1 Diagonal covariance matrix and weighted least squares

Let us consider the situation where the model is

$$\begin{cases} Y = X\beta + \varepsilon \\ E(\varepsilon) = 0, \ Var(\varepsilon) = \Phi = diag(\sigma_1^2, \sigma_2^2, \ldots, \sigma_n^2) \end{cases} \tag{3.2}$$

If $\sigma_i^2\ (i = 1, \ldots, n)$ are known, i.e., Φ is known, then we define the generalized least squares (GLS) estimator of β as

$$\hat{\beta} = (X'\Phi^{-1}X)^{-1}X'\Phi^{-1}Y$$

The Generalized Least Squares (GLS) Estimator was first offered by A.C. Aitken (1934). When Φ is a diagonal matrix, it is easy to get

$$P = diag(\sigma_1^{-1}, \sigma_2^{-1}, \ldots, \sigma_n^{-1})$$

so that

$$P'P = \Phi^{-1}$$

We define the transformation as

$$X^* = PX, \ Y^* = PY, \ \varepsilon^* = P\varepsilon$$

Then the original model turns into

$$\begin{cases} Y^* = X^* \beta + \varepsilon^* \\ E(\varepsilon^*) = 0, Var(\varepsilon^*) = I_n \end{cases}$$

$$\hat{\beta} = (X^{*\prime}X^*)^{-1} X^{*\prime} Y^*$$

Thus we obtain the ordinary least squares estimate.

This is also referred to **Weighted Least Squares Estimator (WLS)**, because the underlying transformation is equivalent to weighting the individual observations by the reciprocal of the standard deviations $\sigma_i^{-1}, i = 1, \cdots, n$. Here the minimized function is

$$\sum_{i=1}^{n} \left(\frac{\varepsilon_i}{\sigma_i} \right)^2 = (Y - X\beta)'\Phi^{-1}(Y - X\beta)$$

We see that relatively smaller σ_i makes the corresponding observation receive a relatively larger weight, while bigger σ_i reduces the importance of the corresponding data point. This point is apparent in the following equation

$$\hat{\beta} = \left(\sum_{i=1}^{n} \sigma_i^{-2} X_i X_i' \right)^{-1} \sum_{i=1}^{n} \sigma_i^{-2} X_i' Y$$

The reasoning above is intuitive. We see that if a person's opinion on a given issue fluctuates to a considerable degree, then one discounts his views, while if a person is clearheaded and has consistent opinions, his opinions are taken seriously. In Section 3.4, we also apply the GMM method to deal with this type of problem.

3.2.2   Model with two unknown variances

Next we turn to the situation of unknown variances. It is evident that there should not be too many unknown variances. For $\Phi = diag(\sigma_1^2, \ldots, \sigma_n^2)$, if all of them are unknown, we cannot estimate all n variances since there are only n sets of data points.

We may assume that there are only two unknown variances σ_1^2 and σ_2^2, so the model is divided into

$$\begin{pmatrix} Y_1 \\ Y_2 \end{pmatrix} = \begin{pmatrix} X_1 \\ X_2 \end{pmatrix} \beta + \begin{pmatrix} \varepsilon_1 \\ \varepsilon_2 \end{pmatrix}$$

Here Y_i, X_i, ε_i are n_i rows, $i = 1,2$; $n_1 + n_2 = n$, $Y' = (Y_1', Y_2')$, $X' = (X_1', X_2')$, $\varepsilon' = (\varepsilon_1', \varepsilon_2')$.

$$Var(\varepsilon) = E\left(\begin{pmatrix} \varepsilon_1 \\ \varepsilon_2 \end{pmatrix}(\varepsilon_1' \varepsilon_2')\right) = \begin{pmatrix} \sigma_1^2 I_{n_1} & 0 \\ 0 & \sigma_2^2 I_{n_2} \end{pmatrix}$$

Thus the model may be divided into two, sharing the same regression coefficient, but having different variances.

$$\begin{cases} Y_1 = X_1\beta + \varepsilon_1, & Var(\varepsilon_1) = \sigma_1^2 I_{n_1} \\ Y_2 = X_2\beta + \varepsilon_2, & Var(\varepsilon_2) = \sigma_2^2 I_{n_2} \end{cases}$$

We certainly cannot imagine that they are completely independent and proceed to estimate them separately.

When σ_1^2 and σ_2^2 are already known, from the preceding GLS method, we have

$$\hat{\beta} = (X'\Phi^{-1}X)^{-1}X'\Phi^{-1}Y = \left(\frac{X_1'X_1}{\sigma_1^2} + \frac{X_2'X_2}{\sigma_2^2}\right)^{-1}\left(\frac{X_1'Y_1}{\sigma_1^2} + \frac{X_2'Y_2}{\sigma_2^2}\right) \tag{3.3}$$

When σ_1^2 and σ_2^2 are unknown we must estimate them. As the variances are separated, it is easy to estimate them in the respective sub-models:

$$\begin{cases} \hat{\sigma}_i^2 = \dfrac{S_{ES}}{n_i - m} = \dfrac{1}{n_i - m}(Y_i - X_i\hat{\beta}_i)'(Y_i - X_i\hat{\beta}_i), i = 1,2 \\ \hat{\beta}_i = (X_i'X_i)^{-1}X_i'Y_i, i = 1,2 \end{cases}$$

Having their respective variance estimators, we replace σ_i^2 with $\hat{\sigma}_i^2$ in (3.3) and return to the estimation of β

$$\hat{\hat{\beta}} = (X'\Phi^{-1}X)^{-1}X'\Phi^{-1}Y = \left(\frac{X_1'X_1}{\hat{\sigma}_1^2} + \frac{X_2'X_2}{\hat{\sigma}_2^2}\right)^{-1}\left(\frac{X_1'Y_1}{\hat{\sigma}_1^2} + \frac{X_2'Y_2}{\hat{\sigma}_2^2}\right)$$

and the asymptotic property of $\hat{\hat{\beta}}$ can be established as:

$$\sqrt{n}(\hat{\hat{\beta}} - \beta) \xrightarrow{d} N(0, (X'\Phi^{-1}X)^{-1})$$

so we may work out the interval estimation and hypothesis test for β.

The two-step method of estimation is used here: First, we estimate the variance, then, the regression coefficient.

3.2.3 Multiplicative heteroscedastic model

In this section, we consider a situation where there may be several unknown variances, but they are written into one special function formula:

$$\begin{cases} Y_i = X_i'\beta + \varepsilon_i \\ E(\varepsilon_i) = 0, Var(\varepsilon_i) = \sigma_i^2 = \exp(Z_i'\alpha), i = 1,\ldots,n \end{cases} \tag{3.4}$$

where $Z_i' = (Z_{i1}, Z_{i2}, \ldots, Z_{ik})$ is a known $(1 \times k)$ vector and $\alpha = (\alpha_1, \alpha_2, \ldots, \alpha_k)'$ is an unknown $(k \times 1)$ vector with k << n (symbol << means much less than). Generally, $Z_{i1} = 1$, and the rest of Z_i are either a subset of all the X_is or functions of some or all of X_is. We need to estimate both α and β. The variance here can be written as

$$\sigma_i^2 = \exp(\alpha_1) \cdot \exp(\alpha_2 Z_{i2}) \cdots \exp(\alpha_k Z_{ik})$$

so the model is called the **multiplicative heteroscedasticity model**.

When $k = 2$, let $\ln x_i = Z_{i2}$, $\ln \sigma^2 = \alpha_1$, $p = \alpha_2$, then we have

$$\sigma_i^2 = \exp(Z_i'\alpha) = \exp(\alpha_1 + \alpha_2 Z_{i2}) = \sigma^2 x_i^p$$

Under general situations,

$$\begin{aligned}
\sigma_i^2 &= \exp(Z_i'\alpha) = \exp(\alpha_1 + \alpha_2 Z_{i2} + \cdots + \alpha_k Z_{ik}) \\
&= \sigma^2 \exp(\alpha_2 Z_{i2} + \cdots + \alpha_k Z_{ik}) = \sigma^2 \exp(Z_i^{*'}\alpha^*)
\end{aligned}$$

where $Z_i^* = (Z_{i2}, \ldots, Z_{ik})$, $\alpha^* = (\alpha_2, \ldots, \alpha_k)'$. We adopt the matrix notation in model (3.2) as follows,

$$\begin{aligned}
\Phi &= \begin{pmatrix} \exp(Z_1'\alpha) & & & \\ & \exp(Z_2'\alpha) & & \\ & & \ddots & \\ & & & \exp(Z_n'\alpha) \end{pmatrix} \\
&= \sigma^2 \begin{pmatrix} \exp(Z_1^{*'}\alpha^*) & & & \\ & \exp(Z_2^{*'}\alpha^*) & & \\ & & \ddots & \\ & & & \exp(Z_{n_1}^{*'}\alpha^*) \end{pmatrix}
\end{aligned}$$

If we figure out an estimate $\hat{\alpha}$, we can get $\hat{\sigma}_i^2$ as well as $\hat{\beta}$. Above all, taking the logarithm of σ_i^2, we may get

$$\ln \sigma_i^2 = Z_i'\alpha \tag{3.5}$$

The residual vector of the model is

$$\hat{\varepsilon}_1 = Y_i - X_i'\hat{\beta}_i, \quad i = 1, \ldots, n$$

where

$$\hat{\beta}_i = (X_i'X_i)^{-1} X_i'Y_i$$

Thus, $\ln \hat{\varepsilon}_i^2 (i = 1, \ldots, n)$ is worked out. Combining this result with (3.5), we get

$$\ln \hat{\varepsilon}_i^2 = Z_i'\alpha - \ln \sigma_i^2 + \ln \hat{\varepsilon}_i^2 = Z_i'\alpha + \upsilon_i, i = 1, \ldots, n \tag{3.6}$$

where $\upsilon_i = \ln \hat{\varepsilon}_i^2 - \ln \sigma_i^2 = \ln(\hat{\varepsilon}_i^2 / \sigma_i^2)$.

The system of equation (3.6) may be regarded as an auxiliary regression model. $\ln \hat{\varepsilon}_i^2$ is the new dependent variable, Z_i is the vector of the design matrix, and α is an unknown $k \times 1$ vector. The model can be expressed in a matrix form below:

$$q = Z\alpha + v \tag{3.7}$$

where $q = (\ln \hat{\varepsilon}_i^2, \ldots, \ln \hat{\varepsilon}_n^2)$, $Z = (Z_1, \ldots, Z_k)'$, $v = (v_1, \ldots v_n)'$. Applying the least squares method, we obtain the OLS estimator of α

$$\hat{\alpha} = (Z'Z)^{-1}Z'q$$

It is difficult to know the properties of this estimator, because $\hat{\alpha} = \alpha + (Z'Z)^{-1}Z'v$ where the expected value of v is not necessarily zero, and furthermore v involves α. We may resort to the asymptotic property. Write

$$\frac{1}{n}X'X = Q, \quad \frac{1}{n}X'\Phi X = V$$

Assuming that Q and V are nonsingular and considering the means and variances of $\hat{\varepsilon}_i - \varepsilon_i$, we have

$$E[\hat{\varepsilon}_i - \varepsilon_i] = -X_i'(X'X)^{-1}X'E(Y) = 0$$

and

$$\begin{aligned}
E((\hat{\varepsilon}_i - \varepsilon_i)^2) &= X_i'(X'X)^{-1}X'E[\varepsilon\varepsilon']X(X'X)^{-1}X_i' \\
&= \sigma^2 X_i'(X'X)^{-1}X'\Phi X(X'X)^{-1}X_i' \\
&= \frac{\sigma^2}{n}X_i'\left(\frac{X'X}{n}\right)^{-1}\frac{X'\Phi X}{n}\left(\frac{X'X}{n}\right)^{-1}X_i'
\end{aligned}$$

When $n \to \infty$, $E[(\hat{\varepsilon}_i - \varepsilon_i)^2] \to 0$, then $(\hat{\varepsilon}_i - \varepsilon_i) \to 0$, namely, $\hat{\varepsilon}_i \to \varepsilon_i, (n \to \infty)$
so

$$v_i = \ln(\hat{\varepsilon}_i^2/\sigma_i^2) \to \ln(\varepsilon_i^2/\sigma_i^2) = v_i^*, (n \to \infty)$$

If we assume that $\varepsilon_i \sim N(0, \sigma_i^2)$, then $\varepsilon_i^2/\sigma_i^2 \sim \chi^2(1)$, and $\ln(\varepsilon_i^2/\sigma_i^2) \approx \ln[\chi^2(1)]$. Thus, although our discussion has been in general algebraic terms so far, with the above distributional assumptions we get specific numerical values for the mean and variance of v_i^*:

$$E(v_i^*) = -1.2704$$

$$Var(v_i^*) = E[(v_i^* - E(v_i^*))^2] = 4.9348$$

$$Cov(v_i^*, v_j^*) = 0, \quad i \neq j$$

It is seen from the asymptotic distribution that the random terms v_i of model (3.7) are uncorrelated and have a constant variance satisfying the assumptions of ordinary least squares model. But the expected value of v_i^* is not zero, but this is not a serious problem. We can put the expected value into the constant term α_1 in the model as follows,

$$\hat{\alpha}^* = (\alpha_1 - 1.2704, \alpha_2, \ldots, \alpha_k)$$

It is already LSE with very good properties. Meanwhile, we also know that

$$\sqrt{n}(\hat{\alpha}^* - \alpha) \xrightarrow{d} N(0, 4.9348\Sigma^{-1})$$

where

$$\Sigma^{-1} = \lim_{n \to \infty} \frac{1}{n} Z'Z$$

Now let us summarize algorithm of the model estimation. From the data matrix $(Y \vdots X) = \{Y_i \vdots X_{1i}, \ldots, X_{mi}\}_1^n$ and $\{Z_{1i}, \ldots, Z_{ki}\}_1^n$, we establish the model (3.4). Having obtained $\hat{\beta} = (X'X)^{-1}X'Y$, $\hat{\varepsilon} = Y - X'\hat{\beta}$, $\ln \hat{\varepsilon}^2 = q$, we may obtain the auxiliary regression model (3.7), from which we obtain $\hat{\alpha} = (Z'Z)^{-1}Z'q$. Then we estimate that $\hat{\sigma}_i^2 = \exp(Z_i'\hat{\alpha})$ and $\hat{\Phi}$, and finally get $\hat{\hat{\beta}}$ and $\hat{\hat{\sigma}}$ as follows:

$$\hat{\hat{\beta}} = (X'\hat{\Phi}^{-1}X)^{-1}X'\hat{\Phi}^{-1}Y$$

$$\hat{\hat{\sigma}} = (Y - X\hat{\hat{\beta}})'\hat{\Phi}^{-1}(Y - X\hat{\hat{\beta}})/(n - m)$$

As there exists the asymptotic distribution

$$\sqrt{n}(\hat{\hat{\beta}} - \beta) \xrightarrow{d} N(0, \hat{\sigma}^2(X'\Phi^{-1}X)^{-1})$$

we may perform the hypothesis test on $\hat{\hat{\beta}}$.

3.3   Autocorrelation in a linear model

Consider the linear model

$$\begin{cases} Y = X\beta + \varepsilon \\ E(\varepsilon) = 0, Var(\varepsilon) = \Phi = diag(\sigma_1^2, \ldots, \sigma_n^2) \end{cases}$$

where Φ is a diagonal matrix, indicating that the stochastic observation terms $Y_i(i = 1, \ldots, n)$ are uncorrelated to each other. In economic applications it is usually very difficult to satisfy this assumption of no correlation. In practical economic applications one of three possibilities arises:

(1) Y_i relies on its previous value. For example, if Y_i is the annual economic indicator, it must have something to do with the previous value, and any change from that value could be small;

(2) X contains the present or lagged numerical value of explanatory variables; implying that dependence of Y on correlated lagged values of X gives rise to correlated Y values;

(3) The stochastic error terms ε_is are correlated (**autocorrelated**) giving rise to correlated Ys.

The first two situations suggest that X is also stochastic, i.e., it is a **random effect**, which we will study later. In this section, we focus on autocorrelated ε. Firstly, we explore the autocorrelation model formed by the stochastic error term ε. We then explore the situation where the variance of ε is also stochastic.

3.3.1   Linear model with first-order residual autoregression

The stochastic error terms of linear model may exhibit different forms of correlations. One very common model is the linear model with first-order residual autoregression.

$$\begin{cases} Y_i = X_i'\beta + \varepsilon_i, i = 1,\ldots,n \\ \varepsilon_i = \rho\varepsilon_{i-1} + v_i, i = 2,\ldots,n \\ E(v_i) = 0, \quad E(v_i^2) = \sigma_v^2, \quad E(v_iv_j) = 0, \quad i \neq j \end{cases} \tag{3.8}$$

It is seen that the error terms ε_i do not satisfy the uncorrelated property required by the ordinary least squares method. Yet we may adopt the second best choice and obtain a Generalized Least Squares (GLS) estimator.

When $|\rho| < 1$, the process of **first order autoregression** is stationary[1],

$$\varepsilon_i = v_i + \rho\varepsilon_{i-1} = v_i + \rho(v_{i-1} + \rho\varepsilon_{i-2}) = v_i + \rho v_{i-1} + \rho^2\varepsilon_{i-2}$$

$$= v_i + \rho v_{i-1} + \rho^2 v_{i-2} + \rho^3 v_{i-3} + \cdots = \sum_{k=0}^{\infty}\rho^k v_{i-k}$$

then

$$E(\varepsilon_i) = \sum_{k=0}^{\infty}\rho^k E(v_{i-k}) = 0$$

$$Var(\varepsilon_i) = \sum_{k=0}^{\infty}\rho^{2k}Var(v_{i-k}) = \sum_{k=0}^{\infty}\rho^{2k}\sigma_v^2 = \frac{\sigma_v^2}{1-\rho^2} \triangleq \sigma_\varepsilon^2$$

$$E(\varepsilon_i\varepsilon_{i-1}) = \rho E(\varepsilon_{i-1}^2) + E(\varepsilon_{i-1}v_i) = \rho \cdot \frac{\sigma_v^2}{1-\rho^2}$$

$$E(\varepsilon_i\varepsilon_{i-2}) = \rho E(\varepsilon_{i-1}\varepsilon_{i-2}) + E(\varepsilon_{i-2}v_i)$$
$$= \rho E((\rho\varepsilon_{i-2} + v_{i-1})\varepsilon_{i-2}) + E(\varepsilon_{i-2}v_i)$$
$$= \rho^2 E(\varepsilon_{i-2}^2) = \frac{\rho^2\sigma_v^2}{1-\rho^2}$$

Similarly

$$E(\varepsilon_i\varepsilon_{i-s}) = \frac{\rho^s\sigma_v^2}{1-\rho^2}, \quad s = 1,2,3,\ldots$$

---

[1] The concept of stationarity in time series will be explained in Chapter 7. It suffices here to note that we are assuming this condition of stationarity.

Note that they all have the common factor σ_v^2. We can obtain the residual covariance matrix:

$$\Phi = E(\varepsilon\varepsilon') = E\begin{pmatrix} \varepsilon_1^2 & \varepsilon_1\varepsilon_2 & \cdots & \varepsilon_1\varepsilon_n \\ \varepsilon_{21} & \varepsilon_2^2 & \cdots & \varepsilon_2\varepsilon_n \\ \cdots\cdots & & & \\ \varepsilon_n\varepsilon_1 & \varepsilon_n\varepsilon_2 & \cdots & \varepsilon_n^2 \end{pmatrix}$$

$$= \frac{\sigma_v^2}{1-\rho^2}\begin{pmatrix} 1 & \rho & \rho^2 & \cdots & \rho^{n-1} \\ \rho & 1 & \rho & \cdots & \rho^{n-2} \\ \rho^2 & \rho & 1 & \cdots & \rho^{n-3} \\ & & \cdots\cdots & & \\ \rho^{n-1} & \rho^{n-2} & \rho^{n-3} & \cdots & 1 \end{pmatrix}$$

If we write the matrix as

$$\Psi = \frac{1}{1-\rho^2}\begin{pmatrix} 1 & \rho & \rho^2 & \cdots & \rho^{n-1} \\ \rho & 1 & \rho & \cdots & \rho^{n-2} \\ & & \cdots\cdots & & \\ \rho^{n-1} & \rho^{n-2} & \rho^{n-3} & \cdots & 1 \end{pmatrix} \tag{3.9}$$

then $\Phi = \sigma_v^2\Psi$. So the linear model with first-order residual autoregression may also be written as

$$\begin{cases} Y = X\beta + \varepsilon \\ E(\varepsilon) = 0, \quad Var(\varepsilon) = \sigma_v^2\Psi \end{cases} \tag{3.10}$$

Comparing with the ordinary least squares model, we replace I_n in that model with Ψ. This is a heteroscedasticity linear regression model with the positive definite covariance matrix Ψ. However, the entire Ψ here depends on just one parameter ρ that can be estimated.

To solve the linear model with first order residual autoregression, we should adopt the form of (3.8) first, then the form of (3.10). In the regression equation

$$Y_i = X_i'\beta + \varepsilon_i, \quad i = 1,\ldots,n$$

We obtain the ordinary least squares estimator of β from the original data

$$\hat{\beta} = (X'X)^{-1}X'Y \tag{3.11}$$

and calculate the residuals

$$\hat{\varepsilon}_i = Y_i - \hat{Y}_i = Y_i - X_i'\hat{\beta}, \quad i = 1,\ldots,n$$

In the regression equation concerning the residual

$$\varepsilon_i = \rho\varepsilon_{i-1} + v_i, \quad i = 2,\ldots,n$$

taking $\hat{\varepsilon}_i$ to run the regression, we get the estimator of ρ:

$$\hat{\rho} = \sum_{i=2}^{n}\hat{\varepsilon}_i\hat{\varepsilon}_{i-1} \bigg/ \sum_{i=2}^{n}\hat{\varepsilon}_i^2$$

We substitute for unknown ρ the estimated $\hat{\rho}$. We now return to the form of model (3.10) and calculate the generalized least squares estimation of β:

$$\hat{\hat{\beta}} = (X'\hat{\Psi}^{-1}X)^{-1}X'\hat{\Psi}^{-1}Y$$

We know that when the order of Ψ is high, the computation of Ψ^{-1} poses a problem. Thus we should diagnose the problem and simplify the calculation. As we know the matrix algebraically we may deduce its inverse matrix as

$$\Psi^{-1} = \begin{pmatrix} 1 & -\rho & 0 & \cdots & 0 & 0 \\ -\rho & 1+\rho^2 & -\rho & \cdots & 0 & 0 \\ 0 & -\rho & 1+\rho^2 & \cdots & 0 & 0 \\ \cdots & \cdots & \cdots & \cdots & \cdots & \cdots \\ 0 & 0 & 0 & \cdots & 1+\rho^2 & -\rho \\ 0 & 0 & 0 & \cdots & -\rho & 1 \end{pmatrix}$$

We can also verify that there exists the **lower triangular factorization**

$$P'P = \Psi^{-1}$$

with the lower triangular matrix

$$P = \begin{pmatrix} \sqrt{1-\rho^2} & 0 & 0 & \cdots & 0 & 0 \\ -\rho & 1 & 0 & \cdots & 0 & 0 \\ 0 & -\rho & 1 & \cdots & 0 & 0 \\ \cdots & \cdots & \cdots & \cdots & \cdots & \cdots \\ 0 & 0 & 0 & \cdots & 1 & 0 \\ 0 & 0 & 0 & \cdots & -\rho & 1 \end{pmatrix}$$

With this treatment, it is easy to proceed with the computation of the GLS estimator. Then we take the following transformation

$$Y^* = PY, X^* = PX \tag{3.12}$$

Then the model (3.10) becomes

$$\begin{cases} Y^* = X^* \beta + \varepsilon^* \\ E(Y^*) = 0, \quad Var(Y^*) = \sigma_v^2 I_n \end{cases}$$

where the unobservable term is $\varepsilon^* = P\varepsilon$. Now the model satisfies the assumptions of ordinary least squares, and the corresponding OLS estimators are

$$\hat{\beta} = (X^{*\prime}X^*)^{-1}X^{*\prime}Y \tag{3.13}$$

$$\hat{\sigma}_v^2 = \frac{1}{n-p}(Y^* - X^*\hat{\beta})'(Y^* - X^*\hat{\beta})$$

Note that the first terms of Y^* and X^* are $\sqrt{1-\rho^2}Y_1$ and $\sqrt{1-\rho^2}X_1$ respectively. This avoids losing the degree of freedom and maintains the effectiveness of parameter estimations.

Here, with respect to matrix decomposition, it is more rational to work out Y_1 and X_1 in this way. This transformation is known popularly as **Cochrane-Orcutt transformation**.

One may ask why we need the generalized least squares $\hat{\hat{\beta}}$ from (3.13) as we already have the ordinary least squares estimator $\hat{\beta}$ from (3.11). The OLS estimator is good no doubt, but the elements of its variance-covariance matrix are too big and will result in relatively bad fits for future data, and also they will result in poor performance of the test statistics.

There are many approaches to test for the first-order residual autocorrelation in a model. The **Durbin-Watson Test** is one of important tests for this. Here we introduce the asymptotic test of first-order residual autoregression.

In model (3.8), we mainly test whether the first-order autoregression holds or not. This is done by setting the null and alternative hypotheses as follows:

$$H_0 : \rho = 0 \leftrightarrow H_1 : \rho \neq 0$$

This hypothesis can be tested making use of the estimator $\hat{\rho}$. Under certain reasonable assumptions, we may deduce that, $E(\hat{\rho}) = \rho$, $Var(\hat{\rho}) = (1 - \rho^2)/n$, and the asymptotic distribution of $\hat{\rho}$ is Normal, namely,

$$\hat{\rho} \sim N(\rho, (1 - \rho^2)/n)$$

Thus we can construct a statistic as follows

$$Z = \frac{\hat{\rho} - \rho}{\sqrt{(1 - \rho^2)/n}} \sim N(0,1)$$

When the null assumption H_0 holds,

$$Z = \sqrt{n}\hat{\rho} \sim N(0,1)$$

If we assume the 5% level of significance, then the hypothesis test has the rejection region $\left|\sqrt{n}\hat{\rho}\right| \geq 1.96$. Generally, the rejection region is

$$\left|\sqrt{n}\hat{\rho}\right| \geq U_{\alpha/2}$$

Where $U_{\alpha/2}$ is the cumulative probability that a standard Normal variable is less than or equal to $\alpha/2$.

The limitation of this test is that it requires a very large sample size. However, it needs no specifically derived (mathematically or empirically) statistical distribution and associated critical values. It is relatively very easy to implement and very pragmatic.

Example 3.2   Linear first-order residual autoregression model: a Cobb-Douglas production function   Table 3.2 presents a sample of 20 observations on one dependent variable and two independent variables. The data refer to a **Cobb-Douglas production function** model. Here Y_i is ln output, X_1 is ln labor force, X_2 is ln capital. We intend to test the linear first-order residual autoregression. We postulate the model:

$$\begin{cases} Y_i = \beta_0 + \beta_2 X_{1i} + \beta_3 X_{2i} + \varepsilon_i \\ \varepsilon_i = \rho\varepsilon_{i-1} + \upsilon_i \\ E(\upsilon_i) = 0, \quad Var(\upsilon_i) = \sigma^2, \quad Cov(\upsilon_i, \upsilon_j) = 0, \ i \neq j \end{cases}$$

Table 3.2   The data of Cobb-Douglas production function.

No.	Y	X_1	X_2	No.	Y	X_1	X_2
1	42.0837	14.53	16.74	11	52.4668	20.77	19.33
2	41.4857	15.30	16.81	12	50.6757	21.17	17.04
3	39.0557	15.92	19.50	13	51.6428	21.34	16.74
4	45.0892	17.41	22.12	14	56.1883	22.91	19.81
5	51.6698	18.37	22.34	15	66.2164	22.96	31.92
6	51.1838	18.83	17.47	16	63.2273	23.69	26.31
7	54.7777	18.84	20.24	17	68.9648	24.82	25.93
8	60.3343	19.71	20.37	18	64.2596	25.54	21.96
9	49.7552	20.01	12.71	19	63.7541	25.63	24.05
10	55.4592	20.26	22.98	20	69.6836	28.73	25.66

First of all, we compute the regression coefficients of original data, and the estimated original model is:

$$\hat{Y}_i = 3.8419 + 1.8110X_{1i} + 0.6343X_{2i}$$

The estimates indicate that there are increasing returns to scale, as the coefficients of the two explanatory variables add to more than 1. It could also mean that there could be some other missing factors whose contribution is captured by labor. We will later see if this phenomenon is carried over when we re-estimate the model taking the first order autocorrelation into account.

After running the first-order autoregression on the estimated residuals $\hat{\varepsilon}_i$

$$\hat{\varepsilon}_i = \rho\hat{\varepsilon}_{i-1} + v_i$$

it works out that $\hat{\rho} = 0.5285$. Taking the asymptotic test, we get the following statistic

$$\sqrt{n}\hat{\rho} = 2.3634$$

and the three critical values under the 1, 5 and 10 % levels of significance are 2.326, 1.645, 1.282. Therefore, we claim that the first-order autoregression is very significant[2]. While building the generalized least squares model, we take transformation in accordance with (3.12), and the corresponding data are shown on the screen. As regards the data after transformation, the model is

$$Y_i^* = 4.0451 + 1.6746X_{1i}^* + 0.7575X_{2i}^*$$

---

[2] It may be noted that the sample size here is only 20 and hence we apply this asymptotic test with tongue in cheek. While the Durbin-Watson test is a small sample test it is not exact and it could lead to inconclusive results. The best alternative in this case is to use the bootstrap method. The bootstrap method is explained in Chapter 11, Section 11.7.

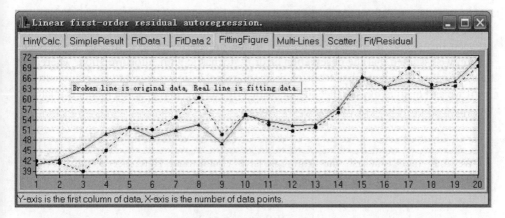

Figure 3.4   Linear first-order residual autoregression for production function.

This regression equation is undoubtedly suitable for Y^* and X^*. See the fitting results shown in Figure 3.4. In terms of the original data without transformation the above estimated regression turns out to be:

$$Y_i = 4.0451 + 1.6746X_{2i} + 0.7575X_{3i}$$

It not only provides good fit to the original data, but also eliminates the influence of autocorrelation. The phenomenon of increasing returns to scales is reflected in these revised estimates also. The main advantage of the first-order residual autoregression is in the prediction out of the sample. The major results are summarized as follows.

The ordinary least squares regression coefficients of original data = 3.8419, 1.8110, 0.6343.

The first-order residual autoregression coefficient = 0.5285.

The asymptotic test for the significance of first-order residual autoregression coefficient.

Statistic = 2.3634, Critical value (0.01) = 2.326 (0.05): 1.645 (0.10): 1.282.

F-statistic= 22.7207, F-critical value F (3, 17) = 3.197.

Total correlation coefficient $R^2 = 0.8004$ ($R = 0.8946$).

The Figure and computation can be shown by clicking DASC→Regression→Other Linear Regression→Linear First-order Residual Autoregression Model.

3.3.2   Autoregressive conditional heteroscedasticity (ARCH) model

Researchers have observed that many financial time series data, such as stock price, inflation rate, foreign exchange rate and so on, assume a simple law that their first differences are random. For some time periods, the variance of the random errors are relatively small, while for some other time periods they are relatively large, and then they are small again in another time period. This phenomenon is called volatility clustering in financial economics. Such a change could be attributed to volatility in financial markets that could be partly due to speculations based on sensitivity to political upheavals and changes in government monetary and fiscal policies. This would suggest that we take into account the variances of observation errors with two features; they are stochastic and have some autocorrelation. The difference between this situation and that mentioned in the previous section is that in the previous section we assumed that the observation error is stochastic with autocorrelation, whereas in this section we assume such autocorrelation in the stochastic variance of observation error.

If we assume that the variance of stochastic error term ε_i in regression model is related to the square of error term of former observation:

$$Var(\varepsilon_i) \propto \varepsilon_{i-1}^2$$

We may then establish the Autoregressive Conditional Heteroscedasticity (ARCH) Model.

$$\begin{cases} Y_i = X_i'\beta + \varepsilon_i \\ \varepsilon_i \sim N(0, (\alpha_0 + \alpha_1\varepsilon_{i-1}^2)) \end{cases}$$

In this model, the variance of ε_i is only related to the squared error of previous term, so it is called ARCH(1), and it is assumed that the errors are normally distributed.

Knowing that the variance of regression model is a linear function of previous squared error, we extend the ARCH model in the following three aspects:

(1) The linear part $X\beta$ of the model may either be a linear function of some explanatory variables or past values of the dependent variable Y_i, for example

$$Y_i = \beta_0 + \beta_1 Y_{i-1} + \beta_2 Y_{i-1} + \cdots + \beta_k Y_{i-k} + \varepsilon_i$$

(2) ε_i is not necessarily subject to normality, but to other kinds of distributions. And we may just know its first and second moments.

(3) $Var(\varepsilon_i)$ is not necessarily a linear function of ε_{i-1}^2 alone, but may be the linear function of several past squared errors, namely,

$$Var(\varepsilon_i) = \sigma_i^2 = \alpha_0 + \alpha_1\varepsilon_{i-1}^2 + \alpha_2\varepsilon_{i-2}^2 + \cdots + \alpha_p\varepsilon_{i-p}^2 \tag{3.14}$$

The model here is referred to as ARCH (p).

In general, we assume that the basic observation data Y_i, $X_i' = (x_{i1}, x_{i2}, \ldots, x_{ik})$, $i = 1, \ldots, n$ satisfy the following linear relation

$$Y_i = X_i'\beta + \varepsilon_i \tag{3.15}$$

where the square of error term ε_i satisfies the p th order **autoregressive process AR(p)**:

$$\varepsilon_i^2 = \alpha_0 + \alpha_1\varepsilon_{i-1}^2 + \alpha_2\varepsilon_{i-2}^2 + \cdots + \alpha_p\varepsilon_{i-p}^2 + \upsilon_i \tag{3.16}$$

The random term υ_i here is a white noise process:

$$E(\upsilon_i) = 0, \quad E(\upsilon_i^2) = \sigma_\upsilon^2, \quad E(\upsilon_i\upsilon_j) = 0, \ i \neq j \tag{3.17}$$

We can deduce condition (3.14) from conditions (3.16) and (3.17). We call the combined model of (3.15), (3.16), and (3.17) as ARCH(p), which is introduced by Engle (1982).

Prior to discussing the methods of estimation and computing the estimates we will study the properties of the model, especially that of variance.

As ε_i^2 is non–negative, we may know from (3.16) that v_i is bounded:

$$-\alpha_0 < v_i < \alpha_0, \quad i = 1, 2, \ldots$$

In order to ensure the steadiness of variance of ε_i^2, we need to further assume that the roots of the following equation

$$1 - \alpha_1 Z - \alpha_2 Z^2 - \cdots - \alpha_p Z^p = 0$$

are outside the unit circle[3]. If all coefficients α_j are non-negative, then it is equal to requiring

$$\alpha_1 + \alpha_2 + \cdots + \alpha_p < 1$$

When all these assumptions are satisfied, the unconditional variance of ε_i is determined by the following formula:

$$\sigma^2 = E(\varepsilon_i^2) = \alpha_0 / (1 - \alpha_1 - \alpha_2 - \cdots - \alpha_p) \tag{3.18}$$

One may note that (3.14) reflects a varying $E(\varepsilon_i^2)$, while (3.18) reflects a constant $E(\varepsilon_i^2)$. This may be explained by the fact that the former is a conditional variance while the latter is unconditional variance under the given assumptions. The conditional variance is given by:

$$E(\varepsilon_i^2 \mid \varepsilon_{i-1}^2, \ldots, \varepsilon_{i-p}^2) = \alpha_0 + \alpha_1 \varepsilon_{i-1}^2 + \cdots + \alpha_p \varepsilon_{i-p}^2 \tag{3.19}$$

Here, the variance is heteroscedastic, depicting the autoregressive nature of the amplitude of economic data in line with p lagged time periods.

We now study the solution of the model ARCH(p) described once more concisely below:

$$\begin{cases} Y_i = X_i'\beta + \varepsilon_i \\ \varepsilon_i^2 = \alpha_0 + \alpha_1 \varepsilon_{i-1}^2 + \cdots + \alpha_p \varepsilon_{i-p}^2 + v_i \\ E(v_i) = 0, \quad E(v_i^2) = \sigma_v^2, \quad E(v_i v_j) = 0, \quad i \neq j \end{cases}$$

We can not rely completely on the solution of the first order autoregressive linear model (3.10). We may estimate $\hat{\beta}$ from the main regression model (first formula) on the basis of original data, and then obtain $\hat{\varepsilon}_i$. We substitute it into the second formula of the model to run the regression for obtaining $\hat{\alpha}_0, \hat{\alpha}_1, \ldots, \hat{\alpha}_p, \hat{v}_i$. But in order to apply GLS we need to know the variance covariance matrix. We do not know the concrete form of

$$Var(\varepsilon_i) = \Phi$$

Statisticians developed methods for ARCH model, based on some additional assumptions. For the rest of the discussion in this section we assume the model to be

$$\begin{cases} Y_i = X_i'\beta + \varepsilon_i, \quad \varepsilon_i = \sqrt{h_i} \cdot v_i, \quad E(v_i) = 0, \quad E(v_i^2) = 1 \\ h_i = \alpha_0 + \alpha_1 \varepsilon_{i-1}^2 + \alpha_2 \varepsilon_{i-2}^2 + \cdots + \alpha_p \varepsilon_{i-p}^2 \end{cases} \tag{3.20}$$

---

[3] This is a condition that will be explained fully when we deal with stationary univariate time series in Chapter 8.

We may deduce (3.19) from (3.20). Hence conditions (3.20) are more general than that of (3.19).

1.   The maximum likelihood estimate under normal distribution

We have n observations in the ARCH(p) model (3.20). For convenience we take the previous p observations to calculate conditional variance, for $i = 1,2,\ldots,n$, we write the following sample set with i as a termination:

$$\tilde{Y}_i = (Y_i, Y_{i-1}, \ldots, Y_1, Y_0, \ldots, Y_{-p+1}; X_i', X_{i-1}', \ldots, X_1', X_0', \ldots, X_{-p+1}')'$$

Since i begins with 1, this sample set must have at least p observations ($p < n$).

Assume that υ_i is $i.i.d.$ to $N(0,1)$, and υ_i, X_i and Y_{i-1} are independent, then the conditional distribution of Y_i is

$$f(Y_i \mid X_i, \tilde{Y}_{i-1}) = \frac{1}{\sqrt{2\pi h_i}} \exp\left(\frac{-(Y_i - X_i'\beta)^2}{2h_i}\right)$$

This is a normal distribution with expectation being $X_i'\beta$ and variance being h_i. As $\varepsilon_i = Y_i - X_i'\beta$, the variance h_i can be written as

$$\begin{aligned}
h_i &= \alpha_0 + \alpha_1(Y_{i-1} - X_{i-1}'\beta)^2 + \alpha_2(Y_{i-2} - X_{i-2}'\beta)^2 + \cdots + \alpha_p(Y_{i-p} - X_{i-p}'\beta)^2 \\
&= (Z_i(\beta))'\delta
\end{aligned} \quad (3.21)$$

where

$$\delta = (\alpha_0, \alpha_1, \alpha_2, \ldots, \alpha_p)'$$

$$Z_i(\beta) = (1, (Y_{i-1} - X_{i-1}'\beta)^2, (Y_{i-2} - X_{i-2}'\beta)^2, \ldots, (Y_{i-p} - X_{i-p}'\beta)^2)'$$

Let $\theta = (\beta', \delta')'$. The log likelihood function of conditional density, conditional on all the predetermined variables (current exogenous and lagged dependent variables) is

$$\begin{aligned}
L(\theta) &= \sum_{i=1}^{n} \log f(Y_i \mid X_i, \tilde{Y}_{i-1}; \theta) \\
&= -\frac{n}{2}\log(2\pi) - \frac{1}{2}\sum_{i=1}^{n} \log h_i - \frac{1}{2}\sum_{i=1}^{n}(Y_i - X_i'\beta)^2 / h_i
\end{aligned} \quad (3.22)$$

Substituting the given sample observations $\tilde{Y}_i, X_i'$ into (3.21), we can derive the sequence h_i, $i = 1,2,\ldots,n$. Substitute $\tilde{Y}_i$, X_i, h_i into (3.3.15) we form a log likelihood function $L(\theta)$ containing parameter θ. Our final goal is to maximize it in order to obtain the estimator of θ, namely,

$$L(\hat{\theta}) = \max_{\theta} L(\theta)$$

Actual numerical computation of MLE can be done by the Powell algorithm (Fletcher and Powell, 1963).

2. Generalized method of moment estimation (GMM) under non-correlation assumption

The generalized method of moments consists of specifying a few conditions that the moments (which are functions of the parameters to be estimated) of the underlying random variable must satisfy, and using those moment conditions to estimate the unknown parameters. If there are more moment conditions than there are parameters to be estimated a loss function is defined and that loss is minimized. For more details one may see Ogaki (1993), and Section 3-2 of the Electronics References for Chapter 3.

We also may assume that the residuals of the regression model have no correlations with the explanatory variables, namely,

$$E((Y_i - X_i'\beta)X_i) = 0$$

Simultaneously, we assume that residual terms in the relation of the Autoregressive Conditional Heteroscedasticity model are not related to the hysteretic mean square residuals, namely

$$E(v_i Z_i) = E((\varepsilon_i^2 - h_i)Z_i) = 0$$

Under these assumptions, Raymond and Butler (1991) applied the **Generalized Method of Moments Estimation (GMM)** to estimate the parameters in the ARCH model.

Write

$$g(\theta, \tilde{Y}_i) = \begin{pmatrix} \dfrac{1}{n}\sum_{i=1}^{n}(Y_i - X_i'\beta)X_i \\ \dfrac{1}{n}\sum_{i=1}^{n}[(Y_i - X_i'\beta)^2 - (Z_i(\beta))'\delta]Z_i(\beta) \end{pmatrix}$$

We then minimize

$$L(\theta) = [g(\theta; \tilde{Y}_i)]' \hat{S}_i^{-1}[g(\theta; \tilde{Y}_i)]$$

where $\hat{S}_i^{-1}$, is the variance covariance matrix of estimators of the parameter. We thus have,

$$L(\hat{\theta}) = \min_{\theta} L(\theta)$$

The first order conditions of this minimization process are taken as the moment conditions for the GMM estimation.

There are some other aspects of the ARCH model which will be discussed in Chapter 8 in detail. Another problem of interest to us is the test to see whether the hypothesis of the ARCH model can be accepted. Fortunately, such a test is deduced by Engle (1982) using the Lagrange Multiplier Method.

Firstly, in the basic relation: $Y_i = X_i'\beta + \varepsilon$, we use the ordinary least squares to calculate $\hat{\beta}$ so as to get the estimator of sample residual ε_i:

$$\hat{\varepsilon}_i = Y_i - X_i'\hat{\beta}, \quad i = -p+1, -p+2, \ldots, 0, 1, \ldots, n$$

Applying the $n + p$ data points, we run the pth order autoregression:

$$\hat{\varepsilon}_i^2 = \alpha_0 + \alpha_1\hat{\varepsilon}_{i-1}^2 + \cdots + \alpha_p\hat{\varepsilon}_{i-p}^2 + v_i, \quad i = 1, \ldots, n \tag{3.23}$$

Under the assumption that

$$\varepsilon_i \sim N(0,\sigma^2), i = 1,\ldots,n$$

the RSS R_ε^2 of autoregression formula (3.23) converges to the χ^2 distribution with p degrees of freedom, namely,

$$R_\varepsilon^2 \to \chi^2(p)$$

Based on this distributional assumption we carry out the hypothesis test to see whether the variance of the residuals ε_i concerning the original data regression changes along with time periods.

If we extend the linear autoregressive relation of conditional variances of error in the ARCH model to an infinite number of lagged terms, namely

$$E(\varepsilon_i^2 \mid \varepsilon_{i-1}^2,\ldots) = \alpha_0 + \alpha_1 \varepsilon_{i-1}^2 + \cdots + \alpha_p \varepsilon_{i-p}^2 + \cdots$$

we obtain the so-called **Generalized Auto-Regressive Conditional Heteroscedasticity (GARCH)** Model. We further extend the relation and write it as that in (3.20):

$$h_i = \alpha_0 + \alpha_1 \varepsilon_{i-1}^2 + \cdots + \alpha_p \varepsilon_{i-p}^2 + \cdots$$

We assume that h_i has linear relations with both ε_{i-p}^2 and its lagged value, namely,

$$h_i = \alpha_0 + \alpha_1 \varepsilon_{i-1}^2 + \cdots + \alpha_p \varepsilon_{i-p}^2 + \gamma_i h_{i-1} + \cdots + \gamma_q h_{i-q}$$

Then we call the model the **GARCH(p,q) model**. The conceptual beauty of this generalization of the model far exceeds its practical utility. We will discuss this model further in Chapter 9.

3.4　Generalized linear model with positive definite covariance matrix

3.4.1　Model definition, parameter estimation and hypothesis tests

We discussed the situation where a covariance matrix is diagonal. In this section, we will further extend it. In reality, if observations are correlated, covariance matrices are usually no longer diagonal. First let us define a **positive definite matrix**. A matrix M is called positive definite, and is denoted as $M > 0$, if given any vector $X \neq 0$; $X'MX > 0$.

Let us consider the following linear model

$$\begin{cases} Y = X \beta + \varepsilon \\ {\scriptstyle n\times1} {\scriptstyle n\times p} {\scriptstyle p\times1} \\ E(\varepsilon) = 0, Var(\varepsilon) = \sigma^2 M, M > 0 \end{cases} \tag{3.24}$$

Here M is a known positive definite matrix, and thus there is only one parameter σ^2 needed for estimation of variance.

As $M > 0$, there exists a **nonsingular matrix** P such that $M = P'P$. Let $Y = P'Z$, $Z = (P^{-1})'Y$, then we obtain the following model after transformation:

$$\begin{cases} E(Z) = (P^{-1})'X\beta = \tilde{X}\beta \\ Var(Z) = (P^{-1})'Var(Y)P^{-1} = \sigma^2(P^{-1})'P'PP^{-1} = \sigma^2 I_n \end{cases} \tag{3.25}$$

This is a model in which the observations are uncorrelated. We may therefore apply the LSE:

$$\tilde{\beta} = (\tilde{X}'\tilde{X})^{-1}\tilde{X}'Z$$

$$\tilde{\sigma}^2 = \frac{1}{n-p}(Z - \tilde{X}\tilde{\beta})'(Z - \tilde{X}\tilde{\beta})$$

This estimator is surely the **Minimum Variance Linear Unbiased Estimator** (or **Best Linear Unbiased Estimate (BLUE)**) in respect of the model (3.25) after transformation. Returning to original data, it is easy to show

$$\tilde{\beta} = (X'P^{-1}(P^{-1})'X)^{-1}X'P^{-1}(P^{-1})'Y = (X'M^{-1}X)^{-1}X'M^{-1}Y$$

$$\begin{aligned} \tilde{\sigma}^2 &= \frac{1}{n-p}((P^{-1})'Y - (P^{-1})'X\tilde{\beta})'((P^{-1})'Y - (P^{-1})'X\tilde{\beta}) \\ &= \frac{1}{n-p}(Y - X\tilde{\beta})'P^{-1}(P^{-1})'(Y - X\tilde{\beta}) \\ &= \frac{1}{n-p}(Y - X\tilde{\beta})'M^{-1}(Y - X\tilde{\beta}) \end{aligned}$$

Thus we obtained the parameter estimates using the data X and Y of original model. Next we consider the tests of hypothesis on parameters. If we assume $\varepsilon \sim N(0, \sigma^2 M)$ in the original model, then in the transformed model is:

$$Z = (P^{-1})'Y \sim N(\tilde{X}\beta, \sigma^2 I_n)$$

As $\tilde{\beta}$ is a linear function of Z, it follows that

$$\tilde{\beta} \sim N_p(\beta, \sigma^2(\tilde{X}'\tilde{X})^{-1})$$

$$S_{ES} = \frac{1}{\sigma^2}(Z - \tilde{X}\tilde{\beta})'(Z - \tilde{X}\tilde{\beta}) \sim \chi^2(n-p)$$

AS $\tilde{\beta}$ and S_{ES} are independent we get the following distributional result:

$$\frac{1}{\sigma^2}(\tilde{\beta} - \beta)'\tilde{X}'\tilde{X}(\tilde{\beta} - \beta) \sim \chi^2(p)$$

Returning to the original model, we have

$$\tilde{\beta} \sim N_p(\beta, \sigma^2(X'M^{-1}X)^{-1})$$

$$S_{ES} = \frac{1}{\sigma^2}(Y - X\tilde{\beta})'M^{-1}(Y - X\tilde{\beta}) \sim \chi^2(n-p)$$

Again, as $\tilde{\beta}$ and S_{ES} are independent we get the result:

$$\frac{1}{\sigma^2}(\tilde{\beta} - \beta)'X'M^{-1}X(\tilde{\beta} - \beta) \sim \chi^2(p)$$

We can thus perform the tests of hypotheses on the parameters using the above distributional results.

3.4.2   Some equivalent conditions

In the Generalized Linear Model, we have introduced the **BLUE** ($\tilde{\beta}$) and **LSE** ($\hat{\beta}$). We would like to know under what conditions the two estimators are equivalent, and when the residuals of BLUE and LSE are equal. We introduce two theorems to answer the questions above. This material is adopted from the work of Rao (1965, 1971) and Zhang and Liu (1992). We only state the propositions here and the detailed proofs are given in the Appendix.

When we discuss the **equivalent conditions of BLUE and LSE** for linear model, we consider a more general situation: the estimation of the linear function $\alpha'\beta$ of parameter β, where α is any p-dimensional vector.

Definition 3.1 If there exists a linear function $b'Y$, so that

$$E(b'Y) = a'\beta$$

we say that the linear function $\rho = \alpha'\beta$ of β is estimable, and $b'Y$ is a **linear unbiased estimator** of $\rho = \alpha'\beta$.

Before probing into the equivalence between BLUE and LSE with regard to parameter estimation of the original model, we will introduce two lemmas on estimable functions.

Lemma 3.1 For some given a, the following six propositions are equivalent:

(1) $a'\beta$ is estimable;

(2) Equation $X'Z = a$ has a solution;

(3) $a \in L(X') = L(X'X)$;

(4) $a'(I - X^+ X) = 0$;

(5) $a'\beta$ is unique for all solutions of a normal equation;

(6) $E(a'\hat{\beta}) = a'\beta$.

Here $L(X')$ denotes the subspace spanned by column vectors of X', X^+ is the '+' generalized inverse of X (**Moore-Penrose generalized inverse**). X^+ is a unique matrix that satisfies the following matrix equations:

$$XX^+ X = X; X^+ XX^+ = X^+; (XX^+)' = XX^+; (X^+ X)' = X^+ X.$$

Lemma 3.2 For any given a, the necessary and sufficient condition for $a'\beta$ to be estimable is $rk(X) = p$, that is, the design matrix has full column rank.

Now we present conditions under which LSE are BLUE.

Theorem 3.1 In model (3.24), the following four propositions are equivalent:

(1) The BLUE and LSE of any estimable function $a'\beta$ are one and the same;

(2) $L(X)$ is formed by r eigenvectors of M, $r = rk(X)$;

(3) $P_X M = M P_X$, where the projection matrix $P_X = X(X'X)^{-1} X'$;

(4) $L(MX) \subset L(X)$.

Now we will consider the conditions under which the residual sum of squares (RSS) calculated by both BLUE and LSE of $X\beta$ will be equal, that is,

$$(Y - X\hat{\beta})'(Y - X\hat{\beta}) = (Y - X\tilde{\beta})M^{-1}(Y - X\tilde{\beta})$$

In particular we will establish that this equality holds if and only if $\tilde{\beta} = \hat{\beta}$, $M = I_n$.

Theorem 3.2 If $X\tilde{\beta} = X\hat{\beta}$, then the following four propositions are equivalent:

(1) $(Y - X\hat{\beta})'(Y - X\hat{\beta}) = (Y - X\tilde{\beta})'M^{-1}(Y - X\tilde{\beta})$;

(2) For all $d \in L^{\perp}(X)$, $\langle d, d \rangle = \langle d, M^{-1}d \rangle$, here $\langle \cdot, \cdot \rangle$ denotes inner product;

(3) For all $d, e \in L^{\perp}(X)$, $\langle d, e \rangle = \langle d, M^{-1}e \rangle$;

(4) For all $d \in L^{\perp}(X)$, $Md = d$.

The proofs of these equivalent conditions are very graceful in mathematics but too difficult to understand. The detailed proofs can be found in Electronic References for Chapter 3.

3.5   Random effects and variance component model

The independent variables in the regression models discussed so far are fixed or non-random, and the models are called fixed effects models. However, in some cases, such as panel data and **Analysis of Variance (ANOVA)**, or in economic problems, independent variables are often random with an uncontrolled design matrix $(X'X)$. We call such a regression model a **random effects regression model** where independent variables are random variables.

3.5.1   Random effect regression model

Let us illustrate the difference between a fixed effects model and random effects model through an example. Let us consider the consumption function that can be written as

$$C = C_0 + b(X - T)$$

where X is income, T is tax, C_0 is basic consumption for survival and b is the coefficient to be estimated. By adding the random disturbance term we obtain the following regression model:

$$C = C_0 + b(X - T) + \varepsilon$$

Whether this is a **fixed effects model** or a **random effects model** depends on the sampling procedure. If we investigate the consumption in terms of families with certain known incomes, then the design matrix is known and fixed, and it is a fixed effects model. On the other hand, if we sample some families randomly and register their income and consumption, regardless of their income, then the design matrix is random and we have the random effects model.

The basic aim of regression is to predict Y given X. In other words we are looking for a function $Y = M(X) = M(X_1,\ldots, X_p)$. The criterion for choosing this prediction function is that the mean or average value of the sum of squared error of this prediction should be minimum. That is

$$E[Y - M(X)]^2 = \min_L E[Y - L(X)]^2 \qquad (3.26)$$

where $\min_L$ is a notation to minimize its right hand side among all measurable functions of $L(X)$ of X. Let

$$M(X) = E(Y \mid X)$$

We know that $E(E(Y \mid X)) = E(M(X)) = E(Y)$, and

$$E[Y - M(X)][M(X) - L(X)] = 0$$

From the above considerations the following equation holds,

$$\begin{aligned}
E[Y - L(X)]^2 &= E[Y - M(X) + M(X) - L(X)]^2 \\
&= E[Y - M(X)]^2 + E[M(X) - L(X)]^2 + 2E[Y - M(X)][M(X) - L(X)] \\
&= E_X\{[Y - M(X)]/X\} + E[M(X) - L(X)]^2 + 0 \\
&= E[M(X) - L(X)]^2
\end{aligned}$$

As $E[Y/X] = M(X)$ and $E[Y - M(X)][M(X) - L(X)] = 0$. To make the above equation minimum, we let $L(X) = M(X) = E(Y \mid X)$.

The result above implies that taking conditional expectation $E(Y|X)$ as the forecasting function we can minimize the prediction error. We also prove below that $M(X) = E(Y \mid X)$ has maximum correlation with Y, that is

$$\rho (Y, M(X)) = \max_L \ \rho (Y, L(X)) \qquad (3.27)$$

where ρ is correlation coefficient.

When $M(X) = E(Y \mid X)$, it is easy to demonstrate $Cov(Y, L(X)) = Cov(M(X), L(X))$, and at the same time $Cov(Y, M(X)) = Cov(M(X), M(X))$, so

$$\begin{aligned}
\rho^2(Y, L(X)) &= \frac{Cov^2(Y, L(X))}{D(Y)D[L(X)]} = \frac{Cov^2(M(X), L(X))}{D(Y)D[L(X)]} \\
&= \frac{Cov^2(M(X), L(X))}{D[M(X)]D[L(X)]} \cdot \frac{D[M(X)]}{D(Y)} \cdot \frac{D[M(X)]}{D[M(X)]} \\
&= \rho^2(M(X), L(X)) \cdot \rho^2(Y, M(X)) \\
&\leq \rho^2(Y, M(X))
\end{aligned}$$

The strict equality in the expression above occurs if and only if $|\rho(M(X), L(X))| = 1$. Then $L(X)$ is the linear function of $M(X)$.

(3.26) and (3.27) express the extremal property of $M(X) = E(Y \mid X)$. We name

$$Y = M(X) = E(Y|X)$$

the regression curve of Y on X.

$L(X)$ appearing above can be set as any function. If we define that $L(X)$ is a linear function of X, which means we should restrict that

$$E[|Y - (\beta_0 + \beta_1 X_1 + \cdots + \beta_m X_m)|^2] = \min_L$$

where $\min_L$ is to minimize overall the linear functions of X. We call this the linear regression of Y on X. We can obtain the least squares solutions of $\beta_0, \beta_1, \ldots, \beta_m$. Let $\beta = (\beta_1, \ldots \beta_m)'$, using the following loss function and minimizing it:

$$L(\beta_0, \beta) = E[|Y - (\beta_0 + \beta_1 X_1 + \cdots + \beta_m X_m)|^2]$$
$$= b^2 + \beta' R_{XX} \beta - 2\beta' R_{XY} + D(Y)$$

where

$$b = E(Y) - (\beta_0 + \beta_1 E(X_1) + \cdots + \beta_m E(X_m))$$

and

$$R_{XX} = E[(X - E(X))(X - E(X))']$$
$$= \begin{pmatrix} D(X_1) & Cov(X_1, X_2) & \cdots & Cov(X_1, X_m) \\ \vdots & \vdots & \vdots & \vdots \\ Cov(X_m, X_1) & Cov(X_m, X_2) & \cdots & D(X_m) \end{pmatrix}_{m \times m}$$

$$R_{XY} = (Cov(Y, X_1), \ldots, Cov(Y, X_m))'$$

Differentiating $L(\beta_0, \beta)$ (derivative formula of the matrix $\frac{\partial}{\partial X}(X'AX) = 2AX$), we obtain

$$\begin{cases} b = 0 \\ R_{XX} \beta = R_{XY} \end{cases}$$

From these we get the following estimators

$$\begin{cases} \hat{\beta}_0 = E(Y) - \hat{\beta}' E(X) \\ \hat{\beta} = R_{XX}^{-1} R_{XY} \end{cases}$$

If R_{XX}^{-1} exists, otherwise we would use generalized inverse in place of that matrix. The predicted variance then is

$$\hat{\sigma}^2 = L(\hat{\beta}_0, \hat{\beta}) = E[|Y - (\hat{\beta}_0 + \hat{\beta}_1 X_1 + \cdots + \hat{\beta}_m X_m)|^2]$$
$$= \hat{\beta}' R_{XX} \hat{\beta} - 2\hat{\beta}' R_{XY} + D(Y) = \sigma_Y^2 - R_{XY}' R_{XX}^{-1} R_{XY}$$

We call

$$\rho_{XY} = (R_{XY}' R_{XX}^{-1} R_{XY})^{1/2} / \sigma_Y$$

multiple correlation coefficient, which indicates the degree of linear correlation between Y and several variables $X = (X_1,...,X_m)$. It may be recalled that the simple correlation coefficient between Y and a single explanatory variable X is given by:

$$r_{XY} = \frac{Cov(X,Y)}{\sqrt{D(X)}\sqrt{D(Y)}}$$

The multiple correlation is the generalization of the simple ordinary correlation between two variables Y and X, and in both cases it is the correlation coefficient between the dependent variable Y and its predicted value from the linear regression.

The above derivations are based on the theory of probability distribution of jointly dependent random variables. The sample analogs of these results are obtained by substituting for the population quantities $E(X)$, $E(Y)$, σ_Y, R_{XX} and R_{XY} the corresponding sample quantities $\bar{X}$, $\bar{Y}$, S_Y, S_{XX}, and S_{XY}, respectively. Then we get

$$\begin{pmatrix} \hat{\beta}_0 \\ \hat{\beta} \end{pmatrix} = (X'X)^{-1} X'Y$$

and the estimator of variance is $\hat{\sigma}^2 = \dfrac{1}{n-m-1}(Y - X\hat{\beta})'(Y - X\hat{\beta})$. So it can be seen that the random effects regression model deduced from the conditional expectation is equivalent to the regression equation of the fixed effects. Hence we will not differentiate between them in calculation in our model here.

3.5.2   The variance component model

Since the concept of random effects has been dealt with by treating the independent variable as a random variable, we can proceed to discuss the **variance component model**.

We take a random sample of the above mentioned regression model of the consumption function. We shall consider classifying the residents by career such as worker, teacher, doctor, lawyer and so on, which are written as X_i, $i = 1,...,m$. We draw n samples from these careers randomly, and then the model can be written as

$$C_{ij} = C_0 + b(X_i - T_i) + \varepsilon_{ij}, \quad j = 1,...,n, \quad i = 1,...,m$$

where X_i can be regarded as the income of the ith career. As what we chose randomly were the households, for any sample household both the observed career and the consumption are random variables. We also assume that the variance of consumption depends on careers. These considerations suggest that we introduce the variance component model. In the fixed effects model the variance of C_{ij} is composed of two parts:

$$Var(C_{ij}) = b^2\sigma_X^2 + \sigma_\varepsilon^2$$

To make our discussion in general terms we suppress the fact that the dependent variable is consumption and make it more generic Y. We rewrite the model as:

$$Y_{ij} = \mu + U_1\xi_{1i} + \varepsilon_{ij}, \quad i = 1,...,m, \quad j = 1,...,n$$

Here we have one fixed effect μ, one random effect ξ_1 and one random error ε. Matrix U consists of 1 and 0, 1 corresponding to presence of the chosen career in a sampled consumer and hence U is given. If the geographic location of the consumer is also expected to have an effect on consumption a second random effect ξ_2 should be added, and then we obtain the model:

$$Y = \mu + U_1\xi_1 + U_2\xi_2 + \varepsilon$$

Here we omit the subscript of the value and the variance of Y is composed of three items. The general formulation of the random effects variance component model is:

$$Y = X\beta + U_1\xi_1 + \cdots + U_m\xi_m$$

Here there is a **fixed effect vector** β and a **random effect vector** $\xi = (\xi_1, \xi_2, \ldots, \xi_m)'$ and the random error item ε is incorporated into the random effect vector. The **design matrix** X and

$$U = (U_1, U_2, \ldots, U_m)'$$

are known. We make the following assumptions regarding the random effects ξ_i, $i = 1, \ldots, m$,:

$$\begin{cases} E(\xi_i) = 0, Cov(\xi_i, \xi_j) = 0, i \neq j \\ D(\xi_i) = \sigma_i^2, i = 1, \ldots, m \end{cases}$$

We assume that each ξ_i is one-dimensional variable. Let

$$V_i = U_iU_i', i = 1, \ldots, m, \quad \Sigma = \sigma_1^2 V_1 + \cdots + \sigma_m^2 V_m$$

The variance component model can now be expressed as:

$$E(Y) = X\beta, \quad Var(Y) = \Sigma$$

The main objective of the model is to estimate the fixed effect vector β and variance components $\sigma_1^2, \sigma_2^2, \ldots, \sigma_m^2$. Compared with general multiple linear regression model, in this model we have more variances to estimate. Along this line, we can build various general linear regression models in economics into variance component models. For example, we can treat the **cross-section effect** and time series effect separately in a **panel data model** by allowing for separate main effects of cross section and time series, along with separate variances for them.

3.5.3 Analysis of variance method to solve variance component model

For variance component model

$$\begin{cases} \underset{n\times1}{Y} = \underset{n\times p}{X} \underset{p\times1}{\beta} + \underset{n\times p_1}{U_1} \underset{p_1\times1}{\xi_1} + \cdots + \underset{n\times p_m}{U_m} \underset{p_m\times1}{\xi_m} \\ E(Y) = X\beta, \quad Var(Y) = \sum_{i=1}^{m}\sigma_i^2 U_iU_i' \triangleq \Sigma \end{cases} \tag{3.28}$$

We generally adopt two-step estimation method. First, we estimate the **variance components** $\sigma_1^2,\ldots,\sigma_m^2$ and then we estimate the fixed effect β. According to the **generalized least squares**:

$$\beta^* = (X'\hat{\Sigma}^{-1}X)^{-1}X'\hat{\Sigma}^{-1}Y \tag{3.29}$$

where

$$\hat{\Sigma} = \sum_{i=1}^{m}\hat{\sigma}_i^2 U_i U_i'$$

Therefore the estimation of variances is the key to the solution of variance component models. The statistical method used for the random effects model such as the above is an analysis of variance.

We illustrate the method of Analysis of Variance through a simple model integrating data structures. Consider the model

$$Y_{ij} = \beta_0 + \xi_i + \varepsilon_{ij}, \quad i = 1,\ldots,m, \quad j = 1,\ldots,k \tag{3.30}$$

where β_0 is the population mean (fixed effect), and $\xi_1,\ldots,\xi_m$ are random effects, $E(\xi_i) = 0$, $Cov(\xi_i, \xi_j) = 0$, $i \neq j$, $Var(\xi_i) = \sigma_A^2$, $i = 1,\ldots,m$.

For the random error ε_{ij}, $Var(\varepsilon_{ij}) = \sigma_\varepsilon^2$. If this model is written as the variance component model, the standard form is

$$Y = X\beta_0 + U\xi + \varepsilon$$

where the design matrix is $X = (1,1, \ldots\ 1)'$, the random effect matrix is

$$U = \begin{pmatrix}
1 & 0 & & & \\
\vdots & \vdots & & 0 & \\
1 & 0 & & & \\
0 & 1 & & & \\
\vdots & \vdots & & & \\
0 & 1 & & & \\
& & \ddots & & \\
& & & 1 & \\
0 & & & \vdots & \\
& & & 1 &
\end{pmatrix}_{m \times k} \tag{3.31}$$

The only available data are $Y = (Y_{11},\ldots, Y_{1k}, Y_{21},\ldots, Y_{2k},\ldots, Y_{m1},\ldots, Y_{mk})$. Therefore we arrange the data Y in a table as follows (Table 3.3):

Table 3.3   Data structure of a simple variance component model.

i \ j	1	2	...	k	Intra-class average
1	Y_{11}	Y_{12}	...	Y_{1k}	$\bar{Y}_1\cdot$
2	Y_{21}	Y_{22}	...	Y_{2k}	$\bar{Y}_2\cdot$
$\vdots$	$\vdots$			$\vdots$	$\vdots$
m	Y_{m1}	Y_{m2}	...	Y_{mk}	$\bar{Y}_m\cdot$

Three steps are essential to analysis of variance. The first step is to calculate intraclass (or within) variances and variances between classes (Inter-class variances), The second step is achieved by performing the decomposition of quadratic sum. Finally, we provide the degrees of freedom associated with each of the estimated variances.

Firstly we calculate the overall sample mean:

$$\bar{Y}_{..} = \frac{1}{mk} \sum_{i=1}^{m} \sum_{j=1}^{k} Y_{ij} \tag{3.32}$$

Second, we calculate the total variance (the square sum of the deviations of all the data from the population mean):

$$S_T = \sum_{i=1}^{m} \sum_{j=1}^{k} (Y_{ij} - \bar{Y}_{..})^2$$

Third, we calculate the **class mean** or average of each class:

$$\bar{Y}_{i.} = \frac{1}{k} \sum_{j=1}^{k} Y_{ij}, \quad i = 1,\ldots,m$$

Fourth, we calculate the **variation between classes** (the sum of squared deviation of the average of each group from the population mean):

$$S_A = k \sum_{i=1}^{m} (\bar{Y}_{i.} - \bar{Y}_{..})^2$$

And finally we calculate the **interclass or within class variance** (the sum of squared deviation of the data in each class from its average):

$$S_\varepsilon = \sum_{i=1}^{m} \sum_{j=1}^{k} (Y_{ij} - \bar{Y}_{i.})^2$$

The decomposition of sum of squared deviations can now be expressed as:

$$S_T = S_A + S_\varepsilon$$

Divide each sum of squares by the respective degree of freedom. S_T is a sum of mk squared deviations with a constraint associated with population mean $\bar{Y}_{..}$ in equation (3.32). The degree of freedom is hence $mk - 1$; S_A has m terms with 1 constraint and hence has degree of freedom $m - 1$; S_ε has mk terms with m constraints and hence its degree of freedom is $mk - m$. We summarize below the **decomposition of sums of squared deviations**

$$S_T = S_A + S_\varepsilon$$

along with the decomposition of the degrees of freedom:

$$mk - 1 = (m - 1) + (mk - m)$$

We can obtain the mean squares as follows:

$$Q_T = \frac{1}{mk-1} S_T$$

$$Q_A = \frac{1}{m-1} S_A$$

$$Q_\varepsilon = \frac{1}{mk-m} S_\varepsilon$$

Under the assumption of random effects model we can express the expected values of these mean squares:

$$E(Q_A) = k\sigma_A^2 + \sigma_\varepsilon^2$$

$$E(Q_\varepsilon) = \sigma_\varepsilon^2$$

Substituting Q_A for $E(Q_A)$ and Q_ε for $E(Q_\varepsilon)$, we can obtain a system of two equations:

$$\begin{cases} k\sigma_A^2 + \sigma_\varepsilon^2 = Q_A \\ \sigma_\varepsilon^2 = Q_\varepsilon \end{cases}$$

We thus get

$$\hat{\sigma}_\varepsilon^2 = Q_\varepsilon, \qquad \hat{\sigma}_A^2 = (Q_A - Q_\varepsilon)/k \tag{3.33}$$

This completes the estimation of variance components. Now we can estimate β using equation (3.33). As components of the variances are estimated using the decomposition of total variance the procedure is called analysis of variance.

When it is extended to general variance component model, the basic principles are similar. We might now return to the random effects model introduced earlier in equation (3.32):

$$\begin{cases} Y = X\beta + U_1\xi_1 + U_2\xi_2 + \varepsilon \\ Cov(Y) = \sigma_1^2 U_1 U_1' + \sigma_2^2 U_2 U_2' + \sigma_\varepsilon^2 I \end{cases}$$

The decomposition of total sum of squares: $Y'Y$ yields:

$$Y'Y = S_\beta + S_{\xi1} + S_{\xi2} + S_\varepsilon$$

where S_β is the regression sum of squares of β in the model $Y = X\beta + \varepsilon$:

$$S_\beta = S_{RS}(\beta) = Y'X(X'X)^{-1}X'Y$$

$S_{\xi1}$ is the sum of squares of ξ_1 with influence of β eliminated in the model $Y = X\beta + U_1\xi_1 + \varepsilon$:

$$S_{\xi1} = S_{RS}(\beta, \xi_1) - S_{RS}(\beta)$$

Similarly, S_{ξ_2} is the sum of squares of ξ_2 with influence of β and ξ_1 eliminated in the model $Y = X\beta + U_1\xi_1 + U_2\xi_2 + \varepsilon$:

$$S_{\xi_2} = S_{RS}(\beta,\xi_1,\xi_2) - S_{RS}(\beta,\xi_1)$$

Finally S_ε is the sum of squares of the residuals

$$S_\varepsilon = Y'Y - S_{RS}(\beta,\xi_1,\xi_2)$$

It can be proved that

$$S_\beta = Y'(I - D)Y$$

$$S_{\xi_1} = Y'(D - D_1)Y$$

$$S_{\xi_2} = Y'(D_1 - D_{12})Y$$

$$S_\varepsilon = Y'D_{12}Y$$

where

$$D = I - X(X'X)^{-1}X' = I - P_X$$

$$D_1 = D - DU_1(U_1'DU_1)^{-1}U_1'D = D - P_{DU_1}$$

$$D_{12} = D_1 - D_1U_2(U_2'D_1U_2)^{-1}U_2'D_1 = D_1 - P_{D_1U_2}$$

with P_* being the projection matrix of Y on*.
We can write the expected value of each sum of squares as follows:

$$\begin{aligned}
E(S_{\xi_1}) &= \beta'X'(D - D_1)X\beta + tr(D - D_1)[U_1U_1'\sigma_1^2 + U_2U_2'\sigma_2^2 + \sigma_\varepsilon^2 I] \\
&= \beta'X'(D - D_1)X\beta + tr(U_1'DU_1)\sigma_1^2 - tr(U_1'D_1U_1)\sigma_1^2 \\
&\quad + tr(U_2'DU_2)\sigma_2^2 - tr(U_2'D_1U_2)\sigma_2^2 + tr(D - D_1)\sigma_\varepsilon^2
\end{aligned}$$

Since $DX = 0, D_1X = 0$, the first item of the equation above is zero. In the third item, there is

$$tr(U_1'D_1U_1) = tr[U_1'DU_1 - U_1'DU_1(U_1'DU_1)^{-1}U_1'DU_1] = 0$$

In the sixth item

$$\begin{aligned}
tr(D - D_1) &= tr[D_1U_1(U_1'D_1U_1) - U_1'D_1] = tr[(U_1'D_1U_1)^{-1}U_1'D_1U_1] \\
&= rk(U_1'D_1U_1) = rk(U_1'D_1) = rk(U_1 \vdots X)' - rk(X') \\
&= rk(U_1 \vdots X) - rk(X)
\end{aligned}$$

So finally we get

$$E(S_{\xi_1}) = c_1\sigma_1^2 + (c_2 - c_3)\sigma_2^2 + r_2\sigma_\varepsilon^2$$

where

$$c_1 = tr(U_1'DU_1)$$
$$c_2 = tr(U_2'DU_2)$$
$$c_3 = tr(U_2'D_1U_2)$$
$$r_1 = rk(X), \qquad r_1 + r_2 = rk(U_1 \mid X)$$

Similarly, we obtain

$$E(S_{\xi 2}) = c_2\sigma_2^2 + r_3\sigma_\varepsilon^2$$

$$E(S_\varepsilon) = (n - r_1 - r_2 - r_3)\sigma_\varepsilon^2$$

$$r_3 = rk(X \vdots U_1 \vdots U_2) - r_1 - r_2$$

We thus have the following system of three equations in three unknowns $\sigma_1^2, \sigma_2^2, \sigma_\varepsilon^2$:

$$\begin{cases} S_{\xi 1} = c_1\sigma_1^2 + (c_2 - c_3)\sigma_2^2 + r_2\sigma_\varepsilon^2 \\ S_{\xi 2} = c_2\sigma_2^2 + r_3\sigma_\varepsilon^2 \\ S_\varepsilon = (n - r_1 - r_2 - r_3)\sigma_\varepsilon^2 \end{cases}$$

Solving them, we can get the estimators of $\sigma_1^2, \sigma_2^2, \sigma_\varepsilon^2$. By substituting these estimators of variances in the least squares solution we obtain the estimator of the fixed effects.

Example 3.3   The Relationship among market rate of return, dividends and turnover rate   The market rate of return (Y) depends on dividend payouts and turnover (variable X). The actual relationship may vary among different stocks. We consider the data given in Table 3.4.

Let us consider a multiple linear random effects model:

$$\underset{n\times 1}{Y} = \underset{n\times p}{X}\,\underset{p\times 1}{\beta} + \underset{n\times m}{U}\,\underset{m\times 1}{\xi} + \varepsilon$$

where the form of U is the same as (3.31).

The model can also be written as

$$Y_{ij} = X'_{ij}\beta + \xi_i + \varepsilon_{ij}, \quad i = 1,\ldots,m, \, j = 1,\ldots,k$$

The data structure and the specific data are as follows, $m = 6$, $k = 6$. These data are collected from *Data Summarization of 1996 Shanghai Stock Market*.

We are interested in determining the effects of the dividend incomes for last year and the turnover rate of current year on the market rate of return of current year. We are also interested in knowing whether there is a potential unobserved random effect specific to each stock, under the specific assumption that each stock price has its own volatility. It is thus quite appropriate here to use the variance component model.

First, we will run the ordinary least squares regression to obtain $\hat\beta = (X'X)^{-1}X'Y$, and then calculate $Y_{ij}^* = Y_{ij} - X'_{ij}\hat\beta$.

At this time for Y_{ij}^* the influence of the fixed effects has been eliminated. Then we shall array Y_{ij}^* into a table of analysis of variance and calculate $\hat\sigma_\varepsilon^2$ and $\hat\sigma_A^2$. The calculation process is from (3.33). The actual computations are given below

Data of variance analysis Y(I,J)

−50.6210	−39.0275	−38.6721	137.5441	−56.0541	−50.4640
−22.4490	−8.9357	−7.8936	8.0546	37.4223	−20.2416
−25.8348	221.1285	−21.4183	83.6328	−4.9701	−18.2668
−46.8722	75.9169	132.1827	−13.6501	51.7486	6.1371
30.6483	−14.9082	−34.5268	−8.9422	−40.1694	−42.8772
33.9744	20.2007	−77.2975	−103.9000	−8.8455	−81.7529

Population mean $\overline{Y}.. = 0.000006$
Average of each class $\overline{Y}_i = -16.216, -2.341, 39.045, 34.244, -18.463, -36.270$.
Calculate all the variations:
Total variance SST(S_T) = 149400.6000,
Interclass variance SSA(S_A) = 27731.9200, variation among classes
SSE(S_e) = 121668.7000.
Total correlation coefficient $R^2 = 0.4686$ ($R = 0.6846$).

If we compare the sum of squared residuals of ordinary least squares (149400.6000), with that of generalized least square (2290.6910) we note that the random effects model is a definite improvement over the simple fixed effects model.

From the numerical calculations above we can see that the resolution of sum of squares is satisfied ($S_T = S_A + S_e$). For the data in this example, the random error of 4055.6 is much larger than random effects variance, and the between class variance is more than variation within classes. More specifically SSA = 27731.92, SSE = 121668.7. Note that $m = 6$ and $k = 6$, so the degree of freedom of SSA is $m - 1 = 6 - 1 = 5$, and the degree of freedom of SSE is $mk - m = 6 \times 6 - 6 = 30$, then F statistic= $\dfrac{SSA/m-1}{SSE/mk-m} = \dfrac{27731.92/5}{121668.7/30} = 1.36$, and F critical value $F(5,30) = 2.53$, F statistic smaller than critical value, so we can conclude that the random effects are not significant, that is, the industry discrimination is not significant. With respect to the selected variance component model.

Estimate of variance components $\Sigma_{AA} = 248.4600$, $\Sigma_{AE} = 4055.6240$

Residual sum of squares = 2290.69   Square sum of regression = 2014.61
Estimate of variance = 63.6303   Standard deviation = 7.9769
F statistic = 14.5113 F critical value $F(2, 33) = 3.285$

The results of the goodness of fit of the model are shown in Figure 3.5. The fit seems to be quite satisfactory.

Readers can see and verify the calculations and figures using DASC software by clicking DASC→Regression Analysis→Other Linear Regression→Variance Component Model by Variance Analysis.

Some analytic details are necessary for carrying out the calculations involved in the above example. Since $\hat{\Sigma} = \sigma_A^2 UU' + \sigma_\varepsilon^2 I_n$, we need to use it and equation (3.29) to calculate β^*:

$$\beta^* = (X'\hat{\Sigma}^{-1}X)^{-1}X'\hat{\Sigma}^{-1}Y$$

Table 3.4 Data of the Stock Market (China) in 1996.

Category	Stock Code	Name of Stock	Rate of Return (%) in 1996	Dividend in 1995 %	Daily Turnover Rate in 1996
Commercial	628	New World	64.769	20	3.12
	631	Shanghai No.1 Department Store	46.845	11.8	1.68
	632	Hualian Department Store	41.958	11.3	1.81
	655	Yuyuan Department Store	16.195	11.2	1.10
	682	Nanjing Xinjiekou Department Store	79.911	5.2	3.36
	694	Dalian Department Store	91.388	5.8	4.26
Electronic	602	Vacuum Electronics	33.112	10	3.52
	651	Feilo Acoustics	8.108	0	1.95
	800	Tianjin Global Magnetic Card	271.763	5	3.74
	839	Sichuan Changhong Electric	381.686	60	4.41
	850	Shaghai East-China Computer	14.638	1	3.27
	870	Xiamen Overseas Chinese Electronic	68.579	3.9	4.20
Chemical	617	Guangdong United Textile & Dyeing	−21.871	0.5	1.53
	618	Chemical engineering of halogen and alkali	22.370	2	2.63
	672	Guangdong Chemical Fiber	11.860	0	4.65
	688	Shanghai Petrochemical	179.817	3.5	4.38
	886	Hubei Xinhua	236.328	52.3	4.45
	889	Nanjing Chemical Fiber	−33.122	2.4	4.64
Medical	664	Harbin Pharmaceutical	191.666	5	4.32
	671	Tian-Mu-Shan Pharmaceutical	111.135	16	4.11
	812	North China Pharmaceutical	152.015	8.4	4.11
	842	SH Zhongxi Pharmaceutical	13.821	2.6	1.71
	849	Daichi Seiyaku	17.892	2.5	1.68
	779	Sichuan Pharmaceutical	−24.744	0	12.28
Steel	608	SH Yi Gang Shaped Steel Tube	8.389	10	2.24
	665	Huchang Special Steel	75.39	1.87	4.01
	674	Sichuan Emei Ferroalloy Group	35.932	3	3.64
	808	Maanshan Iron and Steel	86.528	0.5	4.52
	845	Steel Tube Inc.	−25.170	0	1.61
	894	GZ Iron & Steel	51.371	2.7	7.08
Mechanical	604	SH Erfangji	14.4	10	2.31
	605	Light Industry Machinery	6.122	0	3.50
	610	China Textile Machinery	0.701	0	2.27
	806	Kunming Machine Tool	41.852	1.1	4.22
	841	SH Diesel Engine	66.981	20	2.20
	862	Nantong Stock	41.093	20	1.36

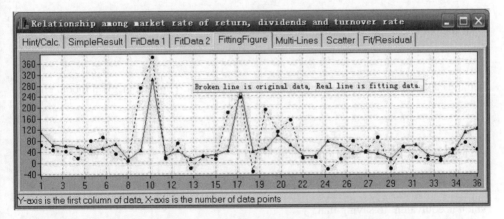

Figure 3.5 Relationship among market rate of return, dividends and turnover rate.

Note that UU' is a block diagonal matrix with m diagonal blocks. Each of these blocks is a $k \times k$ square matrix with all elements being 1, it is easy to calculate Σ. It happens that X is divided into m blocks and each block is a $k \times p$ matrix. Hence,

$$X'\hat{\Sigma}^{-1}X = (X'_1,\ldots,X'_m)\text{diag}(\hat{\Sigma}_1,\ldots,\hat{\Sigma}_m)\begin{pmatrix} X_1 \\ \vdots \\ X_m \end{pmatrix} = X'_1\hat{\Sigma}_1 X_1 + \cdots + X'_m\hat{\Sigma}_m X_m$$

and $\hat{\Sigma}_1 = \cdots = \hat{\Sigma}_m = \sigma_A^2 1_m 1'_m + \sigma_\varepsilon^2 I_m$, where $1_m = (1,1,\ldots,1)'$.

These results simplify the calculation dramatically. Without these it is impossible for a general processor to calculate the inverse of Σ, a 36×36 matrix.

3.5.4 Minimum Norm Quadratic Unbiased Estimation (MINQUE) to solve variance component

Minimum Norm Quadratic Unbiased Estimation (MINQUE) of the variance components in variance component models was proposed by C.R. Rao (1971). The basic idea is similar to the partitioned inverse matrix method which has been used for the generalized linear models with singular variance covariance matrix. It introduces some general properties that the estimation should satisfy and then works out the solution in terms of those properties. The entire procedure is equivalent to formulating an equivalent minimization problem. Now we describe the method briefly.

Consider the general variance component model (3.32). We will estimate variance components $\sigma_1^2,\ldots,\sigma_m^2$ and their linear function

$$\varphi = c'\sigma^2, \quad c = (c_1,\ldots,c_m)', \quad \sigma^2 = (\sigma_1^2,\ldots,\sigma_m^2)'$$

First of all, we shall consider what mathematical form the estimator of φ should be. As it is an estimator of variances, we may consider using the quadratic form $Y'AY$, namely

$$\hat{\varphi} = c'\hat{\sigma}^2 = Y'\hat{A}Y$$

where A is a symmetric matrix to be estimated. Then we will consider the properties that $Y'AY$ should have.

1. Translation Invariance of Parameter β

If the parameter β has translation:

$$\gamma = \beta - \beta_0$$

then the estimation of the variance component is unaltered. Thus the original model changes into

$$Y - X\beta_0 = X\gamma + U\xi$$

and its quadratic form estimation changes into $(Y - X\beta_0)' A(Y - X\beta_0)$. Then we have

$$(Y - X\beta_0)' A(Y - X\beta_0) = Y'AY \tag{3.34}$$

which is equivalent to saying that:

$$-2Y'AX\beta_0 + \beta_0'X'AX\beta_0 = 0$$

Hence, the necessary and sufficient condition on matrix A for the translation invariance (3.34) is

$$AX = 0$$

2. Unbiasedness of the Estimator

Since

$$E(Y'AY) = tr(A\Sigma) + \beta'X'AX\beta = \sum_{i=1}^{m} \sigma_i^2 tr(AU_iU_i')$$

Unbiasedness of the estimator requires the following:

$$E(Y'AY) = \varphi = c'\sigma^2 = \sum_{i=1}^{m} c_i \sigma_i^2$$

Thus the necessary and sufficient condition for unbiasedness is:

$$tr(AU_iU_i') = c_i, \quad i = 1,\ldots,m$$

These two conditions have imposed 2 m conditions on the matrix containing m^2 elements. As there are fewer restrictions than what are required we need to choose among alternate estimators using an optimization criterion.

3. Guidelines for Minimum Norm

If the random effects vector ξ_i, $i = 1,\ldots, m$ are known, the estimation of $\varphi = c'\sigma^2$ should be

$$c_1\left(\frac{\xi_1'\xi_1}{p_1}\right) + c_2\left(\frac{\xi_2'\xi_2}{p_2}\right) + \cdots + c_m\left(\frac{\xi_m'\xi_m}{p_m}\right) \hat{=} \xi'\Delta\xi \tag{3.35}$$

where

$$\Delta = diag(\frac{c_1}{p_1}I_{p_1},\ldots,\frac{c_m}{p_m}I_{p_m})$$

Now we will use $Y'AY$ to estimate $\varphi = c'\sigma^2$. Under the translation invariance condition $AX = 0$, we have

$$Y'AY = (X\beta + U\xi)' A(X\beta + U\xi) = \xi'U'AU\xi \tag{3.36}$$

We must insist that there is equality between (3.35) and (3.36). This requires that matrix $\Delta = U'AU$. We select the matrix norm $\| U'AU - \Delta \|$ to measure the variance between Δ and $U'AU$. In order to select A we minimize $\| U'AU - \Delta \|$. As to the norm, we can choose Euclidean Norm

$$\| B \| = tr(B'B)$$

Let $V = UU'$. As Δ is a block diagonal matrix unbiasedness requires:

$$\| U'AU - \Delta \| = tr[U'AUU'AU - 2U'AU\Delta + \Delta^2]$$
$$= tr(AUU'AUU') - 2tr(AU\Delta U') + tr\Delta^2$$
$$= tr(AV)^2 - 2\sum_{i=1}^{m}\frac{c_i}{p_i}tr(AU_iU_i') + tr\Delta^2$$
$$= tr(AV)^2 - 2\sum_{i=1}^{m}\frac{c_i}{p_i}c_i + tr\Delta^2$$
$$= tr(AV)^2 - 2tr\Delta^2 + tr\Delta^2$$
$$= tr(AV)^2 - tr\Delta^2$$

where Δ is known, so the minimum norm $\| U'AU - \Delta \|$ is equivalent to minimum $tr(AV)^2$.

The solution of the minimum norm unbiased estimator of $\varphi = c'\sigma^2$ turns out to be the solution of the following extremum problem:

$$(L1) \qquad \min tr(AV)^2$$

$$s \cdot t \cdot \begin{cases} AX = 0 \\ tr(AV_i) = C_i, & i = 1,\ldots,m \end{cases}$$

As the objective function is the matrix trace, we call it the minimal trace problem. In order to solve the extremum problem (L1), we can first simplify it. As $V = \sum_{i=1}^{m}V_i$, $V_i = U_iU_i'$, V is therefore positive definite and V^{-1} exists. Let

$$B = V^{\frac{1}{2}}AV^{\frac{1}{2}}, Z = V^{-\frac{1}{2}}X, W_i = V^{-\frac{1}{2}}V_iV^{-\frac{1}{2}} \tag{3.37}$$

Then the model (L1) can be transformed into the following form:

$$(L2) \qquad \min tr(B^2)$$

$$s \cdot t \cdot \begin{cases} BZ = 0 \\ tr(BW_i) = c_i, & i = 1,\ldots,m \end{cases} \tag{3.38}$$

To solve the optimal problem L2, we have following theorem:

Theorem 3.3 The solution of the extremum problem L2 is

$$B^* = P_Z^{\perp}(\sum_{i=1}^{m}\lambda_i W_i)P_Z^{\perp}$$

where $\lambda_1,\ldots, \lambda_m$ are the solutions of the system of equations

$$\sum_{i=1}^{m}tr(P_Z^{\perp}W_iP_Z^{\perp}W_j)\lambda_i = C_j, \quad j = 1,\ldots,m \tag{3.39}$$

where $P_Z^{\perp}$ is the projection matrix on $L^{\perp}(Z)$, the orthogonal complement space of $L(Z)$:

$$P_Z^{\perp} = I - Z(Z'Z)^{-}Z'$$

The proof of above theorem is omitted here and can be found in the Electronic References for Chapter 3.

We discussed the minimum norm quadratic unbiased estimator in terms of the principles on which it was derived. We showed the existence of the MINQUE. And finally we presented the computational algorithm. More issues such as the non-negativity of the solution and some complications of calculation arising in a few special cases are beyond the scope of our present discussion and are omitted.

3.5.5   Maximum likelihood method to solve variance component model

Under the assumption that the random effects ξ_i of the variance component model follow the normal distribution, the parameter estimation can be obtained using the **maximum likelihood method (MLE)**. We assume that the model is

$$Y = X\beta + U_1\xi_1 + \cdots + U_m\xi_m$$

$$\xi_i \sim N(0, \sigma_i^2 I_{p_i}), \quad i = 1, \ldots, m$$

Other symbols are same as before, then

$$Y \sim N(X\beta, \Sigma), \quad \Sigma = \sum_{i=1}^{m} \sigma_i^2 U_i U_i'$$

The conditional density function of Y is

$$f(Y|\beta, \sigma^2) = (2\pi)^{-n/2} |\Sigma|^{-\frac{n}{2}} \exp[-\frac{1}{2}(Y - X\beta)'\Sigma^{-1}(Y - X\beta)]$$

Taking logarithm and eliminating the constant, we obtain the **likelihood function**:

$$L(\beta, \sigma^2) = -\frac{n}{2}\ln|\Sigma| - \frac{1}{2}(Y - X\beta)'\Sigma^{-1}(Y - X\beta) \tag{3.40}$$

Using the matrix derivative formula

$$\frac{\partial |A|}{\partial t} = |A| tr(A^{-1}\frac{\partial A}{\partial t})$$

$$\frac{\partial X'AX}{\partial X} = (A + A')X, \quad \frac{\partial a'X}{\partial X} = a$$

$$\frac{\partial A^{-1}}{\partial t} = -A^{-1}\frac{\partial A}{\partial t}A^{-1}$$

We obtain the system of equations

$$\begin{cases} \dfrac{\partial L}{\partial \beta} = X'\Sigma^{-1}Y - X'\Sigma^{-1}X\beta = 0 \\ \dfrac{\partial L}{\partial \sigma_i^2} = -\dfrac{n}{2}tr(\Sigma^{-1}V_i) + \dfrac{1}{2}(Y - X\beta)'\Sigma^{-1}V_i\Sigma^{-1}(Y - X\beta) = 0, i = 1, \ldots, m \end{cases}$$

As this system of equations has no explicit solution, the statisticians have offered some iterative algorithms. However, with advanced numerical calculation techniques it does not seem necessary to discuss the derivation of the likelihood equations and associated iterative algorithms. For given design matrix $V_i = U_i U_i'$, substituting the sample $Y = (Y_1,\ldots,Y_n)$, $X_i = (X_{it},\ldots,X_{pt})$, $i = 1,\ldots,n$ into the likelihood function (3.40) and using Powell Algorithm improved by Sargent for extremum calculation, we can calculate the maximum likelihood estimators of β, σ^2.

Here we have introduced the MLE estimations and MINQUE estimations, but which one among these two is better? According to the author's work experience, MLE is better when the residual term's effect is significant and has better normal distribution, otherwise, MINQUE is better. In fact, for other regression models, when the effect of error is significant and when it has a normal distribution, the MLE of the parameters is better, otherwise the LSE of the parameters is better. What is a better estimator? We encounter this type of question quite frequently in applied statistical work. With ease in computations we can perform a simulation exercise to answer such questions. We can generate sample data of model according to different error distributions and different ranges of known parameter values. We can replicate generating such simulated samples several times. Then we calculate MLE and LSE using these data respectively. Better estimation method should be more close to known of parameter values. This procedure can be done easily by DASC.

Electronic references for Chapter 3

References

Aitken A.C. (1935) On least squares and linear combinations of observations. *Proceedings of the Royal Society of Edinburgh* **55**, 42–8.

Amemiya T. (1971) The estimation of variances in a variance-components model. *International Economic Review* **12**, 1–13.

Amemiya T. (1984) Tobit models: a survey. *Journal of Econometrics* **24**, 3–63.

Baltagi H.B., Heun S.S. & Cheol J.B. (2001) The unbalanced nested error component regression model. *Journal of Econometrics* **101**, 357–81.

Carlson F.D., Sobel E. & Watson G.S. (1966) Linear relationship between variables affected by errors. *Biometrics* **22**, 252–67.

Chaubey Y.P. (1983) A non-negative estimator of variance component closest to MINQUE. *Sankhya* **45**, 201–11.

Chen M.H. & Dey D.K. (2003) Variable selection for multivariate logistic regression models. *Journal of Statistical Planning and Inference* **111**, 37–55.

Chen Y.M. & Wang S.W. (2001) Frequency-domain regression method for estimating CTF models of building multilayer constructions. *Applied Mathematical Modeling* **25**, 579–92.

Davidson J.W., Savic D.A. & Walters G.A. (2003) Symbolic and numerical regression: experiments and applications. *Information Sciences* **150**, 95–117.

Engle R.F. (1982) Autoregressive Conditional Heteroscedasticity with Estimates of the Variance of United Kingdom Inflation. *Econometrica* **50**, 987–1008.

Fletcher R.M. & Powell J.D. (1963) A Rapidly Convergent Descent Method for Minimization. *Computer Journal* **6**, 163–68.

Garren S.T. & Peddada S.D. (2000) Asymptotic normality in multivariate nonlinear regression and multivariate generalized linear regression models under repeated measurements with missing data. *Statistics and Probability Letters* **48**, 293–302.

Giles D. (1982) The interpretation of dummy variables in semilogarithmic equations. *Economics Letters* **10**, 77–9.

Halvorsen R. & Palmquist R. (1980) The interpretation of dummy variables in semilogarithmic equations. *American Economic Review* **70**, 474–75.

Harville D.A. (1977) Maximum likelihood approaches to variance component estimation and related problems. *J. Amer. Statist. Assoc* **72**, 320–40.

Hartung J. (1981) Nonnegative minimum biased invariant estimation in variance component models. *Ann. Statist.* **9**, 278–92.

Hastie T.J. & Tibshirani R.J. (1990) *Generalized Additive Models*. Chapman and Hall, New York.

Jeong J.-H. (2001) A note on asymptotic efficiency of a regression coefficient parameter under ordinal logistic regression model. *Communications in Statistics—Theory and Methods* **30**, 1257–69.

Judge G.G., Griffiths W.E., Hill R.C., Lütkepohl H. & Lee T.C. (1985) *The Theory and Practice of Econometrics*, 2nd ed. New York: John Wiley & Sons, Inc.

Karni E. & Weissman I. (1974) A consistent estimator of the slope in a regression model with errors in the variables. *J.Am.Statist.Assoc.* **69**, 211–13.

Kelvin K.W. & McGilchrist C.A. (1999) Power family of transformation for Cox's regression with random effects. *Computational Statistics & Data Analysis* **30**, 57–66.

Kleffe J. & Norberg R. (2001) Minimum norm estimation of variance components for life insurance data. *Communications in Statistics* **30**, 1591–1603.

Kmenta J. (1986) *Elements of Econometrics*, 2nd ed. Macmillan, New York.

Koul H.L. & Qian L.F. (2002) Asymptotics of maximum likelihood estimator in a two-phase linear regression model. *Journal of Statistical Planning and Inference* **108**, 99–119.

Koul H.L., Qian L.F. & Surgailis D. (2003) Asymptotics of M-estimators in two-phase linear regression models. *Stochastic Processes and their Applications* **103**, 123–54.

Krivy I., Tvrdík J. & Krpec R. (2000) Stochastic algorithms in nonlinear regression. *Computational Statistics and Data Analysis* **33**, 277–90.

Lee H.S. & Chaubey Y.P. (1996) MINQUE of variance components in generalized linear model with random effects. *Communications in Statistics* **26**, 1375–82.

Liu C.R. & Huang Y.X. (1992) *Linear Model and Statistical Inference*. Wuhan University of Technology Press,Wuhan.

Liu L.M. & Senturia J.N. (1977) Computation of MINQUE variance component estimates. J.Amer. Statist Asso., **72**, 867–8.

Markatou M., Basu A. & Lindsay B. (1997) Weighted likelihood estimating equations: the discrete case with applications to logistic regression. *Journal of Statistical Planning and Inference* **57**, 215–32.

Montgomery D.C. & Peck E.A. (1992) *Introduction to Linear Regression Analysis*. Wiley, New York.

Nawata K. (1997) Estimation of generalised regression models by the grouping method. *Mathematics and Computers in Simulation* **43**, 503–10.

Ogaki M. (1993) Generalized Method of Moments: Econometric Applications. *Handbook of Statistics* **11**, 455–488.

Ohtani K. (2002) Exact distribution of a pre-test estimator for regression error variance when there are omitted variables. *Statistics and Probability Letters* **60**, 129–40.

Olson A., Seely J. & Birkes D. (1976) Invariant quadratic unbiased estimation for two variance components. *Ann. Statist.* **4**, 878–90.

Pukelsheim F. (1981) On the existence of unbiased non-negative estimates of variance-covariance components. *Ann.Statist.* **9**, 293–99.

Ralitza V.G. & Alan A. (2001) A correlated probit model for joint modeling of clustered binary and continuous responses. *Journal of the American Statistical Association* **96**, 1102–13.

Rao C.R. (1965) *Linear Statistical Inference and its Applications*. John Wiley & Sons, Inc., New York.

Rao C.R. (1971) Estimation of Variance and Covariance Components: MINQUE theory. *Journal of Multivariate Analysis* **1**, 257–75.

Rao C.R., Toutenburg H., Shalab H. and Heumann C. (2008) *Linear Models and Generalizations – Least Squares and Alternatives,* New York, Springer.

Rao C.R. & Kleffe J. (1980) Estimation of Variance Components. *In Handbook of Statistics (ed, Krishnaiah, P.R)*, 1–40.

Rich R.W., Raymond J. & Butler J.S. (1991) Generalized instrumental variables estimation of autoregressive conditional heteroskedastic models. *Economics Letters* **35**, 179–85.

Rivers D. & Yuong Q. (1988) Limited information estimators and exogencity tests for simultaneous probit models. *Journal of Econometrics* **39**, 347–66.

Rom M. & Cohen A. (1995) Estimation in the polytomous logistic regression model. *Journal of Statistical Planning and Inference* **43**, 341–53.

Seely J. (1975) An Example of an Inadmissible Analysis of Variance Estimator for a Variance Component. *Biometrika* **62**, 689–90.

Trenkler G. (1998) Methods and applications of linear models - regression and the analysis of variance. *Computational Statistics & Data Analysis* **26**, 378–79.

Van Keilegom I., Akritas M.G. & Veraverbeke N. (2001) Estimation of the conditional distribution in regression with censored data: a comparative study. *Computational Statistics and Data Analysis* **35**, 487–500.

Zhang Y.T. & Fang K.T. (1982) *Introduction to Multivariate Statistical Analysis*. Science Press, Beijing.

4

Discrete variables and nonlinear regression model

The variables in the regression models considered in the previous chapters are all numerical values and are generally continuous. However, we should take note that in an actual situation variables can take on discrete numerical values. In addition, variables with categorical values such as buy and sell, rise and drop, profit and loss, also often arise in economic analysis. We therefore need to introduce **categorical variables** and use discrete numerical values to represent these **discrete variables**. The form of the basic model is a linear regression model:

$$Y = X\beta + \varepsilon, \ E(\varepsilon) = 0, \ Var(\varepsilon) = \Sigma$$

But now Y or X are categorical or discrete, therefore Σ may have some special structure.

In Section 4.1 we introduce a linear model with **categorical or discrete independent variables**. Many economic activities show seasonal changes that are discrete periodic changes. In that situation we can introduce **dummy variables**, called **seasonal dummies**, to account for **seasonal factors** in order to make **seasonal analysis**. More discussion on seasonal analysis such as **seasonal smoothing** can be found under time series analysis.

In Section 4.2 we introduce a linear model with **categorical or discrete dependent variables**. In this case the variance of errors no longer satisfies the homoscedasticity assumption and their distributions may not be normal distributions. We should therefore deal with them employing the generalized least squares model as in the previous chapter. While generalized least squares solve the estimation problem, the statistical testing of hypotheses requires greater attention to the sampling distribution of the estimators of new models with discrete or categorical variables. For a situation involving a dummy dependent variable we develop the Logit and **Probit regression models.** Subsequently we introduce the famous **Tobit regression model** whose algorithm was proposed by the celebrated Economist James Tobin. The Tobit model

Developing Econometrics, First Edition. Hengqing Tong, T. Krishna Kumar and Yangxin Huang.
© 2011 John Wiley & Sons, Ltd. Published 2011 by John Wiley & Sons, Ltd.

deals successfully with **truncated data** of dependent variables. The Tobit model also helps us to comprehend easily **the EM algorithm**.

When we have discrete dependent variables the linear regression may need to be replaced by Probit or Logit models that are nonlinear. Likewise, when there are discrete independent variables the linear regression becomes piece-wise linear or nonlinear.

We make a distinction between two types of nonlinear regression models. A regression model that is nonlinear in variables showing a nonlinear relationship between the dependent variable and the independent variable, and another in which the nonlinearity of regression is in terms of the regression having the parameters appearing in a nonlinear fashion. Various regression models discussed in the previous chapters are linear regression models irrespective of whether the variables are univariate or multivariate, continuous or discrete, with regard to the pattern of the error, and whether they have constraint or not. They were all linear in their parameters. In this chapter, we focus on **regression models that are nonlinear in their parameters**.

In business and economic contexts nonlinear models occur naturally. We discussed in Chapter 2 models that are nonlinear in variables that can be linearized. In other words, models in which variables enter nonlinearly can be transformed into models that are linear in terms of transformed variables. However, in some cases models that are nonlinear are difficult to linearize. In such cases we need to handle regression models that are nonlinear.

In this chapter we discuss many nonlinear regression models such as the **Cobb-Douglas production function model**, **growth curve model** (including Logistic model), **Box–Cox model**, **failure rate model**, measurement model of **Total Factor Productivity (TFP)**, etc. We introduce the evaluation model to measure TFP. The evaluation model is proposed by the principal author of this book. The dependent variable in evaluation model is completely unknown but the evaluation model specifies a **prescription constraint** that all regression coefficients are nonnegative and their sum equals 1. This model is another kind of a generalized linear regression model. Its LSE and MLE are obtained by **alternative projection** between two convex sets.

There is some discussion in statistical theory regarding the properties of nonlinear regression models, on subjects such as the measure of **intensity of nonlinear curvature** which can be seen in the Electronic References for Chapter 4.

We will introduce the algorithms of the nonlinear regression model. The most useful algorithm for the nonlinear regression model is the **Powell algorithm improved by Sargent**, and its detailed description is in the Electronic References for Chapter 4. Besides, there have been some advanced random optimal algorithms for the nonlinear regression model in recent years such as **evolutionary algorithms** (EA), **genetic algorithms** (GA), which can also be seen in the Electronic References for Chapter 4.

4.1   Regression model when independent variables are categorical

In regression models, dependent variables are affected not only by some **continuous independent variables** (such as price, income, output, temperature, distance, weight) which have numerical values in a continuous range, but also by other **categorical independent variables** (such as gender, nationality, race, color, an educational degree, earthquake, strike, recession, change in government, etc). In order to represent the effects of such variables on the dependent variable we can introduce numerical codes for these categories and thus introduce discrete variables in their place. For example, for binary variables (such as gender), we can introduce a dummy variable as follows:

$$D_i = \begin{cases} 1 & \text{when ith sample comes from male} \\ 0 & \text{when ith sample comes from female} \end{cases}$$

Of course, we can also define D_i with (1,1) or (1,2) and the interpretation of results will be different. If some categorical variable assumes more than two states we can also code them by discrete values. For example, if the categorical variable is the level of academic achievement we can represent the variable using discrete variables as follows:

$$D_i = \begin{cases} 1 & \text{bachelor} \\ 2 & \text{master} \\ 3 & \text{doctor} \end{cases}$$

Note that a master's degree may not be just twice as much as bachelor's degree, and a doctoral degree is not thrice as much as bachelor's degree. Hence such coding is not only arbitrary but also confusing with a numerical continuous scale. However, as we will show in the next section it is more useful if we represent such categorical variable through two dummy or dichotomous variables without any implicit numerical ordering.

4.1.1   Problem about wage and gender differences

Suppose for ten sample observations wages are recorded for workers in a specified job who all had equal years of experience, along with the gender of the wage earner. We wish to know if there is any systematic variation in wages by gender. The information collected is listed in the table below (Table 4.1). In this table, the unit of wage is omitted, 1 and 0 in the gender row refer to male and female, respectively.

We can establish a regression model as follows by using gender as independent variable

$$Y_i = \beta_0 + \beta_1 D_i + \varepsilon_i \tag{4.1}$$

Generally, for model (4.1)

$$E(Y_i \,|\, D_i = 0) = \beta_0$$

$$E(Y_i \,|\, D_i = 1) = \beta_0 + \beta_1$$

If β_1 passes the significance tests, it proves that there are significant differences between the wages of male and female employees.

Table 4.1   Wages of some careers.

ID	1	2	3	4	5	6	7	8	9	10
Wage	22.0	19.0	18.0	21.7	18.5	21.0	20.5	17.0	17.5	21.2
Gender	1	0	0	1	0	1	1	0	0	1

According to the data in the table above, we get a regression equation

$$Y_i = 18.00 + 3.28 D_i$$

which means that the average wage of a female is 18, compared to $18 + 3.28 = 21.28$ for male. Because the statistic t of the regression coefficient β_1 is 7.44, which is much greater than the critical value 1.86 under the significance level of 0.05, we can conclude that the wages between male and female of this job are significantly different.

The model above does not consider any other factors except gender. If we take the effects of other factors on wage into account, for example job experience which is represented by a continuous variable (designed as X), the model can be written as:

$$Y_i = \beta_0 + \beta_1 D_i + \beta_2 X_i + \varepsilon_i \tag{4.2}$$

Then

$$E(Y_i \mid X_i, D_i = 0) = \beta_0 + \beta_2 X_i$$

$$E(Y_i \mid X_i, D_i = 1) = (\beta_0 + \beta_1) + \beta_2 X_i$$

If the coefficient β_1 is statistically significant, it means that there is a gender difference about salaries between men and women, even after controlling for the effect of the continuous variable X (job experience).

When we have categorical variables with more than two states we can represent them by dummy/binary/dichotomous variables. We can use two dummy variables to represent three states. In the example above of educational achievement at three levels, Bachelors, Masters, and Doctors we can introduce:

$$D_{1i} = \begin{cases} 1 & \text{Master} \\ 0 & \text{otherwise} \end{cases}$$

$$D_{2i} = \begin{cases} 1 & \text{Doctorate} \\ 0 & \text{otherwise} \end{cases}$$

The intercept term refers to both D_{1i} and D_{2i} being equal to 0 and refers to the degree being a Bachelor's degree.

We thus get the following model:

$$Y_i = \beta_0 + \beta_1 D_{1i} + \beta_2 D_{2i} + \beta_3 X_i + \varepsilon_i$$

Then

$$E(Y_i \mid D_1 = 0, D_2 = 0) = \beta_0 + \beta_3 X_i$$

$$E(Y_i \mid D_1 = 1, D_2 = 0) = \beta_0 + \beta_1 + \beta_3 X_i$$

$$E(Y_i \mid D_1 = 1, D_2 = 1) = \beta_0 + \beta_1 + \beta_2 + \beta_3 X_i$$

In fact, we can use more categorical variables, such as the wage situation of different types of employees, to establish a regression equation as follows:

$$Y = 37.07 + 0.403X_1 - 90.06D_2 + 75.51D_3$$
$$+ 47.33D_4 + 113.64D_5 + 2.26X_6 + \varepsilon$$

where X_1 is the initial starting salary, $D_2 \sim D_5$ are dummy variables associated with different races (white people, nonwhite people), residence (urban district, non-urban district), area (western, non-western) and education level (higher education, non-higher education), X_6 is age.

4.1.2 Structural changes in the savings function (use of categorical variables in combination with continuous variables)

In this section, new variables are defined as products of dummy variables and continuous variables, which take into account possible changes in the slope of regression equation. First, let us look at a concrete example. Table 4.2 lists the savings and income data of the U.K. residents from 1946 to 1963. A million pounds is a unit.

Studying these data closely, we can divide them into two postwar periods: the restoration or recovery period under the Marshall Plan, from 1946 to 1954, and the sustained growth period from 1955 to 1963. We can establish two regression equations one for each period to specify the savings function, with savings (Y) as a function of income (X) respectively:

$$Y_{1i} = \beta_{10} + \beta_{11}X_{1i} + \varepsilon_{1i}, \ i = 1,\ldots,n_1$$

$$Y_{2i} = \beta_{20} + \beta_{21}X_{2i} + \varepsilon_{2i}, \ i = 1,\ldots,n_2$$

Based on the data in this example, we can obtain

$$Y_{1i} = -0.2663 + 0.0470X_{1i} \tag{4.3}$$

$$Y_{2i} = -1.7501 + 0.1504X_{2i} \tag{4.4}$$

Table 4.2   Saving and income data of the UK.

Year	Savings	Income	Year	Savings	Income
1946	0.36	8.8	1955	0.59	15.5
1947	0.21	9.4	1956	0.90	16.7
1948	0.08	10.0	1957	0.95	17.7
1949	0.20	10.6	1958	0.82	18.6
1950	0.10	11.0	1959	1.04	19.7
1951	0.12	11.9	1960	1.53	21.1
1952	0.41	12.7	1961	1.94	22.8
1953	0.50	13.5	1962	1.75	23.9
1954	0.43	14.3	1963	1.99	25.2

The slopes of the two equations above are different, which reflects that the growth of savings accelerated during the second period.

There are some problems associated with this type of regression analysis of splitting the sample into two when the samples share several common structural characteristics. First, we can not statistically compare the regression coefficients from the two regressions, as we do not have a common denominator or pooled error against which the observed differences in regression coefficients can be tested. Such regressions may be called **seemingly unrelated regression** (but related). When they are seemingly unrelated but related by combining the two samples into one we get a larger sample and larger degrees of freedom, and we also get a common error variance using which testing of differences in regression coefficients can be performed.

We can write the following equation for the combined sample:

$$Y_i = \beta_0 + \beta_1 D_i + \beta_2 X_i + \beta_3 (D_i X_i) + \varepsilon_i$$

where Y_i and X_i represent savings and income respectively, and D_i is a dummy variable.

$$D_i = \begin{cases} 1 & \text{while } X_i \text{ belongs to the first period} \\ 0 & \text{while } X_i \text{ belongs to the second period} \end{cases}$$

Then

$$E(Y_i \mid D_i = 0) = \beta_0 + \beta_2 X_i$$

$$E(Y_i \mid D_i = 1) = (\beta_0 + \beta_1) + (\beta_2 + \beta_3) X_i$$

The representation above of the regressions can be shown alternately as in the diagram below:

We are interested in knowing whether the determining equation of savings as a function of income is the same between the two periods. We can have four possibilities that are depicted below in Figure 4.1.

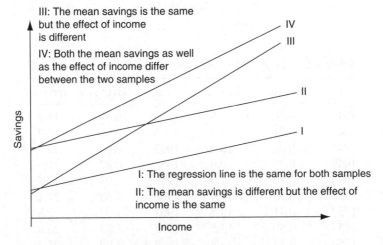

Figure 4.1   Relationship between savings and income.

We demonstrated above how the cases I and II are taken care of by introducing a dummy variable D_i for the period. How do we take care of cases III and IV? For this we interpret the new variable which is a product of X_i and D_i.

We can get a regression equations based on the data of this example:

$$Y_i = -1.7502 + 1.4839 D_i + 0.1505 X_i - 0.1034 D_i X_i$$

Let $D_i = 0$, then

$$Y_i = -1.7502 + 0.1505 X_i \tag{4.5}$$

Let $D_i = 1$, then

$$Y_i = (-1.7502 + 1.4839) + (0.1505 - 0.1034) X_i$$
$$= -0.2663 + 0.0471 X_i$$

Equation (4.5) may be compared with equations (4.3) and (4.4). They differ slightly as the estimated coefficients are based on a different larger sample.

Why do we adopt only one equation instead of two? One big advantage of one equation is that it provides larger **degrees of freedom**, which increases the precision of estimation of parameters. We lose only two degrees of freedom by adding two variables, but gain many more degrees of freedom by pooling the two samples, the net result being a substantial gain in degrees of freedom.

One can establish a similar relationship between unemployment rate (UN) and job-vacancy rate (V) in two industries by introducing a dummy variable (D) to distinguish the data between the two industries:

$$UN_i = \beta_0 + \beta_1 D_i + \beta_2 V_i + \beta_3 (D_i V_i) + \varepsilon_i$$

Similarly one can find a relationship of expenditure on costumes by gender, and education using two dummy variables.

$$Y_i = \beta_0 + \beta_1 D_{1i} + \beta_2 D_{2i} + \beta_3 X_i + \varepsilon_i$$

where Y_i is yearly expenditure on costumes, X_i is the income, D_1 is the dummy variable representing gender, D_2 is the dummy variable representing level of education (two levels). To examine if the yearly expenditure on costumes for women who receive higher education is much more than others, that is to say, gender factor and degree of education have an interaction effect, we can improve the regression equation as follows:

$$Y_i = \beta_0 + \beta_1 D_{1i} + \beta_2 D_{2i} + \beta_3 X_i + \beta_4 (D_{1i} D_{2i}) + \varepsilon_i$$

that is, add one item $(D_{1i} D_{2i})$ to reflect the interaction.

Next, we take the data in Table 4.2 as an example in order to introduce the **Chow test**[1].

---

[1] Although this test is called the Chow test by economists, based on a paper by Chow (1960), this is a special case of the test in linear regression models that statisticians are familiar with from Rao (1952).

Example 4.1   Piecewise regression and Chow test with the yearly saving and income data of the UK residents   Supposing that there are n_1 groups of data (Y_{1i}, X_{1i}), X_{1i} can be multivariate, and n_2 groups of data (Y_{2i}, X_{2i}), X_{2i} must have the same dimension with X_{1i} and refer to the same independent variables, we can establish regression models respectively:

$$n_1 : Y_{1i} = \beta_{10} + X_{1i}'\beta_1 + \varepsilon_{1i}, \quad \varepsilon_{1i} \sim N(0, \sigma_1^2)$$

$$n_2 : Y_{2i} = \beta_{20} + X_{2i}'\beta_2 + \varepsilon_{2i}, \quad \varepsilon_{2i} \sim N(0, \sigma_2^2)$$

The aim of the Chow test is to distinguish whether these two models have a significant difference. The process is as follows:

(1) Merge the data of the two groups to establish a common model:

$$n_1 + n_2 : Y_i = \beta_0 + X_i'\beta + \varepsilon_i$$

and figure out the sum of squared residuals S, with a degree of freedom $n_1 + n_2 - m$.

(2) Compute the sum of squared residuals of the two single models separately, one is S_1 (the degree of freedom is $n_1 - m$) and the other is S_2 (the degree of freedom is $n_2 - m$).

(3) Let $S_3 = S_1 + S_2$ (the degree of freedom is $n_1 + n_2 - 2m$), $S_4 = S - S_3$ (the degree of freedom is m). We define a statistic below,

$$F = \frac{S_4/m}{S_3/(n_1 + n_2 - 2m)}$$

Based on the assumption that the two individual regression models are identical $(\sigma_1^2 = \sigma_2^2, \beta_{10} = \beta_{20}, \beta_{1i} = \beta_{2i})$, the statistic F above should follow F distribution, with the degree of freedom $(m, n_1 + n_2 - 2m)$. Then we can figure out the critical value $F_\alpha(m, n_1 + n_2 - 2m)$ under a significance level of α. The assumption that the two regression models are identical will be rejected if the value of F -statistic exceeds the critical value.

In this case we only know that the two models have a significant difference, but can not confirm whether σ_i^2 are different or β_is are different or both are different. f in the following equations referrers to the degrees of freedom associated with that regression.

According to the data of Table 4.2, we obtain:

$$Y = -1.0821 + 0.1178X, \quad S = 0.5722, \quad f = 16$$

$$Y_1 = -0.2622 + 0.0470X, \quad S_1 = 0.1396, \quad f = 7$$

$$Y_2 = -1.7502 + 0.1504X, \quad S_2 = 0.1931, \quad f = 7$$

$$S_3 = S_1 + S_2 = 0.3327, \quad S_4 = S - S_3 = 0.2395$$

$$F = \frac{0.2395/2}{0.3327/14} = 5.04 > F_{0.05}(2, 14) = 3.74 \tag{4.6}$$

Based on the results above, we can reject the assumption that the two individual regression models are identical. In other words, there is a significant difference in regression of savings

Table 4.3 Yearly saving and income data of the UK residents with categorical variable.

Y	D_1	X_1	X_2
.36	1.0	8.8	8.8
.21	1.0	9.4	9.4
.08	1.0	10.0	10.0
.2	1.0	10.6	10.6
.1	1.0	11.0	11.0
.12	1.0	11.9	11.9
.41	1.0	12.7	12.7
.5	1.0	13.5	13.5
.43	1.0	14.3	14.3
.59	0.0	15.5	0
.9	0.0	16.7	0
.95	0.0	17.7	0
.82	0.0	18.6	0
1.04	0.0	19.7	0
1.53	0.0	21.1	0
1.94	0.0	22.8	0
1.75	0.0	23.9	0
1.99	0.0	25.2	0

on income of residents between the restoration period and the sustained growth period after the war. Next, we introduce a dummy variable for the same example and illustrate the results using the ordinary F test with dummy variables.

We take the same data given in Table 4.2 and prepare the following data sheet in which a dummy variable is added in the second column (Table 4.3).

The following are the main results:

Total regression equation (total number of sample is 18): Y = −1.0821 + 0.1178 X1

The sum of squared residuals: Q = 0.5722, Degree of freedom: 16.

The first regression equation (total number of sample is 9): Y = −0.2663 + .0470 X1.

The sum of squared residuals of the first equation Q1 = 0.1397. Degree of freedom is 7.

The second regression equation (total number of sample is 9): Y = −1.7501 + 0.1504 X1.

The sum of squared residuals of the second equation Q_2 = 0.1931. The degree of freedom is 7.

To test significance of difference between the two regression equations, we use Chow-testing with 0.05 level of significance. The testing values:

The value of the statistic is 5.0371. The critical value: 4.6001.

The results indicate that the two regression equations are significantly different.

Note that the regression equation with the dummy variable is given by:

$$Y = -1.7502 + 1.4839 \, D1 + 0.1505 \, X1 + -0.1034 \, X2.$$

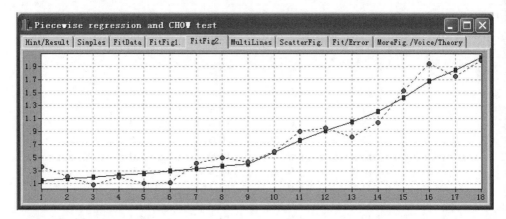

Figure 4.2   Regression with a regime shift using a dummy variable for yearly saving and income data.

The sum of errors squares = 0.33, Regression sum of squares = 6.69.

Estimation of variance: 0.0185, Standard deviation: 0.1360.

The value of F-statistic = 93.8415. The critical value of F-statistic: F (3, 14) = 4.2417.

Coefficient of total correlation $R^2 = 0.9526$ ($R = 0.9760$).

Figure 4.2 and the computation can be seen by clicking DASC→Hypothesis Test→Chow Test of Piecewise Regression. Of course, the user can load or input his or her own data in DASC from any folder with any data form (text, Excel, SQL, and other database form) to calculate this test or other models.

4.1.3   Cross section analysis

The data in Table 4.4 are taken from one of the most famous examples in applied econometric research. This example was given by Y. Grunfeld (1961) to define seemingly unrelated (but related) regressions, as the companies he considered faced the same investment climate and were affected by some unknown common factors. Columns Y, X_1 and X_2 represent the total investment, the value of the physical capital stock of the company, and the value of the common stock of the company, respectively. All the data are divided into two groups from 1935 to 1954. One group is from company A, and the other from company B. The data form a time series of cross-sections, changing with the years. This data can be used to illustrate an interesting switching regression or regime shift (or equivalently an intersecting surface analysis) model. Unfortunately, there are only very few observations for each company.

The means and standard deviations of the three variables are presented below.

Y	X_1	X_2
317.6	3078.5	2.8
12.93	191.5	1.8

According to the data from companies A and B, we can find the time series models independently:

Table 4.4 Data for investment analysis.

	Company A			Company B		
Year	Y	X_1	X_2	Y	X_1	X_2
1935	317.6	3078.5	2.8	12.93	191.5	1.8
1936	391.8	4661.7	52.6	25.90	516.0	8.0
1937	410.6	5387.1	156.9	35.05	729.0	7.4
1938	257.7	2792.2	209.2	22.89	560.4	18.1
1939	330.8	43413.2	203.4	18.84	519.9	23.5
1940	461.2	4643.9	207.2	28.57	628.5	26.5
1941	512.0	4551.2	255.2	48.51	537.1	36.2
1942	448.0	3244.1	303.7	43.34	561.2	60.8
1943	449.6	4053.7	264.1	37.02	617.2	84.4
1944	547.5	4379.3	201.6	37.81	626.7	91.2
1945	561.2	4840.9	265.0	39.27	737.2	92.4
1946	688.1	4900.9	402.2	53.46	760.5	86.0
1947	568.9	3526.5	761.5	55.56	581.4	111.1
1948	529.2	3254.7	922.4	49.56	662.3	130.60
1949	555.1	370.2	1020.1	32.4	583.8	141.8
1950	642.9	3755.6	1099.0	32.24	635.2	13.67
1951	755.9	4833.0	1207.7	54.38	723.8	129.7
1952	897.2	4924.9	1430.5	71.78	864.1	145.5
1953	1304.4	6241.7	1777.3	90.08	1193.5	174.8
1954	1486.7	5593.6	2226.3	68.6	1188.9	213.5

$$A : Y_{1i} = \beta_{10} + \beta_{11} X_{11i} + \beta_{12} X_{12i} + \varepsilon_{1i}$$

$$B : Y_{2i} = \beta_{20} + \beta_{21} X_{21i} + \beta_{22} X_{22i} + \varepsilon_{2i}$$

From the data, we obtain

$$A : Y = -149.7815 + 0.1193 X_1 + 0.3714 X_2$$

$$B : Y = -0.5779 + 0.0529 X_1 + 0.0931 X_2$$

By pooling the data from both A and B companies we get:

$$Y = -58.1096 + 0.0980 X_1 + 0.3765 X_2$$

The sum of squared residuals from the three regressions A, B and Pooled sample are 143205.8, 1774.9 and 164213.8 respectively. The degrees of freedom are 17, 17 and 37 respectively. From the estimated equations we find that there seems to be a significant difference.

Example 4.2 Cross section analysis model (investment analysis data of two companies) We introduce the switching regression (or intersecting surface analysis

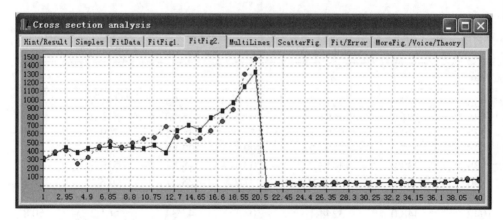

Figure 4.3   Cross section analysis for investment of two companies.

method) using the time series data with categorical dummy variables. We specify the switching regression model as follows:

$$\begin{cases} Y_{it} = \beta_0 + \beta_1 D_{it} + \beta_2 X_{1it} + \beta_3 (D_{it} X_{1it}) + \beta_4 X_{2it} + \beta_5 (D_{it} X_{2it}) + \varepsilon \\ D_{it} = \begin{cases} 1 & Y_{it} \in A, \, while \; 1 \le it \le 20 \\ 0 & Y_{it} \in B, \, while \; 21 \le it \le 40 \end{cases} \quad i = 1,2 \quad t = 1,\ldots,20 \end{cases}$$

Then we have 40 data points and five independent variables. We fit the data to this model and get

$$Y_{it} = -0.5831 - 149.1996 D_{it} + 0.0529 X_{1it}$$
$$+ 0.0664 (D_{it} X_{1it}) + 0.0931 X_{2it} + 0.2784 (D_{it} X_{2it})$$

The error sum of squares = 144980.70, Regression sum of squares = 4876556.0.

Estimation of variance: 3624.5180, Standard deviation: 60.204.

Significance test of the regression equation, H_0: $\beta_0 = \beta_1 = \cdots = \beta_5 = 0$.

The value of F-statistic = 228.724. The critical value of F-statistic: F (5, 34) = 2.494.

So we can get a conclusion: the whole regression equation is significant.

From the equation above, we can get two intersecting surface equations. For example, when D = 1 we get

$$Y_i = -149.7815 + 0.1193 X_{1i} + 0.3714 X_{2i}$$

The sum of error squares of the first regression equation Q_1 = 143205.8000, and the degree of freedom is 17.

It is an intersecting surface analysis, or a switching regression as when D = 0 we get

$$Y_i = -0.5779 + 0.0529 X_{1i} + 0.0931 X_{2i}$$

The sum of error squares of the first regression equation Q_2 = 1774.9010, and the degree of freedom is 17. The coefficient of total correlation R^2 = 0.9438 (R = 0.9715).

The results of model fitting are shown in Figure 4.3.

Figure 4.3 and the computation can be seen by clicking DASC→Regression→Other Linear Regression→Cross Section Analysis Model.

4.1.4   Seasonal analysis model

We now introduce how to use the dummy variables to analyze the seasonal effects in a regression model, the **seasonal analysis regression model**. Although seasonality is a specific feature of time series analysis that is treated in Chapter 8 we present it here as it is handled using dummy variables.

Economic data sway with the seasons. There are two issues here. One is how do we take the seasonal influence into account in the regression model. The other is how do we eliminate the seasonal influence in the regression model.

We can use the dummy variables to address the two problems mentioned above. Suppose we construct a regression model of seasonal analysis:

$$Y_i = \alpha_1 + \alpha_2 D_{2i} + \alpha_3 D_{3i} + \alpha_4 D_{4i} + X_i'\beta + \varepsilon_i \qquad (4.7)$$

where

$$D_{2i} = \begin{cases} 1 & Y_i \text{ belongs to the second quarter} \\ 0 & \text{otherwise} \end{cases}$$

$$D_{3i} = \begin{cases} 1 & Y_i \text{ belongs to the third quarter} \\ 0 & \text{otherwise} \end{cases}$$

$$D_{4i} = \begin{cases} 1 & Y_i \text{ belongs to the fourth quarter} \\ 0 & \text{otherwise} \end{cases}$$

and we set the first quarter as the standard or base, the effect of which is included in the intercept term. If the coefficients α_2, α_3, α_4 are statistically significant, there are significant seasonal influences. The ultimate coefficient β represents the effect of the variable X on Y, after eliminating the seasonal effects on Y. The following model results are based on such a seasonal analysis of time series data.

Example 4.3   Seasonal analysis model (the effect of sales on profit in American manufacturing)   The profit and sale data of American manufacturing from 1965 to 1970 are listed in Table 4.5, counted by four seasons every year with the hundred million dollars as its unit.

We construct the seasonal analysis model as equation (4.7).

The data are arranged by year, and four quarters within each year.

We introduce the seasonal dummy variables into the model and report the regression data of the new model with the seasonal dummy variables as shown in Table 4.6.

The estimation results are given below:

$$Y = 6.688 + 1.323 D_2 - 0.218 D_3 + 0.1839 D_4 + 0.038 X$$

Then we use t-test to check the significance of the regression coefficients. When the level of significance is 0.05 with the critical value of 1.729, the values of t-statistic are 1.97, 0.33,

Table 4.5   The profit and sales data of American manufacturing.

Year	Season	Profit	Sale
1965	I	10.503	114.862
	II	12.092	123.968
	III	10.834	121.454
	IV	12.201	131.917
1966	I	12.245	129.911
	II	14.001	140.976
	III	12.213	137.828
	IV	12.820	145.465
1967	I	11.349	136.989
	II	12.615	145.126
	III	11.014	141.536
	IV	12.730	151.776
1968	I	12.539	148.862
	II	14.849	158.913
	III	13.203	155.727
	IV	14.947	168.409
1969	I	14.151	162.781
	II	15.949	176.057
	III	14.024	172.419
	IV	14.315	183.327
1970	I	12.381	170.415
	II	13.991	181.313
	III	12.174	176.712
	IV	10.985	180.370

0.27, and 3.17. Apparently, the second season coefficient D_2 is significant so is the coefficient of Sales (X). But the coefficients of the third and fourth seasons are not significant. The coefficient of X is 0.038, which has eliminated the seasonal influence. It means that one dollar increase in sale can bring about four cents gain of the average profit, after correcting for seasonal fluctuations in profits.

Because only the second season has a significant effect on profits, we can construct the simplified seasonal analysis model:

$$Y = \alpha_1 + \alpha_2 D_2 + X\beta + \varepsilon$$

We estimate the regression equation using DASC software and get

$$Y = 6.516 + 1.311 D_2 + 0.0393 X$$

The coefficient of X has increased slightly.

The figure below gives the goodness of fit of the model.

Figure 4.4 and the computation can be seen by clicking DASC→Regression→Other Linear Regression→Seasonal analysis Model.

Table 4.6   The profit and sales data with seasonal dummy variables.

Profit	D_2	D_3	D_4	Sales
10.5030	.0000	.0000	.0000	114.8620
12.0920	1.0000	.0000	.0000	123.9680
10.8340	.0000	1.0000	.0000	121.4540
12.2010	.0000	.0000	1.0000	131.9170
12.2450	.0000	.0000	.0000	129.9110
14.0010	1.0000	.0000	.0000	140.9760
12.2130	.0000	1.0000	.0000	137.8280
12.8200	.0000	.0000	1.0000	145.4650
11.3490	.0000	.0000	.0000	136.9890
12.6150	1.0000	.0000	.0000	145.1260
11.0140	.0000	1.0000	.0000	141.5360
12.7300	.0000	.0000	1.0000	151.7760
12.5390	.0000	.0000	.0000	148.8620
14.8490	1.0000	.0000	.0000	158.9130
13.2030	.0000	1.0000	.0000	155.7270
14.9470	.0000	.0000	1.0000	168.4090
14.1510	.0000	.0000	.0000	162.7810
15.9490	1.0000	.0000	.0000	176.0570
14.0240	.0000	1.0000	.0000	172.4190
14.3150	.0000	.0000	1.0000	183.3270
12.3810	.0000	.0000	.0000	170.4150
13.9910	1.0000	.0000	.0000	181.3130
12.1740	.0000	1.0000	.0000	176.7120
10.9850	.0000	.0000	1.0000	180.3700

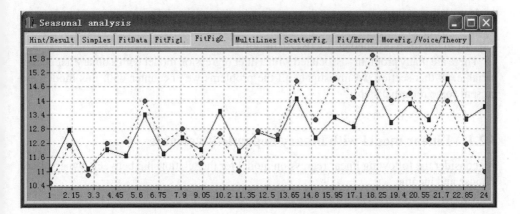

Figure 4.4   Seasonal analysis for profits and sales in American manufacturing.

The regression equation is:

$$Y = 6.6884 + 1.3229 \, D2 + (-.2178) \, D3 + 0.1839 \, D4 + 0.0382X$$

The sum of squared residuals is 22.42. The regression sum of squares: 24.83. The estimate of variance: 0.9342. The standard deviation: 0.9665. The value of F-statistic: 5.2604. The critical value of F-statistic: $F(4, 19) = 2.895$. Coefficient of total correlation $R^2 = 0.5255$ ($R = 0.7249$).

4.2   Models with categorical or discrete dependent variables

The various uses of categorical variables as independent variables were outlined in the previous section. We also find often that the dependent variables are categorical variables. For example, for determining the relationship between ownership of a house and income, we specify a model:

$$Y_i = \beta_0 + \beta_1 X_i + \varepsilon_i \tag{4.8}$$

$$Y_i = \begin{cases} 1 & \text{owning a house} \\ 0 & \text{not owning a house} \end{cases}$$

Here X is the income of the household.

Another example is modeling stock price fluctuation:

$$Y_i = X_i'\beta + \varepsilon_i$$

$$Y_i = \begin{cases} 1 & \text{if there is an increase in stock price} \\ 0 & \text{otherwise} \end{cases}$$

Here X is a multivariate vector determining the factors that influence the stock prices.

Another most commonly encountered statistical model of this nature is that of a weather forecast in the form of whether it will rain or not.

There are many problems associated with a liner regression model with a binary dependent variable. In this section we investigate all the problems we encounter with this model and present some remedial steps.

4.2.1   Linear model with binary dependent variable

We consider the following linear regression model for the relationship between ownership of a house and income.

The standard linear regression model is specified as:

$$Y = X\beta + \varepsilon \qquad E(\varepsilon) = 0, \qquad Var(\varepsilon) = \sigma^2 I_n$$

It can be written in the following equivalent form:

$$E(Y) = X\beta, \quad Var(Y) = \sigma^2 I_n$$

(4.8) can be described as

$$E(Y_i \,|\, X_i) = \beta_0 + \beta_1 X_i$$

The variance of Y_i will be discussed in the next paragraph.

Since the value of Y_i is either zero or one, assume that the probability of $Y_i = 1$ is P_i, and then the probability of $Y_i = 0$ is $1 - P_i$. Thus we have.

$$E(Y_i) = 0 \cdot (1 - P_i) + 1 \cdot P_i = P_i$$

So, in general, there is a constraint as follows:

$$0 \le E(Y_i \,|\, X_i) = \beta_0 + \beta_1 X_i \le 1 \tag{4.9}$$

Because of (4.9) an ordinary specification of the linear regression with binary dependent variable does not guarantee that the estimated values lie between 0 and 1. This is the first peculiar difficulty for ordinary linear regression with a binary or dummy dependent variable.

Consider the residuals

$$\varepsilon_i = Y_i - \beta_0 - \beta_1 X_i$$

Since the value of Y_i is either 1 or 0 with probabilities P_i and $1 - P_i$, we obtain

$$\varepsilon_i = \begin{cases} 1 - \beta_0 - \beta_1 X_i & \text{with probability } P_i \\ -\beta_0 - \beta_1 X_i & \text{with probability } (1 - P_i) \end{cases}$$

So the residual of the linear regression model with binary dependent variable has a binomial distribution. Since ε_i follow the binomial distribution, its variance is:

$$\begin{aligned} Var(\varepsilon_i) &= P_i(1 - P_i) = E(Y_i \,|\, X_i) \left[1 - E(Y_i \,|\, X_i)\right] \\ &= (\beta_0 + \beta_1 X_i)(1 - \beta_0 - \beta_1 X_i) \end{aligned}$$

As we see, the variances of residuals are not constants, but have a relationship with the conditional expectation of Y_i, that is to say, they are heteroscedastic. This is the second peculiar point of departure from the standard regression model.

We can, however, apply weighted least squares to this linear regression model for this binary dependent variable. While that guarantees correction for heteroscedasticity it does not guarantee that the estimated probabilities lie between 0 and 1. We can adopt generalized linear regression to deal with heteroscedastic problems. Letting

$$\sqrt{E(Y_i \,|\, X_i)(1 - E(Y_i \,|\, X_i))} = \sqrt{P_i(1 - P_i)} = \sqrt{\omega_i}$$

the model after transformation becomes

$$\frac{Y_i}{\sqrt{\omega_i}} = \frac{\beta_0}{\sqrt{\omega_i}} + \beta_1 \frac{X_i}{\sqrt{\omega_i}} + \frac{\varepsilon_i}{\sqrt{\omega_i}} \tag{4.10}$$

which is homoscedastic.

Of course, we can not get the theoretical value of $\sqrt{\omega_i}$. We can only estimate it from data through the following computations described in two steps.

Step 1: Use OLS regression for (4.8), obtain y_i, and regard it as the estimation of $E(Y_i | X_i)$. So

$$\hat{\omega}_i = \hat{Y}_i(1 - \hat{Y}_i)$$

Step 2: Use OLS for the transformed model.

For the binary dependent variable the coefficient of total correlation R^2 is quite often relatively small in magnitude, as it is the correlation between highly variable estimated values with actual values that are concentrated at just two points 0 and 1. For the constraint $0 \le \hat{Y}_i \le 1$ in (4.9), we use man-made restrictions by replacing any value of $\hat{Y}_i > 1$ by 1, and replacing any $\hat{Y}_i < 0$ by 0.

We give below a numerical example with real data.

Example 4.4 Model for the relationship between owning a home and income We consider a linear model with a binary dependent variable (ownership of house, $Y_i = 1$, non-ownership, $Y_i = 0$):

$$Y_i = \beta_0 + \beta_1 X_i + \varepsilon_i$$

As the following data are being used just for illustration of the methods, we are not presenting the source of data and specific units. The data on ownership of house (Y) and income (X) for a sample of 20 households are given below in Table 4.7.

$$Y_i = \begin{cases} 1 & \text{owning a house} \\ 0 & \text{not owning a house} \end{cases}$$

Using OLS at the first stage we get:

$$Y_i = -0.9457 + 0.1021X_i$$
$$R = 0.8971$$

Then we can calculate the value $\hat{Y}_i$, $\hat{\omega}_i = P_i(1 - P_i) = \hat{Y}_i(1 - \hat{Y}_i)$. When the estimated Y is greater than 1 we replace it by 1 and when it is less than 0 we replace it by 0. After estimating $\hat{\omega}_i$, thus we use it for the transformation needed to correct for heteroscedasticity. When $\hat{\omega}_i = 0$ or 1, we say that the observed value Y_i are fitted exactly, and thus we need not change them or transform them. In this way, we get the data of (4.10).

$$Y_i / \sqrt{\omega_i}, \quad \beta_0 / \sqrt{\omega_i}, \quad X_i / \sqrt{\omega_i}$$

Table 4.7 Data of owning a house with incomes.

NO.	Y	X	NO.	Y	X
1	0	8	21	1	22
2	1	16	22	1	16
3	1	18	23	0	12
4	0	11	24	0	11
5	0	12	25	1	16
6	1	19	26	0	11
7	1	20	27	1	20
8	0	13	28	1	18
9	0	9	29	0	11
10	0	10	30	0	10
11	1	17	31	1	17
12	1	18	32	0	13
13	0	14	33	1	21
14	1	20	34	1	20
15	0	6	35	0	11
16	1	19	36	0	8
17	1	16	37	1	17
18	0	10	38	1	16
19	0	8	39	0	7
20	1	18	40	1	17

Note that $\beta_0/\sqrt{\omega_i}$ is not a constant, the column number of independent variables is increased by 1 in the second regression, and the constant term (intercept term) no longer exists. In using the regression estimation software we must remember to use the option, with no intercept or constant. This is a generalized linear regression model. However, the independent variables have two columns now in model (4.10). The first column is $\beta_0/\sqrt{\omega_i}$. We have the final regression equation (after reverse transformation of the second stage estimated regression):

$$Y_i = -0.9873 + 0.1048X_i \quad R = 0.9870$$

We see that the coefficient of total correlation has a considerable improvement over the first. The goodness of fit is presented in Figure 4.5. The method illustrated with just one variable can be applied to a multivariate model. The following are the main results.

The result of the first least squares regression: $Y = -0.9457 + 0.1021 X1$.

Coefficient of total correlation $R^2 = 0.8048$ ($R = 0.8971$).

The result of the second least squares regression: $Y = -0.9873 + 0.1048 X1$.

Coefficient of total correlation $R^2 = 0.9743$ ($R = 0.9870$).

The sum of squared residuals: 9.57. Regression sum of squares: 362.58.

Estimation of variance $= 0.2393$. Standard deviation $= 0.4892$.

F statistic $= 1439.0990$. F critical value $F(1, 38) = 4.098$.

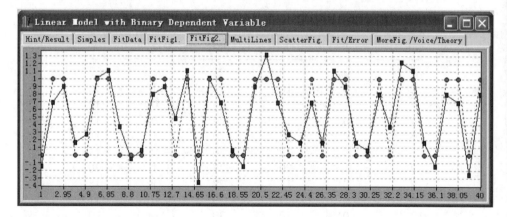

Figure 4.5   Binary dependent variable model for ownership of a house with incomes.

Figure 4.5 and the computation can be seen by clicking DASC→Regression→Other Linear Regression→Binary Dependent Variable Model.

4.2.2   Logit regression model

In the section above, we noted a few special aspects associated with a regression model with a binary dependent variable. One of them is the problem of a binomial distribution for the errors. With large samples we note that the binomial tends to Normal asymptotically and hence in large samples the problem disappears. In the previous section the heteroscedasticity problem was handled by the generalized least squares method. However, in the previous sections the problem of restricting the estimated value of the probability of home ownership to lie between 0 and 1 was not addressed. The problem was that such restriction and linearity of regression are incompatible. In this section we relax the linearity assumption by using a transformation of the linear function on the right hand side of the regression such that after that transformation the range always lies between 0 and 1.

As statisticians we are aware that whatever be the value assumed by a random variable (anywhere between $-\infty$ and $+\infty$), and whatever be its probability distribution, the **cumulative distribution function** (CDF) of that random variable at that point will lie between 0 and 1. Originally, the model is

$$P_i = E(Y = 1 \mid X_i) = \beta_0 + \beta_1 X_i$$

The right hand side being a linear function can not lie between 0 and 1 for all values of X. How do we transform the right hand side so that the transformed value lies between 0 and 1? Let $F(X)$ be the cumulative distribution function (CDF) of $\beta_0 + \beta_1 X_i$ with a density function $f(\beta_0 + \beta_1 X_i)$. Let us now consider a new generic model:

$$Y_i = E(Y = 1 \mid X_i) + \varepsilon_i = F(\beta_0 + \beta_1 X_i) + \varepsilon_i$$

We are now certain that the deterministic part on the right hand side, which must be the probability that Y_i assumes the value 1 given X_i, lies between 0 and 1.

There are two special cases of this very generic model that are very popular. One is called the **Probit Model**, when the underlying CDF is that of a Normal distribution. The other is called the **Logit Model**, when the underlying CDF is that of a **logistic distribution**. We shall present the Logit model in this section, as it is more popular in economics. In the next two subsequent sections we deal with the Probit Model and its variant Tobit Model.

The Logit model is specified as:

$$P_i = E(Y = 1 \mid X_i) = \frac{1}{1 + e^{-(\beta_0 + \beta_1 X_i)}}$$

It can be easily verified that the right hand side expression is nonnegative and has non-negative derivative. Hence it is a non-decreasing function. It can also be verified that when $\beta_0 + \beta_1 X_i$ is extremely small and a large negative number P_i is positive and close to 0 and when $\beta_0 + \beta_1 X_i$ is very large and a large positive number P_i is positive and close to but less than 1. Hence $0 \leq P_i \leq 1$.

Let $Z_i = \beta_0 + \beta_1 X_i$, then

$$P_i = \frac{1}{1 + e^{-Z_i}}$$

$$1 - P_i = \frac{1}{1 + e^{Z_i}}$$

$$\frac{P_i}{1 - P_i} = \frac{1 + e^{Z_i}}{1 + e^{-Z_i}} = e^{Z_i}$$

$$\ln \frac{P_i}{1 - P_i} = Z_i = \beta_0 + \beta_1 X_i$$

As the left hand side is the logarithm of the odd ratio it is called Logit, i.e., log it. The curvilinear relationship between P_i and X_i is the S-type curve. When we have several variables we can replace the number β by a vector β and the variable by a multidimensional vector variable.

We then get the **general Logit regression model**:

$$\ln \frac{P_i}{1 - P_i} = X_i' \beta + \varepsilon_i \tag{4.11}$$

If an estimated value $\hat{\beta}$ of β is obtained, we can estimate the probability P_i of the ith sample. As the dependent variable takes values 0 or 1, we can not compute $\ln(Y_i / (1 - Y_i))$.

There are two ways of handling this problem. First, even when we have individual household data, we can write the likelihood associated with the binomial distribution, and employ the maximum likelihood estimation.

For all those cases where $Y_i = 1$ the probability P_i can be written as: $\dfrac{1}{1 + e^{-(\beta_0 + \beta_1 X_i)}}$.

Likewise for all those cases where $Y_i = 0$ we can write the probability $1 - P_i$ as: $\dfrac{1}{1 + e^{\beta_0 + \beta_1 X_i}}$.

Let us assume that the sample is of size n and let us rearrange the sample in such a way that all samples for which Y = 1 are put together first as observations from $1...n_1$, the remaining $n - n_1$ observations referring to Y = 0. The likelihood of the observed sample can now be written as a function of the unknown parameters β_0 and β_1 as follows:

$$L(Y,X;\beta_0,\beta_1) = \prod_{i=1}^{n_1} \frac{1}{1+e^{-(\beta_0+\beta_1 X_i)}} \prod_{i=n_1+1}^{n} \frac{1}{1+e^{(\beta_0+\beta_1 X_i)}}$$

The unknown parameters could be estimated using the method of maximum likelihood. For this we can use the computer algorithm of Fletcher, Powell, and Davidon.

Second, assuming that we have a very large sample, we can group these households according to some criterion, and proceed with grouped data. This is illustrated below. Suppose X is divided into n groups, with group means $X_1,\cdots, X_n$. Suppose there are n_i samples in the ith group, with N_i of them reporting ownership of the house while $(n_i - N_i)$ report non-ownership. Therefore

$$P_i = \frac{N_i}{n_i}, \quad i = 1,...,n$$

Put this data (P_i, X_i) into the data sheet of Logit regression as follows:

Table 4.8   Home ownership.

No. of year	Sample size	Number of owning houses	Income per month (in '000$)
1	10.0	1.0	2.0
2	20.0	3.0	3.0
3	25.0	4.0	4.0
4	30.0	5.0	5.0
5	40.0	8.0	6.0
6	50.0	12.0	8.0
7	60.0	18.0	10.0
8	80.0	28.0	13.0
9	100.0	45.0	15.0
10	70.0	36.0	20.0
11	65.0	39.0	25.0
12	50.0	33.0	30.0
13	40.0	30.0	35.0
14	25.0	20.0	40.0
15	30.0	27.0	50.0
16	40.0	38.0	60.0
17	50.0	48.0	70.0
18	60.0	58.0	80.0

From this table, we know that if income is $6000 per month the possibility of having house P_i is $8/40 = 0.2$. The next issue is to obtain the distribution of the residuals in (4.11). When the sample is large we can assume that ε_i follows a normal distribution approximately:

$$\varepsilon_i \sim N\left(0, \frac{1}{n_i P_i (1 - P_i)}\right)$$

Notice that this is only an approximate assumption. Under this assumption, the heteroscedasticity of this model is easy to deal with, where we can use a similar transformation as in the previous section.

The Logit regression model estimates the probability of events that follow a binomial distribution. Its applications are not limited to economics and business only. It can be used to predict earthquakes and tsunamis. It can also be used to estimate the probability of survival from open heart surgery.

The Logit model can be extended to fit any S-shaped curve to situations even when the dependent variable is not binary or dichotomous. In those cases the following conditions must be satisfied:

(1) Numerical values of X grow gradually, and Y is an increasing function of X.

(2) Numerical value of Y is bounded, $a \leq Y \leq b$.

(3) Numerical value limit exists: $\lim_{X \to -\infty} Y(X) = a$, $\lim_{X \to \infty} Y(X) = b$

We can describe a generalization of the Logit model for such cases as follows:

$$\ln \frac{Y_i - a}{b - Y_i} = X_i'\beta + \varepsilon_i, \ i = 1, 2, \cdots, n \tag{4.12}$$

If there is only an upper limit $\lim_{X \to \infty} Y(X) = Y_0$, whose value is not known to us, we can estimate it. This is done as follows:

$$\ln \frac{Y_i / Y_0}{1 - Y_i / Y_0} = X_i'\beta + \varepsilon_i, \ i = 1, 2, \ldots, n$$

As Y_0 is not known the user has to specify an initial starting value and search for improvement. The search procedure involves choosing a step direction and step length, and a criterion to stop the search. We can use the estimated variance of the residuals $\hat{\sigma}_k^2$ corresponding to the chosen value of Y_0 at iteration k, let us call it Y_{0k}. We can then use AIC or BIC criteria that minimize either AIC or BIC:

$$\text{AIC}(k) = \ln(\hat{\sigma}_k^2) + \frac{2k}{n}, \text{BIC}(k) = \ln(\hat{\sigma}_k^2) + \frac{k \ln n}{n}$$

The optimal estimation of Y_0 can be taken as the maximum trend value of Y.

A great deal of economic data can be represented by an S-type growth trend that is amenable to modeling using a Logit model such as above. For example, there are many economic growth indices such as the growth of the number of infectious diseases, the growth of population and so on. We used the Logit model to forecast the Wenzhou-Fuzhou Railway growth rate, the increase in the number of infections in 2003, the increase in computer CPU frequency, and so on. We now give a numerical illustration of this last example of growth in CPU.

Example 4.5   Forecasting for computer CPU frequency   We all know the history of the development of computer CPU frequency, from 286, 386, 486, 586 to P2, P3, P4, etc. The CPU frequency can increase, but it can not grow indefinitely. The growth should have a limit. Without either computer expertise about the CPU or a crystal ball for the future, our estimate of that limit to growth must be based only on the data on the historical development of CPU. Computer CPU frequencies data from 1971 to 2005 are presented in Table 4.9.

Using model (4.12) and the AIC criterion, the trend searching being confined to the range 1000, 18000, we find that the limit of the CPU frequency is about 9400, and that it would occur in 2020.

Figure 4.6 and the computation can be seen by clicking DASC→Regression→Linear Regression with Dummy Variable→Logit Model Regression.

The Logit growth model can be seen as a nonlinear regression model (Figure 4.7). Its independent variable is then taken as time period. In this case we only use data with only one column. We use the Logit model as a nonlinear regression model to forecast sales of houses in Section 5.4, Chapter 5.

Table 4.9   Data of the computer CPU frequency (MHz).

1	2	2.5	5	8	12	16	20	33	40	50
60	180	200	233	350	450	733	1000	1300	2000	3000

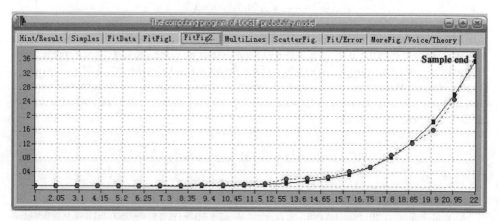

Figure 4.6   Fitting of Logit model for increase of computer CPU frequency.

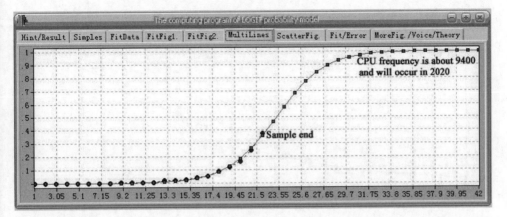

Figure 4.7   Forecasting for increase of computer CPU frequency by Logit model.

4.2.3   Probit regression model

We presented in the previous section a generic model in which the linear regression function is transformed, using a CDF of a random variable. We considered one special case in that section, that of the CDF associated with a logistic distribution. In this section we consider the CDF of standardized normal distribution:

$$F(Y) = \frac{1}{\sqrt{2\pi}} \int_{-\infty}^{Y} e^{-\frac{t^2}{2}} dt$$

This model is called a Probit model. It is also called a Normit model.

First, we should obtain P_i, $i = 1, \ldots, n$. Then we check out the quantile Y_i of each P_i in the $N(0,1)$ distribution function table. At last we make a linear regression about Y_i and X. DASC uses the **electronic software table** for the CDF of a Normal distribution. It is very convenient and user-friendly.

Our next step is to analyze the variance of regression model. The original model is

$$P_i = F(Y_i) + e_i = F(X_i'\beta) + e_i$$

where P_i is the parameter of a binomial distribution. Its variance is $P_i(1 - P_i)$. Therefore

$$X_i'\beta = F^{-1}(P_i - e_i)$$

taking first order Taylor expansion, we have

$$X_i'\beta = F^{-1}(P_i) - \frac{e_i}{f[F^{-1}(P_i)]}$$

where $f(\cdot)$ is the standard normal density function and the derivative of $F(\cdot)$. So

$$F^{-1}(P_i) = X_i'\beta + \frac{e_i}{f[F^{-1}(P_i)]}$$

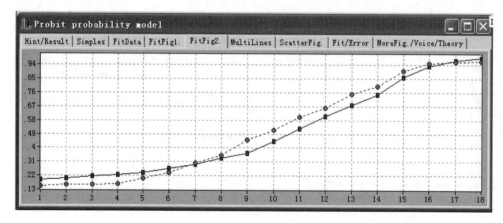

Figure 4.8 Probit regression model with normal distribution function.

Compare this with the OLS model

$$F^{-1}(P_i) = X_i'\beta + \varepsilon_i \tag{4.13}$$

Because the variance of e_i is $P_i(1 - P_i)$, the variance of ε_i is

$$Var(\varepsilon_i) = Var(\frac{e_i}{f[F^{-1}(P_i)]}) = \frac{P_i(1-P_i)}{n_i\{f[F^{-1}(P_i)]\}^2} \tag{4.14}$$

Now we can use the generalized least squares method to develop linear regression.

Example 4.6   Fitting probit model to home ownership data   We illustrate this method using the home ownership data of Example 4.3 with the data given in Table 4.8. First we need to calculate probability P_i, and then get quantiles Y_i from the CDF of $N(0,1)$. These quantiles are used to make a linear regression of independent variables (4.13). Then we calculate heteroscedasticity as given in (4.14) and obtain generalized least squares estimators of the unknown parameters. The process of calculation and the fitting results are similar to the Logit model.

Figure 4.8 and the computation can be seen by clicking DASC→Regression→Linear Regression with Dummy Variable→Probit Model Regression.

4.2.4   Tobit regression model

We often encounter in economic and business applications where no data are available for a part of the population. This situation is called the **truncated sample** problem. On the other hand there are situations where the sample is not truncated and there are observations from all sections of the population but some information on some variables is not available. One may say that the nature or the data collector have censored and what we have is **censored data**.

The Tobit regression model is best suited to deal with censored data. Tobin, a winner of Nobel Prize in economics, who introduced this model, applied it to the demand for automobiles. He postulated that there is an inherent demand for possessing an automobile which is a function of income, but that demand results in the purchase and possession of an automobile only if the price the customer is willing to pay is more than the price at which the automobile dealer is willing to sell. The economic market mechanism censors the hidden willingness to pay for automobiles by those who cannot afford to buy at going prices.

The example we use below is quite similar. We study residents' desire to invest in housing. The income is a continuous independent variable, but the desire to invest in housing may be revealed in the data only if the person buys a house. So, there is a linear relationship between the desired housing investment Y^* and the income as follows:

$$Y_i^* = X_i'\beta + \varepsilon_i, \quad i = 1,\ldots,n \tag{4.15}$$

However, the observation data are indicated by:

$$Y_i = \begin{cases} Y_i^* & \text{if } Y_i^* > c \\ c & \text{if } Y_i^* \le c \end{cases} \tag{4.16}$$

Our goal is to regress with the censored data and estimate the parameters (β and c) of the model.

There are many such problems in economics and business. Many economic activities do not take place or are not recorded unless a threshold is reached. But we wish to take the information contained in the fact that there is such a threshold, as the existence of the threshold and its level has some bearing on the observations we actually record and analyze. This is what is permitted by the Tobit model. This situation often appears in natural sciences as well. Experimental observations are made with equipment with a level of precision. Any actual observation that is below the level of precision is not observed or recorded as zero.

First, we subtract the unknown parameter c from both sides of (4.16), or assume that $c = 0$ (this is also equivalent to assuming that c is absorbed in the intercept term), then the Tobit model is

$$Y_i = \begin{cases} X_i'\beta + \varepsilon_i, & \text{if } X_i'\beta + \varepsilon_i > 0 \\ 0, & \text{otherwise} \end{cases} \tag{4.17}$$

Now, we analyze what will happen if we use the ordinary least squares to estimate the model (4.17). Then we will introduce the maximum likelihood estimation proposed by Tobin.

Suppose there are total n observations, in which n_0 observations refer to $Y_i = 0$ and n_1 observations refer to $Y_i > 0$. If we ignore the n_0 samples of $Y_i = 0$, and regress with the n_1 remaining samples using OLS, we are ignoring the information content on X_i of the other n_0 observations. Then it must be intuitive that the inference we make is based on insufficient information. The estimators are then biased, and they are so even in large samples, implying that they are not even consistent. In fact, denote the conditional expectation of Y_i on the condition of $Y_i > 0$ as

$$E(Y_i \mid Y_i > 0) = X_i'\beta + E(\varepsilon_i \mid Y_i > 0)$$

If the conditional expectation of error term is zero, unbiasness holds. But unfortunately, if we assume ε_i is an independent normal variable whose mean is zero, then

$$E(\varepsilon_i \mid Y_i > 0) = E(\varepsilon_i \mid X_i'\beta + \varepsilon_i > 0) = E(\varepsilon_i \mid \varepsilon_i > -X_i'\beta) \ne 0$$

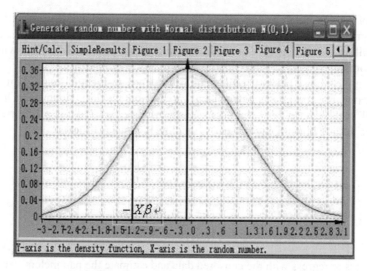

Figure 4.9   A Normal distribution figure.

This result is also clearly visible in the figure of the density function of normal distribution, shown as Figure 4.9. The density function of ε_i is symmetric with Y axis. Thus, only when the interval ε_i lies symmetrically, the conditional expectation may be zero, such as $E(\varepsilon_i \mid -X_i'\beta < \varepsilon_i < X_i'\beta) = 0$.

Figure 4.9 can be seen by clicking DASC→Basic Statistics→Generate Random Data1→ Normal distribution.

Denote the constant as

$$C_X = \int_{-X_i'\beta}^{+\infty} f(t)dt$$

then the density function of the random variable $\varepsilon_i^* = (\varepsilon_i \mid \varepsilon_i > -X_i'\beta)$ is

$$f(\varepsilon_i^*) = \frac{1}{C_X} f(\varepsilon_i), \quad \text{when} \quad \varepsilon_i > -X_i'\beta$$

In order to analyze the corresponding influence on OLS estimator of β in this case, we denote

$$E_i = E(\varepsilon_i^*) = E(\varepsilon_i \mid \varepsilon_i > -X_i'\beta)$$

then $E_i > 0$. If we only use the sample of $Y_i > 0$ to regress, the regression model is

$$Y_i = X_i'\beta + \varepsilon_i^*$$

$$\hat{\beta} = (X'X)^{-1}(X'Y) = (X'X)^{-1}X'(X\beta) + (X'X)^{-1}(X'\varepsilon^*)$$

$$E(\hat{\beta}) = \beta + E\left\{(X'X)^{-1}(X'\varepsilon^*)\right\}$$

$$plim\hat{\beta} = plim(X'X)^{-1}(X'Y) = plim(X'X)^{-1}X'(X\beta) + plim(X'X)^{-1}(X'\varepsilon^*)$$
$$= \beta + plim\{(X'X)^{-1}plim\ (X'\varepsilon^*) \neq \beta$$

as the last *plim* is not equal to 0.

In the following, we will introduce the method of regressing with censored dependent variable, proposed by Tobin, that is the Tobit model. We use the maximum likelihood estimation proposed by Tobin. Assume that the error item is distributed as $N(0,\sigma^2)$, the general formulation of the Tobit model is given by

$$Y_i = \begin{cases} X_i'\beta + \varepsilon_i & \text{If } X_i'\beta + \varepsilon_i > 0 \\ 0 & \text{otherwise} \end{cases}$$
$$\varepsilon_i \sim N(0,\sigma^2)$$

The parameters to be estimated are β, σ^2.

Suppose f_i and F_i denote the values of the density function $f(\cdot)$ and distribution function $F(\cdot)$ of standard normal distribution on $X_i'\beta/\sigma$, respectively, that is

$$f_i = f(X_i'\beta/\sigma) \tag{4.18}$$

$$F_i = F(X_i'\beta/\sigma) \tag{4.19}$$

For $Y_i = 0$, the independent variables satisfy

$$X_i'\beta + \varepsilon_i < 0 \qquad or \qquad \varepsilon_i < -X_i'\beta$$

So the probability of the event $\{Y_i = 0\}$ is

$$P(Y_i = 0) = P(\varepsilon_i < -X_i'\beta) = P\left(\frac{\varepsilon_i}{\sigma} < -\frac{X_i'\beta}{\sigma}\right) = 1 - F_i$$

The probability of $\{Y_i > 0\}$ is also derivable from the normal distribution. Since $E(Y_i) = X_i'\beta$, $\text{Var}(Y_i) = \text{Var}(\varepsilon_i) = \sigma^2$. Thus

$$P(Y_i) = \frac{1}{\sqrt{2\pi}\sigma}e^{-(Y_i - X_i'\beta)^2/(2\sigma^2)}$$

Then the likelihood function of the entire samples is

$$l = \prod^{n_0}(1 - F_i)\prod^{n_1}(2\pi\sigma^2)^{-\frac{1}{2}}\exp(-(Y_i - X_i'\beta)^2/(2\sigma^2))$$

After ignoring the constant item that does not matter when we maximize the function, its logarithmic function is:

$$L = \ln l = \sum^{n_0}\ln(1 - F_i) - \frac{n_1}{2}\ln\sigma^2 - \sum^{n_1}(Y_i - X_i'\beta)^2/(2\sigma^2) \tag{4.20}$$

The **maximum likelihood estimation** is to determine the values of $\hat{\beta}$, $\hat{\sigma}^2$ so that

$$L(\hat{\beta},\hat{\sigma}^2) = \max_{\beta,\sigma^2} L(\beta,\sigma^2)$$

The maximum value of the likelihood function can be obtained by numerical methods, and also by solving the algebraic equations below:

$$\frac{\partial L}{\partial \beta} = -\frac{1}{\sigma}\sum_{}^{n_0}\frac{f_i X_i}{1-F_i} + \frac{1}{\sigma^2}\sum_{}^{n_1}(Y_i - X_i'\beta)X_i = 0$$

$$\frac{\partial L}{\partial \sigma^2} = \frac{1}{2\sigma^3}\sum_{}^{n_0}\frac{(X_i'\beta)f_i}{1-F_i} - \frac{n_1}{2\sigma^2} + \frac{1}{2\sigma^4}\sum_{}^{n_1}(Y_i - X_i'\beta)^2 = 0$$

We can also use Rao's method of scoring (C.R. Rao, 1965) as an iterative method. Let

$$\theta' = (\beta',\sigma^2)$$

then the iterative rule of the method of scoring is

$$\theta_{n+1} = \theta_n + [I(\theta_n)]^{-1}\left(\frac{\partial L}{\partial \theta}\bigg|_{\theta=\theta_n}\right)$$

where the information matrix $I(\theta)$ is

$$I(\theta) = \begin{pmatrix} \sum_{i=1}^{n} a_i X_i X_i' & \sum_{i=1}^{n} b_i X_i \\ \sum_{i=1}^{n} b_i X_i' & \sum_{i=1}^{n} c_i \end{pmatrix}$$

where

$$a_i = \frac{-1}{\sigma^2}\left(Z_i f_i - \frac{f_i^2}{1-F_i} - F_i\right)$$

$$b_i = \frac{1}{2\sigma^3}\left(Z_i^2 f_i + f_i - \frac{Z_i f_i^2}{1-F_i}\right)$$

$$c_i = -\frac{1}{4\sigma^4}\left(Z_i^3 f_i + Z_i f_i - \frac{Z_i^2 f_i^2}{1-F_i} - 2F_i\right)$$

$$Z_i = X_i'\beta/\sigma$$

When the Tobit model is used to regress we should pay attention to the three functions relevant to the model:

$$E(Y_i^*) = X_i'\beta$$

$$E(Y_i \mid Y_i > 0) = X_i'\beta + \sigma f_i / F_i$$

$$E(Y_i) = F_i \cdot E(Y_i \mid Y_i > 0)$$

where the representations of f_i, F_i are shown in (4.18) and (4.19). To explain the influence of independent (dependent) variable corresponding to the unit change of the independent variable, note that

$$\frac{\partial E(Y^*)}{\partial X_j} = \beta_j$$

$$\frac{\partial E(Y_i)}{\partial X_j} = F_i \beta_j$$

$$\frac{\partial E(Y_i \mid Y_i > 0)}{\partial X_j} = \beta_j \left(1 - (X_i'\beta/\sigma)\frac{f_i}{F_i} - \left(\frac{f_i}{F_i}\right)^2 \right)$$

Next, we will analyze the essentials of the computation with specific data.

Example 4.7   Maximum likelihood regression of the censored data   The Tobit model can deal with censored data. This is useful to investigate some economic problems such as tax evasion. In Table 4.10, there are 20 small companies with their incomes (Y), energy consumptions (X_1), and deposits in bank accounts (X_2). In the left column, their incomes (Y) are declared by themselves. We suspect some companies (Number 1 to 5) have false declarations. Meanwhile we believe their data of energy consumptions (X_1) and deposits in bank accounts (X_2) as we can investigate them from the third party. Now we use Tobit model to investigate the authenticity of their incomes. We reconstruct the data in the right columns. The data of incomes for companies (Number 1 to 5) are censored with 0.

For the right data in Table 4.10, we can get computation results using DASC→ Regression→Linear Regression with Dummy Variable→Tobit Model Regression. The maximum likelihood regression equation on the second step is

$$Y = -1.6320 + 0.6641\ X_1 + 3.1106\ X_2$$

The coefficient of total correlation $R = 0.6753$, $R^2 = 0.4560$. The fitting data of incomes for companies (Number 1 to 5) are 0.3273, -1.2340, 0.0649, -0.4057, -0.1595, but their declarations are $-.2087$, -1.8099, -1.2222, -0.1319, -0.9992 respectively, so we need to investigate their incomes further.

For the uncensored data, shown in the left side of Table 4.10, this program is also useful after letting the number of censored data N_0 be zero. In some further research on modeling with censored data, Tobit model was used and estimated employing the EM algorithm (Figure 4.10). The details are not given here. Interested readers can refer to the Electronic References for Chapter 4.

Table 4.10   Censored data for the Tobit model.

Y	X_1	X_2	Y	X_1	X_2
−.2087	.1315	.6018	0.0	.1315	.6018
−1.8099	.4175	.0388	0.0	.4175	.3880
−1.2222	.0535	.5341	0.0	.0535	.5341
−.1319	.8310	.2168	0.0	.8310	.2168
−.9992	.3460	.4660	0.0	.0346	.4660
.0594	.6711	.5261	.0594	.6711	.5261
.4258	.0070	.6954	.4258	.0070	.6954
.7534	.3834	.7658	.7534	.3834	.7658
.8650	.6793	.6578	.8650	.6793	.6578
.8270	.5194	.8946	.8270	.5194	.8946
1.4516	.4587	.8749	1.4516	.4587	.8749
1.3767	.5328	.8912	1.3767	.5328	.8612
1.6312	.2190	.8470	1.6312	.2190	.8470
1.4393	.6789	.7099	1.4393	.6789	.7099
1.0681	.9347	.5896	1.0681	.9347	.5896
1.0839	.3835	.7397	1.0839	.3835	.7397
1.3038	.5297	.9549	1.3038	.5297	.9549
1.9154	.0668	.5312	1.9154	.0668	.5312
2.0924	.7556	.8237	2.0924	.7556	.8237
3.0846	.4700	.8907	3.0846	.470	.8907

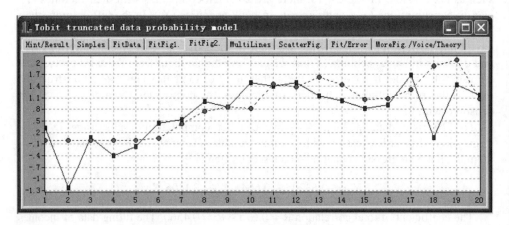

Figure 4.10   Tobit model with censored data.

4.3   Nonlinear regression model and its algorithm

The ordinary nonlinear regression model can be written as

$$Y = f(X, \beta) + \varepsilon \qquad (4.21)$$

where X is the independent random variable (could be a vector consisting of several independent variables) which can be observed, β is the unknown parameter vector, Y is the dependent and observable variable which depends on X and β, ε is random error. $f(\cdot)$ is a known nonlinear function.

The **Cobb-Douglas production function** is a typical example of the nonlinear regression model:

$$Q = \alpha \, L^{\beta_1} K^{\beta_2} + \varepsilon$$

where Q is the output, L is labor, K is the stock of capital, and α, β_1 and β_2 are model parameters to be estimated. Letting $Y = Q$, $X' = (L, K)$, $\beta = (\alpha, \beta_1, \beta_2)'$, and $f(X, \beta) = \alpha L_1^{\beta_1} K_1^{\beta_2}$, the Cobb-Douglas production function can be written in the form of (4.21). Another example is **consumption function**:

$$C = \beta_1 + \beta_2 Y^{\beta_3} + \varepsilon$$

where Y is the household income, C is the household consumption. $\beta_i (i = 1,2,3)$ are model parameters to be estimated. If $\beta_3 \neq 1$, the model is a model nonlinear in parameters; if $\beta_3 = 1$, it reduces to linear model. But the actual data may reject the null hypothesis $\beta_3 = 1$.

The linearization of economic model depends on how the error term enters into the specification of the model. Take the Cobb-Douglas production function for example. Suppose the error is expressed in a multiplicative form as in the following equation:

$$Q = \alpha L^{\beta_1} K^{\beta_2} e^{\varepsilon}$$

It can be **linearized** after taking logarithm:

$$\ln Q = \ln \alpha + \beta_1 \ln L + \beta_2 \ln K + \varepsilon$$

Estimation of a regression model nonlinear in parameters requires solving a nonlinear optimization problem. Many of the linear regression models can also be regarded as nonlinear optimization models when the **method of maximum likelihood** is used. For example, the maximum likelihood estimation of the generalized least squares problem

$$Y = X\beta + \varepsilon, \quad E(\varepsilon) = 0, \quad Var(\varepsilon) = \sigma^2 \psi$$

can be regarded as a nonlinear problem.

This chapter will discuss the nature and the computation for the estimation of the parameters of nonlinear regression model. As special cases we consider nonlinear regression models that represent **growth curves** and **failure rate models**.

There are two ways for the solution of nonlinear regression model. One is least squares method, namely to seek the shortest distance between vector Y and $f(X, \beta)$

$$\|Y - f(X, \beta)\| \xrightarrow{\ \beta\ } \min$$

where $\|\cdot\|$ is a metric that measures distance from the origin.

The other one is the maximum likelihood method. We assume that the probability density function $g(X, \beta, \sigma^2)$ of error is known and write the **likelihood function** (**joint density**

function of sample). Then we need to compute its maximum with respect to the unknown parameters:

$$L(\beta, \sigma^2) = \prod_{i=1}^{n} g(X_i, \beta, \sigma^2) \xrightarrow{\beta, \sigma^2} \max$$

We can see that in either case the method of solution requires the computation of the extremum. Two methods concerning computation of the extremum are introduced in Section 4.1. These methods need the numerical computation of the derivative function $\dfrac{\Delta y}{\Delta x}$ of the objective function. Such computation is meaningful if Δx is equidistant. But the observed data on X are usually not under our control and Δx is not based on equidistant X. When there are repeated observations Δx could be even 0, that leads to arithmetic overflow because the denominator is 0. Hence in our DASC programming we adopt Powell algorithm, improved by Sargent, in which the computation of derivative function and difference is unnecessary and the computation is stable.

4.3.1   The least squares estimate for nonlinear regression model

We consider the multivariate nonlinear regression model ($f(\cdot)$ is known)

$$Y_i = f(X_i, \beta) + \varepsilon_i, \quad E(\varepsilon_i) = 0, \quad Var(\varepsilon_i) = \sigma^2$$

Among them, β is the $m \times 1$ unknown parameter vector. Adopting the matrix notation, the model is

$$Y = f(X, \beta) + \varepsilon \tag{4.22}$$

$$E(\varepsilon) = 0, \quad Var(\varepsilon) = \sigma^2 I_n$$

The sum of residual squares is

$$S(\beta) = \varepsilon' \varepsilon = [Y - f(X, \beta)]' [Y - f(X, \beta)]$$

Its first order condition for minimization is:

$$\frac{\partial S}{\partial \beta} = -2 \left[\frac{\partial f(X, \beta)}{\partial \beta} \right]' [Y - f(X, \beta)] = 0$$

here $\left(\dfrac{\partial f}{\partial \beta} \right)'$ is a $m \times n$ matrix. Write $n \times m$ matrix as

$$Z(\beta) = \frac{\partial f(X, \beta)}{\partial \beta} = \begin{pmatrix} \dfrac{\partial f(X_1, \beta)}{\partial \beta_1} & \cdots & \dfrac{\partial f(X_1, \beta)}{\partial \beta_m} \\ \cdots & \ddots & \cdots \\ \dfrac{\partial f(X_n, \beta)}{\partial \beta_1} & \cdots & \dfrac{\partial f(X_n, \beta)}{\partial \beta_m} \end{pmatrix}$$

Note that β_i with the subscript is a component of the vector β. Therefore the first order condition designating minimum of sum of residual squares is:

$$[Z(\beta)]'[Y - f(X, \beta)] = 0$$

To use the **Gauss-Newton algorithm**, we have to make the multivariate Taylor expansion for multivariate function $f(X, \beta)$ near the initial value β_1.

$$f(X_i, \beta) \approx f(X_i, \beta_1) + \left[\left. \frac{\partial f(X_i, \beta)}{\partial \beta} \right|_{\beta_1} \right]' (\beta - \beta_1)$$

Combining these expressions, we obtain

$$f(X, \beta) \approx f(X, \beta_1) + Z(\beta_1)(\beta - \beta_1)$$

Therefore the nonlinear regression model (4.22) is

$$Y \approx f(X, \beta_1) + Z(\beta_1)(\beta - \beta_1) + \varepsilon$$

If we write

$$\tilde{Y}(\beta_1) = Y - f(X, \beta_1) + Z(\beta_1)\beta_1$$

Then nonlinear model is linearized

$$\underset{n \times 1}{\tilde{Y}(\beta_1)} = \underset{n \times k}{Z(\beta_1)} \underset{k \times 1}{\beta} + \underset{n \times 1}{\varepsilon}$$

We can write down the solution of least squares for this linear regression model, namely the first iterative solution of original nonlinear regression model.

$$\begin{aligned} \beta_2 &= [Z(\beta_1)'Z(\beta_1)]^{-1} Z(\beta_1)' \tilde{Y}(\beta_1) \\ &= \beta_1 + [Z(\beta_1)'Z(\beta_1)]^{-1} Z(\beta_1)'[Y - f(X, \beta_1)] \end{aligned}$$

We obtain the general iterative formula for all subsequent stages of computation:

$$\beta_{n+1} = \beta_n + [Z(\beta_n)'Z(\beta_n)]^{-1} Z(\beta_n)'[Y - f(X, \beta_n)]$$

If $\beta_{n+1} = \beta_n$ appears, it means

$$Z(\beta_n)'[Y - f(X, \beta_n)] = 0$$

That means $\dfrac{\partial S}{\partial \beta} = 0$. In actual computation, however, we do not necessarily aim at equality to zero but set **tolerance levels** both for change in parameter estimates from iteration to iteration and the change in the value of the partial derivative of S, and when both of them become negligibly small we terminate the iterative procedure. What we obtain from such **iterative solution** is a **local minimum of the residual sum of squares** only. In order to ensure that it is a **global minimum** we have to either establish convexity of S or we have to obtain several local extrema with a wide grid of starting values and choose the extremum of those extrema.

4.3.2   Maximum likelihood estimation of nonlinear regression model

There are three very popular algorithms for the computation of maximum likelihood estimators, **Newton-Raphson algorithm**, **Counting algorithm**, **BHHH algorithm** (Berndt, B. Hall, S.G. Hall and Hausman, 1974).

Because **information matrix** $I(\theta)$ here is a block diagonal matrix, we can obtain the estimate of σ^2 once the estimate of β is obtained according to $\hat{\sigma}^2 = \frac{1}{n}S(\hat{\beta})$ (see Section 4.3.3). So we only need to consider the algorithm for estimating β. The general formula for MLE iterative algorithm for β is obtained by the first order condition for the maximum of the likelihood, expanding it in Taylor series, to get the expression:

$$\beta_{n+1} = \beta_n - P_n \frac{\partial L}{\partial \beta}\Big|_{\beta_n}$$

In Newton-Raphson, $P_n = \left(\frac{\partial^2 L}{\partial\beta\partial\beta'}\right)^{-1}_{\beta_n}$ then above expression becomes:

$$\begin{aligned}\beta_{n+1} &= \beta_n - \left(\frac{\partial^2 L}{\partial\beta\partial\beta'}\right)^{-1}_{\beta_n} \frac{\partial L}{\partial\beta}\Big|_{\beta_n} \\ &= \beta_n - \left(\frac{1}{2\sigma^2}\frac{\partial^2 S}{\partial\beta\partial\beta'}\right)^{-1}_{\beta_n}\left(\frac{1}{2\sigma^2}\frac{\partial S}{\partial\beta}\right)_{\beta_n} \\ &= \beta_n - \left(\frac{\partial^2 S}{\partial\beta\partial\beta'}\right)^{-1}_{\beta_n}\frac{\partial S}{\partial\beta}\Big|_{\beta_n}\end{aligned}$$

This is also called Rao's method of scoring (Rao, 1965), where the last term is called the **score** and the matrix before it is the sample information matrix.

Asymptotic variance-covariance matrix of $\hat{\beta}$ in this case can be written as

$$\hat{\Sigma}_{\hat{\beta}} = -\left(\frac{\partial^2 L}{\partial\beta\partial\beta'}\right)^{-1}_{\beta_n} = 2\hat{\sigma}^2\left(\frac{\partial^2 S}{\partial\beta\partial\beta'}\right)^{-1}_{\beta_n}$$

We can see that P_n uses the **Hessian matrix** of logarithm of the likelihood function in the above method. Mathematical expectation of the Hessian matrix, which is the **inverse information matrix**, will be used in the next method. That is

$$P_n = \left(E\frac{\partial^2 L}{\partial\beta\partial\beta'}\right)^{-1}_{\beta_n}$$

Substituting this expression in the equation above we get:

$$
\begin{aligned}
\beta_{n+1} &= \beta_n - \left(E \frac{\partial^2 L}{\partial \beta \partial \beta'} \right)^{-1}_{\beta_n} \left(\frac{\partial L}{\partial \beta} \right)_{\beta_n} \\
&= \beta_n - \left(\frac{-1}{\sigma^2} Z(\beta_n)' Z(\beta_n) \right)^{-1} \left(\frac{-1}{2\sigma^2} \frac{\partial S}{\partial \beta} \right)_{\beta_n} \\
&= \beta_n - \frac{1}{2} \left(Z(\beta_n)' Z(\beta_n) \right)^{-1} \frac{\partial S}{\partial \beta} \bigg|_{\beta_n}
\end{aligned}
$$

This is just the **Gauss-Newton algorithm** of nonlinear regression. Here the estimate of asymptotic variance of $\hat{\beta}$ is

$$
\hat{\Sigma}_{\hat{\beta}} = -\left(E \frac{\partial^2 L}{\partial \beta \partial \beta'} \right)^{-1}_{\beta_n} = \hat{\sigma}^2 \left(Z(\hat{\beta})' Z(\hat{\beta}) \right)^{-1}_{\beta_n}
$$

The third method is the **BHHH algorithm**. We consider the observed logarithm of the likelihood function, namely

$$
L_i = L(\beta, \sigma^2 | Y_i, X_i) = -\frac{1}{2} \ln(2\pi) - \frac{1}{2} \ln \sigma^2 - \frac{[Y_i - f(X_i, \beta)]^2}{2\sigma^2}
$$

The designation of P_n in this algorithm is

$$
P_n = -\left(\sum_{i=1}^n \left(\frac{\partial L_i}{\partial \beta} \right) \left(\frac{\partial L_i}{\partial \beta'} \right) \right)^{-1} \bigg|_{\beta_n, \sigma^2}
$$

We will know why this form is adopted soon. Now

$$
\frac{\partial L_i}{\partial \beta} = \frac{[Y_i - f(X_i, \beta)]}{\sigma^2} \frac{\partial f(X_i, \beta)}{\partial \beta}
$$

This algorithm is obtained according to the following expressions:

$$
\begin{aligned}
\beta_{n+1} &= \beta_n + \left(\sum_{i=1}^n \frac{\partial L_i}{\partial \beta} \frac{\partial L_i}{\partial \beta'} \right)^{-1}_{\beta_n, \sigma^2} \left(\frac{\partial L}{\partial \beta} \right)_{\beta_n} \\
&= \beta_n + \left(\sum_{i=1}^n \frac{[Y_i - f(X_i, \beta)]^2}{\sigma^4} \frac{\partial f(X_i, \beta)}{\partial \beta} \frac{\partial f(X_i, \beta)}{\partial \beta'} \right)^{-1}_{\beta_n} \left(\frac{-1}{2\sigma^2} \frac{\partial S}{\partial \beta} \right)_{\beta_n} \\
&= \beta_n - \frac{1}{2} \sigma^2 \left(\sum_{i=1}^n [Y_i - f(X_i, \beta)]^2 \frac{\partial f(X_i, \beta)}{\partial \beta} \frac{\partial f(X_i, \beta)}{\partial \beta'} \bigg|_{\beta_n} \right)^{-1} \frac{\partial S}{\partial \beta} \bigg|_{\beta_n}
\end{aligned}
$$

This expression, which characterizes BHHH algorithm, is different from the algorithm we presented previously. It may be noted that:

$$E\left[\sum_{i=1}^{n}\left(\frac{\partial L_i}{\partial \beta}\right)\left(\frac{\partial L_i}{\partial \beta'}\right)\right] = \frac{1}{\hat{\sigma}^2}\sum_{i=1}^{n}\left(\frac{\partial f(X_i,\beta)}{\partial \beta}\frac{\partial f(X_i,\beta)}{\partial \beta'}\right) = \frac{1}{\sigma^2}Z(\beta)'Z(\beta)$$

The BHHH algorithm is thus equivalent to the algorithms we mentioned before if $\sum_{i=1}^{n}\left(\frac{\partial L_i}{\partial \beta}\right)\left(\frac{\partial L_i}{\partial \beta'}\right)$ is replaced by $E\left(\sum_{i=1}^{n}\left(\frac{\partial L_i}{\partial \beta}\right)\left(\frac{\partial L_i}{\partial \beta'}\right)\right)$ in iterative formula.

In the BHHH algorithm, **asymptotic variance-covariance matrix** of $\hat{\beta}$ is

$$\hat{\Sigma}_{\hat{\beta}} = \left(\sum_{i=1}^{n}\frac{\partial L_i}{\partial \beta}\frac{\partial L_i}{\partial \beta'}\right)^{-1}_{\hat{\beta},\hat{\sigma}^2} = \hat{\sigma}^4\left(\sum_{i=1}^{n}[Y_i - f(X_i,\beta)]^2\frac{\partial f(X_i,\beta)}{\partial \beta}\frac{\partial f(X_i,\beta)}{\partial \beta'}\right)^{-1}_{\hat{\beta}}$$

4.3.3   Equivalence of maximum likelihood estimation and least squares estimation

Least squares estimation has a long history and precedes the method of maximum likelihood. The **least squares method** gives primary importance to the specified regression and assumes that the errors or disturbances follow a Gaussian distribution. To the contrary the **method of maximum likelihood** gives primary importance to specifying a conditional probability density function of Y given X, and the regression relation turns out to be the mean of that conditional distribution. However, both of these methods are used to estimate the unknown regression parameters. The estimates so obtained from these two methods can be different in general. However, if the conditional distribution is Gaussian or if Y and X are jointly normally distributed then both methods give identical estimates.

Consider the nonlinear regression model with normal error:

$$Y = f(X,\beta) + \varepsilon, \quad \varepsilon \sim N(0,\sigma^2 I_n)$$

Its likelihood function is

$$l(\beta,\sigma^2 \mid Y,X) = \frac{1}{(2\pi\sigma^2)^{n/2}}\exp\left\{-\frac{1}{2\sigma^2}[Y - f(X,\beta)]'[Y - f(X,\beta)]\right\}$$

$$= \frac{1}{(2\pi\sigma^2)^{n/2}}\exp\left\{-\frac{S(\beta)}{2\sigma^2}\right\}$$

Its logarithm likelihood function is

$$L(\beta,\sigma^2 \mid Y,X) = \ln l(\beta,\sigma^2 \mid Y,X) = -\frac{n}{2}\ln(2\pi) - \frac{n}{2}\ln\sigma^2 - \frac{S(\beta)}{2\sigma^2}$$

Generally speaking, it is impossible to seek the solution of $\dfrac{\partial L}{\partial \beta} = 0$, namely the analytical expression of maximum likelihood estimation of β without knowing what σ^2 is. But we can obtain the maximum likelihood estimator of σ^2, namely $\hat{\sigma}^2$ as the analytic expression of function of β. Make the differentiation of L above with respect to σ^2 and let that derivative be 0. Then we get:

$$\hat{\sigma}^2 = \frac{1}{n} S(\beta) \tag{4.23}$$

With this we can simplify the likelihood function as the function of β alone

$$L^*(\beta | Y, X) = -\frac{n}{2}\ln(2\pi) - \frac{n}{2}\ln\frac{S(\beta)}{n} - \frac{n}{2} = C - \frac{n}{2}\ln\frac{S(\beta)}{n}$$

here constant $C = -\dfrac{n}{2}[\ln(2\pi) - 1]$. We can thus see that the maximum likelihood estimation and the least squares estimation introduced previously are the same, as both try to minimize $S(\beta)$.

We should note that the equivalence above of MLE and LSE is based on the normal distribution.

Example 4.8   Estimation of a nonlinear regression model   One basic feature that distinguishes nonlinear regression from linear regression is that while there is only one possible general expression for a linear function there can be several nonlinear functional forms for the nonlinear regression. Each nonlinear regression could have its own nonlinear function and hence the computation algorithm must be specific to each such problem. This can be achieved by providing in the computation algorithm a user-specified nonlinear functional form. The expressions presented in the previous section called for specification of not only the nonlinear regression function but also its first and second derivatives. However most of the computer programs for nonlinear regression can compute the **first and second differences** of the function as approximations to the **first and second derivatives**. Hence it is enough if the user specifies only the nonlinear regression function.[2]

Our program can generate nonlinear regression data block according to given nonlinear regression function and parameters, then estimate the given function from that data, and obtain the estimates of the parameters. The reader can compare the estimates of the parameters with the given parameters. Our program was used to compute the estimates for the nonlinear regression problem with the data provided in Chapter 10 of G.G. Judge, et al. (1982). Our results agree with theirs completely.

For example, when we select the series number of nonlinear function as 0 in DASC, the regression function is a Cobb-Douglas production function:

$$Y = \beta_1 X_1^{\beta_2} X_2^{\beta_3}$$

The data are listed below (Table 4.11).

---

[2] However, it was often noted that the convergence of the iterative procedure is faster if one used the analytically derived first and second derivatives instead of the numerical first and second differences.

Table 4.11 The data of a nonlinear regression model.

No.	y	X_1	X_2	No.	y	X_1	X_2
1	0.2569	0.2280	0.8020	16	0.1687	0.6640	0.1290
2	0.1836	0.2580	0.2490	17	0.0206	0.6310	0.0170
3	1.2129	0.8210	0.7710	18	0.1002	0.0590	0.9060
4	0.5226	0.7670	0.5110	19	0.2523	0.8110	0.2230
5	0.8479	0.4950	0.7580	20	0.1033	0.7580	0.1450
6	0.7634	0.4870	0.4250	21	0.0789	0.0500	0.1610
7	0.6231	0.6780	0.4520	22	0.0058	0.8230	0.0060
8	1.0315	0.7480	0.8170	23	0.7232	0.4830	0.8360
9	0.5695	0.7270	0.8450	24	0.7764	0.6820	0.5210
10	0.8825	0.6950	0.9580	25	0.2165	0.1160	0.9300
11	0.1088	0.4580	0.0840	26	0.5412	0.4400	0.4950
12	0.0264	0.9810	0.0210	27	0.3163	0.4560	0.1850
13	0.0038	0.0020	0.2950	28	0.1238	0.3420	0.0920
14	0.4616	0.4290	0.2770	29	0.3863	0.3580	0.4850
15	0.2684	0.2310	0.5460	30	0.2794	0.1620	0.9340

The main results of the computations as printed by the DASC computer program are as follows:

The Cobb-Douglas functional form above can be rewritten as:

$$Y = \beta_1 \exp\{\log X_1^{\beta_2}\} * \exp\{\log X_2^{\beta_3}\}$$
$$= \beta_1 \exp\{\beta_2 * \log X_1\} * \exp\{\beta_3 * \log X_2\}$$

Iterative results of Powell algorithm lead us to parameter estimates:

$$\hat{\beta}_1 = 1.332696, \quad \hat{\beta}_2 = 0.723546, \quad \hat{\beta}_3 = 0.691670.$$

Sum of Squared residuals = 0.551943.

Readers can verify the computation process by hitting DASC→Regression→Nonlinear Regression→Nonlinear Regression with Designated Regression Function (Figure 4.11).

We conclude this section by emphasizing that nonlinear regression is different from linear regression in some important respects. The solution of a linear regression is in a closed form and can be solved through a single matrix inversion, while the solution of nonlinear regression requires, in general, an iterative procedure. In general, the nonlinear least squares expression or the likelihood function may exhibit multiple local optima. The solution obtained through the algorithms described here may be a local optimum and not necessarily a global optimum. For any data set, and for any problem, it is therefore advisable to use a wide enough grid of initial values and observe how the local optima change. Then find the global optimum among all of them. The iterative process may not converge. Hence the computer program prescribes that the iteration process will stop and the result will be printed after 5000 iterations. There could be several reasons for the non-convergence of the iterative process. The denominator may be 0 and the computation may stop. We used known data and

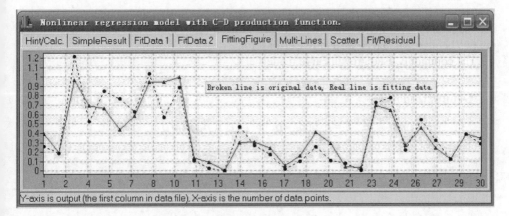

Figure 4.11   Nonlinear regression model with C–D production function.

model parameters generated by data generator of the DASC software. We cannot assure the reader that for any other user-specified regression the corresponding regression parameters can be estimated with the program and the convergence takes place. This non-convergence can arise due to several reasons. The functions written by the user may not admit an optimum; the sample variance of random variable could be too large when we generate the data block; or the number of observation points is too small or the number of parameters may be too large and so on.

In any case, a well-specified model should yield good fitting results.

4.4   Nonlinear regression models in practice

In this section we introduce some useful and practical nonlinear regression models, including the **Growth Curve** model, the **Box–Cox Transformation** model, the **Failure Rate** model, and the model of **Total Factor Productivity**.

4.4.1   Growth curve models

The **Growth Curve** model is widely used in various scientific fields, including economics. The basic feature of the growth curve model is that growth cannot take place in an unbounded fashion. If growth is captured by a linear model then it has to be unbounded. Growth must taper-off until some external impetus is given to the system to raise the growth rate. Even in such instances such impetus cannot create unbounded growth. Hence nonlinear models with shifts are needed to model growth in various real systems. With the increase in number of digits of numbers that can enter into calculation, and with increase in the speed of computation, such models are becoming popular in computer and information science. With increase in total output and the size of population such models are also becoming popular in the field of economics.

The Logit and Probit models introduced in Chapter 4 belong to such a family of growth curve models. Those models were however limited to the notion that probability is bounded between 0 and 1. In this section we introduce general nonlinear models to describe growth curves.

The growth curve models introduced here present a functional relation between a variable and the time t. Generally, we divide this model into empirical model and a theoretical model, the two being separated by an additive error term.

The commonly used growth curve models are:

1. Gompertz model

$$Y = \exp(\beta_1 - \beta_2 \cdot \beta_3^t) + \varepsilon, \quad \beta_2, \beta_3 > 0$$

2. Logistic model

$$Y = \frac{\beta_1}{1 + \exp(\beta_2 - \beta_3^t)} + \varepsilon, \quad \beta_3 > 0$$

3. Weibull model

$$Y = \beta_1 - \beta_2 \exp(-\beta_3 t^{\beta_4}) + \varepsilon, \quad t > 0, \beta_3 > 0$$

For the functions representing the theoretical curve of the Gompertz and Logistic models, as $t \to \pm\infty$, the functions tend to definite finite values, thus making the growth bounded. Just as the figure in the second part of Section 4.2, the basic shape for them is a S curve. The third model described above, Weibull model, requires $t > 0$ and can be regarded as a half S curve.

The theoretical part of the growth curve models above can usually be deduced mathematically from the first principles or axioms of growth phenomena in the underlying process that generates the data

For example, assume that the upper limit to Y is a, and that the rate of growth $\dfrac{dY}{dt}$ is directly proportional to the shortfall $a - Y$, namely the larger the shortfall the faster the rate of growth; then we obtain the following differential equation

$$\frac{dY}{dt} = x(a - Y)$$

After solving the first order linear differential equation and adding the random error, we obtain

$$Y = a(1 - \beta e^{-kt}) + \varepsilon$$

This model can be also called as **single layer growth model**. When $t \to +\infty$, the limit of Y exists and equals a. But when $t \to -\infty$, the limit of Y does not exist. So it is suitable to characterize unidirectional growth from 0 to $+\infty$.

If the real phenomenon suggests that the relative rate of growth of Y, $\dfrac{1}{Y}\dfrac{dY}{dt}$, is directly proportional to relative shortfall $\dfrac{a - Y}{a}$, then we have a differential equation

$$\frac{1}{Y}\frac{dY}{dt} = \frac{k(a-Y)}{a}$$

This is a Bernoulli equation. Let $Z = Y^{-1}$, this leads to a first order linear differential equation in Z: $\frac{dZ}{dt} = -kZ + \frac{k}{a}$. Then substituting $Z = Y^{-1}$ from the solution of this differential equation and adding a random error we obtain the growth curve model:

$$Y = a(1 + \beta e^{-kt})^{-1} + \varepsilon$$

This model can also be called **logarithmic growth model**. In fact, one can see that this is the logistic model.

If the real phenomena can suggest that the relative growth is directly proportional to the logarithm of the proportional shortfall $\ln a - \ln Y$, then Y satisfies the differential equation

$$\frac{1}{Y}\frac{dY}{dt} = k(\ln a - \ln Y)$$

Its solution is the **Gompertz model**

$$Y = a \exp(-\beta e^{-kt}) + \varepsilon$$

It has an S-shape. But if we define $Z = \ln Y$ and use a multiplicative error, then the model transforms into

$$Z = \gamma - \beta e^{-kt} + \varepsilon$$

Then it is not S type growth curve, but it is similar to the single layer growth curve described above.

If only the limit on the right side along the increasing direction of t exists and not on the left side (namely we do not require the perfect S curve) then there are many growth curve models such as the **Holliday model**:

$$Y = (\beta_1 + \beta_2 x + \beta_3 x^2)^{-1} + \varepsilon$$

4. Asymptotic regression models

$$Y = \alpha - \beta \gamma^x + \varepsilon$$

$$Y = \alpha - \exp\{-(\beta + \gamma^x)\} + \varepsilon$$

Finally, we introduce the **Von Bertalanffy model**. This is a four parameter growth curve model. As it will be shown presently, several of the models described above become special cases of the Bertalanffy model.

5. Bertalanffy model

$$Y = (\alpha^{1-m} - \theta e^{-kt})^{\frac{1}{1-m}} + \varepsilon$$

where α, θ, k, m are unknown parameters to be estimated.
Assume $\theta = \alpha\beta$ and $m = 0$, then we get:

$$Y = \alpha(1 - \beta e^{-kt}) + \varepsilon$$

It is the single layer growth model.

Assume $\theta = -\dfrac{\beta}{\alpha}$ and $m = 2$, then we get:

$$Y = \frac{\alpha}{(1 + \beta e^{-kt})} + \varepsilon$$

It is the logistic model.

When $m \to 1$, since $\dfrac{m}{1-m} \approx \dfrac{1}{1-m}$, then we get:

$$\frac{dY}{dt} = \frac{1}{1-m}(\alpha^{1-m} - \theta e^{-kt})^{\frac{m}{1-m}}(\theta k e^{-kt}) \approx \frac{1}{1-m}Y(\theta k e^{-kt})$$

So

$$\frac{1}{Y}\frac{dY}{dt} \approx \frac{1}{1-m}\theta k e^{-kt}$$

It is similar to the Gompertz model. But it is a discontinuous function when $m = 1$. When $m > 1$, then $\theta < 0$; when $m < 1$, then $\theta > 0$. The estimation methods for nonlinear regression described in the previous section did not deal with any parametric constraints. So it is necessary to add the parametric constraints above to the methods described in the previous section for proper estimation.

Example 4.9 Gompertz model and logistic model to forecast sales of houses   This example lists 12 growth curve regression models which we collected. All of them are univariate and nonlinear. Time t is represented as X in the program. If the user of DASC finds that there is no function among the models specified in DASC which meets his or her need, he or she can write a regression function himself or herself. There is one of the drop-down menus for doing so.

Throughout this book we have two types of examples. One type is to use actual data from real situations. The other type of model is the one that is purely pedagogical, in the sense that their data are derived from a pre-specified model with known parameters and known error distribution. Then we pretend as though we do not know the true parameter values and estimate them and compare the model fit with the generated data. Now we use the latter type of example and generate the data from a Gomperz growth curve and estimate it.

Table 4.12 The data of Gompertz growth curve model.

Y	X	Y	X	Y	X
−0.4014	3.2285	0.7887	2.4296	1.5764	1.4957
−0.2893	3.4112	0.8017	2.2850	1.6484	1.5748
0.1008	3.3834	0.9058	1.9497	1.9618	1.4107
0.1433	2.5252	0.9065	2.2223	2.0363	1.3169
0.2254	5.1122	1.1234	1.8118	2.0818	1.3365
0.3403	2.5970	1.1592	2.1031	2.0950	1.5095
0.3813	2.2187	1.1706	2.0992	2.3204	1.1662
0.5714	2.7384	1.3588	1.8916	2.4470	1.0055
0.6428	2.0238	1.4041	1.4958	2.8567	0.9093
0.7416	2.2780	1.4667	1.6602	2.8817	0.9305

Let us generate the regression data block ourselves with the Gompertz model:

$$y = \exp\left(\beta_1 - \beta_2 \exp((x-a)\ln\beta_3)\right) + \varepsilon$$

the parameters $\beta_1 = 2$, $\beta_2 = 2$, $\beta_3 = 2$, $a = 2$, and $\varepsilon \sim N(0, 0.25)$. Because the growth curve considers the independent variable time t, we order the data according to the independent variable in the computation program (Table 4.12).

The main computation results of the models are as follows.

For illustration purposes we choose only one of the models. Our DASC computer program is capable of generating simulated data for other models so that the reader can replicate this computational exercise for other models as well.

Now we select the regression function form of growth curve from among the following types available in DASC software.

Example, Gompertz function (It is equivalent to model 7 below):

0: $Y = \exp(B(1) - B(2)^* B(3)^{**}(X-a)) + \varepsilon$;

1: Empirical type, Gompertz model: $Y = \exp(B(1) - B(2)^* B(3)^{**}X) + \varepsilon$;

2: Empirical type, Logistic model 1: $Y = B(1)/(1 + \exp(B(2) - B(3)^*X)) + \varepsilon$;

3: Empirical type, Logistic model 2: $Y = B(1)/(1 + \exp(B(2) - B(3)^* B(4)^{**}X)) + \varepsilon$;

4: Empirical type, Weibull model: $Y = B(1) - B(2)^* \exp(-B(3)^* X^{**} B(4)) + \varepsilon$;

5: Mechanical type, single layer growth model: $Y = B(1)^*(1 - B(2)^* \exp(-B(3)^*X)) + \varepsilon$;

6: Mechanical type, logarithmic growth model: $Y = B(1)/(1 + B(2)^* \exp(-B(3)^*X)) + \varepsilon$;

7: Mechanical type, Gompertz model: $Y = B(1)^* \exp(-B(2)^* \exp(-B(3)^*X))) + \varepsilon$;

8: Mechanical type, 4 parameters Bertalanffy model:

$Y = (B(1)^{**}(1 - B(2)) - B(3)^* \exp(-B(4)^*X))^{**}(1/(1 - B(2))) + \varepsilon$;

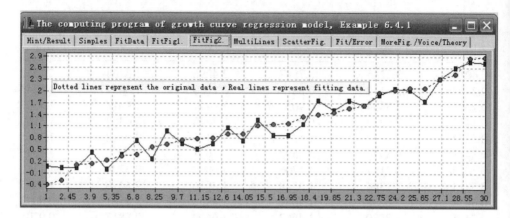

Figure 4.12   Growth curve regression model (Gompertz model).

9: Distributed function: $Y = \exp(-\exp(-(x-B(1))/B(2))) + \varepsilon$;

10: Logit model with single variable: $Y = 1.0/(1 + B[0]^* \exp(-(X[0]^* B[1]))) + \varepsilon$;

11: Logit model with two variables:

$$Y = 1.0/(1 + B[0]^* \exp(-(X[0]^* B[1] + X[1]^* B[2]))) + \varepsilon;$$

12: Logit model with three variables:

$$Y = 1.0/(1 + B[0]^* \exp(-(X[0]^* B[1] + X[1]^* B[2] + X[2]^* B[3]))) + \varepsilon.$$

The Estimation Results are:

Example: Gompertz model, the number of parameters to be estimated = 3.
The estimates of parameters of regression: B(1) = 1.8496, B(2) = 1.8418, B(3) = 2.0684.
Sum of Squares of Residuals = 1.540503.

Comparing with the original parameters $\beta_1 = 2$, $\beta_2 = 2$, β_3 hou = 2, we are satisfied with these estimates. The Goodness of fit is depicted in Figure 4.12 above. We should notice that in this goodness of fit diagram the x-coordinate is the serial number of observation and not X.

The result is quite satisfactory. The percentage error of estimates of three parameters $B(1)$, $B(2)$, $B(3)$ is within 5%. We can see that there is a half S curve. It is also a kind of growth curve. Readers can perform the computation process by hitting DASC→Regression Analysis→Nonlinear Regression→Growth curve regression model.

The most useful growth curve model is the Logistic model. The data of sales area of houses in Hubei Province of China is in Table 4.13. Using Logistic model we fit the data as in Figure 4.13 and Figure 4.14, we can see the trend and make some forecasts from this model. We should notice that the x-coordinate is year number.

Readers can perform the computation process by hitting DASC→Regression→Nonlinear Regression→Logit Growth Curve Regression Model, then hitting menu DASC→Data→Load Other Data Examples, to select \\She\\Wiley Data\\Wiley 4 (Logit)\\ Logit 6212-China Hubei Data\\.

Table 4.13   The sales area of house in Hubei Province of China.

Year	Sales area (10000 m^2)	Year	Sales area (10000 m^2)
1984	2697.2400	1994	9010.1699
1985	2927.3301	1995	12185.2998
1986	2855.3601	1996	14556.5322
1987	2871.5400	1997	18637.1289
1988	3025.4600	1998	22411.9023
1989	4288.8599	1999	26808.2852
1990	6687.9102	2000	33717.6250
1991	7230.3501	2001	38231.6406
1992	7905.9399	2002	55486.2188
1993	7900.4102	2003	61857.0703

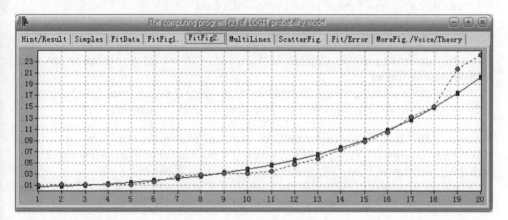

Figure 4.13   Fitting of the Logit model for house sales in Hubei, China from 1987 to 2006.

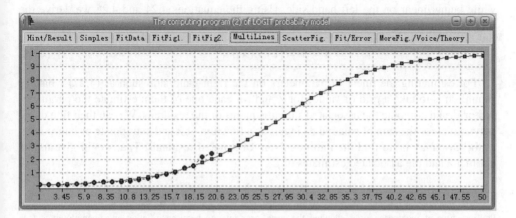

Figure 4.14   Trend and forecast of sales of house by the Logistic model.

4.4.2   Box–Cox transformation model

A transformation regression model has the form

$$H(Y) = X\beta + \varepsilon \tag{4.24}$$

where H is an unknown increasing function, β is an unknown finite dimensional vector of constants, ε is an unobserved random variable, and $Var(\varepsilon) = \sigma^2$. It is assumed here that ε is statistically independent of X. The aim is to estimate H and β. One possibility is to assume that H is known up to a finite-dimensional parameter. For example, H could be the **Box–Cox transformation**

$$H(Y) = \begin{cases} (Y^\lambda - 1)/\lambda, & \text{if } \lambda > 0 \\ \log(Y), & \text{if } \lambda = 0 \end{cases} \tag{4.25}$$

where λ is an unknown parameter. The model combined with (4.24) and (4.25) is the **Box–Cox transformation model**.

Some Box–Cox transformation models have the form

$$H(Y) = f(X, \beta) + \varepsilon \tag{4.26}$$

where f is a nonlinear function. Combining (4.25) and (4.26) we get the **nonlinear Box–Cox transformation model**.

Methods for estimating transformation models in which H is parametric have been developed by Amemiya and Powell (1981) and Foster, et al. (2001) among others.

Example 4.10   Box–Cox transformation   The number of parameters to be estimated in Box–Cox transformation model is $M + 2$, where M is the number of independent variables X, including a constant, a Box–Cox transformation parameter λ, and σ^2.

There are two ways of estimating the linear Box–Cox transformation model. One is the model with linear right hand side but nonlinear left hand side, that is:

$$(Y^\lambda - 1)/\lambda = X\beta \tag{4.27}$$

The other is a model that is completely nonlinear in parameters on the right hand side, while being linear on the left hand side. Using the equations 4.24 and 4.25 we derive the following model:

$$Y = \left\{ 1 + \lambda(X\beta) \right\}^{1/\lambda} \tag{4.28}$$

For estimating the linear in parameters on the right hand side such as (4.27) what we should do is to take a grid of values for λ and for each one of them estimate the parameter vector β, and compute the associated sum of squares of the residuals. We can then fit a cubic polynomial for the sum of squared residuals as a function of λ and extrapolate or interpolate, as the case may be to find the minimum sum of squared residuals. That would give us the optimal λ and the associated estimates of β[3].

---

[3] It is this kind of iterative linear regression models that were used by A.W. Phillips to estimate the famous Phillips curve of macroeconomics showing the curvilinear relation between inflation and unemployment (see Phillips (1958). The functional form however was different in his case but the method is the same.

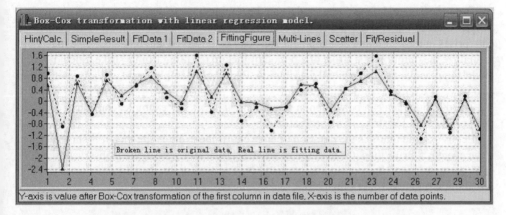

Figure 4.15   Box–Cox transformation with linear model.

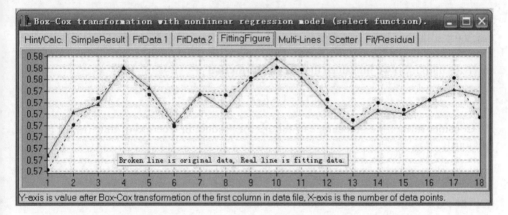

Figure 4.16   Box–Cox transformation with nonlinear model.

In DASC there are three menus for Box–Cox transformation: linear, nonlinear (assigned function), and nonlinear (any function). For each menu there is an example with data to demonstrate how it works. If we hit menu DASC→Regression Analysis→Nonlinear Regression→Box–Cox transformation with linear model, we can get Figure 4.15. The data and calculation result are omitted here.

If we hit DASC→Regression Analysis→Nonlinear Regression→Box–Cox transformation with nonlinear model (assigned function), we can get another data example and another computation result (Figure 4.16). Its nonlinear regression function is $Y = B[0]^*\exp(\log(X[0])^*B[1]+\log(X[1])^*B[2]) + \varepsilon$. The results of parameter estimates are: -1.7208, 0.5597, 0.0081, 0.0091. The first number is Box–Cox transformation parameter λ, the others are parameters to be estimated in nonlinear regression. Residual sum of squares is 1.25461e-05.

4.4.3   Survival data and failure rate model

Duration data models and hazard rate models are used extensively in engineering and technological fields, such as the survival time data of products. The mathematical theory in this field developed quite rapidly with a large amount of work.

Duration data and hazard rate models are becoming increasingly important in economics as well. For example, the life of a corporation, the data for life of medium and small-sized enterprises in the economic development zone can be observed and modeled. One may want to analyze the duration of a strike or a period of lockup resulting from a strike. Such duration models in practice use the Weibull distribution. Period of unemployment and job-waiting can also serve as examples of duration models

The duration data can be written in general as $t_1, t_2, \ldots, t_n$. For example, consider n observations of duration for strike in n corporations.

Let us assume that T is the duration of an event (if the event is life then it is survival time, if the event is a strike then it is duration of strike etc) and let $t_1, t_2, \ldots, t_n$ are n observation values of T. Assume that T has continuous probability distribution, its density function is $f(t)$ and distribution function is $F(t)$, then

$$F(t) = \int_0^t f(s)\,ds = P(T < t)$$

It signifies that the percentage that the sample observed has been alive until t and dead at time t (or strike has been in action until t when the strike ends). Because T signifies the life, $T < t$ signifies that it has survived until t, and hence we show more interest in the number of survivals until t. So we introduce the **survival function**

$$R(t) = 1 - F(t) = P(T \geq t)$$

Consider further the percentage of failure for product in a period of time (t_1, t_2), $l(t_1, t_2)$. Obviously

$$l(t_1, t_2) = P(t_1 \leq T < t_2 \mid T \geq t_1)$$

The percentage of failure in a short time interval is

$$l(t, t + \Delta t) = P(t \leq T < t + \Delta t \mid T \geq t)$$

Now we introduce the concept of **failure rate** which signifies the percentage of failures at time t, it is written as $r(t)$

$$r(t) = \lim_{\Delta t \to 0} \frac{l(t, t + \Delta t)}{\Delta t} = \lim_{\Delta t \to 0} \frac{P(t \leq T < t + \Delta t \mid T \geq t)}{\Delta t}$$
$$= \lim_{\Delta t \to 0} \frac{F(t + \Delta t) - F(t)}{\Delta(t)} = \frac{f(t)}{1 - F(t)}$$

Obviously, failure rate $r(t)$ is the function in which we have most interest. If $r(t)$ is known, we can figure out $f(t)$ and $F(t)$. In fact, according to the expression above, we know

$$r(t) = -\frac{d \ln R(t)}{dt}$$

So

$$R(t) = \exp\left(-\int_{-\infty}^{+\infty} r(t)\,dt\right)$$

And $F(t) = 1 - R(t)$, $f(t) = -R'(t)$.

The **Weibull distribution** is very important in hazard rate models. Weibull distribution can be introduced in many ways. Consider a kind of product life whose failure rate is increasing, such as the lifespan of poor quality leather shoes, or the time of employment of workers under poor labor market conditions. We can describe the failure rate by a positive exponential power function (imagine the picture of $y = x^2$, $x > 0$), namely

$$r(t) = \lambda m t^{m-1}, \quad m > 1$$

Let us compute the distribution function and density function corresponding to this failure rate function. For this we get:

$$\int_0^t r(s)ds = \int_0^t \lambda m s^{m-1} ds = \lambda t^m$$

$$\text{So } R(t) = \exp(-\lambda t^m)$$

$$R(t) = 1 - F(t) = e^{-\lambda t^m}$$

$$F(t) = 1 - R(t) = 1 - e^{-\lambda t^m}$$

$$f(t) = \lambda m t^{m-1} e^{-\lambda t^m}$$

These are none other than the distribution function and density function of Weibull distribution. In fact, the results also hold for $m < 1$. If the lifespan data for certain product indicates that its failure rate decreases, we can describe it by a negative exponent power function (imagine the picture of $y = \dfrac{1}{x}$, $x > 0$), namely

$$r(t) = \lambda m t^{m-1}, \quad m < 1$$

The rest of the derivation for this opposite case is the same as above, except that now $m < 1$.

When $m = 1$, it signifies that the failure rate of product is a constant at all times.

$$r(t) = \lambda$$

Then

$$R(t) = e^{-\lambda t}$$

$$F(t) = 1 - e^{-\lambda t}$$

$$f(t) = \lambda e^{-\lambda t}$$

These are the distribution and density functions of an **exponential distribution**. There are many interesting features of the exponential distribution. One of them is obviously the constant failure rate or the **failure rate having no memory**. The exponential distribution we see here is a special case of the Weibull distribution.

With these conceptual and theoretical models of survival and duration we will now discuss the construction of regression models for estimation of their parameters. From the results of such regression models we can make inferences about the failure rate and survival rate functions. We can also derive the distribution pattern of survival data.

There are three ways of formulating nonlinear regression models for these types of models. First, there is a regression model for the density. Second, there is a regression model for the distribution function. And finally, there is the regression model for the failure rate itself. Certainly, the basic data in hand is life data $t_1, t_2, \dots, t_n$.

If we estimate the density function values $\hat{f}_1, \hat{f}_2, \dots, \hat{f}_n$ from $t_1, t_2, \dots, t_n$, we can then construct the regression model with a multiplicative error term. The key point here is how to obtain the estimated values of density from $t_1, t_2, \dots, t_n$. This point will be taken up later.

$$Y_i = \hat{f}_i = \lambda m t_i^{m-1} e^{-\lambda t_i^m} \varepsilon_i$$

Then parameters can be estimated. This is a nonlinear model which can be linearized by taking logarithms on both sides.

$$\ln \hat{f}_i = \ln(\lambda m) + (m-1)\ln t_i - \lambda t_i^m + \ln \varepsilon_i$$

If the error terms are additives then we get:

$$Y_i = \hat{f}_i = \lambda m t_i^{m-1} e^{-\lambda t_i^m} + \varepsilon_i$$

Then it can not be linearized. We can then use the nonlinear regression modeling methods described in this chapter to seek the solution.

The key point here is, as we said earlier, how to get the estimated values of density from $t_1, t_2, \dots, t_n$. We postpone the discussion of this point until Chapter 6, as the discussion requires nonparametric methods for estimation of densities discussed in that chapter.

Regression modeling is easier from the perspective of distribution function. We can take the estimated distribution function value according to the empirical distribution function value.

$$\hat{F}_i = \frac{i}{n+1}, \quad i = 1, \dots, n$$

Then construct the regression model

$$\hat{F}_i = 1 - e^{-\lambda t_i^m} + \varepsilon_i$$

Alternately one can take the logarithmic version of the theoretical model and add the error term to get:

$$\ln(1 - \hat{F}_i) = -\lambda t_i^m + \varepsilon_i$$

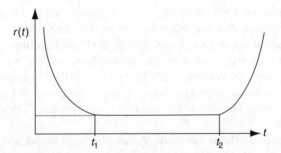

Figure 4.17   Basin curve for failure rate.

In the olden days, prior to the advanced computing, statisticians used **Weibull probability paper** to make nomogram estimation. As yet another alternative one can take double logarithm for the deterministic part and add error terms to yield the model:

$$\ln\ln(1 - \hat{F}_i) = \ln(-\lambda) + m\ln t_i + \varepsilon_i$$

This approach requires fitting a straight line between double log of $(1 - F)$ and $\ln t$. The nomogram approach can be described simply as follows: Draw the scatter point on paper between double log of $(1 - F)$ and $\ln t$. We can then obtain estimate using OLE the intercept and slope. How remarkable is the ingenuity of the method in the absence of advanced computing!

From a failure rate perspective, the third regression method requires estimated values of failure rates

$$\hat{r}_i = \frac{f_i}{1 - F_i}$$

Its merit can be easily seen from the display of the change of failure rate.

We now introduce the **Basin curve** (Figure 4.17).

The deduction of Weibull distribution is based on the assumption that the failure rate is increasing or decreasing or unchangeable. However, the survival time data in practical situations shows that the failure rate is always changing. For example, the mortality rate is high for infants, later it is decreasing. The mortality rate becomes stable from the adolescent period to middle-age period. Then the mortality rate is increasing in older people. The product's life is also often of the same type. The fault rate of an automobile is high in the initial stage; it is stable after the breaking-in period. When the automobile wears out over years the fault rate becomes high again. The image of such phenomenon is a basin curve in the reference frame of the failure rate. Knowing the pattern of the basin curve we can manage the supply and sale of a product well.

4.4.4   Total factor productivity (TFP)

Total factor productivity (TFP) is an important index for development in economics. Given the same inputs such as capital and labor, why the output is different? Many papers explore the effects of macroeconomic factors on TFP in developing countries for recent period

(Fischer, 1993; Harrison, 1996; Edwards, 1998; Anthony, 2006). Meanwhile, TFP affects not only economic growth but also other aspects such as trade (Madsen, 2007), monetary policy and the effect of oil shocks (Leduc & Sill, 2007) in developed countries. Besides, TFP measurement is tightly linked to the measurement of the social return to R&D (Griliches, 1994; Jones & Williams, 1998). Obviously, the measurement of TFP and productive efficiency is an important issue (Fried, Lovell and Schmit, 1993; Jakub & Jaroslav, 2009). The basic ingredient often used for measurement of TFP is the Cobb-Douglas production function.

Cobb and Douglas (1928) described the relation between output and inputs using Cobb-Douglas production function:

$$Y = AK^{\alpha}L^{\beta} \quad (\alpha > 0, \beta > 0) \tag{4.29}$$

where Y is output, K is capital input, L is labor input, α is capital elasticity, β is labor elasticity, and A is the coefficient of technical progress. Today Cobb-Douglas production function is still an impressive economic model in macroeconomics (Paul & Peter, 2007, Nakamura, 2009). If we assume that A is a constant, then there are only two parameters to be determined in C-D production function (4.29). But A is not a constant and it changes over time due to technical progress.

Tinbergen (1942, 1959) stated that all factors in C-D production function change as time series functions. He supposed $\beta = 1 - \alpha$ and $A = A_0 e^{\gamma t}$, so the C-D production function is:

$$Y_t = A_0 e^{\gamma t} K_t^{\alpha} L_t^{1-\alpha} \quad (\alpha > 0) \tag{4.30}$$

where $\gamma (\gamma > 0)$ is the average rate of technical progress in the period. There are only three parameters to be determined in the Tinbergen formula (4.30), but the exponential functional form is too strict a hypothesis.

Solow (1956, 1957) studied the contribution of various factors to economic growth, and proposed the concept of total factor productivity (TFP). He identified, following Edward Denison, that rate of growth in output is due to: (1) rate of improvements of technology and organization management; (2) rate of growth in inputs. He deduced the growth accounting formula:

$$\tilde{a} = y - \alpha k - \beta l \tag{4.31}$$

where $\tilde{a} = \dfrac{dA}{A}$ is rate of growth of technical progress, $y = \dfrac{dY}{Y}$ is rate of growth of output, $k = \dfrac{dK}{K}$ is growth rate of capital input, $l = \dfrac{dL}{L}$ is growth rate of labor input, and the meaning of α and β is the same as before. Solow called $\tilde{a}$ as TFP contribution or rate of technical progress. We notice that there are $N + 2$ parameters to be determined in calculation of Solow formula $\tilde{a}_i = y_i - \alpha k_i - \beta l_i$, $i = 1, \ldots, N$ with N sample observations. In the early research, some countries stipulate both α and β are constants, such as $\alpha = 0.4$ and $\beta = 0.6$.

To solve this problem of the number of unknown parameters being more than the number of sample observation in the Solow formula, United States Bureau of Labor Statistics (BLS) and Organization of Economic Cooperation and Development (OECD) Europe suggested the coefficients α and β should be determined by the weight coefficients of inputs (Englander & Gurney, 1994), i.e.:

$$\alpha = \frac{K}{K+L}, \beta = \frac{L}{K+L} \tag{4.32}$$

where $K = \sum_j K_j$, K_j, $j = 1, 2, \cdots$, are the components of K, and $L = \sum_i L_i$, L_i, $i = 1, 2, \cdots$, are the components of L. Obviously $\alpha + \beta = 1$. This method is simple and convenient, and it was used by many countries and scholars (Madsen, 2007; Leduc, 2007; Yang & Pollitt, 2007). α and β are determined before calculation of production function, and can not reveal the interactive relationship among factors of production input.

In the Solow formula (4.31), we notice that $\alpha + \beta = 1$ and $\alpha > 0$, $\beta > 0$. These impose a condition that the two parameters belong to a convex region. These are the parametric convex constraint conditions in regression model (Fang, 1982, 1985). $\tilde{a}_t$, $t = 1, 2, \cdots$, are unknown and what we have is a generalized linear regression model (Yang, 1982). The evaluation model of Tong (Tong, 1993) is a generalized linear regression model with parametric constraint conditions, and its dependent variable is assumed to be the same piecewise. So in this paper, a new measurement method of TFP by generalized linear regression model with a convex constraint is proposed. This method only assumes that the TFP is the same in each small period, and without any specific functional form.

Some economists discuss the economic meaning of $\alpha + \beta > 1$ or $\alpha + \beta < 1$, while we consider that $\alpha + \beta$ should be equal to 1 exactly, as in the original work of Cobb and Douglas, Tinbergen and Solow $\alpha + \beta$ equals 1. Further more the second order conditions of profit maximization with this production function requires constant returns to scale (or $\alpha + \beta = 1$). We will only discuss the case of $\alpha + \beta = 1$ here.

1.   Data structure of the evaluation model and the Solow model

Before we discuss the regression method of Solow's residual formulation (4.31), we introduce a generalized linear regression model with parametric constraint conditions, i.e., evaluation model.

In the model we assume that there are p indexes and m periods. For each index of each period, there are n observations of input and output. All samples should have $N = mn$ observation records, forming an $N \times p$ matrix. In our model, the weight coefficients are to be determined and have not been given in advance.

The p indexes are variables expressed by $x_{(1)}, \cdots, x_{(p)}$ respectively. Suppose that there are m periods to be observed, and in each period there are n observations. The element x_{ijk} denotes the records given by the ith($i = 1, \cdots, n$) time on the jth($j = 1, \cdots, p$) index of the kth ($k = 1, \cdots, m$) period. Thus, we obtain a matrix $X_{(mn \times p)} = \{x_{ijk}\}$. For the kth period, we must give one and only one terminal score a_k ($k = 1, \cdots, m$) that is the growth rate of technology advancement. These scores are unknown. The model is different from the ordinary regression model where we take a_k ($k = 1, \cdots, m$) as the already given dependent variables.

The date structure of the model is shown in Table 4.14.

In this data structure the dependent variable is unknown, so the model is a generalized linear model (Yang, 1982). In order to use regression model to obtain the estimates of $b_1, \cdots, b_p$ and $a_1, \cdots, a_m$, it is necessary to give a constraint on weight coefficients b_j ($j = 1, \cdots, p$). Obviously, these weight coefficients should satisfy $b_j \geq 0$, ($j = 1, \cdots, p$) and $\mathbf{1}'_p b = 1$,

Table 4.14 Data structure of evaluation model.

	$x_{(1)}$ b_1	$x_{(2)}$ b_2	......	$x_{(p)}$ b_p
a_1	x_{111}	x_{121}	......	x_{1p1}
a_1	x_{211}	x_{221}	......	x_{2p1}
$\vdots$	$\vdots$	$\vdots$	$\vdots$	$\vdots$
a_1	x_{n11}	x_{n21}	......	x_{np1}
$\vdots$	......	......	......	......
$\vdots$	$\vdots$	$\vdots$	$\vdots$	$\vdots$
$\vdots$	......	......	......	......
a_m	x_{11m}	x_{12m}	......	x_{1pm}
a_m	x_{21m}	x_{22m}	......	x_{2pm}
$\vdots$	$\vdots$	$\vdots$	$\vdots$	$\vdots$
a_m	x_{n1m}	x_{n2m}	......	x_{npm}

Table 4.15 Data structure of Solow model.

	y 1	k α	l β
a_1	y_{11}	k_{11}	l_{11}
a_1	y_{21}	k_{21}	l_{21}
$\vdots$	$\vdots$	$\vdots$	$\vdots$
a_1	y_{n1}	k_{n1}	l_{n1}
$\vdots$	......	......	......
$\vdots$	$\vdots$	$\vdots$	$\vdots$
$\vdots$	......	......	......
a_m	y_{1m}	k_{1m}	l_{1m}
a_m	y_{2m}	k_{2m}	l_{2m}
$\vdots$	$\vdots$	$\vdots$	$\vdots$
a_m	y_{nm}	k_{nm}	l_{nm}

where $\mathbf{1}_p = (1,\ldots,1)'$, $b = (b_1,\ldots,b_p)'$, i.e. $b_1 + \cdots + b_p = 1$. This is a prescription constraint (Fang, 1982, 1985; Tong, 1993 and Wang, 2007). Another constraint on the dependent variable is elaborated above, i.e., we can give only one score to each period. We thus define the dependent variable Da, where $Da = a \otimes \mathbf{1}_n$, the definition of D is $D_{mn \times m} = I_m \otimes \mathbf{1}_n$, $a = (a_1,\ldots,a_m)'$, and $\otimes$ is the Kronecker product.

Then the model can be expressed as an evaluation model (4.33) and (4.34) (Tong, 1993):

$$Da = Xb + \varepsilon, \ E(\varepsilon) = 0, \ Var(\varepsilon) = \sigma^2 I \tag{4.33}$$

$$\mathbf{1}_p' \, b = 1, \quad b \geq 0, \quad D_{mn \times m} = I_m \otimes \mathbf{1}_n \tag{4.34}$$

The model can also be expressed as

$$GP \begin{cases} \|Da - Xb\|^2 \xrightarrow{a,b} \min \\ 1'b = 1 \\ b \geq 0 \end{cases} \tag{4.35}$$

If we consider the Solow formula (4.31) according to the evaluation model, we can get the data structure as Table 4.15. We should assume that the TFP is the same in each period in economics, and deal with the variable y in the algorithm because the coefficient of y is a constant 1.

2. The LSE of the evaluation model and the Solow model

We discuss the LSE of the evaluation model in three steps, and get the alternating projection algorithm. Then we apply this algorithm to the Solow model.

First, if Da is known, it is just an ordinary constraint regression model. Only considering the constraint $\mathbf{1}_p' \, b = 1$, we can get an explicit solution by the Lagrange multiplier method. Let

$$Q(a,b) = (Da - Xb)'(Da - Xb)$$

$$\phi(a,b) = Q - 2\lambda(1'_p b - 1)$$

where λ is the Lagrange multiplier. We have

$$\frac{\partial\phi}{\partial b} = -2nX'_0 a + 2X'Xb - 2\lambda 1_p = 0$$

$$\frac{\partial\phi}{\partial a} = 2na - 2nX'_0 b = 0$$

where

$$X'_0 = \frac{1}{n}(I_m \otimes 1'_n)X = \frac{1}{n}D'X$$

It is a compression matrix by taking the average value of each column for each data block in matrix $X_{(mn \times p)}$. Then

$$\hat{a} = X'_0 \hat{b} \tag{4.36}$$

Let

$$P_D = I_{mn} - \frac{1}{n}DD'$$

It is easy to verify that P_D is a projection matrix. Since $(X'X - nX'_0 X_0)b = \lambda 1_p$, let

$$H = X'X - nX'_0 X'_0 = X'P_D X$$

when H is invertible, $\beta = \lambda H^{-1} 1_p$, from $1'_p b = 1$ we have $\lambda 1'_p H^{-1} 1_p = 1$, then the solution of b is

$$\hat{b} = \lambda H^{-1} 1_p = \frac{H^{-1} 1_p}{1'_p H^{-1} 1_p} \tag{4.37}$$

Summarizing the aforesaid, we have the following theorem.

Theorem 4.1. If Da is known and $rk(P_D X) = p$, under the constraint $1'_p b = 1$,

$$Q(a,b) = \| Da - Xb \|^2 \xrightarrow{a,b} \min \tag{4.38}$$

has unique solution (4.36) and (4.37). If each component of $\hat{b}$ is nonnegative, (4.36) and (4.36) are also the solution of the evaluation model (4.33) and (4.4.34).

Second, if some components of $\hat{b}$ are negative, we must consider the constraints $1'_p b = 1$ and $b \geq 0$ simultaneously. We consider the existence and uniqueness of the solution of the model (4.35). When Da is known, (4.35) is just the PR Model of prescription regression studied in detailed by Fang (1982, 1985). According to the Theorem 2.1 in that paper, we have the following theorem.

Theorem 4.2. The existence and uniqueness of model (4.35).

(1) If a is known, then the solution of model (4.35) exists;

(2) If a is known, and $rk(X) = p$, then there exists a unique solution for model (4.4.12);

(3) If a is known, $rk(X) = p$, and the solution of (4.37) $\hat{b} \geq 0$, then it is the solution of model (4.35). If some component of $\hat{b}$ of (4.37) is negative, then the component of $\hat{b}$ of model (4.35) must be the boundary of constraint conditions, i.e., it is 0.

But now the dependent variable is unknown in model, so we continue to discuss issues associated with that problem.

Third, we discuss the algorithm of the model when Da is unknown. We consider the geometric background of (4.38). Denote sets

$$A = \{Da \mid a \in R^m\}$$

$$B = \{Xb \mid 1'_p b = 1, b \geq 0, b \in R^p\}$$

where A is a linear subspace expanded by the column vectors of D, and B is a convex set under the constraint $1'_p b = 1$, $b \geq 0$ in linear subspace Xb. The expression (4.38) means we seek the shortest Euclidean distance between sets A and B. Obviously, A and B are two convex sets and B is bounded.

How does one find the shortest distance between two convex sets? We consider the method of the alternating projection between two sets. A geometric pictorial illustration will be useful here. Let A_0 and B_0 be points in the sets A and B respectively, $d(A_0, B_0)$ be the Euclidian distance between two points A_0 and B_0, and $d(A_0, B)$ be the shortest Euclidian distance between the point A_0 and the convex set B. If $d(A_0, B_0) = d(A_0, B)$, we call B_0 the projection from the point A_0 to the set B. The following is the alternating projection process.

Take an arbitrary initial value $A_0 \in A$, find $B_0 \in B$, satisfying $d(A_0, B_0) = d(A_0, B)$. For B_0, take $A_1 \in A$, satisfying $d(B_0, A_1) = d(B_0, A)$. For $A_i \in A$, take $B_i \in B$, satisfying $d(A_i, B_i) = d(A_i, B)$. For B_i, take $A_{i+1} \in A$, satisfying $d(B_i, A_{i+1}) = d(B_i, A)$, and so on. When $d(A_i, B_i) < \varepsilon$, iterative process is stopped and computation is completed. The meaning of convergence of aforesaid iterative process is:

$$\lim_{i \to \infty} d(A_i, B_i) = d(A^*, B^*)$$

where $A^* \in A$ and $B^* \in B$ respectively. The iterative process may be shown as Figure 4.18.

In this algorithm, the distance between two convex sets may be obtained by making use of successive computation of distance between a point and a convex set. In the model (4.33) and (4.34), for arbitrary a_i, we can get the solution of b_i according to the Theorem 1 and 2. For the solution of b_i, (4.38) becomes a common multivariate regression model which can be solved. The convergence of the alternating projection iterative process has been proved by Tong (Tong, 1993) and hence it is omitted here.

For the Solow model (4.31) and Table 4.13, we need to deal with variable y carefully. For the initial value a_0 of a, Da_0 is known in (4.38), the least squares solution of model is:

$$Q(a, \alpha, \beta) = \| (Da_0 - y) - (-\alpha k - \beta l) \|^2 \xrightarrow{\alpha, \beta} \min \qquad (4.39)$$

where $Da_0 - y$ is a constant vector, α, β have a convex constraint. (4.39) can be solved according to Theorem 1 and Theorem 2, and we can get the estimate α_0, β_0. For known α_0, β_0, the model is a common multivariate linear regression model:

$$Q(a,\alpha,\beta) = \| Da - (y - \alpha_0 k - \beta_0 l) \|^2 \xrightarrow{\ a\ } \min \tag{4.40}$$

where $y - \alpha_0 k - \beta_0 l$ is a constant vector, a has no constraint. We can get a_1, the solution of (4.40) At last we can get the solution of model according to (4.38). The computation process shows that the convergence is very fast.

The above described algorithm has been programmed in DASC. The results of computation with three periods and 30 samples (10 observations in each period) are shown in Figure 4.19, where the dots with connected line are the estimators of a, and the square points with dashed line are the estimations of $\tilde{a} = y - \alpha k - \beta l$.

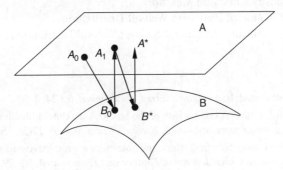

Figure 4.18 Alternative projection between two convex sets A and B.

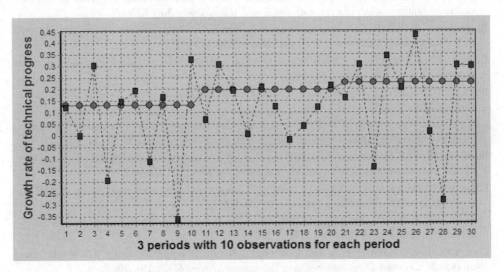

Figure 4.19 Solow model for TFP measurement (LSE).

Electronic references for Chapter 4

References

Amemiya T. (1984) Tobit models: a survey. *Journal of Econometrics* **24**, 3–63.

Amemiya T. & Powell J. (1981) A comparison of the box–cox maximum likelihood estimator and the non-linear two-stage least squares estimator. *Journal of Economerics* **17**(3), 351–81.

Anthony E.A. (2006) Macroeconomic factors and total factor productivity in sub-Saharan African countries. *International Research Journal of Finance and Economics* **1**, 62–79.

Baffi G., Martin E. & Morris J. (2002) Prediction intervals for non-linear projection to latent structures regression models. *Chemometrics and Intelligent Laboratory Systems* **61**(1–2), 151–165.

Berndt E.K., Hall B.H., Hall R.E. & Hausman J.A. (1974) Estimation and inference in nonlinear structural models. *Annals of Economic and Social Measurement* **3**(4), 653–65.

Bhattacharya B. (2001) Csiszar divergence from constant failure rate model for grouped data. *Communications in Statistics—Theory and Methods* **30**, 1131–41.

Bilias Y., Chen S. & Ying Z. (2000) Simple resampling methods for censored regression quantiles. *Journal of Econometrics* **99**(2), 373–86.

Box G.E.P. & Cox D. (1964) An analysis of transformations. *Journal of the Royal Statistical Society Series B* **26**(2), 211–52.

Bull S.B., Mak C.G. & Celia M.T. (2002) A modified score function estimator for multinomial logistic regression in small samples. *Computational Statistics and Data Analysis* **39**, 57–74.

Bunzel H., Kiefer N.M. & Timothy J. (2001) Vogelsang Simple robust testing of hypotheses in nonlinear models. *Journal of the American Statistical Association* **96**(455), 1088–97.

Burguete J.F., Gallant A.R. & Souza G. (1982) On unification of the asymptotic theory of nonlinear econometric models. *Econometric Reviews* **1**, 151–90.

Chen M.-H. & Dey D.K. (2002) Variable selection for multivariate logistic regression models. *Journal of Statistical Planning & Inference* **111**, 37–55.

Choi S.W., Lee D., Park J.H. & Lee I.-B. (2003) Nonlinear regression using RBFN with linear submodels. *Chemometrics and Intelligent Laboratory Systems* **65**(2), 191–208.

Chow G.C. (1960) Tests of Equality Between Sets of Coefficients in Two Linear Regressions. *Econometrica* **28**(3), 591–605.

Clyde M. & Chaloner K. (2002) Constrained design strategies for improving normal approximations in nonlinear regression problems. *Journal of Statistical Planning and Inference* **104**(1), 175–96.

Cobb C.W. & Douglas P.H. (1928) A theory of production. *American Economic Review* 18(Supplement), 139–65.

Cook R.D. & Tsai C.L. (1985) Residuals in nonlinear regression. *Biometrika* **72**, 23–29.

Cook R.D., Tsai C.L. & Wei B.C. (1986) Bias in nonlinear regression. *Biometrika* **73**, 615–23.

Cook R.D. & Witmer J.A. (1985) A notes on parameter-effects curvature. *Journal of Amerecan Statistical Association* **80**, 872–8.

Cordeiro G.M. & Vasconcellos K.L.P. (1997) Bias correction for a class of multivariate nonlinear regression models. *Statistics & Probability Letters* **35**(2),155–64.

Cordeiro G.M., Ferrari Silvia L.P., Uribe-Opazo M.A. & Vasconcellos K.L.P. (2000) Corrected maximum-likelihood estimation in a class of symmetric nonlinear regression models. *Statistics & Probability Letters* **46**(4), 317–28.

Cordeiro G.M. & Montenegro L.C.C. (2001) Bartlett corrected likelihood ratio tests in location-scale nonlinear models. *Communications in Statistics—Theory and Methods* **30**, 1353–72.

Davidson J.W., Savic D.A. & Walters G.A. (2003) Symbolic and numerical regression: experiments and applications. *Information Sciences* **150**, 95–117.

Dempster A.P., Laird N.M. & Rubin D.B. (1977) Maximum likelihood from incomplete data via the EM algorithm(with discussion). *Journal of the Royal Statistical Society*, Series B **39**, 1–38.

Draper N.R. & Smith H. (1981) *Applied Regression Analysis*. John Wiley & Sons, Inc. New York.

Edwards S. (1998) Openness, productivity and growth: What do we really know? *Economic Journal*, **108**, 383–98.

Englander S., Gurney A. (1994) Medium-term determinants of OECD productivity. *OECD Economic Studies* **22**, 49–109.

Fang K.T. & Wang D.Q. & Wu G.F. (1982) A class of constraint regression-fill a prescription regression. *Mathematica Numerica Sinica* **4**, 57–69.

Fang K.T. & He S.D. (1985) Regression models with linear constraints and nonnegative regression coefficients. *Mathematica Numerica Sinica* **7**, 97–102.

Fischer S. (1993) The role of macroeconomic factors in growth. *Journal of Monetary Economics*, **32**, 485–512.

Fried H., Lovell C.A.K. & Schmit S. (1993) The measurement of productive efficiency. *Oxford University Press*, United Kingdom.

Foster A.M., Tial L. & Wei L.W. (2001) Estimation for the Box–Cox transformation model without assuming parametric error distribution. *Journal of the American Statistical Association* **96**(455), 1097–1101.

Fu L.M. & Simpson D.G. (2002) Conditional risk models for ordinal response data: simultaneous logistic regression analysis and generalized score tests. *Journal of Statistical Planning and Inference* **108**, 201–17.

Gallant A.R. (1980) Explicit estimators of parametric functions in nonlinear Regression. *J.Amer Statist. Assoc* **75**, 182–93.

Gallant A.R. (1986) *Nonlinear statistical models*. John Wiley & Sons, Inc. New York.

Geladi P., Hadjiiski L. & Hopke P. (1999) Multiple regression for environmental data: nonlinearities and prediction bias. *Chemometrics and Intelligent Laboratory Systems* **47**(2), 165–73.

Giles D. (1982) The interpretation of dummy variables in semilogarithmic equations. *Economics Letters* **10**, 77–9.

George G.J., Hill C.R., Griffiths W.E., Lutkepohl H. & Lee T.C. (1982) *Introduction to the Theory and Practice of Econometrics*. John Wiley & Sons, New York.

Griliches Z. (1994) Productivity, R&D and the data constraint. *American Economic Review*, **84**(1), 1–23.

Grunfeld Y. (1961) The interpretation of cross section estimates in a dynamic model, *Econometrica*, **29**(3), 397–404.

Gueorguieva R.V. & AA. (2001) A correlated probit model for joint modeling of clustered binary and continuous responses. *Journal of the American Statistical Association* **96**, 1102–13.

Hadjicostas P. (2003) Consistency of logistic regression coefficient estimates calculated from a training sample. *Statistics and Probability Letters* **62**, 293–303.

Hadjicostas P. & Hadjinicola G.C. (2001) The asymptotic distribution of the proportion of correct classifications for a holdout sample in logistic regression. *Journal of Statistical Planning and Inference* **92**, 193–211.

Halvorsen R. & Palmquist R. (1980) The interpretation of dummy variables in semilogarithmic equations. *American Economic Review* **70**, 474–5.

Hamilton D.C., Watts D.G. & Bates D.C. (1982) Accounting for intrinsic nonlinearity in nonlinear regression parameter inference regions. *Annals of Statistics* **10**, 386–93.

Hamilton D.C. & Watts D.G. (1985) A quadratic design criterion for precise estimation in nonlinear regression models. *Technometrics* **27**, 241–50.

Hamilton D.C. (1986) Confidence regions for parameter subsets in nonlinear regression. *Biometrika* **73**, 57–64.

Harrison A.E. (1996) Openness and growth: A time series, cross-country analysis for developing countries. *Journal of Development Economics* **48**, 419–47.

Hastie T.J. & Tibshirani R.J. (1990) Generalized Additive Models. *New York: Chapman and Hall.*

Hauck W.W., Anderson S. & Marcus S.M. (1998) Should we adjust for covariates in nonlinear regression analyses of randomized trials. *Controlled Clinical Trials* **19**(3), 249–56.

Hougaard R. (1982) Parameterization of non.linear models. *J.R.Statist.Soc.B* **44**, 244–252.

Hougaard R. (1985) The appropriateness of the asymptotic distribution in a nonlinear regression model in relation to curvature. *J.R.Statist.Soc.B*, **47**, 103–14.

Huh J. & Carrière K.C. (2002) Estimation of regression functions with a discontinuity in a derivative with local polynomial fits. *Statistics and Probability Letters* **56**, 329–43.

Hu I.C. (1998) Strong consistency of Bayes estimates in nonlinear stochastic regression models. *Journal of Statistical Planning and Inference* **67**, 155–63.

Islam M.Q., Moti L.T. & Yildirim F. (2001) Nonnormal regression. I. skew distributions. *Communications in Statistics – Theory and Methods*, **30**, 993–1020.

Jakub F. & Jaroslav, S. (2009) Towards the measurement of total factor productivity index. *Politická ekonomie* **4**, 544–554.

Johnston J. (1984) *Econometric Methods* 3rd ed.: McGraw-Hill, New York.

Jones C. J. & Williams J.C. (1998) Measuring the social return to R&D, *Quarterly Journal of Economics* **113**, 1119–35.

Jeong J.-H. (2001) A note on asymptotic efficiency of a regression coefficient parameter under ordinal logistic regression model. *Communications in Statistics—Theory and Methods* **30**, 1257–69.

Jovanovic B.D. & Hosmer D.W. (1997) A simulation of the performance of cp in model selection for logistic and poisson regression. *Computational Statistics & Data Analysis* **23**, 373–9.

Kennedy P. (1981) Estimation with correctly interpreted dummy variables in semilogarithmic equations. *American Economic Review* **71**, 801–2.

Kmenta J. (1986) *Elements of Econometrics*, 2nd ed. Macmillan, New York.

Kohler M. (2003) Nonlinear orthogonal series estimates for random design regression. *Journal of Statistical Planning and Inference* **115**(2), 491–520.

Koul H.L. & Qian L.F. (2002) Asymptotics of maximum likelihood estimator in a two-phase linear regression model. *Journal of Statistical Planning and Inference* **108**, 99–119.

Krivy I., Tvrdík J. & Krpec R. (2000) Stochastic algorithms in nonlinear regression. *Computational Statistics and Data Analysis* **33**, 277–90.

Kuhnert P.M., Do K.-A. & McClure R. (2000) Combining non-parametric models with logistic regression: an application to motor vehicle injury data. *Computational Statistics and Data Analysis* **34**, 371–86.

Leduc S. & Sill K. (2007) Monetary policy, oil shocks, and TFP: Accounting for the decline in US volatility. *Review of Economic Dynamics* **10**(4), 595–614.

Li K.-C. (1997) Nonlinear confounding in high-dimensional regression. *The Annals of Statistics* **25**(2), 577–612.

Lu L., Brown B.H., Barber D.C. & Leathard A.D. (1995) A fast parametric modeling algorithm with the Powell method, *Physiological Measurement*. **16**, 39–47.

Madsen J.B. (2007) Technology spillover through trade and TFP convergence: 135 years of evidence for the OECD countries. *Journal of International Economics* **72**(2), 464–80.

Markatou M., Basu A. & Lindsay B. (1997) Weighted likelihood estimating equations: the discrete case with applications to logistic regression. *Journal of Statistical Planning and Inference* **57**, 215–32.

Montgomery D.C. & Peck E.A. (1992) *Introduction to Linear Regression Analysis*. John Wiley & Sons, New York.

Morton R. (1987) Asymmetry of estimators in nonlinear regression. *Biometrika* **74**, 679–85.

Nakamura H. (2009) Micro-foundation for a constant elasticity of substitution production function through mechanization. *Journal of Macroeconomics* **31**(3), 464–72.

Neath A.A. & Cavanaugh J.E. (2000) A regression model selection criterion based on bootstrap bumping for use with resistant fitting. *Computational Statistics and Data Analysis* **35**(2), 155–169.

Noubiap R.F. & Seidel W. (2000) A minimax algorithm for constructing optimal symmetrical balanced designs for a logistic regression model. *Journal of Statistical Planning and Inference* **91**, 151–68.

Paul G. & Peter R. (2007) Theory, measurement and calibration of macroeconomic models. *Journal of Monetary Economics* **54**(2), 460–97.

Phillips A.W. (1958) The Relationship between Unemployment and the Rate of Change of Money Wages in the United Kingdom 1861–1957. *Economica* **25**(100), 283–99.

Poirier D. (1980) Partial observability in bivariate probit models. *Journal of Econometrics* **12**, 209–17.

Qian G.Q. & Künsch H.R. (1998) On model selection via stochastic complexity in robust linear regression. *Journal of Statistical Planning and Inference* **75**(1), 91–116.

Qian W.M. (2000) An application of nonparametric regression estimation in credibility theory, Insurance. *Mathematics and Economics* **27**(2), 169–76.

Rao C.R. (1952) *Statistical Methods in Biometric Research*. John Wiley and Sons, Inc. New York.

Rao C.R. (1965) *Linear Statistical Inference with Applications*, First edition, New York, John Wiley & Sons, Inc.

Rivers D. & Yuong Q. (1988) Limited information estimators and exogencity tests for simultaneous probit models. *Journal of* Econometrics **39**, 347–66.

Rom M. & Cohen A. (1995) Estimation in the polytomous logistic regression model. *Journal of Statistical Planning and Inference* **43**, 341–53.

Schmidt W.H. & Zwanzig S. (1986) Second order asymptotics in nonlinear regression. *J.Multi. Anal* **18**, 187–215.

Sexton J. & Swensen A.R. (2000) ECM algorithms that converge at the rate of EM. *Biometrika* **87**, 651–62.

Simonoff J.S. & Tsai C.L. (1986) Jackknife-based estimators and confidence regions in nonlinear regression. *Technometrics* **28**, 103–12.

Solow R.M. (1956) A contribution to the theory of economic growth. *Quarterly Journal of Economics* **70**, 65–94.

Solow R.M. (1957) Technical change and aggregate production function. *Review Economics and Statistics* **30**, 312–20.

Sundarraman S. (2001) Parameter estimation in regression for long-term survival rate from censored data. *Journal of Statistical Planning and Inference* **99**(2), 211–22.

Tan H. W., Su X.L., Wei W.Z. & Yao S.Z. (1999) Robust complex non-linear regression method for the estimation of equivalent circuit parameters of the thickness-shear-mode acoustic wave sensor. *Chemometrics and Intelligent Laboratory Systems* **48**(1), 71–80.

Tinbergen J. (1942, English translation 1959) On the theory of trend movements. *Weltwirtschaftliches Archiv* **55**, 511–49.

Tiku M.L., Islam M.Q. & Selçuk A.S. (2001) Nonnormal regression. II. symmetric distributions. *Communications in Statistics—Theory and Methods* **30**, 1021–45.

Tong H.Q. (1993) Evaluation model and its iterative algorithm by alternating projection. *Mathematical and Computer Modeling* **18**(8), 55–60.

Vankeerberghen P., Smeyers-Verbeke J., Leardi R., Karr C.L. & Massart D.L. (1995) Robust regression and outlier detection for non-linear models using genetic algorithms, *Chemometrics and Intelligent Laboratory Systems* **28**(1), 73–87.

Vonesh E.F., Wang H. & Dibyen M. (2001) Generalized least squares, Taylor series linearization and fisher's scoring in multivariate nonlinear regression. *Journal of the American Statistical Association* **96**(453), 282–92.

Von Rosen D. (1991) The growth curve model: a review. *Communications in Statistics* **20**, 2791–2820.

Wang C.Y. & Huang Y.J. (2001) Functional methods for logistic regression on random-effect-coefficients for longitudinal measurements. *Statistics and Probability Letters* **53**, 347–56.

Xiang A., Lapuerta P., Ryutov A., Buckley J. & Azen S. (2000) Comparison of the performance of neural network methods and Cox regression for censored survival data. *Computational Statistics and Data Analysis* **34**(2), 243–57.

Yanagihara H.S. & Risa F.Y. (2003) Bias correction of AIC in logistic regression models. *Journal of Statistical Planning and Inference* **115**, 349–60.

Yuen K.C., Zhu L.X. & Tang N.Y. (2003) On the mean residual life regression model. *Journal of Statistical Planning and Inference* **113**(2), 685–98.

5

Nonparametric and semiparametric regression models

The functional forms of the regression models discussed in the previous chapters are known to be either linear or non-linear with unknown parameters that need to be estimated. Those regression models are called **parametric regressions. Nonparametric regression** is the opposite of parametric regression, and its regression functional form is much more flexible with the possibility of being a better fitting model. The general form of nonparametric regression is

$$Y = f(X) + \varepsilon, \, E(\varepsilon) = 0$$

While in notation this model looks similar to the nonlinear regression model, we should recognize that the function $f(\cdot)$ in the nonlinear regression model is known, but the function $f(\cdot)$ here in the nonparametric regression model is unknown. Although the functional form is unknown, it does not mean that it is chosen arbitrarily.

We will introduce the concept and algorithms of nonparametric regression model in detail in Section 5.1. Some more discussion of nonparametric regression models such as the **moment consistency of weight function estimation** can be found in the Electronic References for Chapter 5.

We will discuss in some detail the basic weight function or the kernel function, and the nearest neighbor method of the nonparametric regression model. We place the discussion of some other nonparametric regressions such as spline regression and wavelete **function** in the Electronic References for Chapter 5.

It is not easy to achieve good forecasting accuracy using the pure nonparametric regression model. Hence the **semiparametric models** that combine nonparametric model with parametric

Developing Econometrics, First Edition. Hengqing Tong, T. Krishna Kumar and Yangxin Huang.
© 2011 John Wiley & Sons, Ltd. Published 2011 by John Wiley & Sons, Ltd.

model have been proposed. Such semi-parametric models will also be discussed here. The most basic semiparametric model is the **linear semiparametric model**:

$$Y_i = X_i'\beta + g(X_i) + \varepsilon_i, \quad E(\varepsilon_i) = 0, \quad i = 1, 2, \ldots, n$$

It means that dependent variable Y is affected by both a linear main part $X\beta$ and a nonparametric part $g(X)$. The linear main part may determine the general trend, useful for extra-sample forecasting, and the nonparametric part could adjust that trend locally to make the model fit the data more accurately.

In the **single-indicator regression model**:

$$Y_i = g(\theta_i' X_i) + \varepsilon_i, \quad E(\varepsilon_i) = 0, \quad i = 1, 2, \ldots, n$$

we make univariate index $\theta'X$ by weighting multivariate index X by parameter θ (projection of Y in the X-space), then make univariate nonparametric regression of Y. This model is similar to **projection pursuit regression** (see Electronic References for Chapter 9, Section 1) with a good in-sample fit, but not suitable for out-of-sample forecasting.

The self-modeling regression model is

$$Y_{ij} = g(t_{ij}\theta_i) + \varepsilon_{ij}, \quad E(\varepsilon_{ij}) = 0, \quad i = 1, 2, \ldots, m, \quad j = 1, 2, \ldots, n$$

which shows m curves with n observation points on each curve, and we may obtain m smooth curves whose shape may be similar by using nonparametric regression for every curve. We also have to find the linking parameters to link these smoothing curves, thus leading to what is called the curve forecasting model.

Stochastic frontier regression model:

$$Y_{ij} = X_{ij}'\beta + \alpha_i + \varepsilon_{ij}, \quad E(\alpha_i) \geq 0, \quad E(\varepsilon_{ij}) = 0, \quad i = 1, 2, \ldots, m, \quad j = 1, 2, \ldots, n$$

where Y_{ij} are the outputs of m units (companies, enterprises) at n points in time. Due to the presence of α_i, the efficiency factor associated with each company. The regression curve no longer passes through the average of all observations. The regression models previously studied, whether they are univariate or multivariate, linear or nonlinear, and parametric or nonparametric, are all based on average regression with no stochastic term such as α_i above.

This chapter will present many such nonparametric or semi-parametric models and corresponding complicated computational procedures which can be accomplished by DASC.

5.1   Nonparametric regression and weight function method

5.1.1   The concept of nonparametric regression

In mathematical statistics nonparametric inference and nonparametric regression have different meanings. In **nonparametric inference** the parametric probability distribution is irrelevant. In nonparametric regression the parametric functional form is irrelevant to regression.

As we know, for parametric methods in statistics, it is required that we assume that the probability distribution function of the sample is known, and it is usually assumed to be a normal distribution whose two parameters, the mean and variance, are unknown. In nonparametric statistics, there is no need to know the specific distributional form, that is, it is irrelevant to the statistical inference as to what the underlying probability distribution is. Examples of such nonparametric statistical methods are: **order statistics**, **rank statistics**, *U* **statistics**, etc. These are generally studied in place of specific probability distributions in order to achieve **distribution-free methods**. Likewise there are distribution-free statistical tests of hypotheses. Examples are: **sign test**, **rank sum test**, **runs test**, and so on. In terms of regression, nonparametric regression method does not need a specific functional form for the regression. Thus, **smoothing, kernel density, k-nearest neighbor, wavelet** methods, and other nonparametric methods are usually studied as parameter free methods.

The general form of nonparametric regression is

$$Y = g(X) + \varepsilon, \quad E(\varepsilon) = 0$$

where the form of function $g(\cdot)$ is unknown. Although the functional form is unknown, it does not mean that it is chosen arbitrarily. The basic purpose of the nonparametric regression model is the same as that of parametric regression, which is to estimate a relation between the dependent variable and independent variables by eliminating the influence of random error ε. The commonly used methods for nonparametric regression are the **smoothing method**, **kernel function method**, **k-nearest neighbor method**, **spline method**, and **wavelet method**. Each one of these focuses on different methods for searching for a pattern in the data. Each of these methods requires very few parameters, such as smoothing parameter, window width parameter, etc. We may write the nonparametric regression equation as

$$Y = g(X, \beta) + \varepsilon, \quad E(\varepsilon) = 0$$

where the parameter β refers to the parameters needed in each of these non-parametric methods. We see that the expression is similar to that of the non-linear regression model of the previous chapter. Since there is no unified known function, the methods of the previous chapter are, however, not applicable. The nonparametric regression model in the univariate case can be written as:

$$Y(t) = g(t, \beta) + \varepsilon, \quad E(\varepsilon) = 0$$

As the parameters used in nonparametric regression are inherent in the procedures and not with the specification of the regression function we omit mentioning parameter β from now on.

One simple and practical way to estimate this model is to smooth the data through some smoothing. Regression solutions are often suggested even for smoothing of $Y(t)$, using **smoothing formulas** of 5 points smoothing, 7 points smoothing and 9 points smoothing introduced in the numerical computational methods. If the independent variables are multivariate and equidistant, more complicated methods are required for nonparametric regression.

In general, the functional representations $\hat{g}_n(X)$ of nonparametric regression are the sum of a certain **weight functions** of Y:

$$\hat{g}_n(X) = \sum_{i=1}^{n} W_i(X) Y_i \qquad (5.1)$$

This kind of weight function should meet the following condition:

$$W_i(X; X_1, \ldots, X_n) \geq 0, \quad \sum_{i=1}^{n} W_i(X; X_1, \ldots, X_n) = 1 \qquad (5.2)$$

So, these weight functions may be called **probability weights**. Some familiar weight functions are the **kernel function**, the **closest neighbor function**, **spline function**, and **wavelet function**.

Suppose that Y is a one-dimensional random vector of a dependent variable, and X is a m-dimensional vector of random independent variable. In Chapter 3 that dealt with parametric methods we introduced conditional expectation as regression function. We call

$$g(X) = E(Y|X)$$

as the **regression function** of Y on X. We have shown that such regression function may minimize error sum of squares, that is

$$E[Y - E(Y|X)]^2 = \min_L E[Y - L(X)]^2$$

where L consists of a class of all suitable function types of X. Of course, if L is restricted to a linear function, then $g(X)$ is a linear regression function.

One may say that if the class of functions $L(X)$ has no restrictions, the error sum of squares may be equal to 0 by letting $L(X)$ pass through all observation points (Y_i, X_i). But it doesn't make much sense to give no restriction to fitting function $L(X)$. Just as there is no absolute freedom in the world, we can never say that there are no restrictions on $L(X)$. In the following specific nonparametric regression methods that we study, whether it is the kernel function method, closest neighborhood method, spline method and wavelet method, they all have some restrictions and for each of them we have to select some parameters to restrict the class of functions. (e.g. **window width selection** and **smoothing parameter selection**.)

Therefore, we know the distinction between parametric regression and nonparametric regression is a relative one. Fitting (Y_i, X_i) with a polynomial belongs to parametric regression, and fitting (Y_i, X_i) piecewise with several low power polynomials is called spline regression, which belongs to nonparametric regression.

5.1.2   Weight function method

The basic nonparametric regression methods include the kernel function method, closest neighborhood method, spline method and wavelet method. Although these methods are different and the mathematical forms are entirely different, they all could be considered as a linear combination of Y_i with a certain weight function. In other words, the estimation $\hat{g}_n(X)$ of regression function $g(X)$ can always be expressed in the form of (5.1).

The function $\{W_i(X)\}$ is called the weight function. The expression shows that $\hat{g}_n(X)$ is always the linear combination of Y_i, and one W_i is associated with each Y_i. W_i may depend not only on X_i, but it may also depend on the whole $\{X_i\}$. Hence we must write $W_i(X)$ in detail as $W_i(X; X_1, \ldots, X_n)$. Linear regression can be written in this form. If $Y_i = X_i'\beta + \varepsilon_i$, then $X_i'\hat{\beta} = X_i'(X'X)^{-1}X'Y$, which is also a linear combination of Y_i.

In general for most problems, all weight functions meet the conditions in (5.2). Considering that the prescription regression and evaluation model discussed in Chapter 4 have similar condition, the conditions above might also be called prescription conditions, and the weight function meeting prescription conditions is called **Probability Weight.** The consistency of weight function estimation can be seen in the Electronic References for Chapter 5.

Next we consider various specific nonparametric regression methods.

1. Kernel function method

The kernel function method combines the sample information with a kernel function. $K(X)$, used as the weight function. $K(X)$ is a real number given to each sample point X meeting prescription conditions or probability conditions:

$$K(X) \geq 0 \quad and \quad \int K(X)dx = 1$$

The specific structure of kernel function varies between different kernel estimators. For example, the following functions are all univariate kernel functions:

$$K(x) = \begin{cases} 1/4, & |x| < 2 \\ 0, & |x| \geq 2 \end{cases} \quad K(x) = \begin{cases} \dfrac{3}{4}(1 - x^2), & |x| \leq 1 \\ 0, & |x| > 1 \end{cases}, \quad K(x) = \frac{1}{\sqrt{2\pi}} \exp\left(-\frac{x^2}{2}\right)$$

The first one is a simple rectangle kernel, the second is the famous **Bartlett kernel**, and the third is the normal **probability kernel**.

As for multivariate kernel function, we may obtain it by repeatedly multiplying univariate ones. The first two kernel functions above have window width 4 and 2. We can construct the estimator $\hat{f}_n(X)$ of density function $f(X)$ using kernel function:

$$\hat{f}_n(X) = \frac{1}{nh} \sum_{i=1}^{n} K\left(\frac{X - X_i}{h}\right)$$

The concept of kernel density estimation may be seen in Electronic References for Chapter 5, Section 5-1. We may also construct the weight functions:

$$W_i(X; X_1, \ldots, X_n) = \frac{K\left(\dfrac{X - X_i}{a_h}\right)}{\sum_{j=1}^{n} K\left(\dfrac{X - X_j}{a_h}\right)}$$

Then construct nonparametric regression function:

$$\hat{Y} = \hat{g}_n(X) = \sum_{i=1}^{n} W_i(X)Y_i = \sum_{i=1}^{n} \left\{ \frac{K\left((X - X_i)/h\right)}{\sum_{j=1}^{n} K\left((X - X_j)/h\right)} Y_i \right\}$$

where h is **window width**, X_i, $i = 1, 2, \ldots, n$ are the sample points and X is a real number in the domain of definition of the sample.

2. The closest neighbor method

We now introduce the closest neighbor estimate of density function. In this method, contrary to the kernel method, the number of sample points in each interval is fixed, and we need to measure each interval length which contains the fixed number of sample points.

Suppose that the sample x_i, $i = 1, \ldots, n$ comes from a univariate population with density $f(x)$, and designate an arbitrary point x in R. We estimate the density function value $\hat{f}(x)$ at this point. We first select a number $k = k(n)$, for example, $k(n) = \dfrac{n}{100}$, and when $n = 5000$, $k(n) = 50$. Then we seek the minimum value $\alpha_n(x)$ so that the interval $[x - \alpha_n(x), x + \alpha_n(x)]$ contains $k(n)$ points of the sample, and the density function value $\hat{f}(x)$ is

$$\hat{f}(x) = \frac{k-1}{2n\alpha_n(x)}$$

We call $\hat{f}(x)$ is the closest neighbor estimate of density function.

Now we introduce the closest neighbor regression. We first introduce a distance function, which is used for measuring the distance between two points $u = (u_1, \ldots u_m)$ and $v = (v_1, \ldots v_m)$ in space R_m. Euclidean distance $\left\| u - v \right\|^2 = \sum_{i=1}^{m} (u_i - v_i)^2$ as well as $\left\| u - v \right\| = \max_{1 \leq i \leq m} \left| u_i - v_i \right|$ could be selected. To reflect different degrees of importance of different components, we may introduce weighting factors $C_1, \ldots, C_m$, and make $\{C_i\}$ meet the prescription condition, that is $\sum_{i=1}^{m} C_i = 1$, $C_i \geq 0$. Then the modified distance functions are

$$\left\| u - v \right\|^2 = \sum_{i=1}^{m} C_i (u_i - v_i)^2$$

$$\left\| u - v \right\| = \max_{1 \leq i \leq m} C_i \left| u_i - v_i \right|$$

Then we must give a series of weight functions meeting prescription condition in advance, that is, $w_i \geq 0$, $i = 1, 2, \ldots, n$, $\sum_{i=1}^{n} w_i = 1$. They are sorted from large to small: $w_1 \geq w_2 \geq \ldots \geq w_n > 0$.

Suppose there is a regression sample (Y_i, X_i), $i = 1, \ldots, n$. The basic idea of closest neighbor regression is that the biggest weight w_i should be given to that Y_k whose corresponding X_k is the closest to the point X. For a given point X, sort $X_1, \ldots, X_n$ by the distance to X based on the selected distance $\left\| \cdot \right\|$:

$$\left\| X_{k_1} - X \right\| < \left\| X_{k_2} - X \right\| < \cdots < \left\| X_{k_n} - X \right\|$$

It shows that, X_{k_1} is closest to X with weight function w_1, X_{k_2} is second closest to X with weight function $w_2, \ldots$, and so on. With this ordering we have:

$$W_{k_i}(X; X_1, \ldots, X_n) = w_i, \quad i = 1, \ldots, n$$

Then the closest neighbor regression function is

$$\hat{Y} = \hat{g}(X) = \sum_{i=1}^{n} W_{k_i}(X; X_1, \ldots, X_n) Y_{k_i} = \sum_{i=1}^{n} w_i(X) Y_{k_i} = \sum_{i=1}^{n} w_i Y_{k_i}$$

The intuitive meaning is quite clear that Y is estimated as a weighted average of sample Ys, the weights being functions of all the independent variables of the entire sample, with the (Y, X) pair that is closest to the Y being predicted getting the maximum weight, next closest getting the next best weight and so on.

Although k_i and n are constants, which are selected beforehand, the specific sequence is relevant to X, so it could be written as $k_i(X)$.

If there exist m different sample points that are equally close to X with the same value for $\{\|X_i - X\|, i = 1, ..., n\}$, we may take an average of the m same weights. For instance, if the first two are equal, $\|X_1 - X\| = \|X_2 - X\|$, we adopt $W_1 = W_2 = \frac{1}{2}(k_1 + k_2)$.

We considered polynomial regression in the previous chapter, and closest neighbor method in this section. The so-called **spline function method** could be considered as smoothing method that is a **piece-wise function of low power polynomials**. It can also be interpreted as blending the polynomial smoothing with the nearest neighbor method using information from every point. The detailed discussion of spline regression can be seen in the Electronic References for Chapter 5, Section 2.

The so-called **wavelet function method** is a method developed from the concept of a **Fourier transform**. The Fourier transform is defined over an infinite range. The wavelet method is a Fourier transform method over a finite window width with data **frequency adaptation**. The detailed description of wavelet regression can be seen in the Electronic References for Chapter 5, Section 3.

Example 5.1   Univariate nonparametric regression for macro-economic data of Brazil   This example gives univariate nonparametric regression using kernel estimation. The macro-economic data of Brazil are presented in Table 5.1. The dependent variable Y is the broad money supply (M2), and independent variable X is one-dimensional and it is the Public financial system's credit.

In this program, computer determines the window width by cross verification. The concept of cross verification may be found in the Electronic References for Chapter 5, Section 5-1-5 dealing with the widow width selection of bivariate kernel regression. The kernel function is the Bartlett kernel. The initial value of window width is 0.5 for the iterative selection of the window width, and the final value of window width is 1.98. The iterative algorithm is the Powell Algorithm. The goodness of fit of the kernel regression is shown in the following figure. Readers can verify the computation process by clicking DASC → Regression Analysis → Nonparametric and semiparametric → Univariate nonparametric regression model. Readers can input or load their own data with any form (text, Excel, SQL, and other database form) in DASC to perform calculations using this program (Figure 5.1).

5.2   Semiparametric regression model

In the discussion of nonparametric regression, we mentioned the advantages and disadvantages of parametric regression and nonparametric regression. Parametric regression is easy to estimate, and is appropriate to predict and forecast, but its form is inflexible making it hard to fit complicated curvilinear relationships. On the other hand nonparametric regression has flexible forms, which enable us to fit complicated curves and surfaces. But its estimation is more complicated, and its performance in forecasting or prediction is not very good. We also discussed in the section on spline regression that the differentiation between parametric regression and nonparametric regression is, in fact, relative. We focused on selection of smoothing parameter, such as the window-width parameter in nonparametric regression.

Table 5.1   Macro-economic data of Brazil (1999.1–2006.12) Broad money supply M2 (Thousand millions of Real) Credit operations of public financial system (million Real).

Year-Month	M2	Credit operations	Year-Month	M2	Credit operations	Year-Month	M2	Public Financial System Credit
1999–1	254.930	4054	2001–9	296.575	7018	2004–5	427.762	3619
1999–2	259.568	4058	2001–10	295.901	7062	2004–6	436.469	3589
1999–3	260.900	4013	2001–11	301.951	7003	2004–7	441.904	3676
1999–4	257.075	3963	2001–12	321.612	2857	2004–8	450.248	3800
1999–5	258.345	4087	2002–1	314.519	2439	2004–9	457.264	3948
1999–6	260.973	4141	2002–2	316.189	2399	2004–10	463.012	3770
1999–7	260.036	4144	2002–3	323.975	2507	2004–11	470.778	3751
1999–8	259.187	4165	2002–4	322.668	2507	2004–12	493.497	3693
1999–9	257.450	4141	2002–5	324.542	2535	2005–1	489.052	3668
1999–10	259.628	4035	2002–6	342.029	2333	2005–2	492.621	3660
1999–11	262.755	4006	2002–7	353.510	1958	2005–3	502.562	3666
1999–12	274.770	2720	2002–8	369.202	1975	2005–4	503.109	3672
2000–1	269.834	2850	2002–9	375.894	1990	2005–5	504.302	3765
2000–2	261.494	2954	2002–10	382.187	1524	2005–6	512.485	3648
2000–3	261.427	3617	2002–11	385.610	1530	2005–7	518.085	3626
2000–4	259.793	3432	2002–12	397.503	1567	2005–8	526.645	3595
2000–5	259.850	15409	2003–1	388.506	2353	2005–9	532.469	3581
2000–6	260.097	6691	2003–2	391.101	1960	2005–10	539.183	3400
2000–7	262.670	6708	2003–3	385.238	2506	2005–11	549.489	3404
2000–8	264.099	6135	2003–4	382.255	2509	2005–12	582.464	3370
2000–9	264.759	6146	2003–5	385.368	2554	2006–1	567.253	3283
2000–10	265.691	6156	2003–6	383.248	2541	2006–2	574.855	3451
2000–11	271.618	6164	2003–7	385.674	2987	2006–3	578.795	3430
2000–12	283.785	6291	2003–8	387.611	3529	2006–4	579.657	3404
2001–1	276.498	5998	2003–9	388.097	3505	2006–5	593.981	3400
2001–2	279.763	5998	2003–10	386.023	3499	2006–6	600.442	3388
2001–3	278.378	6193	2003–11	398.425	3479	2006–7	604.813	3390
2001–4	279.599	6466	2003–12	412.895	3464	2006–8	607.033	3372
2001–5	283.478	6599	2004–1	405.056	3443	2006–9	611.875	3340
2001–6	289.059	6738	2004–2	408.096	3520	2006–10	622.409	3321
2001–7	290.466	6882	2004–3	409.758	3742	2006–11	637.456	3321
2001–8	295.619	6949	2004–4	410.978	3737	2006–12	662.896	3267

Along these lines, it is useful to combine parametric regression with non-parametric regression to form what is called a **semi-parametric regression model**.

Stone (1977) may be the first person who thought of the semi-parametric regression problem. He considered the regression model

$$Y_i = X_i'\beta + g(T_i) + \varepsilon_i$$

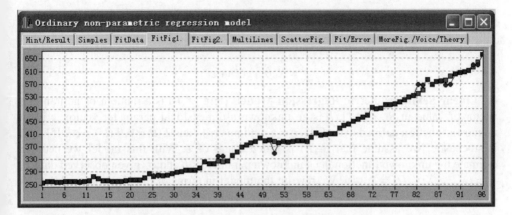

Figure 5.1 Univariate nonparametric regression for macro-economic data of Brazil.

It has a **linear main part** $X\beta$, which can handle the **general trend** and is appropriate to extend and predict, and it also has **nonparametric part** $g(T)$, which can make local adjustment to fit data precisely. Since the parametric and nonparametric methods are combined, it is called the **Semiparametric Regression Model**.

Later, in the statistics literature we also find other forms of semiparametric regression models, such as the **Single-Index Regression Model** (Hardle, 1993):

$$Y_i = g(\theta_i' X_i) + \varepsilon_i$$

The Self-Modeling Regression Model (Kneip, 1988):

$$Y_{ij} = g(t_{ij}\theta_i) + \varepsilon_{ij}$$

We have already put forward the **Stochastic Frontier Semiparametric Regression Model**:

$$Y_{ij} = X_{ij}'\beta + g(T_j) + \alpha_i + \varepsilon_{ij} \tag{5.3}$$

Likewise we have the **Stochastic Frontier Variance Component Regression Model**:

$$Y_{ij} = X_{ij}'\beta + U_{ij}\xi + \alpha_i + \varepsilon_{ij} \tag{5.4}$$

and the **Stochastic Frontier Generalized Linear Model**:

$$Y_{ij} = \mu_{ij} + \varepsilon_{ij}$$
$$g(\mu_{ij}) = X_{ij}'\beta + \alpha_i$$

We should note that there are both parametric and nonparametric terms in (5.3) and (5.4), so they are a semi-parametric regression models. This is also true for **projection pursuit regression** (see the Electronic References for Chapter 9, Section 1).

5.2.1   Linear semiparametric regression model

We call

$$Y = X'\beta + g(T) + \varepsilon$$

Linear Semiparametric Regression Model. Here (X,T) is a random or nonrandom vector of value in $R^p \times [0,1]$, β is an unknown p-dimensional parameter vector, g is an unknown function defined over $[0,1]$, ε is a random error, and $E(\varepsilon) = 0$, $E(\varepsilon^2) = \sigma^2$. If (X,T) is stochastic, we assume that (X,T) is independent of ε. With this model we need to estimate the unknown function $g(\cdot)$, unknown parameters β and σ^2 given observed data Y_i, $X_i = (X_{i1},\ldots,X_{ip})', T_i, i = 1,\ldots,n$. We rewrite the model in terms of the observational data as follows:

$$Y_i = X_i'\beta + g(T_i) + \varepsilon_i, \quad i = 1,\ldots,n$$

We develop the method of estimation of this semiparametric regression in two steps. The intuitive way to describe this two-step method of estimation is that we pretend that the nonparametric part is known to estimate the linear parametric part, and likewise we pretend that the linear parametric part is known when we estimate the nonparametric part, and substitute them together to estimate both parts simultaneously.

First we transpose the equation above to get:

$$Z_i = Y_i - X_i'\beta = g(T_i) + \varepsilon_i$$

The right side is now in nonparametric form, and the left side is some unknown Z_i. We can use the weight function method to estimate the unknown function $g(\cdot)$:

$$\hat{g}_n(T) = \sum_{i=1}^{n} \omega_{ni}(T)Z_i = \sum_{i=1}^{n} \omega_{ni}(T)Y_i - \sum_{i=1}^{n} \omega_{ni}(T)X_i'\beta$$

Let us write the right side in terms of two terms defined as follows:

$$\hat{g}_{1n}(T) = \sum_{i=1}^{n} \omega_{ni}(T)Y_i$$

$$\hat{g}_{2n}(T) = \sum_{i=1}^{n} \omega_{ni}(T)X_i$$

We then have:

$$Y_i - X_i'\beta = \hat{g}_{1n}(T_i) - \hat{g}_{2n}(T_i)'\beta + \varepsilon_i$$

$$Y_i - \hat{g}_{1n}(T_i) = (X_i - \hat{g}_{2n}(T_i))'\beta + \varepsilon_i$$

Also note

$$\tilde{Y}_i = Y_i - \hat{g}_{1n}(T_i)$$

$$\tilde{X}_i = X_i - \hat{g}_{2n}(T_i)$$

So let $\tilde{Y}_i = \tilde{X}_i'\beta + \varepsilon_i$, Least Square Estimator (LSE) of β may be obtained as:

$$\hat{\beta}_n = (\tilde{X}'\tilde{X})^{-1}\tilde{X}'\tilde{Y}$$

$$\hat{\sigma}_n^2 = \frac{1}{n}(\tilde{Y} - \tilde{X}\hat{\beta}_n)'(\tilde{Y} - \tilde{X}\hat{\beta}_n)$$

where $\tilde{Y} = (\tilde{Y}_1,...,\tilde{Y}_n)'$, $\tilde{X}_{n \times p} = (\tilde{X}_1,...,\tilde{X}_n)'$. But these are not known and they depend on $\hat{g}_{1n}(T_i)$ and $\hat{g}_{2n}(T_i)$. These functions can be obtained by choosing:

$$\omega_{ni}(t) = K\left(\frac{t - T_i}{h}\right)\bigg/ r_n(t)$$

$$r_n(t) = \sum_{i=1}^{n} K\left(\frac{t - T_i}{h}\right)$$

where K is a kernel function. As mentioned earlier a probability density function kernel, such as the **Bartlett kernel**, may be chosen for it. $h = h_n > 0$ is window width series, which may be chosen by experience. From the computational point of view, there is no problem in estimating the linear semiparametric regression model.

The rate of convergence of parameter estimators in the linear semiparametric regression model can be seen in Shengyan Hong and Ping Cheng (1994) and also in the Appendix to the Electronic References for Chapter 5.

Although we used t as the variable to represent the nonparametric trend, as time trend is most common, one that can have the nonparametric relation with any independent variable. This is illustrated in the example below, where the nonparametric part is the relationship between the Money Supply M2 and the inter bank rate.

Example 5.2   Linear semiparametric regression model for explaning the money supply in Russia using monthly macro-economic data for Russia   In fact, readers may construct any linear regression model into the semiparametric linear regression model, by adding a curvilinear time trend to be determined in a nonparametric way. In this example, we consider the macro-economic monthly data of Russia from 2000.1–2008.12. The dependent variable Y is Money Supply M2 (billion rubles). The independent variables are Merchandise Trade Import of goods (X_1, USD million), Merchandise Trade Export of goods (X_2, USD million), The Bank of Russia Balance Sheet Total Assets (X_3, millions of rubles), International Reserves (X_4, millions of US dollars), respectively. The nonparametric item is Interbank Rate (t, % per annum). The data of 2000 and 2008 can be seen in Table 5.2. The other data omitted here can be seen in DASC, \\She\\Wiley Data\\ Wiley 5(nonparameter)\\ Figure721-Russia Data.

The kernel function is the Bartlett kernel. The window width of the kernel function is selected as $h = 0.5$. Regression coefficients for independent variables X_1–X_4 are 0.0220, 0.0341, 0.0460, 0.1013. The squared sum of regression is 189176, sum of squared residuals is 879.58, and variance estimate of error is 8.4575. The coefficient of total correlation $R = 0.997683$, $R^2 = 0.995372$. Readers can verify the computation process by clicking DASC→Regression Analysis→Nonparametric and semiparametric→Linear semiparametric regression model (Figure 5.2).

Table 5.2 Linear semiparametric regression model for explaining the money supply in Russia using monthly macro-economic data of Russia.

Y–M	X_1	X_2	X_3	X_4	X_5	T
2000–01	709.6	2889	6801	880912	12948	11.8
2000–02	742	3429	7950	921417	13657	11.3
2000–03	768.4	3662	9142	977731	15532	6.5
2000–04	802.5	3386	8255	1034284	17091	11.1
2000–05	850.1	3402	8469	1090051	19570	7.6
2000–06	905.8	3592	8733	1128192	20996	5.1
2000–07	950.5	3602	8576	1178195	23302	3.4
2000–08	977.6	3775	9106	1186846	23731	4.6
2000–09	1008.8	3750	8954	1230858	25007	3.3
2000–10	1016.4	4132	8897	1266211	25880	5.2
2000–11	1054.6	4352	10052	1318770	27667	8.5
2000–12	1154.4	4891	10101	1346096	27972	7.3
......	......	......	......	......	......	
2008–01	12914.8	15649	34520	12640459	488368	2.8
2008–02	13080.4	21164	35685	12887542	494932	4.3
2008–03	13382.4	23402	39923	12842840	512584	4.3
2008–04	13347.7	25408	40243	13421994	532474	4.2
2008–05	13724.5	24495	42581	13634302	546035	3.7
2008–06	14244.7	25539	43846	14042139	568966	3.7
2008–07	14210	28636	47330	14650349	596566	4.4
2008–08	14530.1	27054	45668	15083153	582212	5.8
2008–09	14374.6	27212	43774	15179168	556813	7.1
2008–10	13519.7	27461	39088	15082421	484590	7.6
2008–11	13226.2	21856	30332	15747914	455730	9.5
2008–12	13493.2	23985	28616	16963714	427080	8.3

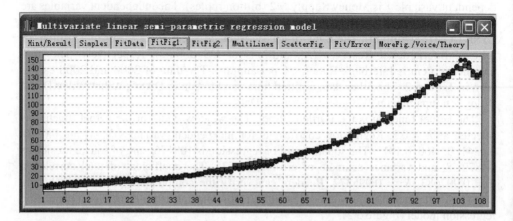

Figure 5.2 Linear semiparametric regression model for money supply in Russia.

5.2.2   Single-index semiparametric regression model

The Single-Index regression model is the expansion of the linear regression model, which has various applications, such as the discrete choice model in economics and the response model in biology. As explained earlier in Chapter 4 the projection pursuit regression model is a dimension reduction method for dealing with regression with high-dimensional data.

Compared to the linear regression model $Y_i = X_i'\beta + \varepsilon_i$, $i = 1, \ldots, n$, and the nonlinear regression model $Y_i = f(X_i, \beta) + \varepsilon_i$ where the right hand side is a known linear or nonlinear function with unknown parameters, a Single-Index Regression Model now considered is

$$Y_i = g(\theta' X_i) + \varepsilon_i, \quad i = 1, \ldots, n$$

where $g(\cdot)$ is an unknown univariate function with much fewer unknown parameters (of the nonparametric procedure). In this model we need to estimate parameter θ and an unknown function g given observed data (Y, X).

We note that the single-index model is like the first step of projection pursuit regression. Considering general p-variate data X, and p-variate function $g_1(\cdot)$, we have a non-parametric regression model

$$Y_i = g_1(X_i) + \varepsilon$$

Then function $g(\theta' X_i)$ is the approximation of the first projection to $g_1(X_i)$, where the function g and parameter θ are taken to minimize $\sum_{i=1}^{n} [g_1(X_i) - g(\theta' X_i)]^2$.

Statistical smoothing is needed to estimate g or θ, and kernel estimation method may be suitable to construct estimator $\hat{g}_n$ of g. Once estimator $\hat{g}_n$ is obtained, substitute it into

$$S(\theta) = E\{Y - g(\theta' X)\}^2$$

Then we choose θ by minimizing $S(\theta)$. However, this method depends strongly on window width selection of estimator $\hat{g}_n(\cdot)$, as it is necessary to choose window width of $\hat{g}_n(\cdot)$ to estimate θ. Wolfgang et al. (1993) suggested a method of selecting a window width for dual-purpose, which is to estimate both g and θ. Now we introduce their method below.

The recorded data are (Y_i, X_i), $1 \leq i \leq n$, and the model is

$$Y_i = g(\theta' X_i) + \varepsilon_i$$

where g is a smooth univariate function, and θ is a p-variate unit vector. We also assume that $(p + 1)$-dimensional (X_i, ε_i) is independently and identically distributed.

Suppose $A \subset R^p$ is a set, which is selected to ensure the denominator of formula in kernel estimation is not 0. Suppose K is a kernel function which may be a symmetric probability function with support $(-1, 1)$. Define

$$A^{2h} = \{x \mid x \in R^p, \|x - y\| \leq 2h, y \in A\}$$

where $\| \cdot \|$ denotes the vector modular length under Euclidean distance.

Assume (X, Y) and (X_i, Y_i) have identical distributions. Define

$$g(u|\theta) = E(Y|\theta' X_i = u)$$

where X_i has conditional distribution $F(X|A)$. The estimation of g is easy to get:

$$\hat{g}(u|\theta) = \left\{\sum_{j=1}^{n} Y_j K_h(u - \theta'X_j)\right\} \bigg/ \left\{\sum_{j=1}^{n} K_h(u - \theta'X_j)\right\}$$

where h is **window width**, and $K_i(\cdot) = K_i(\cdot|h)$. If the ith pair of observation data (X_i, Y_i) are omitted, we have

$$\hat{g}_{hi}(u|\theta) = \left\{\sum_{j \neq i} Y_j K_h(u - \theta'X_j)\right\} \bigg/ \left\{\sum_{j \neq i} K_h(u - \theta'X_j)\right\}$$

Since $g(\cdot|\theta_0) \equiv g$, we may choose the direction of θ to minimize distance $g(\cdot|\theta) - g$. Define cross-efficientation function

$$\hat{S}(\theta, h) = \sum_{i \in A} \left\{Y_i - \hat{g}_{hi}(\theta'X_i|\theta)\right\}^2$$

Our computational task is completed when we choose θ and h to minimize $\hat{S}(\theta, h)$. However, the extremum of bivariate function is not easy to calculate, and we will consider it separately. Of course, we may consider choosing θ to approach θ_0, and h to approach h_0, where θ_0 and h_0 minimize

$$E\{\hat{g}_h(\theta'X|\theta) - g_h(\theta'X)\}^2, x \in A$$

We can realize the minimization of these equations at the same time. In other words, it can be proved that

$$\hat{S}(\theta, h) = \tilde{S}(\theta) + T(h) + O(1)$$

where

$$\tilde{S}(\theta) = \sum_{i \in A} \left\{Y_i - g_h(\theta'X_i|\theta)\right\}^2$$

is a distance measure, which is to replace $\hat{S}$ when $g(\cdot|\theta) \equiv g$ is known, and

$$T(h) = \sum_{i \in A} \left\{\hat{g}_{hi}(\theta_0'X_i|\theta_0) - g_h(\theta_0'X_i)\right\}^2$$

is the mean square distance between $\hat{g}(\cdot|\theta_0)$ and g. Then, choosing minimized parameters θ and h in $\hat{S}(\theta, h)$ simultaneously is equal to choosing θ in $\hat{S}(\theta)$ and h in $T(h)$ respectively. The insignificant item $O(1)$ can be decomposed into two items in detail. One is smaller than $T(h)$'s order and doesn't depend on θ, and the other is smaller than both the order of $\tilde{S}$ and $T(h)$, and this ensures it can be ignored.

According to the description above, we may obtain the estimation $\hat{\theta}, \hat{h}$ of θ and h. $\hat{\theta}$ is the minimized result of $\tilde{S}(\theta)$, and $\hat{h}$ is the minimized result of $T(h)$. Since in such minimizing process parameter values at each stage are irrelevant to each other, they are solved one by one separately. However, when seeking their sum, the subset of parameter space A is to be considered, and the structure of A should be discussed in greater detail.

Wolfgang et al. (1993) gave some theoretical analysis for the single-index model and its algorithm, which is not presented in detail here.

Obviously, single-index regression model $Y_i = g(X_i'\beta) + \varepsilon_i$ can improve the goodness of fit of common linear regression model $Y_i = X_i'\beta + \varepsilon_i$, or a nonlinear regression model $Y_i = f(X_i, \beta) + \varepsilon_i$ because after getting $X_i'\beta$ or $f(X_i, \beta)$ we can use nonparametric function $g(\cdot)$ to improve the goodness of fit of $X_i'\beta$ or $f(X_i, \beta)$.

Example 5.3 Single-index semiparametric regression model for money supply in Russia The data of this example are macro-economic data of Russia, the same as that of Example 5.2, except that the last column X_5 is now treated as another independent variable like others. In order to observe the goodness of fit clearly, we only take 48 points of the data from Jun. 2000. First we take ordinary linear regression model without constant item, and the goodness of fit is as in Figure 5.3. The estimates of the regression coefficients $\hat{\beta} = -6.5771, -0.0039, 0.0576, 0.0417, 0.2413, 0.0908$. The square sum of residuals is 39.7612, the square sum of regression is 1916.39, the variance estimate of error is 0.92468, the standard deviation $= 0.961603$, the statistic F $= 414.498$, the critical value F(5,43) $= 2.8787$, and the coefficient of total correlation $R^2 = 0.9797$. This computation can be verified and seen by clicking the menu DASC→Regression→ Linear Regression→Multi-linear regression (without constant term), then load the data from DASC\\She\\Lizi\\SheHui752 using menu DASC→Data→Load Other Example Data.

Then we take single index regression model for the same data. The iterative initial value of window width is $h = 0.5$, and the last estimation is $\hat{h} = 0.05505$. Estimates of the regression coefficients: $\hat{\theta} = -0.5944, 0.4941, 0.8380, 0.6607, 1.5451$. Residual sum of squares is: 26.133942. Readers can verify the computation process by clicking DASC→Regression→ Nonparametric and semiparametric→Single-index semiparametric regression model. The goodness of fit is as in Figure 5.4. We can see two lines overlap exactly indicating that the goodness of fit is too perfect.

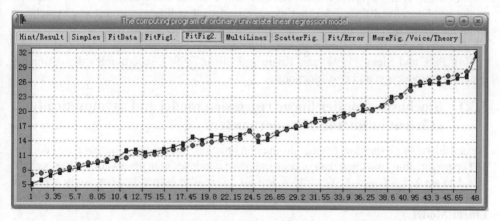

Figure 5.3 Ordinary linear regression model for money supply in Russia.

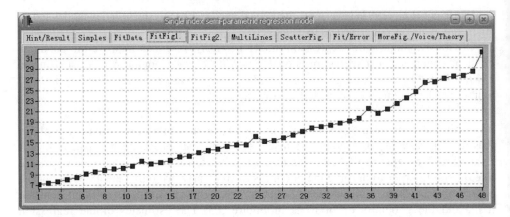

Figure 5.4   Single-index semiparametric regression model for money supply of Russia.

5.3   Stochastic frontier regression model

Production functions and **cost functions** are quite important in economic analysis and business policy. As profit is the revenue less cost, maximization of profit requires maximization of revenue and minimization of cost at the same time. Production function is a technical relation which shows the largest available **output** associated with a given set of **inputs**. The cost function, on the other hand, is an economic relation that shows the minimum cost of producing a given output. These concepts of production function and cost function thus involve an implicit optimization. The ordinary statistical regression method was used in early research on production and cost functions. With such an approach what was estimated was an average relation and not an optimal relation, and as such it is really not a production function or a cost function, as the case may be. There are two ways of incorporating optimality into specification and estimation of a production and cost function, the **Data Envelopment Analysis (DEA)** and the **frontier regression approach**. The Data Envelopment Analysis (DEA) uses the mathematical programming approach to estimate effective production or cost frontier which is an empirical frontier relation. However, the DEA method is not a statistical model and hence is of little use either to make statistical analyses or to test any hypotheses about the production structure.

The stochastic frontier linear model, developed by Statisticians Schmidt and Sickles (1984), Park and Simar (1994) and Kneip and Simar (1996), incorporates the optimality concept of production and cost functions.

5.3.1   Stochastic frontier linear regression model and asymptotically efficient estimator of its parameters

We consider a single-product frontier production function. Suppose that there are n production and operation units, the input data of each unit have d indexes with observations in m periods. The data are $X_{ij} = (X_{ij1}, \ldots, X_{ijd})'$, $i = 1, \ldots, n; j = 1, \ldots, m$. The output data have only one index (a single product), and general observation on inputs is X_{ij}. Then the **Stochastic Frontier Linear Model** is

$$(SFL) \qquad y_{ij} = X'_{ij}\beta + \alpha_i + \varepsilon_{ij}, \quad i = 1, \ldots, n, j = 1, \ldots, m \qquad (5.5)$$

where β is a d-dimensional parameter to be estimated; ε_{ij} is *i.i.d.* and $\varepsilon_{ij} \sim N(0, \sigma^2)$; σ^2 is unknown; α_i is the random data from *i.i.d.* with unknown density h; h has finite support with the **lower boundary** θ_1 and the **upper boundary** θ_2; that is, for points out of interval $[\theta_1, \theta_2]$, $h \equiv 0$. In addition, we also assume that ε_{ij}, X_{ij}, α_i are independent of each other.

The goal here is to estimate parameters β, σ^2, θ_1, θ_2 given observations (X_{ij}, y_{ij}). Once estimates of these parameters are obtained, we may deduce that for a given input X_{ij}, the maximum attainable or most efficient output is $X'_{ij}\beta + \theta_2$ (or the least cost, as the case may be is $X'_{ij}\beta + \theta_1$). We call $X'_{ij}\beta + \theta_2$ $(X'_{ij}\beta + \theta_1)$ as frontier function. Now, the **technical efficiency** of the ith production and operation unit could be measured by α_i, the closer it is to θ_2 the more efficient it is. The concept of technical efficiency here is equivalent to that of general economic literatures, but different from the concept of statistical efficiency.

Combining the two random terms of model SFL (5.5), we have $y_{ij} = X'_{ij}\beta + [random]$, which should belong to a linear model, but the variance of its random items is not $\sigma^2 I$. According to the theory of linear regression model, directly making least squares estimation of β on observation data (X_{ij}, Y_{ij}) will not lead to good estimation due to heteroscedasticity. We will improve the estimation of β focusing on this heteroscedasticity issue in the next section.

The **asymptotically efficient estimation** of a model (SFL) is developed from least squares estimation. The least squares estimator of β is

$$\tilde{\beta} = \frac{1}{mn}(\Sigma_W)^{-1} \sum_{i=1}^{n}\sum_{j=1}^{m}(X_{ij} - \bar{X}_i)(Y_{ij} - \bar{Y}_i)'$$

where

$$\bar{X}_i = \frac{1}{m}\sum_{j=1}^{m}X_{ij}, \quad \bar{X} = \frac{1}{mn}\sum_{i=1}^{n}\sum_{j=1}^{m}X_{ij}.$$

Since the variance of random term $\alpha_i + \varepsilon_{ij}$ in the model is not $\sigma^2 I$, $\tilde{\beta}$ is no longer the best linear unbiased estimation (BLUE). There are many methods to improve the estimator under heteroscedasticity, such as the generalized least squares estimator. We introduce a new nonparametric efficient estimator using the kernel estimator of variance. The method is developed by Park and Simar (1994).

In this method we need to consider the estimation of the density of the random term. We use the notations:

$$Z_{ij}(\tilde{\beta}) = Y_{ij} - X'_{ij}\,\tilde{\beta}, \quad \bar{Z}_i(\tilde{\beta}) = \frac{1}{m}\sum_{j=1}^{m}Z_{ij}(\tilde{\beta}), \quad \text{and} \quad \bar{Z}_j(\tilde{\beta}) = \alpha_i + \sum_{j=1}^{n}\varepsilon_{ij}$$

We construct the kernel density W of $\bar{Z}(\tilde{\beta})$

$$\hat{W}(Z,\tilde{\beta}) = \frac{1}{na_n}\sum_{i=1}^{n}K_0\left(\frac{Z - \bar{Z}_i(\tilde{\beta})}{a_n}\right)$$

and the kernel estimation of its derivative

$$W^{(1)}(Z,\tilde{\beta}) = \frac{1}{na_n^2}\sum_{i=1}^{n}K_1\left(\frac{Z - \bar{Z}_i(\tilde{\beta})}{a_n}\right)$$

where K_0, K_1 are kernel functions, and a_n is the window width of kernel function. The constructions of kernel functions of the estimators of density and its derivative can be seen in the Electronic References for Chapter 5, Section 5-1-2. The kernel estimators have good convergence rates if the kernels use orthogonal polynomials. Noting $U_{ij}(\tilde{\beta}) = Z_{ij}(\tilde{\beta}) - \overline{Z}(\tilde{\beta})$, we can write the estimate $\hat{\sigma}^2(\tilde{\beta}) = \sum_{i=1}^{n}\sum_{j=1}^{m} U_{ij}^2(\tilde{\beta})/n(m-1)$.

Based on the estimators above, we may improve least squares estimation $\tilde{\beta}$ of β as an **Asymptotically Efficient Estimator of** β (Park, 1994):

$$\hat{\beta} = \tilde{\beta} + \frac{1}{n}\hat{I}^{-1}\sum_{i=1}^{n}\left[\frac{1}{\tilde{\sigma}^2}\sum_{j=1}^{m} U_{ij}(\tilde{\beta})X_{ij} - (\overline{X}_i - \overline{X})\frac{\hat{W}^{(1)}(\tilde{Z}_i,\tilde{\beta})}{\hat{W}(\tilde{Z}_i,\tilde{\beta})}\right]$$

where $\tilde{\sigma}^2 = \tilde{\sigma}^2(\tilde{\beta})$, $\tilde{Z}_i = \tilde{Z}_i(\tilde{\beta})$, $\hat{I} = m\hat{\Sigma}_W/\tilde{\sigma}^2 + \hat{I}_0\hat{\Sigma}_B$, $\hat{I}_0 = \frac{1}{n}\sum_{i=1}^{n}(\hat{\omega}^{(1)}/\hat{\omega})^2(\tilde{Z}_i,\tilde{\beta})$, and

$$\hat{\Sigma}_W = \frac{1}{mn}\sum_{i=1}^{n}\sum_{j=1}^{m}(X_{ij} - \overline{X}_i)(X_{ij} - \overline{X}_i)', \quad \hat{\Sigma}_B = \frac{1}{n}\sum_{i=1}^{n}(\overline{X}_i - \overline{X})(\overline{X}_i - \overline{X})'.$$

Noting that $Y_{ij} - X_{ij}'\beta = \alpha_i + \varepsilon_{ij}$, and $\overline{Z}_i(\beta) = \frac{1}{m}\sum_{j=1}^{m}(Y_{ij} - X_{ij}'\beta)$, we take

$$\hat{\alpha}_i = \hat{Z}_i(\hat{\beta})$$

as the estimator of α_i, and

$$\hat{\theta}_2 = \max_{1 \le i \le n}\overline{Z}_i(\hat{\beta})$$

as the estimator of θ_2.

Based on the asymptotically efficient estimators given above, for different input data X_{ij}, for model (SFL) we may obtain the asymptotically efficient estimator of frontier function as $X_{ij}'\hat{\beta} + \hat{\theta}_2$. Some theoretical analysis on why $\tilde{\beta}$ is an asymptotically efficient estimator can be seen in the original work of Park and Simar (1994).

Example 5.4 Stochastic frontier regression model In the data documents of Example 5.4, $n = 8$, $m = 10$, $d = 4$. There are 80 rows and five columns in total data block. The detailed computation process is omitted here. Readers can verify the computation process by clicking DASC→Regression→Nonparametric/semiparametric Regression→Stochastic Frontier Regression Model (Figure 5.5).

5.3.2 Semiparametric stochastic frontier model

The main part of model (SFL) is a linear model. In actual problems, linear regression may possibly deviate too much, and nonparametric regression may be inconvincible. Stone (1982) first designed a model combining linear regression with nonparametric regression, which is the linear semiparametric regression model: $y_i = X_i'\beta + g(T_i) + \varepsilon_i, 1 \le i \le n$. We take advantage of Stone's work and apply it to stochastic frontier problems, and propose the following **Semiparametric Stochastic Frontier Model**

$$(SFS) \qquad y_{ij} = X_{ij}'\beta + g(T_i) + \alpha_i + \varepsilon_{ij}, \quad 1 \le i \le n, 1 \le j \le m \qquad (5.6)$$

where T_i is a random variable in $[0,1]$, g is an unknown function defined in $[0,1]$, and others are the same as in model (SFS). Obviously, the model is more adaptable for actual data

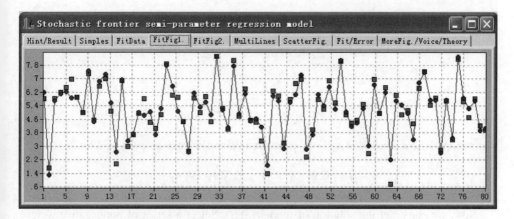

Figure 5.5   Stochastic frontier regression model.

by adding $g(T_i)$ term. We may generally state like this: production function is mostly realized by $g(T_i)$, while the optimality is mainly achieved by α_i density supported by an upper boundary. Of course, they are unified in one model, and the estimation of each item can not be separated from that of other items.

Next we will describe the solution of the model from the simple to the complex. For the nonparametric regression model:

$$y_j = g(T_j) + \varepsilon_j, \quad 1 \le j \le m$$

most commonly the weight function method is used. That is, we choose suitable weight functions $W_{mj}(t) = W_{mj}(t; T_1, \ldots, T_m) \ge 0$, and $\sum_{j=1}^{m} W_{mj}(t) = 1$, then let

$$\hat{g}(t) = \sum_{j=1}^{m} W_{mj}(t) y_i$$

be the estimator of $g(t)$, $t \in [0,1]$. Forms of weight function include kernel function, nearest neighbor weight function, spline function and wavelet function which were proposed earlier. As for the least squares solutions of parameters β, σ^2 in the model:

$$y_i = X_i'\beta + \varepsilon_i$$

is very familiar to us. Let $X = (X_1, \ldots X_n)$, $Y = (y_1, \ldots, y_n)'$, then $\hat{\beta} = (X'X)^{-1} X'Y$, $\hat{\sigma}^2 = \dfrac{1}{n} \sum_{i=1}^{n} (y_i - X_i'\hat{\beta})^2$.

Combining both models above together, the solution of semiparametric regression model is:

$$y_i = X_i'\beta + g(T_i) + \varepsilon_i, \quad 1 \le i \le n$$

First transpose $y_j - X_i'\beta = g(T_i) + \varepsilon_i$, regard it as single nonparametric regression model. Then we obtain the weight function solution of $g(t)$:

$$\hat{g}(t) = \sum_{i=1}^{n} W_{ni}(y_i - X_i'\beta) = \sum_{i=1}^{n} W_{ni}(t) y_i - \sum_{i=1}^{n} W_{ni}(t) X_i'\beta$$

Note that

$$\hat{g}_1(t) = \sum_{i=1}^{n} W_{ni}(t)y_i, \quad \hat{g}_2(t) = \sum_{i=1}^{n} W_{ni}(t)X_i$$

Let

$$\tilde{Y}_i = Y_i - \hat{g}_1(T_i), \quad \tilde{X}_i = X_i - \hat{g}_2(T_i)$$

then the model becomes $\tilde{Y}_i = \tilde{X}_i'\beta + \varepsilon_i$, parameters β and σ^2 may be estimated by

$$\tilde{\beta} = (\tilde{X}'\tilde{X})^{-1}\tilde{X}'\tilde{Y}, \tilde{\sigma}^2 = \frac{1}{n}\sum_{i=1}^{n}(\tilde{Y}_i - \tilde{X}_i'\beta)^2$$

Now, we construct the solution of model (SFS). Select a series of nonnegative weight functions $W_j(t) = W_j(t;T_1,\ldots,T_m)$, $1 \le j \le m$ defined in [0,1], which meet $\sum_{j=1}^{m} W_j(t) = 1, \forall t \in [0,1]$. Transform the model into

$$y_{ij} - X_{ij}'\beta = g(T_j) + \alpha_i + \varepsilon_{ij}$$

And we have the estimator of unknown function $g(t)$:

$$\hat{g}_1(t) = \sum_{j=1}^{m} W_j(t)(y_{ij} - X_{ij}'\beta) = \sum_{j=1}^{m} W_j(t)y_{ij} - \sum_{j=1}^{m} W_j(t)X_{ij}'\beta$$

Note

$$\hat{g}_1(t) = \sum_{j=1}^{m} W_j(t)y_{ij}, \quad \hat{g}_2(t) = \sum_{j=1}^{m} W_j(t)X_{ij}$$

$$\tilde{y}_{ij} = y_{ij} - \hat{g}_1(T_j), \quad \tilde{X}_{ij} = X_{ij} - \hat{g}_2(T_j)$$

and model SFS is transformed into

$$\tilde{Y}_{ij} = \tilde{X}_{ij}'\beta + \alpha_i + \varepsilon_{ij}, \quad 1 \le i \le n, 1 \le j \le m$$

Thus the model formally reduces to model SFR.

Electronic references for Chapter 5

References

Abramovich F. & Steinberg D.M. (1996) Improved inference in nonparametric regression using Lk-smoothing splines. *Journal of Statistical Planning and Inference* **49**, 327–41.

Albert J. & Chib S. (1993) Bayesian analysis of binary and polytomous response data. *Journal of the American Statistical Association* **88**, 669–79.

Amemiya T. & Morimune K. (1974) Selecting the optimal order of polynomial in the almon distributed Lag. *Review of Economics and Statistics* **56**, 378–86.

Borra Simone & Di Ciaccio Agostino (2002) Improving nonparametric regression methods by bagging and boosting. *Computational Statistics and Data Analysis* **38**, 407–20.

Brown P.J. (1982) Multivariate calibration (with discussion). *J. R. Statist. Soc. B* **44**, 287–321.

Burguete J.F., Gallant A.R. & Souza G. (1982) On unification of the asymptotic theory of nonlinear econometric models. *Econometric Reviews* **1**, 151–90.

Casu B. & Molyneux P. (2003) A comparative study of efficiency in European banking. *Applied Economics* **17**, 1866–76.

Cha K.-J. & Schucany W.R. (1998) Nonparametric kernel regression estimation near endpoints. *Journal of Statistical Planning and Inference* **66**, 289–304.

Chang F.-C., Lo H.M.-N., Lin D.K.J. & Yang H.-C. (2001) Optimal designs for dual response polynomial regression models. *Journal of Statistical Planning and Inference* **93**, 309–22.

Cleveland W.S. (1979) Robust locally weighted regression and smoothing scatterplots. *Journal of the American Statistical Association* **368**, 829–36.

Cooper P. (1972) Two approaches to polynomial distributed lag estimation. *American Statistician* **26**, 32–5.

Copas J.B. (1995) Local likelihood based on kernel censoring. *J.R. Statist. Soc. B* **57**, 221–36.

Efron B. (1983) Estimating the error rate of a forecasting rule: improvement on cross-efficientation. *J. Amer. Statist. Asso* **78**, 316–31.

Gallant A.R. (1980) Explicit estimators of parametric functions in nonlinear regression. *J. Amer Statist. Assoc* **75**, 182–193.

Garren S.T. & Peddada S.D. (2000) Asymptotic normality in multivariate nonlinear regression and multivariate generalized linear regression models under repeated measurements with missing data. *Statistics and Probability Letters* **48**, 293–302.

Gutierrez-P.E. & Smith A.F.M. (1998) Aspects of smoothing and model inadequacy in generalized regression. *Journal of Statistical Planning and Inference* **67**, 273–86.

Hardle W., Hall P. & Ichimura H. (1993) Optimal smoothing in single index models, *Annals of Statistics* **21**(1), 157–78.

Holger, D. (2002) A consistent test for heteroscedasticity in nonparametric regression based on the kernel method. *Journal of Statistical Planning and Inference* **103**, 311–29.

Hong S. & Cheng P. (1994) The convergence rate of estimation for parameter in a semi-parammetric model. *Chinese Journal of Probability and Statistics* **10**, 62–71.

Hu I. (1998) Strong consistency of Bayes estimates in nonlinear stochastic regression models. *Journal of Statistical Planning and Inference* **67**, 156–63.

Kneip A. and Engle J. (1995) Model estimation in nonlinear regression under shape invariance. *Annals of Statistics* **23**(2), 551–70.

Kneip A. & Gasser T. (1988) Convergence and consistency results for self-modeling nonlinear regression, *Ann.Statistics* **16**(1), 82–112.

Kneip A. & Simar L. (1996) A general framework for frontier estimation with panel data, *Journal of Productivity Analysis* **7**, 187–212.

Mallat S.G. (1989) Multiresolution Approximations and wavelet orthonormal bases of L.2(R). *Transactions of the American Mathematical Society* **315**, 69–87.

Park B.U. & Simar L. (1994) Efficient semiparametric estimation in a stochastic frontier model. *The Journal of the Acoustical Society of America* **89**(427), 929–36.

Schick A. (1999) Efficient estimation of a shift in nonparametric regression. *Statistics & Probability Letters* **41**, 287–301.

Schmidt P. & Sickles R.C. (1984) Production frontiers and panel data, *Journal of Business and Economic Statistics* **2**, 367–74.

Stone C.J. (1977) Consistent nonparametric regression (with discussion). *Annals of Statistics* **5**, 549–645.

Stone C.J. (1982) Optimal global rates of convergence for nonparametric regression. *Annals of Statistics* **10**(4), 1040–51.

Tian G.L. (1998) The comparison between polynomial regression and orthogonal polynomial regression. *Statistics & Probability Letters* **38**, 289–94.

Tong H.Q. (1996) Convergence rates for empirical Bayes estimators of parameters in multiparameter exponential families. *Communications in Statistics* **25**, 1089–98.

Wu J.S. & Chu C.K. (1993) Kernel-type estimators of jump points and values of a regression function. *Annals of Statistics* **21**, 1546–66.

6

Simultaneous equations models and distributed lag models

In the previous chapters we focused mainly on discussing regression models with a single-equation, each model containing a dependent variable Y, one or more explanatory variables X. These models emphasize estimating or forecasting Y under the condition that X is given. The causality is very clearly from X to Y.

In this chapter we will discuss the general situation in economics requiring regression models with more than one equation, i.e. the **simultaneous equations model**. There are two kinds of variables, **endogenous variables** and **exogenous variables** in an economic model. They are different clearly in a single equation model but they are confusable in a simultaneous equation model. Some endogenous variables which are dependent variables in some equations are independent variables in some other equations, making them stochastic independent variables. Therefore the **ordinary least squares estimator (OLSE)** may be inconsistent. So we need to discuss the issue of improved LSE, including the estimators of **indirect least squares**, and **two stages least squares**. More improved methods of estimation such as **three stages LSE**, maximum likelihood estimation of **limited information and full information** can be found in the Electronic References for Chapter 6. We also need to discuss the issue of **model identification,** detailed discussion of this is also to be found in the Electronic References for Chapter 6, Section 1.

Previously discussed models contained contemporaneous variables, or variables of a given time. In many economic examples there are **lag effects** such as consumption lag, inflation lag, deposit re-creation, etc. We therefore need to consider **lag variables** in a model. We will discuss **finite distributed lag models** and **infinite distributed lag models**, including the determination of **distributed lag length**, **Koyck transformation** and estimation of the **geometric lag model**. More discussion on such as **finite polynomial lag**, the method of **instrumental variables** and maximum likelihood estimation can be found in the Electronic References for Chapter 6, Section 3.

Developing Econometrics, First Edition. Hengqing Tong, T. Krishna Kumar and Yangxin Huang.
© 2011 John Wiley & Sons, Ltd. Published 2011 by John Wiley & Sons, Ltd.

DASC can accomplish the estimation of these systems of simultaneous equations employing suitable estimation methods. In order to test the accuracy of computation in DASC we select data from examples in a famous book. We also use our own examples with data from the BRIC counties.

6.1   Simultaneous equations models and inconsistency of OLS estimators

Multiple equation models arise quite naturally in economics and business. Before introducing the background of simultaneous equations models we will introduce the concept of models and the methods of estimating them from given data.

In a non-experimental situation that characterizes most situations in economics and business, economic variables are interrelated to each other through a set of relations suggested by the underlying economic theory. The variables in a multi-equation econometric model are divided into two groups called endogenous and exogenous variables. Those variables that are determined by the set of equations specified by the model, usually one equation explaining one variable, are called the **endogenous variables** (there are as many equations in the system of equations as there are endogenous variables). These variables can influence each other but do not influence the other set of variables called **exogenous variables**. Exogenous variables (usually independent variables) influence endogenous variables (usually dependent variables) but are not influenced by them. One major problem that arises in simultaneous equations system is that one or more relations may look alike and it is difficult distinguish one from the other, unless one imposes certain *a priori* conditions on each of them to distinguish them from the others. This is the problem of identification in econometric models.

We can always take a single equation from the system of equations with one endogenous variable as the dependent variable and other endogenous variables and the exogenous variables as the independent variables. We can then use the **ordinary least squares** method to estimate the parameters of that equation separately, ignoring the presence of other equations in the system, and thus ignoring the stochastic nature of some of the independent variables. This can be done with each of the equations in the system of equations. This is called the OLS method of estimating a system of simultaneous equations. As some of the independent endogenous variables enter into other stochastic equations they are stochastic and the OLS estimators will turn out to be biased as well as inconsistent (as will be shown in Section 6.1.3 below). For a detailed discussion of these concepts of bias and consistency the reader is referred to Chapter 10, Section 10.4.3.

We shall discuss in this chapter the issues of **identification** and methods of **consistent estimation** of parameters of simultaneous equations.

To illustrate the issue of identification we present a simple two endogenous variables case with two exogenous variables. We can write the equation system as follows:

$$Y_{1i} = \beta_{10} + \beta_{12}Y_{2i} + \gamma_{11}X_{1i} + \gamma_{12}X_{2i} + \varepsilon_{1i} \tag{6.1}$$

$$Y_{2i} = \beta_{20} + \beta_{21}Y_{1i} + \gamma_{21}X_{1i} + \gamma_{22}X_{2i} + \varepsilon_{2i} \tag{6.2}$$

where Y_1 and Y_2 depend on each other and both of them are endogenous variables. X_1 and X_2 are exogenous variables; ε_1 and ε_2 are error terms. Let us say that the first equation is the demand for a product and the second one is the supply of the same product, and that there is

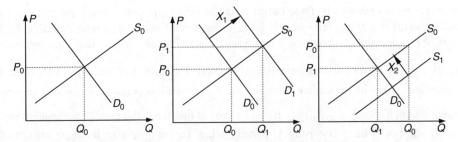

Figure 6.1 Shifts in demand and supply due to shifts in exogenous variables.

an equilibrium in the market so that Y_1 refers to the quantity demanded and supplied, Y_2 is the price of the product, X_1 is the household personal disposable income, and X_2 is the excise duty on the product.

As we do not know the parameters of the above two equations we wish to estimate them from the given data on Ys and Xs. How do we know which of the equations is estimated? We need some *a priori* conditions on the parameters so that we know which of the equations is being estimated, as otherwise equations (6.1) and (6.2) look alike. Economic theory tells us that X_1 affects demand and not supply and X_2 affects supply and not demand. Economic theory also tells us that $\beta_{12} < 0$, $\gamma_{11} > 0$, and $\gamma_{12} = 0$. Similarly, we have from economic theory that $\beta_{21} > 0$, $\gamma_{21} = 0$, $\gamma_{22} < 0$. We can represent the above two equations in two dimensions of Y_1 (quantity-horizontal axis) and Y_2 (price-the vertical axis) as Figure 6.1.

As each equation has different exogenous variables entering into them the two equations are distinguishable or identifiable. For more details on the concept of identification and conditions on the equation system to bring about identification, reader can refer to the Electronic References for Chapter 6, Section 1.

In the model above variable Y_1 is correlated with ε_2 and Y_2 is correlated with ε_1. As we will show in the next section they are thus dependent on each other and the OLS estimators are inconsistent (as will be shown in Section 6.3).

The best way to resolve this problem is to replace the stochastic independent variable by another proxy variable that is strongly correlated with it which is non-stochastic. This is achieved by the **two-stage least squares** (2SLS) procedure suggested by Henry Theil (1954) and Basmann (1957).

The first stage of two-stage least squares method is to regress each dependent variable directly on all the exogenous variables in the entire system of equations. This step would provide estimates of each dependent variable as that linear function of all exogenous variables that has the highest correlation with the dependent variable under question. For example, corresponding to (6.1), designate the dependent variable as Y_1 and the independent variables as X_1 and X_2, all of them having n observations. Through the ordinary least squares regression, $\hat{Y}_1$ is estimated as the linear function of X_1 and X_2 that has the highest correlation with Y_1, similarly $\hat{Y}_2$ is the linear combination of X_1 and X_2 that has the highest correlation with Y_2. Sometimes when the system of equations is too large and the number of observations is few it is possible that the number of independent variables in this first stage are larger than the number of observations, reducing the number of degrees of freedom to zero. In this case one regresses Ys on the principal components of Xs.

The second stage is to regress each equation of the original set of simultaneous econometric relations separately, with the dependent variables viewed as their original values, and the independent endogenous (stochastic) variables being replaced by their estimated values obtained in the first stage. For example in (6.1), designate Y_1 as the dependent variable, $\hat{Y}_2, X_1$, X_2 as the independent variables, then through least squares regression, the estimators $\hat{\hat{\beta}}_{10}, \hat{\hat{\beta}}_{12}, \hat{\hat{\gamma}}_{11}$ of regression coefficients are obtained. The same method is used for (6.2), by designating Y_2 as the dependent variable, $\hat{Y}_1, X_1, X_2$ are independent variables, we obtain regression coefficients $\hat{\hat{\beta}}_{20}, \hat{\hat{\beta}}_{21}, \hat{\hat{\gamma}}_{22}$. It can be proved that the estimators of parameters of the second stage will have consistency, namely when the sample size tends to infinity, the estimators will converge to their true values.

The **three-stage least squares estimator** is based on the two-stage least squares estimator. The error variance covariance matrix $\hat{\Phi}$ may not be $\sigma^2 I_n$. Then we have to apply the generalized least squares method

$$\hat{\hat{\beta}} = (X'\hat{\Phi}^{-1}X)^{-1}X'\hat{\Phi}^{-1}Y$$

to eliminate the influence of the residual variance covariance matrix. It is to be noted that matrix X in the formula above has already contained $\hat{Y}$ on the right of the equation.

We will also consider the **limited information and full information maximum likelihood** estimation. The basic principle behind these methods is similar to that of the two-stage and three-stage least squares. The limited information maximum likelihood is like two stage least squares that takes prior information of the equation that is being estimated, while the full information maximum likelihood uses prior information from the entire system of equations. Two-stage least squares and limited information maximum likelihood are called single equation methods and three-stage least squares and full-information maximum likelihood are called system-wide methods of estimation. It is shown that estimators obtained from both two-stage least squares and limited-information maximum likelihood have the same **asymptotic distributions**, while the estimators obtained from the three-stage least squares and the full-information maximum likelihood have the same asymptotic distributions. More detailed discussion on these methods of estimation and their properties can be found in the Electronic References for Chapter 6, Appendix.

6.1.1 Demand-and-supply model, Keynesian model and Wage-Price model (Phillips curve)

First we consider the classic **demand-and-supply model**.

The commodity price P and the commodity quantity Q are decided by the intersection of the demand-and-supply curves. For simplicity, we assume that the demand-and-supply curves are linear functions with the random terms ε_1 and ε_2, respectively. Then the demand-and-supply function can be written as:

Demand function: $Q^d = \alpha_0 + \alpha_1 P + \varepsilon_1$, $\alpha_1 < 0$,
Supply function: $Q^s = \beta_0 + \beta_1 P + \varepsilon_2$, $\beta_1 > 0$,
Equilibrium condition: $Q^d = Q^s$,

where P is the price, α_0, α_1, β_0, β_1 are the parameters. α_1 is a negative coefficient which denotes that higher the price, smaller is the quantity demanded. β_1 is a positive coefficient which signifies that the higher the price the more products the manufacturer produces.

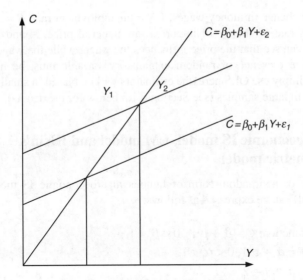

Figure 6.2 Consumption curve shifts while random error term changes.

We can easily find out that P and Q are interdependent variables. For example, ε_1 changes by the effect of other factors (such as income, wealth, and taste), and then the demand curve shifts. These shifts are shown in Figure 6.1.

Figure 6.2 shows that because of the change in ε_1 the demand curve (line D) shifts, which also leads to the change in the price and output Q. Similarly, when ε_2 changes, the supply curve (line S) shifts, and at the same time will affect both P and Q again. Because P, Q, ε_1 and ε_2 are not independent of each other, the basic assumption of the classical least squares method can not be satisfied.

Next, we consider an example from macroeconomics, the simplified Keynesian model:

Consumption function: $C = \beta_0 + \beta_1 Y + \varepsilon,\ 0\ \beta < 1,$

Identity: $Y = C + I (= S),$

where C = consumption expenditure, Y = income, I = investment (assumed as an exogenous variable), S = savings, ε = random error term, β_0 and β_1 are parameters. Parameter β_1 is called marginal propensity to consume (MPC). From economic theory, we have $0 < \beta_1 < 1$, investment I = the savings S and $Y = C + I$ is an identity of national income. Since ε shifts, the consumption curve also shifts as shown in Figure 6.2. When the consumption and investment increase, they affect the income in turn and bring about an increase in income. Because the right-hand side of consumption function has an endogenous (stochastic) variable Y adopting OLS to estimate the consumption function will cause some problems.

Next we look at wage-price model. Consider the following two-equation Phillips model determining money wages and price:

$$\dot{W} = \alpha_0 + \alpha_1 UN + \alpha_2 \dot{P} + \varepsilon_1$$

$$\dot{P} = \beta_0 + \beta_1 \dot{W} + \beta_2 \dot{R} + \beta_3 \dot{M} + \varepsilon_2$$

where $\dot{W}$ = rate of change in money wages, UN = unemployment rate, $\dot{R}$ = rate of change in capital costs, $\dot{M}$ = rate of change of imported raw material price, ε_1 and ε_2 are stochastic disturbances. We can see that the price influences the wage, while the wage also influences the price. Thus the presence of random explanatory variable must be noted in the two equations. If we simply use OLS here, the estimators will be biased in small samples and are inconsistent even in large samples (see Section 6.1.3 below for the details).

6.1.2   Macroeconomic IS model, LM model and Klein's econometric model

The deterministic or nonrandom form of famous macroeconomic IS model (commodity equilibrium model) can be expressed as follows:

Consumption function: $C = \beta_0 + \beta_1 Y_d$, $0 < \beta_1 < 1$,
Tax function: $T = \alpha_0 + \alpha_1 Y$, $0 < \alpha_1 < 1$,
Investment function: $I = \gamma_0 + \gamma_1 r$,
Definition: $Y_d = Y - T$,
Government expenditure: $G = \bar{G}$,
Identity of national income: $Y = C + I + G$,

where Y = national income, C = consumption expenditure, I = planned net investment, $\bar{G}$ = given government expenditure, T = taxes, Y_d = disposable income, r = interest rate. If we make the necessary substitutions from the earlier equations the last formula can be rewritten as the IS equation:

$$Y = \pi_0 + \pi_1 r$$

where

$$\pi_0 = \frac{\beta_0 - \alpha_0 \beta_1 + \gamma_1 + \bar{G}}{1 - \beta_1(1 - \alpha_1)}$$

$$\pi_1 = \frac{1}{1 - \beta_1(1 - \alpha_1)}$$

The IS equation shows the relation between the income and the interest rate (left panel, Figure 6.3).

The other half of the famous IS-LM paradigm is the LM model, or money market equilibrium model. It takes into account the interest rate and income level and constructs a relation between income and interest rate in the money market. The deterministic (nonrandom) form of LM model can be expressed as follows:

Money demand function: $M^d = a + bY - rC$,
Money supply function: $M^s = \bar{M}$,
Equilibrium condition: $M^d = M^s$,

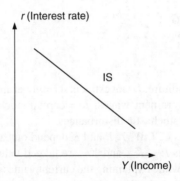

Figure 6.3   IS equation.

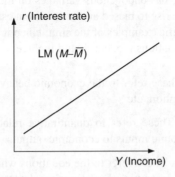

Figure 6.4   LM curve with given $M = \bar{M}$.

where Y = income, r = interest rate, and $\bar{M}$ = assumed money supply, and $\bar{M}$ is usually decided by the government or the central bank. By making the necessary substitutions and bringing Y to the left hand side we get the LM equation:

$$Y = \lambda_0 + \lambda_1 \bar{M} + \lambda_2 r$$

where $\lambda_0 = -\dfrac{a}{b}, \lambda_1 = \dfrac{1}{b}, \lambda_2 = \dfrac{c}{b}$. The LM curve with given $M = \bar{M}$ is shown in Figure 6.4.

The interest rate links the real investment and the money market. Hence the macroeconomic equilibrium between the real and monetary sectors is achieved by the intersection of IS and LM curves. One of the relations is an increasing function, and the other is a decreasing function. Next we focus on Klein's econometric model. The econometricians construct many econometric models of simultaneous equation form. The Klein model was constructed by Lawrence Klein of the University of Pennsylvania:

Consumption function: $C_1 = \beta_0 + \beta_1 P_t - \beta_2 (W + W')_t + \beta_3 P_{t-1} + \varepsilon_{1t}$
Investment function: $I_t = \beta_4 + \beta_5 P_t + \beta_6 P_{t-1} + \beta_7 K_{t-1} + \varepsilon_{2t}$
Demand for labor: $W_t = \beta_8 + \beta_9 (Y + T - W')_t + \beta_{10} (Y + T - W')_{t-1} + \beta_{11} t + \varepsilon_{3t}$

Identity: $Y_t + T_t = C_t + I_t + G_t$

Identity: $Y_t = W'_t + W_t + P_t$

Identity: $K_t = K_{t-1} + I_t$

where C = consumption expenditure, I = investment, G = government expenditure, P = profits, W = private wages, W' = government wages, K = capital stock, T = taxes, Y = disposable income, t = time, ε_1, ε_2, ε_3 are stochastic disturbances.

In this model, the variables C, I, W, Y, P and K depend on each other, and all of them are endogenous variables, whereas P_{t-1}, K_{t-1} and Y_{t-1} are lagged values of endogenous variables, and thus are given and known while explaining the current values of endogenous variables. Six equations in this model (including the three identities) can determine the six endogenous variables assuming that all the six equations are linearly independent. Obviously, each of the first three stochastic equations also has endogenous variables on the right-hand side, hence OLS applied to these equations give rise to biased and inconsistent estimators (see Section 6.1.3).

We have enumerated specific examples of the simultaneous equations models. Generally speaking, the simultaneous equations models should include

(1) *Behavior equations*: These refer to the economic behavior, such as demand, supply, investment or consumption, etc.

(2) *Technical equations*: These refer to quantitative relations, such as technological relations linking economic inputs to economic outputs (production functions).

(3) *Institutional equations*: These refer to the equations which reflect economic statutes and economic system. Institutional relations are determined by an economic institutional mechanism such as the taxation laws etc.

(4) *Identities*: These refer to the equations that must be true based on the definition or a kind of equilibrium condition.

In general, the behavior equations and technical equations contain the error terms. All of these equations express the basic structural relations between economic variables. Hence they are also called **structure equations**.

6.1.3   Inconsistency of OLS estimation

As stated previously, the OLS method may not be suitable to estimate the parameters of a single equation belonging to a system of simultaneous equations. The OLS estimator may be biased in small samples and even in large samples there could be a bias and inconsistency. In other words, when sample size n tends to infinity, the parameter estimates may not converge in probability to the corresponding true value of the parameter.

Let us consider an example to illustrate this. Suppose we want to estimate parameters β_0 and β_1 of the consumption function $C_t = \beta_0 + \beta_1 Y_t + \varepsilon_t$. Assume that $E(\varepsilon_t) = 0$, $E(\varepsilon_t^2) = \sigma^2$, $E(\varepsilon_t \varepsilon_{t-j}) = 0$ (when $j \neq 0$), $Cov(I_t, \varepsilon_t) = 0$.

We show Y_t is correlated with ε_t. Taking the consumption function along with the identity $Y_t = C_t + I_t$, we obtain

$$Y_t = \beta_0 + \beta_1 Y_t + I_t + \varepsilon_t$$

Thereupon

$$Y_t = \frac{\beta_0}{1-\beta_1} + \frac{1}{1-\beta_1}I_t + \frac{1}{1-\beta_1}\varepsilon_t$$

$$E(Y_t) = \frac{\beta_0}{1-\beta_1} + \frac{1}{1-\beta_1}I_t$$

$$Y_t - E(Y_t) = \frac{1}{1-\beta_1}\varepsilon_t$$

$$Cov(Y_t, \varepsilon_t) = E[Y_t - E(Y_t)][\varepsilon_t - E(\varepsilon_t)] = \frac{E(\varepsilon_t^2)}{1-\beta_1} = \frac{\sigma^2}{1-\beta_1} \neq 0$$

Thus we know that Y_t is correlated with ε_t.

Next we show that $\hat{\beta}_1$ is neither an **unbiased estimator** nor a **consistent estimator** of β_1. As

$$\hat{\beta}_1 = \frac{\sum(C_t - \bar{C})(Y_t - \bar{Y})}{\sum(Y_t - \bar{Y})^2} = \frac{\sum C_t y_t}{\sum y_t^2}$$

$$= \frac{\sum(\beta_0 + \beta_1 Y_t + \varepsilon_t)y_t}{\sum y_t^2} = \beta_1 + \frac{\sum y_t \varepsilon_t}{\sum y_t^2}$$

The last step can be obtained because $\sum y_t = \sum(Y_t - \bar{Y}) = 0$ and $\left(\sum Y_t y_t\right)\big/\sum y_t^2 = 1$, where $y_t = Y_t - \bar{Y}$.

Taking expectation on both sides, we obtain

$$E(\hat{\beta}_1) = \beta_1 + E\left(\frac{\sum y_t \varepsilon_t}{\sum y_t^2}\right)$$

We know that $\hat{\beta}_1$ cannot be the unbiased estimator of β_1 as $E\left(\sum y_t \varepsilon_t\right) = E[Y_t - E(Y_t)][\varepsilon_t - E(\varepsilon_t)] = \dfrac{\sigma^2}{1-\beta_1}$, as already demonstrated.

We now take the probability limits on both sides of $\hat{\beta}_1$, and obtain

$$p\lim_{n\to\infty}\hat{\beta}_1 = \beta_1 + p\lim_{n\to\infty}\frac{\sum y_t \varepsilon_t/n}{\sum y_t^2/n} = \beta_1 + \frac{p\lim_{n\to\infty}\sum y_t \varepsilon_t/n}{p\lim_{n\to\infty}\sum y_t^2/n}$$

$$= \beta_1 + \frac{E(y_t \varepsilon_t)}{Ey_t^2} = \beta_1 + \frac{\sigma^2/(1-\beta_1)}{\sigma_y^2} \neq \beta_1$$

which indicates $\hat{\beta}_1$ is not a consistent estimator of β_1.

6.2   Statistical inference for simultaneous equations models

In the preceding sections we presented a few specific examples of simultaneous equations models, showed what kind of statistical inference problems they pose, and demonstrated the importance of *a priori* parametric restrictions on distinguishing one equation of the model from others (identification), etc. It may be pointed out here that there are three different types of situations regarding identifiability. There may be just sufficient prior restrictions on the parameters to identify an equation (just-identified case), or there can be more *a priori* information than what is just sufficient to identify the equation (over-identified case) or there could be insufficient information to identify an equation (the under-identified case). Now we proceed to give statistical methods to solve the statistical inference problem in these three types of identification.

These methods contain **indirect least squares** (ILS), **generalized least squares** (GLS), two-stage least squares (2SLS), three-stage least squares (3SLS), limited information maximum likelihood estimation (LIML), full information maximum likelihood estimation (FIML), etc. The basic objective of all these methods is to obtain consistent estimators of the unknown parameters, thus overcoming the problem posed by the OLS estimators in the context of a system of simultaneous equations.

6.2.1   Indirect least squares and generalized least squares

Let us specify the structural equation system in very general terms. Let the equation system be represented by a set of M structural equations represented by:

$$Y\Gamma + XB + \varepsilon = 0$$

where Y and ε are M dimensional vectors and Γ is a $M \times M$ matrix, B is a $M \times K$ matrix, M being the number of endogenous variables in the system while K being the number of exogenous variables in the system.

We can write a reduced form of the equation system, assuming that Γ is non-singular, as:

$$Y = -\Gamma^{-1}BX - \Gamma^{-1}\varepsilon = \Pi X + \upsilon$$

At the outset we note two important aspects of this equation system. First, there are as many independent equations as there are endogenous variables and thus we can associate one equation with each endogenous variable. Now we proceed to discuss the prior information on the parameters.

Normally one would specify an equation to explain each endogenous variable. We can therefore normalize the equations so that each equation has a coefficient −1 associated with one endogenous variable. This is termed the normalization condition. Second, not all exogenous variables appear in all the equations, and not all endogenous variables appear in all equations. Hence we use the notation m_i for the number of endogenous variables that enter into the ith equation and m_i^* for the number of endogenous variables that are absent from equation i. Similarly we define k_i and k_i^* as the number of exogenous variables that are present and absent from the ith equation.

According to the relationship of these numbers we can say if the equations are just-identified, over-identified or under-identified. This process is called model identification and its detailed discussion can be found in the Electronic References for Chapter 6. We can, however, provide an intuitive meaning as follows. If we can derive the structural parameters of a structural equation from the reduced form parameters in just one way or uniquely then that structural equation is just-identified. If there is more than one way we can derive the structural parameter from the reduced form parameters then we say that the structural equation is over-identified. If we cannot derive the structural parameters of the equation from the reduced form parameters then we say that that structural equation is not identified.

Assume the ith equation of the model is

$$Y\Gamma_i + XB_i + \varepsilon_i = 0, \quad i = 1, \ldots, M$$

If we eliminate those variables whose coefficients are zero and make clear whose normalization coefficient is -1, then the equation can be written as

$$\begin{aligned}
y_i &= Y_i\gamma_i + Y_i^*\gamma_i^* + X_i\beta_i + X_i^*\beta_i^* + \varepsilon_i \\
&= Y_i\gamma_i + X_i\beta_i + \varepsilon_i \\
&= (Y_i, X_i)\begin{pmatrix} \gamma_i \\ \beta_i \end{pmatrix} + \varepsilon_i = Z_i\delta_i + \varepsilon_i
\end{aligned} \tag{6.3}$$

where

$$\Gamma_i = \begin{pmatrix} -1 \\ \gamma_i \\ \gamma_i^* \end{pmatrix} = \begin{pmatrix} -1 \\ \gamma_i \\ 0 \end{pmatrix}, \quad B_i = \begin{pmatrix} \beta_i \\ \beta_i^* \end{pmatrix} = \begin{pmatrix} \beta_i \\ 0 \end{pmatrix}$$

$$Y = (y_i, Y_i, Y_i^*), \quad X = (X_i, X_i^*)$$

$$M = m_i + m_i^*, \quad K = k_i + k_i^*$$

Y_i^* denotes those endogenous variables whose coefficients are zero (or say they do not appear) in the ith equation. There are m_i^* endogenous variables that do not appear in equation i. X_i^* denotes those exogenous variables whose coefficients are zero (or say they do not appear) in the ith equation. While Y_i, X_i are those variables which appear in the ith equation. y_i is the variable whose normalization coefficient is -1, which is a $T \times 1$ vector. Y_i is a $T \times (m_i - 1)$ matrix, γ_i is a $(m_i - 1) \times 1$ vector, X_i is a $T \times k_i$ matrix, β_i is a $k_i \times 1$ vector, ε_i is a $T \times 1$ vector, $Z_i = (Y_i, X_i)$, whereas

$$\delta_i = \begin{pmatrix} \gamma_i \\ \beta_i \end{pmatrix} \tag{6.4}$$

The relation between structural form and the reduced form of the ith equation is $\Pi\Gamma_i = -B_i$, that is

$$\Pi\begin{pmatrix} -1 \\ \gamma_i \\ 0 \end{pmatrix} = \begin{pmatrix} -\beta_i \\ 0 \end{pmatrix}$$

where Γ_i and B_i are the ith column of Γ and B, respectively. The reduced form parameters can be estimated by OLS as the right-hand side of the reduced form equations consist only of exogenous variables and are uncorrelated with the error terms.

$$\hat{\Pi} = (X'X)^{-1}X'Y$$

We may substitute this estimator for the reduced form parameters in the above equation to get the following:

$$(X'X)^{-1}X'(y_i, Y_i, Y_i^*)\begin{pmatrix} -1 \\ \hat{\gamma}_i \\ 0 \end{pmatrix} = \begin{pmatrix} -\hat{\beta}_i \\ 0 \end{pmatrix}$$

where $\hat{\gamma}_i$ and $\hat{\beta}_i$ are the estimators of structural parameters associated with variables Y_i and X_i. Pre-multiplied the formula above by $(X'X)$,

$$-X'y_i + X'Y_i\hat{\gamma}_i = -X'X\begin{pmatrix} \hat{\beta}_i \\ 0 \end{pmatrix}$$

Rearranging this equation, we obtain

$$X'y_i = X'Y_i\hat{\gamma}_i + X'X\begin{pmatrix} \hat{\beta}_i \\ 0 \end{pmatrix} = X'Y_i\hat{\gamma}_i + X'X_i\hat{\beta}_i$$

$$= X'(Y_i, X_i)\begin{pmatrix} \hat{\gamma}_i \\ \hat{\beta}_i \end{pmatrix} = X'Z_i\hat{\delta}_i$$

Notice that X' is a $K \times T$ matrix, Z_i is a $T \times (m_i - 1 + k_i)$ matrix, and

$$\hat{\delta}_i = \begin{pmatrix} \hat{\gamma}_i \\ \hat{\beta}_i \end{pmatrix}$$

where $\hat{\delta}_i = \begin{pmatrix} \hat{\gamma}_i \\ \hat{\beta}_i \end{pmatrix}$ is a $(m_i - 1 + k_i) \times 1$ vector; therefore $X'Z_i$ is a $K \times (m_i - 1 + k_i)$ matrix.

The **indirect least squares method** of estimation is that method which takes the reduced form estimators and derives the estimators of the structural parameters. This can be done uniquely only if the equation is just identified.

If the ith equation is just identified, then we require

$$K = k_i + k_i^* = m_i - 1 + k_i \text{ or } k_i^* = m_i - 1$$

In this just-identified case $X'Z_i$ becomes a square matrix and the indirect least squares estimator is

$$\hat{\delta}_{i(ILS)} = (X'Z_i)^{-1}X'y_i$$

While indirect least squares is used for just-identified case, generalized least squares is used for the over-identified case. The generalized least squares and indirect least squares can be derived from the following two equations in the structural parameters: $X'y_i = X'Z_i\hat{\delta}_i$

$$y_i = Z_i\delta_i + \varepsilon_i$$

If we left multiply the second equation by $\dfrac{1}{T}X'$, replace δ_i by $\hat{\delta}_i$, replace $\dfrac{1}{T}X'\varepsilon_i$ by its probability limit 0, then cancel out T^{-1}, the former equation can be obtained. Accordingly for the equation that is just identified, $\hat{\delta}_i$ is also the **instrumental variables estimator** (see Electronic References for Chapter 6, Section 6-3-2). In this case, the instrumental variable set is the entire set of independent variables X.

We note that when indirect least squares method is used for estimating the parameters of an '**over identified**' equation we use less prior information than what is available to arrive at matrix of reduced dimensions that can be inverted. As only parts of prior information are used for estimating the structural parameters, the indirect least squares estimators are therefore generally not efficient in the over-identified case. We need alternate methods of parameter estimation that utilizes all the information efficiently.

For over-identified equation, in order to obtain a unique estimator of the unknown parameter, K of the X instrumental variables need to be transformed into $m_i - 1 + k_i$ variables. If the error vector $X'\varepsilon_i$ is retained, then it will lead to the following generalized least squares method.

We further consider the ith equation

$$y_i = Y_i\gamma_i + X_i\beta_i + \varepsilon_i = Z_i\delta_i + \varepsilon_i$$

and the statistical model transformed from it is

$$X'y_i = X'Y_i\gamma_i + X'X_i\beta_i + X'\varepsilon_i = X'Z_i\delta_i + X'\varepsilon_i$$

Where X is a $T \times K$ exogenous variable as well as an observation matrix of lagged endogenous variable, $Z_i = (Y_i, X_i)$.

In order to use the generalized least squares method, we need to calculate

$$Var(X'\varepsilon_i) = E(X'\varepsilon_i\varepsilon_i'X) = \sigma_{ii}E(X'X)$$

This matrix is unknown, but our main interest lies in the asymptotic property of the estimator. So we can substitute its limit. We assume $p\lim \dfrac{1}{T}X'X = \lim E\left(\dfrac{1}{T}X'X\right)$.

Under the condition that $\sigma_{ii}X'X$ is given, we can use the generalized least squares method on equation $y_i = Z_i\delta_i + \varepsilon_i$,

$$\tilde{\delta}_i = [(X'Z_i)'(\sigma_{ii}X'X)^{-1}(X'Z_i)]^{-1}(X'Z_i)'(\sigma_{ii}X'X)^{-1}X'y_i$$
$$= [(Z_i'X(X'X)^{-1}X'Z_i]^{-1}Z_i'X(X'X)^{-1}X'y_i$$

where the inverse of matrix $Z_i'X(X'X)^{-1}X'Z_i$ is assumed to exist. The dimension of this matrix is $m_i - 1 + k_i$. If its inverse exists, because $rk(Z_i'X) \le \min\{rkZ_i, rkX\}$, then K, the rank of X, must be equal to or greater than $m_i - 1 + k_i$, the rank of Z_i, Thereby we have $m_i - 1 + k_i \le K$, namely

$$m_i - 1 \le k_i^*$$

where k_i^* is the number of exogenous variables which do not appear in the ith equation. This inequality is a necessary condition to identify the ith equation of the simultaneous equations. Accordingly, in order to estimate $\tilde{\delta}_i$ the structural equation must be just identified or over identified. When it is over identified, the condition is $m_i - 1 < k_i^*$.

If the structure formula is just identified, $X'Z_i$ is a K-order square matrix. Then the generalized least squares estimator $\tilde{\delta}_i$ becomes the indirect least squares estimator,

$$\tilde{\delta}_i = [Z_i'X(X'X)^{-1}X'Z_i]^{-1}Z_i'X(X'X)^{-1}X'y_i$$
$$= (X'Z_i)^{-1}(X'X)(Z_i'X)^{-1}Z_i'X(X'X)^{-1}X'y_i$$
$$= (X'Z_i)^{-1}X'y_i = \hat{\delta}_i$$

where the generalized least squares estimator can be regarded as the instrumental variables estimator, which is $X(X'X)^{-1}X'Z_i$, a $T \times (m_i - 1 + k_i)$ matrix.

The asymptotic properties of the generalized least squares estimator may be found in the Electronic References for Chapter 6.

Example 6.1   Indirect least squares   The structural equations of the simultaneous equations are represented by $Y\Gamma + XB + E = 0$. When Γ is nonsingular, it can be reduced as a simplified formula $Y = X\Pi + V$. The reduced form parameters Π are related to the structural parameters through the equation:

$$\Pi\Gamma = -B, V\Gamma = -E$$

The data in this example require the first M columns as dependent variables (Y) and the next K columns as independent variables. The reader should note that in the structural equations each equation has a Y with -1 as its coefficient, and there are a few independent variables with 0 as their coefficients in each equation.

In the data file of Example 6.1, $N = 171$, $M = 3$, $K = 7$, and the original data are **Consumer Price Index (CPI)** of China with nine other variables. The observations are from January 1995 to March 2009. We select three indexes as dependent variables (CPI, broad money supply, and value added by Industrial production). Other indexes are independent variables (Loans, Total retail sales of social consumer goods, Exchange rate, Residents' deposits, Food price index, Shanghai composite index, corporate goods price index). All indexes are the rates for the same period of two years. The data can be found in Table 6-2-1-1 in the Electronic References for Chapter 6 or in DASC. We assume the number of equations is the same as the number of dependent variables:

$$Y_1 = 0Y_1 + \beta_{12}Y_2 + \beta_{13}Y_3 + \gamma_{11}X_1 + \gamma_{12}X_2 + \gamma_{13}X_3 + \gamma_{14}X_4 + \gamma_{15}X_5 + \gamma_{16}X_6 + \gamma_{17}X_7$$
$$Y_2 = \beta_{21}Y_1 + 0Y_2 + 0Y_3 + \gamma_{21}X_1 + \gamma_{22}X_2 + \gamma_{23}X_3 + \gamma_{24}X_4 + 0X_5 + 0X_6 + 0X_7$$
$$Y_3 = \beta_{31}Y_1 + \beta_{32}Y_2 + 0Y_3 + \gamma_{31}X_1 + 0X_2 + \gamma_{33}X_3 + \gamma_{34}X_4 + 0X_5 + 0X_6 + \gamma_{37}X_7$$

So we write a record matrix for above equations as follows.

1	7	2	3	4	5	6	7	8	9	10	0
2	5	1	4	5	6	7	0	0	0	0	0
3	6	1	2	4	6	7	10	0	0	0	0

In each row of this record matrix, the first number is the column number of dependent variable in original data, and the second number is the number of all variables present in this equation. The numbers from third to the end are the order numbers of variables that appeared in this equation in original data. The record matrix is under the original data in the file Hui831.txt.

We can click DASC→Regression→Simultaneous/Lagging Regress→Indirect Least Squares model to perform the computation process. There are six curves, including three curves of original data and three curves of fitting data, because there are three dependent variables. Figure 6.5 is the figure of CPI of China, in which dot line is the raw data, and real line is the fitting of data. We may feel that fitting is not very good. Since forecasting of CPI is very important for economic policy, we must ask how we can improve the model. We will discuss this problem in Chapter 8 (Section 8.5) where readers can see a much more accurate fitting and forecasting by improving the model that takes note of the time series nature of data.

Of course, the user can load or input his or her own data in DASC from any folder with any data form (text, Excel, SQL, and other database form) to calculate this model or other models.

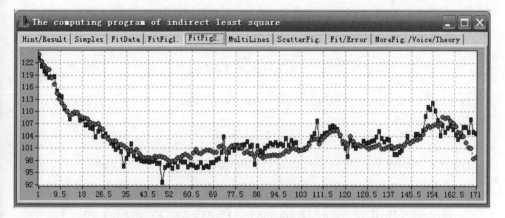

Figure 6.5   Indirect least squares for CPI of China.

6.2.2   Two stage least squares

The generalized least squares estimator $\tilde{\delta}$ can be expressed in many forms and each has their own explanation. The important one is **two-stage least squares (2SLS)** method. In order to derive 2SLS, $\tilde{\delta}_i$ can be rewritten as

$$
\begin{aligned}
\tilde{\delta}_i &= (Z_i' X(X'X)^{-1} X'Z_i)^{-1} Z_i' X(X'X)^{-1} X' y_i \\
&= \left((Y_i X_i)' X(X'X)^{-1} X'(Y_i X_i)\right)^{-1} (Y_i X_i)' X(X'X)^{-1} X' y_i \\
&= \begin{pmatrix} Y_i' X(X'X)^{-1} X'Y_i & Y_i' X(X'X)^{-1} X'X_i \\ X_i' X(X'X)^{-1} X'Y_i & X_i' X(X'X)^{-1} X'X_i \end{pmatrix}^{-1} \begin{pmatrix} Y_i' X(X'X)^{-1} X' y_i \\ X_i' X(X'X)^{-1} X' y_i \end{pmatrix}
\end{aligned}
$$

We have already shown that from the structural equations $Y\Gamma + XB + E = 0$ we can be derive the reduced form

$$
Y = X\Pi + V
$$

Taking the ith equation, we obtain

$$
(y_i, Y_i, Y_i^*) = X(\pi_i, \Pi_i, \Pi_i^*) + (v_i, V_i, V_i^*)
$$

where y_i is the $T \times 1$ vector of ith dependent variable, Y_i denotes the variables which appear in the ith equation. Y_i^* is a $T \times m_i^*$ matrix, which specifically refers to those variables which do not appear in the ith equation. (π_i, Π_i, Π_i^*) are the corresponding coefficients in the simplified formula. The least squares estimator of Π_i is $\hat{\Pi}_i = (X'X)^{-1} X' Y_i)$, thereby

$$
X(X'X)^{-1} X'Y_i = X\hat{\Pi}_i = \hat{Y}_i = Y_i - \hat{V}_i
$$

where $\hat{Y}_i$ is a $T \times (m_i - 1)$ matrix. With $(X'X)^{-1}X'X = I$, the preceding complicated formula of $\tilde{\delta}_i$ can be simplified as

$$
\tilde{\delta}_i = \begin{pmatrix} \hat{Y}_i' \hat{Y} & \hat{Y}_i X_i \\ X_i' \hat{Y}_i & X_i X_i \end{pmatrix}^{-1} \begin{pmatrix} \hat{Y}_i' & y_i \\ X_i' & y_i \end{pmatrix}
$$

So if we denote $\hat{Z}_i = (\hat{Y}_i, X_i)$, then the two-stage least squares estimator of δ_i (for the definition of δ_i the reader can refer to (6.4)) can be written as

$$\tilde{\delta}_i = (\hat{Z}_i'\hat{Z}_i)^{-1}\hat{Z}_i y_i$$

This estimator can also be obtained from the ordinary least squares method of the regression equation

$$y_i = (\hat{Y}_i, X_i)\delta_i + \bar{\varepsilon}_i \tag{6.5}$$

The principles of two-stage least squares estimators are summarized as follows:

(1) Use LSE for the statistical model $Y_i = X\Pi_i - V_i$, adopt $\hat{\Pi}_i = (X'X)^{-1}X'Y_i$ to estimate parameter Π_i of the reduced form and use $\hat{Y}_i = X\hat{\Pi}_i = (X'X)^{-1}X'Y_i$ to predict $\hat{Y}_i$.

(2) Use LSE to estimate structural parameter δ^* in the statistical model $y_i = (\hat{Y}_i, X_i)\,\delta_i + \bar{\varepsilon}_i$.

Repeating the steps above for each structural equation, the estimators of all structural parameters can be obtained.

Example 6.2   Two stage least squares   We give a specific numerical example to demonstrate two stage least squares. Assume there are structural equations as follows:

$$\begin{aligned}
Y_1 &= Y_2\gamma_{21} + Y_3\gamma_{31} + X_1\beta_{11} + \varepsilon_1 \\
Y_2 &= Y_1\gamma_{12} + X_1\beta_{12} + X_2\beta_{22} + X_3\beta_{32} + X_4\beta_{42} + \varepsilon_2 \\
Y_3 &= Y_2\gamma_{23} + X_1\beta_{13} + X_2\beta_{23} + X_5\beta_{53} + \varepsilon_3
\end{aligned} \tag{6.6}$$

They can be arranged in orderly columns as

$$\begin{aligned}
-Y_1 + Y_2\gamma_{21} + Y_3\gamma_{31} + X_1\beta_{11} && +\varepsilon_1 = 0 \\
Y_1\gamma_{12} - Y_2 \qquad + X_1\beta_{12} + X_2\beta_{22} + X_3\beta_{32} + X_4\beta_{42} && +\varepsilon_1 = 0 \\
Y_2\gamma_{23} - Y_3 \; + X_1\beta_{13} + X_2\beta_{23} && + X_5\beta_{53} + \varepsilon_3 = 0
\end{aligned}$$

Denote them in the form of matrix,

$$Y\Gamma + XB + E = 0 \tag{6.7}$$

Among them Y and X have T observations respectively,

$$\begin{pmatrix} Y_{11} & Y_{12} & Y_{13} \\ \cdots & & \\ Y_{T1} & Y_{T2} & Y_{T3} \end{pmatrix} \begin{pmatrix} -1 & \gamma_{12} & 0 \\ \gamma_{21} & -1 & \gamma_{23} \\ \gamma_{31} & 0 & -1 \end{pmatrix} + \begin{pmatrix} X_{11} & X_{12} & X_{13} & X_{14} & X_{15} \\ \cdots & & & & \\ X_{T1} & X_{T2} & X_{T3} & X_{T4} & X_{T5} \end{pmatrix} \begin{pmatrix} \beta_{11} & \beta_{12} & \beta_{13} \\ 0 & \beta_{22} & \beta_{23} \\ 0 & \beta_{32} & 0 \\ 0 & \beta_{42} & 0 \\ 0 & 0 & \beta_{53} \end{pmatrix}$$

$$+ \begin{pmatrix} \varepsilon_{11} & \varepsilon_{12} & \varepsilon_{13} \\ \cdots & & \\ \varepsilon_{T1} & \varepsilon_{T2} & \varepsilon_{T3} \end{pmatrix} = \begin{pmatrix} 0 & 0 & 0 \\ \cdots & & \\ 0 & 0 & 0 \end{pmatrix}$$

Observations can be found in the following table, the data are derived from the reference, Judge et al. (1982).

These observations do not arise out of actual real life data, but are generated by the Monte Carlo method. The Monte Carlo simulations are generated by choosing the following 'true' parameters.

$$\Gamma = \begin{pmatrix} -1 & 0.2 & 0 \\ -10 & -1 & 2 \\ 2.5 & 0 & -1 \end{pmatrix}, B = \begin{pmatrix} -60 & 40 & -10 \\ 0 & -4 & 80 \\ 0 & -6 & 0 \\ 0 & 1.5 & 0 \\ 0 & 0 & 5 \end{pmatrix}$$

Error term ε_i follows a normal distribution with $E(\varepsilon_i) = 0$ and

$$E \begin{pmatrix} \varepsilon_1^2 & \varepsilon_1\varepsilon_2 & \varepsilon_1\varepsilon_3 \\ \varepsilon_{21} & \varepsilon_2^2 & \varepsilon_2\varepsilon_3 \\ \varepsilon_3\varepsilon_1 & \varepsilon_3\varepsilon_2 & \varepsilon_3^2 \end{pmatrix} = \Sigma \otimes I_T$$

$$\Sigma = \begin{pmatrix} 27.55 & 3.91 & -0.89 \\ 3.91 & 0.66 & -1.88 \\ -0.89 & -1.88 & 15.76 \end{pmatrix}$$

For given Γ and B as above we have

$$\Pi = -B\Gamma^{-1} = \begin{pmatrix} -142.50 & 11.50 & 13.00 \\ 110.00 & 18.00 & 116.00 \\ 15.00 & -3.00 & -6.00 \\ -3.75 & 0.75 & 1.50 \\ 6.25 & 1.25 & 7.50 \end{pmatrix}$$

Of course, the elements of Γ, B, Σ, Π listed above are known, but we assume them to be unknown for illustrating the method of estimating the structural parameters. Only X and Y in Table 6.1 are used in the estimation process. The task of first stage is to estimate Π, which is easy. Assume Γ^{-1} exists. From the model (6.7), the simplified formula is

$$Y = -XB\Gamma^{-1} - E\Gamma^{-1} = X\Pi + V$$

namely,

$$(Y_1, Y_2, Y_3) = (X_1, X_2, X_3, X_4, X_5) \begin{pmatrix} \Pi_{11} & \Pi_{12} & \Pi_{13} \\ \cdots & \cdots & \cdots \\ \Pi_{51} & \Pi_{52} & \Pi_{53} \end{pmatrix} + (V_1 + V_2 + V_3)$$

or

$$(Y_1, Y_2, Y_3) = X(\Pi_1, \Pi_2, \Pi_3) + (V_1, V_2, V_3)$$

This is a kind of linear regression model with multiple dependent variables, and the model can be written separately as

$$Y_i = X\Pi_i + V_i, \quad i = 1, 2, 3 \tag{6.8}$$

Table 6.1   The data come from Judge et al. (1982).

Y_1	Y_2	Y_3	X_1	X_2	X_3	X_4	X_5
359.27	102.96	678.49	1.	3.06	1.34	8.48	28.
415.76	114.38	650.86	1.	3.19	1.44	9.19	35.
435.11	118.23	684.87	1.	3.30	1.54	9.9	37.
440.17	120.45	680.47	1.	3.40	1.71	11.02	36.
410.66	116.25	642.19	1.	3.48	1.89	11.64	29.
530.33	140.27	787.41	1.	3.60	1.99	12.73	47.
557.15	143.84	818.06	1.	3.68	2.22	13.80	50.
472.80	128.20	712.16	1.	3.72	2.43	14.50	35.
471.76	126.65	722.23	1.	3.92	2.43	15.47	33.
538.30	141.05	811.44	1.	4.15	2.31	16.61	40.
547.76	143.71	816.36	1.	4.35	2.39	17.40	38.
539.	142.37	807.78	1.	4.37	2.63	18.83	37.
677.60	173.13	983.53	1.	4.59	2.69	20.62	56.
943.85	223.21	1292.99	1.	5.23	3.35	23.76	88.
893.42	198.64	1179.64	1.	6.04	5.81	26.52	62.
871.	191.89	1134.78	1.	6.36	6.38	27.45	51.
793.93	181.27	1053.16	1.	7.04	6.14	30.28	29.
850.36	180.56	1085.91	1.	7.81	6.14	25.40	22.
967.42	208.24	1246.99	1.	8.09	6.19	28.84	38.
1102.61	235.43	1404.94	1.	9.24	6.69	34.36	41.

which is a linear regression model with a single dependent variable. Immediately we can use OLS to estimate regression coefficient Π_i and variance σ_i^2 ($E(V_i) = \sigma_i^2 I_T$),

$$\hat{\Pi}_i = (X'X)^{-1} X'Y_i$$

$$\hat{\sigma}_i^2 = (Y_i - X\hat{\Pi}_i)'(Y_i - X\hat{\Pi}_i)/(T-3)$$

Thus, the estimation task of the first stage is completed.

For the second stage, we return to the original model (6.6), and in each equation we replace Y_i by $\hat{Y}$, $\hat{Y}$ using

$$\hat{Y}_i = X\hat{\Pi}_i$$

to replace Y_i on the right hand side only (not the left) of the equation. Then we can carry out the parameter estimation using OLS. Taking the first equation for example, there is

$$Y_1 = \hat{Y}_2 \gamma_{21} + \hat{Y}_3 \gamma_{31} + X_1 \beta_{11} + \varepsilon_1$$

where $Y_1, \hat{Y}_2, \hat{Y}_3, X_1$ are all known $T \times 1$ vectors. OLS can be used to estimate $\gamma_{21}, \gamma_{31}, \beta_{11}$.

For the second equation, there is

$$Y_2 = \hat{Y}_1 \gamma_{12} + X_1 \beta_{12} + X_2 \beta_{22} + X_3 \beta_{32} + X_4 \beta_{42} + \varepsilon_2$$

where Y_2, $\hat{Y}_1$, X_1, X_2, X_3, X_4 are all known $T \times 1$ vectors. OLS can be used to estimate γ_{12}, β_{12}, β_{22}, β_{32} and β_{42}.

For the third equation, there is

$$Y_3 = \hat{Y}_2 \gamma_{23} + X_1 \beta_{13} + X_2 \beta_{23} + X_5 \beta_{53} + \varepsilon_3$$

thereby γ_{23}, β_{13}, β_{23}, β_{53} can be also estimated.

Those readers who have not read the preceding complicated theoretical analysis, will say that there is no need to perform the first stage regressions and each coefficient of the original set of structural equations can be estimated taking original data and using OLS. Yes, but that is called the direct LS method and it would lead to biased and inconsistent estimates for the structural parameters, as there is mutual dependence between the endogenous variables, which in turn gives rise to correlation between endogenous explanatory variables, and the error term.

We present both the two-stage least squares estimates as well as the direct least squares estimates to show that there is a difference.

The readers who read the preceding theoretical analysis will perhaps be bewildered as to why such a simple two-stage least squares result is expressed by statisticians in a style that is so difficult to understand. The statisticians can use mathematics to express quite complicated things easily, but they also express sometimes what seem to be intuitively simple things in very complicated forms using mathematics![1]

The following are estimators of parameters obtained by OLS directly. We write them in the form of matrix:

$$\hat{\Gamma}_{(OLS)} = \begin{pmatrix} -1 & 0.20 & 0 \\ -6.03 & -1 & 1.38 \\ 1.87 & 0 & -1 \end{pmatrix}$$

$$\hat{B}_{(OLS)} = \begin{pmatrix} -107.27 & 39.53 & -1.34 \\ 0 & -3.87 & 90.97 \\ 0 & -6.07 & 0 \\ 0 & 1.64 & 0 \\ 0 & 0 & 5.80 \end{pmatrix}$$

The estimators obtained from two-stage least squares method are as follows:

$$\hat{\Pi} = \begin{pmatrix} -137.84 & 12.54 & 10.67 \\ 108.54 & 17.41 & 117.77 \\ 14.05 & -3.32 & -7.91 \\ -3.21 & 1.01 & 1.56 \\ 6.17 & 1.21 & 7.47 \end{pmatrix}$$

---

[1] When one of the authors was teaching econometrics a German student in the class was sneezing continuously for a few minutes. When the author made a remark that perhaps he was allergic to the pollen in the tropical city, immediately came his response: 'No Sir, it is not the pollen I am allergic to, it is instead the mathematics you use in econometrics'.

$$\hat{\Gamma}_{(2SLS)} = \begin{pmatrix} -1 & 0.1959 & 0 \\ -9.4047 & -1 & 1.9383 \\ 2.4090 & 0 & -1 \end{pmatrix}$$

$$\hat{B}_{(2SLS)} = \begin{pmatrix} -65.9709 & 39.5511 & -8.7672 \\ 0 & -.8587 & 80.9009 \\ 0 & -6.0693 & 0 \\ 0 & 1.6445 & 0 \\ 0 & 0 & 5.0718 \end{pmatrix}$$

From these results we note that there are some differences between the results of two-stage least squares and ordinary least squares, and the former are closer to original parameters.

Another task for two-stage least squares method is to estimate variance. From the Electronic References for Chapter 6 (6-2-1) $\hat{\sigma}_{ij} = \frac{1}{\tau}(y_i - Z_i\tilde{\delta}_i)'(y_j - Z_j\tilde{\delta}_j)$, we obtain

$$\hat{\sigma}_{ij}^2 = (Y_i - \hat{\hat{Y}}_i)'(Y_j - \hat{\hat{Y}}_j)/\tau$$
$$= (Y_i - Z_i\tilde{\delta}_i)'(Y_j - Z_j\tilde{\delta}_j)/\tau, \quad i, j = 1, \dots, M$$
$$\tau = T - p/M$$

where T is sample size, p is the number of parameters to be estimated. In this example $T = 20$, $p = 12$, $M = 3$. $\hat{\hat{Y}}_i$ is the value calculated by using $\hat{Y}_i$ to replace Y_i on the right and substituting estimated parameters of the two-stage least squares into the original model (6.8). Namely, in this example we find out that

$$\hat{\Sigma} = (\hat{\sigma}_{ij}^2) = \begin{pmatrix} 8.3383 & 2.6128 & 0.0116 \\ 2.6128 & 1.6280 & -0.1211 \\ 0.0116 & -0.1211 & 11.0558 \end{pmatrix}$$

Thus the task of two-stage least squares estimation is completed.

Based on the estimation of Γ and B, we can obtain a series of equations, and accordingly we can make forecasts. In this example by the 2SLS method, we obtain:

$$Y_1 = -65.97X_1 - 9.40Y_2 + 2.41Y_3 + \varepsilon_1$$
$$Y_2 = 39.55X_1 + 0.20Y_1 - 3.86X_2 - 6.07X_3 + 1.64X_4 + \varepsilon_2$$
$$Y_3 = -8.77X_1 + 1.94Y_2 + 80.90X_2 + 5.07X_5 + \varepsilon_3$$

But from the aspect of forecast, perhaps it is more convenient to use the reduced form

$$Y_1 = -142.33X_1 + 110.57X_2 + 14.91X_3 - 4.04X_4 + 6.34X_5 + \varepsilon_1^*$$
$$Y_2 = 11.66X_1 + 17.81X_2 - 3.15X_3 + 0.85X_4 + 1.24X_5 + \varepsilon_2^*$$
$$Y_3 = 13.84X_1 + 115.41X_2 - 6.10X_3 + 1.65X_4 + 7.48X_5 + \varepsilon_3^*$$

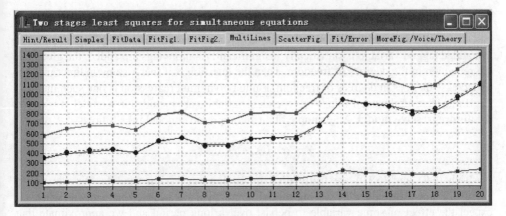

Figure 6.6   Two stage least squares for simultaneous equations.

The process of the calculation is as follows. We need to emphasize the determination of nonzero coefficients in structural equations and the necessary to input matrix Γ (it is C in the program), B (it is still B in the program). In terms of this example,

$$C(2, 1) = 1; C(3, 1) = 1; C(1, 2) = 1; C(3, 2) = 1; C(1, 3) = 0; C(2, 3) = 1$$

but $C(1, 1) = C(2, 2) = C(3, 3) = -1$ is evaluated automatically by the program. Following the example above readers can input the coefficients of these equations correctly.

The computation process can be shown by clicking DASC→Regression→Simultaneous/Lagging Regress→Two Stage Least Squares (Figure 6.6).

In principle the three-stage least squares adds one more stage to the two-stage least squares. After obtaining the two-stage least squares estimates the variance covariance matrix is estimated of the errors and then a generalized least squares estimator is obtained. The method of three-stage least squares is omitted here. Three stage least squares is, however, asymptotically equivalent to the Full-Information Maximum Likelihood (FIML) method. If the reader is interested in obtaining more efficient system-wide estimators he or she can use the FIML estimation technique that is available in DASC program. Go to DASC→Regression→Simultaneous/Lagging Regression→Limited Information and Full Information MLE.

6.3   The concepts of lag regression models

Regression models often use time series data. If both current values and past values of variable X are included in a regression model, we call this model a **distributed lag model** such as

$$Y_t = \alpha_0 + \beta_0 X_t + \beta_1 X_{t-1} + \beta_2 X_{t-2} + \cdots + \beta_N X_{t-N} + \varepsilon_t \tag{6.9}$$

If **lag length** N is known, we can seek the solution directly. However, we note that the first N observations are lost in order to set the initial conditions. The effective sample size for estimation is therefore $n - N$. In other words, the number of degrees of freedom of this model is reduced by N, the maximum lag length used in the model. If lag length N is unknown, we can start with minimum lag length of 1, and keep on adding additional lag lengths until the last added lagged variable is statistically insignificant. As more lags are added, the greater is the reduction in the degrees of freedom. Then the question is if there is any indirect method to decrease the loss in degrees of freedom. Finite polynomial regression is one such method.

If one or several lagged values of dependent variables are included in a model, it is called the **autoregressive model**. An example of an autoregressive model is as follows:

$$Y_t = \alpha + \beta X_t + \gamma Y_{t-1} + \varepsilon_t \tag{6.10}$$

Both (6.9) and (6.10) are **finite distributed lag regression models**. We sometimes encounter an **infinite distributed lag model** in practical situations. This happens when we expect the effect of some variable to persist over a long period and we approximate that situation by permitting an infinite distributed lag. Furthermore, after certain transformations and some manipulations of two kinds of lag adjustment models that are quite popular in economics, *viz.* the adaptive expectations model and the partial adjustment model, we obtain an infinite distributed lag model.

Distributed lag models and autoregressive models both belong to regression models with lagged variables. It is easy to understand that a current indicator is easily affected by certain past economic indicators (including its own lagged values). Before we proceed further it is useful to ask a series of questions related to the presence of lagged variables in economics.

1. What role do the lagged variables play in economic analysis? How lagged variables are important in characterizing the dynamic economic phenomena?

2. Is there any economic theoretical justification for the presence of lagged variables in empirical economic analysis? How do we measure the lag among economic indexes?

3. What is the relationship between the auto-regression and distributed lag? Can we deduce one from another?

4. What statistical problems are posed by the presence of lagged variables?

In economic activity, dependent variable Y almost always is affected by the past values of itself and other economic variables. To explain the common occurrence of such lag relationship we give below a few examples.

6.3.1   Consumption lag

If a consumer's wages will be increased by 2000 Yuan, a once and for all increase, its effect on his consumption will last for a period of time. Generally speaking, the consumer will not spend all of the increase in income in one year. It is probable that he would spend 800 Yuan in the first year, 600 Yuan in the next year and 400 Yuan in the third year, and then he will save the remaining 200 Yuan permanently. His consumption increments by the third year will be 1800 Yuan. So the consumption function can be written as

$$Y_t = C + 0.4X_t + 0.3X_{t-1} + 0.2X_{t-2} + \varepsilon_t$$

where Y is the consumption expenditure, C is a constant, X is the increase in income.

In principle, a finite distributed lag model can be written as

$$Y_t = \alpha + \beta_0 X_t + \beta_1 X_{t-1} + \beta_2 X_{t-2} + \cdots + \beta_k X_{t-k} + \varepsilon_t$$

In this model the lag length is k. Coefficient β_0 is called the **short-run coefficient** as it presents the response of Y to the change in X in the same period. If the change of X maintains, $(\beta_0 + \beta_1)$ presents the change of Y in the next period and $(\beta_0 + \beta_1 + \beta_2)$ gives the change after next, etc. After k periods, we obtain

$$\sum_{i=0}^{k} \beta_i = \beta_0 + \beta_1 + \cdots + \beta_k = \beta$$

β is called the **long-run impact multiplier**.
Infinite distributed lag model can be written as

$$Y_t = \alpha + \beta_0 X_t + \beta_1 X_{t-1} + \beta_2 X_{t-2} + \cdots + \varepsilon_t$$

It is convenient to employ some simple mathematical operations to deal with it. We define

$$\omega_i = \frac{\beta_i}{\sum \beta_i} = \frac{\beta_i}{\beta}$$

where ω_i denotes the normalized coefficients, $\sum \omega_i = 1$; so the distributed lag model can be rewritten as

$$Y_t = \alpha + \beta \sum \omega_i X_{t-i} + \varepsilon_t$$

6.3.2 Inflation lag

Economic theory has a prominent place for inflation as a basic economic phenomenon as the money supply will often surpass the actual demand for money, thereby causing inflation. Certainly, the relation between inflation and money supply is not always simultaneous and inflation always follows an increase in money supply. Analytic research shows that the lag period between money supply and inflation is about 3–20 quarters.

The following table is taken from the research report entitled *The Lag from Money to Prices* authored by Keith M. Carlson (1980). The sample period is from the first quarter in 1955 to the fourth quarter in 1969, namely 60 quarters. We assume that the maximum lag is 20 (quarters), then the lag equation is

$$P_t = -0.146 + \sum_{i=0}^{20} m_i M_{t-i}$$

where M in the equation is the percentage change of money supply (net currency = deposit money) and P is the percentage of price rise. In the long run, $\sum m_i = 1.031 \approx 1$, it is statistically significant ($t = 7.870 > t_{0.01}(20) = 2.528$), which means that the price will increase by 1% if the money supply increases by 1%. In the short run, $m_0 = 0.041$ means the price in that year will increase by 0.041% if the money supply increases by 1%.

The data in Table 6.2 are the American data in the 1950s and 1960s, which is just for illustration purpose only. However, this problem is quite important from a real life macroeconomic policy perspective as well.

Table 6.2 The lag from money to prices.

	Coefficient Value	t value		Coefficient Value	t value
m_0	0.041	1.276	m_{11}	0.065	4.673
m_1	0.034	1.538	m_{12}	0.069	4.795
m_2	0.030	1.903	m_{13}	0.072	4.694
m_3	0.029	2.171	m_{14}	0.073	4.468
m_4	0.030	2.235	m_{15}	0.072	4.202
m_5	0.033	2.294	m_{16}	0.069	3.943
m_6	0.037	2.475	m_{17}	0.062	3.712
m_7	0.042	2.798	m_{18}	0.053	3.511
m_8	0.048	3.249	m_{19}	0.039	3.388
m_9	0.054	3.783	m_{20}	0.022	3.191
m_{10}	0.059	4.305	Σ_{mi}	1.031	7.870

6.3.3 Deposit re-creation

If a central bank infuses 1 billion rupees into the banking system through central bank credit, then what is its impact on the total money supply? Let us say that there is a reserve requirement that the banks should reserve 20% of their deposits (Rs 200 million) with the central bank as the reserve money. The remaining 800 million can be lent by the banks in the first round. The Rs 800 million will be saved back to the bank after the circulation out of the bank for a period of time. Reserving 20% of the 800 million (Rs 160 million) as the reserve money, the bank can lend 640 million. This money will again get back to the banking. Repeating this process we get the money multiplier effect and the total amount of deposit for the bank will be:

$$1 \cdot \frac{1}{1-0.8} = 5 \text{ billion}$$

Described by a lag model is:

$$Y_t = X_t + \beta X_t + \beta X_{t-1} + \beta X_{t-2} + \cdots + \beta X_{t-k} + \cdots$$
$$= X_t + \beta X_t + \beta^2 X_t + \beta^3 X_t + \cdots + \beta^{k-1} X_t + \cdots$$

where $X_t = 1$ (billion rupees), $\beta = 0.8$. Certainly, such 5 billion rupees is not obtained instantly. It is generated over a series of transactions.

These are just a few examples of lag relationships among the economic indicators. Why do lags occur? Whether it is a technological relation or a behavior relation most economic relations have cause and effect relationship and the causation takes place after a time lag, giving rise to lagged variables. Prices prevailing this year would motivate the producer to make production plans but production of output takes time and the output is realized only after a year, let us say. Besides this, psychological factors and social traditions are also responsible for the presence of lags. The new products will be accepted widely after they have been tested and people are convinced by them. Both simultaneous economic relations without lags and recursive relations with lags appear in economic modeling. Ideally one would expect economic relations to be recursive with lags if detailed process analysis is carried out with disaggregation over commodities and in time. Conversely, if one takes a longer period of analysis lags could disappear and simultaneity will set in.

6.4   Finite distributed lag models

6.4.1   Estimation of distributed lag models when the lag length is known and finite

The distributed lag model

$$Y_t = \alpha + \beta_0 X_t + \cdots + \beta_N X_{t-N} + \varepsilon_t$$

where N is given and is called lag length. With the standard notation,

$$Y = X\beta + \varepsilon$$

where

$$Y = \begin{pmatrix} Y_1 \\ Y_2 \\ \vdots \\ Y_T \end{pmatrix}, X = \begin{pmatrix} 1 & X_1 & X_0 & \cdots & X_{-N+1} \\ 1 & X_2 & X_1 & \cdots & X_{-N+2} \\ \cdots & \cdots & & & \\ 1 & X_T & X_{T-1} & \cdots & X_{T-N} \end{pmatrix}, \beta = \begin{pmatrix} \alpha \\ \beta_0 \\ \vdots \\ \beta_N \end{pmatrix}, \varepsilon = \begin{pmatrix} \varepsilon_1 \\ \varepsilon_2 \\ \vdots \\ \varepsilon_T \end{pmatrix}$$

Note that sample values $X_{-N+1}, X_{-N+2}, \ldots, X_0$ are contained in matrix X. We assume that these N observations are available, ε is such that $\varepsilon \sim N(0,\sigma^2 I)$, X_t is regarded as fixed and nonrandom. Then the least squares estimator of β is $\hat{\beta} = (X'X)^{-1} X'Y$ and it is an unbiased estimator based on the information of sample Y and X.

However, there are some problems associated with this estimator in the distributed lag model. Firstly, lag length is seldom known in many practical situations. If we substitute certain upper-bound M for $N(M > N)$, LSE [$\beta^{(M)} = (\alpha, \beta_0, \beta_1, \ldots, \beta_M)$] of $\beta^{(M)}$ will not be an efficient estimator for it overlooks the restriction $\beta_{N+1} = \beta_{N+2} = \cdots = \beta_M = 0$. We will solve this problem later.

Secondly, certain column vectors of X may be linearly dependent, which is a typical multicollinearity situation. If the distributed lag length N is short, say, 3 or 4, the multicollinearity may not be severe. However, it is usual that $N = 10$ in practice. If X_t has small variation from one period to another then serious multicollinearity will occur.

6.4.2   The determination of distributed lag length

If lag length N is unknown, but it has an upper bound M, then we can choose N using a simple method, called Ad Hoc Estimation of a distributed lag model.

We assume X_t is nonrandom, at least it is uncorrelated with ε_t, and X_{t-1}, X_{t-2}, etc are also under the same assumption as X_t, so ordinary least squares can be applied. We can make a regression series:

(1) regress Y_t on X_t,

(2) regress Y_t on X_t, X_{t-1},

(3) regress Y_t on X_t, X_{t-1}, X_{t-2},

......

We terminate this process if the following two conditions hold: (i) the last lagged variable introduced is statistically insignificant, and (ii) compared with the pervious equation, the sign associated with the last lagged variable is changed.

Alt and Tinbergen regressed consumption of petroleum Y on new order quantity X during 1930–39 using the American data. Take a quarter as the lag unit and apply Ad Hoc method.

$$\hat{Y}_t = 8.37 + 0.171 X_t,$$

$$\hat{Y}_t = 8.27 + 0.111 X_t + 0.064 X_{t-1},$$

$$\hat{Y}_t = 8.27 + 0.109 X_t + 0.071 X_{t-1} - 0.055 X_{t-2},$$

$$\hat{Y}_t = 8.32 + 0.108 X_t + 0.063 X_{t-1} + 0.022 X_{t-2} - 0.020 X_{t-3}.$$

As a result, they thought that the third equation with lag length of 2 is the best, because the coefficients of X_{t-2} are not stable in the third and fourth equitation. Besides this, it is not easy to explain the economic meaning of a negative coefficient. Thus it is suitable that the lag length is 2.

The following statistical test leads to the same result as above but it proceeds in the reverse order starting from lagged regressions with a pre-assigned maximum lag length.

We construct a series of sequent hypothesis for testing in that sequence.

$$H_0^1 : \beta_M = 0 \qquad \leftrightarrow \qquad H_a^1 : \beta_M \neq 0$$

$$H_0^2 : \beta_{M-1} = 0 \qquad \leftrightarrow \qquad H_a^2 : \beta_{M-1} \neq 0, \beta_M = 0$$

$$H_0^3 : \beta_{M-2} = 0 \qquad \leftrightarrow$$

......

$$H_0^i : \beta_{M-i+1} = 0 \qquad \leftrightarrow \qquad H_a^i : \beta_{M-i+1} \neq 0, \beta_{M-i+2} = \cdots = \beta_M = 0$$

Each null hypothesis is tested based on the condition that the pervious null hypothesis is accepted. The process of hypothesis testing stops when a certain null hypothesis is rejected. Assuming $\varepsilon \sim N(0, \sigma^2 I)$ we can use F test or t test. Now we construct the statistic. Denote

$$\beta_n = \begin{pmatrix} \alpha \\ \beta_0 \\ \vdots \\ \beta_n \end{pmatrix}, X_n = \begin{pmatrix} 1 & X_1 & X_0 & \cdots & X_{-n+1} \\ 1 & X_2 & X_1 & \cdots & X_{-n+2} \\ \cdots & \cdots & & & \\ 1 & X_T & X_{T-1} & \cdots & X_{T-n} \end{pmatrix}$$

$$\hat{\sigma}_n^2 = \frac{S_{SEn}}{T - n - 2}, \quad S_{SEn} = (y - X_n \hat{\beta}_n)'(y - X_n \hat{\beta}_n)$$

$$\hat{\beta}_n = (X_n' X_n)^{-1} X_n' Y$$

Then likelihood ratio statistic to test the ith null hypothesis H_0^i can be written as

$$\lambda_i = \frac{S_{SEM-i} - S_{SEM-i+1}}{\hat{\sigma}_{M-i+1}^2}$$

If hypotheses $H_0^1, H_0^2, \ldots, H_0^i$ are true, this statistic follows the F distribution with $(1, T - M + i - 3)$ degrees of freedom. Notice that $M - i + 3$ is the number of parameters in the model with $M - i + 1$ as the lag length. Besides F test, t test can be also used to test the significance of the final coefficient β_{M-i+1} in the model:

$$Y = \beta_0 + X_1\beta_1 + \cdots + X_{M-i+1}\beta_{M-i+1} + \varepsilon$$

According to the hypothesis testing procedure described above, lag length N depends on the test level. To be more precise, it depends on probability of type I error. The so-called type I error refers to the error of rejecting the null hypothesis when it is right. However, in a series of tests, the probability of refusing H_0^i is not just the single statistical significance level in the ith test. For example, when H_0^2 is true, the probability to refuse it should be the probability to refuse H_0^1 or H_0^2. If $H_0^1, \ldots, H_0^i$ are true, there are F distributions for each statistic $\lambda_1, \ldots, \lambda_i$, respectively. It can be proved that λ_i is independent of $\lambda_1, \ldots, \lambda_{i-1}$. Applying the basic probability formula

$$P(A \cup B) = P(A) + P(B) - P(AB)$$

We obtain the probability of type I error in the ith test:

$$
\begin{aligned}
p_i &= P\{\lambda_i > F_{\gamma i}(1, T - M - 3 + i) \cup \ldots \cup \lambda_1 > F_{\gamma 1}(1, T - M - 2)\} \\
&= P\{\lambda_i > F_{\gamma i}(1, T - M - 3 + i)\} \\
&\quad + P\{\lambda_{i-1} > F_{\gamma(i-1)}(1, T - M - 4 + i) \cup \ldots \cup \lambda_1 > F_{\gamma 1}(1, T - M - 2)\} \\
&\quad - P\{\lambda_i > F_{\gamma i}(1, T - M - 3 + i)\} \\
&\quad \cdot P\{\lambda_{i-1} > F_{\gamma(i-1)}(1, T - M - 4 + i) \cup \ldots \cup \lambda_1 > F_{\gamma 1}(1, T - M - 2)\} \\
&= \gamma_i + p_{i-1} - \gamma_i p_{i-1} = \gamma_i(1 - p_{i-1}) + p_{i-1}, \quad i = 1, 2, \ldots
\end{aligned}
$$

where γ_i is the statistical significance level of the ith individual testing, $p_0 = 0$. All probabilities are computed on the condition that $H_0^1, \ldots, H_0^i$ are all true. If we use the same significance level to each individual testing, the probability of type I error will increase rapidly. For example, for all k

$$\gamma_k = 0.01$$

then

$$p_1 = 0.01, \quad p_2 = 0.0199, \quad p_3 = 0.029701$$

and so on. In fact, if the maximal lag length M is a large number, then a suitable test strategy is to designate small significance level at the beginning of the test. That is to say the probability of type I error should be controlled at a rational level when the lag length is considerably large.

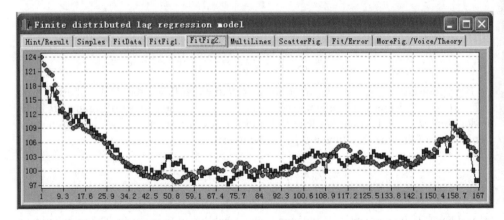

Figure 6.7   Fitting figure of the finite distributed lag model for CPI of China.

Example 6.3   Finite distributed lag model for CPI of China   We continue to use the data of Example 6.1, but we only use the first four columns of the data as the columns will be expanded by lag regression.

We only consider four lags and compute the regression model first by adopting Ad Hoc method. This procedure can be realized by selecting parameter Step 2 in area B of DASC. In the first regression, there are four columns of independent variables, and the data points are 170. Meanwhile, statistic $F = 165.761$, the critical value $F(4,165) = 2.8643$, and coefficient of total correlation $R^2 = 0.8007$. In the second regression, there are eight columns of independent variables, because four lagged variables are added, and the data points are 169. Meanwhile, statistic $F = 89.0065$, the critical value $F(8,158) = 2.2731$, and coefficient of total correlation $R^2 = 0.8184$. In the third regression, there are 12 columns of independent variables, because 8 lagged variables are added, and the data points are 168. Meanwhile, statistic $F = 60.2663$, the critical value $F(12,154) = 2.0302$, and coefficient of total correlation $R^2 = 0.8244$. In the fourth regression, statistic $F = 47.3917$, there are 16 columns of independent variables, because 12 lagged variables are added, and the data points are 167. Meanwhile, the critical value $F(16,150) = 1.8931$, and coefficient of total correlation $R^2 = 0.8349$. We can see the coefficients of total correlation increase along with the lag times.

The computation process can be shown by clicking DASC→Regression→Simultaneous/ Lagging Regression→Finite Distributed Lag Model. Of course, if we select the parameter Step 2 (maximum of lag) more than 4, the lag regression will be continued until statistic F is not significant (Figure 6.7).

We note that we considered here lags in independent variables. If we use lagged dependent variables (autoregression) then the goodness of fit of the regression may improve considerably. We will discuss this aspect in Chapter 8, Section 8.5.

6.5   Infinite distributed lag models

The general form of an infinite distributed lag model is

$$Y_t = \alpha + \beta_0 X_t + \beta_1 X_{t-1} + \beta_2 X_{t-2} + \cdots + \varepsilon_t$$

One might argue that it is quite reasonable to cut off the infinite distributed lag relationship after a finite lag. However, the issue then is how to determine the cut-off point. Instead it is preferable to describe a specific lag structure (the pattern of coefficients of the lagged variables) and keep the infinite lags. In this section, we describe two settings under which infinite distributed lag models with geometrically declining weights arise in economics quite naturally. We then introduce Koyck Transformation to convert such infinite distributed lag models into the finite first-order autoregression models. Finally, we discuss the issue of estimating the parameters of such models.

6.5.1   Adaptive expectations model and partial adjustment model

Let's discuss the adaptive **expectations model** first.

Assume commodity supply Y is related to the market expected price X^*. Let us represent this relationship as follows:

$$Y_t = \alpha_0 + \alpha_1 X_t^* + \varepsilon_t \tag{6.11}$$

where α_0, α_1 are constants, ε_t is a random variable. Let us assume that the price expectations are updates of the previous period price expectations, the updating being based on the observed difference between the expected price and the actual price in the previous period, (and thus it is called the adaptive expectations model). That is

$$X_t^* - X_{t-1}^* = \lambda(X_{t-1} - X_{t-1}^*) \tag{6.12}$$

where $0 < \lambda < 1$, X_{t-1} is the actual price in $t-1$ period. The above equation can be rewritten as:

$$X_t^* = X_{t-1}^* + \lambda(X_{t-1} - X_{t-1}^*) = (1-\lambda)X_{t-1}^* + \lambda X_{t-1}$$

The relation above suggests that under the adaptive expectations model the expectations are formed in such a way that the expected value in period t is a weighted average of the expectation of the previous period and the actual value of the previous period.

In order to substitute observable variable for the unobservable variable X^* in model (6.11), we collect terms in the previous expression, then X_{t-1} is

$$\lambda X_{t-1} = X_t^* - (1-\lambda)X_{t-1}^*$$

We introduce the lag operator L and define

$$LX_t^* = X_{t-1}^*$$

then

$$\lambda X_{t-1} = [1 - (1-\lambda)L]X_t^*$$

It is convenient to use the inverse operator of $[1 - (1 - \lambda)L]$

$$[1 - (1-\lambda)L]^{-1} = 1 + (1-\lambda)L + (1-\lambda)^2 L^2 + (1-\lambda)^3 L^3 + \cdots$$

Using this inverse operator we get:

$$
\begin{aligned}
X_t^* &= [1-(1-\lambda)L]^{-1}\lambda X_{t-1} \\
&= [1+(1-\lambda)L+(1-\lambda)^2 L^2 +\cdots]\lambda X_{t-1} \\
&= \lambda X_{t-1} +\lambda(1-\lambda)X_{t-2} +\lambda(1-\lambda)^2 X_{t-3} +\cdots
\end{aligned}
$$

Thus we demonstrated that the adaptive expectations model becomes an infinite distributed lag model.

$$
Y_t = \alpha_0 + \alpha_1 \lambda[X_{t-1}+(1-\lambda)X_{t-2}+(1-\lambda)^2 X_{t-3}+\cdots]+\varepsilon_t \tag{6.13}
$$

A model like this is also called the geometric lag model. The adaptive expectations model can be transformed into a first-order autoregressive model. We will address it later in the next section.

Now let's discuss the **partial adjustment model**.

The primary point of the model is that the current value of independent variable X determines the expected value of dependent variable Y

$$
Y_t^* = \alpha_0 + \alpha_1 X_t + \varepsilon_t
$$

It is further postulated that the actual difference between the present value and the lagged value is a partial adjustment of the difference between the desired or expected value and the lagged value. This partial adjustment mechanism can be represented by the following equation:

$$
Y_t - Y_{t-1} = \gamma(Y_t^* - Y_{t-1})
$$

where $0 < \gamma < 1$, γ is called adjustment coefficient.

The equation above can also be rewritten as:

$$
Y_t = Y_{t-1} + \gamma(Y_t^* - Y_{t-1}) = (1-\gamma)Y_{t-1} + \gamma Y_t^*
$$

This equation states that under the partial adjustment mechanism the actual value in period t is a weighted average of the lagged value and the current expected or desired value. There is now some similarity between adaptive expectations model and the partial adjustment model. The first model specifies how the expectations are formed while the second specifies how the actual values adjust to the expectations.

A first-order autoregression model can be obtained after the combination of the two expressions above,

$$
Y_t = \alpha_0\gamma + \alpha_1\gamma X_t + (1-\gamma)Y_{t-1} + \gamma\varepsilon_t
$$

Introduce lag operator and its inverse operator, then

$$
\begin{aligned}
Y_t &= \alpha_0 + \frac{\alpha_1\gamma}{1-(1-\gamma)L}X_t + \frac{\gamma}{1-(1-\gamma)L}\varepsilon_t \\
&= \alpha_0 + \alpha_1\gamma X_t + \alpha_1\gamma(1-\gamma)X_{t-1} + \alpha_1\gamma(1-\gamma)^2 X_{t-2} +\cdots+\varepsilon_t^*
\end{aligned} \tag{6.14}
$$

We obtain the infinite geometric lag model again, but the structure of ε^* is now more complex.

At last let's see the **combination of these two models**.

We consider the following model:

$$Y_t^* = \beta_0 + \beta_1 X_t^* + \varepsilon_t \tag{6.15}$$

where Y_t^* is the expected capital stock, X_t^* is the expected output. The problem is that the dependent and independent variables here are unobservable. We have to translate them into observable variables. We can adopt the relationship in adaptive expectations model

$$X_t^* = [1 - (1-\lambda)L]^{-1} \lambda X_{t-1}$$

and the relationship in the partial adjustment model

$$Y_t^* = \frac{1}{\gamma} Y_t - \frac{1-\gamma}{\gamma} Y_{t-1} \tag{6.16}$$

Substitute them into (6.15), and then

$$
\begin{aligned}
Y_t &= \beta_0 \gamma + (1-\gamma) Y_{t-1} + \gamma \beta_1 \lambda [1 - (1-\lambda)L]^{-1} X_{t-1} + \gamma \varepsilon_t \\
&= \beta_0 \gamma + (1-\gamma) Y_{t-1} + \gamma \beta_1 \lambda [X_{t-1} + (1-\lambda) X_{t-2} + (1-\lambda)^2 X_{t-3} + \cdots] + \gamma \varepsilon_t
\end{aligned}
$$

There is no unobservable variable in such a model.

The infinite distributed lag models derived from the adaptive expectations model and partial adjustment model are difficult to use in practice for regression analysis for estimating the underlying economic parameters. This is because there are an infinite number of explanatory variables in the regression. The economist Koyck (1954) developed an ingenious method to convert this infinite dimensional regression into a finite dimensional auto regression model. We describe his method in the next subsection.

6.5.2   Koyck transformation and estimation of geometric lag models

A general infinite lag regression model can be written as:

$$Y_t = \alpha + \beta_0 X_t + \beta_1 X_{t-1} + \beta_2 X_{t-2} + \cdots + \varepsilon_t$$

It is difficult to handle such a regression problem with an infinite set of regressors that demands information on an infinite set of parameters with a finite set of observations. Economic intuition tells us that the only way we can solve the problem is to impose some *a priori* conditions on the infinite set of regression parameters so that the number of independent unknown parameters is reduced to a very small number. In most of the economic examples the lagged influence of a variable declines as the lag length increases. Koyck therefore made the ingenious suggestion of imposing certain *a priori* restrictions that the regression coefficients of the lagged variables follow a geometric distribution.

Koyck suggested writing the equation above as:

$$Y_{t-1} = \alpha + \beta_0 X_{t-1} + \beta_0 \lambda X_{t-2} + \beta_0 \lambda^2 X_{t-3} + \cdots + \varepsilon_{t-1}$$

If we multiply two sides of this later expression by λ, and subtract from the first expression we obtain:

$$Y_t - \lambda Y_{t-1} = \alpha(1-\lambda) + \beta_0 X_t + \varepsilon_t - \lambda \varepsilon_{t-1}$$

Let $\varepsilon_t^* = \varepsilon_t - \lambda\varepsilon_{t-1}$. Rearranging the expression above we have:

$$Y_t = \alpha(1-\lambda) + \beta_0 X_t + \lambda Y_{t-1} + \varepsilon_t^*$$

It is the first-order autoregressive model, which is unlikely to generate multicollinearity among independent variables, but it is likely to create autocorrelation of Y. We can use the method discussed in the previous chapters to solve this.

We adopt the **Koyck transformation** to the adaptive expectations model above. Seeking the solution of basic relational expression (6.12). $X_t^* - X_{t-1}^* = \lambda(X_{t-1} - X_{t-1}^*)$, it follows that

$$X_t^* = \lambda X_{t-1} + (1-\lambda)X_{t-1}^*$$

Substitute it into the original model, then

$$Y_t = \alpha_0 + \alpha_1 \lambda X_{t-1} + \alpha_1(1-\lambda)X_{t-1}^* + \varepsilon_t \tag{6.17}$$

Lagging the original model for one-period,

$$Y_{t-1} = \alpha_0 + \alpha_1 X_{t-1}^* + \varepsilon_{t-1}$$

We can obtain

$$X_{t-1}^* = \frac{1}{\alpha_1}Y_{t-1} - \frac{\alpha_0}{\alpha_1} - \frac{\varepsilon_{t-1}}{\alpha_1} \tag{6.18}$$

Substitute it into (6.18), then

$$\begin{aligned} Y_t &= \alpha_0 + \alpha_1 \lambda X_{t-1} + (1-\lambda)Y_{t-1} - \alpha_0(1-\lambda) - (1-\lambda)\varepsilon_{t-1} + \varepsilon_t \\ &= \alpha_0 \lambda + \alpha_1 \lambda X_{t-1} + (1-\lambda)Y_{t-1} - \varepsilon_t^* \end{aligned}$$

where $\varepsilon_t^* = \varepsilon_t - (1-\lambda)\varepsilon_{t-1}$. This is a first-order autoregressive model of the adaptive expectations model.

Let us consider the combined model of adaptive expectations and partial adjustment as specified by model (6.15). It can be converted into a first-order autoregressive model. Substitute the equation (6.16) and the one-period-ahead, $X_t^* = \dfrac{1}{\alpha_1}Y_t - \dfrac{\alpha_0}{\alpha_1} - \dfrac{\varepsilon_t}{\alpha_1}$ in (6.15), to obtain:

$$\frac{1}{\gamma}Y_t - \frac{1-\gamma}{\gamma}Y_{t-1} = \beta_0 + \beta_1\left(\frac{1}{\alpha_1}Y_t - \frac{\alpha_0}{\alpha_1} - \frac{\varepsilon_t}{\alpha_1}\right) + \varepsilon_t$$

After rearranging the terms we get:

$$\begin{aligned} Y_t &= \frac{\alpha_1\gamma}{\alpha_1 - \gamma\beta_1}\left[\beta_0 - \frac{\beta_1\alpha_0}{\alpha_1} + \frac{1-\gamma}{\gamma}Y_{t-1} + \left(1 - \frac{\beta_1}{\alpha_1}\right)\varepsilon_t\right] \\ &= C_0 + C_1 Y_{t-1} + C_2 \varepsilon_t \end{aligned}$$

Although this last expression is linear in Y, it is nonlinear in the original parameters.

We make the parameter estimation of the first-order autoregression form of a **geometric lag model**:

$$Y_t = \gamma_0 + \gamma_1 X_t + \lambda Y_{t-1} + \varepsilon_t \tag{6.19}$$

If error $\varepsilon_t = (\varepsilon_2, \ldots, \varepsilon_T)$ meets $\varepsilon \sim N(0, \sigma^2 I)$, the least squares estimation of parameter $\gamma = (\gamma_0, \gamma_1, \lambda)'$ can be obtained. However, LSE will not be the best linear unbiased estimators because even if X_t is non-random and Y_{t-1} is correlated with Y_t or ε_t. Formally, we note:

$$Y = \begin{pmatrix} Y_2 \\ Y_3 \\ \vdots \\ Y_T \end{pmatrix}, X = \begin{pmatrix} 1 & X_2 & Y_1 \\ 1 & X_3 & Y_2 \\ \vdots & \vdots & \vdots \\ 1 & X_T & Y_{T-1} \end{pmatrix}$$

then the LSE can be written as:

$$\hat{\gamma} = (\hat{\gamma}_0, \hat{\gamma}_1, \hat{\lambda})' = (X'X)^{-1} X'Y$$

Example 6.4   Geometric lag model and Koyck transformation for stock prices of Brazil, Russia, UK, USA and Japan   Three economic regression models are introduced in this section. They are:

Adaptive expectations model: $Y_t = \alpha_0 + \alpha_1 X_t^* + \varepsilon_t$

$$X_t^* - X_{t-1}^* = \lambda(X_{t-1} - X_{t-1}^*)$$

Partial adjustment model: $Y_t^* = \alpha_0 + \alpha_1 X_t + \varepsilon_t$

$$Y_t - Y_{t-1} = \gamma(Y_t^* - Y_{t-1})$$

The combined model of the two models above: $Y_t^* = b_0 + b_1 X_t^* + \varepsilon_t$

In these models, the expected price or value is marked with an asterisk. By introducing the lag operator these models can be transformed into infinite lag models. Using the Koyck transformation, they can be transformed into the first-order autoregression form (6.19):

$$Y_t = \gamma_0 + \gamma_1 X_t + \lambda Y_{t-1} + \varepsilon_t$$

But in DASC, we arrange the columns of data as follows:

$$Y_t = \gamma_0 + \lambda Y_{t-1} + \gamma_1 X_t + \varepsilon_t \tag{6.20}$$

The data in this example are 'Weekly Stock Price Data for Japan, UK, US, and Brazil', from 7-Jan-2004 to 11-Jul-2007. So the data has 184 rows and four columns. The first two rows and the last two rows of data are shown as follows:

Date	Brazil (Y_t)	US (X_1)	UK (X_2)	Japan (X_3)
7-Jan-2004	23,320.00	6,525.30	4,473.0	10,784
14-Jan-2004	23,398.00	6,559.81	4,461.4	10,461
....	....	....	....	....
4-Jul-2007	55,696.00	10,032.60	6,673.1	18,050
11-Jul-2007	56,356.00	10,014.70	6,615.1	18,050

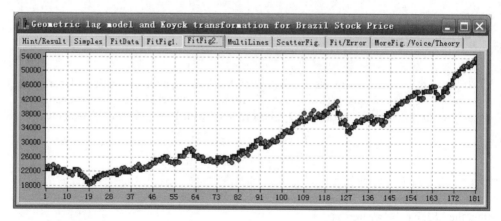

Figure 6.8   Geometric lag model and Koyck transformation for Brazil stock price.

The data can be found in Brazil Data, Appendix, Electronic References for Chapter 6. We use them here.

The results are as follows.

Statistic F = 4890.59. The critical value F(4,176) = 2.8593. Coefficient of total correlation $R^2 = 0.9911$, R = 0.9955. The regression equation is:

$$Y_t = -9600.187 + 0.709Y_{t-1} + 2.267X_1 - 0.167X_2 + 0.153X_3$$

The computation process can be shown by clicking DASC→Regression→ Simultaneous/ Lagging Regression→Geometric Lag Model and Koyck Transformation. Figure 6.8 shows the goodness of fit. In the figure, the dash line with dot points is original data, and continuous line with square points is the regression fit. On the X-axis we have the time, and on the Y-axis we have the price of stock. The goodness of fit reveals that the fit is very good. In Section 8.5 of Chapter 8, we will develop the model further to obtain better forecasts for the stock prices.

We continue to use this model to fit Russian Stock Prices. To input other data in the same model, there are five methods in DASC. Now we use menu 'DASC→(top menu) Load Other Example Data (in Wiley book etc.)', select the folder \\DASC\\She\\WileyData\\WileyData 3(Lag Model)\\Russia Data 2\\, and hit files according to the prompt, then the data can be input automatically.

The data are 'Weekly Stock Price Data for Japan, UK, US, and Russia', from 7-Jan-2004 to 11-Jul-2007. So the data has 184 rows and four columns. The first two rows and the last two rows of original data are shown as follows:

Date	Russia (Y_t)	US (X_1)	UK (X_2)	Japan (X_3)
7-Jan-2004	592.63	6,525.30	4,473.0	10,784
14-Jan-2004	595.16	6,559.81	4,461.4	10,461
....	....	....	....	....
4-Jul-2007	1943.29	10,032.60	6,673.1	18,050
11-Jul-2007	1995.58	10,014.70	6,615.1	18,050

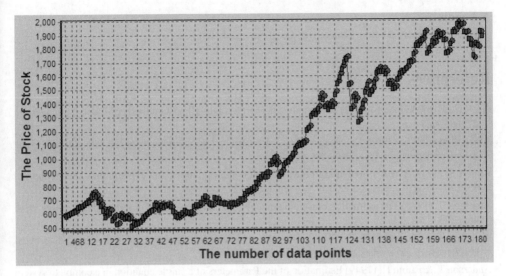

Figure 6.9   Geometric lag model and Koyck transformation for Russia stock price.

The original data can be seen in Russia Data, Appendix, Electronic References for Chapter 6. We use them here in this model.

The results are as follows.

Statistic $F = 5116.49$. The critical value $F(4,175) = 2.8597$. Coefficient of total correlation $R^2 = 0.9915$, $R = 0.9958$. Regression equation is:

$$Y_t = -139.217 + 0.950 Y_{t-1} + 0.030 X_1 + 0.001 X_2 - 0.004 X_3$$

Figure 6.9 is adopted from the second figure system in Area C of DASC.

Electronic references for Chapter 6

Appendix
Asymptotic Properties of the Generalized Least Squares Estimator

References

Adelman F. & Adelman I. (1959) The dynamic properties of the Klein-Goldberger Model. *Econometrica* **27**, 596–625.

Albert J. & Chib S. (1993) Bayesian analysis of binary and polytomous response data. *Journal of the American Statistical Association* **88**, 669–79.

Almon S. (1965) The distributed lag between capital appropriations and expenditures. *Econometrica* **33**, 176–96.

Amemiya T. (1978) The estimation of a simultaneous equation generalized probit model. *Econometrica* **46**, 1193–1205.

Amemiya T. & Morimune K. (1974) Selecting the optimal order of polynomial in the almon distributed lag. *Review of Economics and Statistics* **56**, 376–386.

Anderson T. & Rubin H. (1949) Estimation of the Parameters of a single equation in a complete system of stochastic equations. *Annals of Mathematical Statistics* **20**, 46–63.

Arellano M. & Bover O. (1995) Another look at the instrumental variables estimation of error components models. *Journal of Econometrics* **68**, 29–52.

Baltagi B. H. (1995) *Econometric Analysis of Panel Data*. John Wiley and Sons, Inc, New York.

Basmann R.L. (1957) A generalized classical method of linear estimation of coefficients in a structural equation. *Econometrica* **25**, 76–83.

Berndt E., Hall B., Hall R. & Hausman J. (1974) Estimation and inference in nonlinear structural models. *Annals of Economic and Social Measurement* **3**(4), 653–65.

Brundy J. & Jorgenson D. (1971) Consistent and efficient estimation of systems of simultaneous equations by means of instrumental variables. *Review of Economics and Statistics* **53**, 206–24.

Burt Oscar R. (1989) Testing for the length of a distributed lag with a differencing transformation. *Economics Letters* **29**(3), 221–3.

Chen L.A. & Portnoy S. (1996) Two-stage regression quantiles and two-stage trimmed least squares estimators for structural equation models. *Communications in Statistics* **25**(5), 1005–32.

Cooper P. (1972) Two approaches to polynomial distributed lag estimation. *American Statistician* **26**, 32–5.

Cragg J. (1967) On the relative small-sample properties of several structural-equation estimators. *Econometrica* **35**, 89–110.

Cumby R., Huizinga J. & Obstfeld M. (1983) Two step, two stage least squares estimation in models with rational expectations. *Journal of Econometrics* **21**, 333–55.

Dhrymes P. (1969) Efficient estimation of distributed lags with autocorrelated errors. *International Economic Review* **10**, 46–67.

Dhrymes P. (1971) *Distributed lags: problems of estimation and formulation*. Holden Day, San Francisco.

Dufour Jean-Marie & Olivier Torrès (2000) Markovian processes two-sided autoregressions and finite-sample inference for stationary and nonstationary autoregressive processes. *Journal of Econometrics* **99**(2), 255–89.

Durbin J. (1970) Testing for serial correlation in least squares regression when some of the regressors are lagged dependent variables. *Econometrica* **38**, 410–21.

Fair R. (1970) The estimation of simultaneous equations models with lagged endogenous variables and first order serially correlated errors. *Econometrica* **38**, 506–16.

Fair R. (1972) Efficient estimation of simultaneous equations with autoregressive errors by instrumental variables. *Review of Economics and Statistics* **54**, 444–9.

Franses P.H. & van Oest R. (2007) On the econometrics of the geometric lag model. *Economics Letters* **95**(2), 291–6.

Garry D. & Phillips, A. (2000) An alternative approach to obtaining Nagar-type moment approximations in simultaneous equation models. *Journal of Econometrics* **97**(2), 345–64.

Goldfield S. & Quandt R. (1968) Non linear simultaneous equations, estimation and prediction. *International Economic Review* **9**, 113–36.

Godfrey L. & Poskitt, D. (1975) Testing the restrictions of the Almon lag technique. *Journal of the American Statistical Association* **70**, 105–8.

Griliches Z. (1961) A note on serial correlation bias in estimates of distributed lags. *Econometrica* **26**, 65–73.

Griliches Z. (1967) Distributed lags: A survey. *Econometrica* **35**, 16–49.

Griliches Z. & Rao P. (1969) Small sample properties of several two stage regression methods in the context of autoccorrelated errors. *Journal of the American Statistical Association* **64**, 253–72.

Grether D. & Maddala G. (1973) Errors in variables and serially correlated disturbances in distributed lag models. *Econometrica* **41**, 255–62.

Hassler U. & Wolters Jürgen (2006) Autoregressive distributed lag models and cointegration. *Allgemeines Statistisches Archiv* **90**, 59–74.

Hatanaka M. (1976) Several efficient two-step estimators for the dynamic simultaneous equations model with autoregressive disturbances. *Journal of Econometrics* **4**, 189–204.

Heckman J. & Macurdy T. (1985) A simultaneous equations linear probability model. *Canadian Journal of Economics* **18**, 26–37.

Ip W.C. & Phillips G.D.A. (1998) The non-monotonicity of the bias and mean squared error of the two stage least squares estimators of exogenous variable coefficients. *Economics Letters* **60**(3), 303–10.

Jorgenson D. (1966) Rational distributed lag functions. *Econometrica* **34**, 135–49.

Judge G.G., Hill C.R., Griffiths W.E., Lütkepohl H. & Lee T.C. (1982) *Introduction to the theory and practice of econometrics*, John Wiley & Sons, Inc, New York.

Kang H. (2008) The canonical least squares estimation of large-scale simultaneous equations models. *Economic Modeling* **25**(2), 191–200.

Kiviet J.F. & Dufour Jean-Marie (1997) Exact tests in single equation autoregressive distributed lag models. *Journal of Econometrics* **80**, 325–53.

Koyck L. (1954) *Distributed Lags and Investment Analysis*, North Holland, Amsterdam.

Kim K. il (2006) Sample selection models with a common dummy endogenous regressor in simultaneous equations: A simple two-step estimation. *Economics Letters* **91**(2), 280–6.

Lahiri K. & Schmidt P. (1978) On the estimation of triangular structural systems. *Econometrica* **46**, 1216–21.

McClain K.T. & Wooldridge J.M. (1995) A simple test for the consistency of dynamic linear regression in rational distributed lag models. *Economics Letters* **48**, 235–40.

Pagan A. (1978) Rational and polynomial lags: The finite connection. *Journal of Econometrics* **8**(2), 246–54.

Pagano M. & Hartley M. (1981) On fitting distributed lag models subject to polynomial restrictions. *Journal of Econometrics* **16**, 171–98.

Poskitt D.S. & Skeels C.L. (2007) Approximating the distribution of the two-stage least squares estimator when the concentration parameter is small. *Journal of Econometrics* **139**(1), 216–36.

Su L. & Aman U. (2008) Local polynomial estimation of nonparametric simultaneous equations models. *Journal of Econometrics* **144**(1), 193–218.

Theil H. (1954) Estimation of parameters of econometric models. *Bulletin of International Statistics Institute* **34**, 122–8.

7

Stationary time series models

In economics we deal with economic variables that come to us in three different forms, either as observations made at the same time of different economic variables (**cross-section data**), or as observations of the same variable at different points in time (**time series data**), or as observations of different variables at different points in time (time series of cross-sections or **panel data**). In this and the next chapter we introduce statistical theories and methods that are suitable for dealing with data that come to us as time series of observations on a single variable, or data that come to us as panel data or as vectors of time series.

It is assumed that the reader is already familiar with some of the basic concepts of time series to be discussed here, such as the definition and the characteristics of the **stochastic process**, **time domain** and **frequency domain** analysis of the time series. The reader may refer to the Electronic References for Chapter 7 to find the information needed.

Time series can mainly be divided into the two categories of **stationary time series** and **nonstationary time series**. Nonstationary time series can be converted into stationary time series through **differencing** and **fractional differencing** (to be explained in Chapter 8).

Intuitively, stationarity refers to a situation where the characteristics of the series will not change as time changes. Mathematically, for any positive integer n and for any time points $t_1 < t_2 < \cdots < t_n$ (in this chapter and next chapter we always assume t as discrete integer), the joint distribution function $F(x_{t_1}, x_{t_2}, \ldots x_{t_n})$ is unrelated to the starting point. Such time series are called **strictly stationary time series**. In application, we only require that the mean of the time series is a constant and the auto-covariance function is unrelated to the starting point, and such time series are named **weakly stationary time series**. In fact, this definition gives us the basic method of model identification. More details can be found in the Electronic References for Chapter 7. Unless otherwise specified the stationary time series to be discussed in this chapter are weakly stationary time series.

Intuitively time series analysis is based on **independently and identically distributed** random variables with finite variance, called **white noise**, and relating stationary time series to a transformation of the white noise series. The non-stationary time series are sums or repeated sums or fractional sums of stationary time series and hence by taking the difference

---

Developing Econometrics, First Edition. Hengqing Tong, T. Krishna Kumar and Yangxin Huang.
© 2011 John Wiley & Sons, Ltd. Published 2011 by John Wiley & Sons, Ltd.

or fractional differences of a non-stationary time series one gets stationary time series. Time series modeling consists of transforming the non-stationary time series into stationary time series by appropriate differencing and finding out which transformation of white noise series leads to that stationary time series. In other words, all time series are transformations of white noise series, and our job is to take a real time series and perform reverse engineering to discover which transformation of white noise would lead to those real time series.

Most of the stationary time series belong to one of three types. This chapter describes these three main models of Stationary Time Series. These are **Auto Regressive (AR) Models**, **Moving Average (MA) Models**, and **Auto-Regressive Moving Average Models (ARMA)**. The methods of time series analysis therefore consist of: 1. Converting a non-stationary time series into a stationary series through differencing or fractional differencing; 2. Determining whether the stationary time series so derived is an AR process or a MA process or a ARMA process; 3. To **estimate the parameters** of the model so identified; and 4. **Forecasting future values** of the time series and provide confidence intervals for such forecasts.

The **auto-regression** (or Auto-regressive) model AR(p) describes the relationship between X_t and its past p values, where p could be finite or infinite, and the white noise ε_t. AR(p) is expressed as

$$X_t = \mu + \rho_1 X_{t-1} + \rho_2 X_{t-2} + \cdots + \rho_p X_{t-p} + \varepsilon_t \tag{7.1}$$

That is, given the **initial value** $X_0, X_1, \ldots, X_p$, a white noise series-ε_t, the parameter μ and the values of the autoregressive parameters $\rho_1, \rho_2, \ldots, \rho_p$ the time series X_t can be generated by equation (7.1).

The relationship between **moving average model of** X_t or MA(q), and white noise is described by:

$$X_t = \varepsilon_t + \lambda_1 \varepsilon_{t-1} + \lambda_2 \varepsilon_{t-2} + \cdots + \lambda_q \varepsilon_{t-q} \tag{7.2}$$

Given a white noise series-ε_t, and parameters $\lambda_1, \lambda_2, \ldots, \lambda_q$, one can generate the time series X_t.

A general model that includes a auto-regressive model and moving average model is **auto-regressive moving-average model**, or ARMA(p, q), with the general form

$$X_t = \mu + \sum_{j=1}^{p} \rho_j X_{t-j} + \sum_{j=0}^{q} \lambda_j \varepsilon_{t-j} \tag{7.3}$$

The discussion of these three models follows the same course. First, we discuss the conditions for stationarity. Then we discuss the relationship between their **auto-covariance functions** and the regression coefficients to derive the **Yule-Walker** equations. The next point for discussion is the estimation of parameters, including the method of **moment estimation**, **least squares estimation**, and **maximum likelihood estimation**. Time series can be represented as a magnitude of the variable plotted against time (representation in the **time domain**), or the same amplitude or value of the time series plotted against how frequently that value is assumed (representation in the **frequency domain**), depicted as a probability density function. The latter is called a **spectral density function**. Hence, after estimating the parameters of the identified model we present the properties and estimation of spectral density of the series.

The main points to note are as follows. Econometrics deals primarily with regression analysis and time series analysis. Time series includes two categories: stationary time series and non-stationary time series. Stationary time series includes three categories:

the auto-regression model AR(p), moving average model MA(q), and auto-regression moving-average model, ARMA(p, q). The main tools of analysis in time series are two functions: autocovariance function and spectral density function. The main issues we confront in time series analysis are: identification of the model, estimation of parameters of that model and tests of hypothesis. The method of determining the model is a model selection problem, and **AIC criterion** and **BIC criterion** are useful here. The main goal of time series analysis is prediction, based on a well-fitted model.

7.1 Auto-regression model AR(p)

7.1.1 AR(p) model and stationarity

Auto-regression, as the name suggests, means one variable regressed with itself. **First-order auto-regression model AR(1)** has the form

$$X_t = \mu + \rho X_{t-1} + \varepsilon_t \tag{7.4}$$

where $\{\varepsilon_t\}$ is white noise with $E(\varepsilon_t) = 0$, $D\{\varepsilon_t\} = \sigma^2$, and $\text{Cov}(\varepsilon_t, \varepsilon_s) = 0$ for all $t \neq s$. If the model constant $\mu \neq 0$, it is said to be non-centralized. By subtracting μ from both sides we can make it a centralized model. Hence, without any loss of generality we let $\mu = 0$ to make model a centralized model

$$X_t = \rho X_{t-1} + \varepsilon_t \tag{7.5}$$

Let us examine the stationary solution and stationarity of this AR(1) process. If a stationary time series is the solution to an auto-regression model, we call this the time series **stationary solution**. When $|\rho| < 1$, define

$$X_t = \sum_{j=0}^{\infty} \rho^j \varepsilon_{t-j} \tag{7.6}$$

It can be easily verified that this has a mean zero and a constant variance-covariance matrix $\dfrac{1}{1-\rho^2}\sigma^2 I$. As its mean function is a constant and the auto-covariance function is unrelated to the starting point (a constant), it is **weakly stationary time series**. The discussion of its stationarity can be found in the Electronic References for Chapter 7, Section 1. By writing the terms on the right

$$X_t = \rho \sum_{j=0}^{\infty} \rho^j \varepsilon_{t-1-j} + \varepsilon_t = \rho X_{t-1} + \varepsilon_t$$

we see that (7.6) is the solution to (7.5), so it is a stationary solution.

By introducing the **lag operator** L, namely, $LX_t = X_{t-1}$, we obtain a new form of (7.5),

$$(1 - \rho L)X_t = \varepsilon_t \tag{7.7}$$

We call $(1 - \rho z) = 0$ **lag polynomial** and the characteristic equation of the process. The root of this equation is $z = 1/\rho$, when $|\rho| < 1$, $|z| > 1$. It indicates that when the root z of characteristic equation of AR(1) is outside the unit circle, the model AR(1) process has stationary solution. Usually, the solution of (7.7) can be written as

$$X_t = (1 - \rho L)^{-1} \varepsilon_t$$

and it also explains why (7.6) is so defined, namely, coefficient $\sum_{j=0}^{\infty} \rho^j \varepsilon_{t-j} = (1 - \rho L)^{-1} \varepsilon_t$.

The stationary solution of auto-regressive model is not unique. In fact, (7.5) can be regarded as a difference equation, and then (7.5) has general solution

$$X_t = \sum_{j=0}^{\infty} \rho^j \varepsilon_{t-j} + \xi \rho^t$$

where ε is a random variable with zero mean. It differs from (7.6) for an infinitesimal $\xi \rho^t$. As $t \to \infty$, $\xi \rho^t$ tends to 0. That is to say, when $|\rho| < 1$, any solution of model (7.5) approaches the stationary solution as time approaches ∞, thus the system is stable. As $t \to \infty$, only the first summation of infinite series matters and the variance of series X_t is

$$Var(X_t) = \sigma^2 \sum_{j=0}^{\infty} \rho^{2j} = \frac{\sigma^2}{1 - \rho^2}$$

Next we discuss the more general centralized p-th order auto-regression model. It describes the linear relationship between X_t and its p lagged values, represented by

$$X_t = \rho_1 X_{t-1} + \rho_2 X_{t-2} + \cdots + \rho_p X_{t-p} + \varepsilon_t = \sum_{j=1}^{p} \rho_j X_{t-j} + \varepsilon_t \qquad (7.8)$$

We call (7.8) a pth **order auto-regressive process**, or AR(p).

By introducing lag operator L, namely, $L^j X_t = X_{t-j}$ for $j = 1, 2, \ldots$, (7.8) can be rewritten as:

$$(1 - \sum_{j=1}^{p} \rho_j L^j) X_t = \varepsilon_t$$

Analogous to the characteristic equation of AR(1), given real numbers $\rho_1, \rho_2, \ldots \rho_p$ we define the characteristic equation:

$$1 - \sum_{j=1}^{p} \rho_j z^j = 0 \qquad (7.9)$$

Then the stationary solution for the AR(p) model is

$$X_t = (1 - \sum_{j=1}^{p} \rho_j L^j)^{-1} \varepsilon_t$$

Similar to $(1 - \rho z)^{-1} = \sum_{j=0}^{\infty} \rho^j z^j$, let $(1 - \sum_{j=1}^{p} \rho_j z^j)^{-1} = \sum_{j=0}^{\infty} \psi_j z^j$, then, if the zeroes of the characteristic equation lie outside the **unit circle** (the condition for stationarity), the stationary solution for the AR(p) model can be written as

$$X_t = \sum_{j=0}^{\infty} \psi_j L^j \varepsilon_t = \sum_{j=0}^{\infty} \psi_j \varepsilon_{t-j} \tag{7.10}$$

Here, the coefficients $\{\Psi_j\}$ are named **Wold coefficients** of the stationary time series. Since $\{X_t\}$ is stationary, coefficient $\{\Psi_j\}$ of infinite series will converge to zero definitely. This formula also reflects the relationship between the AR(p) model and infinite order moving average model. It is also called the **Wold decomposition** of a stationary Autoregressive process of order p.

Assume that k distinct roots of polynomial (7.9) are $(z_1, z_2, \ldots, z_k)$, and z_j is repeated $r(j)$ times, then the general solution of the AR(p) model has the form

$$Y_t = \sum_{j=0}^{\infty} \psi_j \varepsilon_{t-j} + \sum_{j=1}^{k} \sum_{i=1}^{r(j)-1} U_{i,j} t^j z_j^{-i}$$

where $\{U_{i,j}\}$ are random variables with zero mean.

The difference between the general solution of the AR(p) model and the stationary solution $\{X_t\}$ satisfies

$$\left| X_t - Y_t \right| = \left| \sum_{j=1}^{k} \sum_{i=1}^{r(j)-1} U_{i,j} t^j z_j^{-i} \right| \leq o(\xi^{-t}), \quad as \quad t \to \infty \tag{7.11}$$

where ξ is between $(1, \min_{1 \leq j \leq k} z_j)$. This inequality indicates that any solution of AR(p) model approaches the stationary solution as t approaches ∞. Thus (7.10) is the unique stationary solution of the AR(p) model.

(7.11) also provides a method of constructing an AR(p) series by using white noise $\{\varepsilon_t\}$ and auto-regression coefficients $(\rho_1, \rho_2, \ldots \rho_p)$. We can choose an arbitrary solution $\{Y_t\}$ and set initial values $Y_0 = Y_1 = \cdots = Y_p = 0$, then use the model

$$Y_t = \sum_{j=1}^{p} \rho_j Y_{t-j} + \varepsilon_t, \quad t = p, p+1, \ldots, m+n$$

to implement recursion computation. Since $Y_t \to X_t$, we let $X_t = Y_{t+m}, t = 1, 2, \ldots, n$, When $m \geq 50$, $\{Y_{t+m}\}$, namely $\{X_t\}$, becomes stationary. For smaller $\min_{1 \leq j \leq k} z_j$, m needs to be larger than 50 to bring about this stationarity. For instance, if $X_0 = 5, X_1 = 10, X_2 = 15$ (input on page 2 in A area of DASC), and $\rho_1 = 0.4, \rho_2 = 0.3, \rho_3 = 0.1$ (input on page 1 in A area of DASC), that is

$$X_j = 0.4X_{j-1} + 0.3X_{j-2} + 0.1X_{j-3} + \varepsilon_t$$

where $Var(\varepsilon) = \sigma^2 = 0.9$ (input in B area of DASC). The time series is constructed by this method, as Figure 7.1 shows.

If we change the input coefficients in area A of DASC as $\rho_1 = 0.1, \rho_2 = 0.1, \rho_3 = 0.1$, then the figure is as Figure 7.2. We can see that the nature of their stationarity is different. These computations can be seen by clicking on the menu DASC → Time Series Analysis → Generate Random Numbers → Generate Random Numbers for AR(3). Readers can input or load other parameters in DASC to calculate and show many forms of AR(p) time series.

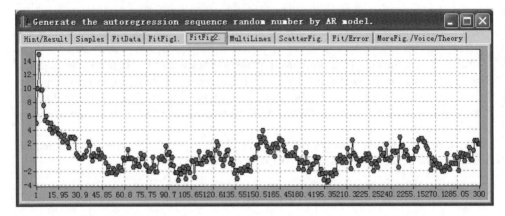

Figure 7.1   AR(3) model and stationarity ($p = 3$, $\rho_1 = 0.4$, $\rho_2 = 0.3$, $\rho_3 = 0.1$).

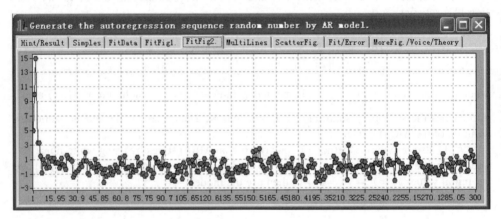

Figure 7.2   AR(3) model and stationarity ($p = 3$, $\rho_1 = 0.1$, $\rho_2 = 0.1$, $\rho_3 = 0.1$).

7.1.2 Auto-covariance function and autocorrelation function of AR(p) model

In general, the **autocovariance function** of a series X_t is

$$\gamma_k = Cov(X_t, X_{t+k}) = \sum_{t=1}^{N-k} (X_t - \overline{X})(X_{t+k} - \overline{X})$$

The **autocorrelation function (ACF)** is obtained by dividing by the variance γ_0 to obtain:

$$\lambda_k = \frac{\gamma_k}{\gamma_0} = \frac{Cov(X_t, X_{t+k})}{Var(X_t)} = \frac{\sum_{t=1}^{N-k} (X_t - \overline{X})(X_{t+k} - \overline{X})}{\sum_{t=1}^{N} (X_t - \overline{X})^2}$$

Their properties can be seen in the Electronic References for Chapter 7. Now we deduce **Yule-Walker equations** from them.

Let $\{X_t\}$ be a series of AR(p) and (7.10) be the stationary solution of AR(p). For any $k \geq 1$,

$$E(X_t \varepsilon_{t+k}) = E\left(\sum_{j=0}^{\infty} \psi_j \varepsilon_{t-j}\right) \varepsilon_{t+k} = \sum_{j=0}^{\infty} \psi_j E(\varepsilon_{t-j} \varepsilon_{t+k}) = 0 \qquad (7.12)$$

It illustrates that the stationary solution of the AR(p) model is such that the value at time t (X_t) is unrelated to the stochastic disturbance items after $t(\varepsilon_{t+k})$. In particular, while $\{\varepsilon_t\}$ is independent white noise, X_t is independent of stochastic disturbance ε_{t+k}.

Multiply both sides of model (7.8) by X_{t+k} and then evaluate the mathematical expectation, we obtain

$$E(X_t X_{t+k}) = E\left(\sum_{j=1}^{p} \rho_j X_{t-j} X_{t+k}\right) + E(\varepsilon_t X_{t+k})$$

Or assuming that γ_k is the k-th auto-covariance in the series X we get:

$$\gamma_k = \rho_1 \gamma_{k-1} + \rho_2 \gamma_{k-2} + \cdots + \rho_p \gamma_{k-p} = \sum_{j=1}^{p} \rho_j \gamma_{k-j}, \quad k \geq 1 \qquad (7.13)$$

This shows that auto-covariance function of the AR(p) model satisfies the homogeneous equation as the X series (see equation 7.8).

The homogeneous equation (7.13) reveals the relationship among the auto-covariance function of the AR(p) model and is very useful. Next we extend the model from t to $t + n - 1$, use a vector matrix notation form for $n \geq p$, and obtain the Yule-Walker equations which are very useful in estimating the parameters of AR(p). We have:

$$\begin{pmatrix} X_t \\ X_{t+1} \\ \vdots \\ X_{t+n-1} \end{pmatrix} = \begin{pmatrix} X_{t-1} & X_{t-2} & \cdots & X_{t-n} \\ X_t & X_{t-1} & \cdots & X_{t+1-n} \\ \vdots & \vdots & \ddots & \vdots \\ X_{t+n-2} & X_{t+n-3} & \cdots & X_{t-1} \end{pmatrix} \vec{\rho}_n + \begin{pmatrix} \varepsilon_t \\ \varepsilon_{t+1} \\ \vdots \\ \varepsilon_{t+n-1} \end{pmatrix} \qquad (7.14)$$

where

$$\vec{\rho}_n = (\rho_{n,1}, \rho_{n,2}, \ldots, \rho_{n,n})' = (\rho_1, \rho_2, \ldots, \rho_p, 0, \ldots, 0)'$$

Multiply both sides of (7.14) by X_{t-1} and evaluate the mathematical expectation. From (7.12) we know the error term vanished and then

$$\begin{pmatrix} \gamma_1 \\ \gamma_2 \\ \vdots \\ \gamma_n \end{pmatrix} = \begin{pmatrix} \gamma_0 & \gamma_1 & \cdots & \gamma_{n-1} \\ \gamma_1 & \gamma_0 & \cdots & \gamma_{n-2} \\ \vdots & \vdots & \ddots & \vdots \\ \gamma_{n-1} & \gamma_{n-2} & \cdots & \gamma_0 \end{pmatrix} \vec{\rho}_n \qquad (7.15)$$

Denote that

$$
\vec{\gamma}_n = \begin{pmatrix} \gamma_1 \\ \gamma_2 \\ \vdots \\ \gamma_n \end{pmatrix}, \Gamma_n = \begin{pmatrix} \gamma_0 & \gamma_1 & \cdots & \gamma_{n-1} \\ \gamma_1 & \gamma_0 & \cdots & \gamma_{n-2} \\ \vdots & \vdots & \ddots & \vdots \\ \gamma_{n-1} & \gamma_{n-2} & \cdots & \gamma_0 \end{pmatrix}
\tag{7.16}
$$

then equation (7.15) can be written in a simplified form

$$
\vec{\gamma}_n = \Gamma_n \vec{\rho}_n, \quad n \geq p
\tag{7.17}
$$

Obviously, (7.16) is generalization of (7.13). But they do not express what γ_0 is. When $k = 0$,

$$
\gamma_0 = E(X_t^2) = E\left(\sum_{j=1}^{p} \rho_j X_{t-j} + \varepsilon_t \right)^2 = E\left(\sum_{j=1}^{p} \rho_j X_{t-j} \right)^2 + E(\varepsilon_t)^2
$$

$$
= E\left(\sum_{j=1}^{n} \rho_j X_{t-j} \right)^2 + \sigma^2 = \vec{\rho}_n' \Gamma_n \vec{\rho}_n + \sigma^2 = \vec{\rho}_n' \vec{\gamma}_n + \sigma^2
$$

or

$$
\gamma_0 = \rho_1 \gamma_1 + \rho_2 \gamma_2 + \cdots + \rho_p \gamma_p = \sum_{j=1}^{p} \rho_j \gamma_j
\tag{7.18}
$$

Since auto-covariance function is symmetric, $\gamma_{-k} = \gamma_k$, so (7.18) is another form of (7.13). Combining (7.17) and (7.18) we obtain **Yule-Walker equations** for auto-covariance function of AR(p) series:

$$
\vec{\gamma}_n = \Gamma_n \vec{\rho}_n, \quad \gamma_0 = \vec{\gamma}_n' \vec{\rho}_n + \sigma^2, \quad n \geq p
$$

If the matrix auto-covariance Γ_p is positive definite, then setting $n = p$ in the Yule-Walker equations above we obtain the unique expressions for the auto-regression coefficients of the AR(p) process, as well as the variance of white noise

$$
\vec{\rho}_p = \Gamma_p^{-1} \vec{\gamma}_p, \quad \sigma^2 = \gamma_0 - \vec{\gamma}_p' \Gamma_p^{-1} \vec{\gamma}_p
\tag{7.19}
$$

This result provides us with method of moments estimators of the p parameters of an AR(p) process, and of the error variance.

Hence for our estimation of autoregression parameters through (7.19) the positive definiteness of Γ_p is crucial. We need to examine the conditions under which the matrix Γ_p is **positive definite**, and if those conditions are likely to be met in most cases.

The condition needed depends on the concept called a **spectral density**. Spectral density and its relationship with autocorrelation function can be found in the Electronic References for Chapter 7, Section 3. We will give an intuitive interpretation of it here. Any time series looks like a wave. Any such wave can be represented in two ways: (i) as a plot

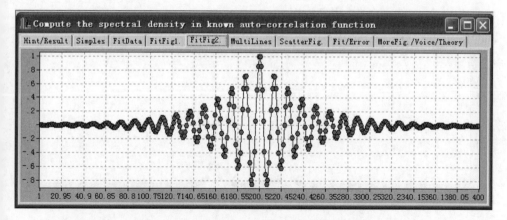

Figure 7.3   The figure of autocorrelation function $\gamma_k(t) = \exp(-a|t|)\cos(\omega_0 t)$.

of the value of the series (amplitude) on the vertical axis and the time on the horizontal axis, or (ii) as a plot of the value (amplitude) on the horizontal axis and the frequency with which the series assumes that value on the vertical axis. The latter is called the spectral density. It is obvious that the frequency depends on the periodicity of oscillations of the time series. It is also obvious that the autocorrelation function depends on the periodicity of oscillations. As both spectral density $f(\omega)$ and autocorrelation function $\gamma(t)$ deal with the same time series, they should be derivable one from the other. In fact the following **Fourier transform** does that:

$$\gamma(t) = \int_{-\infty}^{+\infty} f(\omega) e^{i\omega t} \, d\omega \leftrightarrow f(\omega) = \frac{1}{2\pi} \int_{-\infty}^{+\infty} \gamma(t) e^{-i\omega t} \, dt$$

So they can be used to represent uniquely each other. For example,

$$\gamma(t) = \exp(-a|t|)\cos(\omega_0 t) \leftrightarrow f(\omega) = \frac{a}{a^2 + (\omega + \omega_0)^2} + \frac{a}{a^2 + (\omega - \omega_0)^2}$$

Their figures are in Figure 7.3 and Figure 7.4.

The figures can be seen in DASC → Time Series Analysis → Spectral Analysis. The two figures are beautiful and the two functions are succinct, and they can be derived mathematically. Can we generate the figures of autocorrelation function and spectral density by the data of any time series? In fact, Figure 7.3 and Figure 7.4 are generated by data of a given time series and not according to formula directly.

It can be proved that if the spectral density $f(\lambda)$ of $\{X_t\}$ exists, Γ_n is positive definite with $n \geq 1$; or if $\gamma_k \to 0$ as $k \to \infty$, Γ_n is positive definite with $n \geq 1$. The spectral density exists if the auto covariance function is absolutely additive, that is if $\sum |\gamma_k| < \infty$.

Example 7.1   Calculation of Yule-Walker equations   The DASC software has a toolbar for AR(p) model computation under the time series menu. The computation program for Yule-Walker calculations is in this toolbar. After inputting original data, the program

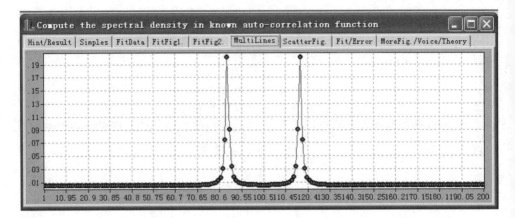

Figure 7.4   The figure of spectral density of $f(\omega) = \dfrac{a}{a^2 + (\omega + \omega_0)^2} + \dfrac{a}{a^2 + (\omega - \omega_0)^2}$.

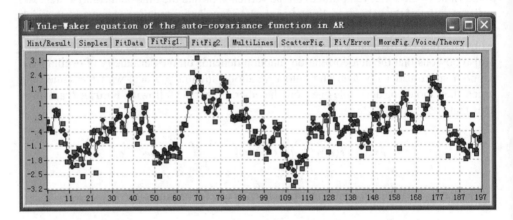

Figure 7.5   The original time series by third-order auto-regression.

calculates the autocorrelation function and solves Yule-Walker equations to estimate the coefficients $\hat{\rho}_j$ of the AR(p) process, for $j = 1, 2, \ldots, p$.

The original data, shown in Figure 7.5 as discrete square points, is a third-order auto-regressive series with coefficients 0.4, 0.3, 0.1, satisfying stationarity condition. Figure 7.6 shows its auto- covariance function values. By using Yule-Walker calculations, we estimate auto-regression coefficients as 0.571, 0.317 and −0.028. Taking the original data as initial values, we can work out the predictions of the series for future periods. Note that each time when we make forecasts, we use the original data but not the estimates. Picture that involves predictive series and original series is shown in Figure 7.5. This computation process can be seen by clicking DASC → Time Series Analysis → Stationary Series → Yule-Walker equations of AR(p).

About the prediction of time series, we should be aware that the predictive range must be limited, and we should not expect to use a new estimate to acquire a newer estimate for a long range by

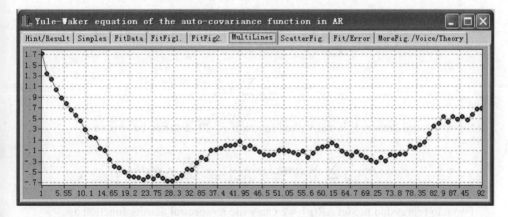

Figure 7.6   The auto-covariance function of third-order auto-regression series.

$$Y_t = \sum_{j=1}^{p} \rho_j Y_{t-j} + \varepsilon_t, \quad t = p, p+1, \ldots, m+n$$

Because as when an AR(p) series is long the principal part $\sum_{j=1}^{p} \rho_j X_{t-j}$ of the model will approach zero, merely random error ε_t taking effect. But random error cannot be predicted accurately.

7.1.3   Spectral density of AR(p) model and partial correlation coefficient

Let $\{X_t\}$ be the stationary solution of the AR(p) model, defined by (7.10). From the properties of linear stationary series we know it has zero mean and auto-covariance function as

$$\gamma_k = Cov(X_{t+k} X_t) = \sigma^2 \sum_{j=0}^{\infty} \psi_j \psi_{j+k}, \quad k = 0, 1, 2, \ldots$$

By using **Cauchy inequality** and the convergence of **Wold coefficients** $\{\psi_k\}$, we obtain

$$|\gamma_k| \le \sigma^2 \left(\sum_{j=0}^{\infty} \psi_j^2 \sum_{j=0}^{\infty} \psi_{j+k}^2 \right)^{1/2} \le c_0 \left(\sum_{j=k}^{\infty} \xi^{-2j} \right)^{1/2} \le c_1 \xi^{-k}$$

where c_0, c_1 are positive constants and ξ is between $(1, \min_{1 \le j \le k} z_j)$. So similar to Wold coefficients $\{\psi_k\}$, auto-covariance function of AR(p) series γ_k also converges to zero. And the larger $\min\|z_j\|$ is, the faster γ_k converges to zero. This phenomenon is called **the short memory of a time series**. More discussion about memory of a time series may be found in the Electronic References for Chapter 7.

As mentioned earlier, the spectral density of stationary time series can be expressed by its auto-covariance function. If auto-covariance function $\{\gamma_k\}$ of stationary time series $\{X_t\}$ is absolutely additive, namely, $\sum |\gamma_k| < \infty$, then $\{X_t\}$ has spectral density

$$f(\lambda) = \frac{1}{2\pi} \sum_{k=-\infty}^{\infty} \gamma_k e^{-ik\lambda} \tag{7.20}$$

Since spectral density is a real-valued function, (7.20) also can be written as

$$f(\lambda) = \frac{1}{2\pi} \sum_{k=-\infty}^{\infty} \gamma_k \cos(k\lambda) = \frac{1}{2\pi}\left[\gamma_0 + 2\sum_{k=1}^{\infty} \gamma_k \cos(k\lambda) \right]$$

For auto-regression model AR(p), we can write its spectral density function as

$$f(\lambda) = \frac{\sigma^2}{2\pi}\left| 1 - \sum_{j=1}^{p} \rho_j e^{-ij\lambda} \right|^{-2}$$

Substituting the estimators of autoregressive parameters and the variance of the error term we obtain the estimator of spectral density of auto-regression model:

$$\hat{f}(\lambda) = \frac{\hat{\sigma}^2}{2\pi}\left| 1 - \sum_{j=1}^{p} \hat{\rho}_j e^{-ij\lambda} \right|^{-2}$$

As the estimators of the AR(p) process $\hat{\rho}_j$ are consistent estimators of the true autoregressive parameters (as will be shown in Chapter 8, section 8.1.4), this estimator of the spectral density is also a **consistent estimator** of the true spectral density.

Let $\{X_t\}$ be a stationary series with zero mean. We consider obtaining a linear forecast of X_{n+1} by using $X_1, X_2,\ldots, X_n$. That means we use the linear combination $\sum_{j=1}^{n} b_j X_{n-j+1}$ to forecast X_{n+1}. Then the question is 'What are the best coefficients $b_1, b_2,\ldots, b_n$?' Let $\vec{X} = (X_n, X_{n-1},\ldots, X_1)'$ and $\vec{b} = (b_1, b_2,\ldots, b_n)'$, then the coefficient of **Yule-Walker** calculation is $\vec{\rho}_n = (\rho_{n,1}, \rho_{n,2},\ldots, \rho_{n,n})$, we have

$$\begin{aligned}
E(X_{n+1} - \sum_{j=1}^{n} b_j X_{n-j+1})^2 &= E(X_{n+1} - \vec{\rho}_n'\vec{X} + \vec{\rho}_n'\vec{X} - \vec{b}'\vec{X})^2 \\
&= E(X_{n+1} - \vec{\rho}_n'\vec{X})^2 + E(\vec{\rho}_n'\vec{X} - \vec{b}'\vec{X})^2 + 2E[(X_{n+1} - \vec{\rho}_n'\vec{X})\vec{X}'(\vec{\rho}_n' - \vec{b})] \\
&= E(X_{n+1} - \vec{\rho}_n'\vec{X})^2 + E(\vec{\rho}_n'\vec{X} - \vec{b}'\vec{X})^2 + 2(\vec{\gamma}' - \vec{\rho}_n'\Gamma)(\vec{\rho}_n - \vec{b}) \\
&= E(X_{n+1} - \vec{\rho}_n'\vec{X})^2 + (\vec{\rho}_n - \vec{b})'\Gamma_n(\vec{\rho}_n - \vec{b})] \geq E(X_{n+1} - \vec{\rho}_n'\vec{X})^2
\end{aligned}$$

then

$$\sigma_n^2 = E(X_{n+1} - \vec{\rho}_n'\vec{X})^2 \leq E(X_{n+1} - \vec{b}'\vec{X})^2$$

$$\hat{X}_{n+1} = \vec{\rho}'\vec{X}$$

This result indicates that in terms of minimum mean squared error, $\hat{X}_{n+1} = \vec{\rho}'\vec{X}$ is the best forecast of X_{n+1}. So it is called **best linear forecasts** of X_{n+1} and σ_n^2 is called the mean squared error of the forecast.

We have shown that the best linear forecast is obtained from the Yule-Walker coefficients. The next question is how to calculate the Yule-Walker coefficients? Although we can get them from Yule-Walker equations $\vec{\gamma}_n = \Gamma_n\vec{\rho}_n$, we'd rather use the following Levinson recursion formula.

If Γ_{n+1} is positive definite, for $1 \le k \le n$, it follows that

$$\rho_{1,1} = \gamma_1 / \gamma_0, \quad \sigma_0^2 = \gamma_0$$

and

$$\begin{cases} \sigma_k^2 = \sigma_{k-1}^2(1-\rho_{k,k}^2) \\ \rho_{k+1,k+1} = \dfrac{\gamma_{k+1} - \gamma_k\rho_{k,1} - \gamma_{k-1}\rho_{k,2} - \cdots - \gamma_1\rho_{k,k}}{\gamma_0 - \gamma_1\rho_{k,1} - \gamma_2\rho_{k,2} - \cdots - \gamma_k\rho_{k,k}} \\ \rho_{k+1,j} = \rho_{k,j} - \rho_{k+1,k+1}\rho_{k,k+1-j}, \quad 1 \le j \le k \end{cases} \qquad (7.21)$$

where

$$\sigma_k^2 \triangleq E(X_{k+1} - \rho_k'\vec{X})^2$$

is the mean squared error when we use $\vec{X} = (X_k, X_{k-1}, \ldots, X_1)'$ to forecast X_{k+1}.

If Γ_n is positive definite, we call $\rho_{n,n}$ as nth order **partial autocorrelation coefficient** (**PACF**) of series $\{X_t\}$. Since the auto-covariance function matrix of AR(p) series is always positive definite, we know from (7.15) its Yule-Walker coefficient is

$$\vec{\rho}_n = (\rho_{n,1}, \rho_{n,2}, \ldots, \rho_{n,n})' = (\rho_1, \rho_2, \ldots, \rho_p, 0, \ldots, 0)', n \ge p$$

namely,

$$\rho_{n,n} = \begin{cases} \rho_p, & \text{when } n = p \\ 0, & \text{when } n > p \end{cases} \qquad (7.22)$$

Here we call partial autocorrelation coefficients $\rho_{n,n}$ **truncated at p**. Conversely, if the partial autocorrelation coefficients of a stationary series with zero mean are truncated at p, this series must be an AR(p) series.

These conclusions are all theoretical results. Actual data, however, cannot always satisfy the constraint that auto-covariance function γ_k is a constant, for any fixed k, due to the random error and deficiency of ergodicity. The following example illustrates this difference.

Example 7.2   Recursive computation by Levison formula and partial correlation coefficient   Let us first calculate estimates of AR(1), theoretically.

Let $\{X_t\}$ be an auto-regression process AR(1) that $X_t = \rho X_{t-1} + \varepsilon_t$, where $\varepsilon_t \sim N(0, \sigma^2)$, and $|\rho| < 1$. Let $X_t = \sum_{j=0}^{\infty} \rho^j \varepsilon_{t-j}$ be the stationary solution of $\{X_t\}$ with auto-covariance functions

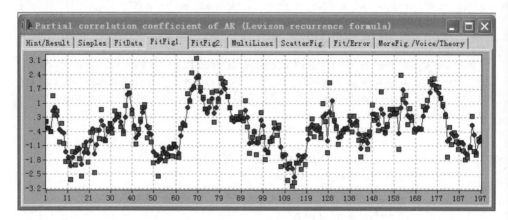

Figure 7.7   Series forecast by Levison formula and partial correlation coefficient.

$\gamma_0 = \sigma^2 \sum_{j=0}^{\infty} \rho^{2j} = \dfrac{\sigma^2}{1-\rho^2}$, for k > 0 $\gamma_k = \gamma_{k-1} = \cdots = \rho^k \gamma_0$ and auto-correlation coefficient

$r_k = \dfrac{\gamma_k}{\gamma_0} = \rho^k$. According to the Levison recursion formula, theoretically, the partial autocorrelation coefficients are

$$\rho_{1,1} = \frac{\gamma_1}{\gamma_0} = \rho, \quad \rho_{2,2} = \frac{\gamma_2 - \gamma_1 \times \rho_{1,1}}{\gamma_0 - \gamma_1 \times \rho_{1,1}} = \frac{\rho^2 - \rho^2}{\gamma_0 - \gamma_1 \times \rho_{1,1}} = 0, \quad \rho_{k,k} = 0, \ (k > 1).$$

One may obtain, likewise, the theoretical Yule-walker equations for AR(3) needed for our illustration.

Software DASC gives an example of 200 data from a third order auto-regressive time series. Regression coefficients of the original series are 0.4, 0.3, 0.1 while the coefficients got by Levison formula are 0.478, 0.316, 0.049.

There are two ways of forecasting. One way is forecasting by successive recursion, namely, using $X_1, X_2, \ldots, X_p$ to forecast $\hat{X}_{p+1}$, and using $X_2, X_3, \ldots, X_{p+1}$ to forecast $\hat{X}_{p+2}$, etc. Each time we use the original data thus the predictive series is $X_1, X_2, \ldots, X_p, \hat{X}_{p+1}, \hat{X}_{p+2} \ldots, \hat{X}_n$ of which the first p data are the same with the original series. In this example, $p = 3$, shown in the Figure 7.7. The goodness of fit is relatively perfect. This computation process can be seen by clicking DASC → Time Series Analysis → Stationary Series → Levison Recursive formulae of AR(p).

Another way is just by using the first p data of the original time series, namely, using $X_1, X_2, \ldots, X_p$ to forecast $\hat{X}_{p+1}$ and then using $X_2, X_3, \ldots, \hat{X}_{p+1}$ to forecast $\hat{X}_{p+2}$, etc. thus every forecast value after $\hat{X}_{p+p}$ is obtained by estimates. Predictive series $X_1, X_2, \ldots, X_p$, $\hat{X}_{p+1}, \hat{X}_{p+2}, \ldots, \hat{X}_n$ obtained in this way is obviously far different from the original data, except for the first three observations. Specific figures can be referred to in the DASC software.

7.1.4 Estimation of parameters for AR(p) model with known order p

Assume that we know that the given time series is an autoregressive series with order p specified as:

$$X_t = \mu + \sum_{j=1}^{p} \rho_j X_{t-j} + \varepsilon_t, \quad \varepsilon_t \sim W(0, \sigma^2)$$

and that we wish to estimate parameters μ, ρ_1, ρ_2,..., ρ_p, and σ^2 from the observed sample.

First, process the observed data $X_1, X_2,..., X_N$ so as to centralize them, which is equivalent to saying that we assume that the auto regression goes through the mean values.

$$x_t = X_t - \overline{X}_N, \quad t = 1, 2, ..., N, \quad where \quad \overline{x}_N = \frac{1}{N}\sum_{j=1}^{N} x_j$$

Second, construct an AR(p) process for series $\{x_t\}$. Now we can assume that the observed data, suitably transformed $x_1, x_2,..., x_N$ already have zero means. The three different commonly used methods for point estimation of parameter are Yule-Walker estimation, least squares estimation, and maximum likelihood estimation.

1. Yule-Walker estimation of AR(p) model

We first calculate the auto-covariance function $\hat{\gamma}_k$ of the sample

$$\hat{\gamma}_k = \frac{1}{N}\sum_{j=1}^{N-k} x_j x_{j+k}, \quad k = 0, 1, ..., p \tag{7.23}$$

then Yule-Walker equations can be written as:

$$\begin{pmatrix} \gamma_1 \\ \gamma_2 \\ \vdots \\ \gamma_p \end{pmatrix} = \begin{pmatrix} \gamma_0 & \gamma_1 & \cdots & \gamma_{p-1} \\ \gamma_1 & \gamma_0 & \cdots & \gamma_{p-2} \\ \vdots & \vdots & & \vdots \\ \gamma_{p-1} & \gamma_{p-2} & \cdots & \gamma_0 \end{pmatrix}\begin{pmatrix} \rho_1 \\ \rho_2 \\ \vdots \\ \rho_p \end{pmatrix}$$

When auto-covariance matrix is positive definite, we can obtain the estimators of autoregressive coefficients

$$\hat{\rho}_p : \hat{\vec{\rho}}_p = \hat{\Gamma}_p^{-1}\hat{\vec{\gamma}}_p \tag{7.24}$$

and the estimator of variance σ^2 of white noise

$$\hat{\sigma}^2 = \hat{\gamma}_0 - (\hat{\rho}_1\hat{\gamma}_1 + \hat{\rho}_2\hat{\gamma}_2 + \cdots + \hat{\rho}_p\hat{\gamma}_p) \tag{7.25}$$

Coefficients of AR(p) obtained in this way also need verification for the stationarity (7.12). If the estimated coefficients do not satisfy the stationarity condition, then this model cannot be used to describe any stationary system and it is also invalid to forecast via this model. Expression (7.19) tells us that as long as the auto-covariance matrix Γ_p of sample is positive definite, the AR(p) process satisfies stationarity condition. Besides, when $N > p$, and $x_1, x_2,\ldots, x_N$ are not identical, auto-covariance matrix of pth order sample $\hat{\Gamma}_p = (\hat{\gamma}_{k-j})$ is positive definite. Therefore we always assume that $N > p$, and $x_1, x_2,\ldots, x_N$ are not identical. After figuring out the estimator (7.22) of the auto-covariance function, for larger p, in order to speed up computation, we can adopt Levinson recursion method (7.21) to calculate the estimator $\hat{\vec{\rho}}_p$ and $\hat{\sigma}^2$.

An estimation based on (7.24) and (7.25) is called the **Yule-Walker estimation** which belongs to method of moments estimation. One advantage of the Yule-Walker estimation is simple in computation and another is that autoregressive coefficients $\hat{\vec{\rho}}_p = (\hat{\rho}_1,\hat{\rho}_2,\ldots,\hat{\rho}_p)$ satisfy the stationarity condition

$$1-\sum_{j=1}^{p} \hat{a}_j z^j \neq 0, \text{ when } |z|\le 1$$

The third advantage is that Yule-Walker estimation is a method that generates consistent estimators which converge in probability to the true parameter values under general conditions. That is, if $\{\varepsilon_t\}$ of AR(p) process is an i.i.d. $W(0, \sigma^2)$ and $E(\varepsilon_t^4) < \infty$, then

$$\hat{\sigma}^2 \xrightarrow{P} \sigma^2, \quad \hat{\rho}_j \xrightarrow{P} \rho_j, \quad \text{when} \quad N \to \infty, \quad 1\le j\le p$$

The symbol $\xrightarrow{P}$ denotes convergence in probability. Furthermore, as this is a method of moments estimation the estimators also have asymptotic Normal distributions under some general conditions. More precisely,

$$\sqrt{N}(\hat{\rho}_1-\rho_1,\hat{\rho}_2 -\rho_2,\ldots,\hat{\rho}_p -\rho_p)' \xrightarrow{L} N(0, \sigma^2\Gamma_p^{-1}) \text{ when } N \to \infty \qquad (7.26)$$

Here the symbol $\xrightarrow{L}$ denotes convergence in distribution and $N(0, \sigma^2\Gamma_p^{-1})$ presents a Normal distribution of p variables.

Using the results of convergence in distribution we obtain the asymptotic interval estimations of parameters ρ_j. Let $\sigma_{j,j}$ denote the $j \times j$th element of $\sigma^2\Gamma_p^{-1}$, from the features of Normal distribution we know $\sqrt{N}(\hat{\rho}_j - \rho_j)$ converges to normal distribution $N(0, \sigma_{j,j})$ in distribution, then the asymptotic confidence interval of ρ_j with confidence level $1 - \alpha$ is:

$$\left[\hat{\rho}_j -u_{\alpha/2} \sqrt{\sigma_{j,j}}\Big/\sqrt{N},\hat{\rho}_j +u_{\alpha/2} \sqrt{\sigma_{j,j}}\Big/\sqrt{N}\right]$$

where $u_{\alpha/2}$ denotes the $100(1 - \alpha/2)$ percent critical value, or quantile of standard normal distribution with significance level $\alpha/2$. If $\sigma_{j,j}$ is unknown, substitute $\hat{\sigma}_{j,j}$ by the $j\times j$th element of $\hat{\sigma}^2\hat{\Gamma}_p^{-1}$, we obtain the approximate confidence interval of ρ_j:

$$\left[\hat{\rho}_j - u_{\alpha/2}\sqrt{\hat{\sigma}_{j,j}}\big/\sqrt{N}, \hat{\rho}_j + u_{\alpha/2}\sqrt{\hat{\sigma}_{j,j}}\big/\sqrt{N}\right]$$

2. Least squares estimator of AR(p) process

Now we consider the residuals of the AR(p) process

$$\varepsilon_t = X_t - \sum_{j=1}^{p} \rho_j X_{t-j}$$

Least squares estimation aims to find estimator $(\hat{\rho}_1, \hat{\rho}_2, ..., \hat{\rho}_p)$ to minimize residual sum of squares. Now we denote this vector by β and residual sum of squares is

$$S(\beta) = \sum_{t=p+1}^{N}\left(X_t - \sum_{j=1}^{p}\rho_j X_{t-j}\right)^2$$

Now our purpose is to find the minimum of $S(\beta)$.

By introducing column vector and matrix

$$Y = \begin{pmatrix} x_{p+1} \\ x_{p+2} \\ \vdots \\ x_N \end{pmatrix}, \quad X = \begin{pmatrix} x_p & x_{p-1} & \cdots & x_1 \\ x_{p+1} & x_p & \cdots & x_2 \\ \vdots & \vdots & & \vdots \\ x_{N-1} & x_{N-2} & \cdots & x_{N-p} \end{pmatrix}, \quad \beta = \begin{pmatrix} \rho_1 \\ \rho_2 \\ \vdots \\ \rho_p \end{pmatrix}$$

Function $S(\beta)$ can be written in distance form of $(N-p)$-dimensional Euclidean space

$$S(\beta) = \|Y - X\beta\|^2$$

which is exactly the same as what we had in the multiple linear regression of Chapter 2. Therefore when $p \times p$ symmetric matrix $X'X$ is positive definite, the least squares estimator of parameter β is

$$\hat{\beta} = (\hat{\rho}_1, \hat{\rho}_2, ..., \hat{\rho}_p)' = (X'X)^{-1}X'Y$$

and the least squares estimator of white noise variance σ^2 is

$$\hat{\sigma}^2 = \frac{1}{N-p}S(\hat{\beta}) = \frac{1}{N-p}(\hat{\beta}-\beta)'(\hat{\beta}-\beta)$$

The excellent performance of least squares estimator $\hat{\beta}$ and $\hat{\sigma}^2$ can be derived from the Gauss-Markov theorem in Chapter 2, namely, if $\{\varepsilon_t\}$ is an i.i.d. white noise, the least squares estimator $\hat{\beta}$ of β is the unique minimum variance linear unbiased estimator.

Besides these, the least square estimator is also a method of moments estimator and as such they both have the large sample property of convergence in distribution to a Normal. Assume that $\{\varepsilon_t\}$ of AR(p) process is an i.i.d. white noise, and $E(\varepsilon_t^4) < \infty$, then when $N \to \infty$,

$$\sqrt{N}(\hat{\beta} - \beta) \xrightarrow{L} N(0, \sigma^2 \Sigma_p^{-1})$$

where $\xrightarrow{L}$ denotes convergence in distribution, and $N(0, \sigma^2 \Sigma_p^{-1})$ represents a p-variate Normal distribution.

It can be proved that for larger N, there is no difference between the least squares estimation and the Yule-Walker estimation.

3. Maximum likelihood estimation of AR(p) process

The Yule-Walker estimation and least squares estimation belong to moment estimation. It's better to use least squares estimation when the random term has a relatively weak effect, while it is better to use the maximum likelihood estimation under the condition that it is strong. However, maximum likelihood estimation requires knowledge of the distribution of error.

Assume that the white noise of the AR(p) process $\varepsilon_t = X_t - \sum_{j=1}^{p} \rho_j X_{t-j}$ has a normal

distribution, then the joint density function of $\varepsilon_{p+1}, \varepsilon_{p+2}, \ldots, \varepsilon_N$ is

$$\left(\frac{1}{2\pi\sigma^2} \right)^{\frac{N-p}{2}} \exp\left(-\frac{1}{2\sigma^2} \sum_{t=p+1}^{N} \varepsilon_t^2 \right)$$

The likelihood function for $x_{p+1}, x_{p+2}, \ldots, x_N$ is

$$L(\vec{\rho}_p, \sigma^2) = \left(\frac{1}{2\pi\sigma^2} \right)^{\frac{N-p}{2}} \exp\left(-\frac{1}{2\sigma^2} \sum_{t=p+1}^{N} \left(x_t - \sum_{j=1}^{p} \rho_j x_{t-j} \right)^2 \right)$$

and the log-likelihood function is

$$\ln L(\vec{\rho}_p, \sigma^2) = -\frac{N-p}{2} \ln(\sigma^2) - \frac{1}{2\sigma^2} \sum_{t=p+1}^{N} \left[x_t - \sum_{j=1}^{p} \rho_j x_{t-j} \right]^2 + c$$

$$= -\frac{N-p}{2} \ln(\sigma^2) - \frac{1}{2\sigma^2} S(\vec{\rho}_p) + c \qquad (7.27)$$

where $c = -\dfrac{N-p}{2} \ln(2\pi)$ is a constant. To find the maximum value of logarithmic like-lihood function, we solve the equation

$$\frac{\partial \ln L(\vec{\rho}_p, \sigma^2)}{\partial \sigma^2} = -\frac{N-p}{2\sigma^2} + \frac{1}{2\sigma^4} S(\vec{\rho}_p) = 0$$

and obtain

$$\sigma^2 = \frac{1}{N-p} S(\vec{\rho}_p) \qquad (7.28)$$

Substituting it in log-likelihood function (7.26), we get

$$\ln L(\vec{\rho}_p, \sigma^2) = -\frac{N-p}{2} \ln(S(\vec{\rho}_p)) + c_0$$

Here c_0 is a constant unrelated to $\vec{\rho}_p$ and σ^2. We can see that the maximum value of $\ln L(\vec{\rho}_p, \sigma^2)$ is actually the minimum value of $S(\vec{\rho}_p)$. Therefore for the AR(p) process, under the assumption that the error terms have a Normal distribution, the maximum likelihood estimator of auto-regression coefficient is the same as least squares estimator, namely,

$$\hat{\vec{\rho}}_p = (\hat{\rho}_1, \hat{\rho}_2, ..., \hat{\rho}_p)' = (X'X)^{-1} X'Y$$

If we substitute maximum likelihood estimator $\hat{\vec{\rho}}_p$ in (7.28), we obtain maximum likelihood estimator of σ^2,

$$\hat{\sigma}^2 = \frac{1}{N-p} S(\hat{\vec{\rho}}_p) = \frac{1}{N-p} (\hat{\vec{\rho}}_p - \vec{\rho}_p)'(\hat{\vec{\rho}}_p - \vec{\rho}_p)$$

4. Box–Pierce test and Ljung–Box test

Since the sample estimates of the autocorrelation function are not likely to be identically zero even when the population values are, we use diagnostic tests to discern whether a time series appears to be nonautocorrelated. Box–Pierce test is a portmanteau test for autocorrelated errors. The **Box–Pierce statistic** (1970):

$$Q = N \sum_{k=1}^{p} \gamma_k^2$$

is computed as the weighted sum of squares of a sequence of autocorrelations. Under the null hypothesis that the series is white noise, Q has a limiting chi-squared distribution with p degrees of freedom.

Another portmanteau test is by the **Ljung–Box statistic** (1978):

$$Q' = N(N+2) \sum_{k=1}^{p} \frac{\gamma_k^2}{N-k}$$

which is a preferred version of the Box–Pierce test, because the Box–Pierce statistic has poor performance in small samples. The limiting distribution of Q' is the same as that of Q.

The Ljung–Box statistic is better for all sample sizes including small ones. In fact, the Ljung–Box statistic was described explicitly in the paper that lead to the use of the Box-Pierce statistic and from which the statistic takes its name.

Example 7.3   The least squares estimation of parameters of AR(p)   It is not difficult to program computation of least squares estimation for AR(p) process parameters. One can refer to DASC software for computations from data and the results. The goodness of fit figure of an example is as in Figure 7.8. In this example, total data points are 400, the order of the

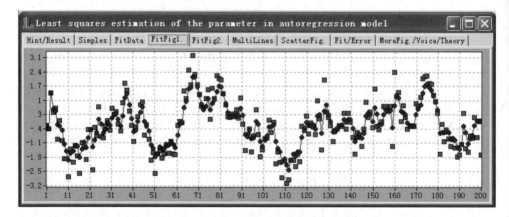

Figure 7.8   The least squares estimation for parameters of AR(p) process.

AR model, p = 3. In the computation of LSE, the number of total samples is 397. The results of LSR are as follows. The estimated regression equation is Y(t) = 0.398 Y(t–1) + 0.297 Y(t–2) + 0.128 Y(t–3); residual sum of squares is 257.95; regression sum of squares is 301.832; error variance estimation is 0.654695; standard deviation is 0.809132; and total correlation coefficient R^2 is 0.5392.

Besides, the program calculated the Box-Pierce statistic and Ljung-Box statistic. The Box-Pierce (1970) statistic is 74.696106, which as a chi-square statistic with 3 degrees of freedom is significant at 1% level. The Ljung-Box statistic is 79.800644, which as a chi-square statistic with three degrees of freedom is significant at 1% level. So we should reject the null hypothesis that the series is white noise.

More detailed computation process can be seen by clicking DASC → Time Series Analysis → Stationary Series → The Least Square Estimation for AR(p).

5.   Interval estimation of AR(p) process

We obtain the interval estimates of the AR(p) model parameters by means of the interval estimation methods of multivariate linear regression.

Suppose that the AR(p) model is

$$X_t = \sum_{j=1}^{p} \rho_j X_{t-j} + \varepsilon_t, \quad \varepsilon_t \sim W(0, \sigma^2)$$

Let

$$Y = \begin{pmatrix} x_{p+1} \\ x_{p+2} \\ \vdots \\ x_N \end{pmatrix}, \quad X = \begin{pmatrix} x_p & x_{p-1} & \cdots & x_1 \\ x_{p+1} & x_p & \cdots & x_2 \\ \vdots & \vdots & & \vdots \\ x_{N-1} & x_{N-2} & \cdots & x_{N-p} \end{pmatrix}, \quad \beta = \begin{pmatrix} \rho_1 \\ \rho_2 \\ \vdots \\ \rho_p \end{pmatrix}$$

then the least squares estimator of parameter β is:

$$\hat{\beta} = (\hat{\rho}_1, \hat{\rho}_2, ..., \hat{\rho}_p)' = (X'X)^{-1} X'Y$$

and the LSE of variance σ^2 of white noise is:

$$\hat{\sigma}^2 = \frac{1}{N-p}S(\hat{\beta}) = \frac{1}{N-p}(\hat{\beta}-\beta)'(\hat{\beta}-\beta)$$

According to the knowledge of multivariate linear regression, we have

$$(\hat{\beta}_j - \beta_j)\Big/\sqrt{C_{jj}\sigma^2} \sim N(0,1)$$

$$t = \frac{\hat{\beta}_j - \beta_j}{\sqrt{C_{jj}S_{ES}/(n-p)}} \sim t(N-p)$$

where $\hat{\beta}_j$ is the jth component of $\hat{\beta}$, C_{jj} is the jth element on the diagonal of the matrix $(X'X)^{-1}$. Substituted σ^2 by $\hat{\sigma}^2$, and the significant level is α, then the interval estimate of ρ_i is:

$$\hat{\rho}_j - \sqrt{C_{jj}}\,\hat{\sigma}\,t_{\alpha/2} < \rho_j < \hat{\rho}_j + \sqrt{C_{jj}}\,\hat{\sigma}\,t_{\alpha/2} \qquad (7.29)$$

Or the upper limit and lower limit of interval estimate of ρ_i

$$\hat{\rho}_j \pm \sqrt{C_{jj}}\,\hat{\sigma}\,t_{\alpha/2} \qquad (7.30)$$

Now we consider the interval estimate of the forecasting AR(p) model.

Taking $X_0 = (X_{01},\ldots, X_{0p})$, letting the forecasting value $\hat{Y}_0 = X_0\hat{\beta}$,[1] because $\hat{\beta} \sim N_p$ $(\beta, \sigma^2(X'X)^{-1})$, we have

$$\hat{Y}_0 = X_0\hat{\beta} \sim N(X_0\beta, \sigma^2 X_0'(X'X)^{-1}X_0)$$

If the value of σ^2 is unknown, substitute with $\hat{\sigma}^2 = S_{ES}/(n-p)$, we have

$$\frac{\hat{Y}_0 - X_0\hat{\beta}}{\hat{\sigma}\sqrt{X_0'(X'X)^{-1}X_0}} \sim t(n-p)$$

The interval estimate of $\hat{Y}_0$ (with significant level α) is:

$$X_0\hat{\beta} \pm t_{\alpha/2}\cdot\hat{\sigma}\cdot\sqrt{X_0'(X'X)^{-1}X_0} \qquad (7.31)$$

If the X_0 is a definite observation value, the interval length of the interval estimate of $\hat{Y}_0$ is $2\,t_{\alpha/2}\cdot\hat{\sigma}\cdot\sqrt{X_0'(X'X)^{-1}X_0}$. If X_0 is a forecasting value with lower limit X_{01} and upper limit X_{02}, then the interval estimate of $\hat{Y}_0$ (with significant level α) is:

$$X_0\hat{\beta} - t_{\alpha/2}\cdot\hat{\sigma}\cdot\sqrt{X_{01}'(X'X)^{-1}X_{01}},\, X_0\hat{\beta} + t_{\alpha/2}\cdot\hat{\sigma}\cdot\sqrt{X_{02}'(X'X)^{-1}X_{02}} \qquad (7.32)$$

---

[1] To keep the familiar notation used in multiple regression model we are replacing the autocorrelation coefficients ρs by βs.

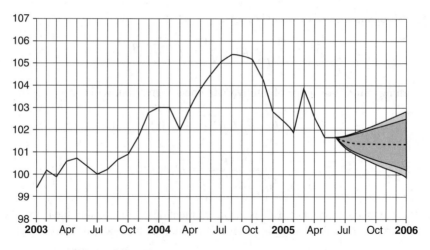

Figure 7.9   The interval forecasting of CPI of China.

Figure 7.9 shows the interval forecasting of CPI of China from June 2005 to January 2006. We should notice the shape of bell-mouthed range for interval forecasting, i.e., the farther the forecasting point is, the bigger the forecasting error is. Meanwhile we note that there are two wide mouths in the right side of diagram, one wider than the other, and the dot line in the middle of mouths is the values of point forecast. The mouths are corresponding to different significant level, i.e., the lower the significant level is, the wider the mouth is.

Figure 7.9 is generated by another figure system using DASC. In fact, DASC not only offers self-contained software through an executable file, but also offers DLL facility to embed the Browser/Server (B/S) or Client/Server (C/S) system for wider use such as cloud computing.

7.1.5   Order identification for AR(p) process

So far, the methods of estimation of the parameters of the AR(p) process are based on knowing a priori the order p of the AR process. In any given real problem, order p is unknown. We have to discuss the determination or identification of p. Three main methods, partial autocorrelation function (PACF), **AIC criterion**, and **BIC criterion**, are mainly used.

A property of AR(p) is that the partial autocorrelation function is **truncated at** p, so a natural choice of p depends on where the sample partial autocorrelation function is truncated at k. If $\{\hat{\rho}_{k,k}\}$ truncated at $\hat{p}$, namely, when $k > \hat{p}$, $\hat{\rho}_{k,k} \approx 0$, whereas $\hat{\rho}_{\hat{p},\hat{p}} \neq 0$, then we choose $\hat{p}$ as the choice for p.

Since for any $k < N$, kth order auto-covariance matrix of sample is positive definite, sample partial autocorrelation coefficient $\hat{\rho}_{k,k}$ can be figured out via Yule-Walker equation

$$\begin{pmatrix} \hat{\gamma}_1 \\ \hat{\gamma}_2 \\ \vdots \\ \hat{\gamma}_k \end{pmatrix} = \begin{pmatrix} \hat{\gamma}_0 & \hat{\gamma}_1 & \cdots & \hat{\gamma}_{k-1} \\ \hat{\gamma}_1 & \hat{\gamma}_0 & \cdots & \hat{\gamma}_{k-2} \\ \vdots & \vdots & & \vdots \\ \hat{\gamma}_{k-1} & \hat{\gamma}_{k-2} & \cdots & \hat{\gamma}_0 \end{pmatrix} \begin{pmatrix} \hat{\rho}_{k,1} \\ \hat{\rho}_{k,2} \\ \vdots \\ \hat{\rho}_{k,k} \end{pmatrix} \qquad (7.33)$$

or via the Levinson recursion formula (7.32) as well.

When we take the limit of a matrix or a vector, it means we take the limit of every element in them. We know that estimators of auto-covariance function are consistent, namely, $\hat{\gamma}_k \xrightarrow{P} \gamma_k, (as\ N \to \infty)$, therefore for any $k > p$, we solve the Yule-Walker equation above (7.33) to obtain $\hat{\vec{\rho}}_k = \hat{\Gamma}_k^{-1} \hat{\vec{\gamma}}_k$ and take the limits of the both side of it,

$$
\lim_{N \to \infty} \begin{pmatrix} \hat{\rho}_{k,1} \\ \hat{\rho}_{k,2} \\ \vdots \\ \hat{\rho}_{k,k} \end{pmatrix} = \lim_{N \to \infty} \begin{pmatrix} \hat{\gamma}_0 & \hat{\gamma}_1 & \cdots & \hat{\gamma}_{k-1} \\ \hat{\gamma}_1 & \hat{\gamma}_0 & \cdots & \hat{\gamma}_{k-2} \\ \vdots & \vdots & & \vdots \\ \hat{\gamma}_{k-1} & \hat{\gamma}_{k-2} & \cdots & \hat{\gamma}_0 \end{pmatrix}^{-1} \times \lim_{N \to \infty} \begin{pmatrix} \hat{\gamma}_1 \\ \hat{\gamma}_2 \\ \vdots \\ \hat{\gamma}_k \end{pmatrix}
$$

$$
= \begin{pmatrix} \gamma_0 & \gamma_1 & \cdots & \gamma_{k-1} \\ \gamma_1 & \gamma_0 & \cdots & \gamma_{k-2} \\ \vdots & \vdots & & \vdots \\ \gamma_{k-1} & \gamma_{k-2} & \cdots & \gamma_0 \end{pmatrix}^{-1} \times \begin{pmatrix} \gamma_1 \\ \gamma_2 \\ \vdots \\ \gamma_k \end{pmatrix} = \begin{pmatrix} \rho_{k,1} \\ \rho_{k,2} \\ \vdots \\ \rho_{k,k} \end{pmatrix}
$$

Then from (7.15) we obtain $\vec{\rho}_n = (\rho_{n,1}, \rho_{n,2}, ..., \rho_{n,n})' = (\rho_1, \rho_2, ..., \rho_p, 0, ..., 0)'$, thus we conclude that when the white noise term $\{\varepsilon_t\}$ of AR(p) process is i.i.d., then for any $k > p$,

$$
\lim_{N \to \infty} \hat{\rho}_{kj} = \begin{cases} \rho_j, & \text{when } j \le p \\ 0, & \text{when } j > p \end{cases}
$$

Since the limiting distribution of $\hat{\rho}_k$ is already established one can use an asymptotic test for the null hypothesis $\rho_{p+1} = 0$. Since this is an asymptotic test and the sample is of a finite size the test cannot be relied upon. As such we may entertain alternate models including the true AR(p) model.

AIC criterion can be used to select one among the competing models. Assume that the order of the AR(p) process is k, less than the upper bound P_0 (chosen from the asymptotic test for partial autocorrelation discussed above). If we have the estimator of variance of the white noise of AR(k) and denote it as $\hat{\sigma}_k^2$, we can introduce **AIC function**

$$
\text{AIC}(k) = \ln \hat{\sigma}_k^2 + \frac{2k}{N}, \quad k = 0, 1, ..., P_0
$$

We may choose that k which minimizes AIC(k) to determine **the order of** AR(p) **process**.

It can be proved that order $\hat{p}$ chosen using AIC criterion is not consistent; namely, it doesn't converge to the true order p in probability. Generally when sample size N is not large enough, AIC order is relatively high.

In order to avoid the inconsistency associated with order chosen by the AIC criterion, we can use the BIC criterion for order identification. The BIC function is:

$$
\text{BIC}(k) = \ln \hat{\sigma}_k^2 + \frac{k \ln N}{N}, \quad k = 0, 1, ..., P_0
$$

We call a positive integer a k **BIC order** of AR(p) process if it is the first local minimum point of BIC(k) in $(0, 1, 2, ..., P_0)$. If the white noise of the AR(p) process is i.i.d., it can be proved that the BIC order is strongly consistent.

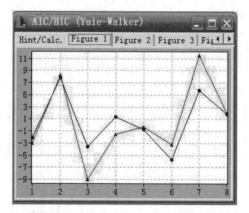

Figure 7.10   AIC/BIC (Yule-Walker).

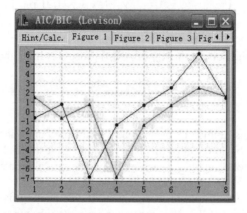

Figure 7.11   AIC/BIC (Levison).

Example 7.4   AIC criterion and BIC criterion   Which choice is the better, AIC **or** BIC for choosing the order p of $AR(p)$? There are many arguments. According to our programming experience, each has its own merits. In the following two figures, dots represent AIC criterion data points, while triangles represent BIC criterion data points. $\hat{\sigma}^2$ in Figure 7.10 are evaluated via the Yule-Walker calculation with AIC order 6 and BIC order 3. $\hat{\sigma}^2$ in Figure 7.11 are obtained by the Levison recursion formula with AIC order 3 and BIC order 4.

In fact, there are many methods to identify the $AR(p)$ model or to test the parameters of the $AR(p)$ model. In this section we only introduced some basic methods such as testing the hypothesis on the significance of partial correlation coefficients $\rho_{n,n}$ ((7.21) and (7.19)), and the AIC and BIC criteria.

7.2   Moving average model MA(q)

7.2.1   MA(q) model and its properties

The moving average process describes the relationship between time series X_t and white noise series ε_t. **The Moving Average process of order q**, or MA(q), is expressed by

$$X_t = \varepsilon_t + \lambda_1 \varepsilon_{t-1} + \lambda_2 \varepsilon_{t-2} + \cdots + \lambda_q \varepsilon_{t-q} = \varepsilon_t + \sum_{j=1}^{q} \lambda_j \varepsilon_{t-j} \qquad (7.34)$$

where $\{\varepsilon_t\}$ is white noise $W(0, \sigma^2)$. If real numbers $\lambda_1, \lambda_2,..., \lambda_q$ $(\lambda_q \neq 0)$ satisfy

$$1 + \sum_{j=1}^{q} \lambda_j z^j \neq 0, \quad |z| < 1 \qquad (7.35)$$

then the series is a stationary time series and is called a moving average series. If we further require polynomial (7.35) has no zeros on unit circle $|z| = 1$, namely, when $|z| \leq 1$, $1 + \sum_{j=1}^{q} \lambda_j z^j \neq 0$, then (7.34) is said to be invertible, and the corresponding stationary time series is called invertible MA(q) series. For an invertible MA(q) process, the relationship between ε_t and X_t can be expressed by

$$\varepsilon_t = \sum_{j=1}^{\infty} \varphi_j X_{t-j}$$

Since MA(q) series is the sum of finite weighted sums of white noise, compared to AR(p) series, the series of a MA(q) oscillates more moderately and hence more stable. These features are embodied in the truncation of auto-correlation function and flatness of spectral density.

We can convert the mean of a MA(q) series to zero, i.e. without any loss of generality assume that $E(X_t) = 0$. Then its auto-covariance function is autocorrelation function. Let $\lambda_0 = 1$, we obtain

$$\gamma_k = E(X_t X_{t+k}) = \begin{cases} \sigma^2 \sum_{j=0}^{q-k} \lambda_j \lambda_{j+k}, & 0 \leq k \leq q \\ 0 & k > q \end{cases} \qquad (7.36)$$

We conclude therefore that auto-covariance function of $\{X_t\}$ of MA(q) series is truncated at q according to

$$\gamma_q = \sigma^2 \lambda_q \neq 0, \quad \gamma_k = 0, \quad |k| > q$$

And its spectral density is

$$f(\omega) = \frac{1}{2\pi} \sum_{k=-q}^{q} \gamma_k e^{-ik\omega}, \quad \omega \in [-\pi, \pi]$$

for all $\omega \in [-\pi, \pi]$, and $f(\omega) \geq 0$.

Conversely, for any stationary time series with zero mean, if the autocovariance function truncates at q, then this stationary time series must be an MA(q) series.

In conclusion, for a stationary time series $\{X_t\}$ with zero mean and auto-covariance function $\{\gamma_k\}$, the necessary and sufficient condition for $\{X_t\}$ being an MA(q) series is

$$\gamma_q \neq 0, \quad \gamma_k = 0, \quad |k| > q$$

7.2.2   Parameter estimation of MA(q) model when the order q is known

We introduce three methods to estimate the parameters of MA(q) when the order q is known: moment estimation, estimation using the inverse correlation function, and estimation based on new information.

1.   Moment estimation of MA(q) process based on auto-covariance function

Suppose that sample $X_1, X_2,...,X_N$ come from moving average process MA(q)

$$X_t = \varepsilon_t + \sum_{j=1}^{q} \lambda_j \varepsilon_{t-j}, \quad \varepsilon_t \sim W(0, \sigma^2)$$

where $\bar{\lambda} = (\lambda_1, \lambda_2,...,\lambda_q)$ and σ^2 are parameters to be estimated. We also assume that $\bar{\lambda} = (\lambda_1, \lambda_2,...,\lambda_q)$ satisfies the invertibility condition

$$1 + \sum_{j=1}^{q} \lambda_j z^j \neq 0, \quad |z| \leq 1 \tag{7.37}$$

After evaluating the auto-covariance function $\{\gamma_k\}$ of the sample, we can estimate the parameters of MA(q) by two methods using $\{\gamma_k\}$.

The method of **moment estimation** is based on (7.36). If we set $\lambda_0 = 1$, $\bar{\lambda}$ should satisfy equations

$$\gamma_k = \sigma^2(\lambda_0 \lambda_k + \lambda_1 \lambda_{k+1} + \cdots + \lambda_{q-k} \lambda_q), \quad 0 \leq k \leq q$$

We can solve this system of $q + 1$ nonlinear equations, in as many unknown parameters, to obtain the estimates of $\bar{\lambda}$ and σ^2. One can solve this equation system algebraically, but the solution may not satisfy the invertibility condition. We find it more convenient, however, to use another iterative procedure for estimation of the parameters of MA(q) that could lead to estimates that do satisfy the invertibility conditions by changing the starting points of the iterative algorithm.

We first calculate the auto-covariance function $\hat{\gamma}_k$, for $k = 0, 1, 2,..., q$, by using the observations. Let the given initial values of $\bar{\lambda}$ and σ^2 be

$$\vec{\lambda}(0) = [\lambda_1(0), \lambda_2(0), ..., \lambda_q(0)]^T, \quad \sigma^2(0)$$

and let the jth values of $\bar{\lambda}$ and σ^2 be

$$\vec{\lambda}(j) = [\lambda_1(j), \lambda_2(j), ..., \lambda_q(j)]^T, \quad \sigma^2(j)$$

then the $(j+1)$th values of $\bar{\lambda}$ and σ^2 are

$$\hat{\sigma}^2(j+1) = \frac{\hat{\gamma}_0}{1 + \hat{\lambda}_1^2(j) + \cdots + \hat{\lambda}_q^2(j)}$$

$$\hat{\lambda}_k(j+1) = \frac{\hat{\gamma}_k}{\hat{\sigma}^2(j+1)} - [\hat{\lambda}_1(j)\hat{\lambda}_{k+1}(j) + \cdots + \hat{\lambda}_{q-k}(j)\hat{\lambda}_q(j)]$$

$$\hat{\lambda}_q(j+1) = \frac{\hat{\gamma}_q}{\hat{\sigma}^2(j+1)}$$

where $j \le k \le q - 1$. With the given iterative precision $\delta > 0$, the iteration stops when the jth iterative $\hat{\lambda}(j)$ and $\hat{\sigma}^2(j)$ satisfy

$$\sum_{k=0}^q \left| \hat{\gamma}_k - \hat{\sigma}^2(j) \sum_{t=0}^{q-k} \hat{\lambda}_t(j)\hat{\lambda}_{t+k}(j) \right| < \delta$$

and the iterated results are regarded as estimators of $\hat{\lambda}$ and σ^2. These estimates need to be checked for the verification of invertibility condition (7.37). If its characteristic polynomial has root in the unit circle, then we need to start the iterations again by changing the initial values until we find that the invertibility conditions are satisfied.

Examples indicate that we cannot guarantee the iterations converges for all MA series,[2] and that even after repeated trials with alternate initial conditions we may not get estimates that satisfy the invertibility conditions. We therefore present an alternate method that can generate estimates satisfying the invertibility condition.

Now we introduce the second methods of estimation of the parameters of MA(q) when the order q is known.

2. Estimation of parameters of MA(q) process based on an inverse correlation function

The disadvantages of the method of moment estimation above are that the estimators cannot guarantee the invertibility condition and that the iterative procedure may not converge. Another method, called inverse correlation function method (Cleveland, 1972), however, can guarantee the invertibility condition. We first introduce the concept of an inverse correlation function. The basic idea behind the inverse correlation function method is that if a MA(q) is invertible there exists a AR(q) process with the same parameters as the MA(q) process, and then one can estimate those parameters using the Yule-Walker equations.

Let $\{X_t\}$ be an invertible stationary MA(q) series:

$$X_t = \varepsilon_t + \sum_{j=1}^q \lambda_j \varepsilon_{t-j}$$

Let $f(\omega)$ be its (positive) spectral density. Then it can be proved that the spectral density of AR(q) series

$$Y_t = -\sum_{j=1}^q \lambda_j Y_{t-j} + \varepsilon_t$$

---

[2] As the iterative algorithm defines a mapping of successive parameter values as functions of the previous iteration values, one can determine under what conditions such mapping will be a contraction mapping. As per a theorem in functional analysis there will be a fixed point if the mapping is a contraction mapping. Convergence is characterized by the mapping having a fixed point. Thus one can derive the conditions under which the iterative procedure in fact converges.

where $\varepsilon_t \sim W(0, \sigma^{-2})$ exists, and it is given by:

$$f_y(\omega) = \frac{1}{4\pi^2 f(\omega)} \tag{7.38}$$

Note that the variance of white noise ε_t is the reciprocal of that of MA(q) series. We call (7.38) **inverse spectral density** of $\{X_t\}$, and call

$$\gamma_y(k) = \int_{-\pi}^{\pi} e^{ik\omega} f_y(\omega) d\omega \tag{7.39}$$

inverse correlation function or inverse autocorrelation function of $\{X_t\}$.

We also note that the auto-covariance function

$$\gamma_y(k) = \int_{-\pi}^{\pi} e^{ik\omega} f_y(\omega) d\omega, \qquad k = 0, 1, \ldots$$

of $\{Y_t\}$ is exactly the inverse correlation function of $\{X_t\}$, as defined in (7.39).

Now if we can estimate the inverse correlation function $\gamma_y(k)$ of $\{X_t\}$, for $k = 0, 1, \ldots, q$, then we can obtain the estimators of parameters in $\bar{\lambda}$ and σ^2 of MA(q) process by solving the Yule-Walker equations using the sample estimates of the lagged correlations up to order q.

$$\begin{pmatrix} \hat{\gamma}_y(1) \\ \hat{\gamma}_y(2) \\ \vdots \\ \hat{\gamma}_y(q) \end{pmatrix} = \begin{pmatrix} \hat{\gamma}_y(0) & \hat{\gamma}_y(1) & \cdots & \hat{\gamma}_y(q-1) \\ \hat{\gamma}_y(1) & \hat{\gamma}_y(0) & \cdots & \hat{\gamma}_y(q-2) \\ \vdots & \vdots & & \vdots \\ \hat{\gamma}_y(q-1) & \hat{\gamma}_y(q-2) & \cdots & \hat{\gamma}_y(0) \end{pmatrix} \begin{pmatrix} -\hat{\lambda}_1 \\ -\hat{\lambda}_2 \\ \vdots \\ -\hat{\lambda}_q \end{pmatrix} \tag{7.40}$$

and

$$\hat{\sigma}^{-2} = \hat{\gamma}_y(0) + \hat{\lambda}_1 \hat{\gamma}_y(1) + \hat{\lambda}_2 \hat{\gamma}_y(2) + \cdots + \hat{\lambda}_q \hat{\gamma}_y(q) \tag{7.41}$$

When the $(q+1)$th order matrix of the inverse correlation function

$$(\hat{\gamma}_y(k-j)), k, j = 1, 2, \ldots, q+1$$

is positive definite, the estimator $\hat{\bar{\lambda}}$ will satisfy the invertibility condition.

As to the estimation of the inverse correlation function, we begin from the AR(p) process. Let $X_t = \sum_{j=1}^{p} \rho_j X_{t-j} + \varepsilon_t$ be an AR(p) process, where $(\rho_1, \rho_2, \ldots, \rho_p)$ are its regression coefficients and σ^2 is the variance of $\{\varepsilon_t\}$, then the inverse correlation function of $\{X_t\}$ is

$$\gamma_y(k) = \frac{1}{\sigma^2} \sum_{j=0}^{p-k} \rho_j \rho_{j+k}, \quad 0 \le k \le p, \quad \rho_0 = -1 $$

when $k > p$, $\gamma_y(k) = 0$.

Therefore we can generalize the method of estimating the parameters $\hat{\lambda}_1, \hat{\lambda}_2, \ldots, \hat{\lambda}_q$ and $\hat{\sigma}^2$ of MA(q) series by calculating inverse correlation function $\hat{\gamma}_y(k)$ of the sample $x_1, x_2, \ldots, x_N$. The procedure involves the following four steps:

Step 1. Create an AR($\hat{p}$) process using the sample of $\{x_t\}$. Here $\hat{p}$ can be identified by the graph of the partial autocorrelation function (PACF) or AIC.

Step 2. Solve Yule-Walker equations for this sample

$$\begin{pmatrix} \hat{\gamma}_1 \\ \hat{\gamma}_2 \\ \vdots \\ \hat{\gamma}_{\hat{p}} \end{pmatrix} = \begin{pmatrix} \hat{\gamma}_0 & \hat{\gamma}_1 & \cdots & \hat{\gamma}_{\hat{p}-1} \\ \hat{\gamma}_1 & \hat{\gamma}_0 & \cdots & \hat{\gamma}_{\hat{p}-2} \\ \vdots & \vdots & & \vdots \\ \hat{\gamma}_{\hat{p}-1} & \hat{\gamma}_{\hat{p}-2} & \cdots & \hat{\gamma}_0 \end{pmatrix} \begin{pmatrix} \hat{\rho}_1 \\ \hat{\rho}_2 \\ \vdots \\ \hat{\rho}_{\hat{p}} \end{pmatrix}$$

and

$$\hat{\sigma}^2 = \hat{\gamma}_0 - (\hat{\rho}_1 \hat{\gamma}_1 + \hat{\rho}_2 \hat{\gamma}_2 + \cdots + \hat{\rho}_{\hat{p}} \hat{\gamma}_{\hat{p}})$$

We thus obtain estimates of coefficients $(\hat{\rho}_1, \hat{\rho}_2, ..., \hat{\rho}_p)$ and $\hat{\sigma}^2$ of AR($\hat{p}$) process.

Step 3. Compute the inverse correlation function of sample

$$\hat{\gamma}_y(k) = \frac{1}{\hat{\sigma}^2} \sum_{j=0}^{p-k} \hat{\rho}_j \hat{\rho}_{j+k}, \quad k = 0, 1, 2, ..., q, \quad \hat{\rho}_0 = -1$$

When $(\hat{\rho}_1, \hat{\rho}_2, \cdots, \hat{\rho}_p)$ are not identical, $q \times q$ coefficient matrix in (7.40) is exactly positive definite.

Step 4. Obtain the coefficient estimators $\hat{\bar{\lambda}} = (\hat{\lambda}_1, \hat{\lambda}_2, ..., \hat{\lambda}_q)'$ and $\hat{\sigma}^2$ of MA(q) by sample Yule-Walker calculation (7.40) and (7.41).

Now we introduce the third method of estimating the parameters of MA(q) when the order q is known.

3. New information estimate for MA(q) process

We call $\varepsilon_t = X_t - \hat{X}_t$ new information or innovation of X_t, where $\hat{X}_t$ is constructed from X_1, $X_2, ..., X_{t-1}$, excluding ε_t.

For an MA(q) series, the estimation of X_t that is constructed by sample series $X_1, X_2, ..., X_{t-1}$ is the same as that by new information series $\{\varepsilon_t\}$, because white noise series $\{\varepsilon_t\}$ is just its new information series. Let ε_m be the predictive error when we forecast X_m by use of all previous data $X_{m-k}(k = 1, 2, ...m - 1)$. Then when m is large, $\hat{\varepsilon}_m = X_m - \hat{X}_m$ is the approximation of ε_m.

Substituting for the right side of MA(q),

$$X_t = \varepsilon_t + \lambda_1 \varepsilon_{t-1} + \lambda_2 \varepsilon_{t-2} + \cdots + \lambda_q \varepsilon_{t-q}$$

from the new information series, we obtain

$$X_t = \hat{\varepsilon}_t + \lambda_1 \hat{\varepsilon}_{t-1} + \lambda_2 \hat{\varepsilon}_{t-2} + \cdots + \lambda_q \hat{\varepsilon}_{t-q}$$

Since $\hat{\varepsilon}_t = X_t - \hat{X}_t$,

$$X_t = X_t - \hat{X}_t + \lambda_1 \hat{\varepsilon}_{t-1} + \lambda_2 \hat{\varepsilon}_{t-2} + \cdots + \lambda_q \hat{\varepsilon}_{t-q}$$

Then

$$\hat{X}_t = \lambda_1 \hat{\varepsilon}_{t-1} + \lambda_2 \hat{\varepsilon}_{t-2} + \cdots + \lambda_q \hat{\varepsilon}_{t-q}$$

Suppose that the mth step estimator for X_t constructed by new information series $\{\hat{\varepsilon}_t\}$ is

$$\hat{X}_{m+1} = \theta_{m,1}\hat{\varepsilon}_m + \theta_{m,2}\hat{\varepsilon}_{m-1} + \cdots + \theta_{m,q}\hat{\varepsilon}_{m+1-q}$$

Comparing these two formulas, we know it is reasonable to estimate λ_j by $\theta_{m,j}$, and this is the new information estimation for MA(q) process. The estimator of $\theta_{m,j}$ is obtained by the recursion formula

$$\hat{\theta}_{n,n-k} = \hat{v}_k^{-1}\left(\hat{\gamma}_{n-k} - \sum_{j=0}^{k-1}\hat{\theta}_{k,k-j}\hat{\theta}_{n,n-j}\hat{v}_j\right), \quad 0 \le k \le n-1$$

If the summation is from zero to -1 then we define the corresponding sum to be zero. As to the estimation of v_j^2, we always obtain by predictive mean squared error

$$v_k = E(\hat{\varepsilon}_{k+1}^2)$$

and recursion formula

$$\hat{v}_n = \hat{\gamma}_0 - \sum_{j=0}^{n-1}\hat{\theta}_{n,n-j}^2\hat{v}_j, \quad 1 \le n \le m$$

At the beginning, we assume that $\hat{v}_0 = \hat{\gamma}_0$, and then the recursion order is

$$\hat{v}_0; \hat{\theta}_{1,1}, \hat{v}_1; \hat{\theta}_{2,2}, \hat{\theta}_{2,1}, \hat{v}_2; \hat{\theta}_{3,3}, \hat{\theta}_{3,2}, \hat{\theta}_{3,1}, \hat{v}_3; \ldots.$$

The justification for the estimation using new information is comparatively complicated (Brockwell and Davis, 1991), and thus it is omitted. Estimation of the parameters using the methods described here in this section can all be performed by DASC software, and they will be illustrated shortly.

7.2.3   Spectral density estimation for MA(q) process

The **spectral density** for a MA(q) process is

$$f(\lambda) = \frac{\sigma^2}{2\pi}\left|1 + \sum_{k=1}^{q}\lambda_k e^{ik\omega}\right|^2$$

By estimating the parameters of the MA(q) process, we obtain the estimate of spectral density function:

$$\hat{f}(\omega) = \frac{\hat{\sigma}^2}{2\pi}\left|1 + \sum_{k=1}^{\hat{q}}\hat{\lambda}_k e^{ik\omega}\right|^2$$

If $\hat{q}, \hat{\lambda}_1, \hat{\lambda}_2, \ldots, \hat{\lambda}_q$ and $\hat{\sigma}^2$ are consistent estimators of $q, \lambda_1, \lambda_2, \ldots, \lambda_q$ and σ^2 respectively, $\hat{f}(\omega)$ is the consistent estimator of $\hat{f}(\omega)$.

Example 7.5   Method of moments estimation and LSE of parameters of MA(q) process   We first consider moving average process MA(1):

$$X_t = \varepsilon_t + \lambda\varepsilon_{t-1}, \quad \varepsilon_t \sim W(0, \sigma^2), \quad \text{and} \quad |\lambda| < 1$$

Since $|\lambda| < 1$, MA(1) is invertible. It is easy to figure out

$$\gamma_0 = \sigma^2(1+\lambda^2), \quad \gamma_1 = \lambda\sigma^2 \text{ and } \gamma_k = 0 \text{ when } |k| \geq 2$$

The autocorrelation coefficients of this MA(1) series are

$$r_1 = \frac{\lambda}{1+\lambda^2}, \quad r_2 = r_3 = \cdots = 0 \tag{7.42}$$

Rewrite (7.42) as a quadratic equation of λ, namely, $r_1\lambda^2 - \lambda + r_1 = 0$, and its discriminant is $1 - 4r_1^2$. There will be real roots of (7.42) only when $|r_1| \leq 0.5$. Because MA(1) process requires that $|\lambda| \leq 1$, only one solution $\lambda = \dfrac{1-\sqrt{1-4r_1^2}}{2r_1}$ meets the requirement. And we know that the moment estimator of r_1 is $\hat{r}_1 = \hat{\gamma}_1/\hat{\gamma}_0$, so the **moment estimator** of λ is

$$\hat{\lambda} = \frac{1-\sqrt{1-4\hat{r}_1^2}}{2\hat{r}_1}$$

If $\{\varepsilon_t\}$ is i.i.d. white noise, then $\hat{r}_1$ is the **strongly consistent estimator** of r_1, namely, $\lim\limits_{N\to\infty} \hat{r}_1 = r_1$, and then

$$\lim_{N\to\infty} \hat{\lambda} = \lim_{N\to\infty} \frac{1-\sqrt{1-4\hat{r}_1^2}}{2\hat{r}_1} = \lambda$$

Therefore, $\hat{\lambda}$ is the strongly consistent estimator of λ. Furthermore, as $N \to \infty$, $\sqrt{N}(\hat{\lambda} - \lambda)$ converges in distribution to normal distribution

$$N\left(0, \frac{1+\lambda^2+\lambda^4+\lambda^6+\lambda^8}{(1-\lambda^2)^2}\right)$$

The spectral density of this MA(1) series is

$$f(\omega) = \frac{\sigma^2}{2\pi}|1+\lambda e^{i\omega}|^2 = \frac{\sigma^2}{2\pi}(1+\lambda^2+2\lambda\cos\omega), \quad \omega \in [-\pi, \pi]$$

and the **partial correlation coefficients** are

$$\rho_{k,k} = -(-\lambda)^k(1-\lambda^2)(1-\lambda^{2k+2})^{-1}, \quad k \geq 1$$

The reverse form is $\varepsilon_t = \sum\limits_{j=0}^{\infty}(-\lambda)^j X_{t-j}$, where a finite order MA process is written as an infinite order autoregressive process.

Next we study another example of the moving average process MA(2):

$$X_t = \varepsilon_t + \lambda_1\varepsilon_{t-1} + \lambda_2\varepsilon_{t-2}, \quad \varepsilon_t \sim W(0, \sigma^2)$$

The characteristic polynomial for this series is $1 + \lambda_1 z + \lambda_2 z^2 \neq 0$, satisfying $|z| < 1$. The auto-covariance functions of MA(2) are

$$\gamma_0 = \sigma^2(1 + \lambda_1^2 + \lambda_2^2), \quad \gamma_1 = \sigma^2(\lambda_1 + \lambda_1 \lambda_2)$$
$$\gamma_2 = \sigma^2 \lambda_2, \quad \gamma_k = 0, \quad \text{when} \quad |k| > 2$$

the autocorrelation coefficients are

$$r_1 = \frac{\lambda_1 + \lambda_1 \lambda_2}{1 + \lambda_1^2 + \lambda_2^2}, \quad r_2 = \frac{\lambda_2}{1 + \lambda_1^2 + \lambda_2^2}, \quad r_k = 0, \quad \text{when} \quad |k| > 2$$

the spectral density is

$$f(\omega) = \frac{\sigma^2}{2\pi} |1 + \lambda_1 e^{i\omega} + \lambda_2 e^{i2\omega}|^2$$

The right side of the MA process is random error without specific data. How do we obtain a predicted or fitted value on the left, having obtained the parameter estimates of the model? There are three series of which one is the original observation data series $\{X_t\}$, another is fitted values using the estimated model $\{\hat{X}_t\}$, and the third is a series of residuals of estimation series $\{\hat{\varepsilon}_t\}$. They satisfy three kinds of relations. Using the concept of **estimation of new information or innovation**, we have

$$\hat{\varepsilon}_t = X_t - \hat{X}_t$$

according to the MA process, the relation is

$$\hat{X}_t = \varepsilon_t + \sum_{j=1}^{q} \lambda_j \hat{\varepsilon}_{t-j}$$

according to the best fitting,

$$\sum_{t=q+1}^{N} (X_t - \hat{X}_t)^2 \xrightarrow{\lambda_1 \cdots \lambda_q} \min$$

Therefore when model coefficients and the first q initial values for fitting are given, with original observation we can obtain the estimated series of residual and the series of model fitted values by successive recursion. Then according to the best fitting requirement, we obtain new estimates for model coefficients. And with these new estimates we can go on to get a next estimate and so on. After a sufficient number of iterations, we choose the coefficients corresponding to the best fitting situation. The detailed computation process can be seen by clicking DASC → Time Series Analysis → Stationary Series → Moment Estimation for MA(q) with Covariance. Figure 7.12 below shows the computation results.

7.2.4 Order identification for MA(q) process

A MA(q) series is characterized by its autocorrelation coefficient r truncating at q, therefore when autocorrelation coefficient of sample $\hat{r}_k = \hat{\gamma}_k / \hat{\gamma}_0$ becomes very small after a certain $\hat{q}$, we may regard $\hat{q}$ as the estimator of q. Then how to judge whether $\hat{r}_k$ is very small? We can judge

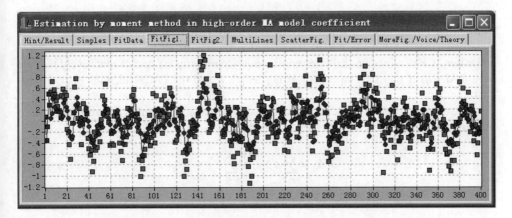

Figure 7.12   Estimation of MA(5) by Moment Method.

either by the figure of $\hat{r}_k$ or approximately by its limiting distribution. When $m > q$, $\sqrt{N}\hat{r}_m$ converges in distribution to normal distribution $N(0,\ 1+2r_1^2+2r_2^2+\cdots+2r_q^2)$.

As in the last section dealing with the AR(p) process we can use both AIC and BIC criteria for selecting the order of the MA(q) process. If the upper bound of order q is Q_0, then for $m = 0, 1, 2,..., Q_0$, we can fit MA(q) process successively by using the foregoing methods. Let $\hat{\sigma}_m^2$ denote the estimator of the variance of white noise σ^2, and we define the **AIC function**

$$\text{AIC}(m) = \ln(\hat{\sigma}_m^2) + \frac{2m}{N}, \quad m = 0, 1, ..., Q_0$$

where N is the number of observations in our sample. The point $\hat{q}$ where AIC(m) reaches its minimum is chosen to be the estimator of order q of the MA(q) process. Similarly we have BIC criterion:

$$\text{BIC}(m) = \ln(\hat{\sigma}_m^2) + \frac{m \ln N}{N}, \quad m = 0, 1, ..., Q_0$$

7.3   Auto-regressive moving-average process ARMA(p, q)

7.3.1   ARMA(p, q) model and its properties

1.   General model of ARMA(p, q) model

In the previous two sections we discussed the AR(p) and MA(q) process. Sometimes we encounter stationary time series that cannot be easily fitted as a AR(p) process or as a MA(q) process. Any such attempt could require estimation of either p or q of a large magnitude with several parameters. It is however found that one can use what is called an Autoregressive Moving Average Process with much fewer parameters giving rise to an equivalent or a better fit.

We have shown earlier in this chapter that an AR(p) can be represented as a MA(∞) and an invertible MA(q) can also be represented as an AR(∞). We also know that it is better to have a model with fewer parameters than more parameters. So, we look at the Auto Correlation Function (ACF) and Partial Auto Correlation Function (PACF) and decide tentatively that we have a AR(p) if the PACF tapers off or truncates at lag length p while the ACF declines or oscillates continuously. Similarly we decide tentatively that we have a MA(q) if the ACF tapers off at lag length q and the PACF declines or oscillates continuously.

An extremely general model that encompasses AR(p) and MA(q) is the **auto-regressive moving average process**, or ARMA(p, q), model:

$$X_t = \sum_{j=1}^{p} \rho_j X_{t-j} + \sum_{j=0}^{q} \lambda_j \varepsilon_{t-j} \tag{7.43}$$

where white noise $\varepsilon_t \sim W(0, \sigma^2)$. At the same time, we still emphasize that time t should be an integer.

The series ARMA(p, q) may not be stationary without some restrictions on coefficients ρ_j and λ_j. In order to guarantee the stationarity, analogous to AR(p) and MA(q) process, we assume that two characteristic polynomials have no roots in the unit circle, namely,

$$1 - \sum_{j=1}^{p} \rho_j z^j \neq 0, \sum_{j=0}^{q} \lambda_j z^j \neq 0 \,|\, z \,|\, < 1 \tag{7.44}$$

Another requirement is that these two characteristic polynomials have no common roots.

2.   Stationary solutions for ARMA(p, q) process

We can write (7.43) in the following equivalent form:

$$X_t - \sum_{j=1}^{p} \rho_j X_{t-j} = \sum_{j=0}^{q} \lambda_j \varepsilon_{t-j} \tag{7.45}$$

When the coefficients satisfy (7.44), we can solve (7.45) to obtain the unique relationship between X_t and $\{\varepsilon_t\}$,

$$X_t = \sum_{j=0}^{\infty} \psi_j \varepsilon_{t-j} \tag{7.46}$$

which is the stationary solution of ARMA(p, q), and $\{\psi_k\}$ are named **Wold coefficients** of $\{X_t\}$. (7.46) also represents the transformation between stationary ARMA(p, q) process and a moving average process with infinite order, the Wold decomposition.

Owing to the stationarity of ARMA(p, q) process, analogous to AR(p) process, we can obtain the ARMA(p, q) series recursively by using white noise $\{\varepsilon_t\}$ and process coefficients. First we choose initial values $Y_0 = Y_1 = \cdots = Y_{p-1} = 0$, and obtain a recursive series $\{Y_t\}$,

$$Y_t = \sum_{j=1}^{p} \rho_j Y_{t-j} + \sum_{j=0}^{q} \lambda_j \varepsilon_{t-j}, \quad t = p, p+1, \ldots, m+n$$

Next we choose an appropriate m, and let

$$X_t = Y_{m+t}, \quad t = 1, 2, \ldots, n$$

then series $\{X_t\}$ can be regarded as ARMA(p, q) series that we need. Similar to the situation we encountered with AR(p) series, when characteristic polynomials (7.45) have roots near to the unit circle, we need larger m.

3. Auto-covariance function for ARMA(p, q) model

We know from Wold coefficients that the auto-covariance function of $\{X_t\}$ of ARMA(p, q) is unrelated to the initial values, but is related to process parameters and can be expressed by Wold coefficient $\{\psi_j\}$ as

$$\gamma_k = \sigma^2 \sum_{j=0}^{\infty} \psi_j \psi_{j+k}, \quad k \geq 0$$

When computing Wold coefficients $\{\psi_j\}$ using parameters $\{\rho_j\}$ and $\{\lambda_j\}$, we apply recursive method. Set $\psi_0 = 1$, and then

$$\psi_j = \lambda_j + \sum_{k=1}^{p} \rho_k \psi_{j-k}, \quad j = 1, 2, 3, \ldots$$

We set $\lambda_j = 0$ when $j > q$ and $\psi_j = 0$ when $j < q$.

4. Yule-Walker equations of ARMA(p, q) model

The **Yule-Walker equations** for ARMA(p, q) series that satisfies the **stationary condition** and **auto-covariance function** $\{\gamma_k\}$ is

$$\begin{pmatrix} \gamma_{q+1} \\ \gamma_{q+2} \\ \vdots \\ \gamma_{q+p} \end{pmatrix} = \begin{pmatrix} \gamma_q & \gamma_{q-1} & \cdots & \gamma_{q-p+1} \\ \gamma_{q+1} & \gamma_q & \cdots & \gamma_{q-p+2} \\ \vdots & \vdots & & \vdots \\ \gamma_{q+p-1} & \gamma_{q+p-2} & \cdots & \gamma_q \end{pmatrix} \begin{pmatrix} \rho_1 \\ \rho_2 \\ \vdots \\ \rho_p \end{pmatrix}$$

It can be proved that the coefficient matrix is invertible when ARMA(p, q) series is stationary, therefore the parameter $\{\rho_j\}$ can be uniquely determined by $\gamma_0, \gamma_1, \ldots, \gamma_{q+p}$.

When parameters $\{\rho_j\}$ have been determined, so is the model, as the series on the left side of (7.45) is an MA(q) series,

$$Y_t = X_t - \sum_{j=1}^{p} \rho_j X_{t-j} = \sum_{j=0}^{q} \lambda_j \varepsilon_{t-j} \tag{7.47}$$

where auto-covariance function $\{\gamma_y(k)\}$ is truncated at q. For those $|k| \leq q$, it follows by $\gamma_y(k) = E(Y_t Y_{t-k})$ that

$$\gamma_y(k) = \sum_{j=0}^{p} \sum_{l=0}^{p} \rho_j \rho_l E(X_{t-j} X_{t-k-l}) = \sum_{j=0}^{p} \sum_{l=0}^{p} \rho_j \rho_l \gamma_{k+l-j}$$

where $\rho_0 = -1$. As we obtained auto-covariance function $\{\gamma_y(k)\}$ of MA(q) series, we can determine the parameters $\{\lambda_j\}$ of MA(q), i.e., the parameters $\{\lambda_j\}$ of ARMA(p, q).

5.   The spectral density of ARMA(*p*, *q*)

The auto-covariance function of ARMA(*p*, *q*) series is absolutely additive and its spectral density is:

$$f(\omega) = \frac{1}{2\pi} \sum_{k=-\infty}^{\infty} \gamma_k e^{-ik\omega} = \frac{\sigma^2}{2\pi} \left| \sum_{k=0}^{\infty} \psi_k e^{ik\omega} \right|^2$$

6.   Invertible ARMA(*p*, *q*) Process

The stationary condition of ARMA(*p*, *q*) is presented by (7.44). Furthermore, if the characteristic polynomial also has no root on the unit circle, namely

$$1 + \sum_{j=1}^{q} b_j z^j \neq 0, \quad |z| \lessgtr 1$$

then this ARMA(*p*, *q*) process is said to be **invertible**, and the corresponding stationary solution is called **invertible ARMA series**. Thus we can solve (7.45) or (7.46) to obtain

$$\varepsilon_t = \sum_{j=0}^{\infty} \varphi_j X_{t-j}$$

This expression indicates that the invertible ARMA(*p*, *q*) series and its white noise series can be linearly expressed by each other.

Figures for an ARMA(*p*, *q*) series, as well as its auto-covariance function and spectral density can all be generated by DASC software.

7.3.2   Parameter estimations for ARMA(*p*, *q*) model

When getting an observation X_1, X_2,..., X_N of a stationary time series, we first centralize it with zero mean by a constant translation, and then try fitting an AR(*p*) or MA(*q*) process. If the results are not satisfactory, and often requiring a very large order of *p* or *q*, we would consider fitting a general ARMA(*p*, *q*) process:

$$X_t = \sum_{j=1}^{p} \rho_j X_{t-j} + \varepsilon_t + \sum_{j=1}^{q} \lambda_j \varepsilon_{t-j}$$

where $\bar{\rho} = (\rho_1, \rho_2,..., \rho_p)'$ and $\bar{\lambda} = (\lambda_1, \lambda_2,..., \lambda_q)'$ satisfy

$$1 - \sum_{j=1}^{p} \rho_j z^j \neq 0, \quad 1 + \sum_{j=1}^{q} \lambda_j z^j \neq 0, \quad |z| \leq 1$$

Besides, two characteristic polynomials have no common roots. We approach the estimation in two steps. First we assume that the orders of *p* and *q* are given. After describing the estimation of autoregressive and moving average parameters for given *p* and *q* we proceed to describe AIC and BIC criteria for choosing *p* and *q*.

The Method of Moments estimation and least squares estimation for $\bar{\rho} = (\rho_1, \rho_2,..., \rho_p)'$ and $\bar{\lambda} = (\lambda_1, \lambda_2,..., \lambda_q)'$ are relatively easy and practical.

1.   Method of moments estimation based on auto-covariance function

We know from (7.43) that the auto-covariance function satisfies Yule-Walker equations. Plugging the estimators of the auto-covariance function in Yule-Walker equations, we can prove that its coefficient matrix is invertible, thus we obtain the estimators of parameter $\vec{\rho} = (\rho_1, \rho_2, \ldots, \rho_p)'$:

$$
\begin{pmatrix} \hat{\rho}_1 \\ \hat{\rho}_2 \\ \vdots \\ \hat{\rho}_p \end{pmatrix} = \begin{pmatrix} \hat{\gamma}_q & \hat{\gamma}_{q-1} & \cdots & \hat{\gamma}_{q-p+1} \\ \hat{\gamma}_{q+1} & \hat{\gamma}_q & \cdots & \hat{\gamma}_{q-p+2} \\ \vdots & \vdots & & \vdots \\ \hat{\gamma}_{q+p-1} & \hat{\gamma}_{q+p-2} & \cdots & \hat{\gamma}_q \end{pmatrix}^{-1} \begin{pmatrix} \hat{\gamma}_{q+1} \\ \hat{\gamma}_{q+2} \\ \vdots \\ \hat{\gamma}_{q+p} \end{pmatrix}
$$

We can prove that the moment estimators of $\vec{\rho}$ are not only unique but also strongly consistent, namely,

$$
p\lim_{N\to\infty} \hat{\rho}_j = \rho_j, \quad a.s., \quad 1 \le j \le p
$$

where a.s. stands for 'almost surely'.

Next by use of the estimators of $\vec{\rho}$, we construct a new series according to (7.47) which satisfies MA(q) process,

$$
\hat{Y}_t = X_t - \sum_{j=1}^p \hat{\rho}_j X_{t-j} = \sum_{j=0}^q \lambda_j \varepsilon_{t-j}
$$

Its auto-covariance function can be estimated by

$$
\hat{\gamma}_y(k) = \sum_{j=0}^p \sum_{l=0}^p \hat{\rho}_j \hat{\rho}_l \gamma_{k+l-j}
$$

where $\rho_0 = -1$. Hence according to any one of the three methods for estimation of the parameters of the MA(q) model, such as the method of moments estimation based on auto-covariance function, or inverse correlation function estimation, or new information estimation, we can obtain the estimators of $\vec{\lambda}$ of an ARMA(p, q) process.

2. Least squares estimation for ARMA(p, q) process

Different from a standard AR(p) process, there are more than one random term in an ARMA(p, q) process. Then in order to minimize the residual sum of squares, we shall first estimate white noise series $\{\varepsilon_j\}$. Construct an AR(p) process by observation,

$$
X_t = \sum_{j=1}^p \rho_j X_{t-j} + \varepsilon_t
$$

Using estimation methods for AR(p) we obtain the estimators $(\hat{\rho}_1, \hat{\rho}_2, \ldots, \hat{\rho}_p)$. We can then arrive at the estimators of residuals,

$$
\hat{\varepsilon}_t = x_t - \sum_{j=1}^p \hat{\rho}_j x_{t-j}, \quad t = p+1, p+2, \ldots, N \tag{7.48}
$$

Then we construct the complete ARMA(p, q) process as

$$
x_t = \sum_{j=1}^p \rho_j x_{t-j} + \sum_{j=1}^q \lambda_j \hat{\varepsilon}_{t-j} + \varepsilon_t, \quad t = L+1, L+2, \ldots, N
$$

where $L = \max(p, q)$, and ρ_j, λ_j are parameters to be estimated.

Minimize (the objective function) the residual sum of squares,

$$Q(\vec{\rho}, \vec{\lambda}) = \sum_{t=L+1}^{N} \left(x_t - \sum_{j=1}^{p} \rho_j x_{t-j} - \sum_{j=1}^{q} \lambda_j \hat{\varepsilon}_{t-j} \right)^2$$

to obtain least squares estimators $\hat{\vec{\rho}} = (\hat{\rho}_1, \hat{\rho}_2, ..., \hat{\rho}_p)'$ and $\hat{\vec{\lambda}} = (\hat{\lambda}_1, \hat{\lambda}_2, ..., \hat{\lambda}_q)'$. Least squares estimator of σ^2 is defined as

$$\hat{\sigma}^2 = \frac{1}{N-L} Q(\hat{\vec{\rho}}, \hat{\vec{\lambda}})$$

Note that (7.48) is a linear model which can be written in form of

$$Y = X\beta + \varepsilon, Y = (x_{L+1}, x_{L+2}, ..., x_N)', \beta' = (\vec{\rho}, \vec{\lambda}),$$

$$X = \begin{pmatrix} x_L & x_{L-1} & \cdots & x_{L-p+1} & \hat{\varepsilon}_L & \hat{\varepsilon}_{L-1} & \cdots & \hat{\varepsilon}_{L-q+1} \\ x_{L+1} & x_L & \cdots & x_{L-p+2} & \hat{\varepsilon}_{L+1} & \hat{\varepsilon}_L & \cdots & \hat{\varepsilon}_{L-q+2} \\ \vdots & \vdots & & \vdots & \vdots & \vdots & & \vdots \\ x_{N-1} & x_{N-2} & \cdots & x_{N-p} & \hat{\varepsilon}_{N-1} & \hat{\varepsilon}_{N-2} & \cdots & \hat{\varepsilon}_{N-q} \end{pmatrix}$$

where Y has $(N - L)$ components, β has $(p + q)$ components, and X is an $(N - L) \times (p + q)$ matrix. Least squares estimator of β is

$$\hat{\beta} = (X'X)^{-1} X'Y$$

which is the familiar form of a LS estimator of a multiple regression model.

Example 7.6   Least squares estimation of parameters of ARMA(p, q) process   Similar to the AR(p) process, data preparation for least squares estimation for an ARMA(p, q) process is relatively easy and the estimators are generally more accurate than others. We again give attention to three series: the original observation series $\{X_t\}$, fitted or estimated values $\{\hat{X}_t\}$, and the estimated residual series $\{\hat{\varepsilon}_t\}$. They satisfy three kinds of relationship. Based on new information estimation, we know that

$$\hat{\varepsilon}_t = X_t - \hat{X}_t$$

according to the ARMA process, we have

$$X_t = \sum_{j=1}^{p} \rho_j X_{t-j} + \varepsilon_t + \sum_{j=1}^{q} \lambda_j \varepsilon_{t-j}$$

and for the requirement of best fitting, we have

$$\sum_{t=q+1}^{N} (X_t - \hat{X}_t)^2 \xrightarrow{q} \min$$

The estimation and goodness of fit are programmed in DASC. Figure 7.13 is the goodness of fit graph for this example. The detailed computation process can be seen by clicking DASC $\rightarrow$ Time Series Analysis $\rightarrow$ Stationary Series $\rightarrow$ Parametric Estimation for ARMA by LSE.

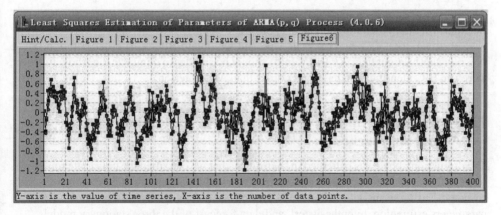

Figure 7.13　Goodness of fit graph of ARMA(p, q) by LSE.

7.3.3　Test for ARMA(p, q) model

After obtaining the estimates of the parameters of an ARMA(p, q) model, we still need to test the model. First we test the stationarity of the model, and then start with the given initial values $x_0 = x_{-1} = \cdots = x_{-p+1} = \hat{\varepsilon}_0 = \cdots = \hat{\varepsilon}_{-q+1} = 0$, calculate recursively the residuals

$$\hat{\varepsilon}_t = x_t - \sum_{l=1}^{p} \hat{\rho}_l x_{t-l} + \sum_{j=1}^{q} \hat{\lambda}_j \hat{\varepsilon}_{t-j}, \quad t = 1, 2, \ldots$$

Choose $m = O(N^{1/3})$ and $m > \max(p, q)$. If the residual $\hat{\varepsilon}_t$, $t = m, m + 1,\ldots, N$ are tested to be white noise, then this model is considered to be suitable, otherwise we attempt other models.

Parameters (p, q) of actual sample data are always unknown. The ranges of orders, p and q, however, can always be determined. Using the autocorrelation coefficient (ACF) and partial autocorrelation coefficient (PACF), we can therefore construct the ARMA(p, q) process for each pair of (p, q) in this range, and any model that can pass the test is a candidate. Then choose the minimum ($p+q$) from all the candidates. One can also use AIC criterion for order identification, and this is explained in the following section.

7.3.4　Order identification for ARMA(p, q) model

The AIC method for choosing the ARMA(p, q) process is similar to that used for the AR(p) process. If the upper bounds of p and q are given, say, P_0 and Q_0, then for each pair of (k, j), $0 \le k \le P_0$, $0 \le j \le Q_0$, minimize the AIC function

$$\text{AIC}(k, j) = \ln(\hat{\sigma}^2(k, j)) + \frac{2(k + j)}{N}$$

to obtain ($\hat{p}, \hat{q}$), and this is the AIC order of (p, q).

When using the AIC method, we mainly consider how to minimize the estimation $\hat{\sigma}^2$ of white noise variance σ^2. But why do we add another term $2(k + j)/N$? In fact, as long as we increase the order of model we will get a smaller $\hat{\sigma}^2$ because $\ln(\hat{\sigma}^2(k,j))$ is a decreasing function. Thus the order we get maybe very large and bring with it so many parameters that makes the model too sensitive to small changes in observation data. But when $2(k + j)/N$ is added to the criterion it increases, thus penalizing increase in order to reduce error variance. AIC function will attain the minimum at an appropriate point.

Substitute $2(k + j)/N$ by $(k + j) \ln N/N$, and we obtain BIC (k, j) order criterion. Since $(k + j) \ln N/N$ is larger than $2(k + j)/N$, $\ln \hat{\sigma}^2$ should be smaller to minimize the whole function, therefore BIC identification has higher order than AIC criterion.

7.3.5   Univariate time series modeling: The basic issues and approaches

The discussion above was patterned in such a way that we classified the univariate time series models first into stationary and nonstationary models, and then within stationary models we identified three models, AR(p), MA(q) and ARMA(p, q). We discussed the issues of parameters estimation, hypothesis test, and data forecast of the three stationary models.

The issues facing a researcher in the real world are:

1. Whether one should use a univariate time series model or a multi-variate time series model?

2. Given a real time series how to identify which model to fit?

3. Once the model is identified how to estimate its parameters?

4. How to test the goodness of fit of the model?

5. How to make (conditional) forecasts of the time series for the future?

6. To establish the degree of credibility of the forecasts by providing confidence intervals for the forecasts.

There is always a subtle difference between the nice theoretical results and methods and which model work best in the real world. The theoretical results and the suggested methods depend on some assumptions that may not really hold with the real world data, requiring some judgment by the user on what model to use and what method of estimation to use etc. One therefore says that statistical practice is an art. We would rather conclude from our experience that it is not art but rather a skill, and the skill is always enriched by scientifically well-justified judgments on what model to use and what estimation method to use and what statistical tests to use and how.

The material covered in this chapter can be used skillfully by a practitioner provided the answer to the first question was to use a univariate time series model. The other questions can also be handled skillfully employing the theory and methods covered in this chapter.

Given any univariate time series we first judge if it is a stationary time series. If it is not stationary, we can try to convert it into a stationary time series by subtracting a function or by differencing. We can test for nonstationarity using the unit root tests that are discussed in Chapter 8. Then we compute the autocorrelation coefficient (ACF) and partial autocorrelation coefficient (PACF). First we see if PACF is getting truncated at a finite lag indicating that the underlying model could be an AR(p) model. The statistical criteria and tests suggested for identification of the order of AR(p) need not be quite definitive, as the results would depend on what level of significance is used or how large is the sample, the statistical tests being only asymptotic. Hence we will choose a range of values for the order and use AIC and or BIC criteria to choose the order of AR(p). If the PACF is not showing truncation we explore the ACF and see if it is getting truncated at a finite lag length. If it does then the MA(q) process may be generating the real data. Again the order q can be chosen by first choosing a range. We then base our final choice based on AIC or BIC criteria.

Sometimes it may so happen that both ACF and PACF do not show truncation at low orders. Then we try an ARMA process with some low orders for p and q. It may be noted that there may not be abrupt truncation in this case, leading to a range of small values for ACF and PACF, and hence small values of p and q together may be better than either an AR(p) with a large p or a MA(q) with a large q. Again we use AIC or BIC to choose p and q of the ARMA(p, q) process.

The ultimate test for the model is how well it fits the data and how well it generates the forecasts for the future. In most of the real life situations, whether it is for business policy or public policy, one would generate the data continuously and use the model repeatedly to make the forecasts and to take necessary corrective steps if necessary for policy intervention. Hence it is necessary to continuously update the model. In fact it may be necessary to move away from the class of single variable parametric models that we covered in this chapter and choose instead the semi-parametric multivariate models dealt with in other chapters.

Electronic references for Chapter 7

References

Abdelhakim A. & Hafida G. (2009) On some probabilistic properties of double periodic AR models. *Statistics & Probability Letters* **3**, 408–13.

Anderson T.W. & Metz, R.P. (1993) A note on maximum likelihood estimation in the first-order Gaussian moving average model. *Statistics & Probability Letters* **3**, 205–11.

Bhansali R.J. (1999) Autoregressive model selection for multistep prediction. *Journal of Statistical Planning and Inference* **1–2**, 295–305.

Bhansali R.J., Giraitis L. & Kokoszka P.S. (2006) Estimation of the memory parameter by fitting fractionally differenced autoregressive models. *Journal of Multivariate Analysis* **10**, 2101–30.

Bondon P. (2009) Estimation of autoregressive models with epsilon-skew-normal innovations. *Journal of Multivariate Analysis* **8**, 1761–76.

Box G.E. P. & Pierce D.A. (1970) Distribution of the Autocorrelations in Autoregressive Moving Average Time Series Models. *Journal of American Statistical Association* **65**, 1509–26.

Brockwell P.J. & Davis R.A. (1988) Simple consistent estimation of the coefficients of a linear filter. *Stochastic Processes and their Applications* **1**, 48–59.

Brockwell P.J. & Davis R.A.(1991) *Time series: Theory and Methods* (Second Edition). Springer-Verlag, New York.

Brockwell P.J. (1994) On continuous-time threshold ARMA processes. *Journal of Statistical Planning and Inference* **2**, 291–303.

Carvalho A.X. & Tanner M.A. (2007) Modeling nonlinear count time series with local mixtures of Poisson auto-regressions. *Computational Statistics & Data Analysis* **11**, 5266–94.

Chan W.S. & Cheung S.H. (2005) A bivariate threshold time series model for analyzing Australian interest rates. *Mathematics and Computers in Simulation* **5–6**, 429–37.

Chen Z.G. & Ni J.Y. (1989) Subset regression time series and its modeling procedures. *Journal of Multivariate Analysis* **2**, 266–88.

Cleveland W.S. (1972) The inverse autocorrelations of a time series and their applications. *Technometrics* **14**, 278–93.

Coakley J., Fuertes A.-M. & Smith R. (2006) Unobserved heterogeneity in panel time series models. *Computational Statistics & Data Analysis* **9**, 2361–80.

De Jong P. & Penzer J. (2004) The ARMA model in state space form. *Statistics & Probability Letters* **1**, 119–25.

Dzhaparidze K. (1986) Parameter estimation and hypothesis testing in spectral analysis of stationary time series, *Springer*, New York.

Fei M.R., Du D.J. & Li K. (2008) A fast model identification method for networked control system. *Applied Mathematics and Computation* **2**, 658–67.

Ferreira E. (1998) Using M-type smoothing splines to estimate the spectral density of a stationary time series. *Statistics & Probability Letters* **2**, 198–205.

Freeland R.K. & McCabe B. (2005) Asymptotic properties of CLS estimators in the Poisson AR(1) model, Statistics & Probability Letters **2**, 148–53.

Ghazal M.A. (2001) Statistical analysis of broanded periodogram for continuous time stationary processes. *Applied Mathematics and Computation* **3**, 343–9.

Gonçalves E. & Nazaré Mendes L. (1998) Some statistical results on autoregressive conditionally heteroscedastic models. *Journal of Statistical Planning and Inference* **1**, 193–202.

Guerrero V.M. (2007) Time series smoothing by penalized least squares. *Statistics & Probability Letters* **12**, 1225–34.

Hall A. & Scotto M.G. (2003) Extremes of sub-sampled integer-valued moving average models with heavy-tailed innovations. *Statistics & Probability Letters* **1**, 98–105.

Hili O. (2008) Hellinger distance estimation of general bilinear time series models. *Statistical Methodology* **2**, 119–28.

Houweling D. & Comeau Y. (2008) A time series model for influent temperature estimation: Application to dynamic temperature modeling of an aerated lagoon. *Water Research* **10–11**, 2551–62.

Jayakumar K. & Kuttykrishnan A.P. (2007) A time-series model using asymmetric Laplace distribution. *Statistics & Probability Letters* **16**, 1636–40.

Kadi A. & Abdelkader M. (1994) Matrix representations of spectral coefficients of randomly sampled ARMA models. *Stochastic Processes and their Applications* **1**, 121–37.

Karakostas K.X. & Wynn, H.P. (1989) Systematic sampling for autocorrelated superpopulations. *Journal of Statistical Planning and Inference* **2**, 181–95.

Lee O. (2000) On probabilistic properties of nonlinear ARMA(p, q) models. *Statistics & Probability Letters* **2**, 121–31.

Lim A.C.K. (2004) Approximating Fourier transformation of orbital integrals. *Journal of Mathematical Analysis and Applications* **2**, 594–602.

Lin T.I. & Ho H.J. (2008) A simplified approach to inverting the auto-covariance matrix of a general ARMA(p, q) process. *Statistics & Probability Letters* **1**, 36–41.

Ljung G.M. & Box G.E.P. (1978) On a measure of a lack of fit in time series models. *Biometrika* **65**, 297–303.

Mauricio J.A. (2008) Computing and using residuals in time series models. *Computational Statistics & Data Analysis* **3**, 1746–63.

McKenzie C.R. (1997) The properties of some two step estimators of ARMA Models. *Mathematics and Computers in Simulation* **3–6**, 451–6.

Mentz R.P., Morettin P.A. & Toloi C.M.C. (1999) On least-squares estimation of the residual variance in the first-order moving average model. *Computational Statistics & Data Analysis* **4**, 485–99.

Monti A.C. (1996) A new preliminary estimator for MA(1) models. *Computational Statistics & Data Analysis* **1**, 1–15.

Nagakura D. (2009) Testing for coefficient stability of AR(1) model when the null is an integrated or a stationary process. *Journal of Statistical Planning and Inference* **8**, 2731–45.

Atakishiyev N.M., Vicent L.E. & Wolf K.B. (1999) Continuous vs. discrete fractional Fourier transforms. *Journal of Computational and Applied Mathematics* **1**, 73–95.

Paparoditis E. (1998) Addendum to bootstrapping periodogram and cross periodogram statistics of vector autoregressive moving average models. *Statistics & Probability Letters* **1**, 109.

Pappas S.Sp., Ekonomou L., Karampelas P., Katsikas S.K. & Liatsis P. (2008) Modeling of the grounding resistance variation using ARMA models. *Simulation Modeling Practice and Theory* **5**, 560–70.

Pollock D.S.G. (1993) On the criterion function for ARMA estimation. *Journal of Statistical Planning and Inference* **2–3**, 413–30.

Qian G.Q. & Zhao X.D. (2007) On time series model selection involving many candidate ARMA models. *Computational Statistics & Data Analysis* **12**, 6180–96.

Qian W. (1987) Gaussian estimation of first order time series models with Bernoulli observations. *Stochastic Processes and their Applications* **27**, 85–96.

Sethuraman S. & Basawa I.V. (1994) Parameter estimation in a stationary autoregressive process with correlated multiple observations. *Journal of Statistical Planning and Inference* **2**, 138–54.

Shin Dong Wan (2004) Estimation of spectral density for seasonal time series models. *Statistics & Probability Letters* **2**, 149–59.

Singh N. & Shelton P.M. (1987) A note on the property of some nonstationary ARMA processes. *Stochastic Processes and their Applications* **1**, 151–5.

Tjøstheim D. (1986) Estimation in nonlinear time series models. *Stochastic Processes and their Applications* **2**, 251–73.

Tran Lanh Tat (1990) Rank statistics for serial dependence. *Journal of Statistical Planning and Inference* **2**, 215–32.

Wang L.Y., Xie Li & Wang X.F. (2009) The residual based interactive stochastic gradient algorithms for controlled moving average models. *Applied Mathematics and Computation* **2**, 442–9.

Wong H., Wai-cheung I., Zhang R.Q. & Xia J. (2007) Non-parametric time series models for hydrological forecasting. *Journal of Hydrology* **3–4**, 338–47.

Yi S. (2005) The asymptotic distribution of the constant behavior of the generalized partial autocorrelation function of an ARMA process. *Statistics & Probability Letters* **2**, 113–8.

Young H.S. (1993) Basawa parameter estimation in a regression model with random coefficient autoregressive errors. *Journal of Statistical Planning and Inference* **1**, 58–67.

8

Multivariate and nonstationary time series models

Econometric research, that commenced more than seven decades ago with a system of simultaneous equations, was under attack for spurious correlations of time series. It was argued that univariate time series analysis, such as that discussed in Chapter 8, can give better economic forecasts than those of the sophisticated models of simultaneous equation systems. However, generating economic forecasts was just one aim of econometric models. Another significant aspect of econometric models is to generate counterfactual simulations that examine what happens to the time profile of economic variables (response) if any variable gets a shock or an arbitrarily chosen impulse. This problem is important both in a business setting and in a public policy setting. In a public policy setting, one would like to know what happens to GNP if there is a **sudden shock** to the system through a reduction in oil prices (Farzanegen and Markwardt, 2007). In a business setting, if the problem facing the business is regarded as a time dependence of interrelated variables such as the price of goods in different regional markets, one might want to know what will be the effect of a sudden increase or decrease (sudden shock) in demand or supply of goods (demand or supply shock) in one regional market on the equilibrium market price of goods in that as well as other regional markets (Sai Prakash, 2007).

One of the main features of economic modeling is dependence of one economic variable on others, such as the **simultaneous equation system** dealt with in Chapter 6. But in that chapter we did not take into account the time series nature of economic data. Chapter 7 dealt with only univariate economic time series. In this chapter we combine these two features, interdependence between economic variables and the time series nature of the variables. The simultaneous equations system that was used earlier was severely criticized by Sims (1980) for what he called the 'incredible' a priori restrictions needed for identification. He introduced the notion of **multiple time series models** with no prior parametric constraints for

Developing Econometrics, First Edition. Hengqing Tong, T. Krishna Kumar and Yangxin Huang.
© 2011 John Wiley & Sons, Ltd. Published 2011 by John Wiley & Sons, Ltd.

identification[1]. According to him even exogeneity or endogeneity is an empirical or statistical question. He argued that all economic variables are related to each other through a **Vector Auto Regressive Model**. He used such a model to study the impact of monetary policy on the real sector of the economy through **impulse-response analysis**, where a policy intervention is treated as giving a shock to one of the equations of the system and observing the dynamic impact of such a shock.

In addition Chapter 7 dealt only with stationary economic variables whereas many economic time series have trends, and some economic variables even have common trends. In this Chapter we will deal with **nonstationary time series** with or without common trends.

Stationary time series require that the mean is constant and the auto-covariance function is a constant, unrelated to the starting point (mean reverting process), whereas a nonstationary time series model doesn't meet either or both of these two requirements. When confronted with nonstationary time series we always consider how to transform them into stationary series. There are two main forms for a nonstationary time series, one is a series with a deterministic trend component and the other is with a stochastic trend, also known as a **unit root process**.

There is serious concern among economists as to whether a given economic time series, say commodity prices such as prices of houses or of oil that show prolonged upward trend, has a constant mean to which it returns (popularly known as as mean reverting). Economists also deal with stocks and flows, such as the stock of capital which is the cumulative sum of all investments made in the past. The investment may include inventories. Inventories added during any period could be stationary. But the stock of inventories held at any point in time may be nonstationary. For a series with a deterministic trend component, a useful way to remove this trend is to subtract a deterministic trend function. For the stochastic trend, or a unit root process, we normally transform the series into the **difference form**, (usually either a first difference or a second difference). Another way is to subtract another series that has the same trend component, making the difference become stationary. This latter procedure is an intuitive way of introducing a more general concept of '**cointegration**'. The cointegration concept is useful in order to model the law of one price (LOP) and long run economic equilibria.

In order to understand all of these issues we need to understand the concept of nonstationarity, and in particular nonstationarity represented by a unit root process or a **random walk**, and the concept of cointegrating equations. All of these aspects form the subject matter of this chapter. First generation econometricians such as Ragnar Frisch, Harold T. Davis, Jan Tinbergen, Tjalling C. Koopmans, and Gerhard Tintner treated nonstationary economic time series as series with deterministic trends, periodic cycles, and a residual error. This was the tradition of business cycle research which was the old name for macroeconomics before Keynes' General Theory changed its nature. The statistical analysis in that case consisted of estimating the long-term trends as long run equilibrium relations. For a discussion of the relation between the old type of analysis and the modern analysis being presented here the reader is referred to Hendry and Morgan (1989) and Kumar (1993).

DASC can accomplish the computational procedures in this chapter and offer some new results developed by us such as more accurate **density curve** of **Dickey-Fuller statistic**, more accurate **significance level table**. **It also has** a program for forecasting with GARCH models, and a program for forecasting complex trend based on the **lagged cointegration process**.

---

[1] Identification can be brought about either through a priori restrictions on the regression coefficients of the model or on the elements of the variance covariance matrix. As pointed out by some critics later Sims after all did make use of certain a priori restrictions on the variance covariance matrix through Cholesky decomposition of that matrix and the choice of the order of the variables.

8.1 Multivariate stationary time series model

8.1.1 General description of multivariable stationary time series model

Economic phenomena sometimes refer to the relations among several interrelated economic variables, and this requires multivariate time series models. We first discuss the multivariate stationary time series. The topics discussed in this section are similar to those of Chapter 7.

Assume that we have m **variate time series**

$$X_t = (X_{1t}, X_{2t}, \ldots, X_{mt})'$$

We continue assuming that t is an integer. We define its expectation as a vector:

$$E(X_t) = \mu = (E(X_{1t}), E(X_{2t}), \ldots, E(X_{mt}))' = (\mu_1, \mu_2, \ldots, \mu_m)'$$

Define its **autocovariance function** as a matrix:

$$G(k) = E\left[(X_{t+k} - \mu)(X_t - \mu)\right]' = (\gamma_{ij}(k))_{m \times n}$$

If the **expectation vector** of multivariate time series and the autocovariance matrix are unrelated to t, then we call this time series the **multivariate weakly stationary time series**. We can define the **autocorrelation coefficient** of multivariate stationary time series:

$$r_{ij}(k) = \frac{\gamma_{ij}(k)}{\sqrt{\gamma_{ii}(0)\gamma_{jj}(0)}}$$

The **autocorrelation coefficient matrix** of the multivariate stationary time series is:

$$R(k) = (r_{ij}(k))_{m \times m}$$

The autocovariance function of multivariate stationary series has some basic characters as follows:

(1) symmetry: $G(-k) = G'(k)$;

(2) Schwarz inequalities: $|\gamma_{ij}(k)| \leq [\gamma_{ii}(0)\gamma_{jj}(0)]^{1/2}$;

(3) semi-definiteness: for any m dimensional real vector $y_1, y_2, \ldots, y_n$, we have

$$\sum_{i=1}^{n}\sum_{j=1}^{n} y_i' G(i-j) y_j \geq 0$$

We can also define the m **dimensional white noise** $\varepsilon = (\varepsilon_1, \varepsilon_2, \ldots, \varepsilon_m)'$ whose expectation is zero, and each of its components is **white noise**:

$$\varepsilon \sim W(0, \sigma^2 I_m) \leftrightarrow \varepsilon_i \sim W(0, \sigma^2), i = 1, 2, \ldots, m, \text{ with mutual independence}$$

The **multivariate moving-average model** is given by the following relation between the m dimensional time series $\{X_t\}$ and the m dimensional white noise $\{\varepsilon_t\}$:

$$X_t = \varepsilon_t + \Lambda_1 \varepsilon_{t-1} + \Lambda_2 \varepsilon_{t-2} + \cdots + \Lambda_q \varepsilon_{t-q}$$

The stationary condition is that the roots of the **determinantal equation** below lie outside the **unit circle**:

$$\det(I_m + \Lambda_1 z + \Lambda_2 z^2 + \cdots + \Lambda_q z^q) \neq 0, |z| < 1$$

If the coefficient matrix of the model satisfies the above condition, then the series is said to be invertible.

The simple autoregressive model AR(p), extends to multivariate situation as the vector autoregressive model VAR(p).

8.1.2   Estimation of mean and autocovariance function of multivariate stationary time series

Consider $\{X_t\}$, an m dimensional stationary series, and suppose that $X_1, X_2, \ldots, X_N$ are observations from that series.

The point estimation of the mean $\mu = E(X_t)$ is defined as

$$\hat{\mu}_N = (\hat{\mu}_1, \hat{\mu}_2, \ldots \hat{\mu}_m)' = \frac{1}{N} \sum_{t=1}^{N} X_t$$

If all of the component series $\{X_{jt}\}, j = 1, 2, \ldots, m$ of the $\{X_t\}$ are **strictly stationary and ergodic series**, then when $N \rightarrow \infty$, $\hat{\mu} \rightarrow \mu$, (a.s.).

The estimation of the **autocovariance function matrix** is

$$\hat{G}(k) = \frac{1}{N} \sum_{t=1}^{N-k} (X_{t+k} - \hat{\mu}_N)(X_t - \hat{\mu})^T, 0 \leq k \leq N - 1$$

while $\hat{G}(-k) = \hat{G}'(k)$.

Using $\hat{\gamma}_{ij}(k)$ to denote the (i, j)th component of the square matrix $\hat{G}(k)$, the estimation of the **correlation coefficient** $r_{ij}(k)$ is

$$\hat{r}_{ij}(k) = \frac{\hat{\gamma}_{ij}(k)}{\sqrt{\hat{\gamma}_{ii}(0)\hat{\gamma}_{jj}(0)}}$$

The estimation of the autocorrelation coefficient matrix is

$$\hat{R}(k) = (\hat{r}_{ij}(k))$$

When a series is a strictly stationary series, we can prove the convergence of the estimations by the ergodic theorem, i.e., when $N \rightarrow \infty$, $\hat{G}(k) \rightarrow G(k)$, (a.s.), $\hat{R}(k) \rightarrow R(k)$, (a.s.).

8.1.3 Vector autoregression model of order p: VAR(p)

Vector autoregression (VAR), generalized from the univariate AR models, is an econometric model used to capture the evolution and the interdependencies between multiple time series. All of the variables in a VAR are treated symmetrically by including for each variable an equation explaining its evolution based on its own lags and the lags of all the other variables in the model. The following discussion on VAR, impulse response and variance decomposition are based on the work initiated by Sims (1980), followed by Runkle (1987) and Lutkepohl (1990). We extend the treatment of a univariate stationary autoregressive model of Chapter 7 and introduce the p-th order centralized stationary auto-regressive process of n-variate random vector X_t, called **Vector Auto Regression or VAR(p)**. Sims (1980) advocated the use of VAR models as a theory-free method to estimate economic relationships, thus being an alternative to the 'incredible identification restrictions' in structural models. The **Granger-causality test**, which will be explained later, can be used to interpret some of the variables as exogenous while the others are endogenous.

The VAR model describes the evolution of a set of n variables over the same sample period ($t = 1,2,\ldots, T$) as a linear function of only their joint past evolution. The variables are collected in a $n \times 1$ vector y_t, which has as the i-th element $y_{i,t}$ the time t observation of variable y_i. For example, if the i-th variable is GDP, then $y_{i,t}$ is the value of GDP at t.

A p-th order VAR, denoted VAR(p), is

$$y_t = c + A_1 y_{t-1} + A_2 y_{t-2} + \cdots + A_p y_{t-p} + \varepsilon_t$$

where c is a $n \times 1$ vector of constants (intercept), A_i is a $n \times n$ matrix (for every $i = 1,\ldots, p$) and ε_t is a $n \times 1$ vector of error terms satisfying

$$E(\varepsilon_t) = 0, E(\varepsilon_t \varepsilon_t') = \Omega, \text{ and } E(\varepsilon_t, \varepsilon_s) = 0 \ \forall s \neq t$$

where Ω (a $n \times n$ positive definite matrix).

The l-periods back observation y_{t-l} is called the l-th lag of y. Thus, a p-order VAR is also called a VAR with p lags.

8.1.4 Wold decomposition and impulse-response

A major issue of interest in business and economic policy is what happens to an economic system when an exogenous shock is given to it. In the time series context this issue translates itself as what happens to the future time profile of a vector of time series of endogenous variables if the system gets an external shock at any given instant. **Impulse-Response** analysis of multiple time series is extremely useful for addressing this issue. We shall discuss the impulse-response analysis in this section.

The **Wold decomposition** theorem constitutes one of the basic tenets of linear time series modeling. It is based on the ability to linearly forecast any stationary process by means of a weighted average of past forecast errors. While this result is convenient, it makes no statement regarding the true form of the data generating process other than the nature of the first and second order moment conditions.

Theorem 8.1 Any mean zero, covariance stationary process, $\{y_t\}_{n\times 1}$ can be represented in the form

$$y_t = \mu_t + \psi(L)\varepsilon_t$$

where $\psi(L)$ is a matrix polynomial in the **lag operator** with $\psi(0) = I_n$, $\sum_{j=1}^{\infty} j|\psi_j| < \infty$ (the summability condition that ensures stationarity). ε_t $_{n \times 1}$ are one-step ahead linear forecast errors in y_t given information on lagged values of y_t. μ_t is linearly deterministic. Usually we consider a constant or a constant and a time trend.

Remark 1 The ε_t are linear forecast errors for y_t. However, this does not necessarily imply that $E(\varepsilon_t | y_{t-1}, \ldots) = 0$. Linear projections are the best linear combination of past y_t that fit y_t while the conditional expectation is the best guess of y_t using linear **and nonlinear** combinations of past y_t. Thus the forecast based on the Wold decomposition could be a biased forecast. It is for this reason that we refer to *MSE* (**Mean Square Error**) of forecasts later in the next section (8.1.5).

Remark 2 It is in general not possible to attach a structural interpretation to the shocks ε_t. Under certain circumstances (linearity, for example) there is a natural correspondence, and in most situations we can think of the linear approximation as probably not a bad approximation.

Remark 3 The Wold representation is a representation of the time series which captures its second moment properties but may not be the representation of the time series y_t. Other representations based on non-forecast errors are perfectly possible.

Remark 4 Two time series with the same Wold representation are the same time series since the Wold representation is unique.

The last two remarks are probably the most important in highlighting the link existing between the properties of the data and the data generating process, which can be equated to the structural economic model. The Wold decomposition theorem is powerful because of its generality and because it enables us to investigate the dynamic properties of any time series on the basis of its second conditional moments. However, it is important to understand that the Wold decomposition can be, at most, a good approximation of the true data generation process. This remark provides a justification for an empirical approach to test for causality in the light of David Hume's dictum that there can never be an empirical verification of a theoretical notion of causality. If a theoretical model were to produce all moment conditions to match those implied by the Wold decomposition theorem, we could conclude that the observed data was generated by our model of the economy with the implied causality. What is harder to evaluate is the success of our model when this match is not exact.

In addition, one can construct economic models that do not have a Wold decomposition, which makes it difficult to use this procedure for choosing a model. In all cases, note that the variance-covariance matrix of the forecast errors ε_t will not be diagonal. This contemporaneous correlation among the forecast errors adds another layer of complication that we will examine when we discuss VARs. The complication has to do with our inability to match the sources of random variation in the data with those identified by our economic model.

Consider the **augmented vector autoregressive model**[2],

$$x_t = \sum_{i=1}^{p} \Phi_i x_{t-i} + \psi w_t + \varepsilon_t, t = 1, 2, \ldots, T \tag{8.1}$$

---

[2] We offer apologies to the reader for occasional changes in the notations. This is often required so as not to conflict with some other variable or symbol in a new section. For example, earlier we used n as the number of inter-dependent variables and now we are assuming that to be m, as n is used in this section for some other purpose.

where $x_t = (x_{1t}, x_{2t}, \ldots, x_{mt})'$ is an $m \times 1$ vector of jointly determined dependent variables, w_t is an $q \times 1$ vector of deterministic and/or exogenous variables, and $\{\Phi_i, i = 1,2,\ldots,p\}$ and ψ are $m \times m$ and $m \times q$ coefficient matrices. We make the following standard assumptions: (see, for example, Lutkepohl, 1991, Chapter 2, and Pesaran, 1997, Section 19.3).

Assumption 1. $E(\varepsilon_t) = 0$, $E(\varepsilon_t \varepsilon_t') = \Sigma$ for all t, where $\Sigma = \{\sigma_{ij}, i, j = 1,2,\ldots, m\}$ is an $m \times m$ positive definite matrix, $E(\varepsilon_t \varepsilon_{t'}') = 0$ for all $t = t'$ and $E(\varepsilon_t | w_t) = 0$.

Assumption 2. All the roots of $\left| I_m - \sum_{i=1}^{p} \Phi_i z^i \right| = 0$ fall outside the unit circle.

Assumption 3. $x_{t-1}, x_{t-2}, \ldots, x_{t-p}, w_t, t = 1,2,\ldots, T$, are not perfectly collinear.

Under Assumption 2, x_t would be covariance-stationary, and (8.1) can be rewritten as the infinite moving average representation,

$$x_t = \sum_{i=0}^{\infty} A_i \varepsilon_{t-i} + \sum_{i=0}^{\infty} G_i w_{t-i}, t = 1,2,\ldots,T \tag{8.2}$$

where the $m \times m$ coefficient matrices A_i can be obtained using the following recursive relations:

$$A_i = \Phi_1 A_{i-1} + \Phi_2 A_{i-2} + \cdots + \Phi_p A_{i-p}, i = 1,2,\ldots$$

with $A_0 = I_m$ and $A_i = 0$ for $i < 0$, and $G_i = A_i \psi$.

An **impulse response function** measures the time profile of the effect of a shock at a given point in time on the (expected) future values of variables in a dynamical system. The best way to describe an impulse response is to view it as the outcome of a conceptual experiment in which the time profile at time $t + n$ of the effect of a hypothetical $m \times 1$ vector of shocks of size $\delta = (\delta_1, \ldots, \delta_m)'$, say, hitting the economy at time t is compared with a base-line profile at time $t + n$, given the economy's history without such a shock. There are three main issues: (i) The types of shocks hitting the economy at time t; (ii) the state of the economy at time $t - 1$ before being shocked; and (iii) the types of other shocks expected to hit the economy from $t + 1$ to $t + n$.

Denoting the known history of the economy up to time $t - 1$ by the non-decreasing information set Ω_{t-1}, the generalized impulse response function of x_t at horizon n, advanced in Koop et al. (1996), is defined by

$$GI_x(n, \delta, \Omega_{t-1}) = E(x_{t+n} | \varepsilon_t = \delta, \Omega_{t-1}) - E(x_{t+n} | \Omega_{t-1}) \tag{8.3}$$

Using (8.3) in (8.2), we have $GI_x(n, \delta, \Omega_{t-1}) = A_n \delta$, which is independent of Ω_{t-1}, but depends on the composition of shocks defined by δ.

Clearly, the appropriate choice of hypothesized vector of shocks, δ, is central to the properties of the impulse response function. The traditional approach, suggested by Sims (1980), is to resolve the problem surrounding the choice of δ by using the **Cholesky decomposition** of Σ:

$$PP' = \Sigma$$

where P is an $m \times m$ lower triangular matrix. Then (8.2) can be rewritten as

$$x_t = \sum_{i=0}^{\infty} (A_i P)(P^{-1} \varepsilon_{t-i}) + \sum_{i=0}^{\infty} G_i w_{t-i} = \sum_{i=0}^{\infty} (A_i P) \xi_{t-i} + \sum_{i=0}^{\infty} G_i w_{t-i}, t = 1,2,\ldots,T$$

such that $\xi_t = P^{-1}\varepsilon_t$ are orthogonalized; namely, $E(\xi_t \xi_t') = I_m$. Hence, the $m \times 1$ vector of the orthogonalized impulse response function of a unit shock to the j-th equation on x_{t+n} is given by

$$\psi_j^0(n) = A_n P e_j, \quad n = 0,1,2,\ldots,$$

where e_j is an $m \times 1$ selection vector with unity as its j-th element and zeros elsewhere.

An alternative approach is to use (8.3) directly, but instead of shocking all the elements of ε_t, we could choose to shock only one element, say its j-th element, and integrate out the effects of other shocks using an assumed or the historically observed distribution of the errors. In this case we have

$$GI_x(n, \delta_j, \Omega_{t-1}) = E(x_{t+n} | \varepsilon_{jt}, \Omega_{t-1}) - E(x_{t+n} | \Omega_{t-1})$$

Assuming that ε_t has a multivariate normal distribution, it is now easily seen (see Koop et al., 1996) that

$$E(\varepsilon_t | \varepsilon_{jt} = \delta_j) = (\sigma_{1j}, \sigma_{2j}, \ldots, \sigma_{mj})' \sigma_{jj}^{-1} \delta_j = \sum_j e_j \sigma_{jj}^{-1} \delta_j$$

where e_j is an $m \times 1$ selection vector with unity as its j-th element and zeros elsewhere. Hence, the $m \times 1$ vector of the (unscaled) generalized impulse response of the effect of a shock in the j-th equation at time t on x_{t+n} is given by

$$\left(\frac{A_n \Sigma e_j}{\sqrt{\sigma_{jj}}} \right) \left(\frac{\delta_j}{\sqrt{\sigma_{jj}}} \right), \quad n = 0,1,2,\ldots$$

By setting $\delta_j = \sqrt{\sigma_{jj}}$, we obtain the scaled generalized impulse response function by

$$\psi_j^g(n) = \sigma_{jj}^{-\frac{1}{2}} A_n \Sigma e_j, \quad n = 0,1,2,\ldots \tag{8.4}$$

which measures the effect of one standard error shock to the j-th equation at time t on expected values of x at time $t + n$.

Finally, the generalized impulses above can also be used in the derivation of the forecast error **variance decompositions**, defined as the proportion of the n-step ahead forecast error variance of variable i which is accounted for by the innovations in variable j in the VAR. For an analysis of the forecast error variance decompositions based on the **orthogonalized impulse responses** see Lutkepohl (1991), Section 2.3.3. Denoting the orthogonalized and the generalized forecast error variance decompositions by $\theta_{ij}^0(n)$ and $\theta_{ij}^g(n)$, respectively, then for $n = 0,1,2,\ldots$

$$\theta_{ij}^0(n) = \frac{\sum_{l=0}^{n}(e_i' A_l P e_j)^2}{\sum_{l=0}^{n}(e_i' A_l \Sigma A_l' e_j)}, \quad \theta_{ij}^g(n) = \frac{\sigma_{ii}^{-1} \sum_{l=0}^{n}(e_i' A_l P e_j)^2}{\sum_{l=0}^{n}(e_i' A_l \Sigma A_l' e_j)}, \quad i,j = 1,\ldots \tag{8.5}$$

Note that by construction, however, due to the non-zero covariance between the original (non-orthogonalized) shocks, in general $\sum_{j=1}^{m} \theta_{ij}^g(n) \neq 1$.

Example 8.1   Impulse response functions in VAR (stock prices of BRIC countries)
Suppose a multivariable time series is $X_t = (X_{1t}, X_{2t},...,X_{mt})'$, and its VAR model is $X_t = A_0 + A_1 X_{t-1} + A_2 X_{t-2} + \cdots + A_p X_{t-p} + \varepsilon_t$. If we partition matrixes $A_1, A_2,..., A_p$ as row vectors, then the VAR model is

$$X_{1t} = A_{01} + A_{11} X_{t-1} + A_{12} X_{t-2} + \cdots + A_{1p} X_{t-p} + \varepsilon_{1t}$$

$$\cdots\cdots\cdots\cdots$$

$$X_{mt} = A_{0m} + A_{m1} X_{t-1} + A_{m2} X_{t-2} + \cdots + A_{mp} X_{t-p} + \varepsilon_{mt}$$

Suppose the MA(q) model of X_t is $X_t = B_0 + \varepsilon_t + B_1 \varepsilon_{t-1} + B_2 \varepsilon_{t-2} + \cdots + B_q \varepsilon_{t-q}$, where multivariable white noise vector is $\varepsilon_t = (\varepsilon_{1t}, \varepsilon_{2t},...,\varepsilon_{mt})'$. If we partition matrixes $B_1, B_2,...,B_q$ as row vectors, then the MA model is

$$X_{1t} = B_{01} + \varepsilon_{1t} + B_{11} \varepsilon_{t-1} + B_{12} \varepsilon_{t-2} + \cdots + B_{1q} \varepsilon_{t-q}$$

$$\cdots\cdots\cdots\cdots$$

$$X_{mt} = B_{0m} + \varepsilon_{mt} + B_{m1} \varepsilon_{t-1} + B_{m2} \varepsilon_{t-2} + \cdots + B_{mq} \varepsilon_{t-q}$$

If the coefficient matrix is diagonal, we can simplify the multivariable moving average model as:

$$X_{1t} = B_{01} + \varepsilon_{1t} + b_{11} \varepsilon_{1,t-1} + b_{12} \varepsilon_{1,t-2} + \cdots + b_{1q} \varepsilon_{1,t-q}$$

$$\cdots\cdots\cdots\cdots$$

$$X_{mt} = B_{0m} + \varepsilon_{mt} + b_{m1} \varepsilon_{m,t-1} + b_{m2} \varepsilon_{m,t-2} + \cdots + b_{mq} \varepsilon_{m,t-q}$$

here $t = 1,..., N$.

We will calculate impulse response functions using the simplified model above by iterative algorithm. Giving some initial value of $\varepsilon_t^{(0)}$, known the value of X_t and using the simplified model above, we can calculate the coefficients of equations and obtain new errors series of $\varepsilon_t^{(1)}$. By repeating this process we can obtain a stable solution of coefficients of equations and ε_t. Before calculation we need to specify the process control parameters: the number of variables of time series (the number of equations); the order of the model of MA(q); the tolerance level for parameter convergence; the maximum number of iterations permitted.

In this example, X_t are the stock prices of BRIC countries (Brazil, Russia, India, China) from 2002 to 2007. The data can be seen in DASC and as Figure 8.1, but we should notice that the data of each series have been divided by 1000 to avoid digital overflow in calculation. The data minus trend is as shown in Figure 8.1. The computational results are as follows.

The data are the original series minus the trend terms (or detrended from original data).

Now we calculate the first impulse response function. The total times of iteration is 3, the best result obtained after the 3-rd time of iteration, the total correlation coefficient is 0.954131. Print the first impulse response function: 0.240219, 0.194363, −0.028616, −0.001824, 1.035598. The estimation of σ2 is 7.668612.

Now we calculate the 2-nd impulse response function. The total times of iteration is 100, the best result obtained after the 2-nd iteration, the total correlation coefficient is 0.921962. Print the 2-nd impulse response function: 0.152843, −0.268649, −0.055853, −0.202046, 0.198355. The estimation of σ2 is 5.316071.

Now we calculate the 3-rd impulse response function. The total times of iteration is 100, the best result obtained after the 3-rd iteration, the total correlation coefficient is 0.918517.

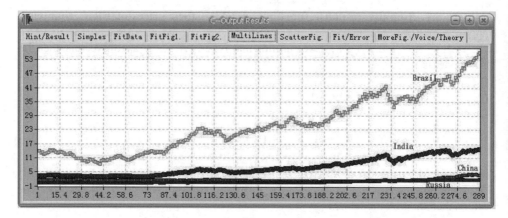

Figure 8.1   The original data of stock prices of BRIC countries (2002–2007).

Print the 3-rd impulse response function: 0.172525, 0.069843, −0.004883, 0.067501, 3.805421. The estimation of σ2 is 21.748737.

Now we calculate the 4-th impulse response function. The total number of iterations is 5, the best result obtained after the 5-th iteration, the total correlation coefficient is 0.953809. Print the 4-th impulse response function: −0.277223, 0.107834, 0.044567, 0.103877, 0.022970. The estimation of σ2 is 0.803493.

The impulse response functions for a unit sd shock to Indian stock price are:

India	−0.240219	0.194363	−0.028616	−0.001824	1.035598
China	−0.152843	−0.268649	−0.055853	−0.202046	0.198355
Brazil	−0.172525	0.069843	−0.004883	0.067501	3.805421
Russia	−0.277223	0.107834	0.044567	0.103877	0.022970

Likewise one can obtain responses to all the four stock prices for unit sd shocks given to the stock prices of other countries. Some business and public policy situations might call for a counter-factual simulation of a situation where shocks of different magnitudes are given to different variables simultaneously. To answer such questions the procedure above can be carried out by defining a shock that is a linear combination of these individual shocks.

The computation can be performed by clicking DASC→Time Series Analysis→ Nonstationary time series →Impulse Response Functions. Besides, there are five ways to load user's data in DASC from any folder with any data form (text, Excel, SQL, and other database form) to calculate this test or other models.

We should note that MA model is designed for, and suitable for, stationary series. So we may need to make a difference for the original data. DASC offers the menu selection for difference in this menu (Figures 8.2–8.5).

8.1.5   Variance decomposition with VAR(p)

Another important business and economic policy issue is to explain how much of an observed variation in response is attributable to each of several shocks that are given to the system simultaneously. This issue is examined by the concept of **Variance Decomposition** of a VAR(p) model.

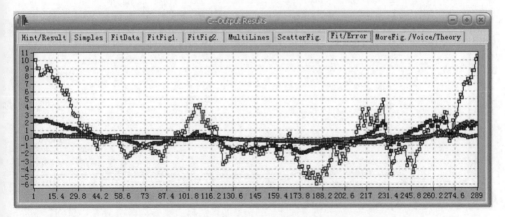

Figure 8.2   The data (minus trend) of stock prices of BRIC countries (2002–2007).

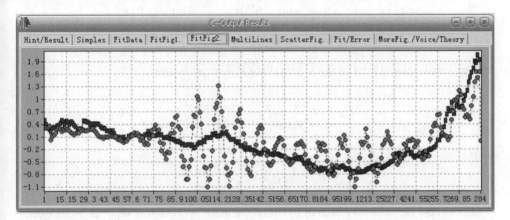

Figure 8.3   The data (minus trend) of stock prices of China with fitting data by MA model.

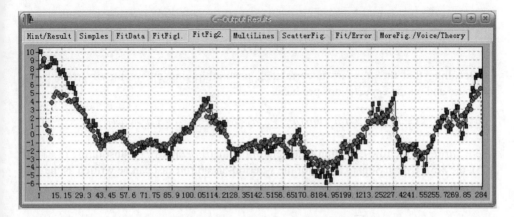

Figure 8.4   The data (minus trend) of stock prices of Brazil with fitting data by MA model.

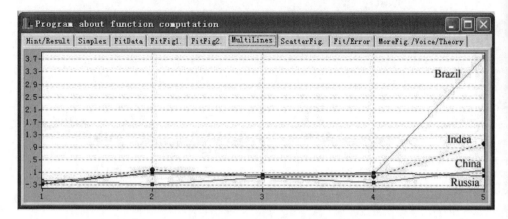

Figure 8.5   Impulse response for one unit sd shock to Indian Stock Price.

We can identify the error in forecasting a VAR s-period into the future as

$$y_{t+s} - \hat{y}_{t+s|t} = \varepsilon_{t+s} + \Psi_1\varepsilon_{t+s-1} + \Psi_2\varepsilon_{t+s-2} + \cdots + \Psi_{s-1}\varepsilon_{t+1}$$

The mean squared error of this s-period-ahead forecast is thus

$$MSE(\hat{y}_{t+s|t}) = E[(y_{t+s} - \hat{y}_{t+s|t})(y_{t+s} - \hat{y}_{t+s|t})']$$
$$= \Omega + \Psi_1\Omega\Psi_1' + \Psi_2\Omega\Psi_2' + \cdots + \Psi_{s-1}\Omega\Psi_{s-1}' \qquad (8.6)$$

where

$$\Omega = E(\varepsilon_t\varepsilon_t')$$

Let us now consider how each of the orthogonalized disturbances $(u_{1t},\ldots,u_{nt})$ contributes to this MSE. Write as

$$\varepsilon_t = Au_t = a_1u_{1t} + a_2u_{2t} + \cdots + a_nu_{nt}$$

where, as before, a_j denotes the jth column of the matrix A given as

$$\Omega = ADA' \qquad (8.7)$$

Recalling that the $u_{jt}'s$ are uncorrelated, postmultiplying the vector of errors by its transpose and taking expectations produces

$$\Omega = E(\varepsilon_t\varepsilon') = a_ja_j' \cdot Var(u_{1t}) + a_2a_2' \cdot Var(u_{2t}) + \cdots + a_na_n' \cdot Var(u_{nt}) \qquad (8.8)$$

where $Var(u_{jt})$ is the row j, column j element of the matrix D in (8.7). Substituting (8.8) into (8.6), the MSE (Mean Square Error) of the s-period-ahead forecast can be written as the sum of n terms, one arising from each of the disturbances u_{jt}:

$$MSE(\hat{y}_{t+s|t}) = \sum_{j=1}^{n} \{Var(u_{jt}) \cdot [a_ja_j' + \Psi_1a_ja_j' \Psi_1' + \cdots + \Psi_{s-1}a_ja_j' \Psi_{s-1}']\} \qquad (8.9)$$

With this expression, we can calculate the contribution of the *jth* orthogonalized innovation to the MSE of the s-period-ahead forecast:

$$Var(u_{jt}) \cdot [a_j a_j' + \Psi_1 a_j a_j' \Psi_1' + \cdots + \Psi_{s-1} a_j a_j' \Psi_{s-1}']$$

Again, this magnitude in general depends on the ordering of the variables.

As $s \to \infty$ for a covariance-stationary *VAR*, $MSE(\hat{y}_{t+s|t}) \to \Gamma_0$, the unconditional variance of the vector y_t. Thus, (8.9) permits calculation of the portion of the total variance of y_i that is duo to the disturbance u_i by letting s become suitably large.

Alternatively, recalling that $a_j \sqrt{Var(u_{jt})}$ is equal to p_j, the *jth* column of the Choleskly factor p, result (8.9) can be written equivalently as

$$MSE(\hat{y}_{t+s|t}) = \sum_{j=1}^{n} p_j p_j' + \Psi_1 p_j p_j' \Psi_1' + \cdots + \Psi_{s-1} p_j p_j' \Psi_{s-1}' \qquad (8.9a)$$

8.1.6 Granger causality with VAR(p) specification

One of the most interesting issues in economic and business policy is how does causality run between economic variables. Another related issue is whether one should treat a variable as an endogenous variable or as an exogenous variable. As we explained earlier an exogenous variable is one that causes an endogenous variable but is not caused by it. Granger introduced the concept of **causality** among time series in terms of one series forecasting another series. We start the investigation by examining the question whether a scalar y can forecast another scalar x. If it cannot, then we say that y does not **Granger-cause** x. More formally, y fails to Granger-cause x if for all $s > 0$ the mean square error of a forecast of x_{t+s} based on $(x_t, x_{t-1},...)$ is the same as the *MSE* of a forecast of x_{t+s} that uses both $(x_t, x_{t-1},...)$ and $(y_t, t_{t-1},...)$. If we restrict ourselves to linear functions, y fails to Granger-cause x if

$$MSE[\hat{E}(x_{t+s}|x_t, x_{t-1},...)] = MSE[\hat{E}(x_{t+s}|x_t, x_{t-1},..., y_t, y_{t-1},...)] \qquad (8.10)$$

Equivalently, we say that x is exogenous in the time series with respect to y if (8.10) holds.

Granger's reason for proposing this definition was that if an event Y is the cause of another event X, then event Y should precede event X. Although one might agree with this position, philosophically there can be serious obstacles to practical implementation of this idea using aggregate time series data, as will be seen in the example considered later in this section. First, however, we explore the mechanical implications of **Granger causality** for the time series representation of a bivariate system.

Econometric test of whether a particular observed series y Granger-causes x uses the autoregressive specification. To implement this test, we assume a particular autoregressive model with lag lengths p and q and estimate

$$x_t = c_1 + \alpha_1 x_{t-1} + \alpha_2 x_{t-2} + \cdots + \alpha_p x_{t-p} + \beta_1 y_{t-1} + \beta_2 y_{t-2} + \cdots \beta_q y_{t-q} + u_t \qquad (8.11)$$

We then conduct F test of the null hypothesis

$$H_0 : \beta_1 = \beta_2 = \cdots = \beta_q = 0$$

One way to implement this test is to calculate the sum of squared residuals from (8.11), (The **residual sum of squares** under the alternative hypothesis)

$$RSS_1 = \sum_{t=1}^{T} \hat{u}_t^2$$

and compare this with the sum of squared residuals under the null hypothesis,

$$RSS_0 = \sum_{t=1}^{T} \hat{e}_t^2$$

where

$$x_t = c_0 + \gamma_1 x_{t-1} + \gamma_2 x_{t-2} + \cdots + \gamma_p x_{t-p} + e_t$$

We then construct the test statistic

$$S_1 \equiv \frac{(RSS_0 - RSS_1)/p}{RSS_1/(T - 2p - 1)} \tag{8.12}$$

If this statistic is greater than the 5% critical value for an $F(p, T - 2p - 1)$ distribution, then we reject the null hypothesis that y does not Granger-cause x; that is, if S_1 is sufficiently large, we conclude that y does Granger-cause x.

The test statistic (8.12) would have an exact F distribution for a regression with fixed regressors and Gaussian disturbances. With lagged dependent variables as in the Granger-causality regressions, however, the test is valid only asymptotically. An asymptotically equivalent test is given by

$$S_2 \equiv \frac{T(RSS_0 - RSS_1)}{RSS_1} \tag{8.13}$$

We would reject the null hypothesis that y does not Granger-cause x if S_2 is greater than the 5% critical values for a $\chi^2(p)$ variable.

The Monte Carlo simulations of Geweke, Meese, and Dent (1983) suggest that the simplest and most straightforward test, namely, that based on (8.13), may well be the best test.

In a bivariate VAR describing x and y, y does not Granger-cause x if the coefficient matrices Φ_j are lower triangular for all j:

$$\begin{bmatrix} x_t \\ y_t \end{bmatrix} = \begin{bmatrix} c_1 \\ c_2 \end{bmatrix} + \begin{bmatrix} \phi_{11}^{(1)} & 0 \\ \phi_{21}^{(1)} & \phi_{22}^{(1)} \end{bmatrix} \begin{bmatrix} x_{t-1} \\ y_{t-1} \end{bmatrix} + \begin{bmatrix} \phi_{11}^{(2)} & 0 \\ \phi_{21}^{(2)} & \phi_{22}^{(2)} \end{bmatrix} \begin{bmatrix} x_{t-2} \\ y_{t-2} \end{bmatrix}$$

$$+ \cdots + \begin{bmatrix} \phi_{11}^{(p)} & 0 \\ \phi_{21}^{(p)} & \phi_{22}^{(p)} \end{bmatrix} \begin{bmatrix} x_{t-p} \\ y_{t-p} \end{bmatrix} + \begin{bmatrix} \varepsilon_{1t} \\ \varepsilon_{2t} \end{bmatrix} \tag{8.14}$$

From the first row of this system, the optimal one-period-ahead forecast of x depends only on itself and its lagged values and not on lagged y. It can be shown that if y fails to Granger-cause x, then the $MA(\infty)$ representation can be written as:

$$\begin{bmatrix} x_t \\ y_t \end{bmatrix} = \begin{bmatrix} \mu_1 \\ \mu_2 \end{bmatrix} + \begin{bmatrix} \psi_{11}(L) & 0 \\ \psi_{21}(L) & \psi_{22}(L) \end{bmatrix} \begin{bmatrix} \varepsilon_{1t} \\ \varepsilon_{2t} \end{bmatrix}$$ (8.15)

where

$$\psi_{ij}(L) = \psi_{ij}^{(0)} + \psi_{ij}^{(1)} L^1 + \psi_{ij}^{(2)} L^2 + \psi_{ij}^{(3)} L^3 + \cdots$$

with $\psi_{11}^{(0)} = \psi_{22}^{(0)} = 1$ and $\psi_{21}^{(0)} = 0$.

The results of any empirical test for Granger causality can be surprisingly sensitive to the choice of lag lengths (p and q) or the methods used to deal with potential nonstationarity of the series. For demonstrations of the practical relevance of such issues, see Feige and Pearce (1979), Christiano and Ljungqvist (1988), and Stock and Watson (1989).[3]

8.2   Nonstationary time series

8.2.1   Stochastic trends and unit root processes

Data of many economic time series such as GDP, money supply, fiscal expenditure and so on, don't possess characteristics of stationary time series in that they always have **trend component**. There are two ways to describe time series with trend. One involves a **deterministic trend** component directly with a mathematical expression of that trend. Another is that of a **stochastic trend**, not shown directly with any trend expression. The latter includes the random walk or unit root process. Both of them (assuming that the deterministic trend is linear in time) can be incorporated into a single model as follows:

$$y_t = a + bt + \rho y_{t-1} + \varepsilon_t$$

where if $b \neq 0$, $|\rho| < 1$ corresponds to a model with deterministic trend. If $a = b = 0$, and $\rho = 1$, we get the random walk or unit root process depicting a stochastic trend without a drift, If $b = 0$ and $\rho = 1$ we get a random walk model with a drift.

The stochastic trend or unit root process without constant terms is written as: $y_t = y_{t-1} + \varepsilon_t$. Although its mean is constant, the variance is not constant, and even it tends to infinity.

The **unit root process** with a constant term called a **random walk** with drift, is expressed as

$$y_t = \mu + y_{t-1} + \varepsilon_t$$

After substituting repeatedly, we obtain

$$y_t = \sum_{i=0}^{\infty} (\mu + \varepsilon_t)$$

---

[3] An interesting example of the importance of this lag length specification in causality testing is the causality between Sunspots and GNP, originally advanced in its simplest form by the eighteenth century economist William Stanley Jevons. Two US economists Sheehan and Grieves (1982) found that US GNP Granger causes Sunspots with a chosen lag length for Sunspots less than 11 years, while it is Sunspots that cause US GNP if the correct lag length of 11 years is chosen for Sunspot series. See Noble and Field (1983), and Sheehan and Grieves (1983).

This obviously indicates increasing tendency. In the processes above the properties of time series depends crucially on whether the parameter $\rho \geq 1$ or $\rho < 1$. Therefore, it is important for us to study the features and generalization of unit root process, as well as the testing of the hypothesis that $\rho = 1$.

The test of a unit root process is very complicated and has several problems associated with it. The derivation of distribution of the test statistic is very difficult.

We discuss first the case of a random walk or unit root without a drift. In general, the form of a simple **random walk process** without constant term or drift is:

$$y_t = y_{t-1} + \varepsilon_t \tag{8.16}$$

where $\{\varepsilon_t\}$ is a white noise series.

The first order differences are

$$x_t = \Delta y_t = y_t - y_{t-1} = \varepsilon_t \tag{8.17}$$

The difference series $\{x_t\}$ is stationary time series, and time series $\{y_t\}$ is called the **unit root process**.

It is called a unit root process as the corresponding stochastic differential equation

$$y_t - \rho y_{t-1} = \varepsilon_t, \quad i.e., \quad (1 - \rho L)y_t = \varepsilon_t$$

has characteristic polynomial in the lag operator L as $1 - \rho z = 0$ with a root $z = \dfrac{1}{\rho}$, and that root $z = 1$ when $\rho = 1$. Hence this is called a unit root process.

This series can be regarded as random walk on a horizontal straight line. Each position y_t is generated by a random walk ε_t from the previous position y_{t-1}. It is a non-stationary process as its variance is not constant although its expectation is constant. Expectation and variance are shown below:

$$E(y_t) = E(y_0 + \varepsilon_1 + \varepsilon_2 + \cdots + \varepsilon_t) = y_0$$

$$V(y_t) = E(y_t - y_0)^2 = E(\varepsilon_1 + \cdots + \varepsilon_t)^2 = t\sigma^2 \tag{8.18}$$

The variance is a function of time t, and diverges to infinity as t approaches infinity. The difference series (8.16) is, however, a stationary process.

More generally, the form of unit root process is

$$y_t = y_{t-1} + u_t$$

where $\{u_t\}$ is a stationary process, $E(u_t) = 0$, $\gamma_k = Cov(u_t, u_{t+k}) < \infty$.

We discuss now the probability limit of least squares estimator of the autocorrelation coefficient for this unit root process. For the first-order auto-regression process

$$y_t = \rho y_{t-1} + \varepsilon_t \tag{8.19}$$

we consider the least squares estimator of parameter ρ. If $\{\varepsilon_t\}$ are i.i.d., and $E(\varepsilon_t) = 0$, $V(\varepsilon_t) = \sigma^2 < \infty$, we use sample $y_1, \ldots, y_T$ to construct the least squares estimator of ρ,

$$\hat{\rho}_T = \frac{\sum_{t=1}^{T} y_{t-1} y_t}{\sum_{t=1}^{T} y_{t-1}^2} \tag{8.20}$$

Substituting (8.19) into y_t in the numerator we obtain

$$\rho_T = \frac{\sum_{t=1}^{T} y_{t-1}(\rho \, y_{t-1} + \varepsilon_t)}{\sum_{t=1}^{T} y_{t-1}^2} = \rho + \frac{\sum_{t=1}^{T} y_{t-1} \varepsilon_t}{\sum_{t=1}^{T} y_{t-1}^2}$$

When $|\rho| < 1$, $\{y_t\}$ is a stationary process. Because $\{\varepsilon_t\}$ are i.i.d. and unrelated to y_{t-1}, $Cov(y_{t-1}, \varepsilon_t) = 0$. When $T \to \infty$, $\hat{\rho}_T$ converges in probability to parameter ρ, so the least squares estimator is a consistent estimator. According to the central limit theorem, $\sqrt{T}(\hat{\rho}_T - \rho)$ has a limiting Normal distribution, namely

$$\sqrt{T}(\hat{\rho}_T - \rho) \xrightarrow{d} N(0, \sigma^2(1-\rho^2))$$

here the symbol $\xrightarrow{d}$ denotes converging in distribution. When $\{y_t\}$ is a stationary process and $|\rho| < 1$, variance $\sigma^2(1-\rho^2)$ is greater than zero and the limiting distribution of $\sqrt{T}(\hat{\rho}_T - \rho)$ is a Normal distribution with a finite non-zero variance. But when $\{y_t\}$ is a unit root process and $\rho = 1$, $\sigma^2(1-\rho^2)$ is zero and then the limiting distribution of $\sqrt{T}(\hat{\rho}_T - \rho)$ tends to a distribution with zero mean and zero variance. In other words, it tends to a degenerate distribution that is no longer normal.

When we describe economic variables with trend, the **random walk process with a constant** term or a **random walk with a drift** is often a suitable candidate. If time series

$$y_t = \mu + \rho \, y_{t-1} + \varepsilon_t \tag{8.21}$$

satisfies $\mu \neq 0$, $\rho = 1$, $\{\varepsilon_t\}$ are i.i.d., and $E(\varepsilon_t) = 0$, $V(\varepsilon_t) = \sigma^2$, then $\{y_t\}$ is called a random walk with a drift. Substituting $\rho = 1$ produces $y_t = \mu + y_{t-1} + \varepsilon_t = \mu + (\mu + y_{t-2} + \varepsilon_{t-1}) + \varepsilon_t$ and after repeated substitution, we get

$$y_t = \sum_{i=0}^{\infty} (\mu + \varepsilon_{t-i}) \tag{8.22}$$

which obviously has increasing trend, and μ gets added with every term. The random variable drifts away from 0. This is obviously a non-mean reverting process.

The least squares estimators $\hat{\mu}$ and $\hat{\rho}$ of parameters μ and ρ for model (8.21) can be expressed jointly as

$$\begin{pmatrix} \hat{\mu} \\ \hat{\rho} \end{pmatrix} = \begin{pmatrix} \mu \\ 1 \end{pmatrix} + \begin{pmatrix} T & \sum_{t=1}^{T} y_{t-1} \\ \sum_{t=1}^{T} y_{t-1} & \sum_{t=1}^{T} y_{t-1}^2 \end{pmatrix}^{-1} \begin{pmatrix} \sum_{t=1}^{T} \varepsilon_t \varepsilon_t \\ \sum_{t=1}^{T} y_{t-1} \varepsilon_t \end{pmatrix}$$

Multiplying $\hat{\mu}$ by $T^{1/2}$ and multiplying $\hat{\rho}$ by $T^{3/2}$, we can deduce the limiting distribution of the estimators (P.C.B. Phillips, 1987),

$$\begin{pmatrix} T^{1/2}(\hat{\mu} - \mu) \\ T^{3/2}(\hat{\rho} - 1) \end{pmatrix} \xrightarrow{d} N(\vec{0}, \sigma^2 Q^{-1}) \tag{8.23}$$

where matrix Q is a positive definite real symmetric matrix, and

$$Q = \begin{pmatrix} 1 & \mu/2 \\ \mu/2 & \mu^2/3 \end{pmatrix} \tag{8.24}$$

8.2.2   Test for unit root hypothesis

For data that looks like a nonstationary economic time series from the data worksheet or table, or from a line graph we cannot statistically infer that whether it is a non-stationary process with only a deterministic trend component (8.25), or if it is a unit root process without drift (8.26), or if it is a unit root process with drift (8.27)

$$y_t = a + bt + \rho y_{t-1} + \varepsilon_t \quad (b \neq 0, |\rho| < 1) \tag{8.25}$$

$$y_t = \rho y_{t-1} + \varepsilon_t \quad \text{with} \quad \rho = 1 \tag{8.26}$$

$$y_t = \mu + \rho y_{t-1} + \varepsilon_t \quad (\mu \neq 0, \rho = 1) \tag{8.27}$$

Hence we need a statistical test for the null hypothesis $\rho = 1$, under these various scenarios.

Research has revealed that even if the data are from (8.27) rather than from (8.25) (i.e. even when $b = 0$), using the traditional t test for testing for no linear trend ($b = 0$), t statistic is likely to show significance. Hence, before testing for time trend, we have to make sure whether unit root exists in time series or not. Only when unit root hypothesis is rejected, we can choose model (8.10) and test hypothesis about its parameters.

For example, assume that the first order auto-regression process

$$y_t = \rho y_{t-1} + \varepsilon_t$$

holds and that $|\rho| < 1$, $\{\varepsilon_t\}$ are i.i.d., and $E(\varepsilon_t) = 0$, $V(\varepsilon_t) = \sigma^2 < \infty$. The hypothesis to be tested is

$$H_0 : \rho = \rho_0 \leftrightarrow H_1 : \rho < \rho_0$$

when $\rho_0 < 1$. The **Dickey-Fuller (DF) statistic** is

$$t_T = \frac{\hat{\rho} - \rho_0}{\hat{\eta}}$$

where $\hat{\rho}$ is least squares estimator of ρ and $\hat{\eta}$ is the standard deviation estimate of $\hat{\rho}$. When the null hypothesis H_0: $\rho = \rho_0 \neq 1$ is true, meaning that data are generated from $y_t = \rho_0 y_{t-1} + \varepsilon_t$, statistic t_T has t distribution with $T - 1$ degrees of freedom. For the α percent significance level, we get the critical value t_α from t distribution tables. If $t_T < t_\alpha$, we accept null hypothesis H_0: $\rho = \rho_0$; otherwise we reject null hypothesis H_0 in favor of alternative hypothesis H_1: $\rho < \rho_0$.

This method is not applicable when testing the hypothesis H_0: $\rho = 1$, because when hypothesis H_0: $\rho = 1$ is true, t_T does not have the t distribution. Now least squares estimator $\hat{\rho}$ of parameter ρ is (8.20). Use $\hat{\eta}$ to denote the estimator of standard deviation of statistic $\hat{\rho}$, it is in the form of

$$\hat{\eta} = \left(\hat{\sigma}^2 \middle/ \sum_{t=1}^{T} y_{t-1}^2 \right)^{1/2} \tag{8.28}$$

where $\hat{\sigma}^2 = \dfrac{1}{T-1} \sum_{t=1}^{T} (y_t - \hat{\rho}\, y_{t-1})^2$ is least squares estimator of variance σ^2. Hence we use $\hat{\rho}$ and $\hat{\eta}$ to construct test statistic t_T for null hypothesis,

$$t_T = \frac{\hat{\rho}-1}{\hat{\eta}} = \frac{T(\hat{\rho}-1)}{\hat{\sigma}^2} \left(\frac{1}{T^2} \sum_{t=1}^{T} y_{t-1}^2 \right)^{1/2} \tag{8.29}$$

The limiting distribution of t_T was derived by Phillips (1987). Phillips showed that

$$t_T \xrightarrow{d} \frac{W^2(1)-1}{2\left\{ \int_0^1 W^2(r)dr \right\}^{1/2}}$$

where $W(r)$ is a continuous time **Wiener process**.[4] The distribution of this limit is not known in closed form and hence the critical values of even this limiting distribution must be obtained through simulation.

If the AR(p) model is:

$$y_t = \rho\, y_{t-1} + \rho_1 \Delta y_{t-1} + \rho_2 \Delta y_{t-2} + \cdots + \rho_p \Delta y_{t-p} + \varepsilon_t$$

then the Augmented Dickey-Fuller (ADF) statistic is

$$t_T = \frac{T(\hat{\rho}-1)}{1 - \hat{\rho}_1 - \hat{\rho}_2 \cdots - \hat{\rho}_p}$$

When we carry out tests of statistical hypothesis, we need to (i) set up a null hypothesis as well as an alternative hypothesis; (ii) derive a test statistics based on the observed sample; and (iii) specify a critical value at a given level of significance. To answer item (iii) above one must know what the statistical distribution of the test statistic is in finite samples. It is difficult many times to obtain the sampling distribution of the test statistic in finite samples. It is also difficult sometimes to get a closed form for the small sample distribution. Hence quite often only a limiting distribution is used. Hypothesis testing for unit root process encounters such problems that we cannot deduce the precise distribution of the statistics. Dickey and Fuller (1979) used random simulation method to calibrate the critical values of the test statistic in finite samples. General reference books present such critical values of **Dickey-Fuller test** at three levels of significance, 1%, 5%, and 10% and for three sample sizes 25, 50, 100. In any

---

[4] Almost everywhere else in this book we are dealing with discrete time stochastic processes. Only when it comes to the limiting distributions of some statistics do we fall back on this continuous time stochastic process.

practical problem one may have to approximate the right critical values through interpolation or extrapolation. In this book we circumvent these problems by providing a very good small sample approximation to the Dickey-Fuller test statistic. This is taken up in the next section.

Example 8.2   Testing for unit root by Monte Carlo method (stock prices of BRIC countries)   We developed a Monte-Carlo algorithm for the probability distribution function of the unit root test statistic. The idea behind this algorithm is quite simple. The theoretical basis is the well known **Glivenko Theorem**: the empirical distribution function of a statistic converges certainly to its distribution function. Now we describe our method of deriving the empirical distribution of Dickey-Fuller statistic under the same set up as our data example.

Our procedure consists of (i) estimating the small sample density of the Dickey Fuller statistic through Monte Carlo simulation of data and fitting a non-parametric kernel density function, (ii) deriving the critical value of the test statistic from this estimated density function, and (iii) testing for unit root from the data example by computing the D-F statistic from data and comparing it against the critical value obtained in step (ii) above.

Suppose a unit root process is $y_t = \rho y_{t-1} + \varepsilon_t$, where $\rho = 1$, $\{\varepsilon_t\}$ are i.i.d., and $E(\varepsilon_t) = 0$, $V(\varepsilon_t) = \sigma^2 < \infty$. In general, we select the distribution of $\{\varepsilon_t\}$ as $N(0,1)$. The steps of our method are as follows:

(1) Generate two series A and B by pseudo random numbers to offer initial values in Step 2. Each series include N numbers, for example, $N = 3000$.

(2) Select an initial value y_0 from set A, and select an initial seed value I_t of pseudo random numbers ε_t from set B.

(3) Get a series $\{\varepsilon_t\}$ by generator of pseudo random numbers, and get a series $\{y_t\}$ by $y_t = y_{t-1} + \varepsilon_t$. Each series include M numbers (M is the sample size of the underlying series), for example, $M = 261$ (Indian data), or $M = 105$ (Russian data).

(4) Get the estimators of parameters $\hat{\rho}$ and $\hat{\eta}$ by (8.20) and (8.28).

(5) Get an estimator of the D-F statistic t_T by (8.29).

We repeat steps (2) to (5) above N times, then we can get a series of estimates of the D-F statistic t_T by changing the initial value y_0 from set A and the initial seed value I_t of pseudo random numbers ε_t from set B. The estimated series of t_T have an empirical distribution (under the null hypothesis and the assumption of model), so we can obtain the rejection area of sample statistic for any significance level. If the sample size of the series t_T is sufficiently large (for example, $N = 3000$), the test should be reasonable. Here we are estimating the sampling distribution using the kernel method of estimating the probability density functions explained in Chapters 5 and 10, and in the Electronic References section for Chapter 5.

The computation can be performed by clicking DASC $\rightarrow$ Time Series Analysis $\rightarrow$ Nonstationary time series $\rightarrow$ D-F Test of Unit Root Process for the First Order AR(p). DASC also offers ADF test of unit root process for higher order AR(p). DASC offers data sets of stock prices of BRIC countries. The data can be loaded by menu 'Data $\rightarrow$ Load other example data' from folder \\She\\Wileydata\\Wiley 7(D-F). The figure of the density curves of D-F test statistic (by kernel method discussed in Chapters 6 and the Electronic References for Chapter 6), are shown in area C and as below (Figures 8.6–8.9). In order to get a better curve for the density function, the selection of suitable window width is important.

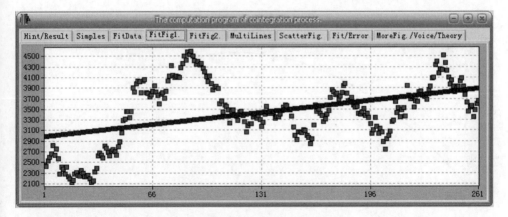

Figure 8.6   The series (dots) of Indian stock prices with its trend (line) (1993–1997).

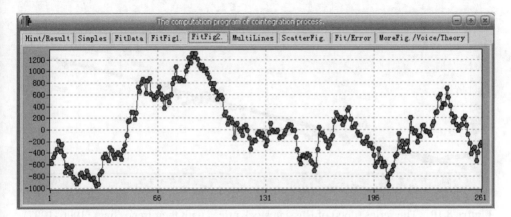

Figure 8.7   The series of Indian stock prices minus its trend.

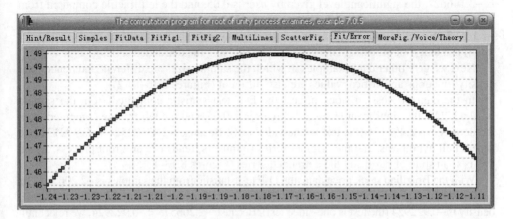

Figure 8.8   The density curve of D-F statistic (with sample size 261, discrete).

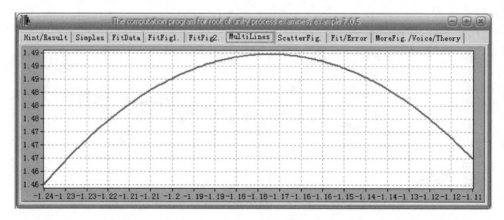

Figure 8.9   The density curve of D-F statistic (with sample size 261, continued).

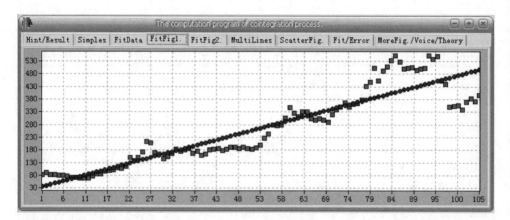

Figure 8.10   The series (dots) of Russian stock prices with their trend (line) (1996–1997).

With the data of Indian stock prices, the D-F test statistic computed from the sample is −2.146627, the significant level given by user is 0.05, and the left fractile computed from the estimated density of the D-F statistic is −1.233780 (the test is one-sided test). Because −2.146627 > −1.233780, we do not reject the null hypothesis. The original series (minus its trend) is a unit root process. (This is so in spite of using the detrended series).

Next we give other data examples in which the sample sizes are different and hence their density functions and critical values are also different (Figures 8.10–8.12).

In the data of Russian stock prices, the D-F test statistic computed from the sample is −2.437225, the significant level given by user is 0.05, and the left fractile computed from the density is −2.492131 (the test is one-sided test). Because −2.437225 > = −2.492131, we accept null hypothesis, and the original series (minus its trend) is a unit root process. Again this is so in spite of our using the detrended series (Figures 8.13–8.15).

With the Brazilian stock price data, the D-F test statistic from the samples is −2.206575, the significant level given by user is 0.05, and the left fractile computed from the estimated kernel density is −0.922924 (the test is one-sided test). Because −2.206575 < −0.922924, we reject null hypothesis, and the original series (minus its trend) is not a unit root process (Figures 8.16–8.18).

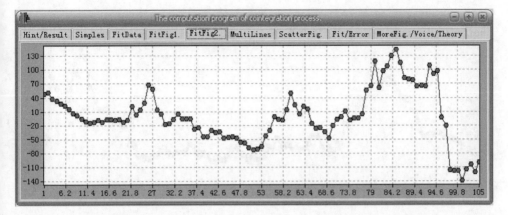

Figure 8.11   The series of Russian stock prices minus their trend.

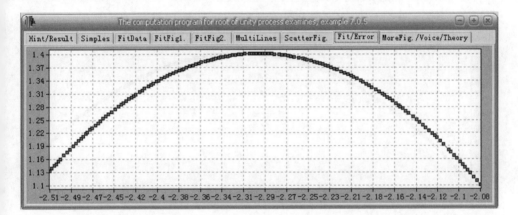

Figure 8.12   The density curve of D-F statistic (with sample size of 105).

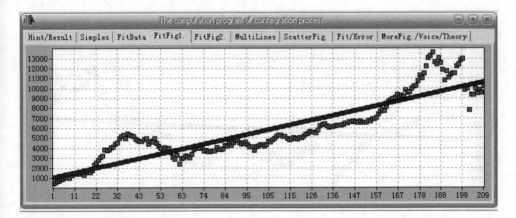

Figure 8.13   The series (dots) of Brazilian stock prices with their trend (line) (1994–1997).

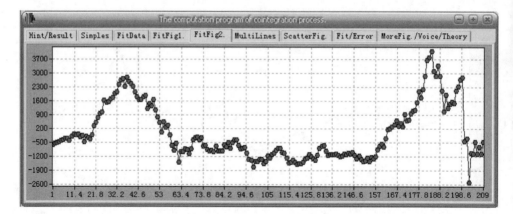

Figure 8.14   The series of Brazilian stock prices minus their trend.

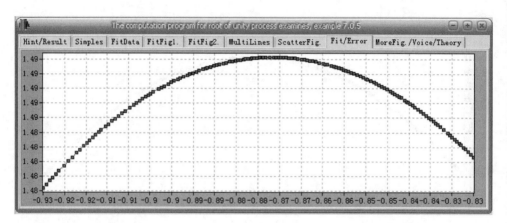

Figure 8.15   The density curve of D-F statistic (with sample content 209).

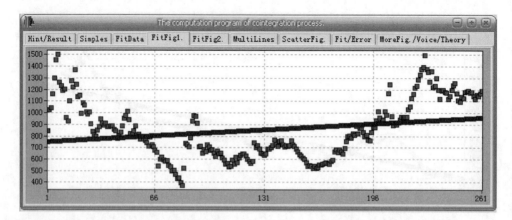

Figure 8.16   The series (dots) of Chinese stock prices with their trend (line) (1993–1997).

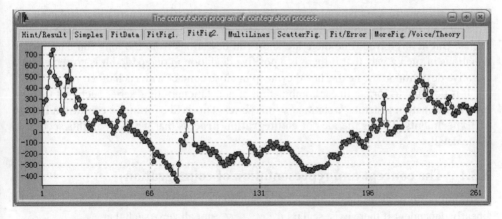

Figure 8.17   The series of Chinese stock prices minus their trend.

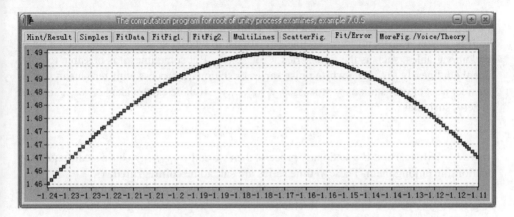

Figure 8.18   The density curve of D-F statistic (with sample content 261).

With the Chinese stock prices data, the D-F test statistic computed from the sample is −2.245482, the significant level given by user is 0.05, and the left fractile computed from the estimated kernel density is −1.233780 (the test is one-sided test). Because −2.245482 < −1.233780, we reject null hypothesis, and the original series (minus its trend) is not a unit root process.

We note that Figure 8.18 is the same as Figure 8.8 because their sample sizes are the same, 261.

More data of stock prices of BRIC counties from 1998 to 2007 are in DASC folder \\She\\ Wileydata\\Wiley 7(D-F). We can use them to make more analysis.

8.3   Cointegration and error correction

Most of the economic time series perform a rhythmic dance in time, like a salsa. They are very dynamic and trendy. They move away from each other but soon come close. Some of the unique moves they make are unexpected, sometimes quite exciting to watch and sometimes quite dangerous to see. This phenomenon is captured by economists by postulating the existence of **long run equilibria** between economic time series, series that have growth trends. But at any given time there are short run deviations from the long run equilibrium equations in such a way that if there is a positive deviation in one period it is corrected by a negative deviation in the next. Thus they keep in close contact with each other.

It is possible to form a linear combination of nonstationary time series such that this linear transformation generates a stationary time series. This is like forming a contrast in **Design of Experiments**. This is the idea of **cointegration process** that we study in this section in some detail.

8.3.1   The concept and representation of cointegration

It is familiar to us from linear algebra that nonrandom variables $y_1, y_2, \ldots, y_m$ are said to be linearly dependent if there exist scalars $\alpha_1, \alpha_2, \ldots, \alpha_m$, not all zero, such that

$$\alpha_1 y_1 + \alpha_2 y_2 + \cdots + \alpha_m y_m = 0$$

In other words, $y_1, y_2, \ldots, y_m$ have a **linear relationship** among them.

It is, however, difficult to find a linear relationship whose value is zero between a set of random variables, such as the time series $y_{1t}, y_{2t}, \ldots, y_{mt}$. But sometimes it is possible to combine them linearly to yield a **white noise series** or stationary process with zero mean. Let us consider a set of non-stationary processes, $y_{1t}, y_{2t}, \ldots, y_{mt}$. If there exist scalars $\alpha_1, \alpha_2, \ldots, \alpha_m$, not all zero, such that

$$\alpha_1 y_{1t} + \alpha_2 y_{2t} + \cdots + \alpha_m y_{mt} = \varepsilon_t$$

where $\varepsilon_t \sim W(0, \sigma^2)$ or ε_t is a stationary process, then we call $y_{1t}, y_{2t}, \ldots, y_{mt}$ have a **cointegrating** relationship among them. These m time series are said to be **cointegrated**.

Many economic time series are nonstationary as they represent a superposition of a long-term growth and short run fluctuations, or they represent long run business cycles superposed by short run business cycles. As economic variables move together in a rhythm, it is but natural that these nonstationary time series move together in a rhythm. This means that long run economic equilibrium is a natural home for cointegration phenomenon.

A typical example is the **Law of One Price** (LOP). According to the Law of One Price the price of a commodity in one market p_{1t} is related to the price of the same commodity in another market to which it is linked through trade, p_{2t} by the following relation:

$$E_t(p_{1t} + t_{12}) = p_{2t}$$

where E is the exchange rate that converts the currency in market 1 to the currency in market 2, in case we are dealing with two different countries, and t_{12} is the transport cost per unit of transporting the commodity from region 1 to region 2. If the markets are in the same country then $E_t = 1$. The basic idea is that there is trade equilibrium between the two markets and if this condition is not satisfied someone could make money through arbitrage of buying in one market and selling in the other, and this process of arbitrage will continue until the gain from such arbitrage is narrowed to zero. However, in real situations there could be some short run disturbances from the equilibrium, and if there were equilibrium then the short run adjustments must have a mean zero and constant variance. Hence the Law of One Price can be stated as a cointegrating equation between the two prices and the exchange rate.

Let p_1 and p_2 be the price level between two countries, and E be the exchange rate between these two countries. Here p_1 and p_2 are endogenous variables and E and t_{12} are exogenous variables. Then the equilibrium state is defined by the following cointegrating equation:

$$E_t(p_{1t}+t_{12})-p_{2t} = \varepsilon_t \tag{8.30}$$

where ε_t are stationary series.

We generalize this example to a situation with m endogenous variables

$$(y_{1t},y_{2t},\dots,y_{mt}) = Y_t'$$

and k exogenous variables

$$(x_{1t},x_{2t},\dots,x_{kt}) = X_t'$$

here each component variable of this m-dimensional vector Y_t is a unit root process. Long-term equilibrium relationship among these variables is given by

$$\alpha'Y_t + \beta'X_t = \varepsilon_t$$

where ε_t is a stationary series, α is a m –dimensional column vector and β is $k \times 1$ column vector.

Here we say that **cointegrating relations** exist in system Y_t, and the system is a **cointegrated system**. Y_t is also called **cointegrated process**, and parameter α is called **cointegrating vector**.

For one system, there possibly exists more than one cointegrating relationship. But for a system containing m unit root processes, it has at most $m-1$ linearly independent cointegrating vectors. The number of linearly independent cointegrating vectors of a system, h, is called the **cointegration rank** of the system.

For example, we consider four variables: nominal money supply m_t, price level p_t, real income y_t, and interest rate r_t, satisfying

$$m_t = \alpha_0 + \alpha_1 p_t + \alpha_2 y_t + \alpha_3 r_t + \varepsilon_t \tag{8.31}$$

Write (8.17) in standard form of cointegration as

$$m - \alpha_0 - \alpha_1 p - \alpha_2 y - \alpha_3 r = \varepsilon$$

and we get a cointegration vector

$$\alpha = (1, -\alpha_0, -\alpha_1, -\alpha_2, -\alpha_3)$$

When we consider the entire macroeconomic system there are other equilibrium relations or other cointegrating equations.

Next we turn to analysis of conditions under which unit root processes will be cointegrated.

Two unit root processes may have upward trend. When these two unit root processes are cointegrated their linear combination eliminates their **common trends**. For instance, suppose we consider a system of two variables and that each variable has a linear trend

$$y_{1t} = a_1 + b_1 t + u_{1t}$$

$$y_{2t} = a_2 + b_2 t + u_{2t}$$

where u_{1t} and u_{2t} are white noises. y_{1t} and y_{2t} can be linearly combined by the vector $\alpha = (1, \theta)$ to produce a new variable as

$$z_t = (a_1 + \theta\, a_2) + (b_1 + \theta\, b_2)t + u_{1t} + \theta\, u_{2t}$$

Generally z_t is non-stationary and only when $\theta = -b_1/b_2$, common linear trend is eliminated, thus z_t becomes stationary.

It was mentioned previously that most of the economic time series have trends, cycles, and random error. Cycles of these series can be expressed as stationary time series and there can be equilibrium relations between them if the common trends are eliminated. Thus the simultaneous equation system we presented in Chapter 6 can be interpreted as a system of Vector Auto Regression (VAR). This is taken up next.

8.3.2   Simultaneous (structural) Equation System (SES) and Vector Auto Regression (VAR)

Write a typical simultaneous equation system with time series data in terms of m endogenous variables Y_t and k exogenous variables X_t as follows:

$$BY_t + \Gamma X_t = \varepsilon_t \tag{8.32}$$

here B is an $m \times m$ non-singular matrix, Γ is an $m \times k$ matrix, and ε_t is an $m \times 1$ vector of stationary time series. Here X_t refers to the list of what are called the predetermined variables that includes the lagged endogenous variables and exogenous variables and their lagged values. Lagged values of exogenous variables also enter into economics as explained in Chapter 7. Let us split the vector X_t into two parts, the lagged endogenous variables and the exogenous and lagged exogenous variables. We can then rewrite the system of equations above as:

$$B_0 Y_t + B(L)Y_{t-1} + \Gamma_0 X_t + \Gamma(L)X_{t-1} = \varepsilon_t \tag{8.33}$$

To the system of equations above we add another system of how the exogenous variables are determined over time through an auto regressive process:

$$X_t + C(L)X_{t-1} = \upsilon_t \tag{8.34}$$

Combining equations (8.33) and (8.34) we can write:

$$\begin{pmatrix} B^* & \Gamma^* \\ 0 & C^* \end{pmatrix} \begin{pmatrix} Y_t \\ X_t \end{pmatrix} = \begin{pmatrix} \varepsilon_t \\ \upsilon_t \end{pmatrix} \tag{8.35}$$

where $B^* = B_0 + B(L)L$; $\Gamma^* = \Gamma_0 + \Gamma(L)L$ and $C^* = I + C(L)L$.

We can write the system of equations above as:

$$A(L)Z_t = \omega_t \tag{8.36}$$

where $A(L) = \begin{pmatrix} B^* & \Gamma^* \\ 0 & C^* \end{pmatrix}$; $Z_t = \begin{pmatrix} Y_t \\ X_t \end{pmatrix}$ and $\omega_t = \begin{pmatrix} \varepsilon_t \\ \upsilon_t \end{pmatrix}$ and $V(\omega_t) = \Omega$. We can write without

any loss of generality $A(L) = A_0 A^*(L)$ with $A^*(0) = I_m$.

Equation (8.36) is a **vector autoregression model**. The **autoregressive distributed lag models (ADL)** and the **structural equation systems** of the Cowles Foundation are included in this specification. The structural simultaneous equations models of the Cowles Foundation variety and structural ADL models imposed a priori restrictions on the parameters of $A(L)$ to identify the model, while Sims called them incredible restrictions and imposed restrictions on the variance covariance matrix Ω. We do not know, in general, if the variables in Z_t are stationary or non-stationary. Some of them could be stationary while others are non-stationary. The representation above (8.36) is equivalent to the vector auto regressive process (8.1).

We shall use this equation of VAR in the next section.

8.3.3   Cointegration and error correction representation

One of the most significant contributions to economic time series analysis is the concept of **cointegration and error correction representation** of economic time series. This was introduced by Engel and Granger (1987). It is for this contribution that they shared the Bank of Sweden prize in economic science in honor of Alfred Nobel.

This concept can be derived and interpreted in a simple way from a concept of a triangular representation introduced by Phillips (1991). Assume that a system is composed of two variables y_t and x_t,

$$y_t = \theta x_t + u_t \tag{8.37}$$

$$x_t = x_{t-1} + \upsilon_t \tag{8.38}$$

where u_t and υ_t are white noises, x_t is a unit root process, and y_t is non-stationary. The system can be cointegrated by the cointegration vector $(1, -\theta)$, if u_t is stationary.

Namely

$$y_t - \theta x_t = u_t \quad \text{where } u_t \text{ is stationary} \tag{8.39}$$

Express (8.38) as

$$\Delta x_t = \upsilon_t \tag{8.40}$$

Then (8.37) and (8.38) are the triangular representation of the simplest cointegration system.

Subtract y_{t-1} from both sides of (8.37), and then plug (8.38) into the first equation, we get

$$y_t - y_{t-1} = -y_{t-1} + \theta x_{t-1} + (\theta \upsilon_t + u_t)$$

which can be written in another form:

$$\Delta y_t = -(y_{t-1} - \theta x_{t-1}) + \varepsilon_t \tag{8.41}$$

This is called the error correction representation of a cointegrated system.

It is so-called the error correction representation because as (8.41) indicates, the increment is mainly produced by correcting the error $(y_{t-1} - \theta x_{t-1})$. When the error is positive, the increment is reduced a bit; while the error is negative, the increment increases a bit. Note that since we know $y_{t-1} - \theta x_{t-1} = u_{t-1}$ from (8.39), the error correction representation is $\Delta y_t = -u_{t-1} + \varepsilon_t$, which is a stationary superposition of the white noises.

With this simple example to illustrate the concept we now present the general Engel-Granger representation. First, we introduce the concept of integration of a given order. We say that a series Y_t is integrated of order d if $\Delta^d Y_t$ is stationary, and it is denoted as the $I(d)$ series. If Y_t is stationary it is a $I(0)$ series, and if ΔY_t is stationary it is called the $I(1)$ series. If the second difference of a series is stationary, it is called the $I(2)$ series. If d is a fraction it is called a fractionally integrated series. In the rest of this section we assume that the time series are either $I(0)$ or $I(1)$. We find in general that logarithms of most of the economic time series are either $I(0)$ or $I(1)$. Many economic time series are also found to have approximately Lognormal distribution.

Let us now assume, based on the discussion in the previous section, that the data generating process can be expressed in terms of a vector auto regression (VAR) of an m-dimensional random variable X_t given by:

$$X_t = \sum_{j=1}^{p} P_j X_{t-j} + \varepsilon_t \tag{8.42}$$

As the series are either $I(0)$ or $I(1)$ the following determinantal equation has at most m unit roots.

$$\det\left(I_m - \sum_{j=1}^{p} P_j z^j\right) = 0 \tag{8.43}$$

When the number of unit roots is less than m, the variables are cointegrated. If there are k unit roots then there are $m - k = r$ cointegrating equations.

Engle and Yoo (1991) provide a detailed derivation of the **cointegration error correction** representation using Smith-McMillan factorization. We present basic features of this factorization here. We define P(z) as follows to represent the following polynomial derived from (8.43):

$$\Pi(z) = I_m - \sum_{j=1}^{p} P_j z^j \tag{8.44}$$

(8.43) can be multiplied both sides by any nonsingular matrix and we cannot distinguish observationally any such transformed model from the original without a priori restrictions on the matrices. Smith-McMillan factorization suggests that there exist non-singular square matrices composed of elementary operations on the matrix $\Pi(L)$ of dimension m, U(L) and V(L) such that

$$U(L)\Pi(1)V(L) = M(L) = \begin{bmatrix} (1-L)I_k & 0 \\ o & I_r \end{bmatrix} \tag{8.45}$$

This factorization stacks together all those variables that are nonstationary at the top. Here r is the number of cointegrating equations and $k + r = m$.

By subtracting X_{t-1} from (8.42) on the left hand side and rearranging terms we get:

$$\Delta X_t = \Pi X_{t-1} + \sum_{i=1}^{p-1} \Gamma_i \Delta X_{t-i} + \varepsilon_t \tag{8.46}$$

where $\Pi = -\Pi(1) = (I_m - P_1 - \ldots P_p)$ and $\Gamma_i = -\sum_{j=i+1}^{p} \Phi_j$ for $j = 1, 2, \ldots p-1$.

In the equation above the terms appearing in difference form and the error are stationary series. Hence the first term involving lagged values in levels must be a set of cointegrating equations. From equation (8.45) it is clear that the rank of $M(L) = $ rank of $\Pi(1) = r$. Thus there exist r independent columns of it that can be written as a $M \times r$ matrix which we label as α'. The matrix $\Pi(1)$ can be written as $\delta\alpha'$.

We can therefore rewrite equation (8.46) above as:

$$\Delta X_t = -\delta\alpha' X_{t-1} + \sum_{i=1}^{p-1} \Gamma_i \Delta X_{t-i} + \varepsilon_t \tag{8.47}$$

and

$$\Delta X_t = -\delta w_{t-1} + \sum_{i=1}^{p-1} \Gamma_i \Delta X_{t-i} + \varepsilon_t \tag{8.48}$$

where $\alpha' X_t = w_t$ constitute the r cointegrating equations, w_t being a stationary series.

Equation (8.48) is the **Vector Error Correction** representation of time series, consisting of nonstationary time series with unit roots. As this equation has both the cointegrating equations and the first differences of nonstationary variables it captures both the long run equilibrium relations between economic variables and the short run fluctuations around those long run equilibrium relations. It can be seen that this is in fact a VAR model in the differences of the unit root processes, which are stationary. Hence one can write the impulse response equations using Wold decomposition formula. The responses of ΔX_t must be integrated to get the responses of the original nonstationary series. The above model can be modified to allow for deterministic terms as we did in deriving the impulse-response functions in the previous section.

Example 8.3   Error Correction Model (ECM) with two time series (India and China stock prices)   Suppose there are cointegrated relationship between two time series $Y(t)$ and $Z(t)$, i.e., there is an **Error Correction Model (ECM)** with two time series:

$$\Delta y_t = X(t)'\beta + a\Delta z_t + c(y_{t-1} - \theta z_{t-1}) + \varepsilon_t$$

where $X(t)$ are exogenous variables. We will compute estimates of coefficients β, a, c, θ in the model by LSE.

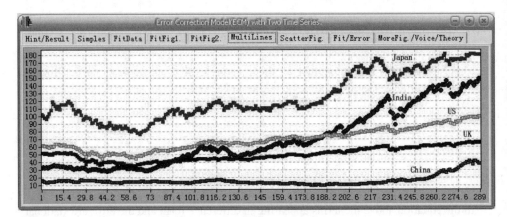

Figure 8.19   The stock prices of India and China with US, UK and Japan (2002–2007).

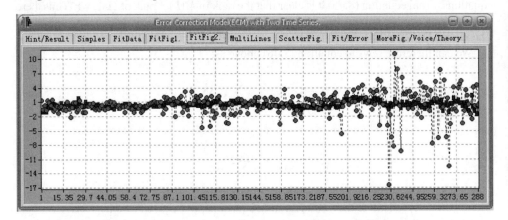

Figure 8.20   The difference of stock prices of India Δy_t and its fitting series.

We should pre process the original data as follows: the first column is $Y(t)$, the second column is $Z(t)$, and others are $X(t)$. Notice that the column number of exogenous variables should equal to the column number of input data minus 2.

In this example, $Y(t)$ is the stock price of India from 2002 to 2007, $Z(t)$ is the stock price of China from the same period, and $X(t)$ are the stock prices of US, UK, and Japan in that order. The data can be seen in DASC and as Figures 8.19 and 8.20, but we should note that the data of each series have been divided by 100 to avoid digital overflow in calculation. The computing results are as follows.

Total number of sample observations is 288, the number of independent variables is 6.

Regression equation: Y = 0.022 X1 −0.139 X2 + 0.065 X3 + 0.561 X4 −0.029 X5 −0.018 X6.

   That is $\Delta y_t = 0.022\,X1 - 0.139\,X2 + 0.065\,X3 + 0.561\,\Delta z_t - 0.029\,y_{t-1} - 0.018\,z_{t-1}$.

Sum of squares of residuals is 1914.6, sum of squares of regression is 101.424.

Estimate of error variance is 6.78937, standard deviation is 2.60564.

Significance level is 0.05; F statistic is 2.48976, the critical value of F(6,282) is 2.4533.

The coefficient of total correlation R^2 is 0.0503 (R is 0.2243).

The critical value of t is 1.9684, the t values of regression coefficients are:

0.452702,	1.935467,	2.990500,	2.262580,	2.398340,	0.589656.

The standard errors of regression coefficients are:

0.048472,	0.071769,	0.021829,	0.247752,	0.012232,	0.029804.

Regression coefficients of exogenous variables β are: 0.021943, −0.138907, 0.065280. Coefficients of other variables: $a = 0.560559$, $c = -0.029337$, $\theta = -0.599034$.

The computation can be performed by clicking DASC → Time Series Analysis → Nonstationary time series → Error Correction Model (ECM) with Two Time Series. Besides, DASC also offer the menu Error Correction Model (ECM) with Many Time Series.

8.3.4   Estimation of parameters of cointegration process

There are different methods of parameter estimation and hypothesis testing for cointegration process. We only discuss the least squares estimation of parameters here. The method of maximum likelihood estimation can be found in the Electronic References for Chapter 8, Appendix.

Suppose that X_t is a m-dimensional random vector which has **cointegration relationship** between all of its components, and α is the **cointegration vector**, then $\alpha' X_t = \varepsilon_t$, where ε_t is a stationary process of a single variable and $E(\varepsilon_t^2) < +\infty$. When $T \to \infty$,

$$T^{-1}\sum_{t=1}^{T}(\alpha' X_t)^2 = T^{-1}\sum_{t=1}^{T}\varepsilon_t^2 \xrightarrow{P} E(\varepsilon_t^2) < +\infty \tag{8.49}$$

But when α is not a cointegration vector, $\alpha' Y_t$ is a non-stationary process, (8.49) fails because $T^{-1}\sum_{t=1}^{T}(\alpha' X_t)^2$ will approach infinity. Therefore we conclude that the cointegration vector α will minimize $T^{-1}\sum_{t=1}^{T}(\alpha' X_t)^2$. Let $\hat{\alpha}$ be the estimator of α, then

$$T^{-1}\sum_{t=1}^{T}(\hat{\alpha} Y_t)^2 = \min_{\alpha} T^{-1}\sum_{t=1}^{T}(\alpha' Y_t)^2 \tag{8.50}$$

and $\hat{\alpha}$ is called the least squares estimator of cointegration vector, and it is a consistent estimator.

The **cointegration rank** of a m-dimensional system is no more than $m - 1$, thus we can assume that cointegration vector α is in the form of

$$\alpha' = (1, -\gamma_2, \ldots, -\gamma_n)$$

Remove T^{-1} from objective function (8.26) and we obtain

$$\sum_{t=1}^{T}(\alpha' Y_t)^2 = \sum_{t=1}^{T}(y_{1t} - \gamma_2 y_{2t} - \cdots - \gamma_n y_{nt})^2$$

which can be regarded as the squared error of regression of y_{1t} on $y_{it}(i = 2, \ldots, n)$. Seeking the minimum is a problem of multivariate linear regression. Regard y_{1t} as a dependent variable and $y_{it}(i = 2, \ldots, n)$ as an independent variable, then least squares solution $\hat{\alpha}$ can be obtained.

If we set other components of the cointegrating vector to be 1 in α, we will get a different least squares solution $\hat{\alpha}$ for finite sample size. There are advantages and disadvantages associated with this method. It is useful to estimate the cointegration vectors when there exist more than one cointegration relationships in the system. If $m - 1$ cointegration vectors are found in this way and are linearly independent, then that is what we seek to get a proper explanation of the economic system. It is disadvantageous, however, as we cannot determine which $\hat{\alpha}$ is a consistent estimator. Hence this least squares estimation procedure cannot provide us consistent estimators of the cointegrating vectors. The Maximum Likelihood method of estimation discussed in the Electronic References to Chapter 8, Appendix provides us the consistent estimators of the cointegrating vectors.

8.3.5   Test of hypotheses on the number of cointegrating equations

We need to test whether a set of nonstationary time series have among them a cointegrating equation or not. We also need to test how many cointegrating equations are there between them. We also need to know if after determining the number of cointegrating equations whether the errors of all of them are stationary or not. The tests of hypotheses rely on the test statistics and their distributions. Mainly there are two methods of estimation – least square method and maximum likelihood method. Corresponding to each one of these estimation methods there is a test statistic, and hence there are different tests of these statistical hypotheses. We only discuss the method of testing based on the least squares estimation of parameter. The method of testing based on the maximum likelihood estimation can be found in the Electronic References for Chapter 8, Appendix.

Let a system be $Y_t = (y_{1t}, y_{2t}, \ldots, y_{nt})'$. First we designate a variable, say y_{1t}, as dependent variable vector, and others as independent variables. The multivariate linear regression of y_{1t} and other variables aims to minimize

$$\sum_{t=1}^{T} (y_{1t} - \gamma_2 y_{2t} - \cdots - \gamma_n y_{nt})^2$$

Then the designated cointegration vector α is in form of $\alpha = (1, -\gamma_2, \ldots, -\gamma_n)$. When getting $\hat{\alpha}$, we can compute the residual

$$\hat{u}_t = y_{1t} - \hat{\gamma}_2 y_{2t} - \cdots - \hat{\gamma}_n y_{nt}$$

If system Y_t is cointegrated, then the residual vector $\hat{u}_t$ should be stationary. Otherwise, it has either non-constant trend or unit root process. So we first separate the trend from $\hat{u}_t$, namely,

$$\hat{u}_t = a + bt + \varepsilon_t$$

and carry out hypothesis test for coefficient b, the null hypothesis is H_0: $b = 0$. If H_0 is true, we eliminate the possibility of a deterministic trend. We have the test for the null hypothesis of a unit root or a stochastic trend. Let

$$\hat{u}_t = \rho \hat{u}_{t-1} + \varepsilon_t$$

where ε_t are normal white noise. We know according to (8.12) that

$$\hat{\rho} = \sum_{t=1}^{T} \hat{u}_{t-1}\hat{u}_t \Big/ \sum_{t=1}^{T} \hat{u}_{t-1}^2 \tag{8.51}$$

Substitute the sample values in (8.51) we obtain the statistic $\hat{\rho}_0$. The null hypothesis of testing for unit root is H_0: $\rho = 1$. When $\rho = 1$, generate T normal pseudo random numbers ε_t from initial value $u_0 = 1$ to produce u_t series. Thus we get ρ_i, one value of ρ, according to (8.51). Repeating the procedure of $\varepsilon_t \rightarrow u_t \rightarrow \rho_i$ by changing the seeds of pseudo random numbers, one can obtain sufficiently many values ρ_i of ρ, $i = 1,2,\ldots, N$, and then the distribution of ρ. We estimate the kernel density function of $\hat{\rho}$ by employing the technique presented earlier in this cahapter. Next based on the significance levels and alternative hypothesis, we can compute the critical values of H_0: $\rho = 1$ and decide whether we accept the hypothesis. If we reject the hypothesis then the residuals are stationary and we have a cointegrating equation.

Example 8.4   Cointegration relationships of stock prices of BRIC countries with some developed countries[5]   DASC offers some data sets of stock prices of BRIC countries with other developed countries: US, UK and Japan respectively. Figure 8.21 shows the stock prices of Brazil with US, UK and Japan from 2002 to 2007. We try to find cointegration relationships of stock prices among them.

We make regressions by letting a series as dependent variable and others as independent variables in turn. The fitting effect of the last regression is shown as Figure 8.22. In this regression, the regression equation is Y = 0.140 X1 −0.411 X2 + 2.363 X3 (Y refers to stock price of Brazil while the X variables refer to the stock prices of US, UK, and Japan, respectively), the sum of squares of residuals is 1.51157e + 08, the sum of squares of regression is 2.5697e + 09, the estimate of variance of error is 528521, the standard deviation is 726.994, and the coefficient of total correlation $R^2 = 0.9444$.

The error series of the above fit of Brazil's stock price data with its trend is shown as in Figure 8.23. The linear fitting equation of the error series is $Y = -21.9103 + 0.2185\,X_1$. For the significance test of the coefficient, the critical value $t(287) = 1.9683$, and t values of regression coefficients are 0.256061, 0.427173, so we accept null hypothesis, i.e. regression coefficients are 0, and there is no linear trend in the last regression, we need to test unit root process.

For the test of unit root process, the Dickey-Fuller statistic of sample is −5.194825, and the fractile of test is −0.997612. The density function curve of D-F statistic (the size of the sample is 287) is shown as Figure 8.24. Because −5.194825 < −0.997612, we reject null hypothesis, and the error series is not unit root process. Therefore we think that there is a co-integrated relationship, and its vector is (−0.139585, 0.411441, −2.363142, 1.000000).

We can print all cointegrated vectors calculated:

−0.051440,	1.000000,	−1.264297,	0.055062
0.042850,	−0.603769,	1.000000,	−0.151113
−0.139585,	0.411441,	−2.363142,	1.000000

From these calculations we know that the co-integrated rank of all series does not exceed 3. But we should check if there is some linear correlation among them. We can calculate

[5] This example is based on a term paper submitted for a course at the Indian Institute of Management, Bangalore in 2007 by Akash Satish Agrawal, Hrishikesh Patil, Udayan Sarkar, and Vikram Balan.

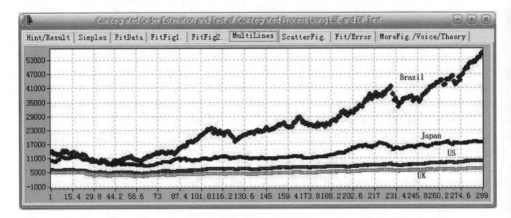

Figure 8.21   The stock prices of Brazil with US, UK and Japan (2002–2007).

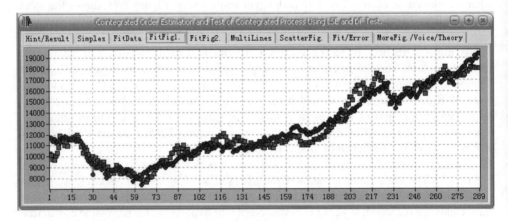

Figure 8.22   The series of Brazil stock prices with its fitting of regression.

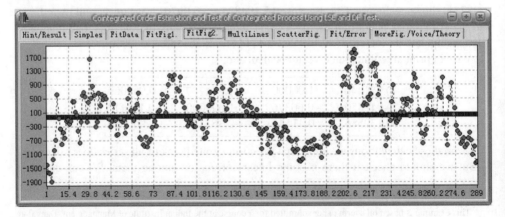

Figure 8.23   The regression errors of Brazil stock prices with its trend line.

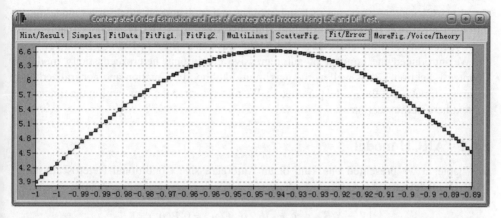

Figure 8.24   The density curve of D-F test for the regression errors of Brazil stock prices.

the rank of above matrix. Print the singular value matrix Σ in A = UΣV' by singular value decomposed of above matrix:

3.165281,	0.000000,	0.000000,	0.000000
0.000000,	0.864579,	0.000000,	0.000000
0.000000,	0.000000,	0.005840,	0.000000

We know the rank of this singular matrix is 3, so the rank of three cointegrated vectors is 3, and the cointegrated rank of all series is 3. So the cointegrated vectors calculated are all cointegrated vectors indeed. But we should be aware that the computation is only an approximation. If we assume that the tolerance value of singular value is 0.01, since 0.005840 < 0.01, so the rank of this singular matrix is 2, and the cointegrated rank of all series is 2 too.

Using our method and the data set in DASC, we can find all three cointegration relationships of stock prices among BRIC countries and other developed countries in periods 1993–1997, 1998–2001, and 2002–2007. Then we can examine how the advanced industrialized countries' stock price fluctuations affect the stock prices of the BRIC countries. The data can be loaded by menu 'Data→Load other example data' from folder \\She\\ Wileydata\\Wiley 8(Cointegration). The computation can be performed by clicking DASC→ Time Series Analysis→Nonstationary time series→Cointegrated Order Estimation and Test of Cointegrated Process Using LSE and DF Test.

8.4   Autoregression conditional heteroscedasticity in time series

It was in France in 1900 that the random walk model for stock price modeling was first proposed by Louis Bachelier, a doctoral student of the famous French mathematician Henry Poincare. He called it a model of speculation. For nearly three quarters of a century that model of random walk remained the main model for stock prices. It was observed in the 1960s that financial time series such as the stock prices exhibit volatility clustering, where large changes are followed by large changes and small changes are followed by small changes.

Engel (1982) was the first one to bring about a major change in stock price modeling by introducing **Autoregressive Conditional Heteroscedasticity (ARCH)** model to capture this phenomenon of volatility clustering. This model was generalized in 1996 by Bolerslev.

We introduced the concept of autoregressive conditional heteroscedasticity model in Chapter 3, Section 3.3, as well as the maximum likelihood estimation and generalized least squares estimation of the model parameters. We now return to the topic within the time series context here in this section.

8.4.1   ARCH model

In Chapter 3 we presented one kind of an Autoregressive Conditional Heteroscedasticity (ARCH) model as:

$$\begin{cases} Y_i = X_i'\beta + \varepsilon_i, \varepsilon_i = \sqrt{h_i} \cdot \upsilon_i, E(\upsilon_i) = 0, E(\upsilon_i^2) = 1 \\ h_i = \alpha_0 + \alpha_1 \varepsilon_{i-1}^2 + \alpha_2 \varepsilon_{i-2}^2 + \cdots + \alpha_p \varepsilon_{i-p}^2 \end{cases}$$

And now we adapt it to another form. Note that the independent variables of the model can be either explanatory variables or the lagged values of dependent variable. We use an AR(p) process as

$$y_t = \sum_{i=1}^{p} \rho_i \ y_{t-i} + \varepsilon_t$$

$$\varepsilon_t = \sqrt{h_t} \cdot \upsilon_t$$

$$E(\upsilon_t) = 0, E(\upsilon_t^2) = 1$$

$$h_t = \alpha_0 + \alpha_1 \varepsilon_{t-1}^2 + \alpha_2 \varepsilon_{t-2}^2 + \cdots + \alpha_m \varepsilon_{t-m}^2 \tag{8.52}$$

h_i gives an mth order lag model, therefore it is called ARCH(m) model. (8.52) also implies

$$E(\varepsilon_t^2 \mid \varepsilon_{t-1}, \ldots, \varepsilon_{t-m}) = \alpha_0 + \alpha_1 \varepsilon_{t-1}^2 + \alpha_2 \varepsilon_{t-2}^2 + \cdots + \alpha_m \varepsilon_{t-m}^2$$

which shows the conditional heteroscedasticity of the residual. In Chapter 3, Section 3.3.2, the maximum likelihood estimation of model parameters was presented.

When υ_t are not normally distributed, we choose t distribution because the probability density curve of t distribution is similar to that of Normal distribution, whereas different in the relatively thick tail. Its limiting distribution is standard normal distribution as well. Assume that the conditional distribution of ε_t is t distribution with k degrees of freedom with a scale parameter, M_t. Its density function is

$$f(x) = \frac{\Gamma[(k+1)/2]}{\sqrt{\pi k} \cdot \Gamma(k/2)} M_t^{-\frac{1}{2}} \left(1 + \frac{x^2}{M_t k} \right)^{-\frac{k+1}{2}} \tag{8.53}$$

When $k > 2$, the expectation of t distribution is zero, and the variance is $M_t k/(k - 2)$. Let scale parameter M_t be

$$M_t = h_t \ (k-2)/k$$

where h_t is defined as (8.52) to make ε_t have conditional variance h_t with ARCH effect. The density function (8.53) then can be written as

$$f(x) = \frac{\Gamma[(k+1)/2]}{\sqrt{\pi} \cdot \Gamma(k/2)} (k-2)^{-1/2} h_t^{-1/2} \left(1 + \frac{x^2}{h_t(k-2)}\right)^{-\frac{k+1}{2}}$$

Let the observed sample data be

$$Y_t = (y_t, y_{t-1}, \ldots, y_1, y_0, \ldots, y_{-p+1})'$$

and parameter set to be estimated be

$$\theta = (\rho_i, \alpha_j, k), i = 1, 2, \ldots, p, j = 1, 2, \ldots, m$$

Then conditional variance h_t can be expressed as the function of sample data and parameter set:

$$h_i = \alpha_0 + \alpha_1 \left(y_{t-1} - \sum_{i=1}^{p} \rho_i y_{t-1-i}\right)^2 + \cdots + \alpha_m \left(y_{t-m} - \sum_{i=1}^{p} \rho_i y_{t-m-i}\right)^2$$

The log-likelihood function with respect to the sample $y_1, y_2, \ldots, y_T$ is

$$L(\theta) = \sum_{t=1}^{T} \ln f(y_t \mid \tilde{Y}_t; \theta) = T \ln \left(\frac{\Gamma\left(\frac{k+1}{2}\right)}{\sqrt{\pi(k-2)} \, \Gamma\left(\frac{k}{2}\right)}\right) - \frac{1}{2} \sum_{t=1}^{T} \ln(h_t)$$

$$- \frac{k+1}{2} \sum_{t=1}^{T} \ln \left(1 + \frac{1}{h_t(k-2)} \left(y_t - \sum_{i=1}^{p} \rho_i y_{t-i}\right)^2\right)$$

We wish to maximize it to generate the estimator of θ, namely

$$L(\hat{\theta}) = \max_{\theta} L(\theta)$$

This maximum likelihood estimator can be computed using the improved Powell algorithm of Sargent.

As to the error distribution of the ARCH(m) model, researchers gave several forms such as Normal-Poisson mixed distribution (Jorion, 1988), power exponential distribution (Baillie, Bollerslev, 1989), Normal-logarithmic and Normal mixed distributions (Hsieh, 1989), generalized exponential distribution (Nelson, 1991) and so on, and the solutions are similar to the foregoing methods with suitable modifications. More detailed materials can be seen in the references cited above.

Example 8.5   Fitting data of ARCH model with forecast   In this example, we first generate random numbers of ARCH(1) model. The model is $y_t = u + \varepsilon_t$, $\varepsilon_t = \sqrt{h_t} \cdot \upsilon_t$, $\upsilon_t \sim N(0, 1)$, $h_t = \alpha_0 + \alpha_1 \varepsilon_{t-1}^2$, where α_0, α_1, u and ε_0 are constants to be specified by the user. The random numbers υ_t needs to be generated by a given seed (any odd number). After these preparations, the series of an ARCH(1) with 300 observations (dots) are generated as in Figure 8.25.

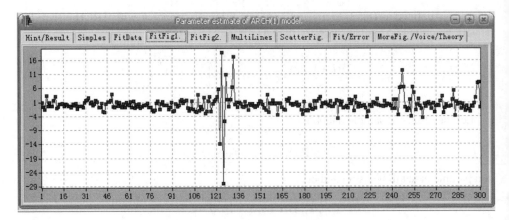

Figure 8.25 The series of an ARCH(1) with 300 dots.

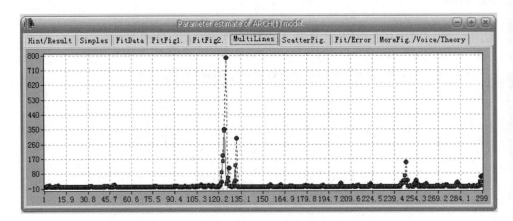

Figure 8.26 ε_t^2 in ARCH(1) model and their fitting data.

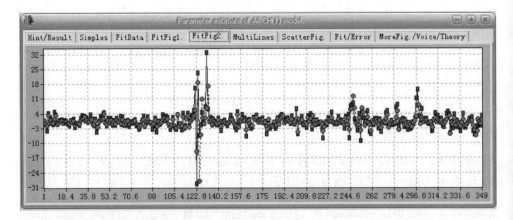

Figure 8.27 The fitting data for ARCH(1) series and 49 forecasting dots.

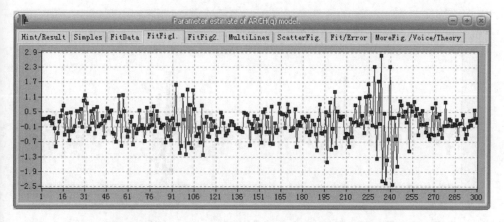

Figure 8.28   The series of an ARCH(5) with 300 dots.

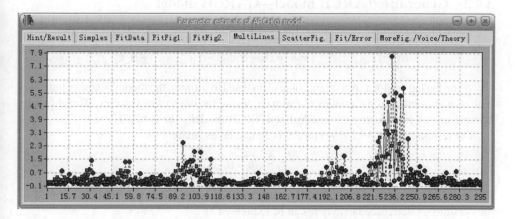

Figure 8.29 ε_t^2 in ARCH(5) model and their fitting data.

To get the parameters estimations of ARCH model, we should first get the data of ε_t from $y_t = u + \varepsilon_t$ by common linear regression, and we estimate mean u. Then we can estimate α_0, α_1 by $\varepsilon_t^2 = \alpha_0 + \alpha_1 \varepsilon_{t-1}^2$. ε_t^2 in ARCH(1) model and their fitting data are as in Figure 8.26.

To fit and forecast the ARCH model, we must know the data of v_t. We can generate a series of random number v_t and calculate the square sum of errors by $\sum (y_t - \sqrt{\alpha_0 + \alpha_1 \varepsilon_{t-1}^2} \cdot v_t)^2$. Changing the seed of v_t, we can get different sum of squares of errors. We take the seed of whom the sum of squares of errors is the minimum. The fitting data for the ARCH(1) series and 49 forecasting dots are as Figure 8.27.

Similarly we can generate random numbers of the ARCH(5) model, get their parameters estimations, and make fitting and forecasting, as in Figure 8.28, Figure 8.29 and Figure 8.30.

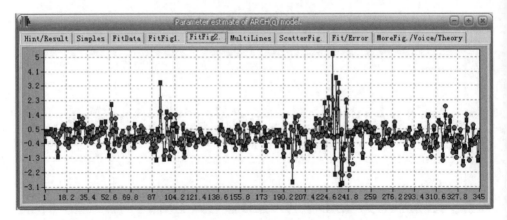

Figure 8.30   The fitting data for ARCH(5) series and 45 forecasting dots.

8.4.2   Generalized ARCH model—GARCH model

We stated in the previous section that the residual ε_t of the ARCH(m) model satisfies

$$E(\varepsilon_t^2 \mid \varepsilon_{t-1}, \ldots, \varepsilon_{t-m}) = h_t = \alpha_0 + \alpha_1 \varepsilon_{t-1}^2 + \alpha_2 \varepsilon_{t-2}^2 + \cdots + \alpha_m \varepsilon_{t-m}^2$$

When the lag length m is too large, and even tends to infinity, the model becomes unwieldy with a large number of parameters to estimate, losing the degrees of freedom. This difficulty is overcome by introducing the **generalized** ARCH **model** – the GARCH model.

The residual of the ARCH(m) model is characterized mainly by

$$\varepsilon_t = \sqrt{h_t} \cdot \upsilon_t$$

where $\{\upsilon_t\}$ are i.i.d., with mean 0 and variance 1. When the order of ARCH model $m \to \infty$, the conditional heteroscedasticity h_t can be expressed as

$$h_t = \alpha_0 + \alpha_1 \varepsilon_{i-1}^2 + \alpha_2 \varepsilon_{i-2}^2 + \cdots = \alpha_0 + H(L)\varepsilon_t^2 \tag{8.54}$$

where $H(L)$ is infinite lag polynomial,

$$H(L) = \sum_{j=1}^{\infty} H_j L^j$$

A natural thought is to express it as the quotient of two finite lag polynomials

$$H(L) = \frac{\alpha(L)}{1 - \delta(L)} = \frac{\alpha_1 L + \alpha_2 L^2 + \cdots + \alpha_m L^m}{1 - \delta_1 L - \delta_2 L^2 - \cdots - \delta_r L^r} \tag{8.55}$$

Let us assume that the roots of characteristic equation $1 - \delta z = 0$ of lag polynomial $1 - \delta(L)$ are outside the unit circle. Substitute (8.55) in (8.54) and multiply by $1 - \delta(L)$ on both sides, to obtain:

$$(1 - \delta(L))h_t = (1 - \delta(1))\alpha_0 + \alpha(L)\varepsilon_t^2$$

Hence h_t can be expressed as

$$h_t = k_0 + \delta_1 h_{t-1} + \delta_2 h_{t-2} + \cdots + \delta_r h_{t-r} + \alpha_1 \varepsilon_{t-1}^2 + \alpha_2 \varepsilon_{t-2}^2 + \cdots + \alpha_m \varepsilon_{t-m}^2$$

where constant k_0 is

$$k_0 = (1 - \delta_1 - \delta_2 - \cdots - \delta_r)\alpha_0$$

In this way we successfully expressed infinite lag h_t as two parts of finite lag.

When h_t in (8.52) is substituted by h_t in (8.55), the model is called the generalized ARCH model, or GARCH model for short, denoted as GARCH(r, m). When $r = 0$, GARCH(r, m) becomes ordinary ARCH(m); when $m = r = 0$, ε_t is a white noise process.

The coefficients H_j and δ_i, α_i follow the recursion $H_i = \alpha_i + \sum_{j=1}^{n} \delta_j H_{i-j}$, for $i = 1, \ldots, m$; when $i = m + 1, m + 2, \ldots, H_i = \sum_{j=1}^{n} \delta_j H_{i-j}$, where $n = \min\{r, i - 1\}$.

GARCH(r, m) process is a stationary process if and only if

$$\alpha(1) + \delta(1) < 1$$

where $\alpha(1) = \sum_{i=1}^{m} \alpha_i$, $\delta(1) = \sum_{i=1}^{r} \delta_i$. Under this condition,

$$E(\varepsilon_t) = 0, D(\varepsilon_t) = k_0(1 - \alpha(1) - \delta(1))^{-1} \text{ and } Cov(\varepsilon_t, \varepsilon_s) = 0 \; (t \neq s)$$

The simplest GARCH process is GARCH(1, 1). In (8.55), let $m = 1, r = 1$. Then

$$h_t = k_0 + \delta_1 h_{t-1} + \alpha_1 \varepsilon_{t-1}^2$$

where $k_0 > 0$, $\delta_1 \geq 0$, $\alpha_1 \geq 0$. GARCH(1, 1) is stationary if and only if $\delta_1 + \alpha_1 < 1$.
GARCH(1, 1) has $2m$th moment if and only if

$$\mu(\delta_1, \alpha_1, m) = \sum_{j=0}^{m} \binom{m}{j} d_j \delta_1^{m-j} \alpha_1^j < 1$$

where m is a positive integer, $d_0 = 1$, $d_j = \prod_{i=1}^{j} (2i - 1)$, for $j = 1, 2, \ldots$. The $2m$th moment of ε_t satisfies

$$E(\varepsilon_t^{2m}) = \frac{d_m}{1 - \mu(\delta_1, \alpha_1, m)} \left[\sum_{n=0}^{m} d_n^{-1} E(\varepsilon_t^{2n}) k_0^{m-n} \binom{m}{m-n} \mu(\delta_1, \alpha_1, n) \right]$$

Next we come to the problems of parameter estimation of the GARCH model. We continue to express the main part of the model in autoregressive form. Thus, the independent variables are just the lagged values of the dependent variable. Let

$$y_t = \sum_{i=1}^{p} \rho_i y_{t-i} + \varepsilon_t$$

$$\varepsilon_i = \sqrt{h_i} \cdot \upsilon_i$$

$$v_t \sim N(0,1)$$

$$h_t = k_0 + \sum_{i=1}^{r} \delta_i h_{t-i} + \sum_{j=1}^{m} \alpha_j \varepsilon_{t-j} \tag{8.56}$$

Since we consider maximum likelihood estimation for parameters, the error is assumed to be normally distributed. Let the observation set of model be

$$\tilde{Y}_t = (y_t, y_{t-1}, \ldots, y_1, y_0, \ldots, y_{-p+1})'$$

and the parameter set of model be

$$\tilde{\delta} = (k_0, \alpha_1, \ldots, \alpha_m, \delta_1, \ldots, \delta_r)', \rho = (\rho_1, \ldots, \rho_p)'$$

and

$$\theta = (\rho, \tilde{\delta}')'$$

Then h_t can be expressed as the function of sample and parameter,

$$h_t = k_0 + \sum_{i=1}^{r} \delta_i h_{t-i} + \sum_{i=1}^{m} \alpha_i (y_{t-i} - \sum_{j=1}^{p} \rho_j y_{t-m-j})^2$$

The log-likelihood function of the GARCH model can be expressed as

$$L(\theta \mid \tilde{Y}_t) = -\frac{T}{2} \ln(2\pi) - \frac{1}{2} \sum_{t=1}^{T} \ln(h_t) - \frac{1}{2} \sum_{t=1}^{T} \varepsilon_t^2 h_t^{-1}$$

Maximize $L(\theta \mid \tilde{Y}_t)$ and we obtain the estimator of θ. The maximum likelihood estimators can be computed by using the framework above and employing the improved Powell algorithm of Sargent.

Example 8.6   Fitting data of GARCH model with forecast   In this example, we first generate the random numbers of GARCH(r, m) model. The model is $y_t = u + \varepsilon_t$, $\varepsilon_t = \sqrt{h_t} \cdot v_t$, $v_t \sim N(0, 1)$, $h_t = k_0 + \sum_{i=1}^{r} \delta_i h_{t-i} + \sum_{j=1}^{m} \alpha_j \varepsilon_{t-j}$, where $k_0, \delta_1, \ldots, \delta_r, \alpha_1, \ldots, \alpha_m, u$ and $\varepsilon_0, \ldots, \varepsilon_m$ are constants to be specified by user. The random numbers v_t needs to be generated by a given seed (any odd number). After these preparation, the series of an GARCH(5, 5) with 300 dots are generated as Figure 8.31.

To get the parameters estimations of GARCH model, we first get the data of ε_t from $y_t = u + \varepsilon_t$ by common linear regression, and estimate the mean u. Then we can estimate $k_0, \delta_1, \ldots, \delta_r$, $\alpha_1, \ldots, \alpha_m$ by $\varepsilon_t^2 = k_0 + \sum_{i=1}^{r} \delta_i h_{t-i} + \sum_{j=1}^{m} \alpha_j \varepsilon_{t-j}$. ε_t^2 in GARCH(5,5) model and their fitting data are as Figure 8.32.

To fit and forecast GARCH model, we must know the data of v_t. We can generate a series of random number v_t and calculate the square sum of errors by

$$\sum (y_t - \sqrt{k_0 + \sum_{i=1}^{r} \delta_i h_{t-i} + \sum_{j=1}^{m} \alpha_j \varepsilon_{t-j}} \cdot v_t)^2.$$ Changing the seed of v_t, we can get different square

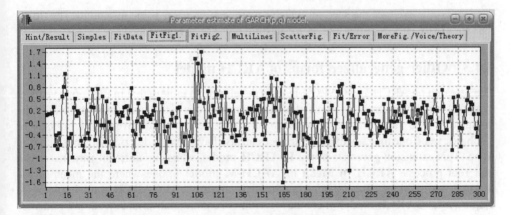

Figure 8.31   The series of an GARCH(5, 5) with 300 dots.

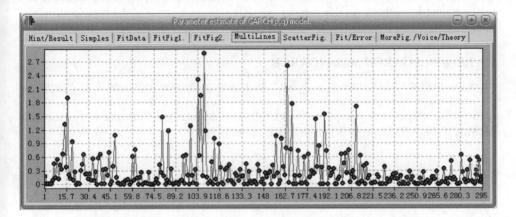

Figure 8.32 ε_t^2 in GARCH(5, 5) model and their fitting data.

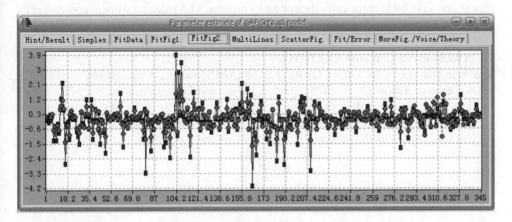

Figure 8.33   The fitting data for GARCH(5, 5) series and 45 forecasting dots.

sums of errors. We take the seed for which square sum of errors is the minimum. The fitting data for GARCH(5, 5) series and 45 forecasting dots are as Figure 8.33.

8.4.3   Other generalized forms of ARCH model

The research on ARCH and GARCH models developed so rapidly that in just a few years, it extended to many other forms, most of which are extensions to different forms of conditional variance h_t. The same way that the mean of a time series could have a deterministic or stochastic trend one may say that the variance can also have either a deterministic or stochastic trend. This extension gave rise to the **IGARCH model**, whose conditional variance h_t is a unit root process. **ARCH in Mean or ARCH-M model** is one where the mean of the dependent variable y_t also contains conditional variance h_t. **EGARCH model** stands for **Exponential GARCH model** where the logarithm of conditional variance h_t, or $\ln h_t$, satisfies the condition of GARCH model. Finally we have multi-variate extensions where vectors of time series are such that each component vector has a GARCH specification. Other extensions include improvements in the estimation of these models by applying non-parametric and semi-parametric methods. In this section, we only introduce some of the basic concepts of these models.

1.   Integrated GARCH model IGARCH

Refer to equation (8.34), since $h_t = \sum_{i=1}^{r} \delta_i h_{t-i}$ is in auto-regression form, and $h_t = \sum_{i=1}^{m} \alpha_i \varepsilon_{t-i}$ is in moving-average form, it implies that u_t^2 follows auto-regression moving average process ARMA. If this ARMA process has unit roots, namely,

$$\sum_{i=1}^{r} \delta_i + \sum_{i=1}^{m} \alpha_i = 1$$

then such a GARCH model is called the **Integrated GARCH model**, **IGARCH** model for short.

Unconditional variance of u_t in an IGARCH model is infinite, therefore the variances of u_t and u_t^2 are not stationary. However, if the unconditional density of u_t is identical for all t, then u_t may also come from a strictly stationary process. This research work is undertaken by Engle and Bolleslev (1986), and Nelson (1990).

2.   ARCH-in-Mean model ARCH-M

The main features of the ARCH, GARCH and IGARCH models discussed earlier are all the same. The expectation $E(y_t) = X_t'\beta$, unrelated to the conditional variance. But in the theory of finance one postulates that the higher the risk of an asset the higher will be its expected yield or returns. The expected yield or expected return is measured by the mean, $E(y_t)$, and the risk is measured by the variance, h_t. Therefore y_t can be expressed as:

$$y_t = X_t'\beta + \lambda h_t + \varepsilon_t$$

where λ is a constant, and the assumptions about ε_t and h_t are:

$$\varepsilon_t = \sqrt{h_i} \cdot \upsilon_t, \upsilon_t \sim N(0, 1)$$

$$h_t = k_0 + \sum_{i=1}^{r} \delta_i h_{t-i} + \sum_{i=1}^{m} \alpha_i \varepsilon_{t-i}$$

h_t can be expressed in the form of ARCH(m) or GARCH(r, m). These three formulae incorporate an ARCH-M model. In practical applications, one may also find it useful to explore alternate specifications of GARCH-M models where y_t can be expressed as $y_t = X_t'\beta + \lambda \sqrt{h_t} + \varepsilon_t$, or $y_t = X_t'\beta + \lambda \ln h_t + \varepsilon_t$.

Since the conditional variance appears in both h_t and ε_t simultaneously, it is relatively complicated to estimate the parameters of an **ARCH-M** model. We just illustrate some main features of **ARCH-M** from a simple example. Let

$$y_t = \lambda h_t + \varepsilon_t$$

where the conditional distribution of ε_t is normal, namely,

$$\varepsilon_t \big| \tilde{Y}_{t-1} \sim N(0, h_t)$$

and

$$h_t = \alpha_0 + \alpha_1 \varepsilon_{t-1}^2 \qquad (8.57)$$

then y_t can be written as

$$y_t = \lambda \alpha_0 + \lambda \alpha_1 \varepsilon_{t-1}^2 + \varepsilon_t$$

Evaluate the expectation of the both sides of (8.34), and we obtain

$$E(\varepsilon_{t-1}^2) = \frac{\alpha_0}{1 - \alpha_1}$$

Thereby the unconditional expectation of y_t is

$$E(y_t) = \lambda \alpha_0 \left(1 + \frac{\alpha_0}{1 - \alpha_1} \right) \qquad (8.58)$$

The unconditional variance of y_t is

$$D(y_t) = \frac{\alpha_0}{1 - \alpha_1} + \frac{(\lambda \alpha_1)^2 \cdot 2\alpha_0^2}{(1 - \alpha_1)^2 (1 - 3\alpha_1^2)} \qquad (8.59)$$

(8.35) and (8.36) make sense only when parameters α_0, α_1 and λ satisfy a certain constraint condition. $E(y_t)$ and $D(y_t)$, however, are nonlinear functions of parameters α_0, α_1 and λ, and this makes parameter estimation more difficult.

3. Exponential GARCH model EGARCH

The assumption of conditional variance of GARCH model expressed by (8.34) is specific to h_t, Nelson (1991) introduced a specific assumption regarding $\ln h_t$:

$$\ln h_t = \alpha_0 + \sum_{j=1}^{\infty} H_j \left\{ \left| v_{t-j} \right| - E \left| v_{t-j} \right| + g \cdot v_{t-j} \right\}$$

That is to say, h_t behaves as an exponential function of v_t, so it is called the Exponential GARCH model, **EGARCH model** for short.

There are two different aspects in the assumption of conditional variance between the EGARCH model and GARCH model. The first is the form on the right side of the expression, which allows h_t to vary with positive or negative value of v_t, thus this model reflects well the price fluctuation of financial products. In the stock market, for example, it is commonly expected that positive and negative deviations from the trend (i.e. positive and negative errors) affect the behavior of investors differently. People react to negative deviations more intensely than to positive deviations. This asymmetry to positive and negative disturbance reaction can be described by EGARCH model. If parameter g is negative, and $-1 < g < 0$, then the change of h_t by the negative disturbance ($v_{t-j} < 0$) is greater than that of positive disturbance ($v_{t-j} > 0$) in the same extent. Conversely, if $g > 0$, the change by positive disturbance is greater. If $g = 0$, then h_t is symmetric to the changes of positive and negative disturbance.

Another situation is when the exponential form of conditional variance h_t is such that h_t is always greater than zero, whatever the values of parameters $H_j(j = 1, 2, \ldots)$. In this case the estimation of the parameters of the EGARCH model does not need imposing any constraints on the values of H_j. It can be proved that, when $\sum_{j=1}^{\infty} H_j^2 < \infty$, $\{\varepsilon_t\}$ of the EGARCH process is a stationary process.

Similar to the approach we used in (8.33), we can express the infinite order lag polynomial $H(L)$ as the quotient of two finite order lag polynomials, namely $H(L) = \alpha(L)/(1 - \delta(L))$, so $\ln h_t$ can be in the form of finite terms as

$$\begin{aligned} \ln h_t = k_0 + \delta_1 \ln h_{t-1} + \cdots + \delta_r \ln h_{t-r} + \alpha_1 \left[|v_{t-1}| - E|v_{t-1}| + g \cdot v_{t-1} \right] \\ + \alpha_2 \left[|v_{t-2}| - E|v_{t-2}| + g \cdot v_{t-2} \right] + \cdots + \alpha_m \left[|v_{t-m}| - E|v_{t-m}| + g \cdot v_{t-m} \right] \end{aligned} \tag{8.60}$$

The estimation of the parameters in the EGARCH model can be done using maximum likelihood method. Nelson (1991) suggests assuming that the random disturbances $\{v_t\}$ follows **generalized error distribution**, with the density function

$$f(x) = \frac{c \exp\left[-\frac{1}{2} |x/\lambda|^c \right]}{\lambda \cdot 2^{[(c+1)/c]} \Gamma(1/c)}; \quad 0 < c \le \infty, \quad -\infty < x < +\infty \tag{8.61}$$

where $\Gamma(\cdot)$ is Γ function, c and λ are constants, and λ has value

$$\lambda = \sqrt{\frac{2^{(-2/c)} \Gamma(1/c)}{\Gamma(3/c)}}$$

λ is called the **tail-thickness parameter.** When parameter $c = 2$, $\lambda = 1$, $f(x)$ is standard normal distribution; when $c < 2$, $f(x)$ has thicker tail than normal distribution; when $c > 2$, $f(x)$ has thinner tail than normal distribution; in particular when $c \to \infty$, $f(x)$ approached the uniform distribution on $[-\sqrt{3}, \sqrt{3}]$. It is easy to show under the density specification above that the mean of this generalized error is 0, and the variance is 1, and that the expectation of absolute value of v_t is:

$$E|v_t| = \frac{\lambda \cdot 2^{1/c} \Gamma(2/c)}{\Gamma(1/c)}$$

Especially for the standard normal distribution when $c = 2$,

$$E|v_t| = \sqrt{2/\pi}$$

Nelson (1991) analyzed the day-to-day rate of return r_t in the stock market by using an EGARCH model. Assume that r_t satisfies

$$r_t = a + br_{t-1} + \delta\, h_t + u_t$$

the residual $u_t = \sqrt{h_t} \cdot v_t$, whereas v_t are i.i.d. by generalized error distribution (8.61). Choose $r = 2$, $m = 2$, in the **GARCH** (r, m), then the logarithm of conditional variance is

$$\ln h_t - \zeta_t = \delta_1(\ln h_{t-1} - \zeta_{t-1}) + \delta_2(\ln h_{t-2} - \zeta_{t-2})$$
$$+ \alpha_1 \left[|v_{t-1}| - E|v_{t-1}| + g \cdot v_{t-1} \right] + \alpha_2 \left[|v_{t-2}| - E|v_{t-2}| + g \cdot v_{t-2} \right]$$

Let ζ_t, the unconditional mean of $\ln h_t$, be a function of the time, namely

$$\zeta_t = \zeta + \ln(1 + \kappa N_t)$$

where N_t denotes the number of non-trade days between the moment t and $t - 1$, ζ and κ are parameters to be estimated. The maximum likelihood function of the sample is

$$L(\theta) = T\left(\ln \frac{c}{\lambda} - (1 + \frac{1}{c})\ln 2 - \ln \Gamma\left(\frac{1}{c}\right) \right)$$
$$- \frac{1}{2}\sum_{t=1}^{T} \left| \frac{r_t - a - br_{t-1} - \delta\, h_t}{\lambda\sqrt{h_t}} \right|^c - \frac{1}{2}\sum_{t=1}^{T} \ln h_t$$

here the series $\{h_t\}_{t=1}^{T}$ is obtained by repeated iteration of (8.60), among which v_t satisfies

$$v_t = \frac{r_t - a - br_{t-1} - \delta\, h_t}{\sqrt{h_t}}$$

The model specification and analysis are clear, although the mathematical expressions look complicated.

4. Multivariate GARCH model

Now we consider the GARCH model of multivariate variable $Y_t = (y_{1t}, y_{2t}, \ldots, y_{nt})$. Extending the multivariate time series process to the ARCH model needs the assumption of the conditional heteroscedasticity form for the model error. Extending to the GARCH model requires conditional variance in ARMA form. The main regression formula of the **multivariate GARCH model** is

$$\underset{n \times 1}{Y_t} = \underset{n \times k}{\Phi'}\, \underset{k \times 1}{X_t} + \underset{n \times 1}{u_t}$$

where Y_t and u_t are all n-dimensional random vectors, X_t are k-dimensional regressors, u_t are i.i.d., and Φ is the coefficient matrix to be estimated. Given the observations $Y_t = (Y_{t-1}, Y_{t-2}, \ldots, X_t, X_{t-1}, \ldots)$, let the conditional expectation and variance of u_t

be $E(u_t \mid Y_t) = 0$ and $E(u_t \vec{u}_t \mid Y_t) = H_t$ respectively. Engle and Kroner presented, in 1993, the vector GARCH(r, m) structure of H_t as

$$H_t = K + \Delta_1 H_{t-1} \Delta_1' + \Delta_2 H_{t-2} \Delta_2' + \cdots + \Delta_r H_{t-r} \Delta_r'$$
$$+ A_1 u_{t-1} u_{t-1}' A_1' + A_2 u_{t-2} u_{t-2}' A_2' + \cdots + A_m u_{t-m} u_{t-m}' A_m'$$

where K, Δ_s and $A_s (s = 1, 2, \ldots)$ are all $n \times n$ coefficient matrices. Such a structure guarantees that H_t is positive definite when K is positive definite, thus we just need $K = PP'$ (P is lower triangular matrix).

In order to simplify the estimation, parameter matrices Δ_s and $A_s (s = 1, 2, \ldots)$ can be assumed to be diagonal matrices. Hence the conditional variance $Cov(u_{it} \cdot u_{jt} \mid \tilde{Y}_t)$ between random variable u_{it} and u_{jt} are functions of $u_{i, t-s} \cdot u_{j, t-s} (s = 1, 2, \ldots)$, not dependent on other cross terms. With this assumption the estimation of parameters can be simplified considerably.

Another commonly used simplification is to assume that the correlation coefficients between each element of random vector $\vec{u}_t$ are not dependent on time t. Use $h_{ii}^{(t)}$ to denote the element in the ith row and the ith column of matrix H_t, and $h_{ii}^{(t)}$ is the conditional variance of element u_{it}, namely

$$h_{ii}^{(t)} = E\left(u_{it}^2 \mid \tilde{Y}_t\right)$$

Each conditional variance can be assumed to follow the GARCH $(1, 1)$ process

$$h_{ii}^{(t)} = k_i + \delta_i h_{ii}^{(t-1)} + \alpha_i u_{i, t-1}^2, \; i = 1, 2, \ldots, n$$

Similarly, use $h_{ij}^{(t)}$ to denote the element in the ith row and the jth column of matrix H_t, and assume that

$$h_{ij}^{(t)} = Cov\left(u_{it}, u_{jt} \mid \tilde{Y}_t\right) = \rho_{ij} \cdot \sqrt{h_{ii}^{(t)}} \cdot \sqrt{h_{jj}^{(t)}}$$

where ρ_{ij} is unrelated to t. Under these assumptions, Bollerslev, in 1990, obtained maximum likelihood estimation of parameters for the multivariate GARCH model.

We have discussed multivariate time series model actually. In the next three sections, we will continue to discuss these models.

8.5 Mixed models of multivariate regression with time series

8.5.1 Mixed model of multivariate regression with time series

Econometric modeling had its early beginnings in 1926 with pioneering work by Ragnar Frisch. Frisch recognized that macroeconomic data come mostly as time series and that there are linear relations among those time series. This is today's concept of cointegration, while Frisch called it confluence analysis. Subsequently most of macroeconometric modeling ignored the time series nature of the data until Newbold and Granger brought to the attention of economists the spurious correlations that can be brought into econometric analysis if regression is carried out when using nonstationary time series. Then for nearly a decade econometric analysis was focused on time series while ignoring simultaneity. Throughout these developments there was however an approach that used regression with time series data that converted the nonstationary time series to stationary series through autoregressive distributed lags.

This section therefore deals with a mixture of multivariate regression and time series. This model was known in the econometrics literature for a long time as the **Autoregressive Distributed Lag model** or simply ADL model. We know that regression analysis seeks the relations between a variable and other variables, while time series analysis seeks the relations between current value and past values. In Section 9.4 we introduced the vector autoregressive model, which is a multivariate relation between several variables but does not have the current values of other endogenous and exogenous variables.

1. We can write a mixed multivariate regression and time series model as

$$y_t = \alpha + \Theta_0 y_t + \Theta_1 y_{t-1} + \Theta_2 y_{t-2} + \cdots + \Theta_p y_{t-p} + \varepsilon_t \tag{8.62}$$

where each y is an n-dimensional vector of endogenous economic variables, Θ_0 is a $n \times n$ matrix which leading diagonal is 0.

$$\begin{pmatrix} 0 & \vartheta_{012} & \cdots & \vartheta_{01n} \\ \vartheta_{021} & 0 & \cdots & \vartheta_{02n} \\ \vdots & \vdots & \ddots & \vdots \\ \vartheta_{0n1} & \vartheta_{0n2} & \cdots & 0 \end{pmatrix}$$

Develop the equations above:

$$\begin{cases} y_{1t} = \alpha_1 + 0 \cdot y_{1t} + \vartheta_{012} y_{2t} + \cdots + \vartheta_{01n} y_{nt} + \vartheta_{111} y_{1t-1} + \cdots + \vartheta_{11n} y_{nt-1} + \vartheta_{211} y_{1t-2} + \cdots \\ \quad + \vartheta_{21n} y_{nt-2} + \cdots + \vartheta_{p11} y_{1t-p} + \cdots + \vartheta_{p1n} y_{nt-p} + \varepsilon_{1t} \\ y_{2t} = \alpha_2 + \vartheta_{021} y_{1t} + 0 \cdot y_{2t} + \cdots + \vartheta_{02n} y_{nt} + \vartheta_{121} y_{1t-1} + \cdots + \vartheta_{12n} y_{nt-1} + \vartheta_{211} y_{1t-2} + \cdots \\ \quad + \vartheta_{22n} y_{1t-2} + \cdots + \vartheta_{p21} y_{1t-p} + \cdots + \vartheta_{p2n} y_{nt-p} + \varepsilon_{2t} \\ \quad \cdots \cdots \cdots \cdots \cdots \cdots \cdots \cdots \cdots \cdots \cdots \cdots \\ y_{nt} = \alpha_n + \vartheta_{0n1} y_{1t} + \vartheta_{0n2} y_{2t} + \cdots + 0 \cdot y_{nt} + \vartheta_{1n1} y_{1t-1} + \cdots + \vartheta_{1nn} y_{nt-1} + \vartheta_{2n1} y_{1t-2} + \cdots \\ \quad + \vartheta_{2nn} y_{nt-2} + \cdots + \vartheta_{pn1} y_{1t-p} + \cdots + \vartheta_{pnn} y_{nt-p} + \varepsilon_{nt} \end{cases}$$

The number of observations of y_t in fact is T, namely for $t = 1, \ldots, T$, For $i = 1, \ldots, n$, let

$$y^{(i)} = \begin{pmatrix} y_{i1} \\ y_{i2} \\ \vdots \\ y_{iT-p} \end{pmatrix}, X^{(i)} = \begin{pmatrix} 1 & y_{11} & \cdots & y_{n1} \\ 1 & y_{12} & \cdots & y_{n2} \\ \vdots & \vdots & \ddots & \vdots \\ 1 & y_{1T-p} & \cdots & y_{nT-p} \end{pmatrix}, \varepsilon^{(i)} = \begin{pmatrix} \varepsilon_{i1} \\ \varepsilon_{i2} \\ \vdots \\ \varepsilon_{iT-p} \end{pmatrix}$$

Therefore we can construct the regression equation:

$$y^{(i)} = X^{(i)} \beta^{(i)} + \varepsilon^{(i)}$$

where $i = 1, \ldots, n$. Note that for different equations, $X^{(i)}$ is $(T-p) \times ((p+1) \times n)$ matrix, but the model is different from the general p dimensional autoregressive model.

2. Identification of the model order

In order to specify the model order, we need two statistics:

$$AIC(p) = \ln \det(\hat{\Sigma}_n) + 2n^2 \, p/T$$

$$BIC(p) = \ln \det(\hat{\Sigma}_n) + m^2 p \ln T/T$$

where n is the number of the variables of the model, T is the number of observations in the sample, $p = 1, 2, 3, \ldots$. $\hat{\Sigma}_n$ is the estimated variance covariance matrix of the residuals of which the ijth entry is

$$\hat{\sigma}_{ij} = \frac{(y^{(i)} - X^{(i)}\hat{\beta}_i)(y^{(j)} - X^{(j)}\hat{\beta}_j)}{T}$$

The order p is the integer p which make the $AIC(p)$ or $BIC(p)$ minimum. We know that we need to know the order p to compute AIC(p) and BIC(p), and we need these statistics to choose p. So what we do is start from $p = 1, 2, 3, \ldots$, evaluate the statistics $AIC(p)$ and $BIC(p)$. And stop when AIC and BIC reach a minimum.

3. Statistical properties of the estimation of the parameters

In the mixed model of multivariate regression and time series, $y_{it}, y_{2t}, \ldots, y_{nt}$ appear as dependent variables on the left of the equation, and they also appear as independent variables on the right of the equation. It can be proved by using the same arguments that advanced for the system of simultaneous equations in Chapter 7 that parameter estimators using OLS are not consistent estimators, namely parameter estimators don't always converge in probability to parameters' true values when the sample size tends to infinity. They are also not efficient estimators in the sense that variances of OLS estimators of parameters do not have minimum values among all linear estimators. We therefore need to improve the general least squares method of estimation of parameters in this mixed model.

We present a two-steps least square method to improve the upon the OLS estimator. First, we do the ordinary least squares regression for original data. That is, we put the original data of the variables on the two sides of the equation and get the ordinary least squares estimators of parameters $\hat{a}_i, \hat{\Theta}_0, \hat{\Theta}_i$; then we make use of these ordinary least squares estimators to compute the estimated values $\hat{y}_{1t}, \hat{y}_{2t}, \ldots, \hat{y}_{nt}$ of right hand side $y_{1t}, y_{2t}, \ldots, y_{nt}$; second we do the second step or second stage regression. In this second step regression, we use the original data of $y_{it}, y_{2t}, \ldots, y_{nt}$ on the left side of the equation and use the estimations $\hat{y}_{1t}, \hat{y}_{2t}, \ldots, \hat{y}_{nt}$ to right side of the equation, and get estimators of the parameters $\hat{\hat{a}}_i, \hat{\hat{\Theta}}_0, \hat{\hat{\Theta}}_i$. These $\hat{\hat{a}}_i, \hat{\hat{\Theta}}_0, \hat{\hat{\Theta}}_i$ we get are two-stage least squares estimators and they do satisfy the consistency property.

We can also use the three stage least squares method to improve the efficiency of the estimators. We use two-stage least squares estimators $\hat{\hat{a}}_i, \hat{\hat{\Theta}}_0, \hat{\hat{\Theta}}_i$ into all the equations to compute the residual errors u, and use these estimates to compute the estimator $\hat{\Sigma}$ of covariance matrix. This $\hat{\Sigma}$ is used to get generalized least square estimators of all the parameters of the mixed model.

We had established in Chapter 3 that in the model $y = X\beta + \varepsilon$, the efficiency of OLS estimators of coefficients of regression $\hat{\beta}_L = (X'X)^{-1} X'y$ will be improved by the generalized least squares estimator $\beta'_G = (X'\Sigma^{-1}X)^{-1} X'\Sigma^{-1}y$. Likewise we mentioned in Chapter 7 that the three stage least squares have in general lower asymptotic variances than the OLS and two stage least squares. Using the same logic we can prove that the three stage estimators of the parameters have in general lower asymptotic variances than the OLS and two-step estimators.

8.5.2 Mixed model of multivariate regression and cointegration with time series

In econometric modeling one often encounters a situation where the endogenous variables, or variables that are being modeled, depend only on the historical information of the variables themselves. There are other cases in which they are modeled as a regression model to model the relations among all the variables. But in the actual economic system, economic variables are affected both by their own historical information, and also on other endogenous economic variables. They may in fact have closer affinity to lagged values of related economic variables than their own lagged values of some distant past. This dependence between economic variables could be described by a model of a dynamic long run economic equilibrium with short run disturbances. It is in this case that we find the mixed model or Autoregressive Distributed lag (ADL) model with cointegration very useful. For such models see Boswijk and Franses (1992).

The patterns of movement of complex economic and financial variables are always better portrayed as non-linear, and even non-parametric models. But it is difficult to determine the appropriate non-linear and the non-parametric model. The linear approximations are quite appropriate to extrapolate and forecast.

We can still use the underlying nonlinear nature of the relation but only in the trend part. In dealing with economic time series, if we want to use the linear model to predict the trend of the complex system, the best way is to assume that the variables both on the right and left hand side of an equation have a sinusoidal trend. The economic model for statistical analysis will then consist of a cointegrating error correction model of these integrated nonlinear sinusoidal variables.

In order to specify the model we need to do some data exploration to determine the leads and lags between various dependent economic variables. The principles to specify the lead and lag are time lag analysis methods that use correlation coefficients, the Kullback-Liebler information method and so on. In our DASC software these selections can be made through the specification of the appropriate parameters of the computer program. We, however, recommend the correlation coefficient method in most cases.

Suppose that the current time series of the dependent variable Y are $Y_t(t = 1, 2,\ldots,n)$, and select the independent variables which are closely related with the dependent variable as $X_1, X_2,\ldots,X_m$, the current time series of the independent variables are $X_{1t}, X_{2t},\ldots,X_{mt}(t = 1, 2,\ldots,n)$ respectively, and the lead or lag $k(k = 0, \pm1, \pm2,\ldots)$ period time series of the independent variables are written as $X_{1(t+k)}, X_{2(t+k)},\ldots,X_{m(t+k)}$ respectively. Our task is to seek the lead or lag time series $X_{i(t+k_i)}$ of X_i which have the greatest relevance with Y_t, that is to specify the optimal lead or the period of lag k_i between the independent variable Y_t and independent variables X_{it}. The specific process to specify the lead or lag period of variables by correlation coefficient method is: in the specified scope of period, calculate the correlation coefficient between the independent variable Y_t and the lead or lag series $X_{i(t+k)}(k = 0, \pm1, \pm2,\ldots)$ of independent variables X_{it} respectively, and select k_i of k which makes the correlation coefficient maximum as the optimal lead or the period of lag. Let $i = 1, 2,\ldots,m$, and we can get $k_1, k_2,\ldots, k_m$, then we can get the series $X_{1(t+k_1)}, X_{2(t+k_2)},\ldots,X_{m(t+k_m)}$. On the other hand, we need to select lag time series $Y_{t-1}, Y_{t-2}, \ldots, Y_{t-p}$ of the dependent variable itself which have the maximum correlation coefficients with Y_t, and calculate the correlation coefficient between Y_t and Y_{t-1}, $Y_{t-2}, \ldots, Y_{t-p}$, if the series Y_{t-p} have the maximum correlation coefficient, then we can select Y_{t-1}, $Y_{t-2}, \ldots, Y_{t-p}$ to join in the model.

When we use series obtained in this way to construct a linear model we will note that the leads and lags for different variables are different. The coefficient matrix of the linear mixed multiple regression of time series will then have several zero elements. In other words the exploratory data analysis we suggested above sets a priori zero-restrictions on the parameter matrix enabling us to identify the models.

Let the current time series of an indicator be X_{1t}, then note the lead or lag k_1 period time series of the indicator as $X_{1(t+k_1)}$, similarly, we have $X_{2(t+k_2)}, \ldots, X_{n(t+k_n)}$, where $k_1, k_2, \ldots, k_n \in \{0, \pm1, \pm2, \ldots\}$. For different periods' vector series $\vec{X}_t = (X_{1(t+k_1)}, X_{2(t+k_2)}, \ldots, X_{n(t+k_n)})$, if there exists a vector $\vec{\alpha} = (\alpha_1, \alpha_2, \ldots, \alpha_n)$, which make

$$\alpha_1 X_{1(t+k_1)} + \alpha_2 X_{2(t+k_2)} + \cdots + \alpha_n X_{n(t+k_n)} = \varepsilon$$

where ε is white noise, then we call the vector series $\vec{X}_t = (X_{1(t+k_1)}, X_{2(t+k_2)}, \ldots, X_{n(t+k_n)})$ are cointegrated, or series X_{it} are lag-cointegrated. Since the vector series are related to the lead or lag time series which are different from current series, we call the cointegration relations between the different period vector series the lag-cointegration of the vector series, and $\vec{\alpha} = (\alpha_1, \alpha_2, \ldots, \alpha_n)$ is the **lag-cointegration vector**.

Lag cointegration relations of the economic variables mean there are some economic mechanisms that restrict the movement of the variables at different periods, which lead to variables at different periods that do not depart by far in the short term, and will go to balance in the long term. This long term balanced relations can be characterized by the lag-cointegration equation of the different period's vector series.

For the test of the lag-cointegration, first we can do unit root test for different periods' variables $X_{1(t+k_1)}, X_{2(t+k_2)}, \ldots, X_{m(t+k_m)}$ and $Y_{t-1}, Y_{t-2}, \ldots Y_{t-p}$, if the vector series above are of the same order of integration we can use lag-cointegration testing based on the ordinary least squares and Johansen testing for the unit root to judge whether there is lag cointegration relations or not.

After the three-stage analysis, we can create the ultimate mixture model, adding the time series $Y_{t-1}, Y_{t-2}, \ldots, Y_{t-p}$ and the lead or lag time series of independent variables $X_{1(t+k_1)}, X_{2(t+k_2)}, \ldots, X_{m(t+k_m)}$ which have close relationships with the dependent variable in the model. We can specify the mixture model of the multivariate time series and lag-cointegration as follows

$$Y_t = \alpha_1 Y_{t-1} + \cdots + \alpha_p Y_{t-p} + \beta_1 X_{1(t+k_1)} + \beta_2 X_{2(t+k_2)} + \cdots + \beta_m X_{m(t+k_m)} + \varepsilon \qquad (8.63)$$

where $\alpha_1, \ldots, \alpha_p, \beta_1, \ldots, \beta_m$ are unknown parameters, and ε is random error. Usually we assume that

$$E(\varepsilon) = 0, \quad Var(\varepsilon) = \sigma^2$$

Example 8.7   Forecasting for Consumer Price Index (CPI) of China   The **Consumer price index (CPI)** reflects consumer goods' prices over time, and is a highly significant economic policy variable that has a direct effect on day to day economic life. CPI is regarded as a standard price measurement the world over.

We therefore try to model CPI for China and hope to obtain better forecasting experience. In fact, forecasting is the final goal using regression or time series. How to get better forecasing? We should select the appropriate model, variables and data, algorithm, and parameters suitably so as to get good forecasts.

1. **Selecting the model**. It is difficult to forecast complex trends of economic phenomena by using only one simple model, regression model or time series model. The mixed multi-variate regression and cointegration model with time series (8.63) is an integrative model, and quite effective for forecasting complex trends. However, it is a linear model.

In this model, the lag data of dependent variable is also used as endogenous (independent) variable. It may improve the forecasting greatly. All variables are extrapolated according to the properties of time series to generate the forecasts. Lag data with some lag period of these variables are used in cointegration, so their combined effect may be better in explaining the dependent variable, CPI.

2. **Selecting variables and data**. All endogenous variables should have an economic relationship with the dependent variable, CPI. They can be obtained from the authoritative official web site. The time period chosen for all the variables must be the same. Exploratory analysis of the data is important.

In this example, we select the right variables as follows: Consumer Price Index (CPI), the broad money supply (M2), the loans of financial institutions (Loan), the total retail sales of consumer goods (Conagg), the corporate goods price index (ECPI), 1-year lending rate (L1Yrate), Yuan / dollar average exchange rate (Exchange), and the Shanghai Stock Index(Shindex).

Then, the model is:

$$CPI_t = \alpha_1 CPI_{t-1} + \cdots + \alpha_p CPI_{t-p} + \beta_1 M2_{(t+k_1)} + \beta_2 Loan_{(t+k_2)} + \beta_3 Conagg_{(t+k_3)}$$
$$+ \beta_4 ECPI_{(t+k_4)} + \beta_5 L1Yrate_{(t+k_5)} + \beta_6 Exchange_{(t+k_6)} + \beta_7 Shindex_{(t+k_7)} + \varepsilon \quad (8.64)$$

3. **Using lag lengths with suitable algorithm**. In the model (8.64), the lag parameters $k_1, \ldots, k_7$ may be positive or negative. As soon as the lag parameters are determined, the data of series need to be extrapolated, including forecasting and back-casting. The relationship of lag cointegration is not easy to be discovered. If there are 10 variables, and 10 time periods to test lag for each variable, then we should calculate 10^{10} times. So selecting a suitable algorithm is important.

4. **Selecting parameters**. There are some parameters in DASC software, such as the lag length being determined by AIC and BIC, the number of all endogenous variables composed by lag dependent variables.

5. **Select the period** over which the forecasts are made. In other commonly used models, the user specifies the data of independent variables to forecast dependent variable. In our model, we only need to specify the number of periods over which the forecasting is made. The program will prolong each independent variable as time series. This prolonging is made by taking the difference for each time series. Even the error of each prolonging cannot be neglected, but the error of their cointegrated combination may be too small to be neglected. Cointegration technology is important to guarantee the precision of forecast.

Figure 8.34 below shows the performance of a mixed model in forecasting CPI. The line with square points is original data, and the line with dot points is fitting data. We can see very

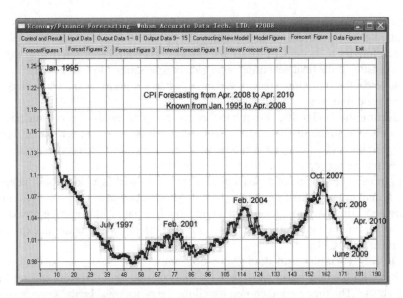

Figure 8.34   Forecasting for CPI of China with 24 months.

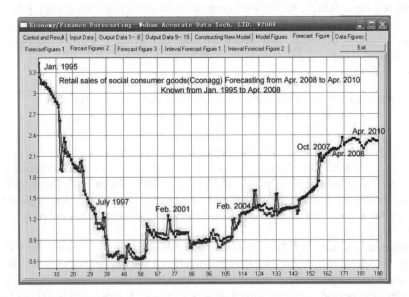

Figure 8.35   Forecasting for Retail sales of social consumer goods of China with 24 months.

good forecasting performance. The most important aspect of this model is that it is linear and is easy to extrapolate and forecast.

Our model can also be used to forecast the trend of other economic variables used in the model. Figure 8.35 shows the forecasting for Retail sales of social consumer goods of China with 24 months. The model and the forecasts generated by the software are wonderful indeed.

These figures are generated by another system that belongs to DASC.

Electronic references for Chapter 8

References

Aknouche A. & Hafida G. (2009) On some probabilistic properties of double periodic AR models. *Statistics & Probability Letters* **3**, 407–13.

Bollerslev T. (1986) Generalized autoregressive conditional heteroskedasticity. *Journal of Econometrics* **31**, 307–27.

Bollerslev T. & Baillie R.T. (1989) Common stochastic trends in a system of exchange rates. *Journal of Finance* **44**(1), 167–81.

Bollerslev T. & Baillie R.T. (1994) Cointegration, fractional cointegration, and exchange rate dynamics. *Journal of Finance* **49**(2), 737–45.

Bollerslev T. & Engle R.F. (1993) Common persistence in conditional variance. *Econometrica* **61**, 167–86.

Boswijk P. & Hans F.P. (1992) Dynamic specification and cointegration. *Oxford Bulletin of Economics and Statistics* **54**(3), 369–381.

Bouissou M.B., Laffont J.J. & Vuong Q.H. (1986) Disequilibrium econometrics on micro data. *Review of Economic Studies* **53**(1), 113–24.

Brown R.G. & Hwang Y.C. (1992) *Introduction to Random Signals and Applied Kalman Filtering.* 2nd edn, John Wiley & Sons, Ltd.

Carvalho A.X. & Tanner M.A. (2007) Modeling nonlinear count time series with local mixtures of Poisson auto-regressions. *Computational Statistics & Data Analysis* **11**, 5266–94.

Chen W.T. & Kuen-Rong H. (1989) A neural network for 3-satisfiability problems. *IJCNN - International Joint Conference on Neural Networks* **2**, 587.

Coakley J., Fuertes A.-M. & Smith R. (2006) Unobserved heterogeneity in panel time series models. *Computational Statistics & Data Analysis* **9**, 2361–80.

Dickey D.A. & Fuller W.A. (1979), Distribution of the estimators for autoregressive time series with a unit root. *Journal of the American Statistical Association* **74**, 427–31.

Engel R.F. (1982) Autoregressive conditional heteroskedasticity with estimates of the variance of U.K. inflation. *Econometrica* **50**, 987–1008.

Engle R.F. & Granger C.W.J. (1987) Co-integration and error correction: representation, estimation, and testing. *Econometrica* **55**(2), 251–276.

Engle R.F. & Kroner K.F. (1995) Multivariate simultaneous generalized ARCH. *Econometric Theory* **11**, 122–50.

Fei M.R., Du D.J. & Li K. (2008) A fast model identification method for networked control system. *Applied Mathematics and Computation* **2**, 658–67.

Feige E.L. & Pearce D.K. (1979) The casual causal relationship between money and income: Some caveats for time series analysis. *The Review of Economics and Statistics* **61**(4), 521–33.

Feige E.L. & McGee R. (1979) Has the federal reserve shifted from a policy of interest rate targets to a policy of monetary aggregate targets? *Journal of Money, Credit and Banking* **11**(4), 381–404.

Freeland R.K. & McCabe B. (2005) Asymptotic properties of CLS estimators in the Poisson AR(1) model. *Statistics & Probability Letters* **2**, 147–153.

Geweke J., Meese R. & Dent W. (1983) Comparing alternative tests of causality in temporal systems: Analytic results and experimental evidence. *Journal of Econometrics* **21**(2), 161–94.

Giovannini A. & Jorion P. (1988) Foreign exchange risk premia volatility once again. *Journal of International Money and Finance* **7**(1), 111–13.

Grewal M.S. & Andrews A.P. (1993) Kalman Filtering Theory and Practice., Prentice-Hall, Englewood Cliffs, New Jersey.

Hendry D.F. & Morgan M.S. (1989) A re-analysis of confluence analysis. *Oxford Economic Papers* **41**, 35–52.

Jacobs R.S., Bober M.A., Pinto I., Williams A.B., Jacobson & M.S. de Carvalho (1993) Pharmacological studies of marine novel marine metabolites. *Advances of Marine Biotechnology* **1**, 77–99.

Jayakumar K. & Kuttykrishnan A.P. (2007) A time-series model using asymmetric Laplace distribution. *Statistics & Probability Letters* **16**, 1636–40.

Hoeting J.A., Madigan D., Raftery A.E. & Volinsky C.T. (1999) Bayesian model averaging: A tutorial. *Statistical Science* **4**(4), 382–417.

Johansen S. & Juselius K. (1990) Maximum likelihood estimation and inference on cointegration–with applications to the demand for money. *Oxford Bulletin of Economics and Statistics* **52**(2), 169–210.

Jorion P. (1988) On jump processes in the foreign exchange and stock markets. *Review of Financial Studies* **1**(4), 427–45.

Kumar T.K. (1995) Cointegration and error-correction models: A historical and methodological perspective. *Journal of Quantitative Economics* **11**(1), 143–54.

Laffont J.-J. & Moreaux M. (1983) The nonexistence of a free entry cournot equilibrium in labor-managed economies. *Econometrica*, **51**(2), 455–62.

Lin Tsung I. & Hsiu J.H. (2008) A simplified approach to inverting the auto-covariance matrix of a general ARMA(p,q) process. *Statistics & Probability Letters* **1**, 36–41.

Lütkepohl H.L. (1991) *Introduction to Multiple Time Series Analysis*. Berlin, Springer.

Meese R. & Rogoff K. (1983) Empirical exchange rate models of the seventies. Do they fit out of sample? *Journal of International Economics* **14**, 3–24.

Murray M.P. (1994) A drunk and her dog: An illustration of cointegration and error-correction. *American Statistician* **48**(1), 37–9.

Nagakura D. (2009) Testing for coefficient stability of AR(1) model when the null is an integrated or a stationary process. *Journal of Statistical Planning and Inference* **8**, 2731–45.

Nelson D.B. (1990) ARCH models as diffusion approximations. *Journal of Econometrics* **45**(1–2), 7–38.

Nelson D.B. (1991) Conditional heteroskedasticity in asset returns: A new approach. *Econometrica* **59**, 347–70.

Noble N.R. & Field T.W. (1983) Sunspots and cycles: Comment. *Southern Economic Journal* **50**, 251–54.

Pappas S.Sp., Ekonomou L., Karampelas P., Katsikas S.K. & Liatsis P. (2008) Modeling of the grounding resistance variation using ARMA models. *Simulation Modeling Practice and Theory* **5**, 560–70.

Pesaran M.H. & Wickens M. (1995) *Handbook of Applied Econometrics: Macroeconomics*, Basil Blackwell, Oxford.

Phillips P.C.B. (1987) Time series regression with a unit root, *Econometrica*, **55**(2) 277–301.

Pierce D.A. & Haugh L.D. (1977) The assessment and detection of causality in temporal systems. *Journal of Econometrics* **5**, 265–93.

Pierce D.A. & Haugh L.D. (1979) Comment on price. *Journal of Econometrics* **10**, 257–60.

Qian G.Q. & Zhao X.D. (2007) On time series model selection involving many candidate ARMA models. *Computational Statistics & Data Analysis* **12**, 6180–96.

Sheehan R.G. & Grieves R. (1982) Sunspots and cycles: A test of causation. *Southern Economic Journal* **48**, 775–77.

Sheehan R.G. & Grieves R. (1983) Sunspots and cycles: Reply. *Southern Economic Journal* **50**(1), 255–6.

Sims C.A. (1980) Macroeconomics and reality. *Econometrica* **48**(1), 1–48.

Sims C.A. (1988) Bayesian skepticism on unit root econometrics. *Journal of Economic Dynamics and Control* **12**(2–3), 463–474.

Sims C.A. (1991) Empirical analysis of macroeconomic time series: VAR and structural models: by M.P. Clements and G.E. Mizon. *European Economic Review* **35**(4), 922–32.

Sims C.A., Jinill K. & Sunghyun K. (2004) Calculating and using second order accurate solution of discrete time dynamic equilibrium models. *Econometric Society 2004 North American Winter Meetings* **4**, 411.

Sims C.A. & Zha T. (1998) Bayesian methods for dynamic multivariate models. *International Economic Review* **39**(4), 949–68.

Stock J.H. & M.W. Watson (1989) New indexes of coincident and leading economic indicators. *NBER Macroeconomics Annual* **4**, 351–409.

9

Multivariate statistical analysis and data analysis

The contents of previous chapters are organized into systematic and sequential development of regression and time series analysis. In this chapter we will discuss multivariate statistical analysis and data analysis applied to economic and financial subjects. Some additional miscellaneous topics in regression analysis including **robust regression**, **projection pursuit regression**, **partial least squares** regression of single equation, **continuum regression**, Bayesian method and empirical Bayesian method etc, have been described in the Electronic References for Chapter 9.

First, this chapter introduces some methods and models of multivariate data analysis, including multivariate **analysis of variance**, **discriminant analysis**, **correlation analysis**, **factor analysis**, **principal component analysis**, and **path analysis**.

Second, the internationally popular analysis of **customer satisfaction index** (CSI) adopts the **structural equations model** (SEM), and the computation uses the **partial least squares** (PLS) method. Confronted with this problem, we have developed a computational method for the choice of best iterative initial value for PLS, and a **definite linear algorithm** for SEM using prescription regression and LSE. These methods greatly improve the algorithm for SEM. We also present **high layer path analysis model** and present its computational algorithm. Because analysis of the customer satisfaction index is required for the ISO9000 standard, an excellent standard for performance, our research is of great significance in terms of both theory and application.

Lastly, most of the models we discussed in this book refer to economic observations of economic indicators observed over time and over different subjects/units of analysis. We have a time series of observations for each subject or unit of analysis, and we have observations like that for different subjects or units of analysis. Such data with both cross section (across units) and time series (over time) are called **Panel Data**. If the data are from a part of the population or truncated population, rather than the whole population, it is called **Truncated Data**. If some indexes of the data are not recorded, such data are called **Censored**

Developing Econometrics, First Edition. Hengqing Tong, T. Krishna Kumar and Yangxin Huang.
© 2011 John Wiley & Sons, Ltd. Published 2011 by John Wiley & Sons, Ltd.

Data. If the original data are life data or duration data, it could be named **Duration Data**. When we are trying directly or indirectly to reveal the original form or transformed form of high dimensional data in three-dimensional or two-dimensional space, it is **high dimensional data visualization** in lower dimensions. This chapter introduces processing and analysis techniques for these kinds of data, including cross-section, time series, and panel data.

9.1   Model of analysis of variance

Analysis of Variance (ANOVA) is a method used to **test** the **significance** of a **factor** in an **experiment**. Usually we assume that there are several **levels** for a factor. ANOVA is a very powerful method of analysis between one dependent variable and several related independent variables. It is based on examining the relationship of the sums of squared deviations of the variables. To make the two types of squared sums comparable the independent variables' contribution is multiplied by the square of the regression coefficients. The reader may find some discussion of variance components in Chapter 3. We must clarify that there we dealt primarily with regression models and showed how the variance component analysis is carried out within a regression analysis. In this chapter our primary emphasis is on design of experiments and analysis of variance and we use the regression model only to explain the same.

ANOVA was first developed by R.A. Fisher to study the effects of various treatments applied in agricultural field experiments on agricultural yield. As the effects of such treatments on yield may not be simply additive, he introduced the notion of interactions between treatments, and such interactions could make the effects super-additive or sub-additive depending on whether the interactions are positive or negative. Thus ANOVA is used with experimental, quasi-experimental, and non-experimental data to analyze the effects of different independent variables on a dependent variable. The model can be considered either with **fixed-effects** or with **random effects**. Owing to the similarity of the underlying basic methodological issues, ANOVA is another way of doing regression analysis. Each of these ANOVA problems corresponds to a regression model and hence ANOVA could be performed by regression method. In this section we discuss ANOVA through regression methods.

9.1.1   Single factor analysis of variance model

Consider only a **single factor** A, which has α levels. Every level repeats n_i times. The test data are represented by $Y = (y_{ij}, i = 1,\ldots,a, j = 1,\ldots,n_i)$. When $n_i = n, i = 1,\ldots,a$, the design is called a **balanced design**, otherwise it is called an **unbalanced design**. The structure of a balanced design is given in the table below (Table 9.1):

Table 9.1   Single factor ANOVA model data.

i \ j	1	2	...	j	...	n	Intra-class Average
1	y_{11}	y_{12}	...	y_{1j}	...	y_{1n}	$\bar{y}_1$
⋮	......					⋮	⋮
i	y_{11}	y_{i2}	...	y_{ij}	...	y_{in}	$\bar{y}_i$
⋮	......					⋮	⋮
a	y_{a1}	y_{a2}	...	y_{aj}	...	y_{an}	$\bar{y}_a$

For the single factor ANOVA method, the following regression model may be constructed:

$$y_{ij} = \mu + \alpha_i + \varepsilon_{ij}, \quad i = 1,\ldots,a, \quad j = 1,\ldots,n_i \tag{9.1}$$

where μ is the overall mean, α_i is the effect of the ith level, ε_{ij} is a random error, and assume $\varepsilon_{ij} \sim N(0,\sigma^2)$, all ε_{ij} are independent of each other. If we designate

$$Y' = (y_{11},\ldots,y_{1n_1},y_{21},\ldots,y_{2n_2},\ldots,y_{a1},\ldots,y_{an_a})$$
$$\beta' = (\mu,\alpha_1,\ldots\alpha_a)$$
$$\varepsilon' = (\varepsilon_{11},\ldots\varepsilon_{1n_1},\varepsilon_{21},\ldots,\varepsilon_{2n_2},\ldots,\varepsilon_{a1},\ldots\varepsilon_{an_a})$$

$$X = \begin{pmatrix} 1_{n_1} & 1_{n_1} & 0 & \cdots & 0 \\ 1_{n_2} & 0 & 1_{n_2} & \cdots & 0 \\ \cdots\cdots & & & \ddots & \\ 1_{n_a} & 0 & 0 & \cdots & 1_{n_a} \end{pmatrix}$$

Then the **single factor ANOVA model** could be expressed as the common form of linear regression model

$$Y = X\beta + \varepsilon \tag{9.2}$$

where the rank of design matrix is a, because the first series of X could be reduced to 0 by an elementary transformation.

Now we discuss the estimation problem of a single factor ANOVA model (9.1), namely to estimate μ and α_i, $i = 1,\ldots,a$ in model (9.2). For the deficiency in the rank of X, we can't directly use formula $\hat{\beta} = (X'X)^{-1} X'Y$, as that inverse does not exist, but we could obtain normal equations as $(X'X)\beta = X'Y$:

$$N\mu + \sum_{i=1}^{a} n_i a_i = y.. \tag{9.3}$$

$$n_i\mu + n_i a_i = y_i., \quad i = 1,\ldots,a \tag{9.4}$$

where

$$y.. = \sum_i \sum_j y_{ij}, \quad y_i. = \sum_j y_{ij}, \quad N = \sum_i n_i$$

It can be seen that in the set of normal equations, by adding a equations in the second line (9.4) together, we obtain the first line (9.3). Therefore (9.3) is a redundant equation. But from (9.4) we may see that stipulating **total average**

$$\hat{\mu} = \frac{1}{N}y.. = \frac{1}{N}\sum_i \sum_j y_{ij} = \bar{y}..$$

is equal to imposing a constraint condition on the parameters

$$\sum_{i=1}^{a} n_i \alpha_i = 0$$

We may also say that we need to solve normal equations under the parametric constraint condition given above. We have

$$\hat{\alpha}_i = \frac{1}{n_i} y_i. - \hat{\mu} = \bar{y}_i. - \bar{y}.., \ i = 1,\ldots,a$$

Next we examine the issue of testing of hypothesis whether the effects of factor A are the same at all of its a levels. This may be expressed as:

$$H_0 : \alpha_1 = \alpha_2 = \cdots = \alpha_a$$

or equivalently as:

$$H_0 : \alpha_1 - \alpha_a = \alpha_2 - \alpha_a = \cdots = \alpha_{a-1} - \alpha_a = 0$$

If H_0 is true, let $\alpha_1 = \alpha_2 = \cdots = \alpha_a = \alpha$. Put it in μ (i.e. $\mu' = \mu + \alpha$), and we obtain reduced model

$$y_{ij} = \mu + \varepsilon_{ij}, \ i = 1,\ldots,a, \ j = 1,\ldots,n_i$$

The best estimate of μ is $\hat{\mu} = \frac{1}{N} \sum_i \sum_j y_{ij}$

Now we present the ANOVA method by regression analysis. We already gave estimators of μ and α_i. We can now write:

$$\hat{Y} = X\hat{\beta}, \ \hat{y}_{ij} = \hat{\mu} + \hat{\alpha}_i = \bar{y}_i., \ i = 1,\ldots,a$$

In regression analysis there is **Corrected Total Sum of Squares** S_{TS} = **Regression Sum of Squares** S_{RS} + **Residual Sum of Squares** S_{ES}, that is,

$$\sum_{i=1}^{N} (y_i - \bar{y})^2 = \sum_{i=1}^{N} (\hat{y}_i - \bar{y})^2 + \sum_{i=1}^{N} (y_i - \hat{y}_i)^2$$

Using the present notation:

$$\sum_i \sum_j (y_{ij} - \bar{y}..)^2 = \sum_i n_i (\bar{y}_i. - \bar{y}..)^2 + \sum_i \sum_j (y_{ij} - \bar{y}.)^2$$

That is the ANOVA method, **decomposition of variance**:
Total Variation S_T + **Variation Between Classes** S_A + **Within Class Variance** S_e
Meanwhile, there is **associated decomposition of degrees of freedom**:

$$N - 1 = (N - a) + (a - 1)_N$$

The testing statistic concerning H_0 is:

$$F = \frac{S_{RS}/(a-1)}{S_{ES}/(N-a)} = \frac{Q_A}{Q_e} \sim F(a-1, N-a)$$

here $Q_A = S_{RS}/(a-1)$, $Q_e = S_e/(N-a)$. If H_0 is rejected, then the assumption that the effects of all levels of treatment A are equal is not correct. Thus, we infer that there are significant differences in the effects of levels of application of factor A.

We have the following ANOVA table (Table 9.2).

We discussed the ANOVA method through the linear regression model above. This covered the point estimation of parameters and the test of significance for differences in effects of treatment applied at various levels. We now move on to a two-factor ANOVA.

9.1.2 Two factor analysis of variance with non-repeated experiment

In **two-factor ANOVA** we assume that there are two factors A and B that have an effect, independently and simultaneously on the final result Y, affecting Factor A has a levels, while factor B has b levels. Let us assume that we have only one observation for each combination of the two treatments. Then the following model can be set up

$$y_{ij} = \mu + \alpha_i + \beta_j + \varepsilon_{ij}, \quad i = 1,\ldots a, \quad j = 1,\ldots,b \tag{9.5}$$

where μ is total average, α_i and β_j respectively stand for the effect of A_i and B_j, $\varepsilon_{ij} \sim N(0,\sigma^2)$, independent from each other. We have only data $\{y_{ij}\}$ available, and the test results are as Table 9.3.

Table 9.2 Single factor ANOVA table.

Variance Sources	Degree of Freedom	Sum of Squares	Mean Squares	F test
Variation Between Classes(Factor A)	a-1	$S_A = \sum_{i=1}^{a} n_i(\bar{y}_{i\cdot} - \bar{y}_{\cdot\cdot})^2$	$Q_A = S_A/(a-1)$	$F = Q_A/Q_e$
Within Class Variance(Error)	N-a	$S_e = \sum_{i=1}^{a}\sum_{j=1}^{n_i} (y_{ij} - \bar{y}_{i\cdot})^2$	$Q_e = S_e/(N-a)$	
Total Sum	N-1	$S_T = \sum_{i}\sum_{j} (y_{ij} - \bar{y}_{\cdot\cdot})^2$		

Table 9.3 Two-factor ANOVA with non-repeated experiment, data structure.

A \ B	B_1	$\cdots$	B_j	$\cdots$	B_b	Average
A_1	y_{11}	$\cdots$	y_{1j}	$\cdots$	y_{1b}	$\bar{y}_{1\cdot}$
$\vdots$		$\cdots\cdots$		$\vdots$		
A_i	y_{i1}	$\cdots$	y_{ij}	$\cdots$	y_{ib}	$\bar{y}_{i\cdot}$
$\vdots$		$\cdots\cdots$		$\vdots$		
A_a	y_{a1}	$\cdots$	y_{aj}	$\cdots$	y_{ab}	$\bar{y}_{a\cdot}$
Average	$\bar{y}_{\cdot 1}$	$\cdots$	$\bar{y}_{\cdot j}$	$\cdots$	$\bar{y}_{\cdot b}$	$\bar{y}_{\cdot\cdot}$

We transform the ANOVA model into common linear regression model. We use the following notations:

$$Y' = (y_{11},\ldots,y_{1b},y_{21},\ldots,y_{2b},\ldots,y_{a1},\ldots,y_{ab})$$

$$\varepsilon' = (\varepsilon_{11},\ldots,\varepsilon_{1b},\varepsilon_{21},\ldots,\varepsilon_{2b},\ldots,\varepsilon_{a1},\ldots,\varepsilon_{ab})$$

$$\gamma' = (\mu,\alpha_1,\ldots,\alpha_a,\beta_1,\ldots\beta_b)$$

$$X = \begin{pmatrix} 1 & 1 & 0 & \cdots & 0 & I \\ 1 & 0 & 1 & \cdots & 0 & I \\ \cdots & \cdots & \cdots & \ddots & \cdots & \cdots \\ 1 & 0 & 0 & \cdots & 1 & I \end{pmatrix}$$

where $\mathbf{1}$ is the vector consisting of 1 amounting to b, I is bth order unit matrix, X is $[ab \times (a+b+1)]$ matrix, then model (9.5) could be transformed into

$$Y = X\gamma + \varepsilon$$

where $\varepsilon \sim N(0,\sigma^2 I_N)$, $N = ab$

We can make a parameter estimation by the regression analysis method. Here the rank of X is $a+b-1$, but the unknown parameters amount to $a+b+1$. Therefore, the following two constraint conditions are required,

$$\sum_i \alpha_i = 0, \quad \sum_j \beta_j = 0$$

The normal equation set of regression model $X'X'\hat{\gamma} = X'Y$ are

$$\begin{cases} ab\mu + b\sum_i \alpha_i + a\sum_j \beta_j = y_{..} \\ b\mu + b\alpha_i + \sum_j \beta_j = y_{i.}, \quad i = 1,\ldots,a \\ a\mu + \sum_i \alpha_i + a\beta_j = y_{.j}, \quad j = 1,\ldots,b \end{cases}$$

Adding the constraint conditions, the normal equations become:

$$\begin{cases} ab\mu = y_{..} \\ a\mu + b\alpha_i = y_{i.}, \quad i = 1,\ldots,a \\ a\mu + a\beta_j = y_{.j}, \quad j = 1,\ldots,b \end{cases}$$

Then solving them we get LSE:

$$\hat{\mu} = \frac{1}{ab}y_{..} = \bar{y}_{..}$$

$$\hat{\alpha}_i = \frac{1}{b}y_{i.} - \hat{\mu} = \bar{y}_{i.} - \bar{y}_{..}, \quad i = 1,\ldots,a$$

$$\hat{\beta}_j = \frac{1}{a}y_{.j} - \hat{\mu} = \bar{y}_{.j} - \bar{y}_{..}, \quad j = 1,\ldots,b$$

Now there are two hypotheses to be tested. First we have the hypothesis of testing whether the effects of factor A at different levels are different. For this the Null Hypothesis is:

$$H_{01} : \alpha_1 = a_2 = \cdots = \alpha_a$$

Second, test to see whether b effects of factor B are different. For this the null hypothesis is:

$$H_{02} : \beta_1 = \beta_2 = \cdots = \beta_b$$

Let us deduce test statistics for H_{01} and H_{02}. Decompose total error sum of squares of regression model

$$S_T = \sum_{i=1}^{a}\sum_{j=1}^{b}(y_{ij} - \bar{y}..)^2 = \sum_{i=1}^{a}\sum_{j=1}^{b}[(y_{ij} - \bar{y}_{i}. - \bar{y}._{j} + \bar{y}..) + (\bar{y}_{i}. - \bar{y}..) + (\bar{y}._{j} - \bar{y}..)]^2$$

$$= \sum_{i=1}^{a}\sum_{j=1}^{b}(y_{ij} - \bar{y}_{i}. - \bar{y}._{j} + \bar{y}..)^2 + b\sum_{i=1}^{a}(\bar{y}_{i}. - \bar{y}..)^2 + a\sum_{j=1}^{b}(\bar{y}._{j} - \bar{y}..)^2 = S_e + S_A + S_B$$

We easily derive the following results:

$$E(S_A) = (a-1)\sigma^2 + b\sum_{i=1}^{a}\alpha_i^2$$

$$E(S_B) = (b-1)\sigma^2 + a\sum_{j=1}^{b}\beta_j^2$$

$$E(S_e) = (a-1)(b-1)\sigma^2$$

Hence we choose statistics

$$F_A = \frac{S_A/(a-1)}{S_e/(a-1)(b-1)}$$

$$F_B = \frac{S_B/(b-1)}{S_e/(a-1)(b-1)}$$

Under the null hypothesis H_{01}, F_A has a central F-distribution with $(a-1)$, $(a-1)(b-1)$ degrees of freedom with mean 1, and hence F_A statistic can be used to test the null hypothesis H_{01}. Similarly F_B, under the null hypothesis, has a central F-distribution with $(b-1)$ only, here $(a-1)(b-1)$ degrees of freedom with mean 1, and hence F_B statistic can be used to test the null hypothesis H_{02}.

We can deduce the distributions of F_A and F_B. When hypotheses H_{01} and H_{02} are true

$$\sum_{i=1}^{a}\sum_{j=1}^{b}(y_{ij} - \mu)^2 = S_A + S_B + S_e + ab(\bar{y}.. - \mu)^2$$

They all belong to the class of nonnegative definite quadratic forms. Their ranks are respectively $a-1$, $b-1$, $(a-1)(b-1)$, and 1. The decomposition equation of the ranks is

$$ab = (a-1) + (b-1) + (a-1)(b-1) + 1$$

The last number 1 may be transferred to the left hand side to reflect the degrees of freedom of the total corrected sum of squares.

When hypotheses H_{01} and H_{02} hold simultaneously, S_A/σ^2, S_B/σ^2, S_e/σ^2 are independent random variables, with $\chi^2(a-1)$, $\chi^2(b-1)$, $\chi^2((a-1)(b-1))$ distributions. Therefore, the statistics F_A, and F_B have the following distributions: $F_A \sim F(a-1,(a-1)(b-1))$, $F_B \sim F(b-1,(a-1)(b-1))$.
The testing procedures are depicted in the standard ANOVA table as below Table 9.4.

9.1.3   Two factor analysis of variance with repeated experiment

It is often doubted that **interaction between two factors** could exist. One then has to make a test with repeated observations, i.e., use multiple replications of each combination of the two factors A and B. Designate γ_{ij} as the interaction effect of level A_i and B_j, then we obtain the ANOVA model

$$y_{ijk} = \mu + \alpha_i + \beta_i + \gamma_{ij} + \varepsilon_{ijk}$$
$$i = 1,\ldots,a, \quad j = 1,\ldots,b, \quad k = 1,\ldots,c$$

Here level combinations A_i and B_j are observed or replicated c times, and the kth time observed value is y_{ijk}. We assume the same number of replications for each treatment pair. The meanings of μ, α_i, β_j are the same as the last paragraph. Random error $\varepsilon_{ijk} \sim N(0,\sigma^2)$, and all are independent of each other. The data structure is as follows (Table 9.5).

Table 9.4   Two-factor ANOVA table for non-repeated experiment.

Variance Sources	Degree of Freedom	Sum of Squares	Mean Squares	Value of F
Factor A	$a-1$	$S_A = b\sum_{i=1}^{a}(\bar{y}_{i\cdot} - \bar{y}_{\cdot\cdot})^2$	$Q_A = S_A/(a-1)$	$F_A = \dfrac{Q_A}{Q_e}$
Factor B	$b-1$	$S_B = a\sum_{j=1}^{b}(\bar{y}_{\cdot j} - \bar{y}_{\cdot\cdot})^2$	$Q_B = S_B/(b-1)$	$F_B = \dfrac{Q_B}{Q_e}$
Error	$(a-1).(b-1)$	$S_e = \sum_{i=1}^{a}\sum_{j=1}^{b}(y_{ij} - \bar{y}_{i\cdot} - \bar{y}_{\cdot j} + \bar{y}_{\cdot\cdot})^2$	$Q_e = S_e/(a-1)(b-1)$	
Total Sum	$ab-1$	$S_T = \sum_{i=1}^{a}\sum_{j=1}^{b}(y_{ij} - \bar{y}_{\cdot\cdot})^2$		

Table 9.5   Two-factor ANOVA with repeated experiment, data structure.

A \ B	B1	...	B_j	...	B_b	Average
A_1	$y_{111},\ldots,y_{11c}$	...	$y_{1j1},\ldots,y_{1jc}$	...	$y_{1b1},\ldots,y_{1bc}$	$\bar{y}_{1\cdot\cdot}$
A_i	$y_{i11},\ldots,y_{i1c}$	...	$y_{ij1},\ldots,y_{ijc}$	...	$y_{ib1},\ldots,y_{ibc}$	$\bar{y}_{i\cdot\cdot}$
A_a	$y_{a11},\ldots,y_{a1c}$	...	$y_{a11},\ldots,y_{a1c}$	...	$y_{ab1},\ldots,y_{abc}$	$\bar{y}_{a\cdot\cdot}$
Average	$\bar{y}_{\cdot 1 \cdot}$	...	$\bar{y}_{\cdot j \cdot}$	...	$\bar{y}_{\cdot b \cdot}$	$\bar{y}_{\cdot\cdot\cdot}$

where

$$\bar{y}_{i}.. = \frac{1}{bc}\sum_{j=1}^{b}\sum_{k=1}^{c} j_{ijk}$$

$$\bar{y}._{j}. = \frac{1}{ac}\sum_{i=1}^{a}\sum_{k=1}^{c} y_{ijk}$$

$$\bar{y}_{ij}. = \frac{1}{c}\sum_{k=1}^{c} y_{ijk}$$

$$\bar{y}... = \frac{1}{abc}\sum_{i=1}^{a}\sum_{j=1}^{b}\sum_{k=1}^{c} j_{iyk}$$

Of course the parameters in this model meet the constraint condition

$$\sum_{i=1}^{a}\alpha_i = \sum_{j=1}^{b}\beta_j = \sum_{i=1}^{a}\gamma_{ij} = \sum_{j=1}^{b}\gamma_{ij} = 0$$

There are independent constraint equations numbering to $a + b + 1$.

In order to transform ANOVA model into regression model form, the parameter can be defined as

$$\delta_{ij} = \mu + \alpha_i + \beta_j + \gamma_{ij}, \quad i = 1,...,a, \quad J = 1,...,b$$

Consider the following four models:

(1) $E(y_{ijk}) = \delta_{ij}$;

(2) $E(y_{ijk}) = \delta._{j}$;

(3) $E(y_{ijk}) = \delta_{i}.$;

(4) $E(y_{ijk}) = \delta$ (irrelevant to i, j)

Let $Y = (y_{111},...,y_{11c};y_{121},...,y_{12c};......;y_{ab1},...,y_{abc})'$. Then different X can be used. If write the four models above in $E(Y) = X\beta$ form, X and β can be expressed, respectively, as follows.

For model (1), $E(y_{ijk}) = \delta_{ij}$,

$$X = \begin{pmatrix} \mathbf{1} & 0 & \cdots & 0 \\ 0 & \mathbf{1} & \cdots & 0 \\ \cdots & \cdots & \ddots & \cdots \\ 0 & 0 & \cdots & \mathbf{1} \end{pmatrix}_{(abc)\times(ab)}$$

$$\beta = (\delta_{11},...,\delta_{1b},\delta_{21},...,\delta_{2b};...;\delta_{a1},...,\delta_{ab})'$$

where $\mathbf{1} = (1,1,...,1)'$. $\mathbf{1}$ appears c times. Then
$$E(Y) = X\beta$$
For model (2), $E(y_{ijk}) = \delta._{j}$,

$$X_0 = \begin{pmatrix} 1 & 0 & \cdots & 0 \\ 0 & 1 & \cdots & 0 \\ \cdots & \cdots & \ddots & \cdots \\ 0 & 0 & \cdots & 1 \end{pmatrix}_{(bc) \times b} , X = \begin{pmatrix} X_0 \\ X_0 \\ \vdots \\ X_0 \end{pmatrix}_{(abc) \times b}$$

$$\beta = (\delta_{.1}, \delta_{.2}, \ldots, \delta_{.b})'$$

For **1**, 1 amounts to c. For X_0, **1** amounts to b. For X, X_0 amounts to a, then
$$E(Y) = X\beta$$
For model (3), $E(y_{ijk}) = \delta_{i..}$,

$$X = \begin{pmatrix} 1 & 0 & \cdots & 0 \\ 0 & 1 & \cdots & 0 \\ \cdots & \cdots & \ddots & \cdots \\ 0 & 0 & \cdots & 1 \end{pmatrix}_{(abc) \times a}$$

$$\beta = (\delta_{1.}, \delta_{2.}, \ldots, \delta_{a.})'$$

For **1**, 1 amounts to bc. For X, **1** amounts to a. Then
$$E(Y) = X\beta$$
For model (4), $E(y_{ijk}) = \delta$,
$$X = \mathbf{1}, \beta = \delta$$
where the number of 1 is abc for **1**, then
$$E(Y) = X\beta$$

For a multiple replication model of two-factor with interaction, we could write the sum of squared deviations and decompose it as follows:

$$\sum_{i=1}^{a}\sum_{j=1}^{b}\sum_{k=1}^{c}(y_{ijk} - \bar{y}...)^2$$
$$= \sum_{i.j.k}[(\bar{y}_{i..} - \bar{y}...) + (\bar{y}_{.j.} - \bar{y}...) + (\bar{y}_{ij.} - \bar{y}_{i..} - \bar{y}_{.j.} - \bar{y}...) + (\bar{y}_{ijk} - \bar{y}_{ij.})]^2$$
$$= \sum_{i}bc(\bar{y}_{i..} - \bar{y}...)^2 + \sum_{j}ac(\bar{y}_{.j.} - \bar{y}...)^2 + \sum_{i.j}c(\bar{y}_{ij.} - \bar{y}_{i..} - \bar{y}_{.j.} - \bar{y}...)^2 + \sum_{i.j.k}(y_{ijk} - \bar{y}_{ij.})^2$$

We have

$$S_T = S_A + S_B + S_{A \times B} + S_e$$

Where the corresponding sum of squares of S_A, S_B, $S_{A \times B}$, S_e are showed in sequence. The decompositions of the degrees of freedom are as follows:

$$f_A = a - 1, \ f_B = b - 1, \ f_{A \times B} = (a-1)(b-1),$$
$$f_e = ab(c-1), \ f_T = abc - 1, \ f_T = f_A + f_B + f_{A \times B} + f_e$$

When interaction is suspected verifying whether the interaction effect exists should be done first. In other words we need to test the hypothesis:

$$H_{0c} : \gamma_{ij} = 0, \ i = 1, \ldots, a; j = 1, \ldots, b$$

Because of the linear constraint between factors, we designate

$$\omega_{ij} = \gamma_{ij} - \overline{\gamma}_{i\cdot} - \overline{\gamma}_{\cdot j} + \overline{\gamma}_{\cdot\cdot}, \quad i = 1,\ldots,a-1; j = 1,\ldots,b-1$$

The original hypothesis is modified as

$$H_{0c} : \omega_{ij} = 0, \quad i = 1,\ldots,a-1; \ j = 1,\ldots,b-1$$

Now the test statistic is

$$F_c = \frac{S_{A\times B}/(a-1)(b-1)}{S_e/(ab(c-1))}$$

When H_{0c} holds, $F_c \sim F((a-1)(b-1),ab(c-1))$. Then using this statistic we are able to test whether interaction effects are zero.

If we wish to test each **factor effect** when interactions are present, we should take into account the effects of other factors. To test the effect of factor A, for example, we could average the effects of B. The original hypothesis for testing the effect of factor A could be designated as

$$H_{0A} : \alpha_1 + \overline{\gamma}_{1\cdot} = \cdots = \alpha_a + \gamma_a.$$

Likewise the hypothesis of testing the effect of factor B could be written as

$$H_{0B} : \beta_1 + \overline{\gamma}_{\cdot 1} = \cdots = \beta_b + \overline{\gamma}_{\cdot b}$$

The test statistics are respectively

$$F_A = \frac{S_A/(a-1)}{S_e/(ab(c-1))}$$

$$F_B = \frac{S_B/(b-1)}{S_e/(ab(c-1))}$$

When H_{0A} holds, $F_A \sim F(a-1,ab(c-1))$. When H_{0B} holds, $F_B \sim F(b-1,ab(c-1))$. Thus we are able to test the significance of the effect of each factor using these statistics and their distributions when the null hypotheses are true.

The detailed ANOVA table is presented in Table 9.6.

It is possible to set up other models of ANOVA analysis. If there are more than two factors, a **multi-factor ANOVA model** could be developed. But as the number of factors and the number of levels at which the factors are used increase, and if interactions are suspected to be present, the total number of observations needs to increase enormously. It is then that one would like to introduce some *a priori* restrictions such as some (higher order) interactions are absent and use **orthogonal designs**. These are specialized as advanced topics that will not be discussed in this book.

Example 9.1   Variance analysis with single factor   We prepared computational programs for ANOVA, programs for single factor model, two-factor model with a single observation for each treatment pair, two-factor model with replications, and multi-factor model. In the example data of single factor model of variance analysis, there are five levels, and for each level the numbers of replications are: 6, 5, 4, 6, 4 respectively (shown in Figure 9.1).

Table 9.6 Two-factor ANOVA table with repeated experiment.

Variance Sources	Degree of Freedom	Sum of Squares	Mean Squares	Value of F
Factor A	$a-1$	$S_A = \sum_{i=1}^{a} bc(\bar{y}_{i..} - \bar{y}_{...})^2$	$Q_A = \dfrac{S_A}{(a-1)}$	$F_A = \dfrac{Q_A}{Q_e}$
Factor B	$b-1$	$S_B = \sum_{j=1}^{b} ac(\bar{y}_{.j.} - \bar{y}_{...})^2$	$Q_B = \dfrac{S_B}{(b-1)}$	$F_B = \dfrac{Q_B}{Q_e}$
Interaction Effects	$(a-1)\cdot(b-1)$	$S_{A\times B} = \sum_{i,j} c(\bar{y}_{ij} - \bar{y}_{i..} - \bar{y}_{.j.} + \bar{y}_{...})^2$	$Q_{A\times B} = \dfrac{S_{A\times B}}{(a-1)(b-1)}$	$F_{A\times B} = \dfrac{Q_{A\times B}}{Q_e}$
Error	$ab(c-1)$	$S_e = \sum_{i,j,k}(y_{ijk} - \bar{y}_{ij.})^2$	$Q_e = \dfrac{S_e}{ab(c-1)}$	
Total sum	$abc-1$	$S_T = \sum_{i,j,k}(y_{ijk} - \bar{y}_{...})^2$		

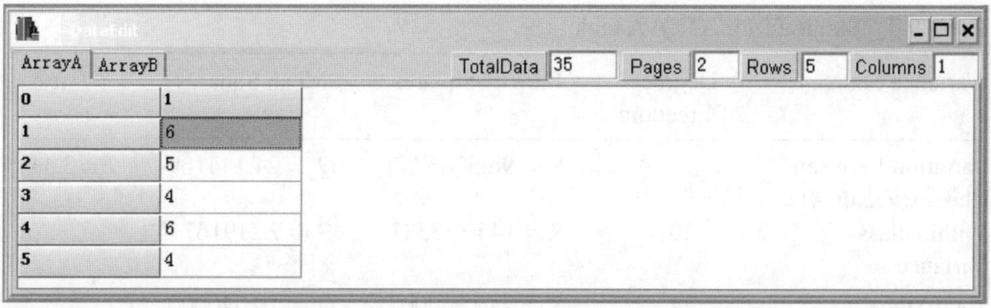

Figure 9.1   The number of replications for each level.

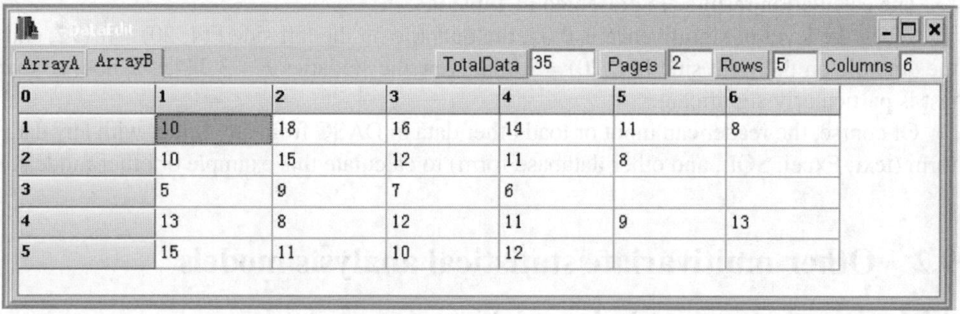

Figure 9.2   The outputs of the replications at each level.

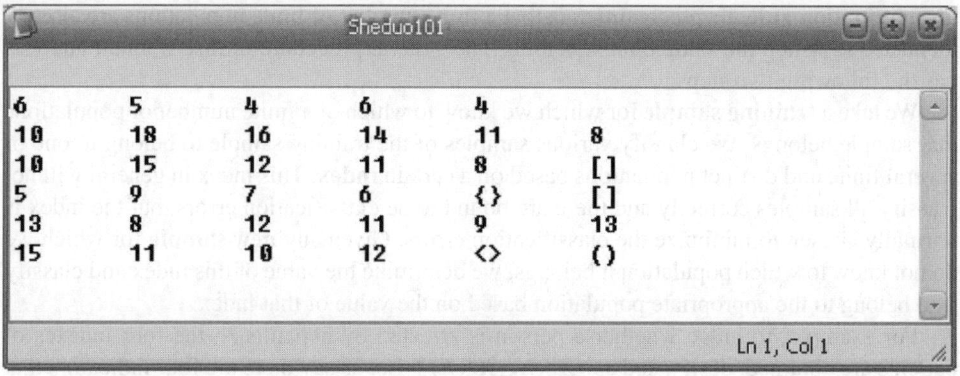

Figure 9.3   The input data of single factor model of variance analysis.

The test results of each level are as in Figure 9.2. We can see the numbers of replications are not equal, and hence it is not a balanced design.

We note that there are some blank spaces in the grid. In order to implement this form, we may input the text of data as Figure 9.3. The first row is the number of replications at each level. The other rows are the results of replication at each level, and using any parentheses ({}, [], (), <>) in the place of blank spaces.

Table 9.7   Single factor ANOVA table.

Variance Sources	Degree of Freedom	Sum of Squares	Mean Squares	F test
Variation Between Classes(Factor A)	4	$S_A = 96.576675$	$Q_A = 24.144169$	$F = 3.3445$
Within class Variance	20	$S_e = 144.383331$	$Q_e = 7.219167$	
Total Sum	24	$S_T = 240.960007$	$Q_T = 10.040000$	

The calculation results are presented in Table 9.7.

When the level of significance is 0.05, the quantile on the left side F(4, 20) = 0.172, and the quantile on the right side F(4, 20) = 2.866. Now the statistics $F = 3.3445 > 2.866$, so the test is particularly significant.

Of course, the reader can input or load other data in DASC from any folder with any data form (text, Excel, SQL, and other database form) to calculate this example or other models.

9.2   Other multivariate statistical analysis models

9.2.1   Discriminate analysis model

Discriminant analysis deals with determining to which population a sample belongs among a pre-specified finite number of populations. It is a method to **classify sample** by **discrimination rule**. Its precondition is that a finite number of finite populations are already identified to which the sample must belong. The general procedure of discriminant analysis has the following two steps.

We take a **training sample** for which we know to which of a finite number of populations that sample belongs. We classify various samples of the training sample to belong to one of several finite and distinct populations based on a certain **index**. This index in general will not classify all samples correctly and there are bound to be classification errors, but the index is normally chosen to minimize the classification errors. Given any **new sample** for which we do not know to which population it belongs, we determine the value of this index and classify it to belong to the appropriate population based on the value of that index.

For example, to judge whether a person is affected by hepatitis A, the four indexes of patients are obtained, designated as $(X_1^0, X_2^0, X_3^0, X_4^0)$. Let us say there are four indicators that tell us whether a patient has hepatitis A or not. For example we may consider his biochemical indexes (icterus index, aminotransferase) and clinical symptoms (vomit, anorexia). Thus there are four variables, designated as (X_1, X_2, X_3, X_4). We should collect n training samples $(X_{1i}, X_{2i}, X_{3i}, X_{4i})$, $i = 1, \ldots, n$ beforehand for which we know whether the patients have hepatitis A or not. Then we calculate discrimination rules according to these training samples to classify them into those having hepatitis A or not. Now let us say we have a new patient and we do not know if he has hepatitis A or not. So we collect these four indicator values and calculate the **discriminating index value**. Based on that index we could classify whether he is affected by hepatitis A.

Judging to which geologic age a rock belongs; judging whether it is going to rain tomorrow; judging whether a company would go bankruptey, to predict whether a credit card applicant would default on his payment schedules, etc., may all be handled by discriminant analysis.

There are mainly three different methods of discriminant analysis. These include (i) discriminant analysis based on some generalized distance concept; (ii) discriminant analysis based on Bayes Loss Function; and (iii) discriminant analysis based on the first principal component as introduced by Fisher.

9.2.1.1   Generalized distance approach

In this approach one is required to compute the **distance between multivariate samples**. The sample is designated to belong to the class that is nearest. The distance usually used is the **Mahalanobis distance**:

$$d^2(X,Y) = (X-Y)' \Sigma_{XY}^{-1} (X-Y)$$

where Σ_{XY} is the sample covariance matrix of X and Y.

9.2.1.2   Bayes loss function approach

This approach is based on minimization of Bayesian loss function. **Bayes discrimination rules** are derived so as to minimize average losses of error of classification or discrimination. Assume that the density functions of populations $G_1,...,G_k$ are $f_i(x), i = 1,...,k$. The discrimination rules are

$$X \in G_1, \quad if \ X \in D_i, i = 1,...,k$$

Then the probability of error of classifying a sample actually from G_i to G_j is

$$P_{ij} = \int_{D_i} f_i(x)dx$$

If the prior distribution of each population is $q_1,..., q_k$ (we always have $q_1 + \cdots + q_k = 1$), then the total average loss due to errors of classification/ discrimination is

$$ECM = \sum_{i=1}^{k} q_i \sum_{j=1}^{k} C_{ij} P_{ij}$$

C_{ij} is the loss function of wrongly classifying a sample from G_i to G_j, and of course $C_{ii} = 0$. Our goal is to find discriminant regions D_i that minimize the expected losses of errors of discrimination/classification. It can be shown through simple algebra that the Bayes solution of discriminant function is

$$D_i = \{x | h_i(x) < h_j(x), j \neq i, j = 1,...,k\}$$

where

$$h_i(x) = \sum_{j=1}^{k} q_i f_j(x) C_{ij}, \quad i = 1,...,k$$

To simplify the problem, we may assume that

$$C_{ij} = 1, \text{ if } i \neq j; \ C_{ij} = 0, \text{ if } i = j$$

$$q_i = \frac{1}{k}, i = 1,\ldots,k$$

In the state of the two populations, assume that

$$h_1(x) = q_2 p_2(x) C_{12}$$
$$h_2(x) = q_1 p_1(x) C_{21}$$

Then the discrimination rules are

$$\begin{cases} x \in G_1, & \text{if } h_1(x) < h_2(x) \\ x \in G_2, & \text{if } h_1(x) > h_2(x) \end{cases}$$

9.2.1.3   Fisher's principal component approach

There were two basic principles behind **Fisher discrimination**. First is the idea of **reduction of dimension**, i.e., to reduce the information content of multivariate data to one dimension. Second, one sought to choose the linear function of all the multivariate data that would maximize the discriminatory power of that index. Under the assumption that different populations are characterized by different multivariate Normal distributions with varying means and a constant variance, we determined the linear function of the multivariate data that minimizes the expected error of wrong classification or that discriminates the populations best. Alternately, we chose the linear function of the observations which **makes dispersion among samples as large as possible** for best possible classification. The answer obtained was the classification based on the first **principal component**, a concept we have discussed in Chapter 2. We shall now describe this method in detail.

Assume that there are k populations $G_i \in R^p$, $i = 1,\ldots,k$. From G_i we collect n_i groups of p-dimensional data:

$$G_i : x_1^{(i)},\ldots,x_{n_i}^{(i)}, i = 1,\ldots,k$$

Let α be an arbitrary p-dimensional vector, and $u(x) = \alpha'x$ is the projection of x in direction α, then the data after projection are

$$G_i : a'x_1^{(i)},\ldots,a'x_{n_i}^{(i)}, i = 1,\ldots,k$$

It is just the data of univariate ANOVA method, whose variation between classes is

$$S_{RS} = \sum_{i=1}^{k} n_i (a'\overline{x}^{(i)} - a'\overline{x})^2$$

The within class or intraclass variance is

$$S_{ES} = \sum_{i=1}^{k} \sum_{j=1}^{n_i} (a'x_j^{(i)} - a'\overline{x}^{(i)})^2$$

To make this projection as dispersed as possible one considers to maximize the following statistic

$$F_o = \frac{S_{RS}}{S_{ES}}$$

Equivalently it is to let

$$F = \frac{S_{RS}/(k-1)}{S_{ES}/(n-k)}$$

maximum. Notice that under the assumption of Normality of errors, statistic F has F distribution whose degrees of freedom are $(k-1, n-k)$.

Now we discuss which direction α can make statistic F maximum. S_{RS} and S_{ES} are both quadratic, which could be expressed as

$$S_{RS} = a'Ba, \quad B = \sum_{i=1}^{k} n_i (\overline{x}^{(i)} - \overline{x})(\overline{x}^{(i)} - \overline{x})'$$

$$S_{ES} = a'Ea, \quad E = \sum_{i=1}^{k} \sum_{j=1}^{n_i} (x_j^{(i)} - \overline{x}^{(i)})(x_j^{(i)} - \overline{x}^{(i)})'$$

In addition, the selection of direction α can be always in terms of a unit vector in that direction. Then we must have:

$$\max F = \max_{\|a\|=1} \frac{a'Ba}{a'Ea}$$

We have been familiar with this form in the section on principal component regression, whose solution α is the corresponding characteristic vector of the maximum characteristic root of the characteristic equation

$$|B - \lambda E| = 0$$

Having thus determined α we calculate

$$a'x_1^{(i)}, \ldots, a'x_{n_i}^{(i)}, i = 1, \ldots, k$$

and the mean indexes of all classes:

$$a'\overline{x}^{(i)} = \frac{1}{n_i} \sum_{j=1}^{n_i} a'x_j^{(i)}$$

Now, given the observations on a new sample that needs to be classified into one of the k groups we compute the projection $a'x^{(0)}$ of that sample. Then according to the Fisher distance principle, $x^{(0)}$ is judged to belong to that class which is nearest among all the mean indexes $a'\overline{x}^{(i)}$, $i = 1, \ldots, k$ to $a'x^{(0)}$.

It is also possible to perform discriminant analysis with regression model. For the discriminant problem with just two populations one can use a linear probability function model with Binomial dependent variable using Probit or Logit regression discussed in Chapter 4.

Having estimated the logit regression we can put the sample information for the sample to be classified in the regression equation. We then obtain the estimated probabilities that the sample belongs to either of the two populations. We classify the sample to that group which carries a higher probability.

For the discriminant analysis problem with more than two populations, we can use the **evaluation model** introduced by the principal author (Tong, 1993). The evaluation model is a **prescription regression model** with unknown dependent variable, so it is a kind of **generalized linear model** and is suitable to describe discriminant analysis for several categories.

The detailed model and the associated method of calculation could be seen in Chapter 4, Section 4.4, and the Electronic References for Chapter 4, Section 4. It is similar to Fisher's projection idea. We estimate the regression coefficients $\beta_1,...,\beta_p$ by sample in evaluation model, and calculate the evaluated values $y_1,..., y_k$. Then for given point $x^{(0)}$, we compute

$$y^{(0)} = \beta_1 x_1^{(0)} + \cdots + \beta_p x_p^{(0)}$$

Finally, the given point is judged to belong to the category that is nearest among $y_1,..., y_k$ to $y^{(0)}$.

Example 9.2   Discrimination by evaluation model for integrated circuit enterprises
The DASC software for this book includes discriminant analysis, which includes Stepwise discriminant analysis, Fisher discriminant analysis, Logit discriminant analysis and Discriminant analysis by evaluation model. There are theoretical descriptions for these discrimination methods in DASC.

In the example of discriminant analysis by evaluation model, there are three Chinese companies of integrated circuit. They are Zongyi Gufen company, Shanghai Beiling company, and Huatian Keji company. They are a typical IC design enterprise, IC manufacture enterprise, and IC encapsulation enterprise respectively, and all are listed companies. We consider six indexes of these companies: Main business income $(x_{(1)})$, Integrated circuit service $(x_{(2)})$, Total property amounts $(x_{(3)})$, Intangible asset $(x_{(4)})$, Net amount of fixed asset $(x_{(5)})$, Running cost $(x_{(6)})$. For each company with each index, there are records for 10 years from 2000 to 2009. The units of these records are ten million Yuan (RMB). The data of the example are presented in Table 9.8.

Computation of the results leading to Figure 9.4 can be performed by clicking DASC $\rightarrow$ Regression $\rightarrow$ Biased/Compress Regression $\rightarrow$Evaluation Model with LSE. Regression coefficients β_i namely weighted coefficients are 0.0000, 0.0361, 0.0000, 0.0000, 0.0000, 0.9639. Dependent variables y_i namely evaluation scores are 15.0826, 8.9066, 5.4208.

Meanwhile, there are six numbers which are the data of a company A. The numbers are input from the last six data in block A: 9.3640, 1.9508, 7.2756, 0.3394, 2.7287, 0.3469. Now we hope to judge which type of enterprise company A belongs to. We can use the evaluation model and calculate the predicted value as 0.404858 by these six numbers. Because 0.404858 is nearest to 5.4208, we judge that company A is an encapsulation enterprise. In fact, these numbers are from company Sanjia Keji in 2002. Sanjia Keji is an encapsulation enterprise indeed.

More detailed contents for the evaluation model can be found in Section 1, Chapter 5 of the Electronic References.

Table 9.8   Data of achievement of three integrated circuit companies of China.

	Year	$x_{(1)}$	$x_{(2)}$	$x_{(3)}$	$x_{(4)}$	$x_{(5)}$	$x_{(6)}$
y_1	2009	51.6469	16.8115	70.8589	2.86179	21.1019	2.59754
	2008	58.8073	13.3359	26.2462	1.51367	5.25764	1.89136
	2007	73.4608	10.1021	18.6210	0.936951	2.46856	1.19119
	2006	63.3821	8.76040	19.4263	0.422554	2.13562	1.02232
	2005	57.3267	8.04391	18.6803	0.320257	2.53501	1.04519
	2004	50.6306	7.12283	18.7129	0.338971	2.15152	1.10509
	2003	38.7617	6.92936	23.7840	0.519277	2.16927	1.16604
	2002	27.2784	3.57022	15.4572	0.384646	1.41891	0.849435
	2001	29.7125	2.80141	9.43784	0.280793	1.01636	0.536273
	2000	37.5217	2.19815	5.69815	0.191182	0.71197	0.304106
y_2	2009	51.2542	30.6272	109.981	1.07926	8.31028	6.69484
	2008	51.2269	33.5266	131.861	1.29138	16.3014	7.07259
	2007	46.3763	24.6160	109.204	1.12459	15.1837	4.57327
	2006	42.0744	27.2683	128.328	1.49157	8.55996	4.76752
	2005	63.8135	18.9605	60.7225	0.742282	4.06498	1.42852
	2004	73.7232	15.7643	44.7199	0.557939	2.63291	1.41000
	2003	75.6927	19.5650	53.1659	0.689079	3.28095	1.98202
	2002	76.2993	24.3689	51.0926	0.898587	10.0459	3.26349
	2001	78.3608	34.4787	67.7819	1.30376	13.0531	4.04949
	2000	79.2385	34.8649	64.2897	1.36959	12.7878	3.86273
y_3	2009	77.7437	77.7437	131.151	4.91084	51.9794	8.87904
	2008	74.2498	74.2498	115.261	4.83473	49.0154	7.36162
	2007	68.2079	68.2080	118.602	2.10749	39.7272	6.20045
	2006	51.2695	51.2695	63.4600	1.57480	32.6750	3.77581
	2005	31.3816	31.3817	42.0480	1.60666	23.8707	2.96329
	2004	21.4625	21.4626	30.7161	1.57801	17.6682	2.07155
	2003	16.3539	16.3539	22.3983	0.789762	14.1800	1.59292
	2002	12.4612	12.4612	16.3330	0.575899	11.3804	1.25112
	2001	9.49509	9.49509	11.9101	0.419949	9.13358	1.00098
	2000	7.23500	7.23500	8.68492	0.306229	7.33034	0.813412

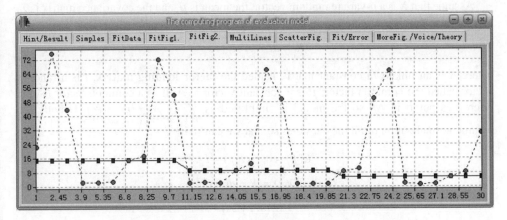

Figure 9.4   Evaluation scores with three IC companies.

9.2.2   Factor analysis model

The **Factor Analysis Model** was first used for statistical analysis in the field of psychology or psychometrics. It is a method designed to **seek fewer factors behind more indexes of samples**. So it is a method to **reduce dimensions**. We present an example from educational measurement. For a period of time the university entrance examination included seven subjects: politics, Chinese, foreign language, mathematics, physics, chemistry, and biology. The grade score X is a seven-dimensional random vector $X = (x_1, x_2, \ldots, x_7)'$, $p = 7$. Generally, we deem that politics, Chinese and foreign language reflect the arts capability of students, while mathematics, physics, chemistry, and biology reflect their science capability. In other words, the seven subjects are mainly determined by two factors, and then we can build a mathematical model

$$\underset{7\times1}{X} = \underset{7\times1}{\mu} + \underset{7\times2}{\Lambda}\,\underset{2\times1}{f} + \underset{7\times1}{\varepsilon}$$

In the model, X is known, and μ and Λ are unknown. f is not only unknown, but it is also not measured. Just assume that f_1 is the arts capability, and f_2 is the science capability. ε is the random error item. First we have to ask whether it is reasonable to assume such a model. Why are there two factors, and not three (or all seven)? Second, we need to estimate μ, Λ and other model parameters.

Let's turn to arbitrage pricing theory. Assume that there are three stocks ($p = 3$). Their yields are affected by two common factors ($k=2$). They may be the regional effect or industry effect. Then we have the model

$$\underset{p\times1}{X} = \underset{p\times1}{\mu} + \underset{p\times k}{\Lambda}\,\underset{k\times1}{f} + \underset{p\times1}{\varepsilon}$$

This is the general form of factor analysis model. Here X is observable, and $\mu, \Lambda, f, \varepsilon$ are unobservable. Comparing this with the following general multiple linear regression model we note that the main difference lies in the **explanatory variables** being unobservable that are linearly related to the observable X.

$$\underset{p\times1}{Y} = \underset{p\times1}{\beta_0} + \underset{p\times k}{X}\,\underset{k\times1}{\beta} + \underset{p\times1}{\varepsilon}$$

where Y and X are known, and β is to be estimated.

Now we give the general form of the factor analysis model.

Assume that X is a p-variate random vector, the mean is μ, and the covariance matrix is Σ. Hypothesize that X is affected by k factors. The model is

$$\underset{p\times1}{X} = \underset{p\times1}{\mu} + \underset{p\times k}{\Lambda}\,\underset{k\times1}{f} + \underset{p\times1}{\varepsilon}$$

where Λ is an unknown constant matrix named the **factor loading matrix**; f is a random vector called the common factor; μ is a constant vector as well as a common factor (Some references put μ in Λf, so the model is simplified as $\underset{p\times1}{X} = \underset{p\times(k+1)}{\Lambda}\,\underset{(k+1)\times1}{f} + \underset{p\times1}{\varepsilon}$). Usually we assume normalization of all the variables so that we can write

$$E(f) = 0, \quad D(f) = I_k$$

$$E(\varepsilon) = 0, \quad D(\varepsilon) = \Psi = diag(\varphi_1^2, \ldots, \varphi_p^2)$$

$$Cov(f, \varepsilon) = 0$$

Under the assumptions above it follows that

$$E(X) = \mu$$
$$D(X) = \Lambda\Lambda' + \Psi = \Sigma$$

The latter equation can be rewritten as:

$$\sigma_{ii} = \sum_{j=1}^{k} \lambda_{ij}^2 + \varphi_i^2 = h_i^2 + \varphi_i^2, i = 1, \ldots, p$$

where the newly cited variables are the elements of the corresponding matrices in the equation above.

$$h_i^2 = \sum_{j=1}^{k} \lambda_{ij}^2$$

reflects the influence of **common factors** on X_i, namely **communality variance**.

The tasks before us are mainly: (1) Test whether the specification of the model is reasonable, especially that there are only k common factors; (2) Estimate the parameter μ and Σ from the sample X, and further estimate Λ and Ψ.

The model has following characteristics:

(1) The model is not affected by the dimension of variable X. If we make a transformation $Y = CX$, $C = diag(C_1, \ldots, C_p)$, then

$$Y = CX = C\mu + C\Lambda f' + C\varepsilon$$
$$E(Y) = C\mu, D(Y) = C\Lambda\Lambda'C' + C\Psi C' = C\Sigma C'$$

Of course $C' = C$. Thus substituting $C\mu$ for μ, $C\Lambda$ for Λ, $C'\Sigma C$ for Σ, and $C'\psi C$ for ψ, we get the original model form.

(2) The factor loading is not unique. If Γ is a arbitrary $k \times k$ orthogonal matrix, the model can also be written as

$$X = \mu + \Lambda\Gamma\Gamma' f + \varepsilon$$

Here regarding $\Gamma' f$ as a common factor, the loading matrix becomes $\Lambda\Gamma$. Equally

$$E(\Gamma' f) = 0, \ D(\Gamma' f) = I_k$$
$$Cov(\Gamma' f, \varepsilon) = \Gamma' Cov(f, \varepsilon) = 0$$
$$(\Lambda\Gamma)(\Lambda\Gamma)' + \Psi = \Lambda\Lambda' + \Psi = \Sigma$$

Because the factor loading is not unique under orthogonal transformation, we can make an orthogonal rotation for the factor loading matrix. Of course the common factor f has made an orthogonal rotation at the same time, so that the common factor obtains a new explanation or interpretation. As will be explained later in this section we can choose an appropriate orthogonal transformation until we get a set of factors that have a meaning as a common factor.

Now we move on to the issue of the estimation of the model parameters. We have, let us say, n observations of a p-variate vector variable X, $X^{(1)}, \ldots, X^{(n)}$. For example, using the entrance examination we may have n pieces to university entrance examination papers, and each piece consists of the marks on seven subjects. Using the other example of stock prices observed yields of three stocks over n periods, and so on. Then we derive the following sample estimates of the p-variate mean μ and an estimate the $p \times p$ variance covariance matrix Σ:

$$\underset{p \times 1}{\hat{\mu}} = \frac{1}{n}\sum_{i=1}^{n} X^{(i)}$$

$$\underset{p \times p}{\hat{\Sigma}} = \frac{1}{n-1}\sum_{i=1}^{n}(X^{(i)} - \hat{\mu})(X^{(i)} - \hat{\mu})'$$

The question now is how to estimate Λ and Ψ from the relation equation $\hat{\Sigma} = \Lambda\Lambda' + \Psi$

We should estimate Ψ first. Since Ψ is a diagonal matrix.

We can estimate Ψ as follows:

$$\hat{\Psi} = diag(\hat{\varphi}_1^2, \ldots, \hat{\varphi}_p^2)$$

$$\hat{\varphi}_i^2 = \frac{1}{\sigma_{ii}}, \quad \hat{\Sigma}^{-1} = (\sigma_{ij})$$

Thus, the principal diagonal element of $\hat{\Psi}$ is the reciprocal of the principal diagonal element of $\hat{\Sigma}^{-1}$. With $\hat{\Psi}, \hat{\Sigma}$, now known, and with the relation $\Sigma - \Psi = \Lambda\Lambda'$, we are able to estimate Λ. Because $\Lambda\Lambda'$ is a nonnegative definite matrix and the rank is k, according to basic knowledge of linear algebra, it could be transformed by orthogonal matrix Γ:

$$\Gamma'(\Sigma - \Psi)\Gamma = diag(\lambda_1, \ldots, \lambda_k, 0, \ldots, 0) = \Phi$$

Assume that Γ_1 is the first k series of Γ, $\Phi_1 = diag(\lambda_1, \ldots, \lambda_k)$, then

$$\Lambda\Lambda' = \Sigma - \Psi = \Gamma\Phi\Gamma' = \Gamma_1\Phi_1\Gamma_1' = (\Gamma_1\Phi_1^{\frac{1}{2}})(\Gamma_1\Phi_1^{\frac{1}{2}})'$$

We have the estimation

$$\hat{\Lambda} = \Gamma_1\Phi_1^{\frac{1}{2}}$$

We can see that orthogonal transformation of $\Sigma - \Psi$ may not only estimate the parameter Λ but also know the rationality of the model, because the nonzero characteristic roots of $\Sigma - \Psi$ only amount to k. Certainly, if there is any root that is close to 0 in nonzero characteristic roots $\lambda_1, \ldots, \lambda_k$, we may delete it also.

In actual computation we may substitute correlation matrix R for the covariance matrix Σ in the above-mentioned procedure, depending on practical considerations. Using DASC software we can calculate and present all this without much difficulty.

In arbitrage pricing theory, the number p of inspection stocks could be more, such as 5 to 10. The number of common factors could be 2 to 3. The number n of observations may be much more, e.g. 20 to 100. The computation is easy. The essence of factor analysis is to reduce dimensions, it is trying to find only k factors for explaining most of the variation in the p-variate data ($k < p$). We have mentioned already that the factor loading matrix is not unique. One can obtain one factor loading matrix from another through a factor rotation. If model $X = \mu + \Lambda f + \varepsilon$ holds, so does model $X = \mu + (\Lambda\Gamma)(\Gamma'f) + \varepsilon$, (with $\Gamma\Gamma' = I$) and all the statistical parameters of the model are the same. Then we could make orthogonal rotation for factor loading matrix in order to obtain the better actual explanation or interpretation of the new common factor $\Gamma'f$ after rotation.

One persuasive method is **varimax rotation**. Its subjective goal is to make the index contributions from all factors as dispersed as possible after rotation. Let

$$\Lambda^* = \Lambda\Gamma = (\lambda_{ij}^*)$$

$$d_{ij} = \lambda_{ij}^*/h_i$$

$$\bar{d}_j = \frac{1}{p}\sum_{i=1}^{k} d_{ij}^2$$

where $h_i^2 = \sum_{i=1}^{k}\lambda_{ij}^2$ is defined as previously. Dividing λ_{ij}^* by h_i is to eliminate the effect of scale of different factors. The varimax rotation is to choose the orthogonal transformation Γ that makes

$$\Phi = \sum_{j=1}^{k}\sum_{i=1}^{p}(d_{ij}^2 - \bar{d})^2$$

maximum.

The rotation of matrix is on the basis of two-dimensional rotation. The two-dimensional rotation matrix is

$$\Gamma = \begin{pmatrix} \cos\theta & \sin\theta \\ -\sin\theta & \cos\theta \end{pmatrix}$$

There is a computing formula that obtains the rotation angle θ of varimax. For $k > 2$, take 2 of k factors in turn to proceed with the rotation of that plane. We are required to perform such rotations of planes with $\frac{1}{2}k(k-1)$ times. After each rotation, the variance doesn't decrease but increase. Then the rotation matrix Γ of varimax can be obtained. However, generally, with the rotation of three factors a lot of maximization of the variation is achieved.

Example 9.3   *P*-style and *Q*-style factor analysis   The factor analysis aiming at indexes is called ***P*-type factor analysis**, and the factor analysis aiming at samples is named ***Q*-type factor analysis**. The factor analysis considering indexes and samples simultaneously is called the correspondence analysis.

Now we continue to use the data of Table 9.7 in Example 9.1. It contains 30 rows and six columns, and factor analysis is *P*-type. The calculation results are as follows.

Data have been standardized. The correlation matrix R is 6×6 matrix:

1.0000	0.4718	0.4552	0.3927	0.2340	0.4339
0.4718	1.0000	0.7866	0.8455	0.9292	0.8851
0.4552	0.7866	1.0000	0.6664	0.6421	0.9346
0.3927	0.8455	0.6664	1.0000	0.8936	0.7677
0.2340	0.9292	0.6421	0.8936	1.0000	0.7720
0.4339	0.8851	0.9346	0.7677	0.7720	1.0000

The characteristic roots of correlation matrix are:

0.6242,	0.3410,	−0.0308,	0.0708,	−0.0383,	4.4025

The eigenvectors (column vectors) are:

0.7766	0.5286	0.1416	−0.0191	0.2050	0.2345
−0.0791	0.1500	−0.3193	−0.6679	−0.4577	0.4623
0.2735	−0.5703	0.5167	0.1380	−0.3804	0.4115
−0.2206	0.3425	−0.2472	0.7137	−0.2927	0.4218
−0.5041	0.2297	0.5423	−0.1517	0.4384	0.4287
0.1140	−0.4503	−0.5058	0.0457	0.5709	0.4476

The arranged characteristic roots, from largest to the smallest are:

4.4025	0.6242	0.3410	0.0708	−0.0308	−0.0383

Print the arranged eigenvectors in the same order as above (column vectors)

0.2345	0.7766	0.5286	−0.0191	0.1416	0.2050
0.4623	−0.0791	0.1500	−0.6679	−0.3193	−0.4577
0.4115	0.2735	−0.5703	0.1380	0.5167	−0.3804
0.4218	−0.2206	0.3425	0.7137	−0.2472	−0.2927
0.4287	−0.5041	0.2297	−0.1517	0.5423	0.4384
0.4476	0.1140	−0.4503	0.0457	−0.5058	0.5709

According to the parameter in step 5 of process parameters, three characteristic roots will be left. They are 4.4025, 0.6242, 0.3410. The cumulative contribution rate of the left three characteristic roots is 0.97461. Print the left eigenvectors (row vectors)

0.2345	0.4623	0.4115	0.4218	0.4287	0.4476
0.7766	−0.0791	0.2735	−0.2206	−0.5041	0.1140
0.5286	0.1500	−0.5703	0.3425	0.2297	−0.4503

Print the load matrix Λ of factors (row vector)

0.4920	0.9699	0.8633	0.8850	0.8995	0.9391
0.6136	−0.0625	0.2161	−0.1743	−0.3983	0.0901
0.3087	0.0876	−0.3330	0.2000	0.1342	−0.2630

Print the standardized (module of each column vector is 1) load matrix of factors Λ:

0.5824	0.9939	0.9086	0.9579	0.9060	0.9589
0.7262	−0.0640	0.2274	−0.1886	−0.4012	0.0919
0.3653	0.0897	−0.3504	0.2165	0.1351	−0.2685

Load variance of initial factors VA = 0.330136.

Q-type factor analysis will use the transpose matrix of Table 9.7 in Example 9.1. It contains six rows and 30 columns. The computation process and results are omitted here, and are easily performed by DASC.

9.2.3   Principal component analysis and multidimensional scaling method

To understand the relation between regression and **principal component analysis**, there is nothing better than principal component regression and latent root regression. These have been introduced in Chapter 2. This section is designed mainly to introduce principal component analysis.

Principal component analysis is a method for seeking some **combination of variables**, and tries to use fewer variables to explain most of the variation of all the variables in the sample. Assume a p-variate variable $X = (X_1,\ldots,X_p)'$, e.g. p economic indexes. We feel that the correlation between the variables is too high, and the number of variables is too large. We would like to combine these variables through linear transformations and reduce the number of variables. This can be realized by principal component transformation.

Assume that the index variable $X = (X_1,\ldots,X_p)'$, and $\mu = E(X)$. Consider the linear transformation of $l_i(i = 1,\ldots, p)$ in p directions.

$$Y_i = l_i' X, \quad i=1,\ldots,p$$

Then $Y_i(i = 1,\ldots,p)$ is univariate, and

$$Var(Y_i) = l_i' \Sigma l_i$$

$$Cov(Y_i,Y_j) = l_i' \Sigma l_j \quad i,j = 1,2,\ldots,p$$

Of course l_i has one direction, and a unit vector in that direction has a length equal to 1. Let us limit to such unit vectors. Then

$$l_i' l_i = 1, \quad i=1,\ldots,p$$

With this constraint, we hope it is best to substitute one variable Y_1 for p variables $X_1,\ldots,X_p$, so that the variance of Y_1 is enough to explain the variance of the original p variables. Even if it is not enough to explain most of the variation of the original variables it can at least make the variance of Y_1 maximum. Namely

$$Var(Y_1) = \max_{l_1' l_1 = 1} l_1' \Sigma l_1$$

Now consider another direction l_2 orthogonal to the direction of l_1, simultaneously, select a variable combination Y_2 in this second direction to maximize the variance of Y_2

$$Var(Y_2) = \max_{\substack{l_2' l_2 = 1 \\ l_2' l_1 = 0}} l_2' \Sigma l_2$$

Keep doing this until p new combinations are selected at most. The first variable combination Y_1 is called first principal component, and the second variable combination Y_2 is named second principal component, etc. Note that $l_i' l_i = 1$ and $l_i' l_j = 0$ for $i \neq j, j = 1,\ldots,p$.

We have deduced these directions $l_i(i = 1,\ldots,p)$ mathematically in Chapter 2. These are just the eigenvector of covariance matrix Σ, and the variance of these transformed variables are just the latent roots of Σ, which are

$$|\lambda_i I - \Sigma| = 0, \quad i = 1,\ldots, p, \quad \lambda_1 \geq \lambda_2 \geq \cdots \geq \lambda_p$$
$$Var(Y_1) = \lambda_1, Var(Y_2) = \lambda_2,\ldots, Var(Y_p) = \lambda_p$$

Since the objective is to decrease the number of variables, we usually adopt the principal components amounting to $m(m < p)$, and make the explanation of the m principal components to variances reach 70%–80%. Usually we call

$$\lambda_j \bigg/ \sum_{i=1}^{p} \lambda_i$$

the **contribution rate of principal components** Y_j. Choose m to make

$$\sum_{j=1}^{m} (\lambda_j / \sum_{i=1}^{p} \lambda_i) > 0.7 \sim 0.8$$

We present next the method of computing these principal components given a sample. Suppose we have n observations on p-variate index variable. The data matrix is

$$\underset{n \times p}{X} = \begin{pmatrix} x_{11} & x_{12} & \cdots & x_{1p} \\ x_{21} & x_{22} & \cdots & x_{2p} \\ \cdots & \cdots & \ddots & \cdots \\ x_{n1} & x_{n2} & \cdots & x_{np} \end{pmatrix}$$

The sample covariance matrix is:

$$S = \frac{1}{n-1} \sum_{j=1}^{n} (X^{(k)} - \bar{X})(X^{(k)} - \bar{X})'$$

where $X^{(k)}$ is the k th row vector in X, and $\bar{X}$ is the average vector of X. The elements of S is

$$S_{ij} = \frac{1}{n-1} \sum_{k=1}^{n} (X_k^{(i)} - \bar{X}^{(i)})(X_k^{(j)} - \bar{X}^{(j)})$$

where $X_k^{(i)}$ is the kth element of ith column in X, and $\bar{X}^{(i)}$ is the i th element in average vector. The sample correlation matrix is:

$$R = (r_{ij}), \quad r_{ij} = \frac{S_{ij}}{\sqrt{S_{ii}}\sqrt{S_{jj}}}$$

Consider S as the estimator of Σ, or R as the estimator of the population correlation matrix. Then the principal components could be derived.

Now let's look at the relation between the principal components and regression. Take first m principal components $Y_1,\ldots,Y_m$ arbitrarily, regard $Y^* = (Y_1,\ldots Y_m)$ as the independent variable in the regression model, and consider index variable X as the dependent variable in the regression model. We can now write the regression equation:

$$X = Y^* \beta + \varepsilon$$

Or the estimated regression is

$$\hat{X} = Y^* \hat{\beta}$$

Here the regression coefficient β is the $m \times p$ matrix. Then least square estimation of β is

$$\hat{\beta} = (Y^{*\prime} Y^*)^{-1} Y^{*\prime} X$$

Let

$$T^* = (l_1, \ldots, l_m)$$

Then $Y^* = XT^*$, $RT^* = T^* \, diag(\lambda_1, \ldots, \lambda_m)$. We have

$$\hat{\beta} = [diag((n-1)\lambda_1, \ldots, (n-1)\lambda_m)]^{-1} T^{*\prime} \, X' \, X = \frac{1}{n-1} diag(\lambda_1^{-1}, \ldots, \lambda_m^{-1}) T^{*\prime} \, (n-1)R$$

$$= diag(\lambda_1^{-1}, \ldots, \lambda_m^{-1}) [\lambda_1 l_1, \ldots, \lambda_m l_m]' = (l_1, \ldots, l_m)' = T^{*\prime}$$

The regression coefficient is just the transposition of the matrix composed of the first m eigenvectors. These are the loading factors associated with the first m principal components.

We should note that this is not the principal components regression in Chapter 2, Section 2.5.

The concept of **multidimensional scaling** can be illustrated by a simple example. Suppose that we have the distances between N cities of India and these cities have geographic locations in East-West and North-South directions. Suppose we ask the question how these cities are ordered with respect to these two dimensions (East-West and North-South) and at the same time to keep the cities that are close to each other together. The multidimensional scaling method seeks the coordinates of the N cities with the (Euclidean) distance between the N cities known. It is the opposite problem from seeking the Euclidean distance between points with the coordinates of the points known.

Let us now present a detailed outline of the multidimensional scaling method. A user provides the distances from point to point between N points, which is d_{ij}, $i,j = 1,2,\ldots,N$. And we have a real symmetric matrix D:

$$D = (d_{ij})_{N \times N}$$

Based on D we may construct matrix

$$A = (a_{ij})_{N \times N}, \ a_{ij} = -d_{ij}^2 / 2$$

Then design $N \times N$ matrix H:

$$H = I_N - 1_N 1_N' / N$$

Here I_N is a Nth order unit matrix, 1_N is a N-dimensional vector, and each element is 1. Make $N \times N$ matrix

$$B = HAH$$

Calculate the principal components of B. In general it is possible to consider just $k = 1, 2$, or 3 principal components. Let us say we choose $k = 2$ as in the distances between cities. The corresponding values assumed by the components of the first two principal components are the coordinates of the points to be sought. Of course, the solution of the coordinates is not unique. Translation and rotation of directional axes to let us say Northeast-Northwest, and Southeast and Southwest don't change the distance between cities.

The DASC software has the program menu for principal component analysis and the method of multidimensional scaling.

9.2.4   Canonical correlation analysis

To study the correlation between two random variables, the **Correlation Coefficient** (or simple correlation coefficient) is used. The computing formula is as follows:

$$r = \frac{Cov(X,Y)}{\sqrt{V(X)}\sqrt{V(Y)}}$$

where

$$Cov(X,Y) = E[(X - E(X))(Y - E(Y))]$$

$$V(X) = E(X - E(X))^2 \quad V(Y) = E(Y - E(Y))^2$$

To understand the correlation between one random variable, the dependent variable, on the one hand and several random variables, the independent variables, on the other **Multiple Correlation Coefficient** (or **Total Correlation Coefficient**) is employed, as discussed in Chapter 2. Extending these concepts one may now ask how one measures the degree of correlation between one set of random variables on one side and another set of random variables on the other side. In 1936 Hotelling extended the simple and multiple correlation coefficients to the correlation between two sets of random variables, and introduced the concept of Canonical **Correlation.** This concept is not just an extension of the concept of correlation, but it is also quite useful. Suppose we wish to compare the degree of human development of two countries. The human development concept has several dimensions such as infant mortality, per capita consumption expenditure, female literacy rate, etc. One country may have more of one dimension and less of another. We may like to know how close one country is to the other in terms of overall human development. Canonical correlation between the various dimensions of human development is an indicator of how close the two countries are with respect to overall human development.

The canonical correlation coefficient describes the degree of the correlation between two groups of random variables $X = (X_1, X_2, \ldots, X_p)$ and $Y = (Y_1, Y_2, \ldots, Y_q)$. The first step is to convert the two sets of variables into just two variables by considering a linear transformation of all the variables in each set. More precisely we form two variables U and V as follows:

$$U = a'X = \sum_{i=1}^{p} a_i X_i, \quad V = b'Y = \sum_{i=1}^{q} b_i Y_i$$

Then think of the correlation coefficient r_{UV} of U and V, Projection vectors a,b influence the value of r_{UV}. The next question is how do we choose a and b? Suppose that for some a^* and b^* we observe

$$r_{U^*V^*} = \max_{\substack{a'\Sigma_{XX} a=1 \\ b'\Sigma_{YY} b=1}} r_{UV}(a,b)$$

where $U^* = a^{*'} X$ and $V^* = b^{*'} Y$, then $r_{U^*V^*}$ is called the **Canonical Correlation Coefficient** between the two sets of variables X and Y.

Partition the covariance matrixes of the two groups

$$Cov\begin{pmatrix} X \\ Y \end{pmatrix} = \begin{pmatrix} Var(X) & Cov(X,Y) \\ Cov(Y,X) & Var(Y) \end{pmatrix} = \begin{pmatrix} \Sigma_{XX} & \Sigma_{XY} \\ \Sigma_{YX} & \Sigma_{YY} \end{pmatrix}$$

Then

$$r_{UV} = \frac{Cov(a'X, b'Y)}{\sqrt{D(a'X)}\sqrt{D(b'X)}} = \frac{a'\Sigma_{XY}b}{\sqrt{a'\Sigma_{XX}a}\sqrt{b'\Sigma_{YY}b}} = a'\Sigma_{XY}b$$

Therefore, the problem is transformed to seek the maximum of $a'\Sigma_{XY}b$ when $a'\Sigma_{XX}a = 1$ and $b'\Sigma_{YY}b = 1$.

Using the **method of Lagrange multipliers** for constrained maximization we need to maximize:

$$S(a,b) = a'\Sigma_{XY}b - \frac{\lambda}{2}(a'\Sigma_{XX}a - 1) - \frac{v}{2}(b'\Sigma_{YY}b - 1)$$

where λ, v are Lagrange multipliers.

By the necessary conditions of extremum, we obtain equations:

$$\begin{cases} \dfrac{\partial S}{\partial a} = \Sigma_{XY}b - \lambda\Sigma_{XX}a = 0 \\ \dfrac{\partial S}{\partial b} = \Sigma_{YX}a - v\Sigma_{YY}b = 0 \end{cases} \tag{9.6}$$

Left multiply the two equations above by a' and b' respectively, then

$$\begin{cases} a'\Sigma_{XY}b = \lambda a'\Sigma_{XX}a = \lambda \\ b'\Sigma_{YX}a = vb'\Sigma_{YY}b = v \end{cases}$$

Notice that $\Sigma_{XY} = \Sigma_{YX}$, thus

$$\lambda = v = a'\Sigma_{XY}b$$

Substitute it in equation (9.6), then

$$\begin{cases} \Sigma_{XY}b - \lambda\Sigma_{XX}a = 0 \\ \Sigma_{YX}a - \lambda\Sigma_{YY}b = 0 \end{cases} \tag{9.7}$$

Multiplying the second equation in (9.7) by Σ_{YY}^{-1} we get is $\lambda b = \Sigma_{YY}^{-1}\Sigma_{XY}a$, so

$$b = \frac{1}{\lambda}\Sigma_{YY}^{-1}\Sigma_{XY}a$$

Substitute it in the first equation in (9.7), we have

$$(\Sigma_{XY}\Sigma_{YY}^{-1}\Sigma_{YX} - \lambda^2\Sigma_{XX})a = 0$$

Likewise,

$$(\Sigma_{YX}\Sigma_{XX}^{-1}\Sigma_{XY} - \lambda^2\Sigma_{YY})b = 0$$

Write

$$A = \Sigma_{XX}^{-1}\Sigma_{XY}\Sigma_{YY}^{-1}\Sigma_{YX}, \quad B = \Sigma_{YY}^{-1}\Sigma_{YX}\Sigma_{XX}^{-1}\Sigma_{XY} \tag{9.8}$$

then

$$Aa = \lambda^2 a, \; Bb = \lambda^2 b \tag{9.9}$$

It indicates that λ^2 is the latent root of A as well as B, and a and b are the corresponding eigenvectors of A and B. The latent roots of A and B are nonnegative and lie between 0 and 1. The equal nonnegative latent roots amounts to $\min(p,q)$. Let it be p.

Assume that the latent roots of $Aa = \lambda^2 a$ are arranged as $\lambda_1^2 \geq \lambda_2^2 \geq \cdots \geq \lambda_p^2 > 0$, and other $q - p$ roots are 0. We call $\lambda_1, \lambda_2, \ldots, \lambda_p$ are typical correlation coefficients. Correspondingly, the unit eigenvectors solved from $Aa = \lambda^2 a$ are $a_1, a_2, \ldots, a_p$, the eigenvectors solved from $Bb = \lambda^2 b$ are $b_1, b_2, \ldots, b_p$. Then we obtain p pairs of linear combinations:

$$U_i = a_i' \, X, \; V_i = b_i' \, Y, \; i = 1, 2, \ldots, p$$

Each pair of variables is called **Typical Variable**. Seeking typical correlation coefficients and typical variables boils down to seeking the latent roots and eigenvectors of A and B.

We can also prove that, for $i \neq j$

$$Cov(U_i, U_j) = Cov(a_i' \, X, \, a_j' X) = a_i' \, \Sigma_{XX} a_j' = 0$$
$$Cov(V_i, V_j) = Cov(b_i' \, Y, \, b_j' Y) = b_j' \, \Sigma_{YY} b_j' = 0$$
$$Cov(U_i, U_j) = E(U_i U_j) = \delta_{ij}$$
$$Cov(V_i, V_j) = E(V_i V_j) = \delta_{ij}$$

where

$$\delta_{ij} = \begin{cases} 1, & i = j \\ 0, & i \neq j \end{cases}$$

The correlation coefficients, between the same pair of typical variables U_i and V_i of X and Y, are λ_i. The typical variables U_i and $V_j (i \neq j)$ which are not in the same pair are irrelevant, which means the covariance is 0. Then

$$Cov(U_i, U_j) = E(U_i V_j) = \begin{cases} \lambda_i \neq 0, & i = 1, \ldots, p \\ 0 & i > p \end{cases}$$

When the average vector μ and covariance matrix Σ in the population are unknown, the typical correlation coefficients and typical variables of the population can be sought.

Assume that $X_{(1)}, \ldots, X_{(n)}$ and $Y_{(1)}, \ldots, Y_{(n)}$ are the samples from population volume. Now we have the maximum likelihood estimation of the covariance matrix:

$$\hat{\Sigma}_{XX} = \frac{1}{n} \sum_{i=1}^{n} (X_{(i)} - \bar{X})(X_{(i)} - \bar{X})'$$

$$\hat{\Sigma}_{YY} = \frac{1}{n} \sum_{i=1}^{n} (Y_{(i)} - \bar{Y})(Y_{(i)} - \bar{Y})'$$

$$\hat{\Sigma}_{XY} = \hat{\Sigma}_{YX} = \frac{1}{n}\sum_{i=1}^{n}(X_{(i)} - \bar{X})(Y_{(i)} - \bar{Y})'$$

where $\bar{X} = \frac{1}{n}\sum_{i=1}^{n}X_{(i)}$, $\bar{Y} = \frac{1}{n}\sum_{i=1}^{n}Y_{(i)}$. Substituting $\hat{\Sigma}$ for Σ, and according to (9.8) and (9.9), estimate $\hat{\lambda}_i$ and $\hat{a}$, $\hat{b}$. Here $\hat{\lambda}_i$ is called the **typical correlation coefficients of the sample**. $\hat{U}_i = \hat{a}_i X$, $\hat{V}_i = \hat{b}_i Y$, $(i = 1,\ldots, p)$ are called the **typical variables of the sample**.

When computing, we could start from the correlation matrix of the sample to seek the typical correlation coefficients and typical variables of the sample. Substitute the correlation matrix R for covariance matrix Σ, and the computing process is the same.

If one variable in canonical correlation coefficients is one-dimensional, it could be called the **partial correlation coefficient**. The partial correlation coefficient describes the relation between one random variable Y and many random variables (a group of random variables) $X = (x_1, x_2, \ldots, x_p)'$, whose aim is to combine linearly the group of random variables in order to obtain one random variable that has the maximum correlation with the other random variable:

$$U = a'X = \sum_{i=1}^{p}a_i x_i$$

Then study the correlation coefficient r_{YU} of Y and U. Since U is relevant to the projection vector a, r_{YU} is relevant to a, and $r_{YU} = r_{YU}(a)$. When a maximize r_{YU} with $a'\Sigma_{XX}a = 1$, then we designate the correlation coefficient, obtained by a as a projection vector, as a multiple correlation coefficient.

$$r_{YU} = \max_{a'\Sigma_{XX}a=1} r_{YU}(a)$$

Other derivation and computing process are similar to that of the multiple correlation coefficients. DASC software has included the computation of this correlation analysis model.

9.3   Customer satisfaction model and path analysis

This section introduces the **Customer Satisfaction Index** (CSI), **Path Analysis**, **Structural Equations Model** (SEM), and computation of partial least squares (PLS) estimators. This section also reports some recent research findings of the principal author (Tong, 2010), such as a definite linear algorithm for SEM, and multi-layer CSI model.

9.3.1   Customer satisfaction model and structural equations model

Measurement of 'Customer Satisfaction' and taking necessary corrective actions to improve customer satisfaction are essential for economic and business development. In the new economy sustainable economic growth not only depends on the productivity of economic resources but it also on the quality of the output. The famous quality scholar Joseph Juran says: 'The past 20th century is the century of productivity, while the 21st century is the century of quality.' Upon an examination of the course of development of quality control, we see that customers'

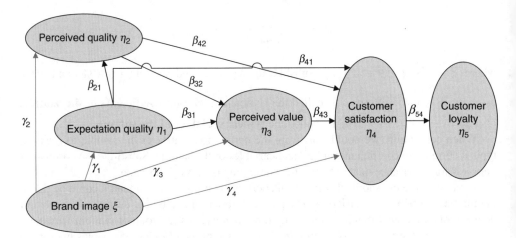

Figure 9.5   The structure of customer satisfaction index model of China.

demands form the beginning of concerns about quality. Thus maximization of the customer satisfaction index can be termed the main goal of quality control. This is embodied in ISO9000 standard, version 2000, which may find the first of eight principles of quality control: 'Focus on customers'.

In the last 20 years, the most influential customer satisfaction model has been the structural equation model (SEM), introduced by Fornell at the National Quality Research Center of Ross School of Business, University of Michigan, United States. It represents the main-stream for research on the customer satisfaction index (CSI) at present, which has been the international universal model.

The structural equation model consists of two equation sets. One is a set of relations (equations) between structural variables or latent variables or unobserved variables. These are called **structural equations**. The other is a set of relations (equations) between structural unobserved or latent variables and observed or measured variables. These are called **observa-tional equations**. Figure 9.5 is a CSI model, in which there are observational equations, and structural equations. It includes six structural variables (latent variables) ξ, $\eta_1,\ldots,\eta_5$, and 11 relations. The relations of the effect of independent observed variables on the unobserved structural variables are reflected through the parameters of a linear system by $\gamma_1,\ldots,\gamma_4$. The effect of structural variables on other structural variables are measured in a linear model by the parameters β_{ij}. The relations between each structural variable and its corresponding obser-vational variables, and the relations among structural variables are called path coefficients. So solving SEM, i.e. to calculate structural variables and path coefficients, is called path analysis.

In SEM, the observational variables are known, and the structural variables and path coef-ficients are unknown.

For the group of relations, we could obtain the following **structural equations**:

$$
\begin{pmatrix} \eta_1 \\ \eta_2 \\ \eta_3 \\ \eta_4 \\ \eta_5 \end{pmatrix} = \begin{pmatrix} 0 & 0 & 0 & 0 & 0 \\ \beta_{21} & 0 & 0 & 0 & 0 \\ \beta_{31} & \beta_{32} & 0 & 0 & 0 \\ \beta_{41} & \beta_{42} & \beta_{43} & 0 & 0 \\ 0 & 0 & 0 & \beta_{54} & 0 \end{pmatrix} \begin{pmatrix} \eta_1 \\ \eta_2 \\ \eta_3 \\ \eta_4 \\ \eta_5 \end{pmatrix} + \begin{pmatrix} \gamma_1 \\ \gamma_2 \\ \gamma_3 \\ \gamma_4 \\ 0 \end{pmatrix} \xi + \begin{pmatrix} \varepsilon_1 \\ \varepsilon_2 \\ \varepsilon_3 \\ \varepsilon_4 \\ \varepsilon_5 \end{pmatrix} \qquad (9.10)
$$

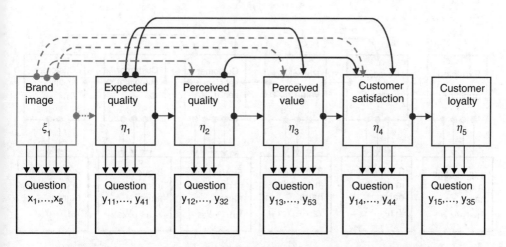

Figure 9.6   The variables of customer satisfaction index model of China.

Each structural variable corresponds to several observed variables, assuming M observations in all. These observations are intended to grade customers. Let us assume that the number of customers is N in total. Assume the mark for each question from each customer ranges from 1 to 10 points, where the most unsatisfied is 1 point, and most satisfied is 10 points. Then we have a $N \times M$ matrix, of which each element is $1 - 10$. The numbers of observed variables in the example above corresponding to the structural variables ($\xi, \eta_1, \ldots, \eta_5$) are 5, 4, 3, 5, 4, 3 respectively.

The relation between structural variables and observed variables could be expressed by equations. We designate the observed variables, corresponding to the independent variable ξ in structural variables, as $x_i, i = 1, \ldots, 5$, and the observed variables, corresponding to the dependent variables η_i in structural variables, as $y_{ji}, i = 1, \ldots, 5$. The observational equations from structural variables to observed variables in Figure 9.6 could be expressed as:

$$\begin{pmatrix} x_1 \\ \vdots \\ x_5 \end{pmatrix} = \begin{pmatrix} \lambda_1 \\ \vdots \\ \lambda_5 \end{pmatrix} \xi + \begin{pmatrix} \delta_1 \\ \vdots \\ \delta_5 \end{pmatrix}$$

$$\begin{pmatrix} y_{1i} \\ \vdots \\ y_{ji} \end{pmatrix} = \begin{pmatrix} \lambda_{1i} \\ \vdots \\ \lambda_{ji} \end{pmatrix} \eta_i + \begin{pmatrix} \sigma_1 \\ \vdots \\ \sigma_j \end{pmatrix}, i = 1, \cdots, 5$$

where λ_i and λ_{ji} are loading coefficients, and δ_i and σ_i are error terms. The equations from observed variables to structural variables could be written as:

$$\xi = \sum_{j=1}^{5} \psi_j x_j + \varsigma, \eta_i = \sum_{j=1}^{L(i)} \omega_{ij} y_{ji} + \tau_i \tag{9.11}$$

Here $L(i)$ is the observed variables number relevant to the ith structural variable. ς, τ_i are random error items.

The observational equation from structural variables to observed variables is $Y = \Lambda \eta + \varepsilon$ in vector form, where Λ and η are both unknown. However, it is different from the factor analysis model, where Λ was not constrained. But the form of Λ here is constrained. Some

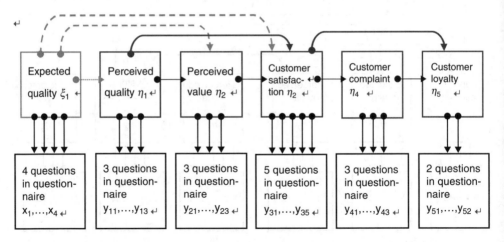

Figure 9.7   Customer satisfaction index model of America.

of its elements are required to be 0. Of course the equation is still different from the general regression model $Y = X\beta + \varepsilon$, where Y and X are known, and β unknown. This equation also differs from the evaluation model $Y = X\beta + \varepsilon$ introduced by Tong (1993), where only X is known with Y and β unknown, but $Y = y \otimes I_n$, $\beta_i > 0$ and $\sum_i \beta_i = 1$. The discussion of the multiple linear regression model introduced in Chapters 2 and 3 is now complete with the inclusion of unobserved variables by the introduction of the path analysis model, evaluation model, general regression model, and factor analysis model.

Example 9.4   American customer satisfaction index (ACSI) analysis   The number of the structural variables of ACSI analysis is also six with an item of customer complaints. The structural equation model is shown in Figure 9.7.

In this model, the numbers of observed variables corresponding to each structural variable in turn are 3, 3, 3, 2, 3, 1, which respectively are expected quality ξ, perceived quality η_1, perceived value η_2, customer satisfaction η_3, customer complaint η_4 and customer loyalty η_5. The structural equations may be expressed as:

$$
\begin{pmatrix} \eta_1 \\ \eta_2 \\ \eta_3 \\ \eta_4 \\ \eta_5 \end{pmatrix} = \begin{pmatrix} 0 & 0 & 0 & 0 & 0 \\ \beta_{21} & 0 & 0 & 0 & 0 \\ \beta_{31} & \beta_{32} & 0 & 0 & 0 \\ 0 & 0 & \beta_{43} & 0 & 0 \\ 0 & 0 & \beta_{53} & \beta_{54} & 0 \end{pmatrix} \begin{pmatrix} \eta_1 \\ \eta_2 \\ \eta_3 \\ \eta_4 \\ \eta_5 \end{pmatrix} + \begin{pmatrix} \gamma_1 \\ \gamma_2 \\ \gamma_3 \\ 0 \\ 0 \end{pmatrix} \xi + \begin{pmatrix} \varsigma_1 \\ \varsigma_2 \\ \varsigma_3 \\ \varsigma_{43} \\ \varsigma_5 \end{pmatrix} \tag{9.12}
$$

The corresponding observed variables of independent variables are expressed as $x_i, i = 1,2,3$, and the corresponding observed variables of dependent variables are expressed as $y_j, j = 1,\ldots,12$. The equation connecting structural variables and observed variables corresponding to independent variables is

$$
\begin{pmatrix} x_1 \\ x_2 \\ x_3 \end{pmatrix} = \begin{pmatrix} \lambda_1 \\ \lambda_2 \\ \lambda_3 \end{pmatrix} \xi + \begin{pmatrix} \delta_1 \\ \delta_2 \\ \delta_3 \end{pmatrix}
$$

The equation relating to structural variables and observed variables corresponding to dependent variables is

$$
\begin{pmatrix} y_1 \\ y_2 \\ y_3 \\ y_4 \\ y_5 \\ y_6 \\ y_7 \\ y_8 \\ y_9 \\ y_{10} \\ y_{11} \\ y_{12} \end{pmatrix} = \begin{pmatrix} \lambda_{11} & 0 & 0 & 0 & 0 \\ \lambda_{21} & 0 & 0 & 0 & 0 \\ \lambda_{31} & 0 & 0 & 0 & 0 \\ 0 & \lambda_{12} & 0 & 0 & 0 \\ 0 & \lambda_{22} & 0 & 0 & 0 \\ 0 & \lambda_{32} & 0 & 0 & 0 \\ 0 & 0 & \lambda_{13} & 0 & 0 \\ 0 & 0 & \lambda_{23} & 0 & 0 \\ 0 & 0 & 0 & \lambda_{14} & 0 \\ 0 & 0 & 0 & \lambda_{24} & 0 \\ 0 & 0 & 0 & \lambda_{34} & 0 \\ 0 & 0 & 0 & 0 & \lambda_{15} \end{pmatrix} \begin{pmatrix} \eta_1 \\ \eta_2 \\ \eta_3 \\ \eta_4 \\ \eta_5 \end{pmatrix} + \begin{pmatrix} \varepsilon_1 \\ \varepsilon_2 \\ \varepsilon_3 \\ \varepsilon_4 \\ \varepsilon_5 \\ \varepsilon_6 \\ \varepsilon_7 \\ \varepsilon_8 \\ \varepsilon_9 \\ \varepsilon_{10} \\ \varepsilon_{11} \\ \varepsilon_{12} \end{pmatrix}
$$

where $\lambda_1, \lambda_2, \lambda_3, \lambda_{11}, \ldots, \lambda_{15}$ are loading coefficients, and $\delta_1, \delta_2, \delta_3, \varepsilon_1, \ldots, \varepsilon_{12}$ are error terms.

We wrote a computer program for this model. It incorporates all the computations needed. Refer to the DASC software for the detailed computational process. What we need to point out here, however, is that the DASC software could be modified by users. Users may define their own CSI models in line with their own requirements.

9.3.2   Partial least square and the best iterative initial value

As mentioned in the previous section path analysis using SEM technique, PLS and LISREL modeling techniques have very wide applications. We first discuss the common form of SEM.

The structural variables are latent variables without observation data. Each structural variable has some corresponding observation variables as shown above in Figure 9.7. Suppose there are M observation variables, and N observation values for each variable. Then we have an $N \times M$ data matrix.

The observation equations are relationships between the structural variables and observation variables. Suppose there are k independent structural variables and m dependent structural variables. The observation variables corresponding to the independent structural variable ξ_t are denoted as x_{tj}, $t = 1,\ldots,k, j = 1,\ldots,K(t)$, where $K(t)$ is the number of observation variables corresponding to the independent structural variable ξ_t. Figure 9.7, $k = 1$ and $K(1) = 4$. The observation variables corresponding to the dependent variable η_i are denoted as y_{ij}, $i = 1,\ldots,m, j = 1,\ldots,L(i)$, where $L(i)$ is the number of observation variables corresponding to the dependent structural variable η_i. In Figure 9.7 $m = 5$ and $L(i) = 3, 3, 5, 3, 2$.

The observational equations in Figure 9.7 can be expressed as the relationship from the observed variables to the structural variables:

$$\xi_t = \sum_{j=1}^{K(t)} \psi_{tj} x_{tj} + \varepsilon_{xt}, t = 1,\ldots,k \tag{9.13}$$

$$\eta_i = \sum_{j=1}^{L(i)} \omega_{ij} y_{ij} + \varepsilon_{yi}, i = 1,\ldots,m \tag{9.14}$$

where ψ_{ij}, ω_{ij} are the summarizing coefficients, and ε with subscripts are random error items.

On the contrary, the observational equations in Figure 9.7 can also be expressed as the relationship from the structural variables to observed variables:

$$
\begin{pmatrix} x_{t1} \\ \vdots \\ x_{tK(t)} \end{pmatrix} + \begin{pmatrix} \upsilon_{t1} \\ \vdots \\ \upsilon_{tK(t)} \end{pmatrix} \xi_t + \begin{pmatrix} \varepsilon_{xt1} \\ \vdots \\ \varepsilon_{xtK(t)} \end{pmatrix}, t = 1,\ldots,k \tag{9.15}
$$

$$
\begin{pmatrix} y_{i1} \\ \vdots \\ y_{iL(i)} \end{pmatrix} = \begin{pmatrix} \lambda_{i1} \\ \vdots \\ \lambda_{iL(i)} \end{pmatrix} \eta_i + \begin{pmatrix} \varepsilon_{yi1} \\ \vdots \\ \varepsilon_{yiL(i)} \end{pmatrix}, i = 1,\ldots,m
$$

where υ_{ij} and λ_{ij} are the load coefficients, and ε with subscripts are random error terms.

We use vector and matrix notation to describe the structural equations. Let $\xi' = (\xi_1,\ldots\xi_k)$ and $\eta' = (\eta'_1,\ldots,\eta'_m)$. The coefficient matrix of η is denoted as $m \times m$ matrix B, and the coefficient matrix of ξ is denoted as $m \times k$ matrix Γ. The residual vector is $\varepsilon'_\eta = (\varepsilon'_1,\ldots, \varepsilon'_m)$. The structural equations can be expanded as:

$$
\eta = B\eta + \Gamma\xi + \varepsilon_\eta \tag{9.16}
$$

Now we simply introduce the **linear structural relationship (LISREL) algorithm** for SEM.

LISREL is an algorithm to fit the sample covariance matrix to the model covariance matrix. In this method we suppose that $E(\xi) = E(\eta) = 0$, $E(\varepsilon_X) = E(\varepsilon_Y) = 0$, $E(\xi\varepsilon'_X) = E(\eta\varepsilon'_Y) = 0$, $E(\eta\varepsilon'_X) = E(\xi\varepsilon'_Y) = 0$, here 0 is a vector or matrix. For variance matrix and covariance matrix, we note that $Var(\varepsilon_X) = \Theta_X$, $Var(\varepsilon_Y) = \Theta_Y$, $Var(\xi) = \Phi$, $Var(\varepsilon_\eta) = \Psi$. The covariance matrix of the model is

$$
Cov(X,Y) = \begin{pmatrix} \Sigma_{XX} & \Sigma_{XY} \\ \Sigma_{YX} & \Sigma_Y \end{pmatrix} = \begin{pmatrix} E(XX') & E(XY') \\ E(YX') & E(YY') \end{pmatrix} = \begin{pmatrix} \Lambda_X\Phi_\xi\Lambda'_X + \Theta_X & \Lambda_X Cov(\xi,\eta)\Lambda'_Y \\ \Lambda_Y Cov(\eta,\xi)\Lambda'_X & \Lambda_Y Var(\eta)\Lambda'_Y + \Theta_Y \end{pmatrix}
$$

From structural equations $\eta = B\eta + \Gamma\xi + \varepsilon_\eta$, we get $\eta = B_1^{-1}\Gamma\xi + B_1^{-1}\varepsilon_\eta$, where $B_1 = I - B$. So $Cov(\xi,\eta) = Cov(\eta,\xi) = E(\eta\xi') = E[(B_1^{-1}\Gamma\xi + B_1^{-1}\varepsilon_\eta)\xi'] = B_1^{-1}\Gamma\Phi$. In the same way we calculate $Var(\eta) = E(\eta\eta') = E((B_1^{-1}\Gamma\xi + B_1^{-1}\varepsilon_\eta)(B_1^{-1}\Gamma\xi + B_1^{-1}\varepsilon_\eta)') = B_1^{-1}(\Gamma\Phi\Gamma' + \Psi)B_1^{-1}$.

Substituting these results in $Cov(X,Y)$, we can get the expression of $Cov(X,Y)$ with unknown parameters.

The covariance matrix S of the sample may be calculated from the observed sample $(X : Y)$. Then we can calculate the estimators of the parameters by use of a fitting function to get its minimum value. A suitable fitting function is $F = 0.5\{tr[V(S - Cov(X,Y))]\}^2$. Scientific Software Internal that distributes LISREL has abundant information on LISREL (see http://www.ssicentral.com).

Now we simply introduce the **partial least square (PLS) algorithm** for SEM.

PLS is a useful and concise algorithm but is a typical iterative algorithm. Firstly, by giving arbitrary initial values to ψ_{tj} and ω_{ij} in (9.13) and (9.14), the estimation of ξ_t and η_i can be obtained according to the known observed variables x_{tj} and y_{ij}. Once ξ_t and η_i are known, we can estimate the parameters in (9.16) based on OLS, and obtain the structural relationships γ_{ij} and β_{ij}, and then ξ_t and η_i are replaced by estimators $\hat{\xi}_t$ and $\hat{\eta}_i$. Secondly, we return (9.13) and (9.14), in which the numerical values of the latent variables ξ_t, η_i and observed variables x_t, y_i are known now, we can solve (9.13) and (9.14) to obtain the estimates of ψ_{1i} and ω_{ij}. With the estimators of ψ_{1i} and ω_{ij}, a new iterative process begins. The iterative process above mentioned can be described as follows:

$$(\psi_{tj}, \omega_{ij})^{(0)} \xrightarrow{\ (11.4.4)(11.4.5)\ } (\hat{\xi}_t^{\,(EXO)}, \hat{\eta}_i^{\,(EXO)})^{(0)} \xrightarrow{\ (11.4.8)\ }$$

$$(\gamma_{ij}, \beta_{ij})^{(0)} \xrightarrow{\ (11.4.8)\ } (\hat{\xi}_t^{\,(END)}, \hat{\eta}_i^{\,(END)})^{(0)} \xrightarrow{\ (11.4.4)(11.4.5)\ } (\psi_{tj}, \omega_{ij})^{(1)}$$

where endogenous (END) means the parameter estimation is obtained from structural equation, and exogenous (EXO) means the parameter estimation is obtained from observational equation.

Now we introduce **the best initial value of iterative** in PLS (Tong et al., 2007).

Take observation vectors $x_t' = (x_{t1}', \ldots, x_{tK(t)}')$, $y_i' = (y_{i1}', \ldots, y_{iL(i)}')$, and take the initial starting values of coefficients $\psi_t' = \psi_{t1}, \ldots, \psi_{tK(t)}$, $\omega_i' = (\omega_{i1}, \ldots, \omega_{iL(i)})$. Combine equations (9.16) (9.13) (9.14) for positive observations as:

$$SEM^+ \begin{cases} \eta = B\eta + \Gamma\xi + \varepsilon_\eta \\ \xi_t = \psi_t' x_t + \varepsilon_{xt}, t = 1, \ldots k \\ \eta_i = \omega_i' y_i + \varepsilon_{yi}, i = 1, \ldots, m \end{cases} \tag{9.17}$$

We call SEM^+ the structural equations model with positive observations.

Noting $\upsilon_t' = (\upsilon_{t1}, \ldots, \upsilon_{tK(t)})$, $\lambda_i' = (\lambda_{i1}, \ldots, \lambda_{iL(i)})$, then the observational equation (9.15) can be expressed as:

$$x_t = \upsilon_t \xi_t + \varepsilon_{xt}, t = 1, \ldots, k \tag{9.18}$$

$$y_i = \lambda_i \eta_i + \varepsilon_{yi}, i = 1, \ldots, m \tag{9.19}$$

We combine equations (9.16) (9.18) (9.19) as:

$$SEM^- \begin{cases} \eta = B\eta + \Gamma\xi + \varepsilon_\eta \\ x_t = \upsilon_t \xi_t + \varepsilon_{xt}, t = 1, \ldots, k \\ y_i = \lambda_i \eta_i + \varepsilon_{yi}, i = 1, \ldots, m \end{cases} \tag{9.20}$$

and call SEM^- the structural equations model with the roles of observable and unobservable variables as dependent and independent variables being reversed.

If we analyze the observation equations of SEM carefully, we can discover the relationship between each structural variable and its corresponding observation variables, and obtain the least squares solution of the structural variable by the modular constraints on the structural variables vector. We give some basic properties of observation equations.

Lemma 1. The structural equations model has some basic properties.

1. The solutions of SEM^+ or SEM^- are not unique, and may differ by a multiple.

2. zero is a solution to SEM^+, but not to SEM^-.

3. The solutions of SEM^+ and SEM^- are equivalent in terms of LSE and the constraint condition on the coefficients $(\psi'_t v_t = 1, \omega'_i \lambda_i = 1, t = 1,...,k, i = 1,...,m)$.

The proof is straightforword and hence omitted. The these properties indicate that, if (η,ξ) is a solution of SEM, $(c\eta,c\xi)$ is also a solution, where c is a nonzero constant. So we can solve SEM by the modular constraint of structural variable vector.

A common PLS algorithm in use is one that is based on SEM^+ but not SEM^-. If we derive the solution of SEM by SEM^-, we get a new algorithm.

We consider (9.15). There are m equation sets in (9.15), and there are $L(i)$ equations in each equation set:

$$y_{ij} = \lambda_{ij}\eta_i + \varepsilon_{yij}, j = 1,...,L(i), i = 1,...,m$$

We notice that equations (9.15) are contradictive equations in which a structural variable must satisfy many linear relationships with the observation variables. We easily think of finding the relationship of the least squares with contradictive equations, and adopting the solution of the least squares. We know that each structural variable is a vector with N components, and that each component satisfies $L(i)$ relationships. Write out the relationship corresponding to i'th structural vector and its observation vector with each component:

$$y_{ijs} = \lambda_{ij}\eta_{is}, j = 1,2,...,L(i), s = 1,2,...,N$$

That is:

$$\begin{pmatrix} y_{i1s} \\ y_{i2s} \\ \vdots \\ y_{iL(i)s} \end{pmatrix} = \begin{pmatrix} \lambda_{i1} \\ \lambda_{i2} \\ \vdots \\ \lambda_{iL(i)} \end{pmatrix} \eta_{is} + \begin{pmatrix} \varepsilon_{yi1s} \\ \varepsilon_{yi2s} \\ \vdots \\ \varepsilon_{yiL(i)s} \end{pmatrix}, s = 1,2,...,N$$

It is a relationship of transverse vector of the observation data matrix.

Using a vector $(\lambda_{i1}, \cdots, \lambda_{iL(i)})$ to multiply both sides of equations above and omitting the error items, we can get $A_i\eta_{is} \approx \lambda_{i1} y_{i1s} + \cdots + \lambda_{iL(i)} y_{iL(i)s}$, where $A_i = \lambda_{i1}^2 + \cdots + \lambda_{iL(i)}^2$. If In terms of the standard multivariate linear regression model, the dependent variables are $\eta_{is}, s = 1,2,...,N$, independent variables are $y_{i1s}, y_{i2s},..., y_{iL(i)s}, s = 1,2,...,N$, and regression coefficients are $\lambda_{i1}, \lambda_{i2},..., \lambda_{iL(i)}$ divided by number A_i. At present dependent variables are unknown, so the equations cannot be solved immediately. But if we assume that the modular length of dependent variables is 1, i.e. $\eta_1^2 + \eta_2^2 + \cdots + \eta_N^2 = 1$ according to Lemma 1, the equations can be solved.

We give a simpler derivation below. We consider (9.20) and assume that each observation variable has N observations, then y_i is an $L(i) \times N$ matrix. Making product $y_i y'_i \approx \lambda_i \eta_i \eta_i' \lambda'_i = \eta_i \eta_i' \lambda_i \lambda'_i$, if the structural variables are regarded as unit vectors, namely $\eta_i \eta_i' = 1$, then $y_i y'_i \approx \lambda_i \lambda'_i$. Both matrixes of $L(i) \times L(i)$ are almost equal under the normal terminology of the least squares, and they are described in detail as follows:

$$\begin{pmatrix} y_{i1}y_{i1}' & y_{i1}y_{i2}' & \cdots & y_{i1}y_{iL(i)}' \\ y_{i2}y_{i1}' & y_{i2}y_{i2}' & \cdots & y_{i2}y_{iL(i)}' \\ \cdots & \cdots & \cdots & \cdots \\ y_{iL(i)}y_{i1}' & y_{iL(i)}y_{i2}' & \cdots & y_{iL(i)}y_{iL(i)}' \end{pmatrix} \approx \begin{pmatrix} \lambda_{i1}^2 & \lambda_{i1}\lambda_{i2} & \cdots & \lambda_{i1}\lambda_{iL(i)} \\ \lambda_{i2}\lambda_{i1} & \lambda_{i2}^2 & \cdots & \lambda_{i2}\lambda_{iL(i)} \\ \cdots & \cdots & \cdots & \cdots \\ \lambda_{iL(i)}\lambda_{i1} & \lambda_{iL(i)}\lambda_{i2} & \cdots & \lambda_{iL(i)}^2 \end{pmatrix}$$

Note that the elements in the left matrix are the products of two vectors but the elements in the right matrix are the products of two numbers. Choosing the equal elements in the diagonal, we get:

$$\hat{\lambda}_{ij}^2 = y_{ij}y_{ij}', \ j = 1, \ldots, L(i) \tag{9.21}$$

Independent variables ξ_t have the similar results. Then we get the estimates of coefficients between structural variables and observed variables under the normal least squares terminology, namely we get the estimator $\hat{\lambda}_i = (\hat{\lambda}_{i1}, \ldots, \hat{\lambda}_{iL(i)})'$ of vector λ_i with their directions.

Now we continue to estimate the structural variable $\eta_i = (\eta_{i1}, \eta_{i2}, \ldots, \eta_{iN})'$, and estimate its elements one by one. Based on the least squares method in (9.21), we have

$$\lambda_i \lambda_i' \eta_{is} = \sum_{j=1}^{L(i)} \lambda_{ij}^2 \eta_{is} = (\lambda_{i1}, \ldots, \lambda_{iL(i)}) \begin{pmatrix} y_{i1s} \\ \vdots \\ y_{iL(i)s} \end{pmatrix} = \lambda_i' Y_s$$

where $Y_s' = (y_{i1s}, \ldots, y_{iL(i)s})$. So we get the estimators:

$$\hat{\eta}_{is} = \frac{\hat{\lambda}_i' Y_s}{\hat{\lambda}_i \hat{\lambda}_i'}, s = 1, \ldots, N \tag{9.22}$$

We can also estimate υ_{ij} and ξ_t in the same way. Then we get the modular constrained least squares solution (MCLS) of all structural variables (with the constraints that the structural vector is a unit vector), and they satisfy:

$$\| \eta_i - \sum_{j=1}^{L(i)} \omega_{ij} y_{ij} \| \to \min$$

Its geometrical meaning is to seek the distance between a unit sphere and a hyper-plane.

Summarizing the aforesaid derivation we have the algorithm for MCLS.

Algorithm 1. The **modular constraint least squares solution** (MCLS) of structural vector in SEM.

Step 1. In *SEM⁻*, suppose ξ_t, η_i all are unit vectors, calculate the least squares estimates of the coefficients between each structural variable and its corresponding observation variables:

$$\hat{\upsilon}_{ij}^2 = x_{ij}x_{ij}', j = 1, \ldots, K(t), t = 1, \ldots, k$$

$$\hat{\lambda}_{ij}^2 = y_{ij}y_{ij}', j = 1, \ldots, L(i), i = 1, \ldots, m$$

Step 2. In *SEM⁻*, calculate the least squares estimates of structural variables by using of $\hat{\upsilon}_{ij}, \hat{\lambda}_{ij}$:

$$\hat{\xi}_{ts} = \frac{\hat{\upsilon}'_t X_{ts}}{\hat{\upsilon}_t \hat{\upsilon}'_t}, \quad \hat{\eta}_{is} = \frac{\hat{\lambda}'_i Y_{is}}{\hat{\lambda}_i \hat{\lambda}'_i}, \quad s = 1,\ldots,N, t = 1,\ldots,k, i = 1,\ldots,m$$

where X_{ts}, Y_{is} are the transverse vectors of the observed data matrix, $X'_{ts} = (x_{t1s},\ldots,x_{tK(t)s})$, $Y'_{is} = (x_{i1s},\ldots,x_{iL(i)s})$.

Step 3. In SEM^+, make use of $\hat{\xi}_t, \hat{\eta}_i$ obtained in Step 2 to calculate regression coefficients ψ_{tj}, ω_{ij} according to common linear regression method.

Step 4. In SEM^+, make use of $\hat{\xi}_t, \hat{\eta}_i$ obtained in Step 2 to calculate the estimates of coefficient matrix B, Γ.

Notice that (9.16) is a common linear regression equations, we can use the two-stage least squares method to calculate it.

In the derivation given above we actually ignored the variance of the error item of (9.21). In the transformed model used in the algorithm above, $y_i y'_i$ is incorrectly specified by ignoring the variance.

Now we suggest some improvements of MCLS.

If we assume the structural variables η_i are independent of the error items ε_{yi}, that is, $E(\eta_i \varepsilon_{yi}) = 0$, then from (9.19) we have:

$$E(y_i y'_i) = E(\lambda_i \lambda'_i \eta_i \eta'_i) + E(\varepsilon_{yi} \varepsilon'_{yi}) = \lambda_i \lambda'_i + E(\varepsilon_{yi} \varepsilon'_{yi})$$

$E(\varepsilon_{yi} \varepsilon'_{yi})$ is a diagonal matrix:

$$E(\varepsilon_{yi} \varepsilon'_{yi}) = diag(\sigma^2_{yi1}, \sigma^2_{yi2}, \cdots \sigma^2_{yiL(i)})$$

So we have

$$y_{ij} y'_{ij} = \hat{\lambda}^2_{ij} + \hat{\sigma}^2_{yij}, j = 1,\ldots,L(i) \quad (9.23)$$

Comparing with (9.21) there is an additive item σ^2_{yij} to be estimated. According to the method of factor analysis, we let the matrix $\Sigma_{yi} = E(y_i y'_i)$ and $\hat{\Sigma}_{yi} = y_i y'_i$. Suppose the diagonal elements of $\hat{\Sigma}^{-1}_{yi}$ be $\hat{\phi}_{yij}, j = 1,\ldots,L(i)$, we can take the estimates

$$\hat{\sigma}^2_{yij} = \hat{\phi}^{-1}_{yij}, j = 1,\ldots,L(i)$$

As soon as we have $\{\hat{\sigma}^2_{yij}\}$, we can easily estimate $\{\lambda^2_{ij}\}$ from (9.23).

Summarizing aforesaid deduction we can improve the algorithm of MCLS.

Algorithm 2. (An Improvement on Step 1 of Algorithm 1).

Step 1. In SEM^-, suppose ξ_t, η_i are unit vectors, calculate the least squares estimates of the coefficients between the structural variable and its observation variables:

$$\hat{\upsilon}^2_{tj} = x_{tj} x'_{tj} - \hat{\sigma}^2_{xij}, j = 1,\ldots,K(t), t = 1,\ldots,k$$

$$\hat{\lambda}^2_{ij} = y_{ij} y'_{ij} - \hat{\sigma}^2_{yij}, j = 1,\ldots,L(i), i = 1,\ldots,m$$

where $\hat{\sigma}^2_{xij} = \hat{\phi}^{-1}_{xij}, \hat{\sigma}^2_{yij} = \hat{\phi}^{-1}_{yij}, \hat{\phi}_{xij}$ and $\hat{\phi}_{yij}$ are diagonal elements of matrix $\hat{\Sigma}^{-1}_{xi}$ and $\hat{\Sigma}^{-1}_{yi}$ respectively, here $\hat{\Sigma}_{xi} = x_i x'_i$, $\hat{\Sigma}_{yi} = y_i y'_i$.

As the initial values of ω_{ij} are chosen using some kind of a generalized least squares method that yields best linear unbiased estimators. This method is called the best iterative method in least squares sense.

For the final computational formula problems of CSI, the steady and comprehensive final computational formula of CSI proposed is as follows:

$$\text{CSI} = \frac{\sum_{i=1}^{n1} \omega_i \gamma_i X_i + \sum_{i=n1}^{n2} \omega_i \beta_i Y_i + \sum_{i=n2}^{n3} \omega_i Y_i}{\sum_{i=1}^{n1} \omega_i \gamma_i + \sum_{i=n1}^{n2} \omega_i \beta_i + \sum_{i=n2}^{n3} \omega_i}$$

We can give the following intuitive interpretation for this formula of CSI.

First determine all the influence coefficients of observation variables impacting on the structural variables of the CSI variables. The size of these influence coefficients will show which observational variables are more important. We must note that an observational variable can affect more than one structural variable. One must take into account the direct impact of that variable on a structural variable and the indirect effect through other structural variables, as the structural variables are related to each other through SEM. The predetermined or exogenous variable X has its effects on CSI through Y, and those effects are captured by the coefficients γ_i. The weights of the variables used in the numerator of CSI denote the direct and indirect effects of observed variables on the structural variables, and the denominator is just the sum of all weights that normalize the index.

The structural variables of CSI won't affect CSI. Comparing with the formula proposed by some researchers:

$$CSI = \frac{E(\xi) - \min(\xi)}{\max(\xi) - \min(\xi)}$$

where

$$\max(\xi) = \sum_{i=1}^{n} \omega_i \max(X_i), \quad \min(\xi) = \sum_{i=1}^{n} \omega_i \min(X_i)$$

our formula is apparently more steady as well as comprehensive.

Example 9.5   Europe Customer Satisfaction Index (ECSI) analysis The structural variables of ECSI analysis include four independent variables, three dependent variables, and 10 relations. The structural equation model is shown in Figure 9.8.

Its structural equations are:

$$\begin{pmatrix} \eta_1 \\ \eta_2 \\ \eta_3 \end{pmatrix} = \begin{pmatrix} 0 & 0 & 0 \\ \beta_{21} & 0 & 0 \\ 0 & \beta_{32} & 0 \end{pmatrix} \begin{pmatrix} \eta_1 \\ \eta_2 \\ \eta_3 \end{pmatrix} + \begin{pmatrix} \gamma_{11} & \gamma_{12} & \gamma_{13} & \gamma_{14} \\ 0 & \gamma_{22} & \gamma_{23} & 0 \\ \gamma_{31} & 0 & 0 & \gamma_{34} \end{pmatrix} \begin{pmatrix} \xi_1 \\ \xi_2 \\ \xi_3 \\ \xi_4 \end{pmatrix} + \begin{pmatrix} \varepsilon_1 \\ \varepsilon_2 \\ \varepsilon_3 \end{pmatrix}$$

The numbers of the corresponding observed variables of each structural variable are 2, 3, 4, 2, 3, 3, 3 in turn. The ordering of structural variables is image ξ_1, expected quality ξ_2, perceived quality software ξ_3, perceived quality hardware ξ_4, perceived value η_1, CS η_2 and customer loyalty η_3.

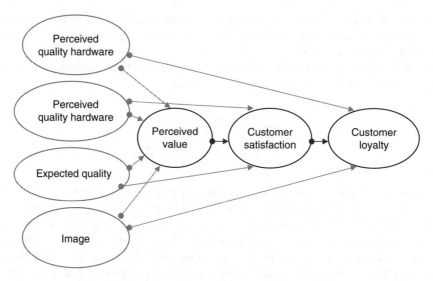

Figure 9.8 Customer satisfaction index of Europe.

The corresponding observed variables of independent variables are expressed as $x_i, i = 1,\ldots,11$, and the corresponding observed variables of dependent variables are expressed as $y_j, j = 1,\ldots,9$. The relation equation of structural variables and observed variables corresponding to independent variables is:

$$
\begin{pmatrix}
x_1 \\ x_2 \\ x_3 \\ x_4 \\ x_5 \\ x_6 \\ x_7 \\ x_8 \\ x_9 \\ x_{10} \\ x_{11}
\end{pmatrix}
=
\begin{pmatrix}
\lambda_{11} & 0 & 0 & 0 \\
\lambda_{21} & 0 & 0 & 0 \\
0 & \lambda_{12} & 0 & 0 \\
0 & \lambda_{22} & 0 & 0 \\
0 & \lambda_{32} & 0 & 0 \\
0 & 0 & \lambda_{13} & 0 \\
0 & 0 & \lambda_{23} & 0 \\
0 & 0 & \lambda_{33} & 0 \\
0 & 0 & \lambda_{43} & 0 \\
0 & 0 & 0 & \lambda_{14} \\
0 & 0 & 0 & \lambda_{24}
\end{pmatrix}
\begin{pmatrix}
\xi_1 \\ \xi_2 \\ \xi_3 \\ \xi_4
\end{pmatrix}
+
\begin{pmatrix}
\varepsilon_1 \\ \varepsilon_2 \\ \varepsilon_3 \\ \varepsilon_4 \\ \varepsilon_5 \\ \varepsilon_6 \\ \varepsilon_7 \\ \varepsilon_8 \\ \varepsilon_9 \\ \varepsilon_{10} \\ \varepsilon_{11}
\end{pmatrix}
$$

The relation equation of structural variables and observed variables corresponding to dependent variables is:

$$
\begin{pmatrix}
y_1 \\ y_2 \\ y_3 \\ y_4 \\ y_5 \\ y_6 \\ y_7 \\ y_8 \\ y_9
\end{pmatrix}
=
\begin{pmatrix}
\rho_{11} & 0 & 0 \\
\rho_{21} & 0 & 0 \\
\rho_{31} & 0 & 0 \\
0 & \rho_{12} & 0 \\
0 & \rho_{22} & 0 \\
0 & \rho_{32} & 0 \\
0 & 0 & \rho_{13} \\
0 & 0 & \rho_{23} \\
0 & 0 & \rho_{33}
\end{pmatrix}
\begin{pmatrix}
\eta_1 \\ \eta_2 \\ \eta_3
\end{pmatrix}
+
\begin{pmatrix}
\varepsilon_1 \\ \varepsilon_2 \\ \varepsilon_3 \\ \varepsilon_4 \\ \varepsilon_5 \\ \varepsilon_6 \\ \varepsilon_7 \\ \varepsilon_8 \\ \varepsilon_9
\end{pmatrix}
$$

where λ_{ij} and ρ_{ij} are loading coefficients, and ε_i are error terms. Note that this model is peculiar. Its independent variables are more than one, so we have to pay attention to determinant restriction when we write the model matrix.

The reverse relation equations are:

$$\xi_i = \omega_{i1}x_{i1} + \cdots + \omega_{ij}x_{ij} + \varepsilon_i, i = 1,\ldots,4$$

$$\begin{pmatrix} \eta_1 \\ \eta_2 \\ \eta_3 \end{pmatrix} = \begin{pmatrix} \omega_{11}y_{11} + \omega_{12}y_{12} + \cdots + \omega_{1j}y_{1j} \\ \omega_{21}y_{21} + \omega_{22}y_{22} + \cdots + \omega_{2j}y_{2j} \\ \omega_{31}y_{31} + \omega_{32}y_{32} + \cdots + \omega_{3j}y_{3j} \end{pmatrix} + \begin{pmatrix} \varepsilon_1 \\ \varepsilon_2 \\ \varepsilon_3 \end{pmatrix}$$

How many coefficients ω_{ij} are there? The number is the same as that of observed variables (including independent variables and dependent variables). What is the ordering of ω_{ij}? The ordering is the same as that of observation variables, one-to-one. What are the functions of ω_{ij}? There are three functions: 1. Variables assembling function that converts several observation variables to corresponding structural variables, as the equation above. 2. Path transmission function: Combining internal coefficients β_i of structural equations, and the effects of coefficients from arbitrary structural variables to arbitrary observation variables. 3. Formula computation function: ultimately CSI is calculated by ω_{ij}, not by λ_i.

We wrote computer programs in DASC that can perform all of these computations. Please refer to the DASC software for detailed computation process. Of course, DASC is user-friendly and all the variables, relations and the parameters of the model could be modified by users.

9.3.3 Definite linear algorithm for SEM

In the previous section we described the modular constraint least squares solution based on modular constraint (with the constraints that the structural vector is a unit vector). In the structural equation (9.16), if each structural variable is multiplied by the same multiplier, its coefficient solutions are the same according to the Lemma 1. From this point of view, the solution of structural equations does not really depend on the modular constraint. But it is not reasonable to stipulate that modular length of each structural variable is 1. What is reasonable is to normalize one structural variable to a unit length.

We need to find a more reasonable constraint to replace modular constraint, and get a **definite linear algorithm** for SEM (Tong et al., 2010). After getting MCLS, we can change the modular length of structural variables in observation equations to make the path coefficients which are between each structural variable and its corresponding observed variables satisfy some conditions. In equations (9.13) and (9.14), the prescription conditions are:

$$\sum_{j=1}^{K(t)} \psi_{tj} = 1, \psi_{tj} \geq 0, t = 1,\ldots,k$$

$$\sum_{j=1}^{L(i)} \omega_{ij} = 1, \omega_{ij} \geq 0, i = 1,\ldots,m$$

There are two cases to compute the prescription condition.

If the corresponding path coefficients of MCLS are non-negative at the beginning, we just need to divide a constant at the two sides of the equation (9.13) and (9.14). This constant should be the sum of corresponding path coefficients in MCLS. For example, in equation (9.13), if $\sum_{j=1}^{K(i)} \psi_{ij} = c_i$, two sides of equation (9.13) are divided by the constant c_i, so modular length of structural variables becomes $1/c_i$, and $\sum_{j=1}^{K(i)} \psi_{ij} = 1$.

If the corresponding path coefficients of MCLS are negative at the beginning of the algorithm, we cannot completely use the method of **prescription regression** proposed by Fang (1982, 1985), because we do not completely know the dependent variables of regression. Now we know the direction of regression dependent variables, but modular length is undecided. According to the theorem in Fang (1982), if the initial regression coefficients have negative values then the prescription regression coefficient should be 0. So we can make ordinary regression about MCLS first, here modular length of dependent variables is 1. If there are some non-positive items in the initial regression coefficients, we can get rid of those variables by forcing the corresponding regression coefficients to equal 0. Then two sides of equations (9.13) and (9.14) can be divided by a constant that should be the sum of the corresponding path coefficients in MCLS, as discussed in the previous section.

Of course we can improve the constraint of prescription condition. As mentioned previously, if some regression coefficients are 0, the corresponding variables may be removed from the model. But this is a pity. To avoid this situation, we may change prescription condition and let $\psi_{tj} \geq \delta$, $\omega_{ij} \geq \delta$, here $\delta > 0$ but not $\delta = 0$. That is:

$$\sum_{j=1}^{K(t)} \psi_{tj} = 1, \quad \psi_{tj} \geq \delta, t = 1,\dots,k$$

$$\sum_{j=1}^{K(t)} \omega_{ij} = 1, \quad \omega_{ij} \geq \delta, i = 1,\dots,m$$

If some initial regression coefficients are less than δ, they are all changed with δ, and the corresponding independent variables multiplied by coefficient δ should be removed to the left of the equation in the regression process.

Summarizing the modification suggested here in replacing the modular condition by a more general prescription condition we can improve the algorithm of MCLS.

Algorithm 3. No modular case with best choice of initial values and improvement on Step 3 of Algorithm 1.

Step 3'. After getting the estimated values as $\hat{\xi}_t$, $\hat{\eta}_i$ of the structural variables ξ_t, η_i in Step 2 of Algorithm 1, we calculate the summarizing coefficients ψ_{tj}, ω_{ij} by prescription regression, and recalculate the estimated values of ξ_t, η_i.

Step 3'-1. Make use of $\hat{\xi}_t$, $\hat{\eta}_i$ directly in Step 2, calculate $\hat{\psi}_{tj}$, $\hat{\omega}_{ij}$ in SEM^+ by common regression.

Step 3'-2. For any t, if for all j there are $\hat{\psi}_{tj} \geq \delta$ ($\delta \geq 0$) and $\sum_{j=1}^{K(t)} \psi_{tj} = c_t$, then both sides of equation (9.13) are divided by c_t. In the same way, for any i, if for all j there are $\omega_{ij} \geq \delta$ ($\delta \geq 0$) and $\sum_{j=1}^{L(i)} \omega_{ij} = c_i$, then the both sides of equation (9.14) are divided by c_i.

After checking all t, i, go to Step 4 in Algorithm 1.

Step 3'-3. For any t, i, if there is j to make $\hat{\psi}_{tj} < \delta$, or $\omega_{ij} < \delta (\delta \geq 0)$, then let corresponding item be fixed, i.e. $\hat{\psi}_{tj} = \delta$ or $\hat{\omega}_{ij} = \delta$. After checking all of j, go to Step 3'-1 and Step 3'-2 in this algorithm.

Note that if some regression coefficients are fixed in common regression, the corresponding independent variables with the coefficient δ should be removed to the left of the equation, and combined with the dependent variable to regress. After regression, the corresponding independent variables with the coefficient δ should be removed to the right of the equation.

Table 9.9 The original data (10 rows and 20 columns).

ξ_1				η_1			η_2			η_3					η_4			η_5	
4	8	7	7	9	9	8	3	5	5	9	4	6	8	4	7	8	7	8	7
7	9	8	5	5	9	7	5	7	7	2	9	8	9	5	2	5	9	2	5
3	5	8	4	5	8	4	2	9	2	6	6	9	9	7	7	3	4	7	7
2	8	7	8	9	9	7	6	2	2	9	4	9	9	4	3	7	3	7	8
4	3	2	9	2	9	3	8	2	4	6	2	8	2	9	3	3	9	2	6
7	8	7	7	7	6	9	6	3	3	7	2	7	5	5	6	3	7	2	2
5	8	8	6	7	3	2	5	3	6	5	4	3	4	4	5	5	4	3	9
4	3	7	7	5	7	7	9	5	9	3	5	5	6	4	6	9	2	7	4
5	5	8	9	3	6	5	9	3	9	3	8	7	5	8	9	2	7	7	4
6	7	9	7	3	7	2	9	5	9	2	9	8	7	4	9	6	5	9	5

Table 9.10 The estimation values of the parameters of the structural equations.

β_{ij}						γ_i
0.000000	0.000000	0.000000	0.000000	0.000000		6.836155
−0.271872	0.000000	0.000000	0.000000	0.000000		8.025583
0.929838	1.394757	0.000000	0.000000	0.000000		1.394757
0.000000	0.000000	0.584309	0.000000	0.000000		0.000000
0.000000	0.000000	0.272769	0.268439	0.000000		0.000000

Example 9.6 Customer satisfaction index analysis of China   The row of the data matrix is $N = 10$. The numbers of the observation variables for each structure variable are 4, 3, 3, 5, 3, 2, so the column count of the data matrix is 20. The number of structural variables is 6. The original data are presented in Table 9.9.

The results of calculation of CSI are summarized in Table 9.10. The left part in Table 9.10 is the matrix $B(\beta_{ij})$, and the right part in Table 9.10 is the matrix $\Gamma(\gamma_i)$.

The estimated values of the structural variables are shown in Table 9.11. The first column is the independent variable, and the other columns are dependent variables.

If we do not use our definite algorithm, then some estimated values of the structural variables may be negative. That is not reasonable. The other results of the calculation are omitted here.

Our algorithm is a linear algorithm without repeated iterations. Its calculation process is well-defined and the computations result in a unique solution. Some potential problems of computation, such as multicollinearity, are common problems in LSE, and are not unique to our algorithm. Compared with two known algorithms, LISREL and PLS of SEM, our algorithm has a non-contestable advantage, because it is a definite linear algorithm without any convergence problem which is a serious problem with LISREL or PLS. Our algorithm process has been programmed and the computation procedure is very fast. The program has been included in our DASC software.

Table 9.11   The estimation values of the structural variables.

$\hat{\xi}_1$	$\hat{\eta}_1$	$\hat{\eta}_2$	$\hat{\eta}_3$	$\hat{\eta}_4$	$\hat{\eta}_5$
0.668898	0.867064	0.432110	0.620453	0.733009	0.749979
0.725599	0.702217	0.632110	0.661388	0.533495	0.350064
0.519251	0.569323	0.427331	0.741121	0.467476	0.700000
0.658026	0.834128	0.335780	0.701436	0.432038	0.750021
0.453397	0.471540	0.470828	0.539919	0.500972	0.400086
0.725836	0.731785	0.401835	0.520628	0.534467	0.200000
0.688890	0.398975	0.468628	0.399581	0.466505	0.600129
0.539718	0.634044	0.770097	0.460604	0.565047	0.549936
0.692640	0.468131	0.705145	0.619976	0.601943	0.549936
0.737218	0.403409	0.770097	0.601250	0.666991	0.699914

9.3.4   Multi-layers path analysis model

In general, what the CSI literature narrates is usually a single layer model. Those are structural variables which are directly correlative with observation variables. When the present writer was giving lessons in CSI model classes across the country, some large enterprises proposed that their work needed a multilayer path analysis model. For example, the perceived quality of cell phone is a structural quality, and has some derivative quality types as well, such as appearance quality, speech quality, reliability quality, etc. Then each type of quality is correlated with several observation variables. Thus, research into the multi-layer structural model is required.

As we demonstrated below we incorporated such a **multilayer path analysis model** as Figure 9.9 through a SEM.

In the structural equations, the independent variables (only affect other variables, not be affected by other variables) consist of 8: brand image ξ_1, expectation quality 1 ξ_2, expectation quality 2 ξ_3, perceived quality 1 ξ_4, perceived quality 2 ξ_5, perceived quality 3 ξ_6, perceived value 1 ξ_7 and perceived value 2 ξ_8.

In the structural equations, the dependent variables (either affect other variables, or be affected by other variables) still include 5: expectation quality η_1, perceived quality η_2, perceived value η_3 (η_1, η_2, η_3 are not directly correlated with observation variables), CSI η_4, customer loyalty η_5. The basic structural equations are as follows (ς_i are random error items)

$$
\begin{pmatrix} \eta_1 \\ \eta_2 \\ \eta_3 \\ \eta_4 \\ \eta_5 \end{pmatrix} = \begin{pmatrix} 0 & 0 & 0 & 0 & 0 \\ \beta_{21} & 0 & 0 & 0 & 0 \\ \beta_{31} & \beta_{32} & 0 & 0 & 0 \\ \beta_{41} & \beta_{42} & \beta_{43} & 0 & 0 \\ 0 & 0 & 0 & \beta_{54} & 0 \end{pmatrix} \begin{pmatrix} \eta_1 \\ \eta_2 \\ \eta_3 \\ \eta_4 \\ \eta_5 \end{pmatrix}
$$

$$
+ \begin{pmatrix} \gamma_{11} & \gamma_{12} & \gamma_{13} & 0 & 0 & 0 & 0 & 0 \\ \gamma_{21} & 0 & 0 & \gamma_{24} & \gamma_{25} & \gamma_{26} & 0 & 0 \\ \gamma_{31} & 0 & 0 & 0 & 0 & 0 & \gamma_{37} & \gamma_{38} \\ \gamma_{41} & 0 & 0 & 0 & 0 & 0 & 0 & 0 \\ 0 & 0 & 0 & 0 & 0 & 0 & 0 & 0 \end{pmatrix} \begin{pmatrix} \xi_1 \\ \xi_2 \\ \xi_3 \\ \xi_4 \\ \xi_5 \\ \xi_6 \\ \xi_7 \\ \xi_8 \end{pmatrix} + \begin{pmatrix} \varsigma_1 \\ \varsigma_2 \\ \varsigma_3 \\ \varsigma_4 \\ \varsigma_5 \end{pmatrix}
$$

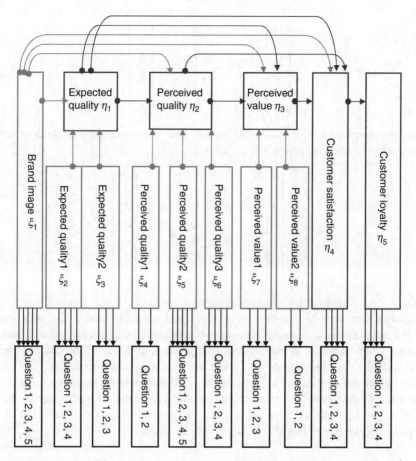

Figure 9.9 Multi-layers path analysis model.

In this model, the numbers of observation variables corresponding to each structural variable are in turn 5, 4, 3, 2, 5, 4, 3, 2, 0, 0, 0, 4, and 4. The ordering is ξ_1, ξ_2, ξ_3, ξ_4, ξ_5, ξ_6, ξ_7, ξ_8, η_1, η_2, η_3, η_4, η_5. We should notice that above ordering decides the column sequence in observation data matrix.

The corresponding observation variables of independent variables are expressed as x_i, $i = 1,\ldots, 6$, and the corresponding observation variables of dependent variables are expressed as y_j, $j = 1,\ldots,12$. The relation equation of structural variables and observation variables corresponding to independent variables is

$$
\begin{pmatrix} x_1 \\ \vdots \\ x_{r(i)} \end{pmatrix} = \begin{pmatrix} \mu_1 \\ \vdots \\ \mu_{r(i)} \end{pmatrix} \xi_i + \begin{pmatrix} \delta_1 \\ \vdots \\ \delta_{r(i)} \end{pmatrix}
$$

$i = 1,2,\ldots,8$. $r(i)$ are respectively 5, 4, 3, 2, 5, 4, 3, 2. The relation equation of structural variables and observation variables corresponding to directly dependent variables is

$$
\begin{pmatrix} y_1 \\ \vdots \\ y_4 \\ y_5 \\ \vdots \\ y_6 \end{pmatrix} = \begin{pmatrix} \lambda_{11} & 0 \\ \vdots & 0 \\ \lambda_{41} & 0 \\ 0 & \lambda_{12} \\ 0 & \vdots \\ 0 & \lambda_{42} \end{pmatrix} \begin{pmatrix} \eta_1 \\ \eta_2 \end{pmatrix} + \begin{pmatrix} \delta_1 \\ \vdots \\ \delta_4 \\ \delta_1 \\ \vdots \\ \delta_4 \end{pmatrix}
$$

The relation equation of structural variables and low layer structure independent variables corresponding to indirectly dependent variables is

$$
\begin{pmatrix} \xi_2 \\ \xi_3 \\ \xi_4 \\ \xi_5 \\ \xi_6 \\ \xi_7 \\ \xi_8 \end{pmatrix} = \begin{pmatrix} \alpha_{11} & 0 & 0 \\ \alpha_{21} & 0 & 0 \\ 0 & \alpha_{12} & 0 \\ 0 & \alpha_{22} & 0 \\ 0 & \alpha_{32} & 0 \\ 0 & 0 & \alpha_{13} \\ 0 & 0 & \alpha_{23} \end{pmatrix} \begin{pmatrix} \eta_1 \\ \eta_2 \\ \eta_3 \end{pmatrix} + \begin{pmatrix} \delta_1 \\ \delta_2 \\ \delta_3 \\ \delta_4 \\ \delta_5 \\ \delta_6 \\ \delta_7 \end{pmatrix}
$$

where $\mu_{ij}, \lambda_{ij}, \alpha_{ij}$ are loading items, and δ_i are error items.

The algorithm scheme for the multi-layers path analysis model has been given in Figure 9.9 and the equations above. It raises two points. First we treat all latent variables that affect other latent variables as independent variables, i.e. all lower latent variables are independent variables, and denote them as ξ_i. Second, we can get the estimate value of all latent variables by our definite algorithm from the data of the observation variables, only the value of higher layer latent variables needs to be calculated from the estimate value of the lower layer latent variables but not from observation variables directly. The calculation of multi-layers path analysis model can also be completed by DASC.

9.4   Data analysis and process

9.4.1   Panel data analysis

The basic character of **panel data** is that it combines time series of cross sectional data. For example, suppose that a study involves 6000 families consisting of 15 000 persons. They have been followed-up through surveys for 30 years. The index records of these consist of panel data of 450 000 panel data observations.

For example, in Section 6.3, in Chapter 6, we presented a **Stochastic Frontier Model**. Assume that there are n production operation units. The input data of each unit have d indexes referring to d different inputs, and the output data have only one index. They are observed in T periods of time. The data set is $(y_{it}, X_{it}) = (y_{it}, X_{it1}, \ldots, X_{itd})$, $i = 1,2,\ldots, n$, $t = 1,2,\ldots, T$. Then the data set is panel data. The stochastic frontier linear model we set up is

$$
y_{it} = X'_{it}\,\beta + \alpha_i + \varepsilon_{it}, i = 1,\ldots,n, \ t = 1,\ldots,T
$$

where β is the d-dimensional parameters to be estimated, $\varepsilon_{it} \sim i.i.d.\ N(0, \sigma^2)$ and σ^2 is unknown. α_i is a random influence that is invariant in time. This is a typical expression of the panel data linear regression model.

In Section 6.2, in Chapter 6, we studied the **Self Modeling Regression Model**, reviewing the output of the ith company at the tth moment, the price of the ith stock at the tth moment, the reaction of the ith patient at the tth moment, the height of the ith child at the tth moment, etc. The nonlinear or nonparametric regression model we set up is as

$$y_{it} = f_i(x_{it}) + \varepsilon_{it}, \ i = 1,\ldots,n, \ t = 1,\ldots,T$$

This is again a typical expression of nonlinear or nonparametric analysis for panel data.

The panel data analysis includes, like most of the methods discussed in this book, parameter estimation or hypothesis testing. Panel data modeling and analysis is actually an extension of multiple regression analysis to special problems arising from the panel data nature. These problems are whether the data are pooled or not, whether heteroscedasticity is related with cross sectional data only or with time series data only or with both (error component models), and how to test for nonstationarity when the data are cross section of time series or time series of cross section. For more detail on these topics the reader may consult Baltagi (2008).

We wrote computer programs in our DASC software for estimation and hypothesis testing with panel data modeling. These are illustrated for two types of panel data models, multiple parametric liner regression analysis (stochastic frontier regression model), and nonparametric and nonlinear regression model with panel data (self-modeling model).

9.4.2   Truncated data analysis

If data are from a part of population, an especially truncated population instead of the whole population, it poses some special problems of analysis called **Truncated Data Analysis**.

Tong (1994) studied the problem of analyzing gear life by gear noise, which is a typical truncated data problem, as when the gear noise is not heard the gear life is not monitored. Let us consider, for example, a situation where the stock price varies in such a way that the variance of stock price increases over time, but if this variance exceeds a threshold the stock exchange would not permit any trade. Assume that in a short time the stock price variance K is governed by the law:

$$K = rt$$

Here r is affected by many independent factors both within and outside, and outside the stock market. Thus we may say that r is a random variable with a distribution similar to normal distribution truncated at zero, whose mean is $\bar{r}$ and variance is σ^2. With the condition $r > 0$, the distribution is actually truncated normal, the density function of which is a **distribution of gear life**:

$$f_r(r) = \begin{cases} \dfrac{C}{\sqrt{2\pi}} \exp\left(-\dfrac{(r-\bar{r})^2}{2\sigma^2}\right), & when\, r > 0 \\ 0, & when\ r \leq 0 \end{cases}$$

where the concept of typical truncated data has been introduced. The constant C of density function can be easily calculated by the property that the integral of density function of the truncated density is 1. $C = \dfrac{1}{\Phi(\bar{r}/\sigma)}$, where Φ is a standard normal cumulative distribution function.

Assume the operating time before the limit of stock, then

$$T = \frac{K_{max}}{r}$$

is also a random variable. By the derivation of the probability density of a function of a random variable in probability theory, we can derive the density function of T:

$$f(t) = \begin{cases} \dfrac{k}{\sqrt{2\pi}\sigma\,\Phi(\bar{r}/\sigma)}\exp\left(-\dfrac{(k-\bar{r}t)^2}{2\sigma^2 t^2}\right), & when\ r > 0 \\ 0, & when\ r \le 0 \end{cases}$$

where $k = K_{max}$. The distribution function of T is

$$F(t) = \frac{1-\Phi(k/(\sigma t)-\bar{r}/\sigma)}{\Phi(\bar{r}/\sigma)}$$

Now let us look at the picture of $f(t)$. Let $t \to 0^+$.

Since $t^2\exp\left[\dfrac{1}{2\sigma^2}\left(\dfrac{k}{t}-\bar{r}\right)^2\right] \to +\infty$, $f(t) \to 0^+$. Let $t \to +\infty$, namely, $f(t) \to 0^+$.

Differentiate $f(t)$, and we obtain:

$$f'(t) = f(t)\left(-\frac{2}{t}+\frac{k(k/t-\bar{r})}{t^2\sigma^2}\right)$$

The solution of equation $f'(t) = 0$ is

$$t = \frac{k}{4\sigma^2}\left(-\bar{r}\pm\sqrt{\bar{r}^2+8\sigma^2}\right)$$

When $t > 0$, the solution of equation $f'(t) = 0$ is unique. Meanwhile, $f(t)$ has a unique peak value, or the picture of the density function is unimodal. Its left limit is the origin, and the horizontal asymptote is t axis. Its mode is determined by the equation above.

We might as well call this distribution **Stocks Free Stroke Distribution**. We discussed the analysis in the Electronic References, Example 3-2-1 Negative Order Moment Estimation, Section 2, Chapter 3.

9.4.3   Censored data analysis

It is quite common in the field of economics, sociology, and psychology that we make observations only if an underlying variable is above a threshold. This kind of data is called **Censored Data**. For example, suppose we are interested in recording the expenditure on any durable goods such as a refrigerator or a house by a household with the independent variable being the income of the household. While the households have both low and high incomes we record data only for those who buy either the refrigerator/house, the dependent variable being the expenditure on the refrigerator/house. For all those households that did not buy the durable goods we do not have information on either expenditure on the durable good or income of the household.

There are many such problems in economics and other social sciences. We can now formalize the model as follows: Assume that the expenditure on housing (housing investment) Y^* and the income X have the linear relation

$$Y_i^* = X_i'\,\beta+\varepsilon_i, \quad i = 1,...,n$$

But what we have observed is truncated data:

$$Y_i = \begin{cases} Y_i^* & \text{if } Y_i^* > c \\ c & \text{if } Y_i^* \le c \end{cases}$$

Our goal is to construct a regression model based on this truncated data, estimate its parameters, and to perform tests of hypotheses.

Tobin (1958) realized the importance in economics for generalizing the regression model in order to deal with such real-life situations and introduced his model, which is now called the Tobit model. He introduced maximum likelihood estimation method for parameters. Please see Paragraph 4, Section 2, Chapter 5 in this book for details.

9.4.4 Duration data analysis

Duration data are some of the important types of data that need econometric modeling. The duration of a strike or a lock out of a company, the duration of unemployment of a person, the duration of a recession, etc. are some examples. We studied in Section 6.3, in Chapter 6 duration data models. Some important concepts used in duration modeling are duration time t, distribution density function $f(t)$ and distribution function $F(t)$ and survival function $S(t)$:

$$S(t) = 1 - F(t)$$

Hazard Rate function $r(t)$ and the relations link all these terms.

$$r(t) = \frac{f(t)}{1 - F(t)} = \frac{f(t)}{S(t)}$$

$$S(t) = \exp\left(-\int_0^t r(t)dt\right)$$

$$f(t) = -S'(t)$$

For some common distributions, we list the density, hazard rate, and survival functions in the following table.

Table 9.12 Density functions, hazard rate functions and survival functions.

Distribution	Density Function $f(t)$	Hazard Rate Function $r(t)$	Survival Function $S(t)$
Exponential	$\lambda \exp(-\lambda t)$	λ	$\exp(-\lambda t)$
Weibull	$\lambda m\, t^{m-1} \exp(-\lambda t^m)$	$\lambda m\, t^{m-1}$	$\exp(-\lambda t^m)$
Weibull	$\lambda p(\lambda t)^{p-1} \exp(-(\lambda t)^p)$	$\lambda p(\lambda t)^{p-1}$	$\exp(-(\lambda t)^p)$
Logarithmic Normal	$\dfrac{p}{t}\phi(p\ln(\lambda t))$	$\dfrac{t}{p} \cdot \dfrac{\phi(p\ln(\lambda t))}{\Phi(-p\ln(\lambda t))}$	$\Phi(-p\ln(\lambda t))$
Logarithm Logistic	$\dfrac{\lambda p(\lambda t)^{p-1}}{(1+(\lambda t)^p)^2}$	$\dfrac{\lambda p(\lambda t)^{p-1}}{1+(\lambda t)^p}$	$\dfrac{1}{1+(\lambda t)^p}$

In the table above, $\Phi(\cdot)$ is the distribution function with standard normal distribution, and $\phi(\cdot)$ is the density function with standard normal distribution. If $\ln(t)$ has normal distribution then variable t has log normal distribution. If $\ln(t)$ has logistic distribution then variable t has logistic distribution.

Example 9.7   Bond data duration fitting   We consider the problem of fitting a model to **bond duration data**. Let P_i^* represent the theoretical price of the ith bond. P_i represents the actual price of the ith bond. $CF_t^{(i)}$ represents the cash flow for the period t, where the ith bond generates. $D(t)$ represents discount function corresponding to time t. $R(0,t)$ represents the interest rate prevailing at time t. Dur_{Mi} represents the duration (duration for which the bond is held or is it the maturity period of the bond?) of the ith bond.

The duration weighted objective function is

$$\min_{\theta} \sum_{i=1}^{n} \omega_i^2 \frac{(P_i^* - P_i)^2}{n}$$

where

$$\omega_i = \frac{1/Dur_{Mi}}{\sum_{i=1}^{n} 1/Dur_{Mi}}$$

Therefore, the weighted coefficients meet the normalization condition:

$$\sum_{i=1}^{n} \omega_i = 1$$

The discount function $D(t)$ is relevant to the theoretical price P_i^*:

$$P_i^* = \sum_t CF_t^{(i)} \cdot D(t)$$

The interest rate $R(0, t)$ is relevant to Discount function $D(t)$:

$$D(t) = \exp(-t \cdot R(0,t))$$

Interest rate $R(0, t)$ depends on six parameters:

$$R(0,t) = \beta_0 + \beta_1 h\left(\frac{t}{\tau_1}\right) + \beta_2 \left[h\left(\frac{t}{\tau_1}\right) - \exp\left(-\frac{t}{\tau_1}\right)\right] + \beta_3 \left[h\left(\frac{t}{\tau_2}\right) - \exp\left(-\frac{t}{\tau_2}\right)\right]$$

where the function

$$h\left(\frac{t}{\tau}\right) = \frac{1 - \exp(-\frac{t}{\tau})}{\frac{t}{\tau}}$$

The parameters to be estimated are represented as a six dimensional vector as follows:

$$\theta = (\tau_1, \tau_2, \beta_0, \beta_1, \beta_2, \beta_3)$$

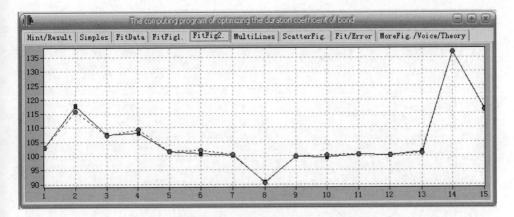

Figure 9.10   Bond data for duration fitting.

The parameters have constraint conditions:

$$5 \le \tau_1 \le 25, \ 2 \le \tau_2 \le 17$$
$$-0.1 \le \beta_0 \le 0.1, \ -0.1 \le \beta_1 \le 0.1$$
$$-1 \le \beta_2 \le 1, \ -1 \le \beta_3 \le 1$$

Our goal is to make use of the observation index data which are the actual price P_i of bonds, duration Dur_{Mi} of bonds and current flow $CF_t^{(i)}$ at the time t, to optimize 6 parameters in order to minimize the objective function. The actual observation data, including 15 bonds and 192 observations, can be found in DASC→Regression→Nonlinear regression→Bond Duration Data Fitting.

After users input the number of bonds, prepare observations data according to the form in the table above, and input constraint conditions and initial value of parameters to be estimated, computing can begin. As a result, the square sum of residual is 0.00060558, and the estimated parameters are: $\hat{\tau}_1 = 12.899740$, $\hat{\tau}_2 = 15.869612$, $\hat{\beta}_0 = -0.057663$, $\hat{\beta}_1 = 0.090730$, $\hat{\beta}_2 = -0.382015$, $\hat{\beta}_4 = 0.576445$.

In Figure 9.10, bullets with a dotted line are the original values of bond price, and square points with a solid line are fitted values. Figure 9.11 is the second system of figures in DASC. Other calculation and test results are omitted here. The figure and computation can be performed by clicking DASC→Regression→Nonlinear Regression→Bond Data Duration Fitting.

9.4.5   High dimensional data visualization

There are many approaches **to High-dimensional Data Visualization**. One is to compress high-m-dimensional data into low-two-dimensional data to display it, such as **Projection searching**:

$$Y_{2 \times n} = u'_{2 \times m} \, X_{m \times n}$$

This can be displayed on a two-dimensional plane. By changing projection vector u, the display varies, from which we could discover the internal relation of data, such as cluster, etc.

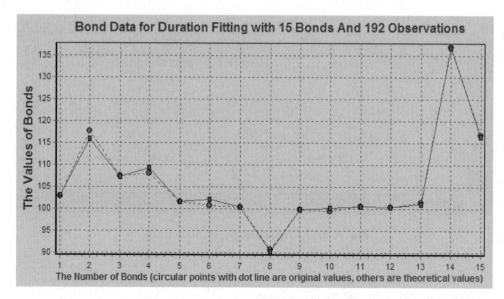

Figure 9.11   Bond data for duration fitting.

The projection searching method was introduced in Section 9.1. When we discussed the **Single Index Model** in Section 6.2, in Chapter 6, the problems of compressing high-dimensional vector also are appeared. For the **Partial Least Squares** method in Section 2 of the Electronic References, in Chapter 8, the basic idea to compress high-dimensional data into one-dimensional data then makes regression as well.

In fact, all of the multivariate linear regression models $y = X\beta + \varepsilon$ are intended to compress high-dimensional data, in order to minimize the distance between compressed one-dimensional vector $X\beta$ and one-dimensional vector y. From this point of view, the algorithms of SEM, including PLS and our definite linear algorithm in this chapter, are all intended to compress high-dimensional data into one-dimensional vector.

There are other situations where one can use the idea of projection and compression, such as the discriminant analysis in Section 9.3 involving Fisher's idea of projecting high-dimensional data into one-dimensional data so as to maximize the variance.

The radar picture is a device for high-dimensional data visualization. Designate a point as a center on a plane. If the dimension of high-dimensional data is m, make m pieces of radial from the center, and divide the round angle into m equal parts. Choose appropriate scales on radials. For each point, mark the m coordinates on radials in turn, and then several polygons are formed. These polygons provide high-dimensional data visualization, as displayed in Figure 9.12.

As with radar there are other lower dimensional visualization tools such as Polar, Wind Rose, and Smith. These are illustrated in Figures 9.13, 9.14, and 9.15. The figures can be accessed by clicking DASC → Figures → Reticulation Figures.

Data visualization is one of the main intuitive research ideas to which this book attaches great importance. But it doesn't have to be limited to the high-dimensional. Whether the data are high-dimensional or low-dimensional, we recommend that the internal relations within

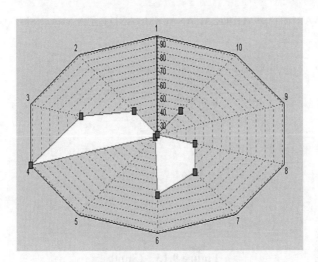

Figure 9.12 (Radar).

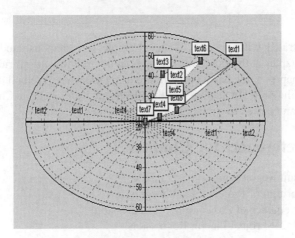

Figure 9.13 (Polar).

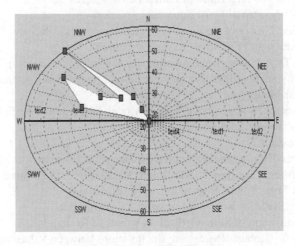

Figure 9.14 (WindRose).

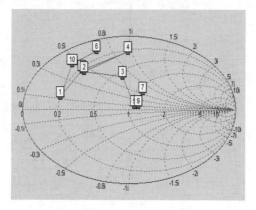

Figure 9.15   (Smith).

the data be illustrated with pictures. Some examples are demonstrated in this book. In Section 2.3, in Chapter 2, the ridge trace figure can be used to confirm ridge parameters. In Section 5.3, in Chapter 5, the basin curve figure using piecewise Weibull distribution can be used to analyze failure rate. In Section 3 of the Electronic References, in Chapter 6, the signal detection figure can be used to explain wavelet regression.

Electronic references for Chapter 9

References

Baltagi B.H. (2008) *Econometric Analysis of Panel Data*, John Wiley & Sons, Ltd. 4th edn, Chichester.

Brown P.J. (1982) Multivariate calibration (with discussion). *J. R. Statist. Soc. B* **44**, 287–321.

Causeur D., Dhorne T. & Antoni A. (2005) A two-way analysis of variance model with positive definite interaction for homologous factors. *Journal of Multivariate Analysis* **95**, 431–48.

Efron B. (1983) Estimating the error rate of a prediction rule: improvement on cross-validation. *J.Am.Statist.Assoc* **78**, 316–31.

Fang K.T., Wang D.Q. & Wu G.F. (1982) A class of constraint regression—fill a prescription regression (in Chinese). *Mathematica Numerica Sinica* **4**, 57–69.

Fang K.T. & He S.D. (1985) Regression models with linear constraints and nonnegative regression coefficients. *Mathematica Numerica Sinica* **7**, 97–102.

Fang K.T., Quan H. & Chen Q.Y. (1988) *Practicaly Regression Analysis*, Science Press, Beijing.

Helland L.S. (1988) On the structure of partial least square regression. *Communs. Statist. Simuln* **17**, 581–607.

Hjorth U. (1989) On model selection in the computer age. *J. Statist. Planng Inf* **23**, 101–15.

Hogg R.V. & Randles R.H. (1975) Adaptive distribution free regression methods and their applications. *Technometrics* **17**, 3910–407.

Hogg R.V., Fisher D.M. & Randles R.H. (1975) A two-sample adaptive distribution-free test. *Journal of the American Statistical Association* **70**, 656–61.

Hsu N.-J., Bonnie R. & Breidt K. F. (2001) Long-range dependent common factor models: a bayesian approach. *Communications in Statistics—Theory and Methods* **30**, 1047–61.

Jarque C.M. & Bera A.K. (1981) Efficient tests for normality, homoscedasticity and serial independence of regression residuals: Monte Carlo evidence. *Economics Letters* **7**(4), 313–18.

Juran J.M. (1954) Universals in management planning and control. *Management Review* **10**, 748–61.

Jureckova J. (1971) Nonparametrice etimate of regession coeffiecients. *Annals of Mathematical Statistics* **42**, 1328–38.

Kleibergen F. & Zivot E. (2003) Bayesian and classical approaches to instrumental variable regression. *Journal of Econometrics* **114**, 210–72.

Kocherlakota S. & Kocherlakota K. (2001) Regession in the bivariate poisson distribution. *Communications in Statistics—Theory and Methods* **30**, 815–25.

Kundu D. & Murali G. (1996) Model selection in linear regression. *Computational Statistics & Data Analysis* **22**, 461–69.

Levine A., Liukkonen J. & Levine D.W. (1992) Pridicting power changes under transformations in ANOVA tests. *Communications in Statistics* **21**, 679–92.

Li B., Morris J. & Martin E.B. (2002) Model selection for partial least squares regression. *Chemometrics and Intelligent Laboratory Systems* **64**, 710–89.

Li H. (2001) Nested designs with multivariate measurement: an illustration of the structural approach to random effects multivariate analysis of variance. *Communications in Statistics – Theory and Methods* **30**, 887–95.

Lin W.B. (2007) The exploration of customer satisfaction model from a comprehensive perspective. *Expert Systems with Applications* **33**, 110–21.

Ortiz M.C., Arcos J. & Sarabia L. (1996) Using continuum regression for quantitative analysis with overlapping signals obtained by differential pulse polarography. *Chemometrics and Intelligent Laboratory Systems* **34**, 245–62.

Refik S. & Kadir T. (2006) Bayesian portfolio selection with multi-variate random variance models. *European Journal of Operational Research* **171**, 977–90.

Tong H.Q. (1993) Evaluation model and its iterative algorithm by alternating projection *Mathematical and Computer Modelling* **18**(8), 55–60.

Wang C.M. & Tong H.Q. (2007) Best iterative initial values for PLS in a CSI model, *Mathematical and Computer Modelling*, **46**(3–4), 439–44.

Tong Q.L., Zou X.C., Wang C.M. & Tong H.Q. (2010) A definite linear algorithm for structural equation model, *Mathematical and Computer Modelling* **52**(5–6), 744–51.

Tong H.Q. (1994) Gear wear life model by noise properties and its statistical inference. *Mathematical and Computer Modelling* **20**(7), 13–18.

Tong H.Q. (1996) Convergence rates for empirical Bayes estimators of parameters in multiparameter exponential families. *Communications in Statistics* **25**(5), 1089–98.

Tong H.Q. (1996) Convergence rates for empirical Bayes estimators of parameters in linear regression models. *Communications in Statistics* **25**(6), 1325–34.

Verdini R.A., Zorrilla S.E., Rubiolo A.C. & Nakai S. (2007) Multivariate statistical methods for Port Salut Argentino cheese analysis based on ripening time, storage conditions, and sampling sites. *Chemometrics and Intelligent Laboratory Systems* **86**, 60–7.

Vinod H.D. (1976) Canonical ridge and econometrics of joint production. *Journal of Econometrics* **4**(2), 147–66.

Wang C.M. & Tong H.Q. (2007) Best iterative initial values for PLS in a CSI model. *Mathematical and Computer Modelling* **46**(3–4), 4310-444.

Wang W.S. & Peter Schmidt (2009) On the distribution of estimated technical efficiency in stochastic frontier models. *Journal of Econometrics* **148**, 36–45.

Wilcox R.R. (1995) ANOVA: the practical importance of heteroscedastic methods, using trimmed means versus means, and designing simulation studies. *British Journal of Mathematical and Statistical Psychology* **48**, 99–114.

William Greene (2005) Reconsidering heterogeneity in panel data estimators of the stochastic frontier model. *Journal of Econometrics* **126**, 2610–303.

Yang J.B. & Peng S.C. (2008) Development of a customer satisfaction evaluation model for construction project management. *Building and Environment* **43**, 458–68.

Yang S.C. (2003) Uniformly asymptotic normality of the regression weighted estimator for negatively associated samples. *Statistics and Probability Letters* **62**, 101–10.

Yang Z.Q. (1994) Algorithm for nonlinear L_1 regression. *Digital Calculation and Computer Application* **1**, 18–23.

Zhong Z.M., Wang G.F. & Geng M. L. (2006) Probing strong adsorption of individual solute molecules at solid/liquid interfaces with model-based statistical two-dimensional correlation analysis. *Journal of Molecular Structure* **799**, 204–10.

10

Summary and further discussion

After going through all the preceding nine chapters and covering various topics, an inquisitive reader may wonder if there is any common thread that unites them all into one. Likewise he or she might want to find most of the answers to typical questions on credibility that one faces when applying the statistical procedures dealt with in this book. The scientific credibility of our modeling efforts is established in two different ways. First we show that the results we obtain through the modeling are objective, reproducible, and verifiable or testable. We provide a blue print of statistical procedures and any one can reproduce the results we produce with the same data and the same assumptions. Second, we demonstrate how well the model performs. It is the main objective of this chapter to give a brief integrated account of the statistical theories and methods that are developed in the first nine chapters and how they meet the two objectives of scientific credibility cited above. Some of the difficult topics and additional details on some topics are presented in the Electronic References to this chapter.

The reader may refer to Figure 1.11 in Chapter 1 which describes the general scheme for the modeling exercise. Given any typical problem we use domain knowledge and **exploratory data analysis** to arrive at a choice of models. We select one on the basis of certain scientific criterion. This procedure of **model selection** is explained in Section 10.6. A large number of models are based on **regression models**. In Section 10.2 the regression models are derived as parametric or non-parametric models depending on the nature of the underlying probability distribution. Model specification depends on **prior information** and the nature of the prior information is dealt with in Section 10.3. On the basis of the chosen model we derive various results such as predictions of the dependent variable and make credible probability statements about how good those predictions are. Likewise we use our sample evidence either to support or to deny some hypotheses on the underlying data generation process. This is permissible only if we have statistical theories that provide us with probability distributions for the estimators of the parameters of the model and of our predictions. The classical theory of statistical inference that provides that basis is covered in Section 10.4.

Developing Econometrics, First Edition. Hengqing Tong, T. Krishna Kumar and Yangxin Huang.
© 2011 John Wiley & Sons, Ltd. Published 2011 by John Wiley & Sons, Ltd.

This theory is explained in such a way that some of the fundamental statistical concepts are given intuitive interpretation so that if it becomes necessary the practitioner can explain to the ultimate user of the study the terms that we use in statistics.

The models could assume either deterministic unknown parameters or unknown parameters with known probability distributions. In the first case we apply the classical theories of statistical inference and these are presented in Section 10.4. The method of maximum likelihood plays a major role in modeling. Section 10.5 presents that theory in some detail along with computational methods. In the second case we use the **Bayesian inference**. The Bayesian inference, which deals with the situation where the prior information on parameters is probabilistic in nature, is covered in Section 10.8.

There are several situations where we do not have adequate statistical theory regarding the estimates, particularly when we have small samples or when we have complicated models. In such cases we still require some credible methods for making valid inferences. We must lift ourselves up with our own bootstraps in that case with our sample information. The method of **bootstraps** in statistical inference is covered in Section 10.7.

10.1 About probability distributions: Parametric and non-parametric

10.1.1 Distributions of functions of random variables

One of the standard problems that arise in statistical theory and methods is to find the distributions of random variables that are functions of random variables. The following result is quite useful in this regard.

Suppose that random variables Y_1, Y_2,...,Y_k have a **joint probability density function** given by $p(y_1, y_2,........y_k)$. Let there be k functions of these k random variables given by:

$$Z_i = f_i(Y_1, Y_2,..., Y_k) \quad for \ i = 1,2,...,k \tag{10.1}$$

Suppose that the partial derivatives of f_i are well behaved to admit a one-to-one transformation from Y to Z and Z to Y with a non-singular **Jacobian matrix**:

$$J = \begin{pmatrix} \dfrac{\partial f_1}{\partial Y_1} & \dfrac{\partial f_1}{\partial Y_2} & \cdots & \dfrac{\partial f_1}{\partial Y_k} \\ \dfrac{\partial f_2}{\partial Y_1} & \dfrac{\partial f_2}{\partial Y_2} & \cdots & \dfrac{\partial f_2}{\partial Y_k} \\ \cdots & \cdots & \cdots & \cdots \\ \dfrac{\partial f_k}{\partial Y_1} & \dfrac{\partial f_k}{\partial Y_2} & \cdots & \dfrac{\partial f_k}{\partial Y_k} \end{pmatrix} \tag{10.2}$$

The joint probability density of Z_1, Z_2,...,Z_k is given by:

$$q(z_1, z_2,..., z_k) = |J|^{-1} p(f_1^{-1}(z_1, z_2 ..., z_k), f_2^{-1}(z_1, z_2,..., z_k),... f_k^{-1}(z_1, z_2,... z_k)) \tag{10.3}$$

over a set of values of Z that are mapped by the transformation from the range of values that the Y variables take. This result is very useful to derive the probability density function of any function of a random variable. As a special case with this result one can obtain the probability distribution of any function of random variables, such as the mean, by using that function as one of the k transformations and defining arbitrarily some simple and other convenient k-1 transformations to integrate them out easily. Many of the results obtained in deriving the sampling distributions of sample statistics use this technique.

10.1.2   Parametric, non-parametric, and semi-parametric specification of distributions

Most statistical modeling deals with either the probability distribution of random variables, or with the moments of those distributions. Most of the classical theory of probability was developed under the old prevailing situation of understanding the probabilistic structure from limited small sample information. It then became necessary to make some prior assumptions regarding the nature of the underlying joint probability density function. The statistical analysis and statistical methods were developed for a variety of situations by assuming a priori that the underlying probability densities belonged to a class of parametric densities, namely densities that depend on a finite number of unknown parameters. As statistical theories and methods evolved the parametric family of density functions became larger. In the parametric density case one specifies, through prior information, a class of probability density functions to which the density is likely to belong with unknown values of the parameters and then estimates the parameters using the observed sample values. Once the unknown parameters are estimated one gets the parametric estimate of the density function.

If there are several such families of distributions one can use the **Pearsonian goodness of fit Chi-Square** as a measure of goodness of fit. Starting with simple univariate probability density functions a variety of other parametric density functions can be derived, either as densities of functions of random variables or as joint distributions of those variables.

In the development of classical statistical theory parametric probability distributions played a significant role. The **Pearsonian system** of frequency curves represents many probability density functions (bell shaped J-shaped and U-shaped and see Johnson, Kotz and Balakrishnan, 1994). A class of density functions belonging to an **exponential family** played an important role in classical theories and methods of statistics. If the probability density function belongs to the exponential family then there exist minimal sufficient statistics that attain the minimum variance limit set by the **Cramer-Rao bound**, which is discussed in some detail later in this chapter (Section 10.4). In actuarial statistics, dealing with failure rates, it is found to be inadequate to have regression models with errors distributed as a Normal distribution. The Normal distribution is replaced, in such cases, by a distribution belonging to an exponential family giving rise to what is termed the **Generalized Linear Model**.

In classical probability theory the probability density functions are specified with unknown but deterministic parameters. In Bayesian statistics one assumes a prior probability distribution for the unknown parameters and obtains a new probability density function derived by combining the information from the prior densities and the sample information. This new probability density function is called a posterior density function. Bayesian inference is developed later in Section 10.8. The exponential density functions have an important role in Bayesian inference. If the prior density belongs to an exponential family then the posterior density also belongs to the same exponential family. The exponential parametric family of density functions thus plays an important role both in classical inference and Bayesian inference. Most of the commonly used probability density functions of statistical inference, such as the Binomial, Poisson, Normal, Chi-square, exponential, Gamma, Beta, etc distributions belong to this exponential family.

The parametric probability density function of a continuous random variable Y can be written as:

$$P(y - \frac{\delta y}{2} < Y < y + \frac{\delta y}{2}) = f(y; \theta)\delta y \qquad (10.4)$$

for infinite small δy.

The probability density function of a single parameter exponential family can be written as:

$$f(y; \theta) = Exp\{A(\theta) + B(y) + C(\theta)B(y)\} \qquad (10.5)$$

As statisticians began dealing with different and large data sets this class of parametric densities, which seemed to include several popular distributions, was found to be inadequate. This gave rise to the notion of **nonparametric density** functions. The notion of a non-parametric density function comes from that of the **histogram** of a sample. The histogram of a sample is constructed by grouping the sample observations into different intervals (windows) and observing the relative frequencies in each of those intervals. This can be understood more clearly by writing a functional form for the histogram. The **naïve density estimator** or the histogram estimator of the density is given in terms of the empirical or sample cumulative relative frequency function $F_n(x)$ by:

$$f_n(x) = \frac{1}{2h}(F_n(x+h) - F_n(x-h)) \qquad (10.6)$$

As can be seen this specification depends only on the sample and it has no unknown parameters, and hence it is a nonparametric density. Models based on such nonparametric specifications are called nonparametric models.

Sometimes it may be desirable to reduce the inferential load on the sample by using a few parameters and keeping the rest of the density function in a nonparametric form. One typical example of this is to have a hybrid nonparametric model which is a linear mix of two non-parametric specifications, the mixing coefficient being a parameter. This gives rise to what is called a semi-parametric model. Another example of a **semi-parametric model** is one where a regression model is specified with a known parametric specification, but the error of the regression is assumed to have a non-parametric density, or the regression equation is expressed as a **non-parametric regression** with an error having a parametric distribution.

10.1.3   Non-parametric specification of density functions

The Naïve estimator of the density given in (10.6) can be viewed as being generated by creating a small **window** of width of $2h$ around x, counting the sample observations falling in that window and taking an average. Here there are two important elements, the width of the chosen window and the weight function chosen for each potential observation that can fall in that window (in this case it is equal weight for all of them). Rosenblatt (1956, 1971) generalized this and introduced the notion of a general class of non-parametric density estimators called **kernel density** estimators.

A general kernel density estimator can be defined as:

$$\hat{f}_n(x) = \frac{1}{nh}\sum_{j=1}^{n} w\left(\frac{x - x_j}{h}\right) \qquad (10.7)$$

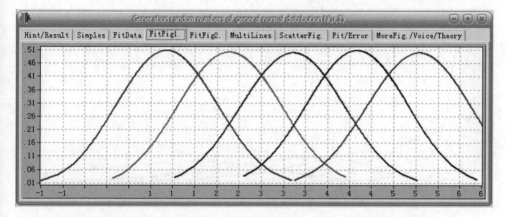

Figure 10.1 Density curves of Normal distribution with different mean.

where $w(x)$ is a suitable kernel function with a window width h, and $x_j, j = 1,\dots,n$ are the sample. The integral of $w(x)$ should be 1.

The naïve histogram estimator can be easily shown to be a special case of this. It can be obtained from it by defining the weight function $w(x)$ as that of the density of a Uniform distribution in the interval $-1 < x < 1$ as follows:

$$w(x) = \begin{cases} 1/2 & for \; -1 < x < 1 \\ 0 & elsewhere \end{cases} \tag{10.8}$$

One can define a variety of kernel density functions by choosing different weight functions $w(x)$.

If one determines the optimal weight function among the set of all continuous density functions with mean zero and unit variance then we get **Epanechnikov kernel density** with the weight function (Epanechnikov, 1969),

$$w(x) = \begin{cases} \dfrac{3}{4} * 5^{-\frac{1}{2}} \left(1 - \dfrac{x^2}{5}\right) & if \; |x| \le 5^{\frac{1}{2}} \\ 0 & Otherwise \end{cases} \tag{10.9}$$

If one considers a h times the Normal density with mean zero and standard deviation h as the weight function we get the **Specht kernel density** estimator (Specht, 1971),

$$w(x) = \begin{cases} \dfrac{1}{\sqrt{2\pi}} Exp\left(-\dfrac{x^2}{h}\right) & for \; x - h < x < x + h \\ 0 & Otherwise \end{cases} \tag{10.10}$$

We can use the method of kernel density estimation to generate the continuous approximations to the empirically determined density curves of any known density function. This can be done by generating a very large number of pseudo random numbers with given distribution such as Normal distribution (Figure 10.1), Chi-square distribution (Figure 10.2), t distribution (Figure 10.3), and F distribution (Figure 10.4). These figures can be shown in

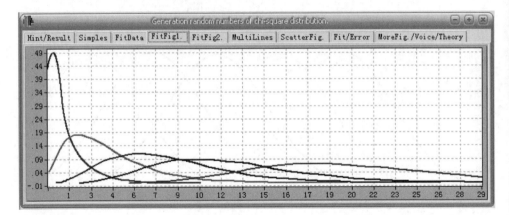

Figure 10.2   Density curves of Chi-square distribution with different degrees of freedom.

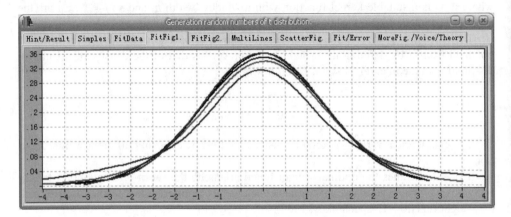

Figure 10.3   Density curves of t distribution with different degrees of freedom.

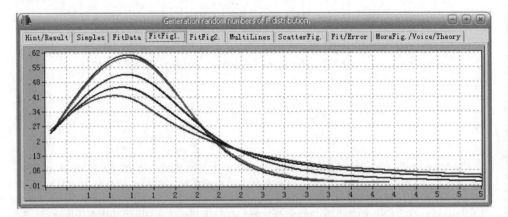

Figure 10.4   Density curves of F distribution with different degrees of freedom.

DASC by clicking menu Basic Statistics→Multi-line Density Curve for Given Distribution. Of course we can change these figures by changing the parameters in software.

10.2   Regression

10.2.1   Regression as conditional mean of the dependent variable

The conditional probability density function of an economic variable given the values assumed by certain related economic variables is of great interest to us. In the previous section we described how those distributions can be specified as parametric or nonparametric distributions. However, as a distribution, whether it is parametric or nonparametric it is too complex to comprehend in general. Thus, one tries to condense the information by concentrating on the first two moments of this distribution. There are three common justifications for limiting to the first two moments. First, under some general conditions the limiting distribution with large samples will be a Normal distribution. Second, one may assume that sufficient care is taken to transform the variables so that their marginal, joint, and conditional distributions are all Normal. Third, even if these distributions are not normal through suitable transformations we can make them approximately normal. Then we know that the Normal distribution is completely characterized by first two moments.

Assume that the conditional probability density function of an economic variable Y given the exogenous variables $X_1, X_2,...,X_k$ is given by:

$$p(y \mid x_1, x_2,...,x_k) \tag{10.11}$$

The regression of Y on $X_1, X_2,...,X_k$ is given by the mean or the expected value of this conditional probability density function:

$$E(Y \mid X_1 = x_1, X_2 = x_2,...,X = x_k) = \int_{-\infty}^{\infty} yp(y \mid x_1, x_2,...,x_k)dy \tag{10.12}$$

One may consider building an econometric model from the stage of specifying the conditional probability density function (10.11) or from specifying the mean or the regression function (10.12). Given a conditional probability density function there is a unique derivable regression function. Given a regression function, however, there could be several probability density functions that could have generated that regression function. This distinction is important when we discuss the issue of identification of the structure of an econometric model later in Section 10.3.

We get parametric regression functions if the probability density function in (10.11) is in parametric form. We get non-parametric or semi-parametric regression functions, such as those covered in Chapter 6 if the density in (10.11) is in either nonparametric or semiparametric forms. Likewise we get a linear regression model, such as those in Chapters 2, 3, and 4 if (10.12) is linear in parameters. We get a **nonlinear regression** model, such as what we covered in Chapter 5, if the regression model (10.12) is nonlinear in parameters.

10.2.2   Regressions with homoscedastic and heteroscedastic variance

The conditional variance could be constant or it could depend on the values assumed by the independent variables $X_1, X_2,...,X_k$. If the conditional variance is constant we get regression functions with homoscedastic variance, such as that which we covered in Chapter 2. If the conditional variance is not constant we get the heteroscedastic variance, such as those discussed in Chapter 3.

Conditional variance of Y given $X_1 = x_1, X_2 = x_2, \ldots, X_k = x_k$ in homoscedastic case is given by:

$$E\{Y - E(Y / X_1 = x_1, X_2 = x_2, \ldots, X_k = x_k)\}^2 = \sigma^2 \tag{10.13}$$

Conditional variance of Y given $X_1 = x_1, X_2 = x_2, \ldots, X_k = x_k$ in a heteroscedastic case is given by:

$$E\{Y - E(Y / x_1, \ldots, x_k)\}^2 = \sigma^2(x_1, x_2, \ldots, x_k) \tag{10.14}$$

There are some variance stabilization transformations that when applied to the dependent variable Y then what is originally a heteroscedastic regression can be converted to a homoscedastic regression. But in the process a regression that was linear in parameters with heteroscedastic variance may become a regression that is nonlinear in parameters with homoscedastic variance. Quite often variance stabilization and conversion of the model to a form, where the errors are normally distributed and reduction of error variance, can all be achieved through adding of relevant variables, transformation of variables, and exploratory data analysis.

A most extensively used regression model (developed in greater detail in Chapters 2 and 3) is what is called a linear regression model which is linear in the parameters. It can be written as:[1]

$$E(Y / (X_1 = x_1, \ldots, X_k = x_k)) = \beta_0 x_1 + \beta_1 x_2 + \beta_2 x_3 + \cdots + \beta_{k-1} x_k$$
$$V(Y / (X_1 = x_1, \ldots, X_k = x_k)) = \sigma^2(x_1, \ldots, x_k) \tag{10.15a}$$

or

$$y_i = \beta_0 x_{1i} + \beta_1 x_{2i} + \beta_2 x_{3i} + \ldots \beta_{k-1} x_{ki} + u_i \tag{10.15b}$$

where $x_{1i} = 1$ for all i, $E(u_i) = 0$ and $V(u_i) = \sigma^2(x_1, \ldots, x_k)$, $Cov(u_i, u_j) = 0$ for $i \neq j$. If $\sigma^2(x_1, \ldots, x_k)$ is constant we have a homoscedastic linear regression model (as in Chapter 2), and otherwise a heteroscedastic linear regression model (as in Chapter 3).

Most of the statistical inference regarding the testing of hypothesis in small samples is based on an assumption that the error terms u_i have a Normal distribution. It is however found that this distributional assumption is untenable when one deals with fat tailed distributions that one encounters in actuarial studies and in financial economics. The linear regression model such as above is extended to a Generalized Linear Model (GLM) where the error term u has a distribution belonging to the exponential family (such as equation 10.5). These regressions include the cases where the conditional distribution of the dependent variable is binomial, Poisson, negative binomial, and exponential. For more detailed discussion on Generalized Linear Model one may see Nelder and Wedderburn (1972).

---

[1] In this chapter where we try to provide a unified approach to statistical modeling we use simple models with one dependent variable and a finite set of independent variables.

10.2.3   General regression functions: Quantiles and quantile regression

The regression function or the conditional mean of Y given values $x_1, x_2,...,x_k$ given in (10.12) can be interpreted as the outcome of an optimal decision. If we ask the question, given $x_1, x_2,...,x_k$, what is a function of $x_1, x_2,...,x_k$, $R(x_1, x_2,...,x_k)$ that has the least expected squared deviation from Y, and the answer is the conditional mean of Y. This can be expressed as

$$\min \int \{y - R(x_1, x_2,...,x_k)\}^2 \, p(y / x_1, x_2,...,x_k) dy$$
$$= \int \{y - E(Y / x_1, x_2,...,x_k)\}^2 \, p(y / x_1, x_2,...,x_k) dy \tag{10.16}$$

One can generalize the concept of regression by considering a general class of optimizing functions. For instance, if one were to use the mean of absolute deviations $\int \| y - R(y/x_1, x_2,...,x_k) \|$ $p(y/x_1, x_2,...,x_k) dy$ as the criterion then the median of the conditional distribution will be the regression function. More generally, one may consider a weighted sum of squared deviations, given below, as the criterion to optimize, giving rise to quantile regression.

$$\min \int w_q \{y - R(y / x_1, x_2,...,x_k)\} p(y / x_1, x_2,...,x_k) dy$$
$$= \int w_q \{y - Q_q(y / x_1, x_2,...,x_k)\} p(y / x_1, x_2,...,x_k) dy \tag{10.17}$$

where $w_q\{z\} = z\{q - I(z < 0)\}$, $0 < q < 1$ and I is an indicator function. i.e. $I(z < 0) = 1$ *if* $z < 0$, $I(z < 0) = 0$ *if* $z > 0$. $Q_q(y/x_1, x_2,...,x_k)$ is q^{th} **quantile regression** of Y on $X_1 X_2,...,X_k$, i.e. the qth quantile of conditional distribution of Y given $X_1, X_2,...,X_k$.

The weight function $w_{q(z)}$ can be shown to be the absolute value function of z for $q = 0.5$. For any general $q(0 < q < 1)$ $w_q(z)$ can be shown in a diagram as below:

In ordinary regression the rate of change of the response variable y for a unit change in one of the conditioning variables is assumed to be the same for all observations in the sample, where as in quantile regression these rates of change of response variable with respect to each of the conditioning variables could vary depending on the quantile of the distribution of the response variable. Thus quantile regression is quite useful if one expects the response rates to be different for different parts of the distribution. For more detail see Koenker (2005).

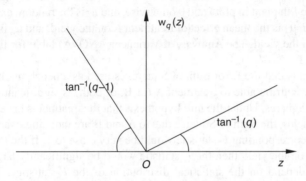

Figure 10.5   The weight function $w_q (z)$ in quantiles and quantile regression.

10.2.4   Design of experiments, regression, and analysis of variance

Fisher laid the foundations to scientific application of statistics in 1925 through his pioneering contribution (Fisher, 1925). In that book he developed the **design of experiments** and the **analysis of variance**. They were developed as tools for statistical analysis of agricultural experiments at Rothamsted Experimental Station. The basic scientific question being asked was 'What are the individual effects when different nutrients were added to the soil while growing different agricultural crops, and what should be an optimal application of those nutrients?'

The principles behind the design of experiments and analysis of variance are actually drawn from the statistical theory of a standard multiple regression model. As mentioned above in equation (10.15) the standard linear multiple regression model can be represented in vector-matrix notation as:

$$y = X\beta + u \tag{10.18}$$

$E(u) = 0$, $E(uu') = \sigma^2 I$ (homoscedastic case). Here y and u are $n \times 1$ vectors, β is a $k \times 1$ regression parameter vector, X is a $n \times k$ design matrix, and I is an $n \times n$ identity matrix.

It was shown in Chapter 3 that the precision of the least squares estimator of β depends on $X'X$, the precision being best if $X'X$ is an orthogonal matrix. In this case it also follows that the total sum of squares of the response variable, expressed as a deviation from its own mean value, can be decomposed into $k - 1$ independent parts plus an error sum of squares, each of the $k - 1$ independent parts being the contribution of each of the $k - 1$ explanatory variables. This aspect was dealt in greater detail in Chapter 2 and Chapter 9. The Design of Experiments deals with an experimental method that makes the matrix $X'X$ orthogonal to estimate the individual effects of k different treatments efficiently.

The statistical model used in the design of experiments (DOE) and analysis of variance (ANOVA) for two treatments is as follows, assuming that there are two nutrients A and B whose effects on the yield is what one is interested in estimating:

$$Y_{ij} = \alpha + \mu_A X_{Aij} + \mu_B X_{Bij} + u_{ij} \tag{10.19}$$

where Y_{ij} is the yield of jth plant in plot i, α is the mean yield with naturally available nutrients in the soil, μ_A is the mean effect of (one unit) of nutrient A, and μ_B is the mean effect of (one unit) of nutrient B, X_{Aij} (X_{Bij}) is a dummy variable that assumes a value equal to 1 if treatment A (B) is applied to j-th plant in plot i and 0 otherwise, and u_{ij} is the random experimental error for plant j in plot i. μ_A is the mean effect of treatment A on the yield, and μ_B is the mean effect of treatment B on the yield. The Analysis of Variance (ANOVA) table for this example will be as in Table 10.1.

The basic idea is that the Error Sum of Squares is used as a bench mark to test whether the sum of squares attributable to treatment A (or B, or both) is significantly different from the Error Sum of Squares. Under the null hypothesis that the treatments have no effect on the response (plant yield), the Sum of Squares due to A and B are indistinguishable from that of the error and the corresponding F-statistic would be very close to 1. If the treatments have a significant effect on the yield then the F-statistic would be significantly larger than 1. How large? That will depend on the statistical distribution of the F-statistics. This aspect was covered in greater depth in Chapters 2 and 9.

Design of experiments is becoming increasingly important in economics and business for two reasons. First, in the field of marketing, before a new product is introduced it is useful to conduct marketing experiments with a few potential customers by offering them different kinds of that product, such as a bundled product where the main product is bundled with some other products or services, or offering products at different prices, etc. The customer response to these different 'treatments' can be observed and analyzed to choose the best marketing strategy that maximizes the sales revenue. Second, in a practical business analytic problem one could encounter both a regression model specification as well as a Design of Experiments situation. In one actual business analytic application we had a large data set to determine what factors affect and by how much the probability that a credit card issued is active. The client however wanted to know how to improve the probability of credit card use once issued. For this some new marketing strategies were ascertained from the marketing executives for improving the probability of credit card use and the same were tried experimentally on a selected list of credit card applicants employing an experimental design. The marketing strategies that were found to be most effective experimentally were tried out on a much larger sample of customers and the results monitored to demonstrate the usefulness of the analytic approach.

10.3   Model specification and prior information

Whether it is modeling the entire probability distribution of a variable, treated as random, or whether it is modeling the mean or other characteristics of that distribution, such as quantiles, one requires specification of the mathematical form of the model with certain unknown parameters. The information provided by the sample observations is then combined with the prior specification of the model to make inferences about the stochastic process that could have generated the data (the data generating process). The basic ingredients of a statistical modeling process are described below schematically in a diagram:

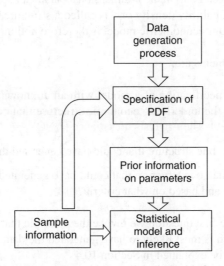

Figure 10.6   The problem of statistical inference.

10.3.1   Data Generation Process (DGP) and economic structure

Statistics is predominantly an applied science and it is applied to make inferences from data pertaining to the field of application. It is therefore essential to understand the underlying phenomenon that generates the data. One major advantage of understanding the **data generation process** (DGP) is that it is that process that can identify which variables depend on what other variables, and what variables are independent, and what is the possible nature of dependence between some of the variables. For example, in regression type of models we need to specify the conditional mean of the dependent variable as a function of the variables on which it depends. Without a proper understanding of the data generation process one might misspecify the regression model.

The pre-existing knowledge of the domain of application has two major components, a general component as it applies approximately to a variety of situations in the domain, and a specific component with specific variations from such a general structure that may have occurred in the present case at hand. The latter are too numerous and not organized into definite patterns and hence are ignored. One is therefore content with a general model. One must take the general pattern of data generation process from the underlying theory pertaining to that domain, and update or modify it to make it more specific to the actual situation that generated the data. This is done by examining the data through exploratory data analysis such as line graphs, scatter plots, zero-order and partial correlations etc. All this understanding (depicted in the left box and the top Box of Figure 10.6) is made use of in specifying what Fisher said, the population of which the given sample is a random sample (depicted in the second box from the top of Figure 10.6).

Suppose that we specify, based on DGP and exploratory data analysis, the conditional p.d.f. as a parametric probability density as follows:

$$p(y \mid x_1, x_2, \ldots, x_k) = f(y, x_1, x_2, \ldots, x_k; \theta_1, \theta_2, \ldots, \theta_p) \qquad (10.20)$$

The distribution above is known completely only if the value assumed by each of the p parameters is known. Each point in the p-dimensional parameter space that generates a fully specified conditional probability density of y is called a structure, the economic structure that generated the data. Our econometric model is therefore nothing but a set of all possible structures.

The econometric problems are:

(1) Given the prior specification of a model with an unknown structure, and the sample data, what is the underlying economic structure that could have generated the data?

(2) Is there more than one structure that could have generated the data?

(3) If there is more than one structure that could have generated the data which of them should be chosen and based on what criteria?

In order to answer the first question we invoke the principle that the structure that generated the data is that which is most likely to have generated the data. This is the **principle of maximum likelihood** to be explained in Section 10.4.

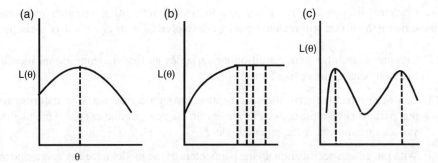

Figure 10.7   Three shapes of likelihood.

In order to simplify the exposition suppose that the specified density function has only one parameter and we represent the likelihood of obtaining (joint probability of obtaining the n samples) of $k + 1$ dimensional vector, *viz.* the sample $y, x_1, x_2, ..., x_k$ under the given specification by $L(\theta)$. The likelihood could take several possible shapes. Consider the following three shapes:

The maximum likelihood principle identifies a single structure when the likelihood function has a single discrete peak as in Figure 10.7a.

When the **likelihood function** is flat, as in Figure 10.7b there are an infinite number of structures, within a continuous range, that could have generated the data. When the likelihood function has more than one peak all of the same height, as depicted in Figure 10.7c, there are as many distinct structures that could have generated the data as there are such peaks. In situation such as Figure 10.7a we say that the model is identified as there is only one structure that could have generated the data.[2]

Suppose the regression model is written as:

$$y_i = \beta_0 x_{1i} + \beta_1 x_{2i} + \beta_2 x_{3i} ... + \beta_{k-1} x_{ki} + u_i \tag{10.21}$$

where $x_{1i} = 1$ for all i, $E(u_i) = 0$ and $V(u_i) = \sigma^2(x_1,...,x_k)$, $Cov(u_i, u_j) = 0$ for $i \neq j$.

We can write the likelihood and obtain maximum likelihood estimates only by making certain assumptions that the random variable u_i has some distribution, such as a Normal as in the case of standard multiple regression models or a distribution belonging to the exponential family in the Generalized Linear Model (GLM). The regression model is a function of the unknown parameters of the likelihood function, given $x_1, x_2,...,x_k$.

The likelihood depends both on the conditioning variables used to obtain the conditional distribution of Y and on the values assumed by the parameter. The problem of identification

---

[2] Strictly speaking the shapes of these likelihood functions depend on the sample, and hence what is being discussed above is the estimability of parameters in finite samples. The econometric concept of identification refers to a situation where such sample problem is dispensed with by assuming that there is an infinite sample. Hence identification in econometrics is a problem of specification of the statistical model and the resulting shape of the likelihood function with respect to the parameter, and is not a finite sample phenomenon.

of the structure discussed above gives rise to several interesting research problems in econometric methods that still remain broadly unexplored.[3] Let us cite a few of them here:

(1) Can one search for new conditioning variables so that the conditional likelihood function behaves more like Figure 10.7a?

(2) Can one re-parameterize the specification through a parametric transformation so that with respect to the new specification (in the new parameter space) the likelihood surface does not show these pathologies?

(3) With the given specification do the parameters of the model have any economic interpretation? Can a transformation of parameters enable one to give economic interpretation and also identifiability?

(4) Can one partition the parameters into two types, one of major policy interest and hence need to be estimated with greater precision and the other not so important? Can one then introduce parameter transformation so that the parameters of policy interest can be estimated precisely?

(5) Any specification is only an approximation to reality and the real structure is not known. If a given specification has unidentified parameters is it possible to find another specification, as close as possible to the original unidentified specification that is identified?[4]

(6) Can a model with larger number of parameters be approximated by another model with fewer parameters?

(7) Can different possible alternate specifications be embedded in a single specification? (This is called encompassing)

(8) How to search for prior restrictions on the parameters so that these pathologies disappear?

10.3.2 Deterministic but unknown parameters and model specification as a maintained hypothesis

If one follows the steps indicated above at the beginning of this section in specifying a model (understanding DGP) it may very well turn out that some or all of the parameters have an interpretation as parameters of the underlying economic process. It is but natural to expect that the model builder, or the client for whom the model is built (and who is going to use the model for economic and business decision), may have some prior 'belief' about the value assumed by the parameters. That belief could be of the form that the parameter assumes a specific but unknown value. It could be that the parameter assumes an unknown value within a range of values, implying parametric inequality restrictions. That belief could also be in terms of some kind of linear or non-linear dependency between parameters in terms of a functional equality constraint. In all these case we have the situation of having deterministic prior information of some kind.

---

[3] Manski (2003) deals with some of the issues mentioned below. One may see also Phillips (1989) on the issue of partial identification.

[4] For a clearer statement of this problem and its solution the reader may refer to a paper by Le Cam (1964).

Statistical inference is thus based on combining prior information with sample information. If the prior information is deterministic with unknown parameters the statistical inference leads to classical approach. Suppose we choose a particular parametric specification for the conditional distribution of y given $X_1 = x_1, X_2 = x_2, \ldots, X_k = x_k$, such as:

$$p(y / x_1, x_2, \ldots, x_k) = f(y, x_1, x_2, \ldots, x_k; \theta_1, \theta_2, \ldots, \theta_p) \qquad (10.22)$$

Here θ is an unknown parameter vector of dimension p[5]. We call this the **maintained hypothesis** based on prior (deterministic) information on the functional form of the conditional probability density function with unknown p-dimensional parameter vector 'θ'.

We may also consider, instead, a regression model implied by such a conditional probability density function such as (10.21).

Statistical inference now consists of taking a sample of size n from y and $x_1, x_2, \ldots, x_k$ to:

(1) Estimate the unknown parameter vector θ, for each of the alternate models and call the estimator (estimate treated as a function of the sample values) $\hat{\theta}$.

(2) Choose one of the alternative models as the best-fitting model on the basis of some criterion.

(3) Obtain the **sampling distribution** of $\hat{\theta}$, the distribution of the values assumed by the estimator in repeated samples from the same specified conditional probability density function.

(4) Make certain hypotheses, called testable hypotheses, on the unknown parameter θ.

Test the testable hypothesis using the **Neyman-Pearson theory of testing of statistical hypothesis**.

10.3.3   Stochastic prior information on unknown parameters

The prior information could be stochastic. For instance, the researcher may wish to consider alternate statistical models, each with its own unknown parameter vector. He or she may attach a prior subjective probability for each one of those models being the true model.[6] On the other hand for any one of those chosen models he or she may have some prior information that is probabilistic on the unknown parameters. For instance one might say that the parameter lies within a range with equal probability i.e. having a uniform distribution within that range. If the range is finite we get what one calls a proper prior probability density, and if the range is infinite one gets an **improper prior** probability density.[7] This is a very commonly used prior belief in Bayesian analysis and it is called the **diffuse prior**. The prior belief could also be of a histogram type, stating that the probability that the parameter lies in different ranges are different but specified a priori. Bayesians did not know how to handle such very general prior probability density functions until statistical computing developed. They assumed, for analytic

---

[5] If there are equality or inequality constraints on the parameters the statistical inference procedures need to be suitably modified using Lagrangian and programming techniques.

[6] In situations like this instead of selecting any one of the models a Bayesian would consider a Bayesian average for the marginal posterior distribution of a parameter. This will be covered later in Section 11.8.

[7] The concepts of prior and posterior densities that are mentioned here will be explained in Section 11.8. Suffice it to say here that information consists of prior probabilistic information incorporated in a prior density and the sample information.

convenience, that the prior belief is of a particular type which gives rise to a posterior density function that is also of the same type.[8] Such priors are called **conjugate priors**. It has been found that if the prior probabilistic belief can be described as belonging to an exponential family then the posterior density would also belong to the same exponential family. In the early phases of Bayesian analysis one therefore tried to contend by approximating any prior belief in terms of an arbitrary histogram by the closest member of an exponential family.

The prior probability distribution on the parameters could be of two types. First it could be purely subjective and given by the researcher or his or her client, based on his or her gut feeling. Second, a very common way of getting the prior information is to gather it from the earlier studies on the same or similar problems that throw light on the underlying DGP. Such information can be obtained through meta-analysis. The relative frequency distribution of parameter estimates in the earlier studies could serve as the prior distribution for the parameter. This latter case is referred to as the **empirical Bayes' procedure**, and is discussed in Section 10.8.

10.4   Classical theory of statistical inference

10.4.1   The likelihood function, sufficient statistics, complete statistics, and ancillary statistics

Under the assumption that there is a random sample of n independent observations on a $k + 1$ dimensional vector (y, x) we can write the likelihood function, as a function of both the sample realizations of y and $x_1, x_2,...,x_k$ and the unknown parameters $\theta_1, \theta_2,..., \theta_p$ as follows:[9]

$$L(y_1, y_2,..., y_n; x_{11},..., x_{1n}; x_{21},..., x_{2n};...,x_{k1},...,x_{kn};\theta_1,...,\theta_p)$$
$$= \prod_{i=1}^{n} L(y_i, x_{1i}, x_{2i},..., x_{ki}; \theta_1,...,\theta_p) = L(y, x; \theta) \qquad (10.23)$$

The likelihood function is a powerhouse of information. The information has three components. First, we have some prior information on the DGP that is used to specify the functional form of the likelihood function. Second, we have prior information on the possible values the parameters take along with their probabilities. Third, there is sample information from the realized sample. The Likelihood function can be viewed as being symmetric in its treatment of parameters and sample data. The Likelihood function provides information that the parameter structure has on the probability of occurrence of the sample. It provides information the realized sample has on the probability of occurrence of the parameter.

The information provided by a sample about the unknown parameter can be classified into the following types:

(1) Information that is relevant for a parameter (falling within parts of regions I and II below in Figure 10.8);

(2) Information that is relevant for the parameter but is redundant in view of other information already available in other parts of the sample (falling in region II in Figure 10.8);

---

[8] More detail on these concepts are given in Section 10.8 below.

[9] As we will be dealing with a multiple regression model as a workhorse we consider that we have a sample of observations on a dependent variable Y and k independent or explanatory variables $X_1, X_2,........X_k$. In econometric models involving simultaneous explanation of several economic variables the dependent variable y itself will be a vector.

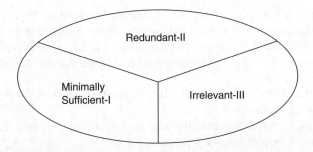

Figure 10.8   Partitioning the sample space into three regions.

(3) Information sufficient to make inference about the parameter (falling in all of region I and parts of regions II and III in Figure 10.8); Information that is minimally sufficient about the parameter (information falling into the entire region I);

(4) Information irrelevant for the parameter (falling in region III of Figure 10.8).

These can be represented by partitioning the sample space into three regions shown schematically in the above diagram.

One would expect on intuitive grounds that the best possible information on a parameter would be contained by that function of the sample that takes all relevant information, regions I and II, omits all irrelevant information (region III), and purges the redundant information (region II) from the relevant information. This is what is done by what is called a complete sufficient statistic and **minimal sufficient statistic**. Let us therefore discuss these terms in some detail.

Let us denote in vector matrix notation $(Y \mid X)$ the random variable representing the random sample of size n from the dependent variable Y and the k independent variables (of which the first one is by definition the variable assuming the constant unit value), and by θ the p-dimensional parameter. Any function $T(Y \mid X)$ of $(Y \mid X)$ is a statistic. While $(Y \mid X)$ is of dimension $n \times (k + 1)$, $T(Y \mid X)$ could be of a lower dimension. In particular $T(Y \mid X)$ could refer to a scalar and an estimator of one of the p components of the p-dimensional parameter θ. Thus statistics or functions of the sample could be means by which data are condensed or reduced in dimension in order to estimate the unknown parameters.

Definition 10.1: Assume that the random sample $(Y \mid X)$ is governed by a conditional probability distribution given in (10.20). A statistic $S(Y \mid X)$ is called a **sufficient statistic** If the conditional probability density of Y given X, given $S(Y \mid X)$ does not depend on θ.

It is extremely important to note that the definition above is conditional on (10.20) being the true model. This definition can be suitably modified to define a sufficient statistic for any component of the p-dimensional parameter vector θ. Note that $S(Y \mid X)$, while having all the information we need on the parameter θ, could also have some redundant information as well. A sufficient statistic could cover all of region I, and parts of regions II and III.

Sometimes identifying a sufficient statistic from the above definition may be difficult because calculations involving conditional probabilities could be cumbersome. Fortunately, one can show that if a distribution admits a sufficient statistic $S(Y \mid X)$ for the parameter θ, then the joint probability distribution $L(y, x \mid \theta)$ of the sample can be expressed as a product of two factors one of which is independent of θ and depends only on (y, x) partitioned and written as:

$$L(y, x; \theta) = g\{S(y \mid x), \theta\} h(y, x) \tag{10.24}$$

Another intuitive notion is irrelevance of sample information for a given parameter. Suppose we are interested in the mean μ of a distribution. Suppose there are two samples X_1 and X_2 drawn from this distribution. The statistic $X_1 - X_2$ has no information on the mean, as the distribution of $X_1 - X_2$ is independent of μ. Such a statistic is called an ancillary statistic.

Definition 10.2: A statistic $A(Y \mid X)$ is called an **ancillary statistic** for θ if its distribution is independent of the parameter θ.

As was the case for the sufficient statistic an ancillary statistic can be defined with respect to any component of the p dimensional parameter θ.

An example will be useful here. Suppose we have a random sample of size 2 from a Normal distribution with mean μ and unit variance. Let X_1 and X_2 be the sample. It can be shown that $X_1 + X_2$ is a sufficient statistic for μ, and the statistic $X_1 - X_2$ is an ancillary statistic for μ.

In order to establish these results we need to obtain the distributions of the two transformed variables $X_1 + X_2$ and $X_1 - X_2$. In this case of Normal distribution we know that $X_1 + X_2$ has a Normal distribution with a mean 2μ and variance 2 and that $X_1 - X_2$ has a Normal distribution with zero mean and variance 2. However it will be useful to present the general approach for any distribution.

Let $Z_1 = X_1 + X_2$ and $Z_2 = X_1 - X_2$, The Jacobian matrix of this transformation is $\begin{pmatrix} 1 & 1 \\ 1 & -1 \end{pmatrix}$, then its determinant is $J = -2$. We can also write $X_1 = \dfrac{Z_1 + Z_2}{2}$ and $X_2 = \dfrac{Z_1 - Z_2}{2}$. This is a one-to-one transformation and we can use the result mentioned in equation (10.10).

$$q(z_1, z_2) = \frac{1}{2} \times \frac{1}{2\pi} e^{-\frac{1}{2}\left(\frac{Z_1 + Z_2}{2} - \mu\right)^2} e^{-\frac{1}{2}\left(\frac{Z_1 - Z_2}{2} - \mu\right)^2} \tag{10.25}$$

The probability density function of the marginal distribution of z_1 is obtained by integrating (10.25) with respect to z_2. Likewise the probability density function of z_2 is obtained by integrating (10.25) with respect to z_1.

The resulting probability density functions of z_1 and z_2 are:

$$q(z_1) = \frac{1}{\sqrt{2\pi}} e^{-\frac{1}{2}\left(\frac{z_1 - 2\mu}{\sqrt{2}}\right)^2} \tag{10.26a}$$

$$q(z_2) = \frac{1}{\sqrt{2\pi}} e^{-\frac{1}{2}\left(\frac{z_2}{\sqrt{2}}\right)^2} \tag{10.26b}$$

The joint distribution of observed sample X_1 and X_2 is:

$$p(x_1, x_2) = \frac{1}{2\pi} e^{-\frac{1}{2}(x_1 - \mu)^2} e^{-\frac{1}{2}(x_2 - \mu)^2} \tag{10.27}$$

We can show (10.27) can be factorized into two multiplicative factors such that one of them is a function of the sample alone, while the other is a function of the statistic and the unknown parameter.

Writing $x_i - \mu = x_i - (x_1 + x_2) + (x_1 + x_2) - \mu$ for $i = 1, 2$, we can rewrite equation (10.27) as follows:

$$
\begin{aligned}
p(x_1, x_2) &= \frac{1}{2\pi} e^{-\frac{1}{2}\{x_1 - (x_1 + x_2) + (x_1 + x_2) - \mu\}^2 + \{x_2 - (x_1 + x_2) + (x_1 + x_2) - \mu\}^2} \\
&= \frac{1}{2\pi} e^{-\frac{1}{2}\{x_1^2 + x_2^2\}} e^{-\{(x_1 + x_2) - \mu\}^2}
\end{aligned}
\tag{10.28}
$$

Equation (10.28) is factorized, the first term being a function of the sample alone while the second being a function of the statistic $(x_1 + x_2)$ and the unknown parameter μ, as in (10.24). $Z_1 = (X_1 + X_2)$ is therefore a sufficient statistic for the unknown parameter μ.

As this statistic is a one to one transform of the sample mean, the sample mean is a sufficient statistic for μ. From equation (10.26b) it is clear that Z_2 is independent of μ and hence $Z_2 = X_1 - X_2$ is an ancillary statistic.

There are some other concepts quite useful in statistical inference. These are minimal sufficiency and completeness.

Suppose a random variable $(Y \mid X)$ has a probability distribution belonging to a known family of joint or conditional probability distributions f parameterized by $\theta \in \Theta$. $C(Y \mid X)$ be any statistic based on $(Y \mid X)$.

$C(Y \mid X)$ is called a **complete statistic** if and only if for every measurable function g,

$$
E[g\{C(Y\mid X)\}] = 0 \text{ for all } \theta \in \Theta \Rightarrow f[g\{C(Y\mid X); \theta\} = 0] = 1 \text{ for all } \theta
\tag{10.29}
$$

$C(Y \mid X)$ is called **boundedly complete** if (10.29) holds for all bounded g. This concept of completeness narrows the range of statistics to parts of region I of Figure 10.8.

The intersection of the set of all complete statistics and the set of all sufficient statistics is the **complete sufficient statistic**. A complete sufficient statistic is also the minimal sufficient statistic. The minimal sufficient statistic refers to all of Region I of Figure 10.8. Completeness does not necessarily imply sufficiency and sufficiency does not necessarily imply completeness. The reason for this is obvious from the interpretation of these concepts given above in Figure 10.8. A complete statistic lies in parts of region I of Figure 10.8, whereas a sufficient statistic covers all of region I and parts of region II and III, and minimal sufficient statistic lies in the entire region I.

One of the basic results with very wide applications in statistical inference is **Basu's theorem.**

Basu's Theorem: If $C(Y \mid X)$ is a complete sufficient statistic for a parameter θ, and if $A(Y \mid X)$ is an ancillary statistic for θ then these two statistics are independent.

This theorem is used to derive the sampling distributions and critical regions of best test statistics based on minimal sufficient statistics. These play a very crucial role in the theory of statistical inference.[10]

---

[10] For a variety of applications of Basu's theorem one may see Ghosh (2002) and Dasgupta (2006). Dasgupta shows the importance of the concept of approximate independence, approximate sufficiency, and approximate ancillarity and approximate Basu's Theorem in situations when we are not sure about a model and use quasi-maximum likelihood methods.

10.4.2   Different methods of estimation of unknown parameters

Usually the sample size n is much larger than the number of parameters p in a model. Hence one tries to find a data reduction through a transformation of n-dimensional sample to p-dimensional parameter estimates. Such transformation is a data reduction and called a p-dimensional statistic in the previous section, each component of the statistic providing an estimate of a component of the parameter vector. There are different methods for obtaining such estimators of parameters. These alternate methods of estimation of parameters can be classified mainly into two types, regression type methods and distribution type methods. In a regression type of methods the model is a regression model with a stochastic error, and the methods of estimation here refer to using different measures of distance of the estimated sample error from a theoretical error. The distribution type method uses the specified probability distribution as the model and tries to minimize some measure of distance between the observed distribution and the theoretical distribution.

To illustrate the alternate methods of estimation we present below four different types of specification of econometric models.

Single equation regression model:

$$Y_i = f(X_{1i}, X_{2i}, \ldots, X_{ki}; \theta_1, \theta_2, \ldots, \theta_p) + \varepsilon_i \tag{10.30}$$

Single variable conditional distribution model:

$$
\begin{aligned}
P(Y_i = y_i \, / \, X_{1i} &= x_{1i}, X_{2i} = x_{2i}, \ldots, X_{ki} = x_{ki}) \\
&= f(y_i, x_{1i}, x_{2i}, \ldots, x_{ki}; \theta_1, \theta_2, \ldots, \theta_p)
\end{aligned}
\tag{10.31}
$$

Multiple equations regression model:

$$
\begin{aligned}
\alpha_{11} Y_{1i} + \alpha_{12} Y_{2i} + \cdots + \alpha_{1G} Y_{Gi} + \beta_{11} X_{1i} + \beta_{12} X_{2i} + \cdots + \beta_{1K} X_{ki} &= \varepsilon_{1i} \\
\alpha_{21} Y_{1i} + \alpha_{22} Y_{2i} + \cdots + \alpha_{2G} Y_{Gi} + \beta_{21} X_{1i} + \beta_{22} X_{2i} + \cdots + \beta_{2K} X_{ki} &= \varepsilon_{2i} \\
\cdots\cdots\cdots\cdots\cdots & \\
\alpha_{G1} Y_{1i} + \alpha_{G2} Y_{2i} + \cdots + \alpha_{GG} Y_{Gi} + \beta_{G1} X_{1i} + \beta_{G2} X_{2i} + \cdots + \beta_{GK} X_{ki} &= \varepsilon_{Gi}
\end{aligned}
\tag{10.32a}
$$

These equations can be written as

$$AY_i + BX_i = \varepsilon_i \tag{10.32b}$$

where A is a square $G \times G$ nonsingular matrix and B is a rectangular $G \times K$ matrix, and Y_i is $G \times 1$ column vector of G endogenous variables, and X_i is a $K \times 1$ vector of exogenous variable, and Y_i is a $G \times 1$ vector of equation errors.

Multiple endogenous variable conditional probability distribution models:

$$
\begin{aligned}
P(Y_{1i} = y_{1i}, Y_{2i} &= y_{2i}, \ldots, Y_{Gi} = y_{Gi} \, / \, X_{1i} = x_{1i}, X_{2i} = x_{2i}, \ldots, X_{Ki} = x_{Ki}) \\
&= f(y_{1i}, y_{2i}, \ldots y_{Gi}, x_{1i}, x_{2i}, \ldots, x_{Ki}; \theta_1, \theta_2, \ldots, \theta_p)
\end{aligned}
\tag{10.33}
$$

for $i = 1, 2, \ldots, n$. Where there are G economic variables that are explained by K exogenously determined variables.

This last specification is a typical specification for a simultaneous equation econometric model that is used to determine the underlying statistical pattern of interdependence between G economic variables in terms of those as well as K exogenously determined variables.

Least Squares Estimator:

The method of the **least squares estimation** (LSE) suggests that we minimize the sum of squared errors of equation (10.31).

Let $y_i - f(x_{1i}, x_{2i}, \ldots, x_{ki}; \theta_1, \theta_2, \ldots, \theta_p) = u_i$, Then the Least Squares estimates of parameters $\theta_1, \theta_2, \ldots, \theta_p$, denoted by $\hat{\theta}_1, \hat{\theta}_2, \ldots, \hat{\theta}_p$, are such that

$$\sum_{i=1}^{n} \{y_i - f(x_{1i}, x_{2i}, \ldots, x_{ki}; \hat{\theta}_1, \hat{\theta}_2, \ldots, \hat{\theta}_p)\}^2$$

$$= \min_{\theta} \sum_{i=1}^{n} \{y_i - f(x_{1i}, x_{2i}, \ldots, x_{ki}; \theta_1, \theta_2, \ldots, \theta_p)\}^2 \tag{10.34}$$

Minimum Risk Estimator:

One may consider any loss or risk function associated with the estimation error.

One method of estimation is that of minimization of expected risk defined as follows:

$$\min \int R\{y - f(y, x_1, x_2, \ldots, x_k; \theta_1, \theta_2, \ldots, \theta_p)\} p(y / x_1, x_2, \ldots, x_k) dy \tag{10.35}$$

The special cases of this are worth noting. When R is the absolute value function we get the **Mean Absolute Deviation** (MAD) estimator and when R assumes the value w_q as defined in equation (10.17) we get the quantile regression estimator.

Minimum Chi-Square Estimator:

Suppose the conditional distribution is given by equation (10.32b), and suppose in addition that the sample is grouped into m intervals in the $k + 1$ dimensional space and the sample observations are sufficiently large and the intervals are course enough to have a minimum of five observations in each interval. The **minimum Chi-square estimator** is defined as that estimator which minimizes the following Chi-square measure of discrepancy between observed relative frequency and theoretical frequency:

$$\chi^2 = \sum_{i=1}^{m} \frac{\{n_i - np_i(y, x_1, x_2, \ldots, x_k; \theta_1, \theta_2, \ldots, \theta_p)\}^2}{np_i(y, x_1, x_2, \ldots, x_k; \theta_1, \theta_2, \ldots, \theta_p)} \tag{10.36}$$

where n refers to the total number of observations, n_i the number of sample observations in the interval i, and p_i is the theoretical probability for that interval.

Method of Moments Estimator:

Suppose the probability density is given by equation 10.4.10. Assume that the first p raw moments of the distribution exist and can be expressed as functions of the p unknown parameters.

$$E(Y^r / X_1 = x_1, X_2 = x_2, \ldots, X_k = x_k) = \mu_r' = g_r(x_1, x_2, \ldots, x_k; \theta_1, \theta_2, \ldots, \theta_p) \tag{10.37}$$

for $r = 1, 2, \ldots, p$.

The **Method of Moments Estimator** is obtained by equating the p sample raw moments m_r to the population raw moments μ_r' (assuming that the p g_r functions are functionally independent), and solving the p equations for the p unknown parameters.

Maximum Likelihood Estimator:

An estimator $\hat{\theta} = (\hat{\theta}_1, \hat{\theta}_2, \ldots \ldots \hat{\theta}_p)$ is called a **maximum likelihood estimator** if it satisfies the condition:

$$L(y_1, y_2, \ldots, y_n; x_{11}, \ldots, x_{1n}; x_{21}, \ldots, x_{2n}; \ldots, x_{k1}, \ldots, x_{kn}; \hat{\theta}_1, \ldots, \hat{\theta}_p)$$
$$= \max_{\theta} L(y_1, y_2, \ldots, y_n; x_{11}, \ldots, x_{1n}; x_{21}, \ldots, x_{2n}; \ldots; x_{k1}, \ldots, x_{kn}; \theta_1, \ldots, \theta_p) \tag{10.38}$$

Minimum Distance Estimators:

The least squares estimator can be taken as a special case of a very general class of minimum distance estimators. We may define a measure of distance (discrepancy or separation) between a sample statistic and the theoretical parametric function of which it is an estimator. It is usually defined in terms of the corresponding probability density functions. The minimum distance estimator is that choice of the statistic which minimizes the distance between them. There are several minimum distance estimators that are suggested. Assume that we have grouped the sample into m intervals in $k + 1$ dimensional space spanned by the single dependent variable and k explanatory variables, and let the estimated and theoretical relative frequencies in the *ith* interval are represented by a suffix *i*.

Some examples of minimum distance estimators are:

Minimum Hellinger Distance Estimator:

It is that estimator which minimizes the Hellinger Distance

$$Cos^{-1} \sum_{i=1}^{m} \sqrt{f(y_i, x_{1i}, x_{2i}, \ldots, x_{ki}; \hat{\theta}_1, \hat{\theta}_2, \ldots, \hat{\theta}_p) f(y_i, x_{1i}, x_{2i}, \ldots, x_{ki}; \theta_1, \theta_2, \ldots, \theta_p)} \tag{10.39}$$

Minimum Kullback-Liebler Distance Estimator:

It is the estimator which minimizes the Kullback-Liebler Distance

$$\sum_{i=1}^{m} f(y_i, x_{1i}, x_{2i}, \ldots, x_{ki}; \theta_1, \theta_2, \ldots, \theta_p) \log \frac{f(y_i, x_{1i}, x_{2i}, \ldots, x_{ki}; \theta_1, \theta_2, \ldots, \theta_p)}{f(y_i, x_{1i}, x_{2i}, \ldots, x_{ki}; \hat{\theta}_1, \hat{\theta}_2 \ldots, \hat{\theta}_p)} \tag{10.40}$$

Minimum Generalized Distance Estimator:

Suppose that there are m estimated parameters or estimated functions of parameters. Let us take the second alternative and represent the m functions of parameters by: $g_i(\theta_1, \theta_2, \ldots, \theta_p)$ for $i = 1, 2, \ldots, m$, the corresponding estimator being denoted by $g_i(\hat{\theta}_1, \hat{\theta}_2, \ldots, \hat{\theta}_p)$. Let A be a $m \times m$ positive definite matrix then the minimum generalized distance estimator is defined as that estimator which minimizes the generalized distance

$$[g(\hat{\theta}) - g(\theta)]' A [g(\hat{\theta}) - g(\theta)] =$$
$$\sum_{i=1}^{m} \sum_{j=1}^{m} \{g_i(\hat{\theta}_1, \hat{\theta}_2, \ldots, \hat{\theta}_p) - g(\theta_1, \theta_2, \ldots, \theta_p)\} A_{ij} \{g_i(\hat{\theta}_1, \hat{\theta}_2, \ldots, \hat{\theta}_p) - g(\theta_1, \theta_2 \ldots, \theta_p)\} \tag{10.41}$$

Generalized Method of Moments Estimator:

Many of the estimators discussed above can be reinterpreted as the estimators that satisfy a moment condition such as:

$$E\{g(y, x_1, x_2, \ldots, x_k; \theta_1, \theta_2, \ldots, \theta_p)\} = 0 \tag{10.42}$$

where g could be a vector of dimension m, and functions of the sample and unknown parameters.

By replacing the theoretical expected value in equation (10.42) by the sample equivalent we get m equations in p unknowns to obtain the estimators.

If the number of moment equations in (10.42) is the same as the number of unknown parameters ($m = p$) and if the functions g are functionally independent then there are p equations in p unknowns, and we get unique estimates under certain conditions.

If $m > p$, however, there is conflicting information from more than p equations on p parameters.[11] In that case one may use a generalized distance such as (10.41) that can be minimized to get a unique set of p estimates for p unknown parameters. This procedure is referred to as the **Generalized Method of Moments (GMM) estimator**.

Single Equation and System-wide Methods of Estimation in a System of Equations:

As described in equations (10.32a), (10.32b), an econometric model may be specified either as a system of G independent equations in G endogenous economic variables that are being explained by the model in terms of those G variables and K exogenous variables (not explained by the model). In such **simultaneous equation models** the **identification** of the underlying probabilistic structure requires imposing some prior restrictions on the parameters. The method of estimation could be performed either separately for each equation or for all equations together. Methods of estimation for each equation that utilize the prior information on the parameters of the equation being estimated are called **single equation methods**, while methods of estimating that use the prior information on the parameters of all equations are called **system-wide methods of estimation**.

Having presented a wide array of methods of estimation we must pose the question 'Which method should be chosen?' The answer to this depends on the context, whether one is interested in a single point estimate of the parameter, or whether one is interested in testing the hypotheses on the parameters, whether one is estimating an entire probability density or one or more parameters of that density, etc. The choice depends on some properties of the sampling distribution of the estimator, properties such as unbiasedness, minimum variance, rate of convergence of the distribution, mean-squared error, etc. These topics are discussed next.

10.4.3   Biased and unbiased estimators, consistency of estimators

The choice between estimators is often made on the properties of the sampling distribution of the estimator, under the assumption that there can be, at least in concept or principle, repeated samples and the estimator could assume different values in the repeated samples. In the limiting case when there are an infinite number of repeated samples we get a probability density function for the estimator. Let us denote that probability density of the estimator $\hat{\theta}$ by $f(\hat{\theta}; \theta)$

We say that $\hat{\theta}$ is an **unbiased estimator** if its sampling distribution has the true value of the parameter as its mean:

$$E(\hat{\theta}) = \int \hat{\theta} \, f(\hat{\theta}; \theta) d\hat{\theta} = \theta \qquad (10.43)$$

In general bias of an estimator $\hat{\theta}$ of θ is defined by $E(\hat{\theta}) - \theta$.

The variance of the estimator is defined by:

$$V(\hat{\theta}) = E\{(\hat{\theta}) - E(\hat{\theta})\}^2 = \int \{\hat{\theta} - E(\hat{\theta})\}^2 f(\hat{\theta}; \theta) \qquad (10.44)$$

---

[11] This would be the case when we have a system of equations to estimate and the system of equations is over-identified. The identification issue was discussed in detail in the electronics reference Section 6.1 of Chapter 6.

The most commonly used criterion for choosing an estimator among few competing ones is unbiasedness with minimum variance. One may take the two components, bias and variance, and minimize both. This is normally done by converting them to comparable units by taking bias square and variance and giving them equal weight. Thus we get a new criterion for choosing an estimator that of minimum **mean squared error** defined as follows:

$$MSE(\hat{\theta}) = \{E(\hat{\theta}) - \theta\}^2 + V(\hat{\theta}) \qquad (10.45)$$

There is no single criterion that is the best criterion and which criterion one must use depends on the purpose for which the estimate is used. The criteria mentioned above are special cases of a more general criterion of minimizing the risk $R(\hat{\theta};\theta)$ associated with an estimator defined through a loss function $L(\hat{\theta};\theta)$ when $\hat{\theta}$ is used to estimate θ,

$$R(\hat{\theta};\theta) = \int L(\hat{\theta},\theta) f(\hat{\theta};\theta) d\hat{\theta} \qquad (10.46)$$

Let us denote the estimator based on a sample of size n by $\hat{\theta}_n$. We say that an estimator $\hat{\theta}_n$ is a **consistent estimator** if the probability limit of $\hat{\theta}_n$ as the sample size n tends to infinity is the true parameter 'θ'.

In other words,

$$P\left\{\left|\hat{\theta}_n - \theta\right| < \delta_n\right\} > 1 - \varepsilon_n \qquad (10.47)$$

where both δ_n and ε_n tends to zero as $n \to \infty$.

One of the properties of the estimator most widely used in econometrics is this property of consistency. As we often deal with small samples it is however necessary to know the extent of departure from the true value at any sample size, *viz.*, finite sample bias, and the rate of convergence at any finite sample size. The property of consistency is of little use when we deal with finite samples. The bootstrap method of estimating the small sample bias and variance, to be described later in Section 10.7, will be very helpful in small sample situations.

10.4.4   Information limit to variance of an estimator, Cramer-Rao bound, and Rao-Blackwell theorem

We can consider the problem of classical statistical inference as that of making inferences from the sample about the probability distribution that is specified to belong to a family of probability distributions with a specification $f(x \mid \theta)$, where both x and θ could be vectors, and $\theta \in \Theta$. The moment we make inference about the unknown parameter θ we have more knowledge and less ignorance about the underlying probability distribution. In this section we go deeper into the concept of information. This concept can be explained by first appealing to simple intuitive notions.

In an extreme case suppose there is one unique and distinguishable sample associated with each value assumed by the parameter. Then we have full or maximum information about the parameter from the sample. At the other extreme suppose that the probability distribution of the sample is the same whatever be the value of the parameter, as in Figure 10.7b. The information content of a sample on a parameter is reflected by the sensitivity of the sampling distribution of the sample to variation in the parameter. Suppose the distribution of the sample is described by the likelihood function $L(y, x \mid \theta)$ as given in (10.23). The sensitivity of the sample to variation in the parameter θ_i is defined by $\dfrac{\partial L(y,x;\theta)}{\partial \theta_i}$. The percentage change in likelihood due to a marginal change in θ_i is given by $\dfrac{1}{L(y,x:\theta)} \dfrac{\partial L(y,x;\theta)}{\partial \theta_i}$. We may say that we give the same weight to positive percentage change and negative percentage change. Then we can take as a measure of sample information on the parameter θ_i the expression $\left(\dfrac{1}{L(y,x\mid\theta)} \dfrac{\partial L(y,x;\theta)}{\partial \theta_i} \right)^2$. But this depends on the sample likelihood for that particular sample. By taking the expected value of the sample measure above we get the following information measure:

$$I_{ii} = E\left(\left(\frac{1}{L(y,x\mid\theta)} \frac{\partial L(y,x;\theta)}{\partial \theta_i} \right)^2 \right) \qquad (10.48)$$

When we deal with the information content of the sample with respect to variations in two parameters θ_i and θ_j simultaneously we are interested in the sign of co-movement in parameters in either direction. Hence we have as the information measure for co-variation of parameters θ_i and θ_j

$$I_{ij} = E\left\{ \left(\frac{1}{L(y,x\mid\theta)} \frac{\partial L(y,x;\theta)}{\partial \theta_i} \right)\left(\frac{1}{L(y,x\mid\theta)} \frac{\partial L(y,x;\theta)}{\partial \theta_j} \right) \right\} \qquad (10.49)$$

The $p \times p$ matrix $I = (I_{ij})$ is called the **information matrix**. The concepts of information and information matrix were introduced by R.A. Fisher and exploited further by C.R. Rao, and hence are referred to as Fisher-Rao information measure.

In a single parameter case the following result is established by Rao and Cramer.

Rao-Cramer Information Limit to Variance:

Let $T(y, x)$ be a statistic that is an unbiased estimator of a parametric function $g(\theta)$. Then under certain regularity conditions on the sensitivity of the probability density function or the likelihood function with respect to changes in the parameter, the following inequality on the variance of $T(y, x)$ holds (Rao, 1945):

$$V(T(y,x)) \geq \frac{[g'(\theta)]^2}{I(\theta)} \qquad (10.50a)$$

In particular if $g(\theta) = \theta$ we get:

$$V(T(y,x)) \geq \frac{1}{I(\theta)} \qquad (10.50b)$$

The intuitive meaning is quite obvious. The greater the Fisher information of the sample on a parameter the lower is the minimum variance of the set of all unbiased estimators. It has been established that if the specified probability density function belongs to the exponential family then the lower bound is attained.[12]

When the parameter is not a scalar but a vector of p **orthogonal parameters** we have a $p \times p$ Fisher information matrix $I = (I_{ij})$ and the information limit to variance is given by:

$$V\{T(y,x)\} \geq I_{ii}^{-1} \tag{10.51}$$

where I_{ii}^{-1} is the *ith* diagonal element of the inverse of the information matrix. For the case where the parameters are not orthogonal the inequality for the variance covariance matrix one may see Theorem 3.3 in Shao (2003).

One may ask a pertinent question, if we have an estimator $T(y, x)$ of a parameter that may not be of minimum variance, and if one has a sufficient statistic $S(y, x)$ is it possible to obtain from the two a better estimator with lower mean squared error? The answer in the affirmative was provided by Rao (1945) and Blackwell (1947) and is given by the following theorem:

Rao-Blackwell Theorem:

If $T(y, x)$ is an estimator, biased or unbiased, of a function $g(\theta)$, and $S(y, x)$ a sufficient statistic for θ, then $E\{T(y, x) - g(\theta)\}^2 \geq E[\{T(y, x)/S(y, x)\} - g(\theta)]^2$. The reader may refer to Rao (1973, page 321 for the proof).

In econometrics we do not see much application of this important theorem as econometricians invariably deal with distributions that belong to the exponential family and with maximum likelihood estimators that do give rise to asymptotically efficient and minimum variance estimators. But in the emerging business analytics research that deals with large data sets which could come from a mixture of distributions one may have to depend on new methods for improving the efficiency of estimators and this theorem could be very useful.

10.4.5   Approximate sufficiency and robust estimation

Fisher information depends on the specification chosen for the probability density which determines the likelihood. If one chooses a slightly different specification of that density the information limit to variance of unbiased estimators would be affected. In fact the methods of estimation and testing of statistical hypotheses that are based on the assumed specification would all be affected if the assumed specification is not true and if one replaces it by another one. At the same time it is intuitive that the sample empirical distribution can be approximated by two different parametric density functions, the distance between the two densities, according to any distance metric such as Kullback-Liebler measure (Kullback and Liebler (1951)), being small. Then one might say that the likelihood associated with one specification is close to the likelihood associated with the other. Each is an approximate likelihood to the other.

We may find it useful at times, particularly when the likelihood function is ill-behaved with flatness in the direction of some parameter, to consider another distribution that approximates the original distribution with fewer parameters. This would give rise to quasi-maximum likelihood estimators. With such quasi or approximate likelihood one may define the concept of an approximate sufficiency (see Le Cam, 1964, Section 7), and presume that some kind of limit theorem applies if the approximation satisfies some regularity conditions. Using such

---

[12] In fact it has been shown by Joshi that the lower bound is attained even for a larger class of densities (Joshi, 1976).

limit theorems we might conclude that if the approximation is sufficiently close we get approximately efficient estimators, the Cramer-Rao bound with approximate likelihood being close to the true Cremer-Rao bound.

On other occasions we may be interested only in some parameters and not all and wish to consider efficient estimation only of those parameters, neglecting the efficiency of the other irrelevant parameters. A typical example is that of parameters of interest on the one hand and nuisance parameters on the other. In econometrics the analog is that we may be interested in the parameters of the endogenous variables or the parameters associated with the control or policy variables. In such instances one may partition the sample or sample statistics into two sets, one set being sufficient to estimate the parameters of interest and the other set being sufficient to estimate the not so relevant parameters. We can then use the concepts of marginal, conditional, and partial likelihood as suggested by Cox (1975). If the class of density functions chosen is quite general enough to approximate a very wide class of density functions we get robust modeling, as in the case of Wedderburn (1974).

One may take the negative of logarithm of the likelihood and approximate it by a quadratic form in unknown parameters using Taylor series. The estimators obtained using these procedures are called quasi-likelihood estimators and they are shown to be consistent (White, 1994).

10.5   Computation of maximum likelihood estimates

The method of maximum likelihood estimation plays a very important role in statistical theory and practice. The computation of maximum likelihood estimates requires a computational procedure that is simple to use and is efficient. While there are several computational methods used in practice we mention just two that are quite popular and are used in this book and our statistical software DASC. This discussion will provide sufficient background to understand what actually happens within statistical computer software that provides maximum likelihood estimates. All of these methods depend on optimization of a function, the likelihood function. These methods are mostly iterative algorithms that start with an initial guess at the unknown parameters being estimated, increase or decrease these initial guesses in a chosen direction up to a step length. The stopping rule for the algorithm consists of insignificant change, from iteration to iteration, either of the parameter values or of the log likelihood, or both. Different algorithms differ in the choice of the direction of search and the step length chosen.

When there are restrictions on the parameters one replaces the log likelihood by a Lagrangian function with a penalty function for violation of the constraint. Most of the algorithms require the computation of the first derivative of the optimizing function at each step (iteration), computation of the second derivatives of the optimizing function, vector matrix multiplication and matrix inversion. As matrix inversion involves several operations and often might lead to problems with near singularity of that matrix some refinements are suggested, such as inverting the matrix only once in a while, and not during every iteration, and adding a diagonal matrix to the information matrix before inversion etc. In addition, it is observed that when one is far from the optimum the steepest ascent or descent works quite well, but as we approach the optimum the steepest ascent or descent takes much longer to reach the optimum. To overcome the latter problem Davidon, Fletcher, Powell, and Reeves suggested the **Conjugate Gradient method** that suggests that one use sequentially directions that are perpendicular to each other in a zigzag fashion. This procedure is explained later in more detail.

It is also suggested that whatever be the nonlinear objective function (logarithm of the likelihood) it can be approximated by a quadratic function and one can then use any of the methods described above. We shall now describe briefly two major computational algorithms.

10.5.1 Newton-Raphson method and Rao's method of scoring

The likelihood function is given by equation (10.23). As statisticians deal with exponential family of distributions it is often more convenient to deal with maximization of log likelihood denoted as:

$$
Log \quad L(y_1, y_2, \ldots, y_n; x_{11}, \ldots, x_{1n}; x_{21}, \ldots, x_{2n}; \ldots; x_{k1}, \ldots, x_{kn}; \theta_1, \ldots, \theta_p)
$$
$$
= \sum_{i=1}^{n} Log\{L(y_i, x_{1i}, x_{2i}, \ldots, x_{ki}; \theta_1, \ldots, \theta_p)\} = Log \quad L(y, x; \theta) = \ell(y, x; \theta) \tag{10.52}
$$

The necessary condition for the maximization of the likelihood or the logarithm of the likelihood is:

$$
\left(\frac{\partial \ell(y, x; \theta)}{\partial \theta} \right) = 0 \tag{10.53}
$$

This is a vector equation of dimension $p \times 1$. We may now assume that we have an initial guess for $\theta = \theta_0$, again a $p \times 1$ vector equation.

Expanding the equation above around the initial guess θ_0 we get the following Taylor series expansion:[13]

$$
\frac{\partial \ell(y, x; \theta)}{\partial \theta} = \left(\frac{\partial \ell(y, x; \theta)}{\partial \theta} \right)\Bigg|_{\theta = \theta_0} + \left(\frac{\partial^2 \ell(y, x; \theta)}{\partial \theta^2} \right)\Bigg|_{\theta = \theta_0} (\theta - \theta_0) = 0 \tag{10.54}
$$

In equation (10.54) the expression $- \dfrac{\partial^2 \ell(y, x; \theta)}{\partial \theta^2}$ is a $p \times p$ matrix ϑ of negative of second partial derivatives of the sample likelihood function, called the sample information matrix, and $S = \dfrac{\partial \ell(y, x; \theta)}{\partial \theta}$ is called **Rao's score**.

Following equation (10.54) we can write:

$$
\theta_1 = \theta_0 + \{\vartheta\}_{\theta = \theta_0}^{-1} s_0 \tag{10.55}
$$

From (10.55) we get an iterative algorithm for computing maximum likelihood estimates starting with an initial guess θ_0 using the iterative formula:

$$
\theta_{i+1} = \theta_i + \vartheta_i^{-1} s_i \tag{10.55a}
$$

The iterative process can be stopped when either subsequent values of θ differ insignificantly or when the subsequent values of ℓ differ insignificantly or both differ insignificantly.

---

[13] This is the Newton-Raphson method for solving a set of simultaneous equations.

The method above is known as **Rao's method of scoring**. From (10.55a) we see that in this procedure the score is the steepest ascent (in place of the word descent normally used in minimizing an objective function), and the second term (the elements of the information matrix that have information on the rates of change of score or ascent) determines the step length.

10.5.2 Davidon-Fletcher-Powell-Reeves Conjugate Gradient procedure

Maximization of the likelihood is equivalent to the minimization of the negative of logarithm of the likelihood. This leads to, in the standard multiple regressions, the problem of minimization of a quadratic function of the unknown parameters. Even in quasi-maximum likelihood where the likelihood function is approximated by a quadratic function we minimize the quadratic function of the parameters. Conjugate Gradient (CG) method was designed as an alternative to the quickest descent method of optimization of a general nonlinear function (Davidon, 1959; Fletcher and Powell, 1963; and Fletcher and Reeves, 1964). We illustrate the method through minimization of a positive definite quadratic form in unknown parameter, θ.

Let us denote the quadratic function in unknown parameters by:

$$f(y, x; \theta) = f(\theta) = \frac{1}{2}\theta'A\theta - b'\theta \qquad (10.56)$$

Minimization of $f(\theta)$ requires that:

$$\frac{df(\theta)}{d\theta} = A\theta - b = 0 \qquad (10.57)$$

Assuming A to be non-singular in a p-dimensional parameter space the point that satisfies equation (10.57) is a point that is the intersection of p independent hyper planes. Let us denote the solution as θ^*. Our objective is to reach θ^* starting from any arbitrarily chosen $\theta = \theta_0$.

The Conjugate Gradient method suggests that given θ_0 we must proceed in the steepest descent direction until we reach a point where we encounter a contour of the equal likelihood surface and where the line joining the initial parameter guess and the new parameter value is a tangent to that surface, as, if we go any further we will be reducing the likelihood instead of increasing it. We then move perpendicular to the first direction until we reach the equal likelihood surface where this second direction is a tangent to it and so on. This is illustrated in Figure 10.9 below.

As an iterative algorithm we write:

$$\theta_{i+1} = \theta_i - s_i\left(\frac{df(\theta)}{d\theta}\right)_{\theta=\theta_i} \qquad (10.58)$$

here s_i is the step length taken in the direction of steepest descent from point θ_i. The optimal step length is that which makes $f(\theta_{i+1})$ minimum in that direction.

Let us define error at iteration i by $\varepsilon_i = \theta_i - \theta^*$ and the direction taken at iteration i by

$$\delta_i = -\frac{df(\theta)}{d\theta_i}$$

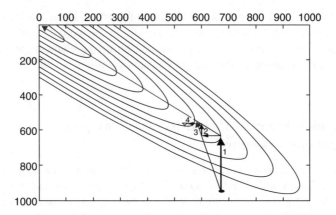

Figure 10.9   Powell Conjugate Gradient procedure.

The Conjugate Gradient procedure described above implies the following:

(1) $\delta'_{i+1}\delta_i = 0$ (Hence the word conjugate gradient)

(2) $(b - A\theta_{i+1})'\delta_i = 0$

(3) $b - A(\theta_i + s_i\delta_i)'\delta_i = 0$

(4) $(b - A\theta_i)'\delta_i - s_i\delta'_i \ A'\delta_i = 0$

(5) $(b - A\theta_i)'\delta_i = s_i\delta'_i \ A'\delta_i$

(6) $\delta'_i\delta_i = s_i\delta'_i A'\delta_i$

$$s_i = \frac{\delta'_i\delta_i}{\delta'_i A\delta_i} \tag{10.59}$$

Having thus determined the initial steepest descent direction, the step length needed to reach the next orthogonal direction, the iterative procedure stops when ε_i reaches a small ε-neighborhood around zero. This procedure is known to converge in a finite number of iterations in most cases. In the standard case of a linear multiple regression model the matrix turns out to be the sample information matrix. This procedure does not require any inversion of a matrix.

When we approximate a general nonlinear negative of likelihood function by a quadratic function the matrix A is no longer constant from iteration to iteration. It may be replaced by A_i.

We all know that LSE and MLE involve the basic problem of statistical computation to solve an extremum problem. Davidon-Fletcher-Powell-Reeves algorithm (for short as Powell algorithm) is very useful for nonlinear problem in statistical computation and is adopted by DASC.

10.5.3   Estimates of the variance covariance matrix of maximum likelihood estimators

As most of the densities normally used by statisticians belong to the exponential family, and as for such densities the information limit to variance is attained, such variances are treated as the asymptotic variances. There are also limit theorems for the distributions of maximum likelihood estimators that establish that such estimators do have asymptotic Normal distributions with information limit to variance as the asymptotic variance. Whatever maximum likelihood estimation method we use, whether it is the method of scoring, or Fletcher-Powell-Reeves conjugate gradient method, the last iteration in the iterative algorithms computes the sample estimate of the information matrix. By calculating its inverse these programs provide the asymptotic variance covariance matrix of the maximum likelihood estimators.

Thus the estimate of the asymptotic variance covariance matrix of the m.l.e. $\hat{\theta}$ obtained using the method of scoring after T iteration is given by

$$\hat{V}(\hat{\theta}) = \hat{\vartheta}_T^{-1} \tag{10.60}$$

Similarly the estimate of the asymptotic variance covariance matrix of the m.l.e. $\hat{\theta}$ obtained by the Fletcher-Powell conjugate gradient method after T iterations is given by

$$\hat{V}(\hat{\theta}) = A_T^{-1} \tag{10.61}$$

here A_T is the negative of the second partial derivative of the likelihood function, which is an estimate of its expected value which is the information matrix.

Two practical questions confront us in this case. First, how large should be the sample to treat these estimates of the asymptotic variances and covariances as applicable with reasonable accuracy? Second, if the sample size is not large enough through such a criterion how one should estimate the variances and covariances of the MLE $\hat{\theta}$? The answer to the first question depends on the rate of convergence of the finite sample distribution of m.l.e. to its asymptotic distribution. This rate of convergence can vary from one problem to another and hence it is not easy and meaningful to have any one rule of thumb and say that a sample size of 30, 40, or 50 is large enough to use the asymptotic variances and covariances. For some ill-behaved problems even a sample size of 1000 may not be large enough.

The second question is answered by the method of obtaining bootstrap estimates described in Section 10.7. Essentially the bootstrap method uses resampling from the given sample, often through **Monte Carlo simulation**, and obtains several replications of the estimated parameters and obtains the sampling distribution of the estimator. From this estimated empirical probability distribution the variances and covariances are calculated. Thus the bootstraps method provides estimates of variances and covariances suitable for finite samples such as the one we normally have.

10.6   Specification searches

10.6.1   Choice between alternate specifications: Akaike and Schwarz information criteria

Any statistical model is a decomposition of information into two components, **signal** and **noise**. What one calls a signal is a systematic part, while the noise is the random part. This decomposition is somewhat arbitrary and complimentary as it depends on how one specifies the systematic part, the noise being just the residual between the observation and the systematic part. In four chapters (Chapters 2–5) we dealt with different types of specifications for the systematic part of single equation models. Given that there can be several possible specifications for the systematic part it becomes necessary to make a choice between alternate specifications. There are two types of choices between models. First, we choose between various possible linear models that one with only those variables that we reasonably expect to describe the underlying data generation process. The model choice criterion in this case is discussed in detail in Chapter 2. Second, one may choose the best model between two or more mathematical and statistical specifications, including nonlinear, parametric, semi-parametric, and non-parametric specifications. The choice is based on some criterion that improves the signal and reduces the noise. To make this **model choice** the basic criteria we use are based on the degree of uncertainty associated with the noise and choose that specification that has least degree of uncertainty.

The data generation processes might suggest a wide variety of specifications for describing the signal component and the probability distributions of the residual error or noise. The signal part can have a mathematical form that depends on a constant but unknown parameter(s) (parametric), or it can have a functional form that does not depend on any such parameters (non-parametric). Non-parametric and semi-parametric regressions are covered in detail in Chapter 5. The parametric model could be linear or non-linear. The nonlinear models are also discussed in Chapter 4. The probability distribution of the noise or error can be specified in different ways.

(1) It could be a mixture of two or more distributions.

(2) It could refer to the distribution of serially correlated variables.

(3) It could refer to several serially and contemporaneously correlated variables.

(4) It could be symmetric distribution with thin tails.

(5) It could be a symmetric distribution with fat tails.

(6) It could be a skewed distribution with thin tails.

(7) It could be a skewed distribution with fat tails.

(8) The underlying probability distribution is semi-parametric or non-parametric. Suppose the true model is:

$$y = g(x;\theta) + u \tag{10.62}$$

where u has a pdf f(u) that may not be that of a pure white noise. For the observed y, given x and g (including the parameter θ) there is a signal $g(x;\theta)$. If θ does not appear then it is a non-parametric form.

We can now create bins in which $y - g(x;\theta)$ lie. The farther from zero $y - g(x;\theta)$ lies the low is the signal strength and high is the noise. Suppose we create 'n' such bins and record the relative frequency of the estimated errors or estimated noise in each of those, and label them as p_i, $i = 1, 2, \ldots, n$. We can then write entropy, a measure of noise in the system, defined as average or expected information as:

$$E = \sum_{i=1}^{n} p_i \ln\left(\frac{1}{p_i}\right) = -\sum_{i=1}^{n} p_i \ln(p_i) \tag{10.63}$$

The entropy above is a function of the distribution of the estimated errors u_i. It is obvious that the above expression is the negative of log likelihood.

Once we limit our choice of models to a finite number we can calculate the entropy as defined above and choose that model which has minimum entropy (noise) or maximum likelihood. One of the early approaches suggested consists of assuming a true probability structure of which each alternative specification is an approximation, uses Kullback and Leibler information distance criterion (KLIC) between the true structure and the model, and chooses that model which has the least divergence from the true model (Kullback and Leibler, 1951). Two very popular criteria used for model selection that depend on the sample size 'n' and number of parameters 'k', are Akaike and Schwarz Information criteria. Akaike Information Criterion (AIC), Schwarz Information Criterion (SIC), and Adjusted R^2 criteria penalize a model if it has more parameters than another one, all others being the same. These criteria are defined as follows:

$$Adjusted \ \ R^2 = \bar{R}^2 = -\frac{k-1}{n-k} + \frac{n-1}{n-k}R^2 \qquad (10.64)$$

Akaike Information Criterion

$$AIC = -2\log(Likelihood) + 2k \qquad (10.65)$$

Schwarz Information Criterion (SIC)

$$SIC = -2\log(Likelihood) + k\log(n) \qquad (10.66)$$

The suggested model choice criteria are:[14]

1. Choose a model with High Adjusted R^2

2. Choose a model with least AIC

3. Choose a model with least SIC

10.6.2   Generalized information and complexity-based model choice criterion

Statisticians develop their theories and methods under a general perspective so that they can be applied in a variety of situations. However, when these methods are applied in practice they should be suitably modified to suit the situation. The information criteria mentioned in the previous section are based on extracting the best/maximum overall signal or minimizing the noise, and penalizing for using more parameters for doing so. Many of the models we use are multivariate models which can be interpreted as the conditional mean of the dependent variable, given that the independent variables assume some known values. Even if the number of parameters is the same in two models, there could be reasons to prefer one model over another based on the precision with which some parameters are estimated. Suppose we are interested in predicting the per capita food consumption given the household size and the per

---

[14]The models should be transformed so that the dependent variable is the same in all models. When the model is nonlinear in parameters one may define R^2 as the square of correlation between predicted values and the actual values of the dependent variable.

capita monthly total expenditure of the household. A policy maker may be more interested in knowing what would be the impact of change in income or total expenditure on per capita food consumption than on the impact of a change in the household size. Hence between two models that have the same overall prediction the one that gives a better conditional prediction of per capita food consumption for a given level of total expenditure is preferred. The criteria mentioned in the previous section do not take this aspect into account.

Between two models that give the same overall prediction the one that estimates the parameters more precisely is to be preferred to the one that estimates them less precisely. The precision with which different parameters are estimated may have different importance in different contexts, depending on the sensitivity of the business decision to changes in those parameter values. In view of these considerations the model choice criteria must be generalized to include a weighted loss function that depends on the variance covariance matrix of the estimates of the parameters. Bozdogan developed such a generalized model selection criterion (Bozdogan, 2000). His method takes into account the variance covariance matrix of the parameter estimates through the inverse of Fisher information matrix or the Cramer-Rao Lower Bound. When we specify a model and estimate it we encounter two kinds of errors. First, there is a specification error, which is the error due to the specified model being different from the true model that must have generated the data. Second, we have an estimation error or a sampling error, which is the error that the estimated parameter is different from the true parameter that must have generated the data. Any choice of a model must be based on minimizing a weighted average of these two errors, the weights being the relative costs of these two errors in making decisions.

10.6.3   An illustration of model choice: Engel Curve for food consumption in India[15]

The relation between expenditure on a specific commodity (or commodity group) and income of a person (or a household) is called an Engel Curve. Economists use different functional forms for Engel Curves. These are:

$$Allen-Bowley\,(AB): \quad q_i = \alpha + \beta z_i + \gamma y_i \tag{10.67a}$$

$$Working-Leser\,(WL): q_i = \alpha + \beta z_i + \gamma y_i + \delta y_i loq(y_i) \tag{10.67b}$$

$$Modified\;W-L\;(MWL): q_i = \alpha + \beta z_i + \gamma y_i + \delta \log(y_i) \tag{10.67c}$$

$$Praise-Houthacker\;(PH): q_i = \alpha + \beta z_i + \gamma \log(y_i) \tag{10.67d}$$

$$Banks-Blundell-Lewbel\,(BBL): q_i = \alpha + \beta z_i + \gamma y_i + \delta y_i^2 + \varepsilon y_i^3 \tag{10.67e}$$

$$Kumar-Gore-Sitaramam\;(KGS): q_i = \alpha + \beta z_i + \frac{\gamma y_i}{(\delta + y_i)} \tag{10.67f}$$

where q_i refers to expenditure on a specific commodity, y_i refers to income (here total expenditure used as a proxy), and z_i refers to other household characteristics (here taken as household size). The last specification is suited for concave Engel Curves that admit a saturation level for the expenditure on an essential commodity, cereals. All the six Engel Curve

---

[15] This example is based on Kumar, Mallick, and Holla (2009)

specifications were used as alternatives. The raw data used is that of a sub-sample of 679 households of Andhra Pradesh in India drawn from the National Sample Survey Organization's sample survey data on consumer expenditure for Urban India in 1999–2000 (the format of the raw data is the one given in Table 1.2 of Chapter 1). The data are processed to smooth out fluctuations from household to household due to factors other than the variables of interest using the following procedure. The variables are first multiplied by the multiplicative factor of the sample design to represent the population characteristics. The households are then grouped into 12 expenditure classes and the variables are mean values in each of the 12 expenditure classes. The results of goodness of fit of these alternatives are presented below in Table 10.1.

Some better fitting curves are as shown in Figure 10.10 and Figure 10.11. Figure 10.12 depicts the Engel Curve by Kumar-Gore-Sitaramam (KGS) extended to forecast.

The figures can be shown by DASC software by clicking DASC→Regression→Nonlinear Regression→Engel Curve. For all menus or figures in DASC, if the user wants to use his or her own data, there are five ways. These are: (1) Input the data directly in the area A. (2) In area B in the block 'Data Source', select user1 (or user 2 to user 9), the data in that folder will be input if user prepares some data in that folder. (3) In the 'Select Source' box of area B, select 'Arbitrary Data' item; or use the menu 'Data(top menu) →Load Text or Excel Data', then the user can select his or her data in text or Excel format. (4) Use the menu 'Data(top menu) →Load Data from Database', user can input data from the database that has been

Table 10.1   Computation results of Engel Curve.

Engel Curve Type	n	k	Error SS	Error Variance	R^2	Adj R^2
Allen-Bowley	96	3	0.372232	0.0040025	0.7325	0.7268
Working-Leser	96	4	0.362684	0.0039422	0.7396	0.7311
Modified Working-Leser	96	4	0.371223	0.0040350	0.7333	0.7246
Praise-Houthacker	96	3	0.331008	0.0035592	0.7622	0.7571
Banks-Bundell-Lewbell	96	5	0.369906	0.0040649	0.7341	0.7225
Kumar-Gore-Sitaramam	96	4	0.359102	0.0037800	0.86798	0.86367

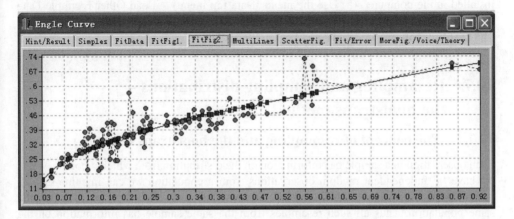

Figure 10.10   Engel Curve by Praise-Houthacker (PH) specification with sample.

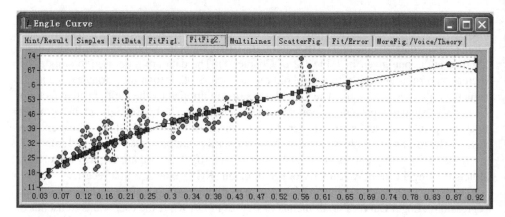

Figure 10.11   Engel Curve by Kumar-Gore-Sitaramam (KGS) specification with sample.

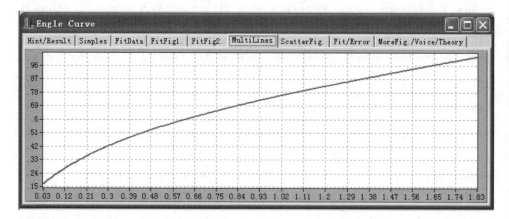

Figure 10.12   Engel Curve by Kumar-Gore-Sitaramam (KGS) extended to forecast.

installed in the computer. (5) Use the menu 'Data(top menu) →Load Other Example Data (Wiley book)'. The user can select the data of this book that are loaded into DASC software. The DASC operations are simple and very user-friendly.

10.7   Resampling and sampling distributions – the bootstraps method

10.7.1   The concept of resampling and the bootstraps method

Each observation in a sample has information on the distribution from which it comes. When we have 'n' independent random observations from a population we can imagine that all possible ways in which that 'same sample' could have been drawn are other samples from the same population. Thus all such resamples from the same sample has information on the distribution that generated the sample. This is the principle behind **resampling** or **bootstraps**.

While a sample from a population gives information on the unknown population distribution, resampling from the sample gives more information. A bootstrap is a method of resampling from the sample. J.A. Hubback, a British Civil Servant working in India was the first person to have used bootstraps as a sampling method in 1927 (see Hubback, 1945). The design of agricultural experiments of Fisher and the sample survey experiments of Mahalanobis were inspired by Hubback's studies. Mahalanobis used resampling methods in his sample survey experiments in the 1930s to estimate the sampling variance. For a greater detailed account of history of bootstrap one may see Hall (2003). There are mainly two types of bootstraps that are often studied; one where given a sample several resamples of the same sample size or smaller are obtained from it using random sampling with replacement, the other, given a sample and its empirical distribution several samples from that empirical distribution are obtained using the Monte Carlo technique and computers. The most useful version of bootstraps is of the second type as suggested by Efron (1979b). This method has become extremely useful in statistical inference in econometrics due to the ease with which modern computers can generate very large number of samples and calculate estimates, including estimates of the entire sampling distribution itself based on them.

Before the bootstraps method was introduced by Efron (1979a), Kumar and Gapinski (1974, 1975) used almost a similar version to study the small sample properties of nonlinear estimators of CES production function parameters using data generated by Monte Carlo simulation. Instead of using the empirical sampling distribution itself they smoothed it using a wide class of parametric densities and chose the best fitting smooth density using Pearson's goodness of fit criterion. That procedure was guided by their assumption that the population density was smooth and belonged to the family of Pearsonian density functions, and that the kinkiness or roughness in the sample must be corrected if it were to be taken as an estimate of the unknown probability density. Markmann and Kumar (1975), and Kumar and Markmann (2011) replaced the fitting of Pearsonian densities by fitting nonparametric densities to the Monte Carlo simulation data, replicating the two endogenous equation model of Anderson and Sawa (1973). The main point of their 1975 study was to demonstrate that where an exact finite sample density is not available one can use the simulation method to estimate numerically the entire sampling distribution of the estimator in small samples. This is today the main aim of bootstraps method.

Two of the most popular bootstrap estimates are the estimates of bias and variance or standard error of an econometric estimator of an unknown parameter. These are functions of the first two moments of the underlying true probability distribution. The basic principle behind bootstrap estimator is that the bootstrap estimator is the same function with the population density being replaced by the empirical density obtained from resampling.

Let us now explain the bootstraps method. Suppose we have a sample $Y_1, Y_2,\ldots,Y_n$ coming from a known distribution $F(Y;\theta)$ with unknown parameter θ. From the sample and the resamples from it we can obtain a sample estimate of the empirical probability distribution function $\hat{F}$. This is a cumulative distribution function derived from the empirical relative frequency distribution of the given sample that attaches a probability of $\frac{1}{n}$ at each realized value of Y (y_i). But our interest is in θ or functions of θ. We need both point and interval estimates of θ. Suppose we have an **estimating equation** that expresses the estimator as a function of the sample:

$$\hat{\theta} = T(Y_1,Y_2,\ldots,Y_n) \tag{10.68}$$

While this is a point estimator that may have desirable properties depending on what method of estimation we use, and depending on the data generating process, in general such nice properties of those estimators are only asymptotic properties.

Until the bootstraps method was developed statistical inference used to rely on the asymptotic theory involving some form of the central limit theorem with a tongue-in-cheek approach of applying the asymptotic distribution results even in small sample situations. To answer the question how large a sample should be for such asymptotic approximation to be reasonable one need to study the rates of convergence of the estimators. This was very rarely undertaken. For statistical inference in econometrics one would like to know what the small sample properties of the estimator are. Theoretical small sample distributions of econometric estimators are derived only in a few special cases, and in some of those cases the expressions turned out to be difficult to comprehend doubly infinite series (Basman, 1955; Bergstrom, 1962; Anderson and Sawa, 1973). The question then arises if one can develop a method that can be applied in general. Efron (1979b) is an excellent article that shows the power of modern computing in gaining more statistical knowledge of the unknown small sample distributions. This was not possible earlier without that computing power.

The bootstraps method calls for resampling from the original sample of $Y_1, Y_2, ..., Y_n$ through replacement, usually with the same sample size n, and estimating the parameter for each of those re-sampled samples. Suppose there are B such replicated resamples of size n. Then we have B such estimates, $\hat{\theta}_1, \hat{\theta}_2, ..., \hat{\theta}_B$. If the number of replications B is very large we have an empirical distribution of the estimator. From that empirical distribution we can estimate the mean of the estimator and the variance of the estimator. It may not be the case that the mean of these B estimates will be the same as the mean of the empirical distribution or its limit.

10.7.2   Bootstraps in regression models

For simplicity of exposition let us assume that we have a simple linear regression with a dependent variable Y and an independent variable X. Suppose we have a sample of size n on a dependent variable Y and the independent variable X; and let:

$$\hat{\theta} = T(Y, X)$$

where Y and X are $n \times 1$ vectors.

Associated with our sample of size n from Y and X we have a sample joint CDF of Y and X as:

$$F_n(y : x) = \frac{1}{n} \sum_{i=1}^{n} I(y_i \leq y) \times I(x_i \leq x)$$

The Monte Carlo method described in the Electronic References for Chapter 10 gives more details on how to obtain a Monte Carlo sample from the above empirical joint distribution. Given the several such samples of Y and X, B in number, say, generated by the Monte Carlo method we get B estimates of $\hat{\theta}_i = T(Y, X); i = 1, 2, ..., B$. From these bootstrap estimates of the estimator we obtain an empirical distribution of the unknown sampling distribution of the estimator. We can study the small sample properties of the estimator $\hat{\theta} = T(Y, X)$ using this empirical distribution.

The bootstraps procedure described above for a simple linear regression model can be suitably modified to describe in general any bootstraps approach to the study of small sample distributions of estimators in econometrics, such as nonlinear least squares estimator, instrumental variable estimator and so on.

Example 10.1   Numerical example of estimating parameters of a CES production function for gross output of an economy between 1961–1987   It is useful to illustrate two main estimation methods described in this chapter so far; the method of maximum likelihood and the bootstraps method. We use CES Production function as the econometric model.

The data used for this example is in the Electronic References accompanying this book. The data consists of gross output in Rs lakhs (Q), Capital in machine-years (K), and labor in man-years (L). The relation between these economic variables is postulated to be a Constant Elasticity of Substitution (CES) production function given by the following formula:

$$Q = \alpha\{\beta K^{-\gamma} + (1-\beta)L^{-\gamma}\}^{-\frac{1}{\gamma}} \tag{10.69}$$

The function is generalization of the Cobb-Douglas production function given by $Q_0 = a_0 K_0^b L_0^{1-b}$. The Cobb-Douglas form is a special case of CES form when $\frac{1}{1+\gamma} = 1$. We further impose the following parametric restrictions imposed by economic theory of production:

$$0 \le \beta \le 1; \quad \gamma \ge -1 \tag{10.70}$$

The econometric model is postulated as a nonlinear regression model derived from the above mathematical form as follows:

$$Q_i = \alpha\{\beta K_i^{-\gamma} + (1-\beta)L_i^{-\gamma}\}^{-\frac{1}{\gamma}} + \varepsilon_i \tag{10.71}$$

where ε_i are i.i.d. as a Normal distribution with a mean zero and a constant variance.

The econometric model is a nonlinear regression model: the CES production function that is nonlinear in parameters. We estimate this using maximum likelihood method.

The results are reproduced below in Tables 10.2 and 10.3.

The optimum of the likelihood was obtained in 8 iterations and the proportion of total sum of squares explained by the model is 0.984.

Table 10.2   Iteration History.

Iteration	Residual Sum of Squares	$\hat{\alpha} = a$	$\hat{\beta} = b$	$\hat{\gamma} = c$
0	282654.569	10.000	.250	.750
1	72226.280	10.136	.250	.750
2	40088.960	10.452	.250	2.634
3	29032.013	10.480	.379	.847
4	28921.558	10.455	.379	.741
5	28904.820	10.450	.376	.793
6	28810.002	10.422	.390	.617
7	28792.890	10.431	.387	.667
8	28792.887	10.431	.386	.667

Table 10.3   Maximum likelihood estimates of the parameters.

Parameter	MLE	SE	Lower CB	Upper CB
Asymptotic Standard Errors and Confidence Bounds				
A	10.431	.113	10.198	11.664
B	.386	.043	.298	.475
C	.667	.661	−.697	2.031
Bootstrap estimates for standard error and confidence bounds for small samples*				
A	10.431	.064	10.303	11.558
B	.386	.028	.330	.443
C	.667	.442	−.217	1.551

*The bootstrap estimates are based on 60 samples.

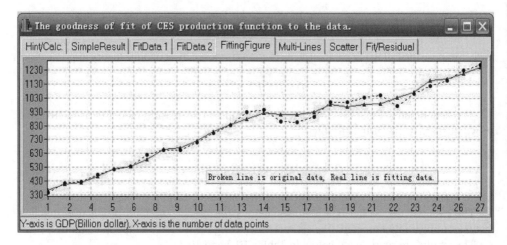

Figure 10.13   The goodness of fit of CES production function to the data.

The maximum likelihood estimates of the parameters, their asymptotic standard errors, confidence bounds are given above. We also give below the small sample bootstrap estimates, their standard errors and confidence bounds are presented in Table 10.3 above.

Figure 10.13 presents the goodness of fit of CES production function to the data. The figure can be shown in DASC software by hitting menu 'DASC→Regression→Nonlinear Regression→Fit of CES production function'.

10.8   Bayesian inference

10.8.1   The Bayes rule

Business and economic decisions almost always involve some subjective information based on unrecorded information gathered out of experience and some recorded objective quantitative information. Hence one of the most useful statistical tools for economic and business decisions is Bayesian inference. However its development and use were inhibited by the mathematical and computational complexity that the procedure involves. Fortunately, thanks to physicists for their initiative, a new method called **Markov Chain Monte Carlo (MCMC)** or Metropolis-Hasting algorithm was developed to perform numerical integration needed to apply the Bayesian procedure (Metropolis et al.,1953; Hastings, 1970). With this development now there is no excuse for not using Bayesian methods in economics and business. The fundamental tool in Bayesian analysis is the Bayes Rule. Let us explain that Rule. For illustration purposes let us assume a simple case of a probability distribution of a random variable X that can be described by its probability density function $f(x;\theta)$, where x is the point in sample space of X where the density is observed and θ is the unknown scalar parameter of the probability distribution. Statistical inference consists of using a sample observation from the distribution to make inferences about the unknown parameter θ. Classical approach to statistics assumes that the unknown parameter is a fixed number whereas Bayesian approach assumes that θ is not deterministic and instead that it is stochastic. It can be represented by a random variable Θ with a 'subjective' **prior probability density** $p(\theta)$.

Given the interpretation above one can say that both X and Θ are random and have a joint probability distribution with a joint density $f(x;\theta)$. We can then write:

$$f(x;\theta) = f(x|\Theta = \theta)p(\theta) = f(\theta|X = x)f(x) \quad \text{or}$$

$$f(\theta \mid X = x) = \frac{f(x|\Theta = \theta)p(\theta)}{\int f(x|\Theta = \theta)p(\theta)d\theta} \tag{10.72}$$

Equation (10.72) is called the **Bayes Rule** or **Bayes Formula** and it is the keystone for Bayesian approach. Here $p(\theta)$ is called the prior probability density of the unknown parameter, while $f(\theta/X = x)$ is called the **posterior probability density** of θ after obtaining the information about θ from the sample x. Note that the denominator in (10.72) is independent of the parameter. Hence one can write (10.72) equivalently as:

$$f(\theta / X = x) \propto f(x / \Theta = \theta)p(\theta) \tag{10.73}$$

That is equivalent to saying that the posterior density of the parameter is the likelihood times the prior density, where the likelihood function has the evidence from the sample. Equation (10.72) can be regarded as a method by which one takes a prior probability density of parameter $p(\theta)$, augments that information with sample information $X = x$, and obtains an improved knowledge of the probability density of θ, the posterior density of θ. One may use this formula recursively when there is a sequential acquisition of sample information, whereby the posterior density at an earlier stage will serve as the prior density of the subsequent stage. Hence this formula is also the basis of what is called as **Bayesian updating**. Empirical Bayes approach is the one that corresponds to replacing the subjective prior probability distribution by an empirically justified distribution such as the relative frequency distribution of estimates of the parameters obtained by others or the relative frequency distribution of the parameter obtained from a group of experts using a Delphi technique.

10.8.2   Choice of prior probability distribution for the parameter

Statistics is a decision science, and decisions are taken by individual persons based on their initial subjective opinion about the unknown parameter, supplemented by the sample information obtained from the sample. Classical statistical inference assumed that the parameter is deterministic and hence there is no meaning to the notion of having a prior opinion about it in a probabilistic sense. The Bayesians interpreted the classical position in their terminology by saying that the classical position is equivalent to saying that there is an equal ignorance, implying any value in the range of the parameter is equally likely, or equivalently that the prior probability density implicit in the classical approach is a uniform density. In the initial phases of the development of Bayesian inference it was also found convenient to assume that the prior probability density is of the same functional form belonging to an exponential family as the one postulated in writing the likelihood but with a different parameters. This leads to a posterior density that is also of the same form whose parameters are a weighted average of the parameters of the prior density and that of the sample estimates. This was called a conjugate prior.

With the development of Metroplis-Hastings algorithm and Monte Carlo Markov Chain approach now it is possible to elicit subjective probabilities through interviews and use them as the priors. For more detail on this one may see Garthwaite et al. (2005).

10.8.3   Bayesian concepts for statistical inference

In Bayesian inference one has the luxury of being able to provide the entire posterior density of the unknown parameter that combines information from the prior probability density and the sample information. However, if one finds that cumbersome or difficult to comprehend, or if one was used to classical inference and wants an equivalent point estimate then the Bayesian equivalent of a point estimate is the posterior mean, or mean of the posterior distribution:

$$E(\theta|X = x) = \int_\theta \theta f(\theta|X = x) d\theta \tag{10.74}$$

Likewise, the Bayesian equivalent of variance of the estimator is the posterior variance or the variance of the posterior distribution:

$$Var(\theta|X = x) = \int_\theta [\theta - E(\theta|X = x)]^2 f(\theta|X = x) d\theta \tag{10.75}$$

Corresponding to the confidence interval of the classical approach, the Bayesian approach uses what is called a credible interval. Suppose that (θ_L, θ_U) is an interval in the parameter space. We say that (θ_L, θ_U) is a $100(1-\alpha)$ % credible interval if:

$$Posterior \text{ Probability } (\theta_L \le \theta \le \theta_U | X = x) = 1 - \alpha \tag{10.76}$$

In view of the concepts above a Bayesian prediction consists of deriving the posterior probability density of the random variable that is being predicted, and then to present the posterior mean and the credible interval.

We will now present the Bayesian equivalent of testing a Null Hypothesis that $\theta = \theta_0$ against the alternative $\theta = \theta_1$. Suppose we observe that $X = x$ and ask what does this sample evidence has to say regarding our choice between the two hypotheses. We calculate the posterior probability under the two hypotheses: $f(\theta_0|X = x)$ and $f(\theta_1|X = x)$. It is obvious that one should choose that hypothesis which has greater posterior probability. This is more formally expressed in terms of posterior odds (ratio):

$$OR \text{ in favor of } \theta_0 = \frac{f(\theta_0|X = x)}{f(\theta_1|X = x)} \tag{10.77}$$

The Bayes factor is defined as follows:

$$BF(H_0, H_1) = \frac{\int_{\theta \in H_0} f(x|\theta) p_0(\theta) d\theta}{\int_{\theta \in H_1} f(x|\theta) p_1(\theta) d\theta} \qquad (10.78)$$

where $p_i(\theta)$ for $i = 0,1$ is a proper density with $\int p_i(\theta) d\theta = 1$, and they are the prior densities of θ under H_0 and H_1.

Let π_0 and π_1 be the prior probabilities for $\theta \in \Theta_0(H_0)$ and $\theta \in \Theta_1(H_1)$ ($\pi_0 + \pi_1 = 1$). The posterior odds (ratio) can now be written as:

$$\frac{\pi_0}{1 - \pi_0} BF(H_0, H_1)$$

The Bayes factor can be taken as a measure of evidence; the larger the value of BF, the stronger is the evidence in favor of H_0 and vice versa. The Bayes factor and posterior odds are equal if $\pi_0 = 1/2$.

The Bayesian approach to model choice or model selection is through the Odds Ratio in favor of Model 1 over Model 2:

$$OR_{12} = \frac{\pi_1 \int f_{M_1}(y|\theta_1, M_1) p_1(\theta_1|M_1) d\theta_1}{(1 - \pi_1) \int f_{M_2}(y|\theta_2, M_2) p_2(\theta_{21}|M_2) d\theta_2} \qquad (10.79)$$

where π_1 is the probability of model M_1 being true and $p_i(\theta_i|M_i)$ are the prior densities.

If one has to make a prediction with two competing models Bayesians consider model averaging of predictions. In other words, they consider the weighted averages of predictions from each of the models, the weights being the prior probabilities associated with the model being true.

Electronic references for Chapter 10

References

Anderson T.W. & Sawa T. (1973) Distributions of estimates of coefficients of a single equation in a simultaneous system and their asymptotic expansions, *Econometrica* **41**(4), July, 683–714.

Arminger G., Stein P. & Wittenberg J. (2006) Mixtures of conditional mean- and covariance-structure models. *Psychometrika* **64**, 475–94.

Barnard G.A. (1949) Statistical inference. *Journal of the Royal Statistical Society. Series B* **11**, 115–49.

Basman R.L. (1961) Note on exact finite sample frequency function of generalized classical linear estimators in two leading over-identified case. *Journal of American Statistical Association* **56**, 619–36.

Bergstrom A.R. (1962) The exact sampling distributions of least squares and maximum likelihood estimators of the marginal propensity to consume. *Econometrica* **30**, 480–90.

Blackwell D. (1947) Conditional expectation and unbiased sequential estimation, *Ann. Math. Statistics* **18**, 105–10.

Bozdogan, H. (2000) Akaike Information Criterion and Recent Developments in Informational Complexity. Journal of Mathematical Psychology **44**, 62–91.

Breusch T.S. & Pagan A.R. (1979) A simple test for heteroscedasticity and random coefficient variation. *Econometrica* **47**, 1287–91.

Breusch T.S. & Pagan A.R. (1980) The Lagrange multiplier test and its applications to model specification in econometrics. *The Review of Economic Studies* **2**, 39–53.

Buehler R.J. (1959) Some validity criteria for statistical inferences. *The Annals of Mathematical Statistics* **30**, 845–63.

Chen Z.H. (1993) Fitting multivariate regression functions by interaction spline models. *Journal of Royal Statistical Society* **55**, 473–91.

Cox D.R. (1958) Some problems connected with statistical inference. *The Annals of Mathematical Statistics* **29**, 357–72.

Cox D.R. (1975) Partial Likelihood. *Biometrika* **62**, 269–76.

Davidon W.C. (1959) Variable Metric Methods for Minimization. *A.E.C. Research and Development Report*, ANL-5990 (Rev)

Dasgupta A. (2006) Extensions to Basu's theorem, factorizations, and infinite divisibility. *Journal of Statistical Planning and Inference* **137**, 945–52.

Dzombak D.A., Fish W., Francois M. & Morel M. (1986) Metal-humane interactions: Discrete ligand and continuous distribution models. *Environ. Sci. Technol.* **20**, 669–75.

Efron B. (1979a) Bootstrap methods: another look at the jackknife. *Annals of Statistics* **7**, 1–26.

Efron B. (1979b) Computers and the theory of statistics: thinking the unthinkable. *SIAM Review* **21**, 460–80.

Epanechnikov, V.A. (1969) Nonparametric Estimates of a Multivariate Probability Density. *Theoretical Probability and Application*, **14**: 153–8.

Fisher R.A. (1922) On the mathematical foundations of theoretical statistics. *Philosophical Transactions of Royal Society of London* **222**, 309–68.

Fisher R.A. (1925) *Statistical Methods for Research Workers*. Oliver and Boyd, London.

Fletcher R. & Powell M.J.D. (1963) A rapidly convergent descent method for minimization. *Computer Journal* **6**, 163–68.

Fletcher R. & Reeves C.M. (1964) Function minimization by conjugate gradients. *Computer Journal* **7**, 149–54.

Garthwaite P.H., Kadane J.B. & O'Hagen A. (2005) Statistical methods for eliciting probability distributions. *Journal of American Statistical Association* **100**(470), 680–701.

Ghosh M. (2002) Basu's theorem with applications: A personalistic review. *Sankhya* **64**, 509–31.

Hall P. (2003) A short prehistory of the bootstrap. *Statistical Science* **18**(2), Silver Anniversary of the Bootstrap (May, 2003), 158–67.

Hastings W.K. (1970) Monte Carlo sampling methods using Markov chains and their applications. *Biometrika* **57**, 97–109.

Holger D. & Munk A. (1998) Testing heteroscedasticity in nonparametric regression. *Journal of Royal Statistical Society* **60**, 693–708.

Hubback J.A. (1946) Sampling for rice yield in Bihar and Orissa. *Sankhyā* **7**, 281–294. (First published in 1927 as Bulletin 166 of Imperial Agricultural Research Institute, Pusa, India.)

Johnson N.L., Kotz S. & Balakrishnan N. (1994) *Continuous Univariate Distributions*. 2nd Ed., John Wiley & Sons, Inc, New York.

Jones M.C. (1990) The performance of kernel density functions in kernel distribution function estimation. *Statistics & Probability Letters* **9**, 129–32.

Joshi V.M. (1976) On the attainment of Cramer-Rao bound. *Annals of Statistics* **4**, 998–1002.

Koenker R. (2005) *Quantile Regression*. Cambridge University Press, New York.

Kullback S. & Leibler R.A. (1951) On Information and Sufficiency. *Annals of Mathematical Statistics* **22**(1), 79–86.

Kumar T.K. & Gapinski J.H. (1974) Nonlinear Estimation of CES Production Parameters: A Monte Carlo Study. *Review of Economics and Statistics* **56**(4), 563–7.

Kumar T.K. & Gapinski J.H. (1975) Estimating the Ex-Ante Elasticity of Substitution from Miss-specified Factor Proportion Equations: A Monte Carlo Study. *Sankhya* **37**(C), 160–72.

Kumar T.K. & Markmann J.M. (2011) Importance of Nonparametric Density Estimation in Econometrics with Illustrations. *Journal of Quantitative Economics*, New Series **9**(1), 18–40.

Kumar T.K. Sushanta K. Mallick & Jayarama H. (2009) Estimating Consumption Deprivation in India Using Survey Data: A State-Level Rural-Urban Analysis Before and during reform Period. *Journal of Development Studies* **45**(4), 441–70.

Le Cam L. (1964) Sufficiency and approximate sufficiency. *Annals of Mathematical Statistics* **35**, 1419–55.

Manski C. (2003) *Partial Identification of Probability Distributions*, Springer Verlag, New York.

Metropolis N., Rosenbluth A.W., Rosenbluth M.N., Teller A. & Teller H. (1953), Equations of state calculations by fast computing machines. *Journal of Chemical Physics* **21**, 1087–91.

Nelder J.A. & Wedderburn R.W.M. (1972) Generalized linear models. *Journal of Royal Statistical Society* **135**, 370–84.

Phillips P.C.B. (1989) Partially identified economic models. *Econometric Theory* **5**, 181–240.

Purushottam W.L. and Ibrahim J.G. (1996) Predictive specification of prior model probabilities in variable selection. *Mathematics & Physical Sciences* **83**, 267–74.

Rao C.R. (1945) Informational accuracy attainable in the estimation of statistical parameters. *Bulletin of Calcutta Mathematical Society*, Vol. 37, and pp. 81–91. Republished in N.L. Johnson and S. Kotz, *Breakthroughs in Statistics,* 1889–1990, Vol. 1.

Rao C.R. (1973) *Linear Statistical Inference, and its Applications*, John Wiley & Sons, Inc, New York.

Rosenblatt M. (1956) Remarks on Some Nonparametric Estimates of Density Functions, Annals of Mathematical Statistics **27**(3), 832–7.

Rosenblatt M. (1971) Curve estimates. *Annals of Mathematical Statistics* **18**, 15–42.

Shao J. (2003) *Mathematical Statistics*. Second Edition, Springer, New York.

Specht D.F. (1971) Series estimation of a probability density function. *Technometrics* **40**, 9–24.

Wedderburn R.W.M (1974) Quasi-likelihood functions, generalised linear models and Gauss-Newton method. *Biometrika* **61**, 439–47.

White H. (1982) Maximum likelihood estimation of misspecified models. *Econometric* **50**, 1–25.

White H. (1994) *Estimation, Inference, and Specification Analysis*. Cambridge University Press, New York.

Wolfowitz J. (1957) The minimum distance method. *The Annals of Mathematical Statistics* **28**, 75–88.

Yuille A.L. (1994) Statistical physics, mixtures of distributions, and the EM algorithm. *Division of Applied Sciences* **6**, 334–40.

Index

adjusted R^2, 20, 51
AIC criteria, 255, 274
AIC function, 275, 285
alternative projection, 130
analysis of variance, 109, 357, 358, 424
ancillary statistic, 432
associated decomposition of degrees of freedom, 360
asymptotically efficient estimation, 209, 210
asymptotic distributions, 218
asymptotic regression models, 171
asymptotic variance-covariance matrix, 164, 166
augmented vector autoregressive model, 302
autocorrelation coefficient, 299
autocorrelation coefficient matrix, 299
autocovariance function, 254, 287, 299
autocovariance function matrix, 300
autoregression, 254
autoregressive (AR) models, 236, 254
autoregressive conditional heteroscedasticity, 85, 334
autoregressive distributed lag model, 325, 347
auto-regressive moving average models, 254
auto-regressive moving average process, 286
autoregressive process, 102

balanced design, 358
Bartlett kernel, 197
basin curve, 181
Basu's theorem, 433
Bayes discrimination rules, 371
Bayesian analysis, 4
Bayesian inference, 416
Bayesian updating, 455
Bayes rule/Bayes formula, 455

Bertalanffy model, 172
best linear forecasts, 265
best linear unbiased estimate, 107
BHHH algorithm, 164, 165
BIC criteria, 255
BIC criterion, 274
bond duration data, 408
bootstraps, 450
boundedly complete, 433
Box-Cox model, 130
Box-Cox transformation, 169, 176
Box-Cox transformation model, 176
Box–Pierce statistic, 271
Breusch-Pagan-Godfrey (BPG) test, 89
business analytics, 2

canonical correlation coefficient, 384
categorical/discrete dependent variables, 129
categorical independent variables, 130
categorical variables, 129
Cauchy inequality, 263
censored data, 154, 357, 406
Cholesky decomposition, 303
classify sample, 370
close curve-fitting, 195
closest neighbor, 193
closest neighbor function, 196
Cobb-Douglas production function, 99, 161
Cobb-Douglas production function model, 130
Cochrane-Orcutt transformation, 99
cointegrated process, 323
cointegrated system, 323
cointegrating, 322
    relations, 323
    vector, 323

Developing Econometrics, First Edition. Hengqing Tong, T. Krishna Kumar and Yangxin Huang.
© 2011 John Wiley & Sons, Ltd. Published 2011 by John Wiley & Sons, Ltd.